TRUANTS FROM LIFE

The Rehabilitation of Emotionally Disturbed Children

TRUANTS FROM LIFE

――――――― ―――――――

THE REHABILITATION OF
EMOTIONALLY DISTURBED CHILDREN

――――――― ―――――――

By *Bruno Bettelheim*

THE FREE PRESS, *New York*
COLLIER-MACMILLAN LIMITED, *London*

Collier-Macmillan Canada, Ltd., Toronto, Ontario

Library of Congress Catalog Card Number: 55–7331

FIRST FREE PRESS PAPERBACK EDITION 1964

printing number
4 5 6 7 8 9 10

TO THE SCHOOL'S STAFF

Contents

ACKNOWLEDGMENTS   xv

PART I

INTRODUCTION   1
   Residential Treatment and Therapeutic Success   9
THE SCHOOL   17
   Physical Setting   17
   . . . And Life Within It   25
   The School Becomes a Shelter   28
   . . . And a Home   39

PART II

"LITTLE THINGS AND TIME":
Paul, A Case of "Institutionalism"   43
   Psychological Institutionalism   43
   Paul's Parents and His Early Life   46
   His Personality   55
   From "Wild Critter" to "Great Dictator"   62

The Beginning of, and the Fight Against, Self-Control   72
Infantile Pleasures and a Changing Outlook on Life   87
The World Becomes Populated   97
Paul Finds Himself as a Person   112
He Makes Peace with Himself and the World   125
. . . And Leaves Us   140
Paul's Counselor   147
Out in Life   149

PART III

EMOTIONAL DEATH AND REBIRTH:

Mary, A Schizophrenic Girl   155
    Mary's Childhood   155
    She Comes to the School   158
        DISCUSSION   161
    Anger and Hope   162
        DISCUSSION   169
    She "Adjusts"   170
        DISCUSSION   181
    Breakdown and First Efforts at Integration   184
        DISCUSSION   202
    Between Two Traumas   208
        DISCUSSION   232
    Emotional Rebirth   242
        DISCUSSION   252
    Mary's Leaving   253
    Her Counselors   254
        SUMMARY   256
    The Next Three Years   266
    Mary Looks Back   268

PART IV

"ICE CREAM IS BETTER THAN GOD":

John, Phantasy Life and Rehabilitation of a Boy with Anorexia   271
    John's Oral Trauma   271
    The Father   273

The Mother 275

John's First Years 279

He Comes to the School 286

Breaking the Anaclitic Ties 287

John and the Staff 290

His First Experience in the School 291

John's Phantasies 296

First Achievements 303

John's Progress Evaluated 322

The Third Year 327

The Fourth Year: A New Friendship Takes Root 346

His Last Years in School 363

In Conclusion 378

John's Worker 384

After Leaving Us 386

PART V

"I NEVER KNEW YOU CARED SO MUCH":

Harry, A Delinquent Boy 389

Harry and His Family 389

Initial Evaluation 393

Disintegration of Delinquent Symptoms 401

AGGRESSION—INITIAL PHASE 402

RUNNING AWAY 409

CONTROL OVER AGGRESSION 425

Personality Integration 431

DISCOVERING HUMAN BEINGS 431

DEVELOPING A CONSCIENCE 439

WORKING THROUGH 445

DEVELOPING A NEW PERSONALITY 450

SOMATIC SYMPTOMS: THE LAST TURMOIL 453

HARRY LEAVES US 465

Out in Life 467

Epilogue 470

APPENDIX

On Writing Case Histories 473

The Children's Families 478
    FAMILY STATUS 483
    EMOTIONAL DISTURBANCE OF PARENTS 486
The Children 495
    SOMATIC DISTURBANCES 495
    INTELLIGENCE 495
    EMOTIONAL DISTURBANCES 498
    TREATMENT BEFORE ENROLLMENT 499
    SIBLINGS 500
    AGE AND LENGTH OF STAY 502

INDEX 505

List of Illustrations

MAPS

Buildings and Playgrounds   *20*

The Dormitory Building   *21-22*

The School Building   *23*

MARY'S DRAWINGS   *Following page 176*

First Year

    I. Self-portrait: "Just any girl, a girl without a name"

    II. Attempt at cheerfulness

    III. Self-portrait

    IV. Mother panda providing food for her baby

Second Year

    V. The School becomes a home—fencing the world out

    VI. Self-portrait

    VII. Attempt to overcome the trauma of mother's death

    VIII. Mastering death through morbid humor

Third Year

    IX. Mother and baby

    X. Incorporating the mother

    XI. Her mother, independent of herself

[xi]

XII. How the baby experiences her mother
XIII. The father's penis, with damaging claws
XIV. Her rebirth

Last Two Months
XV. Self-portrait
XVI. She thinks of becoming a dancer
XVII. A happy girl with her dog
XVIII. "Fun on the Beach"

Tables

I. Success of Treatment — 15
II. Length of Staff Association with School — 36
III. Family Status — 484
IV. Fathers' participation in Family Life — 485
V. Mothers' participation in Family Life — 485
VI. Diagnoses of Mothers — 487
VII. Diagnoses of Fathers — 488
VIII. Therapy of Mothers — 489
IX. Therapy of Fathers — 490
X. Fathers' Occupations — 494
XI. Geographical Distribution — 494
XII. Physical Symptoms — 496
XIII. Intelligence — 497
XIV. Psychiatric Diagnoses — 498
XV. Presenting Symptoms — 499
XVI. Psychotherapy Preceding Placement—I — 500
XVII. Psychotherapy Preceding Placement—II — 500
XVIII. Number of Children in Family — 501
XIX. Position Among Siblings — 501
XX. Age Distribution — 502
XXI. Length of Stay — 503

Acknowledgments

First and foremost I wish to express my gratitude to all staff members, past and present, of the Sonia Shankman Orthogenic School. Only their extraordinary devotion to the cause for which the School stands has made and continues to make possible the rehabilitation of the children who are brought to us for help. As a small token of my appreciation this, which is really our, book is dedicated to them.

In each of the four histories reported here, the staff members who, to the best of my knowledge, contributed most to the rehabilitation of the child are mentioned by name; usually they are also the ones whose reports on their work were most valuable in preparing the histories. This book is as much the history of their untiring efforts as it is a chronicle of certain years in the children's lives. In addition to these staff members, I owe thanks to all the other professional, clerical and technical workers who have made so many contributions, the importance of which is hard to overestimate. My gratitude is also due the children; the parents; and the two social agencies, the Chicago Child Care Society and the Jewish Children's Bureau of Chicago, for their permission to publish these accounts of the children's lives.

To the University of Chicago, which conducts this institution, children, staff and author are deeply indebted. Without the University there would be no Orthogenic School; the children would not be helped; staff and author would not find the self-realization that comes to them through their work.

The work of compiling the data used in writing the histories was supported in part by a research grant (Grant MH-81) from the United States National Institute of Mental Health, of the National Institutes of Health, Public Health Service.

The writing of the histories stretched over many years. In this task I was helped first by Ruth Soffer Marquis; and later, for a shorter time, by Kathleen Ray. Most of the histories took their present shape thanks to Laura Bergquist. Their final form is the result of Paula R. Nelson's efforts. I am most grateful to all of them, not only for the battle they waged for clarity of organization and style, but also for their many helpful suggestions.

Many staff members and several other friends were kind enough to read one or another of the histories in one of its various editions and to make many helpful suggestions. Not all are mentioned here, lest the list of names become unduly long. Major improvements are due to suggestions received from Jules Henry, Gayle Shulenberger Janowitz, Morris Janowitz, David Rapaport, Joan Little Treiman, Milton Wexler, Florence White and Josette Dermody Wingo.

Part of "Harry" has been previously published by the *Journal of Abnormal and Social Psychology,* while a short account of "Mary" has previously appeared in the *Scientific American.* Some parts of the material used in a few of the case histories have appeared in the *American Journal of Orthopsychiatry* and the *Psychoanalytic Review.* The permission of these journals to use this material again is gratefully acknowledged.

PART I

Introduction

THE SONIA SHANKMAN ORTHOGENIC SCHOOL of the University of Chicago is a residential treatment institution devoted to the rehabilitation of children with very severe emotional disturbances; to research into the causation and treatment of primary behavior disorders of childhood; and to the training of persons who wish to specialize in the education and treatment of disturbed children or in child-care work generally. This is the second volume of a planned series of three explaining the work of the School. Each volume is self-contained, but those who wish to gain a comprehensive picture of the School's purpose and work should read all three.

In the first book of the series, *Love Is Not Enough* (published in 1950), an effort was made to describe the School's educational and therapeutic philosophy as it is set into practice throughout the activities of a more or less typical day. No attempt was made, however, to present a full account of the School's work within the limitations of the first volume. Accordingly, many of its readers were stimulated to inquire about the children's lives after they leave the School, about their readjustment to the world outside and their eventual success in life; and some wished to be told more about the School's staff.

These two questions that interested my readers are naturally of even greater importance to all of us on the staff. Even after our basic philosophy had been developed and its application illustrated in practice, there remained the necessity of critically evaluating its results upon the children who live under its influence. This volume tries to answer the several questions implicit in the first of these two general queries, namely: How does the rehabilitation of individual children actually proceed? How do they manage after they have left the School?

The second general question asked by the readers of *Love Is Not Enough* suggests such problems as: How are staff members selected and trained? How are they introduced to their work? What enables them to survive the over-all hardships of the work and to carry on their activities with the children for years despite the harassments to which they are often exposed? What rewards make it possible for the workers to maintain their own integration though they are continually confronted with potentially disintegrating experiences?

The answers to this second group of questions must wait until publication of the projected third volume in this series. It will report research, presently in progress, on the problems of staff training, interaction and integration.[1]

Another question that may come to mind when reading the case histories in this book must also be reserved for the coming volume. How is it possible, it may be asked, for staff members who differ in personality and professional training to function as an integrated unit in creating a unique therapeutic universe for the children under their care? This important aspect of the School's work seems to have been rarely noted by readers of *Love Is Not Enough*. Since it is basic to our work it should at least be mentioned here, although it also will be fully treated only in the coming book.

To put our philosophy in practice we had to create a very specific environment, a particular social organism, which would be the matrix within which the children might begin and develop a new life. This particular society has developed mores of its own. Some of these are identical with or parallel to the mores of our larger society. But others are sometimes at variance with the surrounding standards. For example, tolerance and even temporary encouragement of asocial or regressive tendencies often takes preference over the encouragement of academic progress. In respect to sex behavior, verbal expressions, orderliness, and cleanliness, polite conventions yield to emotional honesty. Protection of property takes second place to emotional needs. These are well-known standards of thera-

---

1. A first paper describing one part of this research will appear shortly in the *American Journal of Orthopsychiatry*.

pist-patient relations and particularly of therapist-child relations. But matters become much more complex as we realize that life for the staff of a treatment institution such as ours is life in a goldfish bowl. Workers are under the children's persistent and very sensitive scrutiny. It would never do to encourage the children to live by one set of mores while the staff abides by quite a different set.[2] In general, the staff is forced to live in line with a much more exacting and honest morality than is required by society.

Some problems of staff selection and work assignment were touched upon in the first volume—for example, I mentioned that in a treatment institution such as the School the particular talents and idiosyncrasies, emotional assets and even emotional problems of a staff member must be matched with the treatment needs of a particular child. This is necessary for the child's benefit above all, but is often to the advantage of the worker as well. In the present volume I am able to elaborate on this somewhat, since the children's histories would be incomplete without any comment on why a particular staff member wished to work with the child whose case is presented, and was able to do so successfully.

In *Love Is Not Enough* I tried to suggest how the School's philosophy is put into action primarily by using examples of events in the lives of the children. Similarly, in the coming book devoted to the staff and to the School as a social organism, it will be necessary to refer again and again to experiences with particular children as they touch upon and illuminate problems of staff training, attitudes, and integration. Thus, in all three volumes, the children will occupy the center of attention. This is as it should be. The universe of the School was created and continues to exist for them.

This concentration on the children is most conspicuous, however, in the present book. The stories of these four children can only roughly illustrate the nature and scope of our work but it is hoped that they will show how the rehabilitation of severely disturbed children proceeds at the School. Each history speaks for itself alone and sheds light on others only by implication. This is necessarily true, since in this institution we try, as far as humanly possible, to gear all efforts to the specific requirements of each child, to the peculiarities presented by his individual disturbance and emerging personality. We try to meet, not his general needs, but always the needs of the particular moment, situation, and personal relation.

---

2. For a first and tentative discussion of the way certain mores of our society impinge on the development of mental health, see the author's "Mental Health and Current Mores," *The American Journal of Orthopsychiatry*, XXII (1952), 76-88.

One way to present a picture of our work as reflected in the children's lives with us would be to describe a great many children. Another way would be to devote an entire book to one child—to show in minute detail how his rehabilitation proceeded and what experiences influenced the unfolding of his new personality.

To present a complete account of just one case would not be possible even if the whole book were devoted to it. In addition, using a single history might suggest that we had arbitrarily selected a particularly successful case or one making a special point in favor of our theories and methods. The reader might even suppose that we work with only one type of disturbance.

On the other hand, to present a great many cases would permit only a brief account of any one child's life with us. My own reaction to the relatively short case studies that are so abundant in the clinical literature speaks out against this procedure. The picture afforded by such brief descriptions of an individual and his treatment, the interpretations of the causes and development of his disturbance, often seem to be superficial. Events are presented either in isolation or in what appears to be arbitrary juxtaposition. The critical reader is not convinced that the author has made the correct or the only possible interpretation of complex life experiences that extended over or were separated by weeks—perhaps years. Without adequate data from which to form an independent judgment, the reader finds it possible to believe that the author may have selected for presentation only those aspects of his work that fitted the points he wanted to make. Material contradicting his theses or suggesting entirely different interpretations may have existed but had been unnoticed or unreported.

On the whole, I have felt convinced of the validity of case histories and their authors' conclusions only where so many potentially verifiable data were presented that the individual came alive in my imagination as a three-dimensional person, moving in time and space. In these rare instances I felt that I knew much more than was actually stated. The patient became a human being, not merely a case. I did not feel entirely at the author's mercy in arriving at an understanding of his subject, but could ask myself whether his discussion of the patient's development in treatment seemed to follow the intrinsic logic of the total personality I had captured in my imagination. If the author's actions and reasoning were suited to what I believed this inherent logic to be, I felt that his statements must be correct; I did not have to accept them on faith.

Others must have similar reactions. The danger of distortion and biased interpretation in presenting clinical material has been recognized and has led to efforts to assemble complete case records, by making electrical transcriptions of all interactions or by other means. But when large quantities of data are presented in their entirety, the individual often gets buried under a mass of detail, which all the reader's empathy cannot weave into a consistent picture of a human being.

The end result of presenting too few and too many data thus is the same. The reader, confronted with a task beyond the ability of his creative imagination, gives up, and accepts or rejects the author and his thesis without adequate grounds for either reaction: in one instance because he has learned too little about the person whose development and treatment he is supposed to understand, and in the other because the overabundance of detail has destroyed his potentiality for spontaneous empathy. In neither case can the reader critically evaluate the author's assertions by testing them against what seems to him to be the essential logic of the case.

These considerations explain why several long, though not exhaustively complete, case histories are presented in this book. For a description of the data on which these histories are based and a further discussion of the problems encountered in writing case histories see pages 473 to 478 in the Appendix.

Once the decision was reached to present a few long histories, the difficult problem arose of selecting the children who should represent the School's work when many had been in the center of our lives for long periods of time. Among the motives for the final choice was the hope that these histories would help to answer the question asked by many readers of *Love Is Not Enough*: How lasting are the School's successes? Despite the best intentions of answering this legitimate question, I cannot do so satisfactorily at this moment. These few cases provide only a stopgap answer.

The reason why a direct and clear-cut reply to this query is not possible at present is that up to the Fall of 1944, when I joined the School's staff as principal, the School had been conducted on the basis of an entirely different philosophy, had applied different methods, and served different types of children. The ten-year period that has passed since then may seem a long time in our fast-living, fast-changing age, but it is not a long time in which to rehabilitate these very disturbed youngsters or assess the permanent outcome of our work. It took some time to assemble staff members able and ready to embark on the difficult venture of reorganizing the School along radically new lines. The staff had to be introduced to the new philosophy and trained to put it in action; they had then to experiment with creating the physical and psychological setting necessary for implementing that philosophy. We all had to learn, and did learn a great deal, from our early years of trial and error. Almost three years went by before we achieved even tentatively the feeling that we had sufficiently tested and improved our ideas, and were putting them into practice. Hence we feel that the School has actually been operating within the framework of its present philosophy only since the second half of 1947.

Children need to remain at the School for three or four years, or longer, before we can consider them rehabilitated. Those who left the School before 1950 had not lived long enough under the impact of our philosophy and the influence of our methods to make their histories useful in illustrating the School's work. Therefore, I wished to present case histories of only those children who were exposed for this minimum of three years to what we considered our full efforts. Some of these children were with us while we were reorganizing the School; but all of them benefited for some three years from what we then viewed as the best we knew about rehabilitation and were able to put into practice.

We have learned a great deal since 1947, and can now serve our children much better. We have a larger and more adequately trained staff as well as a much improved physical plant.[3] Thus children who have left us more recently would serve as better examples of the results of our present efforts. Even their histories, however, would not show the School as we would like it to be. We shall never be wholly satisfied with the School and its work, since our idea of perfection and our wish to help the children always surpass our ability to achieve.

Had I chosen to report our most obvious if not most dramatic successes, I might have selected other case histories. For example, two children, a boy and a girl, came to us after prolonged child psychiatric treatment in one case and psychoanalytic treatment in the other had failed to produce positive results. These children were schizophrenic—one of them had been diagnosed repeatedly as an untreatable, hopeless case. They were complete failures in school, home, and life. The girl, at the age of nine, was unable even to walk or to talk rationally. Later we realized that all her mental activity had been concentrated on wild delusions of grandeur, which compensated for her feelings of deep deprivation and utter despair. The boy, aged ten, had all-pervasive delusions of persecution. While

---

3. Our old buildings were modernized in 1952 and a new dormitory wing was erected, which permits smaller and better groupings in much larger dormitories, gives the children and us ample and comfortable living space, and in many other ways facilitates our work.

the girl could hardly move, he was so hyperactive that he could not
sit still even for a minute. He constantly jumped up and down excitedly, hitting himself and wildly grimacing.

Both remained with us for nearly six years. During this time
they had to face several difficult problems from which we could
not entirely shield them, since their families were involved. The
mother of one had to be committed to an institution twice because
of acute and dangerous paranoiac breakdowns, and this child had
to master, in addition, the anxieties produced by the mother's marked
personality changes after shock treatment.

They made exceedingly slow progress at first, as is often the case
with very disturbed children. Little real integration took place during their first two or three years with us. Then in the fourth year
they began to make excellent progress in integration, which continued with ever-increasing vigor. In their last two years they attended an outside high school (while continuing to live at our
School) and, after initial difficulties of adjustment, did very well
there. They left us in the middle of 1952. Since then they have
graduated from high school with very good academic and social
records and have entered one of our greatest universities, which
they are continuing to attend. There they compare well in integration with the average youngster of their age group, more than holding their own in the company of those who never seemed to need
help with emotional difficulties.

I did not select their case histories for inclusion here because
my purpose is not to demonstrate the optimum that can be achieved
for very disturbed children. I hoped, rather, by means of an unselected sample (except that I have not chosen to use histories of
children who have left the School only recently) to show what can
be done on the average. Since our philosophy has not changed
essentially since 1947, it seemed suitable to present the histories
of the first group that left the School after our basic principles had
been in operation for a considerable period. I decided, therefore,
to devote this volume to *all* children who left the School during
the second half of 1950. This decision prevented our selecting successfully treated cases or disregarding others that were only moderately successful.

Most of the histories (with the exception of parts of Harry's)
were written in 1952 and 1953, and brought up-to-date regarding
the children's present stage of development in the Spring of 1954.
How the children have fared during the first three years after leaving us has been briefly related. Although these histories do not
necessarily illustrate most effectively our thinking on re-education

and therapy, they do show what the results have been during the longest follow-up period now available for study.

Our enrollment turnover is limited by the long duration of the rehabilitation period and by the School's restricted capacity (thirty-four children before the new building was completed in 1952, and forty on the average since then). For this reason, only four children left the School during the half-year period. Yet any selection of a small, continuous series out of a larger continuum should be as representative as any other; so the children who left the School during the last six months of 1950 may be considered representative of the types of children with whom we work. We shall call them Paul, Mary, John and Harry.

Diverse as these four children are, they represent only a good cross section of the wide variety of disturbances with which we deal; they are by no means completely representative. This book should permit the reader to form an opinion of the nature of the problems that confront us and of the way we try to meet them, but the histories exemplify rather than fully describe our work. Considering the scarcity of clinical case material on children with severe emotional disturbances, it is hoped that the histories will have the additional merit of illustrating particular aspects of the rehabilitation of such children.

On the basis of some diagnostic and many important structural considerations, most of our children can be classified as schizophrenic. But on the basis of the presenting symptomatology and more traditional classifications, many children are referred to the School because they are considered delinquent or otherwise unmanageable. Some have severe motor or intellectual blocks, and many function on a level akin to feeble-mindedness. Others suffer from severe psychosomatic disturbances, or from what Kanner[4] has described as infantile autism. Many children present personality pictures similar to those of severe character neuroses; and we have also worked with transvestites, fire setters, and so forth. More information about the nature of the disturbances of all our children is to be found in the Appendix on pages 495 to 499.

The four cases presented here offer a sampling of this variety, though they all, to a marked degree, showed schizophrenic symptoms also. When they were referred to the School, one of them was definitely considered a delinquent (Harry), another psychosomatic (John), a third showed an "institutional" psychosis (Paul), and the fourth was repeatedly diagnosed as schizophrenic (Mary).

---

4. L. Kanner, "Autistic Disturbances of Affective Contact," *The Nervous Child,* II (1943), 217-250.

To those interested mainly in the study of girls, this may seem to be an unfair selection. The fact that three of the four children are boys is not due simply to chance factors at work in this particular series. Until very recently the arrangement of our dormitory building (together with a few technical reasons, none of any intrinsic importance) forced upon us, much against our wish, a boy-girl ratio of approximately three and a half to one. This undesirable situation was corrected in 1952 with the erection of a new dormitory building. Since then the ratio has been more equal.

John is unique in this group in that he is the only child who had come to the School before I was appointed to its staff and began its reorganization. Harry's history also differs from the rest in that I began writing it while he still lived with us, and it has been published previously in part.[5]

Residential Treatment and Therapeutic Success

THE FOUR CHILDREN who left the School in the second half of 1950 and who are described in this book do not represent what we should now consider outstanding results of our efforts. As a matter of fact, we should have preferred to continue our work with two of them for at least another year. The final outcome, we believe, would have been considerably better if we had been permitted to do so. However, in this sense, too, this group is typical, since our experience has been that only about two-thirds of our children remain with us as long as we feel is necessary for their full rehabilitation or for approaching this goal as closely as their natural endowment, the original difficulty, and our methods permit.

Also, not all children, on leaving us, return immediately to their families or to a "normal" home; only about one-third to one-half of our children do so. The rest, while well able to live outside a very special institution, are not yet ready to return to the environment in which the original traumatization took place. These children may spend a year or two in boarding schools before they are ready to return to their families. In this respect also the group of four is typical. Two of the children (Harry and John) returned to their families. The other two went to special homes, which might be likened to special boarding schools, because they had no families: one of them (Mary) was an orphan; the other (Paul) had lost his father in infancy and his mother was not able to offer him a home.

---

5. B. Bettelheim, "Harry—A Study in Rehabilitation," *The Journal of Abnormal and Social Psychology*, XLIV (1949), 231-265.

In evaluating their gains at the School, it is well to remember that the adjustments these children must make on returning to their families, or on going to a new home, are tremendous. Their return cannot be likened to the homecoming of a child who has been away at camp, on a long vacation, or in a boarding school. The child who leaves the School is a child who once had totally failed in life and who now returns home as a radically different person. He may have been able to explore his ability to live at home during visits, which in his last years with us may have become more frequent and extended. But both parents and child can "take" a lot on a visit. While visiting during the first or second year of his stay with us, the child and the parents tend to test one another. Thereafter, they put their best foot forward. The difference, however, between such visits and the permanent return home is similar to that between courtship and marriage—everyone concerned knows that the new living arrangement is permanent.

As to the child who does not go back to living at home (often because he has none), not even long visits can prepare him adequately for what is to come. Disappointment at not having a home— though we do all we can to help him with his feelings about having no parents or about his parents' inability to create a suitable home —is again most keenly experienced. After all, he feels, he has done everything he can to rehabilitate himself. Unconsciously he clings to a hope that the reward for his efforts will be a good father and mother. Our experience suggests that before the end of adolescence no child can really or fully accept having to live without a home and family of his own. This deprivation strikes him very acutely when he leaves the School for boarding school or foster home and adds to his emotional strain as he ventures out into the world.

But it is not only returning to their parents or facing once more the fact that they have none that places our children under great stress when they leave, making their first months in society a severe trial of their newly acquired integration. Children who come to the Orthogenic School have failed not merely to learn to live in a home or with their parents. They have failed completely at life itself. Other means of treatment have not helped them. If they could have profited from out-patient treatment, such as is offered by child guidance clinics or ambulatory child psychiatric or child psychoanalytic practice, they would not have been candidates for the School. We concentrate solely on children who need twenty-four-hour-a-day institutional care. It is easy, therefore, to understand their anxiety about whether they can now master a life that had previously proved to be too much for them. Entering life in the outside world is for them the supreme test. Though it is a great challenge, it also places a terrible strain on their energies. The tasks confronting these children in their readjustment to the world must be viewed in this perspective. It is a difficult and anxiety-loaded adjustment, which might prove overtaxing even for a "normal" child. We feel pleased that, even with these handicaps, nearly all our children (except, of course, those whom we have to send back to their parents prematurely because they are beyond our ability to help) master successfully a new way of life.

The experiences of the four children whose lives at the School are described in this book illustrate these points. Life after leaving us was easy for none of them. In at least one case (Harry's) it was so difficult that it might well have broken even a normal child. In this sense these four children are not representative—fortunately, most of our children meet much less complex and detrimental life settings when they leave the School. We can never depend, however, on life to be extremely favorable for our children. At best, the parents—though making conscious and valiant efforts to be good parents—will probably still be difficult people to live with. At worst, the parents' neuroses will lead them to repeat mistakes similar to those that originally caused or aggravated their child's difficulties. (Fortunately the effect on the child will be very different since he is no longer so vulnerable, but is older, better integrated, and prepared to defend himself against the impact of the parents' neuroses.) Though it may make the parents happy to have their child home again and to see him do well, the great hurt caused them by the fact that their child once needed the School will not have disappeared entirely. On the other hand, if a child does not immediately return to his family, either because a period of boarding school placement is indicated or because the family is not intact, he will suffer from the emotional difficulties experienced by all children who cannot live "normal" lives with their parents.

Given these and many other potentially negative factors, our aim must be to strengthen the child to such a degree that he is able, by himself, to master adverse circumstances with relative success. Technically speaking, we must realize that the "substructure" of the child's personality will always remain weak. The foundation for his personality development was laid in infancy and early childhood. We may be able to strengthen it here and there, to buttress it, so to speak, but we cannot give the child a new substructure. On this basically weak and only partly "remodeled" foundation, we must try to help the child develop sufficient ego strength and personality integration to enable his limited inner resources to carry him along, even if external conditions fail him.

This does not mean that we can hope that these children will always succeed. Whether their integration will be maintained and strengthened depends on how traumatic or benign their later life experiences prove to be. Over these we can exercise relatively little influence beyond planning the next steps of each child's life with his parents or guardians. But the children should retain much of what they acquired during their years at the School, although how much they retain will depend on how far the conditions of their lives permit the treatment results to mature. So far as we are able to judge at this time, and as, for example, Harry's recent life history illustrates, such a maturing has generally taken place.

How these four children who are described in this volume got along in the outside world during a period of slightly more than three years is, of course, no measure of the permanency of their rehabilitation. It is not yet possible to say how well they will retain the gains made at the School, or whether the improvement will last a lifetime. At present it seems more important to find out whether these youngsters, after some initial loss on leaving us, have continued to make progress independently. We feel, for example, that their ability to do well in this respect, even though at least three of them have had to live under unusually adverse circumstances, is a good measure of the School's success.

In any case, the success or failure of our treatment methods must be evaluated in the light of the fact that we work with the most disturbed children—children who from an early age have been totally unable to function in society. Our success, therefore, must be gauged mainly by comparing the child's state of integration on leaving the School with the integration he displayed when he entered. We can be satisfied if the children who are successfully rehabilitated at the School do as well, later in life, as the average population.

The question of the School's therapeutic success must be viewed also within a larger frame of reference—that of the success of psychotherapy in general. It has been stated that, despite the abundance of psychoanalytic publications, "practically no articles have been devoted to the results of psychoanalytic treatment."[6] Also: "The efficacy of the treatment of mental conditions is more difficult to estimate because we are confronted with a great number of im-

---

6. C. P. Oberndorf, "Unsatisfactory Results of Psychoanalytic Therapy," *The Psychoanalytic Quarterly*, XIX (1950), 394.

ponderables both in the patient and in changing external conditions which may profoundly affect the outcome."[7]

These comments relate to psychoanalysis, the best known and presently most widely applied method of psychotherapy, which serves mainly persons who are much less severely disturbed than our children. Furthermore, most psychoanalytic patients are adults, who enjoy relatively great freedom to change their external environment. How much more difficult it is, then, to evaluate the success of treatment in children, who are infinitely more vulnerable than grown-ups to the effects of their environment. Statistical data will hardly suffice for such an evaluation. "The statistical approach to this challenging problem does not seem likely to yield constructive information. The variables in all cases are so numerous and multiform that mathematics alone is not enough and is not only unlikely to give clues as to causes but may be actually misleading."[8]

I do not share this pessimistic outlook, but it is true that at this moment statistical analysis is not sufficiently refined to shed much light on questions of treatment success. The first step toward objective analysis of the results of psychotherapy would be to separate and clearly define the essential factors that would form the basis of a statistical analysis and lead to the development of appropriate statistical methods. Until, for example, the constituent processes of intelligence had been analyzed (processes such as memory, recognition of similarities, problem solving, etc.) and significant factors of social environment considered, no representative samples could be selected for measuring intelligence, or statistical analyses applied for establishing norms and degrees of deviation. While we have many treatises analyzing the processes that make for emotional disturbances, and a few that describe or distinguish significant phenomena observable during the process of therapy, hardly any studies are available that provide the raw material for a significant statistical study of success in psychotherapy.

This being so for psychoanalysis—which has a vast literature, a history of half a century of practice and research, and is a widely practiced discipline with several hundred practitioners—I hope my readers will not expect me to submit conclusive statistical data on the success of our treatment methods at the School. Residential treatment of children is practiced by so few, and some of the most significant experiments in this form of therapy (such as Aichhorn's in Vienna and Redl's in Detroit) have been so short-lived, that little

---

7. *Ibid.*, p. 395.
8. *Ibid.*, p. 406.

knowledge about results is thus far available. We must be satisfied for the moment with our subjective impressions of treatment success. Even this kind of appraisal seems significant to those of us who have seen a child of eight or ten who rarely spoke at all and never in comprehensible sentences, who appeared and was diagnosed as hopelessly feeble-minded, slowly acquire the ability to speak, play, learn, and eventually live a normal life. Those who have been able to participate directly in the unfolding of an integrated personality where formerly there was none, who have helped to liberate a mind so frozen it seemed not to exist—those who have watched closely the emergence of human relations, positive emotions, and enjoyment of life where before there was nothing but defiant or hopeless isolation, hatred, angry anxiety, or homicidal violence—will experience a greater conviction about the efficacy of our methods than could be derived from any statistical treatment.

Persons who cannot observe the children and their development may find useful information in the following table, which sets forth tentatively our achievements and failures. During the five academic years from 1948 until 1953 a total of thirty-one children who had been living with us for more than twelve months left the School. (During these years we enrolled for short periods of three to twelve months four children whom we considered doubtful treatment risks, in order to decide with more certainty whether our pessimism was justified. These four are not included in the table, since we became convinced that we could not rehabilitate them and returned them to their parents within less than a year's time.) As the table shows, we feel that half the children with whom we worked for more than a year left us fully rehabilitated. This opinion is based both on our impression when they left and on what we have been able to learn about their later adjustment. In addition, there were six children whose progress justified the hope that eventually they could have achieved full recovery. But since they left the School —either against our advice or because of the age limit—before they had been with us long enough to be fully rehabilitated, they have to be listed only as much improved. All six maintained or continued their improvement after leaving us.

I should much prefer that the reader base his evaluation of the School's work on *Love Is Not Enough* and on the case histories in this book rather than on these figures and general remarks about treatment success. The two volumes should permit him to form his own opinion about the results of our efforts. As mentioned above, we do not consider the four cases reported here illustrative of our more spectacular successes. We believe that we could have done

e, and not only the staff, but also quite a few of the older children
o are well ahead in their rehabilitation, take advantage of what
campus has to offer. Most of us who work at the School are very
ch a part of campus life, be it as graduate students, as members of
University's research staff, or as faculty members. The School
its staff not only benefit from, but also contribute to, University
and take a vital interest in it.10

The School is located directly on the east end of the main campus,
is, close to the large recreational area of Jackson Park and within
walking distance of its bathing beaches on Lake Michigan and its
eum of Science and Industry. Only two short blocks away is the
st Illinois Central station, from which fast electric trains take us
elve minutes to the Loop, the center of the city. Directly in front
e School is the wide park area of the Midway. The children have
to step out the front door, cross a relatively narrow street, and
re on a lawn one block wide and a mile long. In warm weather
are played there; in winter, part of this area is flooded and used
-skating. Across the Midway and slightly to the east is the Inter-
al House, directly across is Sunny Gymnasium, and slightly to
st are the Educational Quadrangle and the University High
All of these are familiar places to the children and, in part,
eir purposes. In the International House is a barber and beauty
hich they use; they go twice a week to the Sunny Gymnasium
r swimming; and a few children go to the University High
during the transitional period when they are ready to attend a
rapeutic day school but are not yet ready to leave permanently
ection of the Orthogenic School.

main activities are carried on within three buildings and three
playgrounds. The three buildings originally formed the head-
of the Universalist Church. The Church proper and the con-
creation and library buildings now serve as class and play
ooms. In addition, they contain an art and craft shop, a large
mnasium, and, under the big nave, a basement, which has
ted for use as a rumpus room with billiards and ping-pong
ball machines, shuffleboard courts, etc. During bad weather
is also used for roller skating and tricycle riding. Active
h as basketball, are played either in the gymnasium or on

ot by chance that of the seven staff members who, during the last few
arried while working at the School, three married graduate students,
graduate student, and two faculty members, while only one married,
iversity, his former college sweetheart. Three of the seven continued
School after their marriage.

TABLE I—

Success of Treatment

	Number	Per Cent
REHABILITATED		
Children rehabilitated on leaving the School. These children are presently doing well in life	15	48
MUCH IMPROVED		
Children withdrawn prematurely and against advice. We felt that continuation of our work would have led to their full rehabilitation. Their improvement has been either maintained or advanced since they left	3	
Children who left because of age limit (15). Full rehabilitation could have been achieved had the children come to us earlier. Improvement has been either maintained or advanced since they left	3	
Children who left because continued residence did not promise much further improvement. Improvement has been maintained, and the children function relatively well though with some difficulty	2	
Children who were much improved on leaving but whose improvement has not been fully maintained because of deleterious external circumstances	3	
TOTAL MUCH IMPROVED	11	35
SOMEWHAT IMPROVED		
Children who were improved but not enough to warrant hope for adequacy in society. Improvement fully or partly maintained to present	3	10
NO LASTING IMPROVEMENT		
These two children improved while with us to such a degree that they were able to maintain themselves in one case for two, in the other for three years within society. On their leaving, however, we feared that they would not be able to maintain permanently what seemed only very tenuous and inadequate integration. This fear turned out to be justified	2	7
TOTAL	31	100

considerably more for each of these children if they had remained with us longer, and only two of them, Harry and Paul, are listed in the category "fully rehabilitated." John is listed among those who left the School much improved though not fully rehabilitated; in his case we felt that further residential treatment did not promise much greater or faster improvement than out-patient therapy while living at home. Mary is listed among those who left because of age, and were considered much improved but not yet fully rehabilitated. These four examples help to illustrate the degree of treatment success indicated by the categories.

When thinking of emotionally disturbed children, the pertinent question of the relation of the origin of their disturbances to their parents invariably comes to mind. The parents of our children are certainly a fascinating topic for discussion. But this subject is relegated to the Appendix (pages 478 to 492) since this volume is devoted to only four of our children, rather than to all of them. For the same reason some general remarks on all our children are also placed toward the book's end (see Appendix, pages 495 to 503).

In following the histories of the four children, some readers may find it useful to know a little more about the School, its physical setting, and its philosophy. To help them place what happened to the children into the setting in which it occurred, a short discussion of the School is presented in the next chapter.

The School

ANY ATTEMPT to portray an institution merely a static enumeration of buildir devoid of life. Therefore, in describing be overstressed that it is the eternal acterizes a truly human institution, p dren. Any description fails that doe continuous movement and pulsating li

Physical Setting

THE IMPORTANCE of the fact that t of Chicago can hardly be overestir briefly why this is important for th repeat it here. But I should like for the staff. The University offer congenial social contacts and ir are very important as correlate entailed by working at the Scho other aspects of campus life are

9. See *Love Is Not Enough*, pp. 28

the outdoor playing fields. Two of the playgrounds are enclosed by School buildings, while the third, the largest, is across a side street.[11] Each playground is a different size, which provides the large area that some children need for running as well as the more confined area within which others feel safe. Having three playgrounds also permits smaller and more congenial group formations, avoids contagion among the children, and makes it easier for us to give individual attention to each child. Our playgrounds are equipped for such grown-up activities as tennis, baseball, or basketball. But there are also swings, seesaws, sand boxes, a milk wagon, and other equipment used by children of all ages. In addition, there is a small garden on the grounds, where the children may grow flowers or vegetables if they so desire.

Particularly, the main, or dormitory, building is "home" to the School's forty children and some fourteen staff members. Originally it served as the minister's house and as a seminary, later being adapted for the School's purposes. To it was added in 1952 a new dormitory building, which was integrated with the old one so as to form a large unit that still retains the look and feel of a private home. This addition to the main building contains as its most important feature six large dormitories, three on each of the first two floors. Each dormitory is large enough for six or seven children, and is equipped with its own separate bathroom and storage space. Adjacent to the three dormitories on the first floor is a counselor's room, which is a self-contained living unit with private bathroom. Another living unit on this floor is for the counselor on night duty. On the second floor are two similar units. Thus on each floor two adults live and sleep in immediate proximity to the three dormitories. Of course, the rest of the counselors, altogether fourteen, who live in the house are also within easy reach, but their living quarters are several yards away, in the older part of the building.

The photographs of dormitory situations in *Love Is Not Enough* were intended to help the reader form ideas about the School. But these pictures are no longer completely valid since the erection of the new, much more spacious dormitory wing.[12] Among the changes made possible by the new building was the elimination of double-decker beds, which we never liked but which were necessary then to permit sufficient floor space for playing. Now we have single beds, more individual furniture, and freedom to arrange it as the children like—with still more space for playing than before. The new bathrooms are also

11. The approximate size and location of the buildings and playgrounds may be seen from the map on p. 20.
12. Specifically, Plates 1, 5, 6, 13, 14, 15 and 16 are no longer valid.

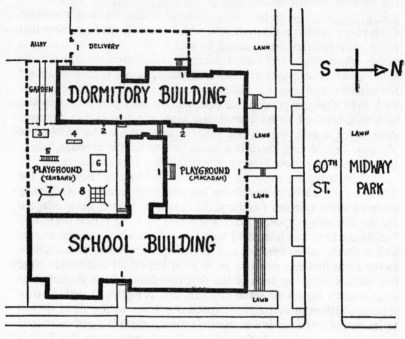

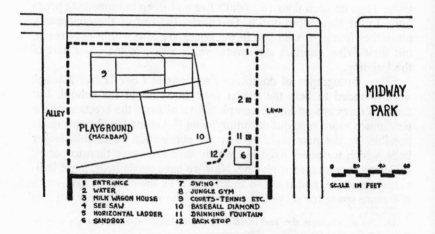

1 ENTRANCE	7 SWING
2 WATER	8 JUNGLE GYM
3 MILK WAGON HOUSE	9 COURTS-TENNIS ETC.
4 SEE SAW	10 BASEBALL DIAMOND
5 HORIZONTAL LADDER	11 DRINKING FOUNTAIN
6 SANDBOX	12 BACK STOP

ORTHOGENIC SCHOOL

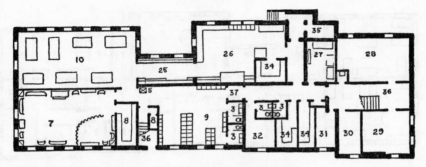

ENGLISH BASEMENT

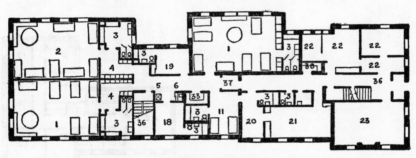

FIRST FLOOR

NUMERICAL IDENTIFICATION FOR DRAWINGS OF SCHOOL BUILDING INTERIORS pp. 21-23

1. Girl's Dorm
2. Boy's Dorm
3. Bathroom
4. Lockers
5. Water Fountain
6. Kitchenette
7. Playroom
8. Toy Closet
9. Locker Room
10. Dining Room
11. Sick Room
12. Schoolroom
13. Play Session Room
14. Craft Shop
15. Wood Shop
16. Rumpus Room
17. Gymnasium
18. Night Counselor
19. Staff Bedroom
20. Medical Room

21. Staff Living Room and Library
22. Office
23. Living Room
24. Dictation Room
25. Pantry
26. Kitchen
27. Laundry
28. Utilities
29. Janitor
30. Seamstress
31. Dietician
32. Maid and Cook Rest-room
33. Laundry Cupboard
34. Storage
35. Garbage
36. Stairhall
37. Fire Vestibule
38. Mail Room

SCALE IN FEET

DORMITORY BUILDING

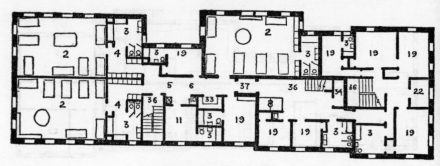

SECOND FLOOR

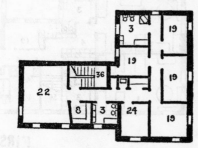

THIRD FLOOR

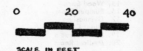

SCALE IN FEET

DORMITORY BUILDING

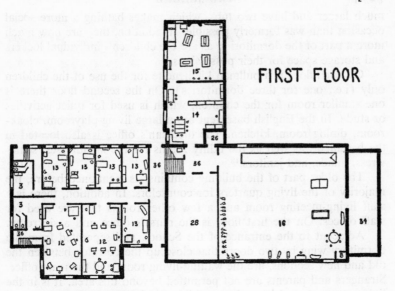

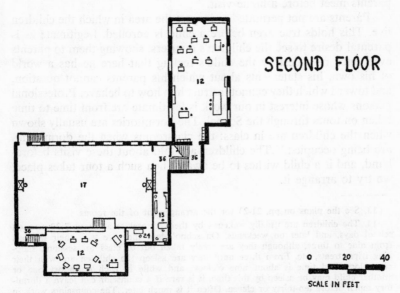

much larger and have two tubs, which makes bathing a more social occasion than was formerly possible. In addition, they are now much more a part of the dormitories, as are the children's individual lockers and storage space for their possessions.

On each floor is a pullman kitchenette for the use of the children only (i.e., one for three dormitories). On the second floor there is one smaller room for the children, which is used for quiet activities or study. In the English basement are a large living-playroom, cloakroom, dining room, kitchen. The dietician's office is also located in the basement, as well as the utility rooms for the laundresses, seamstress, maids, and janitors.[13]

The older part of the building contains, as mentioned before, the majority of the living quarters for counselors. In addition, there is a staff living-meeting room and a few other rooms that are used for staff offices. On the first floor is the nurse's office and a sickroom.

Adjacent to the entrance of the School, and separated from the dormitory wing by two doors that close up the corridor between the old and new sections, are the waiting-living room and the main office. Strangers and parents are not permitted beyond this area. It is in the living room that visits with the children take place or children and parents meet before a home visit.

Parents are not permitted to inspect the area in which the children live. This holds true even before a child is enrolled. Legitimate as is parental desire to see the children's quarters, showing them to parents even once may destroy the child's feeling that here he has a world of his own, his statements about which his parents cannot question, and toward which they cannot instruct him how to behave. Professional persons whose interest in our work is legitimate are from time to time taken on tours through the School. The dormitories are usually shown when the children are in class; the classrooms when the dormitories are being occupied.[14] The children are told about these visits beforehand, and if a child wishes to be away when such a tour takes place, we try to arrange it.

---

13. See the plans on pp. 21-23 for the arrangement of the rooms.

14. The children are usually wakened by their counselors at about 7:30 A.M. on school days, and later on weekends. On school days they are with their teachers from nine to three, although they are freely taken out of class for sessions, shopping trips, treats, etc. From three until they are asleep the children are with their counselors. Bed time is about nine o'clock, and while in each dormitory one or another child may be asleep by this time, it is rare if a counselor can leave a dormitory much before ten-thirty or eleven. Often it is much later. The counselors work in turns; for the details of this arrangement, see *Love Is Not Enough*, footnote on pp. 72-73.

. . . And Life Within It

SO MUCH ABOUT the buildings and their use in general. But what about the spirit that reigns within them? To begin with, noise and movement cannot easily be described in writing. Rooms in a children's institution should not only be colorful and pleasant, but often, also, full of voices and movement. Individual expressions of personality and feeling should never be hushed or, worse, suppressed into stagnant silence; neither should they be drowned out by a chaos of noise. It must be possible at any moment for every child to express freedom and self-assertion in action and sound; but how this happens, though it constitutes the difference between good and bad institutions for children, defies description.

What is true about noise also applies to orderliness and cleanliness. We see to it that only enough of these are maintained to be fully compatible with true comfort. No child is expected to do any housework or daily chores.[15] The educational value of housework as such is questionable, and to enforce such activities is not worth the price of disturbing the relations between counselors and children. Rationalizations about the value of housework in building character or in education do not change the stultifying or obsessional propensities of routine tasks, and children know well whether they are asked to do chores because it helps them or because it makes running the institution less expensive or simpler for the staff. Actually, they resent nothing more than to be sold "a bill of goods" about how good it is for them to work around the house. "Working around the house" does not make children attached to it. Yet because the children at the School are never forced to do such chores, at a certain point in their rehabilitation some children develop proprietary feelings about the School and then like to perform a few household tasks. This is an entirely different matter. Just because we never force them to work, we always have many volunteers in an emergency—for instance, if a heavy snowfall occurs on Sunday when our janitors are off duty.

On the other hand, when a child who, we feel, can well control his actions deliberately and spitefully spills liquids, for example, on the dining room floor, it may be more therapeutic to request him to help clean up the mess than to overlook it or clean it up for him. On the other hand, if a child who cannot yet express his hos-

---

15. All housecleaning, making of beds, and straightening up of rooms is done by the janitors and maids, and all cooking and serving of meals by the kitchen staff.

tility and anxiety in other ways in desperation throws dishes and
glasses on the floor, nothing is done about it beyond cleaning up
the mess and bringing new china and food to the table, so that the
meal can proceed with as little interruption as possible. But if we
feel that a child no longer needs such outlets, and is able to express
his emotions or do his testing of us verbally and interpersonally
rather than by destroying inanimate objects, then we will stop
him from breaking our equipment, or, if he persists, will send him
(naturally with his full fare) out of the dining room to eat by himself.

Our seeming inconsistency, which all the children can observe,
in letting some children break several dishes each meal, sometimes
for a period of months, and others none, makes them wonder. When
they are ready, they begin to think and talk about it. They find in
this experience, and in other similar ones, a demonstration of the
fact that each child is handled differently, that no child is expected
to control himself beyond his ability just for our convenience, but
that self-control and more socialized behavior will be expected of
a child once he is ready and able to exercise them.

Decisions about what we shall and shall not expect of a child
are made, not on the basis of convenience or a preconceived notion
about what is always "right," but only on the basis of what we believe is most likely to help the child. In general, negativistic behavior disappears faster when it is ignored and hence loses its
nuisance value. Once the child has learned that misbehavior does
not irritate the adult, the criticism of other children who have outgrown such conduct is usually sufficient to keep it within bounds.

Although attitudes about noise and orderliness are difficult to
describe, steering a flexible middle course among them is of great
importance in promoting the children's well-being. It is somewhat
easier to convey how finding oneself as an individual is aided when
all personal belongings are respected and no one has a right to
touch them without permission. Each child has a private living
area within his dormitory, with a chest of drawers, shelves, and
lockers all his own. Even his counselors enter this area only when
invited to do so.

The children's clothing, toys, and other very personal belongings are not put away by the maids. Such things are handled only
by a child's own counselors. Whenever feasible they are put away
in the child's presence in accordance with his suggestions. If these
belongings were handled or put away without the child's knowledge, it would tend to create fear that sometime we might not only
put away but also take away some of his possessions. In any case,

we must avoid any orderliness that might be compulsively imposed, since this would be nothing else for the child than another experience of being pushed around by adults. Our protection of the child's privacy and right to his own possessions helps him to develop a feeling of responsibility and self-respect.

Group living becomes acceptable and can contribute to the development of one's own personality only if individuality can continuously be expressed in all important activities and experiences. Therefore, the children must be able to exercise personal choice in matters influencing their lives. And given their insecurity, they feel ready to do this only if they are surrounded at all times by visible, tangible evidence of their ability to influence the physical conditions of their lives. No one can feel that he is master of his fate if he cannot decide even such simple matters as the color of his walls or the design of his curtains. As a matter of fact, only a person who is already convinced of his ego strength can afford to forego making decisions about such externals without loss of self-esteem. On the other hand, a person totally lacking in self-respect, as many of our children are, can never acquire it without being able to participate significantly in such decisions.

Care must be taken, however, that the children's decisions are not so injudicious that their execution would only demonstrate once more to the children that they are unable to become masters of themselves, that making their own decisions only tends to make their lives more undesirable. For example, we will not follow the suggestions of a group of depressive children that the walls of their dormitory be painted black. They would only suffer hardship if this were done. Therefore, we prefer to present to the children an ample variety of reasonable selections from which they can choose. As far as wall colors are concerned, for example, they may select any color except white, black, or extremely dark hues of brown; within this limitation their choice is free and will be faithfully executed by us. Since there are four walls in each dormitory there is ample space to express individuality. If the result is a different color for each wall, this adds to the gaiety of the surroundings. It is our task to see to it that the colors selected do not clash, but rather enhance the cheerful appearance of the rooms. Our stair hall, for example, is presently painted in hues of yellow, red, blue, green, and gray, with the result that what otherwise might be a boring place has been changed into one that is quite attractive and certainly lively.

Each room has different curtains, bedspreads, and furniture. When, for example, new drapes are bought for a dormitory, we present to the children living in it several reasonable patterns from which to choose. If they do not like any of these, we present another series of samples, until they find one on which they all can readily agree. Thus the children's freedom to select, though large, is limited. We find it unimportant to offer unlimited choices, which tend only to be confusing, if not outright overpowering; but it is very important to offer a relatively wide margin of reasonable choices.

The children also participate in arranging the furniture by selecting the location of their beds and chests within the dormitory. In addition, each child is entirely free to decorate, or not to decorate, his wall space. He selects the objects or pictures he wishes to put up and changes them whenever he pleases.[16] Similar freedom extends to many other situations, such as the selection of a day's menu, which is the children's prerogative at least six times every month.

For this reason, every effort is made to insure that neither the child's own private living space nor the entire dormitory building becomes impersonal or uniform. We try very hard to have each room bear the distinctive marks of the particular personalities who use it or live in it, of their interests and, when necessary, their bad taste as well. Buildings and their furnishings should fit the children and their lives, not like a spanking new but a very comfortable, old shoe, which, nevertheless, receives good care. It may not be good looking, but it has served its owner well, and by now is so easy on his foot that he does not even know he is wearing a shoe at all.

The School Becomes a Shelter

THE PHYSICAL SETTING of an institution acquires its greatest personal significance for the children only as it increasingly becomes the framework within which constructive living can proceed—the safe center of their lives, to whose security they can return from excur-

---

16. An incidental, but often significant, aid to therapy is a consequent of this freedom. Some very disturbed children first reveal what is taking place within them by tearing down pictures on their wall space, by putting out of sight or throwing away some of their personal belongings, or suddenly changing their arrangement. This is often done long before these children are able to express the emotions underlying their actions in facial expression, in play, or through words. Such changes in feelings about an object are of great value in gaining insight into what is going on in the child so that we can help him with his emotions. These actions are especially helpful in assessing the feelings of non-speaking or autistically withdrawn children. But they are also of aid in the case of children who, in less emotionally tense situations, can well express themselves. For example, one of our boys took down the pictures on his wall space and did not replace them. Only after we had told him that this suggested to us that he feared he would soon leave the School, could he speak of his feeling that nothing in his life would ever be permanent. When he realized his anxiety, he was able to understand how he suffered from depriving himself of the pleasure of arranging things to his liking when he could do so.

sions into the outside world, and within whose walls they have the
feeling that nothing really bad can happen.

To a disturbed child, any new environment is a potential danger
since he deeply fears and cannot master the unknown. He meets a
strange physical setting with all the anxious expectations derived
from his former threatening experiences and his defenses against
them. Some children, when they first come to us, are especially
fearful of the very things they later learn to cherish as protective
attributes of their new environment. The doors and fences, for
example, arouse anxiety in many children when they enter the
School. To begin with, they fear that they might be locked in. They
explore all the doors to see whether they are really always unlocked
from the inside, as they have been told. In the process of gaining
security, such concern changes characteristically: many a child who
is delighted to learn that all our doors must remain unlocked from
the inside, later becomes concerned about the possibility of unwanted
intrusion. He can feel safe from kidnappers, truant officers, policemen, and other individuals who seem dangerous to him only after
he is convinced that these doors cannot be opened from the outside against our will, and that no intruder can enter the School
without our knowledge or permission.

Soon after coming to the School, one of our children, with much
hesitation, dared to confide his fear of giants. "They are bad people,"
he said. "They have knives. They cut little boys and stick them in
the stomach." Though this anxiety remained with him for quite
some time, a few months later it had become less pressing. "We can
lock the door to our dormitory and no giant can come in." Other
children deal more directly with their concern about interference
from their parents, as did, for example, the seven-year-old boy
mentioned in *Love Is Not Enough*. His aggressive anxiety resulted
largely from his mother's excessive domination as expressed in
rigorous demands for routine physical care. He told his counselor
on his first day at the School, "You know, I love to brush my
teeth." Later he asked, "What happens around here if you don't
brush your teeth?" Assured that there would be no bad consequences, he still worried on the following day, "But my mother
might move in here with me." This fear left him only as he repeatedly
saw that no one but his own counselors and I could enter his dormitory without his permission. (Other staff members enter a dormitory only with the children's permission.)

Just as doors and fences at first give the children a sense of
restriction but eventually are seen as protections against undesirable
outsiders, so may the children object initially to window guards

and safety screens. They ask whether they are like the bars of a jail. Later, however, they enjoy their advantages: the children can play freely on the window sills without fear of accidents. Thus their rebellion against restrictions gives way, as they realize the motives for our actions, to an appreciation of the precautions we take for their safety.[17]

The freedom of the children to arrange their space in the dormitory entirely according to their own inclinations is bound by the limitations necessary for physical safety. Since our insistence on safety reassures the child that he will not lose protection when he exercises his freedom of individual expression, such restrictions as must be imposed are usually readily accepted. Sharp instruments and dangerous toys are locked up by the counselors unless the child is actually using them in the counselors' presence. But they are locked up in a special closet within the dormitory, so that they

---

17. Of course, children's statements on such matters can only be accepted with great caution. This may be illustrated by an experience I had on visiting a girls' school, which, though much advertised for its humane and progressive philosophy, was actually a glorified reformatory. What impressed me first was the huge wire fence surrounding the grounds, and I immediately asked the officials how the girls felt about it. I was told that they liked it because it protected them—with a side remark that I certainly should know that youngsters feel protected by such safety devices, since I had repeatedly made this point myself. When I asked from what dangers this fence protected the children, since the institution was located in what are commonly called the wide open spaces of the West, I was told, "Against stray horses that might wander in." A while later I asked an honor girl who took me around why there were fences and received exactly the same answer. In reply to my question about how she knew this was the purpose, she said that the girls were told that it was. I then asked her how she and the other girls would feel if a horse were to walk in, and she said that they would just love it, that she personally was crazy about horses. When I now inquired why they then needed protection against horses, she admitted that they really did not, but since they were told that this was the purpose of the fence, if she were to say otherwise she would lose her honor status.

Thus, whether a fence is experienced as protection or restriction depends not on the object itself or on how it is explained, but only on its role within the over-all structure of the institution. If, as in the girls' school, the fence is part of a system under which all doors of the cottages, with the exception of the honor cottage, are locked against anyone's leaving or entering; if there is a guard watching the only gate to the outside and the girls know that if they try to run away—"go over the fence," they call it—they will be brought back by the police, deprived of their clothes, and put for a month in solitary confinement, then efforts to explain away these security devices as protection will be experienced simply as another degradation, which makes the institution even more of a jail to them.

Things are quite different in our School. When a child climbs over the fence he is told, concernedly or laughingly, depending on the situation, that it seems strange to prefer climbing over the fence when the gate is wide open at all times; there is no need to risk hurting himself by climbing over a fence when he can walk out at any moment. After a child has repeatedly tested out the veracity of our statement that he can leave any time he wishes and is not punished when he returns, then and only then do fences, safety screens, and doors locked against the outside begin to acquire the connotations of protective rather than restraining devices.

remain easily available. This protects a child from hurting himself, and gives him a sense of security from the hostile actions of himself and of others.

The children's security is further consolidated by the simple, compact, and easily comprehensible layout of the School's physical structure. Even normal children find it difficult to integrate their opposing wishes for physical closeness and emancipated distance. For emotionally disturbed children, distance often implies an anxious or hostile defiance, an angry or depressive isolation, while closeness is merely anxious or hostile clinging. Such children have to learn to dare to experiment flexibly with these contrary inclinations in their feelings about space, before they can tackle them in personal relations. A rigidly closed institution enforces an oppressive and hence anxiety-creating confinement, which prevents any experimentation with distance. A widely dispersed, open institution permits experimentation with distance, but makes it difficult to know the security of closeness. Only a cohesive but definitely open institution permits experimentation with both. But it is much more important for our children to experiment with closeness, since what they need is to learn to seek and find security in the intimacy of human relations.

The spatial closeness of our dormitories, classrooms, recreational facilities, and offices is an important factor in the establishment of security. Cottage-type institutions with wide garden spaces between the buildings, while very pretty and possibly desirable for the normal child, create in the severely disturbed child the fear of getting lost, of losing the way, of meeting many dangers when walking from one building to the other. Our children are relieved that our buildings and playgrounds are all within easy reach. Going to the treatment or school rooms, or playing outside, becomes less disruptive because the children do not have to walk very far, cross dangerous streets, or meet strangers. Relative independence of action can thus be achieved without having to master physical distances, separation anxieties, or fear of strangers—any of which might prove overwhelming. The closeness of all facilities enables many children to make their first steps in overcoming school phobias, truancy, or consistent withdrawal from group play.

One of our children, a nine-year-old girl, had always lived in institutions. Her life had never coalesced into a unity. She had experienced only partial gratification of different functions that seemed to her to have little or nothing to do with each other. At first she saw the School in the same way: "A nursery like this is a place where you get clean clothes, where you take a nap upstairs, and where you go to a dining room to eat." Fear of distances had made her school attendance extremely irregular and she had to endure constant harping and much external pressure because of this. After a short time with us, however, she set out for her classroom on her own. The venture was successful. At that, for the first time, she made a positive comment about the School: "I like this house. You don't have to walk many blocks to school—everything is just here." For her, as for many other children, going to class was simply an aspect of being at home.[18]

Of course, such security as can be derived from buildings depends on whether they are stable and reliable. Many a child expresses his fears about this by questioning us about the School buildings' solidity. Some are concerned that part of our buildings are old and feel reassured only when we stress their soundness by demonstrating, for example, the thickness of their walls. For the well-being of a disturbed child, such immediate impressions about solidity are more essential than aesthetic considerations, which make their appeal to critical, but secure, adults. The protection offered by the building is, however, eventually experienced aesthetically by the children, who express their sense of contentment in such proprietary statements as, "Our dormitory is beautiful."

The behavior of very disturbed children shows clearly how they find their asylum in the School's physical security. For some time after they first come to us, the most disturbed children will play crouched in a corner, covered by blankets, or otherwise protected and enclosed. They actually hug the walls; they like to sit or lie on the floor. It is as if they press against the wall or the floor in order to gain support in withstanding the stresses of life. Only later does the counselor's lap become their refuge.

Other children float around vaguely for days or months before they settle on the first object of attachment. This is usually their bed—the only space they have mastered and within which they feel a minimum of security. There they keep, day and night, all their possessions, in order to be able to find them readily without having to venture into the dangerous world beyond. Only later can they

18. Young children have a difficult time feeling secure in an unfamiliar setting. Particularly when mastery of a difficult task, such as learning, is required of them, they should not also be expected to master an unfamiliar setting. In some cities, a shortage of school buildings led to the use of private homes as temporary classrooms for primary grades. First and second graders adjusted much more easily to classroom routine in these familiar settings and enjoyed going to school much more. The teachers found that teaching was much easier. Though the layout of the houses created handicaps for normal classroom procedures, these shortcomings hardly mattered when compared with the much greater ease of learning that was made possible by familiar surroundings.

include the space around the bed in their ventures: their dormitory, its equipment, and finally the School as a whole. From this point on, the children are rarely destructive of our furniture and equipment because they recognize its serviceable or protective functions.

In their initial quest for security, our children thus spontaneously re-enact the most primitive experiences of infants. Infants normally make their first attempts at growth and mastery within the well-known physical setting of their cribs. Only after they have mastered getting about in the crib are they ready to master the play pen. Our children recapitulate those infantile experiences in which the baby derives security from the firm support of his crib, from being held safely in his mother's arms, and even from the floor itself, which protects him from the primitive fear of falling as he begins to move about by crawling rather than walking. The children seem to need to recapture this sequence of experiences in order to achieve growth within the safe, stable, clearly understandable and unchangeable space of the School.

Darkness and light are also of paramount importance in the development of our children's feelings of security, just as they are for the infant. During periods of sleep, the infant experiences his first separation from the mother, which is bearable to him only if his cry brings her presence and a consequent relief from tension. As she appears when needed during the night, the infant learns to expect with certainty her reappearance in the morning, and thus becomes more able to relinquish her for longer spans of time during the night. When there is an increase in tension, such as during teething, physical illness, or changes in the physical and personal structure of his environment, the infant's need for the mother's presence at night increases.

Similarly, disturbed children, who are chronically under the pressure of fearful expectations, become more tense at night. If they have not yet learned to trust those on whom they depend, they are particularly vulnerable to anything that further weakens their tenuous security. To such children the darkness of night is a constant threat. It deprives them of the visible presence of protective figures and known, safe objects at a period in their lives when they still need such tangible proofs of security. They cannot see whether an imagined, threatening figure is actually approaching. They feel deserted, and the pressure of their anger, as well as their longing wishes, adds to their sense of isolation. This arouses the fear of being separated from human contact, which is heightened in the dark. Many children struggle to keep awake because they cannot tolerate the threat of loss of contact, which for them starts with experiencing darkness. Darkness means helpless abandonment to their own hostile tendencies, which many a child can hold in check only in the immediate presence of protective figures who visibly demonstrate to him that his angry feelings do not lead to actual destruction.

All this is at least reduced when there is always sufficient light to see that nothing has been changed since daytime, and that one can easily find the way to the bathroom, the night counselor on duty, or to the room of one's own counselor. Therefore, the physical features of the School have to be arranged accordingly. In corridors, lights are never turned off during the night, and dim, dark blue lights burn all night in the dormitories and bathrooms. In addition, the children have free use of their individual flashlights.

Nocturnal incontinence is often the expression of a distorted balance between destructive and dependent wishes. The comfort of having freely accessible areas of light protects many children from experiencing recurrent loss of bowel or bladder control. The lighted, friendly bathroom, in which they have spent time during the day playing with their counselor, facilitates going to the toilet at night. When, with such help, a child obtains control of elimination, he has not merely given up a symptom, but has mastered the underlying fear of abandonment, which was a central issue in his disturbance.

The security of emotionally disturbed children depends on the tangible presence of protective figures. But since these children generally invest those on whom they depend with magical powers of omnipotence and omniscience—which is in line with the children's own overwhelming feelings of helplessness—the presence of even a protective figure at times becomes a threat to them. The authority invested in the adults becomes a burden when, for example, a child wishes to masturbate at night. For these reasons we prefer not to have adults sleep in the same room with the children—not to mention the fact that to do so permanently would be an imposition on the freedom of the adult, which he would resent and, as likely as not, take out on those who are under his care.

Similarly, for many children eliminative functions have become a means of expressing hostile phantasies, and disturbances of their toilet habits have resulted. It is necessary for these children to be protected from undue intrusion in such situations. This has determined our bathroom policy. While bathrooms are accessible to the children without their having to overcome fears of distance and darkness, any child is at all times entitled to perform eliminative functions without the threat of having anyone barge into his destructive or sexual preoccupations. His privacy is ensured, since he can lock the toilet stalls, but he is at no time deprived of the presence of an adult if he indicates his desire or need for it. Many irregularities in the children's toilet habits disappear because of our consistent compliance with this principle.

Some children, especially in the early stages of their adjustment to us, are extremely sensitive to changes in the School's physical appearance. Any structural changes, though they all may be improvements that will eventually facilitate our work, set some of the children back. For example, when the children moved from the old into the new wing, which has much bigger dormitories and better equipment, it took some children months to regain the degree of inner security that had been theirs. Having to master the new physical setting, extremely simple though it is, taxed all their energy, which was withdrawn temporarily from mastering emotional difficulties or achieving higher integration in learning and relating.

Even improvements that are requested or desired by the children, such as redecorating or replacing worn-out furniture, arouse anxiety. For example, the children had asked for new desks in the classroom. It had been planned to replace all desks on the same day, but only part of the shipment arrived. We were afraid that the children who still had to use their old desks would feel discontented and jealous. Instead, those who worked at the old desks had a definite advantage over those who received new ones. This was clearly expressed by a boy who had been most outspoken in asking for a new desk because he claimed that he had outgrown the old one, that it was rickety, and in danger of collapsing under him. Yet when the new desks arrived and he was immediately offered one, he did not want it. Instead he became full of praise for the worn beauty of the old desk, and protested vehemently that he could continue to learn only if he could go on using it.

The physical stability of the School makes the children less vulnerable to unavoidable changes in staff personnel. The children can accept and assimilate new counselors or teachers more easily because they are able to fall back on the safe basis of permanency that they find in the structure of the house and in the consistent scheme of values determining their physical existence. These remain the same even if persons do not. This, of course, is true only if changes in staff are infrequent.[19]

The children's fear that they will lose their ability to master the tasks confronting them if the physical framework of their lives

---

19. Human relations can make a positive contribution to a child's security only if they are relatively permanent. The following table shows how long the staff mem-

is altered becomes most acute when they temporarily leave the School grounds. They are afraid that the School may change during their absence, and they are only slightly reassured by our definite promise that, when they return, they will find the house in the same shape as when they left. Before they are fully settled, even short absences weaken their feeling of security toward the building, and the fear that they will not be able to find their way about reappears.

This transference of feelings about the task of emotional mastery to the physical setting is illustrated by typical statements made by children who have reached the point where they are ready to deal with their environment. As long as a child is autistically withdrawn, he hardly responds to the School—at least not visibly. But when the children become ready to try to master living at the School, then the School strikes them as enormous. They frequently make such statements as "I bet this is the biggest school in the world," or "This is the greatest house there is." For these children, trying to master living in such a simple and moderately sized structure as the School is a nearly insurmountable task, the difficulty of which is expressed in their feeling that the buildings are of tremendous size.

Sooner or later, however, the simple, solid, and unchangeable qualities of the physical setting, which is so entirely organized

---

bers who work most directly with the children had been at the School at the time the other statistical data were compiled.

TABLE II—*Length of Staff Association with School*

Less than one year	3
Less than two years	4
Less than three years	5
Less than four years	2
Less than five years	3
Less than six years	3
Less than seven years	1
Less than eight years	1
Less than nine years	1
Less than ten years	1

Thus the median length of time during which staff members significant to the children have been with us is between three and four years. This is not long as time and human relations go. But since the median length of time the children had spent with us was three years, (see Table No. XXI on p. 503) this made it possible for a child to spend most if not all his time at the School with the same persons. The picture is even more favorable when we consider how long the staff members who, in the minds of the children, represent the "School" have been with us. Hardly any staff members who have been with us less than two years are viewed by the children as standing for the School. Fortunately seventeen of us have been at the School for more than two years. Those who are most important to the children have been with us for three years or more.

around the children's needs and desires, help them to gain confidence. After their familiarity with the buildings is firmly established, an opposite phenomenon to that described above can be
observed. When the children return from a trip during which they
have been confronted with strange surroundings, then, by comparison, the old, familiar environment of the School seems very simple.
As the children in amazement express it, "When I used to come
back to the School it seemed so big, but now when I come back
the School is so small."

Once the School has become a shelter, though not yet a home,
its physical features are potential sources of strength because the
child is free to use them according to his needs. As long as he is
still deeply insecure (or later in times of crisis) he can stay close
to the house or not leave it at all, thus protecting himself against
encounters with the outside world as long as they threaten him
with defeat or overwhelming anxiety. But once secure in the protection of the School, a child can experiment with his inner strength
by testing himself in ventures of exploration outside its confines.
The counselors protect the child against prematurely going too far
in such excursions, but with the exception of this qualification, the
timing and regulation of such attempts is left to the child.

Again, the children's spontaneous actions illustrate how they
use the house as their basis of safety. Children who are particularly
fearful of the unknown—for example, those who also suffer from
severe reading difficulties—venture on excursions only if they are
permitted to establish landmarks that will guide them safely back.
Treasure hunts, we find, are one of the best ways to help anxious
children venture away from the house. In these hunts, the more
daring ones set landmarks very short distances apart from each
other. All the anxious children have to do is follow them. Since
these signs are made by children they trust to some degree, and the
hunt takes them eventually back to the house, they can afford to
leave it for a short time. The well-known physical structure of the
School thus is the base line for their security, a reliable frame of
reference from which they may venture with greater courage into
a "dangerous world" outside. This world they cannot yet meet successfully, but they can now at least make some evaluation of it by
comparing it with the School they know well.

Even then, the children at first have to carry with them some
tangible evidence of the security that in its totality is symbolized
by the "School." Such props are necessary when the children are
geographically distant from the School as long as they do not trust

themselves or the outside world. Many insecure children take a variety of their prized possessions with them on every walk. Other possessions, which often represent the children themselves, are stored in a safe place in the house or entrusted to a reliable adult before they dare to leave the confines of the institution. Then, and only then, are they free to explore the new environment without making anxious requests to return home.

One boy, for example, during his first months at the School, insisted on putting all his toys safely away in his chest in the dormitory before taking a walk. A few months later a person seemed to him to be a safer repository; he asked his counselor to keep his most important toys in her room, and showed no concern about the rest of his possessions. After he had sufficiently tested her reliability by repeatedly checking to see that his toys were safe with her and that he could have them back whenever he wanted, his trust in her permitted him to go on walks without any measures of precaution. Initially, physical aids are important for the establishment of security; later, unconditional trust in those with whom relations have been formed and successfully tested by the child makes them unnecessary.

When a child is securely established at the School and accepts it as a reliable frame of reference for his life, he becomes able to deal constructively with the experiences he had in a less secure world, with past failures and disappointments. Not until then can he safely visit his parental home without detriment to his progress in rehabilitation. Visits to the home are very different from short visits with parents at the School. The latter may be desirable soon after a child comes to us; for example, it may become necessary for a child to see his parents in order to reassure himself that his destructive wishes have not made them disappear from the world. Visits in the parental home have to be handled much more carefully. If they are made before a child has begun to feel at home at the School, they tend to make him feel more acutely that he has no real home of his own and prolong the time it takes for him to find his home at the School, which is essential for his rehabilitation.[20] On the other hand, as a child becomes more at home at the School, his visits to the parental home can become longer and more frequent, provided, of course, that they are not misused by the parents in efforts to destroy the security the child is finding at the School.

20. See also John's history.

... And a Home

AS THE SHELTERING FUNCTION of the School demonstrates to the
child that his basic needs for physical protection, for warmth, food,
and rest, will always be satisfied, the strange buildings slowly become "his home." This is particularly true as meaningful relations
to protecting adults are added to the satisfaction of all his other
needs. A parental abode becomes a true home for the child as he
learns to love and depend on his parents, as he forms his personality
under their impact. What kind of home it will become depends on
the particular nature of the parent-child relations existing within
it and on the experiences that are shared. But at the School this
process is often reversed. We have seen that the physical setting
may acquire meaning for a new child before he is able to relate to
the staff members and share experiences with them. For example,
sensitivity to changes in objective surroundings manifests itself
sooner in our children than reactions to changes in the staff, such
as staff vacations. Only after a child is able to feel "at home" in
the physical environment of the School does he begin to recognize
and accept other children, to establish contact with his counselors,
and gradually to form close relations with them.

Once these goals have been achieved, rehabilitation can proceed
comparatively fast. But it takes time for a child to make this new
home his—if he is severely disturbed, easily a year or more. The
child's freedom to manipulate, and even modify, his environment,
by arranging and rearranging his own area of the dormitory, is of
the utmost importance to him in truly finding his "home" at the
School. The case of an eight-year-old boy gives us an example of this.

In our technical age, the anxiety of quite a few children centers
around cars, trains, and engines. While he still lived with his parents, such fears never left the boy, even when he was away from
home. He had to watch trains compulsively for hours during the
day. As we learned much later, this was to make sure that they
would not jump the tracks and run over him. He accumulated a
vast stock of detailed knowledge about trains, apparently in an
attempt to control them and thus deliver himself from his regularly
recurring nightmares about train accidents and their murderous
consequences.

Several months after he came to the School, he decided to out-
fit the space around his bed, and particularly the bed itself, as a
railway depot. He worked on this, in the most elaborate way, for

several weeks. While he was carrying out this plan, his compulsion to watch trains diminished somewhat. Finally, his bed became for him a symbolic train station—a place where all trains must stand still. Now he was able to sleep peacefully because he felt secure against being run over. He let us know about his anxieties only after the use of this self-chosen protective device had considerably decreased their intensity. Nightmares about trains vanished after he became ready to communicate his fears about them, and perhaps even more important, after the freedom to handle his fears demonstrated to him that he was not as powerless to do something about them as he had felt before.

He could fix his living space and bed as a depot because we provide all children with basic materials for gratifying their essential needs, not only for rest or food, but also for spontaneous activity. The free and ingenious use of the boy's imagination in using these materials made it possible for him to meet his difficulties on their own battle ground. These basic materials for living and gratification were shaped by him in such a way that they became the self-chosen matrix for his developing personality. It is this freedom to influence the conditions under which they live that makes the children really feel "at home" at the School. It is a therapeutic side result that the children's autonomous, creative modification of their environment occasionally reveals the content of their emotional difficulties; what is more important is that it gives them the opportunity of making a spontaneous contribution to their dissolution.

How a seven-year-old girl thought of the School during the time it was gradually becoming her home can be illustrated by a series of her drawings. After being with us for one month, she made a drawing of the School, which she criticized as follows: she felt that the picture of the dormitory building was not beautiful enough because she had forgotten to draw the lock on the door. As she added it to her picture, she explained, "So that all kinds of people do not come in." What "people" she had in mind was suggested by her side remark, "Do not tell my mother I said that. I do not mean her—just people." Two months later she drew the School as a house, to which she added a yard with "nice" flowers. More secure now about the protective function of her newly-found shelter, she could envisage purely enjoyable details; the shelter was in the process of changing into a home. Perhaps even more significant was the fact that in this second drawing the house belonged to "a good lady." She had felt that she was "nobody's child" when she came to the School; now she had begun to attach herself to her counselor, whose importance to her was exaggerated to the point where she portrayed this counselor as owning the School. The building became populated as a result of this beginning relation, and thus was becoming more and more like a home.

Later, when upsetting events threatened this emerging security, this was again depicted in a drawing. A visit to the dentist, which at this time was a deeply disturbing event to this child, had been aggravated by a temporary misunderstanding with her favorite counselor. Again she drew a picture of the dormitory building, but made it clear that it was "not the School, just any house." Flowers and trimmings were lacking this time, and locks and guards were stressed. A frightening experience imposed upon her by the staff had made the building appear less beautiful to her and motivated her to overstress its physical safety, as her emotional safety was temporarily threatened. The building also had become depopulated again because her trust in her counselor was not sufficiently established to withstand such a test.

But her disillusionment did not last long. Before going on a short trip several months later, she again drew the dormitory building, but this time with additional features—details that she particularly appreciated. In its restored and improved form, the house would be ready and waiting for her when she returned. It would always be there for her whenever she returned from any place. The shelter had become a home.

Obviously, it is staff philosophy and attitudes, and not physical objects and their arrangement, that determine and create the life that goes on within the physical setting of the School. The best designed institution would not be much good if its over-all plan and all its details did not reflect the right philosophy and attitudes. Buildings become important only as they are endowed with human meaning—only as they acquire significance and dignity as settings for constructive living. We feel that our buildings have acquired such meaning and hence have described them here. The much more important staff philosophy, attitudes, and behavior we hope will become clear in the case histories that follow.

PART II

"LITTLE THINGS AND TIME":

Paul, A Case of "Institutionalism"

Psychological Institutionalism

THE INTENT OF this volume of case histories is to show how emotionally disturbed children can be treated in a special kind of institutional setting, where every activity is directed toward fostering the goals of rehabilitation. Such a setting, we feel, is eminently suited for helping children with severe emotional disturbances.

Contrarily, the objection is often made that institutions, as such, are unsuitable and harmful residences for children. Usually the reason given is that living in them has a bad effect on some children. This charge may be quite justifiable in the case of an incompetent and inadequate institution, but it certainly does not hold true for a good one.

It seems appropriate, therefore, to present as the first of the four histories forming this volume a report showing how one child's disturbance, which had been badly aggravated by certain kinds of "homes" and institutions, was later measurably helped by another kind, as represented by the Orthogenic School. The real issue thus is not whether a child should live in an institution, but whether it is the right kind.

Living in an institution, in itself, did not cause Paul's troubles. As a matter of fact, had his mother really cooperated with some of the agencies and followed their advice, Paul's early life might have been quite different. The main source of Paul's difficulties was the fact that his parents could not give him a normal family life. While this was the major root of his troubles, it is also true that the various children's homes, nurseries, and finally the orphanage in which he lived out his first ten and a half years, failed to satisfy his emotional needs. They gave him adequate physical care, but their drab and empty emotional life, still so typical of many institutions, could only aggravate his disturbance.

The prime reason why these institutions could not help Paul, and why life in them seemed like a nightmare to him, was that the persons in charge were either unaware of, or unable to combat, his profound unhappiness. Not only were the staff members insensitive to his loneliness and despair, and apt to favor routines over emotional needs, but they failed to protect him against the force of his mother's hostility toward these institutions (although he knew she had placed him there of her own volition), and this important additional factor made it impossible for the boy to find any satisfaction in them.

A study of the institutional features that augmented Paul's difficulties may throw light on what can go wrong in nurseries, orphanages, children's centers, and the like, and suggest remedies. After all, there is no reason why a good institution cannot supply the corrective experiences necessary for combating the harmful influences that reach out to a child from his own past life. If we could make Paul receptive to good "mothering" at an age when he was actually fighting off our help because of previous bitter experiences, it should have been relatively easy to work with him during his earlier years, when the past had not yet handicapped his ability to relate.

This over-all problem has been discussed at some length in a previously published paper based partly on Paul's history, which was considered as a sort of object lesson, highlighting certain features of "psychological institutionalism."[1]

In this paper, psychological institutionalism was defined as a "deficiency disease" in the emotional sense. The lack of meaningful and continuous personal relations in a child's life leads to impoverishment of his personality. One can observe what this process does to children who have lived in institutional settings for a long

1. B. Bettelheim and E. Sylvester, "A Therapeutic Milieu," *The American Journal of Orthopsychiatry*, 18 (1948), pp. 191 ff. I am greatly indebted to the American Orthopsychiatric Association for permission to quote from this paper.

time; but the "disease" is not confined to such children. It also occurs in those who live in disorganized family settings or in a series of unsuccessful foster homes.

A child whose frame of reference consists in depersonalized rules and regulations may become an automaton in his passive adjustment to them. He need not and cannot make independent decisions because his physical existence is amply protected and cared for and his activities are arranged for him. His testing of reality does not cover the variety of conditions found in life. Complete regulation of his life by external rules keeps him from developing both inner controls and spontaneous, autonomous reactions. His inner conflicts do not promote personality growth because their resolution cannot result in the shaping of meaningful personal relations. Neither do conflicts resulting from external experiences result in personal development, since they are not conflicts between people, but simply clashes between the child's instinctual tendencies and the impersonal rules of an institution.

Such a child, therefore, lives both emotionally isolated and physically distant from adults. Even where there is some closeness of contact with grown-ups, the intimacy does not promote the child's personality growth if significant characteristics of the normal parent-child relation are not present. For without a "knowing" of the adult, the child is deprived of a chance to identify with adults, to emulate their higher integration, to develop more mature ego ideals. He cannot form a conception of the coherence of life or the rational organization of time, space, and personality, and has no feeling for the deeper logic of events. For him, one day is like any other; as some of these children have told us, they feel that "everything is all the same."

Life becomes simply a matter of performing routine activities —washing, dressing, eating, resting—which are experienced as pleasurable or not purely in terms of the child's own body. Such a regimen is only loosely connected with the adults who are responsible for it. Frequently the child cannot even call staff members by name but, rather, calls them by their function, such as "nurse," "cook," or "supervisor." Thus he is apt to distinguish one from another not as persons, but according to the particular aspects of physical routine that they supervise.

This kind of deviation in personality development points up the danger in rearing a child by caring for his isolated functions rather than by caring for his whole being. Moreover, this danger is heightened in an institution where a number of adults are executing alike the routines set down for them by others, rather than using their own particular personalities in implementing a common philosophy, thus adding individual character to their experiences with the children. In observing children who have been deprived of this, it becomes apparent that every youngster must have the opportunity of forming a continuous, central relation with at least one adult in the institution, as a means of unfreezing his personality. This is achieved not only through the emotional warmth emanating from the adult, but even more because the child acquires, in this relation, a flexibility in his emotional and intellectual interactions, which was previously lacking in his life.

Paul's Parents and His Early Life

PAUL'S PARENTS were separated before his birth. As a small child, he scarcely had any contact with his father—certainly none he could recall—and when Paul was six, his father died after a prolonged illness.

The father came from a middle-class family. Ailing or ill all his life, he was never healthy enough to work and had to be supported by his family, which violently opposed his marrying. Rather naturally, in the light of his financial dependence, their opinions influenced him greatly. Their resentment of his marriage and rejection of his wife poisoned their relations to both child and mother.

Apart from his family's opinion, Paul's father himself felt that he had been maneuvered by his wife into marrying, and had never really wanted the marriage. She was much too domineering, he complained; life with her was unbearable.

When he eventually left her, his family came out quite openly with their hatred, maintaining that "it was all right to let her suffer." Within the family circle she was called "that witch." Later, when she repeatedly sued her husband for alimony, they felt quite justified in their complaints; she was supposed to have been the one who "threw him out of the house." They felt particularly aggrieved because she "dragged their good name" into court, thus disgracing them. The family were also incensed when, during the suit's progress, she purportedly told Paul his father was dead.

Those who had any contact with Paul's father described him as being quite immature. He took no responsibility whatever for his child and showed no interest in him. He never visited Paul in either the nurseries or the foster homes in which Paul lived before his placement in the orphanage (after his father's death). Only with court help could the father be forced into paying his wife alimony, and court records show that he was chronically in arrears in Paul's support.

Neither the boy nor his mother were notified when the father died; his mother learned of it only by chance, months later.

As for Paul's mother, she had always been a profoundly unhappy woman. Her own mother, Paul's grandmother, was an extremely disturbed person. Both of these women thought the other was mentally deranged, and they fought each other over Paul. Both often became confused in their talk, and, at times, even incoherent. They told us completely conflicting stories of their family history, and changed their stories with each telling. It seemed that this mother and daughter maintained themselves precariously, barely avoiding a schizoid break. The grandmother, with whom Paul stayed for short periods, accused the mother in front of Paul of neglecting him. The mother, who had been forced to support herself from the age of thirteen, habitually denied her role as wife and mother; she preferred to be a "professional woman," although she was not trained in a profession and had never had any such position. She said that she had married her husband, who was some ten to sixteen years younger than she (her age varied with each telling), only because she thought "there was money in it."

Paul never knew a family life. He scarcely knew what being loved meant. Although his birth was normal, the mother was under great mental strain, and recovered from her confinement "slowly, due to domestic discord." From the maternity ward of the hospital in which he was born, Paul went directly to a nursery, where he lived out his first four years of life. Both the social agency that had become concerned about the baby and the nursery's social worker urged a foster home placement for Paul, but his mother would not agree to this. The idea simply was not acceptable, in part because she was "afraid his father would lower the amount of support if Paul lived in a foster home." Observations made on the occasions of her visits to the nursery describe her as intelligent but bitter, and quite unable to view situations realistically. The workers in the nursery felt that she "was very insecure in her relation to herself and the baby." Toward Paul she was "impatient and quick-tempered."

The occasional night spent with his mother meant very little to Paul. She worked so late that when she did bring him home he was half asleep, and in the morning she deposited him again at the nursery before he was really awake. Most of the time, he lived round the clock at the nursery, and worse, a life that was regulated only by the clock.

His mother saw Paul rather often in the nursery, but irregularly and with little interest. Once, she devoted the entire time of her visit to teaching him to say "Paul loves mama." On subsequent visits she tutored him in other such phrases.

We know little about Paul's life during this period, except that it must have been unhappy (by the time his history was being compiled by us, the nursery had been closed by the city because it did not meet minimal standards). He sucked his thumb incessantly from the age of seven months, but his physical development at this time was otherwise normal.

When Paul was four, his mother suddenly withdrew him from the nursery, which had been home for him since birth, although she had no other plans for his care in mind. All efforts to forestall this irrational action were to no avail. First she brought him home, but since she worked both days and evenings, she had to "park" him with an assortment of friends and relatives for a day at a time. These many uncertainties and the constantly changing surroundings and routines must have proved very traumatic to an infant who had previously known only an unvarying and deadly nursery regimen. After two months, the mother had quite exhausted her list of acquaintances, and realized that this could not go on. Then she moved herself and the boy in with her mother, but all three hated this arrangement. Finally the grandmother insisted that Paul leave; so that at the age of four and a half, he was placed in yet another nursery—his second—where he lived about six months. This was a much better institution, where the children and their parents were observed and records kept. The staff there considered him a very disturbed child who had undergone "far too many changes," with bad results for his well-being. And although—or perhaps because —his mother was strongly advised against any further shifts, she withdrew Paul from this nursery, too. Again she rejected foster home plans, which were most strongly recommended. Instead, there ensued another hectic nine months of "parking" in assorted homes and environments. Small wonder that when Paul entered kindergarten other children called him "crazy," while his teachers found him a seriously unbalanced child, totally isolated from other children and the world—whose drawings nonetheless showed great talent.

When he was not yet six, his mother had again exhausted her ability to "take" Paul, as well as all the available "parking places," so she placed him in an orphanage. The social worker who studied the situation preceding the placement, asked Paul where he would like best to live. "I'd like a good place to eat, clothes, a nice house,

like a bird house," he said. With whom would he like to live? He
would like to be all alone. The worker was struck by his inability
to discriminate between people who he should have known well and
total strangers. All human beings seemed alien to him, or perhaps
it would be more correct to say that he was totally alienated from
all other human beings.

The orphanage accepted Paul, but only after the mother was
again strongly advised that foster home placement would be much
preferable—advice that she again rejected. In this orphanage Paul
remained four years.[2] During this time events took place within
his family that were traumatic for him: his mother remarried, and
a year later bore her second child, a girl. Paul intensely resented
the fact that this baby was obviously her favorite, and could live
with his mother, although she had failed to established a home for him.

From the beginning, he got along very poorly at the orphanage;
as time passed, matters grew increasingly worse. Soon it became
apparent that Paul was having serious difficulties in communicating.
The elliptical nature of his speech became marked; his pronunciation of syllables was poor and he did not seem to care whether or
not anyone could understand him. He spoke in short, incomplete
sentences so that it was impossible to understand him until he had
repeated these hesitant, garbled groups of words several times. Even
then, one had to know Paul and the situation in order to guess what
he wanted to say. Moreover, he easily lost interest in talking at all.
Any contact established with him was soon lost.

For four years, during her visits to the orphanage, Paul's mother
discharged her contradictory feelings upon him. Typical of her
ambivalence toward the boy was the way she made lavish plans with
him for celebrating his birthday, and then forgot both plans and
birthday when the day came. Later she attempted to continue this
behavior while Paul was living at the School. But her visits to the
School were regulated and rare, and her efforts to act out her
guilt, resentment, and paranoid delusions somewhat controlled by
us. Even so, she still managed to upset Paul terribly, and this gave
us a good notion of what their meetings at the orphanage must
have been like.

Ridden by guilt for having neglected him, she portrayed her
own existence to him in the gloomiest vein. Since she actually led
a submarginal life, this was not difficult. She complained that she
and her daughter went hungry and could not buy adequate clothing; that they suffered because they had no heat or plumbing in

---

2. A few years after Paul left, this orphanage also was closed because of the
inadequate nature of its operations.

their home; that they were persecuted by the landlord, the neighbors, and the Negroes, who were "moving in on them." Unsuccessful in a number of business ventures, she recounted the persecutions she suffered from her competitors. She blamed the relatives of Paul's father (and thus Paul indirectly) for her misfortunes. How much better off Paul was, living comfortably in the orphanage! Thus she burdened him with guilt, not only for the advantages he presumably enjoyed while his mother and sister were suffering, but even more for resenting her and her complaints.

At the same time, her own guilt made her wish to appear as a concerned and protecting mother. In this role she attacked and depreciated everything the orphanage and its staff did for Paul. She carped about the food, the clothing, the program, the living quarters. She fought and argued with staff members in front of him, to his great embarrassment; in this way, any possible, budding attachment he might form to the orphanage was destroyed, and he began to see it in the most miserable light. He was torn by a conflict of loyalties—caught between mother and orphanage. As a result, he could form no attachments at all, and detested everything about his life.

Driven by her guilt and delusions of persecution, his mother's destructiveness sought other targets. She berated Paul for his lack of academic progress, only to become more guilty, for which she tried to compensate by leveling irrational criticisms at Paul's teachers, who were "lazy," "stupid," and prejudiced against her son because he was poor. Thus she destroyed also his chances of success in public school.

Still impelled by unconscious motives, her complaints branched out against society at large. The state and city officials were "all a bunch of crooks" out to rob her and her son. The boy was left with no recourse at all, no institution of society to which he could turn for help or redress. Since the orphanage seemed incapable of counteracting his feeling that he was mistreated, he completely withdrew from the world and wished solely and passionately to be left alone. Any intrusion on his privacy was fought off with increasing violence.

Even after Paul had lived at the Orthogenic School for two or three years, it took only a brief visit from his mother to plunge him back into deepest depression and to increase his guilt unbearably. Although, as time went on, she became less open about her criticism of us and the way of life we were helping Paul to develop for himself, he remained keenly aware of her fanatic suspicion of the School, which fed his paranoid tendencies. Just how extreme her distortions were, was hard for us to assess. To give one example: after she had visited Paul at the School two or three times and admitted that he seemed content and in better health, she was still dead certain that we had taken him only because we wanted to perform some terrible experiments on him, such as vivisection. (At the time, the Hearst papers were campaigning against the University's medical experiments involving the use of dogs.) After all, she said, the University was famous for this type of research, and what other reason could we have for keeping a poor boy?

How Paul really felt about his mother came to light slowly, little by little, and in disjointed fashion. Only then could we understand that his actions were often closely related to his feelings about her. For instance, on first coming to the School (and perhaps at the orphanage), Paul's characteristic reaction to any frustration was to throw himself on the floor and scream and kick. On one occasion, after he had been with us for a year and a half, he acted out a scene that permitted us to fathom what this falling to the floor might mean. It began immediately after he was informed that he would have a short visit with his mother and half sister. He told us how terribly upset he felt when his mother described, so graphically, her deprived way of life. He also realized how much better off he was living at the School and how miserable life with his mother would be. Then, in the course of talking, he abruptly threw himself to the floor from the chair, something he had not done for nearly a year, and began to scream and kick, as he had done so frequently during his first months with us.

When we asked why he had suddenly fallen to the floor, Paul screamed, "Because you pushed me!" Then he checked himself, as if he were astonished by his own remark; he realized that no one had pushed him. Speaking under great stress, he tried to explain that he felt pushed, emotionally "thrown around," by the conflict between his allegiance to his mother and his loyalty to the School. He had fallen to the floor, literally thrust down by an inner struggle that was too much for him to manage.

Reassurance was no help. We told him we had no wish to create such a conflict in him and that he did not have to feel guilty about his divided allegiance; but Paul only claimed that he knew we really were angry with him for his feelings. When he finally could realize that perhaps we were not, he still was certain that we would be angry someday, and that was sufficient reason for feeling unhappy now.

Paul had to fight not only against his ambivalent attachment to his mother, but also against his suspicion of our motives, which was the result both of his past experiences in institutions and of his mother's tirades against us. So it became understandable that any visit with his mother, however rare, should throw him into a terrific state of emotional turmoil, by reviving his anger about past deprivations and activating his ambivalence not only toward her, but also toward the School. These meetings were also trying because they forced him to realize how disturbed his mother really was.

Although Paul would not admit that the visits bothered him, he did his best to avoid them. For example, when informed that his mother was coming to see him the next day, Paul made plans to be at the movies at that time, and he actually attempted to leave before she came. He tried to curtail each visit by leaving the room early, thus cutting down the time he had to spend with her.

Paul was acutely aware of the emotional demands his mother made on him. As he grew stronger, her hopes and expectations that he would look out for her became quite obvious. This made Paul fear that she might force him to leave the School to care for her. Following one visit, which took place after Paul had been with us about two years, he acted out these feelings in play with his counselor. Placing toy father and mother figures in front of a house, he had them shot by a group of soldiers. The whole family was killed; only the little boy survived. He had walked away from his parents in time, said Paul, and the soldiers thereafter took good care of him. But then Paul felt guilty and had to punish the soldiers for killing the family. So he had them shoot each other until they, too, were all dead. Apparently, he had forgotten the little boy. When asked about his fate, Paul said, "Oh, the soldiers shot him, too, a while ago. I forgot. He's dead, too." Then with a forced grin, "Isn't that funny?"

What really perturbed him came out only after much soothing and reassurance. After some ten minutes of silence had gone by, he began complaining about another child's leaving some time before. When the counselor reassured him that he would not be leaving, but would remain in School for a long time, Paul replied very defensively, "I don't care."

Changing the subject, he picked up the toy telephone, and asked what the School's number was. In pretending to call the School, he managed to dial the wrong number and therefore, he said, nobody answered. He just could not seem to dial correctly. Growing frightened, he exclaimed, "How come I always get the wrong number?" He mustered courage to try just once more, and he finally dialed the right number, though it still was not the right connection. Instead, he got the Museum of Science and Industry nearby, where he had actually spent many enjoyable hours. Pleased about this "wrong" connection, he dialed again. At last, in his play, he made the call correctly, and said happily, "Oh, this is the Orthogenic School." Whereupon he launched on a story, whose essence he repeated again and again: "I'm calling to tell you Paul must return right away to School." This was said with practically perfect speech, although as I shall later indicate, his habitual manner of speaking was halting, forced, and infantile. Why must Paul return directly? "Because he has to learn his lessons. It is very important for him to learn and stay in the School." Having made this clear, he rushed from the playroom toward the nearby classroom, where, he repeated, he wanted to stay and learn. Upon entering it, he looked back at his counselor and as a parting shot said, "And you know—know very well—so don't ask."

Such was Paul's typical reaction to a visit from his mother: the play-acting and phantasies took different forms, but the content was always characterized by the anxiety these meetings provoked.

As time went on, their visits became less frequent, partly because of the agency's success in working with the mother. Also, despite her grandiose hopes that Paul would take over and rescue her from her substandard life, the mother must have become aware that Paul actually had little use for her. In growing stronger as a person, he showed her more consideration, but he also indicated more unmistakably that he wanted to lead an independent life of his own.

During the brief meetings with his mother, Paul maintained great control over himself, but he grew very anxious before they occurred, and felt angry, anxious, and guilty afterward. As time went on, he frequently became totally unreachable before and after a meeting with his mother, erecting a wall between himself and the emotional reactions he feared.

Just how traumatic these visits were was expressed by Paul one day after his mother had left. Accusing us of wishing the worst for him, he screamed, "Why don't you do it right now? Go ahead and kill me!" We felt that Paul's anger at us for exposing him to her presence was justified. But we had to give in to his mother occasionally to prevent her from exercising her legal right of withdrawing Paul from the School. She might have done just that, had we not—with the agency's help—steered a very cautious course.

After one of his mother's last visits, shortly before Paul left the School, he put into words his feeling that their relation was linked with his previous inability to spell and write, which was only now clearing up toward the end of his stay with us. Every time he met his mother, both at the orphanage or at the School, she asked him to write her. On this occasion, pressed by guilt, he finally got around to doing so. As was always the case, he managed to misspell his mother's name and address, although on other occasions he spelled these words perfectly. The letter was returned. Rather than correct the address, he threw the letter away. But before tossing it aside, he gave it a long, thoughtful look, and said, "That's why I never learned to spell." His relation with his mother had broken down so badly, and with such painful results for him, that he had no wish to acquire either the clear speech or the adequate spelling necessary for communicating with her.

Nothing characterized their relation more aptly than his reaction on being told of his impending departure from the School. For many months, since first realizing that he would soon reach our usual age limit,[3] he had wanted to be sent to an out-of-town boarding school, far, far from Chicago, where his mother lived. Unfortunately, financial concerns made this impossible. When he realized that he would have to stay in Chicago, he sought reassurance that his mother would not be able to exercise any influence over his life. I told him about the precautions the agency was taking in this respect, and assured him that he was now old enough to have a voice in his future plans. This was a great relief to him, although he was still anxious. Later, when I asked him shortly before he left what I could do for him, Paul had but one request: that his mother be kept uninformed of his future whereabouts, so that she would be unable to reach him. He repeated this request several times to various staff members, to be sure that all of us knew what he wanted. And on his first return visit to the School, he asked whether I had kept my promise not to reveal his secret.

This did not mean that Paul was callous. By this time he felt genuinely sorry for his mother and for her depressed and deprived state of life. Someday, when he was securely established, he meant to help his mother and his half sister. But he wanted to make sure that he could achieve his goals in life without his mother's interference.

As early as Paul's second year at the orphanage his temper outbursts became so intense that they were considered unusual in an environment where serious tantrums were daily events. Long before his most extreme acts of destructiveness took place, which led to his placement in the School, he had been violent with other chil-

---

3. At that time our age limit was fourteen. With the additional space provided by the erection of a new dormitory wing, we are able to keep children with us beyond this age.

dren and adults. Throughout his four years of residence in the orphanage he was unable to form any relations worth mentioning with either adults or children—except perhaps for one extramural social worker, who, he realized, was successfully making plans for his departure. Opening up a bit with her, he confided that he could not bear to look at another child; he felt they were all his deadly enemies.

Just before his referral to us, his behavior at the orphanage indicated that his disturbances were increasing at an ever faster pace. In his last six months there he made several suicidal attempts, during which he screamed that he wanted to die. He tried to jump out of windows. He knocked out two teeth of one child and a week later seriously hurt another while fighting. Finally a third youngster was so seriously injured by him that it might be considered a homicidal attempt. As these violent and self-destructive acts grew in frequency and severity, the orphanage no longer felt able to cope with Paul; they finally requested emergency placement from the agency, which then assumed responsibility for him.[4] Psychiatric evaluation corroborated the grave view taken by the orphanage, and immediate placement in a treatment institution was recommended. Paul then came to live with us.

His Personality

WHEN WE MET HIM, Paul was ten years old. The psychiatric examination that was given him when he entered the School did not so much reveal murderous and depressive phantasies—as might have been expected from his suicidal and homicidal attempts—as emptiness, great flatness and instability of emotion, inability to relate, extreme detachment, and markedly infantile feelings and behavior. His defenses were very primitive and inadequate. With us he played "smarty" to conceal his inability to express himself, and called us "stupid" for not understanding what he was saying.

He was aggressive during the first interview, and interpreted our offer of candy and other efforts to make him feel at ease as stemming from our fear of him, or as attempts to bribe him. Whatever toys we gave him, he broke, but seemingly less out of destructiveness than a desire to cover up with a show of superior aggressiveness his inability to use them; he had simply never learned

---

4. This agency gave us the most splendid cooperation throughout Paul's stay with us, and should receive full recognition for it. It also carried on the difficult work with his mother; just preventing her interference was a major achievement for which much credit is due. Finally, the agency planned for Paul's departure from the School and ever since has been taking care of him (see pp. 142 ff.)

how to play. Similarly, when being tested he handled the test material destructively in order to cover up his inadequacy. For example, he grabbed the test blank on which his score was being recorded and tore it up; then, realizing that he was not doing well, he accused the examiner of cheating and deliberately falsifying his performance. Grandiloquently, he told her that he wanted no more of this silly stuff, and would tell me that she had cheated—after which I would surely fire the examiner for treating him so shabbily.

The I.Q. test indicated that he had normal intelligence (it was exactly 100). While this seemed a correct measure of his average abilities, it by no means gave a fair picture of how uneven his performance was, particularly on the verbal level. In this area he barely scored as an eight-year-old. On the basis of his verbal performance alone, he would have been classified as borderline, hardly reaching the lowest level of the dull normal classification. Only his superior reasoning ability and memory brought his score up to normal.

Paul's academic retardation was related to his poor verbal performance. He proved to be more than three grades below the norm for his age. His performance was significantly lowest in word meaning, spelling, and reading; in these he was not yet ready to begin first grade. But his over-all score was boosted by his competence in arithmetic, in which he more nearly matched his age level.

Thus, although his mother had done her utmost to set Paul against his teachers, he had learned best the subject they alone had taught him: arithmetic. He could not master language, particularly its usage—that is, word meaning and enunciation (as well as spelling and reading, which are based on verbal usage); these skills the child normally acquires through the persons who care for his immediate needs in infancy. Paul's loss of the use of language—and with it, adequate communication and the development of interpersonal relations—took place so early, and with such drastic consequences, that even during his stay at the School he did not fully acquire the verbal skills adequate for his age. But he was perfectly able to master those skills that a child learns later, in class. In these he did much better than is usually expected.

The effects of this early impediment to Paul's intellectual growth were felt all through his years in School. For example, on leaving us at the age of fourteen and a half, his placement in arithmetic was well into the eleventh grade, i.e., more than two years above age expectancy. In social studies he did even better; he knew as much as students who take these subjects are required to know on graduating from high school. Thus, his greatest progress was in subjects he had never been taught before; he did less well in those he had started before coming to us. But in skills like vocabulary, which he should have absorbed from his parents or their substitutes, he was able to reach only the beginning of the sixth grade level by the time he left us. In this area, therefore, he still lagged some two years behind the normal.

THE FIRST RORSCHACH TEST

Even more revealing than the evaluations based on our initial interviews with Paul, which were handicapped by his inability to communicate, were the projective test results. A Rorschach test[5] showed a disorder of thinking manifested in infantile perceptions, some of which were far deviations, which occasionally approached distortion. Some of the relations were bizarre and the thinking fluid, as when a steamboat was equated to the pole of a tree; but there were also perseverations. The ego appeared so immature that it raised the question of a permanent fixation at the infantile level.

Affectively, Paul manifested inadequate contact. On the other hand, he engaged in disproportionately high phantasy living. Some of this was latently rigorous, and based on normal contact. To this extent there appeared to be a potential for personality growth. However, very passive and decidedly resigned attitudes were also projected. It was evident that Paul used his phantasy for withdrawal purposes; this seemed especially serious in the light of his lagging ego development and the inadequate affective contact. He exhibited anxiety of a deep character. The principal dynamics, however, appeared to be feelings of inferiority, although other responses showed emphasis on violence.

For all his immature thinking, the intellectual structure showed that Paul had achieved a grip on reality only moderately below the critical minimum and that his conformity in thinking was actually above average.[6] There was thus some potential that could lead to adaptation at a peripheral intellectual level.

As a whole, the impression received from the test performance was consistent with a schizophrenic process; the test further suggested that Paul would utilize autistic solutions for his difficulties.

THE FIRST TAT

A few months later, Paul was given a Thematic Apperception

---

5. Rorschach evaluation by S. J. Beck.

6. This exaggerated conformity to social canons has also been observed in other "institutional" children. It consists in an empty compliance with "rules and regulations," which is both a social disability and a serious impediment in developing personal integration.

Test. By then he had become free enough to open up more about his phantasies to at least one of his counselors; but as far as his personality was concerned, we had made relatively little progress. The feelings reflected in the test, therefore, were consistent with those he brought to the School. His answers were very curt throughout, and were made unwillingly, although we had delayed giving the TAT until he had formed some fairly good contact with the counselor who administered it.

She prefaced her report of his test with a comment about Paul's inability to communicate: "Paul's speech is so garbled that in order to make any sense of what he said I had to rearrange his remarks. Usually he started at the end of his sentences, and also of his stories, or in the middle, and struggled from there on both forward and then again backward. It was impossible to listen to him or to take down what he said without mentally sorting the words, and interpreting them with the help of his facial expressions and bodily contortions and their possible meaning. Only in this way could I make any sense of what he tried to say."

Paul's story to picture one[7] was: "Boy sad; look like sumpthin' broke, or don't want play. Don't look happy. Ain't gonna play violin. Mad, prob'ly." The depressive mood permeating his whole life is revealed in his very first remark. He repeats, as if for emphasis, that the emotional tone is not a happy one, and ends by suggesting that anger motivates the boy's unhappiness and his resistance to performing.

Anxiety about death and desertion, fear that he will not be cared for and that his life will get progressively worse, seem evident in his story about the third picture:[8] "What's this? Boy cryin' cause sumpthin' sad happen. Prob'ly somebody die—relative, friend of his—oh, father, mother. Won't 've much playin'; he'll 've work very hard, make the livin'. They grow poor and poor, day after a day. Don't feel good."

At first Paul had little to say about picture four.[9] His main reaction was, "Can't make nuttin' out-a this." But eventually he offered: "They was engage. Now don't like each other. Don't know. Sumpthin' must-a happen. Well, prob'ly marry and gonna get divorce." In telling this story he became quite excited and at its

---

7. This picture shows a young boy contemplating a violin, which rests on a table in front of him.

8. Picture three (BM) shows the huddled form of a boy on the floor against a couch with his head bowed on his right arm. Beside him on the floor is a revolver.

9. This picture shows a woman clutching the shoulders of a man, whose face and body are averted as if he were trying to pull away from her.

conclusion left in a hurry for the bathroom. Vague feelings about his parents' marriage and separation seemed here to find expression, together with his lack of understanding of what it all meant.

Anxiety and violence marked his story about the next picture,[10] in which there is a possible suggestion of his conception of the truth about his parents' incomprehensible relations. Paul's story was: "Woman goin' [in] room; she look like [some]body [is] there. She look like she scared afore, like [some]body gonna threaten [her]. She look [and] saw horrible sight—don't know. . . . She gonna call police—don't know. . . . Then he gonna call police. An' they'll try to find who [is] the murder[er]." The switch from the "she" to a "he" who is going to call the police suggests that in his own mind he is not sure who the murderer in his phantasy is, or who is going to do something about the murder—whether a "she" or a "he." He does not even know who has been murdered. Might it not be that it was Paul himself who felt murdered by the fight between his parents, into which he had been innocently drawn?

In addition to his depression and its origin in anxiety about his parents' relations, Paul's main anxiety centered about his most primitive need, for food. This fear that his hunger would go unsatisfied, as well as other depressive feelings, reflecting, perhaps, the complaints his mother made to him, colored his remarks about picture six:[11] "A man tellin' woman sumpthin' very sad. Lady thinkin' sumpthin' about job; she hadda quit a job 'cause she's too old. She'll die from starvin'; she won't have no food."

From the old woman (possibly representing his mother) who was in peril of starvation, Paul switched to a father as the main figure in his story about the next picture:[12] "Old man's tellin' man sumpthin' that should like be secret. So he shouldn't tell nobody 'til he's real old." The counselor asked what the secret was. "Don't know. Can't guess." Then, after a long pause, Paul went over the same story again, as follows: "Well, man makin' good business, got like heart attack, sort of. You're gonna die [in] three week, so he tell one [of] his sons secret. That he'll tell next person, and next person tell next, and next tell next, 'till somebody don't tell that person, one of his sons." Paul seemed to feel that his father should have confided some secret in him but could not because he

---

10. Picture five shows a middle-aged woman standing on the threshold of a half-opened door and looking into a room.

11. Picture six (BM) shows a short, elderly woman standing with her back turned to a tall young man. The latter is looking downward with a perplexed expression.

12. Picture seven (BM) shows a gray-haired man looking at a younger man who is sullenly staring into space.

died prematurely, and that perhaps now, with the breaking of the chain of generations who were handing down the important knowledge, he would be left stranded and alone.

The story that followed (picture eight)[13] seemed an effort to overcompensate for his present feelings of inferiority and deprivation by making plans for great achievements in the future: "Show man being operated. Boy thinkin' this, that he'll be great doctor. Man must-a been fightin' and must-a got shot. Well, boy thinkin' about savin' man's life. Be great doctor. Scare [he] won't make it—be great doctor." There was a desire to save the father figure and reach great heights of achievement, but there was also a depressive feeling that he might not make it.

The main themes of most of the other stories were deprivation, sadness, anxiety (particularly about starvation), and a gloomy outlook on the future; all this was interrupted only by sudden phantasies of homicidal violence. Typical, were Paul's stories about pictures thirteen[14] and fourteen.[15] The first of these was: "Little boy sittin' front-a his house. Thinkin'-a sumpthin' good to eat—like I. They poor—couldn't do nuttin', so move here where tell food good makin'. They'll start-a get poor again. 'Cause there's sumpthin' bad happen [to] farm. Father could-a die and [some]body else could-a die, and [they] need farmer to work. Nobody want work for them—they'll [be] poor and won't make livin' and die from starvin'." Death, poverty, and starvation—around these topics his phantasies revolved.

The second story began: "All black—an' that all. All look like sun come in black room. Figure on floor—dead body." After a long pause: "Don't know what is. There's dead body on floor." Then Paul gave a mumbled and involved account of how various people had been murdered. The end of this rambling and very confused story was: "Killer thinkin' to hisself, 'Now I'm free of murder done. I'm happy.' He very happy 'cause he kill him. That night he go [to] some friend [and] get drunk [and] say, 'Know who kill man and servant and maid and wife; I got away with murder,' and he go home singin' 'cause he so happy he got away with murder." Another long pause. "Then people call police and murder[er] get sentence and go to jail fifty-four years hard labor."

---

13. Picture eight (BM) shows an adolescent boy looking straight out of the picture. The barrel of a rifle is visible at one side, and in the background is the dim scene of a surgical operation, like a reverie-image.

14. Picture thirteen (B) shows a little boy sitting on the doorstep of a log cabin.

15. Picture fourteen shows the silhouette of a man (or woman) against a bright window. The rest of the picture is totally black.

Who were these people who were murdered? Since they employed servants, they may have been his well-to-do relatives, whom he hated for not taking care of him. Or, in phantasy, he may also have been acting out his mother's hostility to her husband's family. Perhaps the friend to whom he boasted of his murders represented his mother, to whom he may have wished to report proudly his act of vengeance; yet since he bragged about how dangerous he had been to the orphanage children and, later at the School, told us that he was a crazy killer, these figures may have represented all the people to whom he made such boasts. But he also felt that in the end they would betray him to the police.[16]

Here, then, in these tests, as in Paul's behavior during his first days with us, were projected the consequences of his lack of opportunity to form lasting personal relations, and of his many traumatic experiences. But there were some hopeful signs, too. Paul disclosed some isolated islands of feeling about past events, so that he did not seem altogether dead, emotionally. He could recognize certain crises in his emotional life, such as the death of his father. His very violence was evidence of some ego strength insofar as it led to desperate attempts to change his environment (through fighting against it) or to escape it (through attempting suicide). The suicidal attempts, moreover, were indecisive, and he seemed to be aware of their secondary advantages, for instance, the attention he got as an individual who was different from others, which was the very attention he needed most to escape his anonymity, his isolation. In dim fashion he might even have thought they would lead to a better placement, as indeed they did. Thus his fighting for a way out— occasional, eruptive, and destructive though it was—showed him to be a person who was not yet ready to submit passively and totally to an unbearable environment.

In view of the institutional anonymity that had contributed so much to his disturbance, we felt that, in addition to the services, personal and otherwise, offered by the School to all children, Paul needed one person who would concentrate on him. Her aim would be to help him to relate, to escape his isolation, and become, through the very attention she would devote to him, a distinct individual.[17]

---

16. Paul did not invent a story about the blank card sixteen. He was unable or unwilling to say anything beyond "Can't see nuttin'."

17. Gayle Shulenberger Janowitz undertook this difficult task. She became the person of greatest importance to Paul throughout his stay at the School. Much credit for his progress is due to her. In addition, Dr. Emmy Sylvester's advice was of great help in planning and evaluating Paul's progress. Significant contributions to his rehabilitation were also made by his teachers, Anna Lukes and George Kaiser, and his other counselors, Patty Pickett McKnight and Lou Harper. In addition, several other staff members continuously or for certain periods helped Paul through their devoted services.

From "Wild Critter" to "Great Dictator"

PAUL'S PROGRESS, whether it was displayed in his growing ability to acquire some measure of self-confidence, or in his progress toward becoming less pessimistic about life, is difficult to describe. For basically he remained a non-communicative person. Even when he wanted to, he could only rarely express himself in words. Therefore, much of our help had to be non-verbal, or he would not accept it. His responses often could be gauged only by watching his facial or bodily expressions.

He was very skillful in using his body to show his feelings. At first he gave vent to anger and frustration chiefly through temper tantrums, kicking, inarticulate screaming; by throwing himself and his playthings about; and by destroying objects through breaking or tearing them. As time passed, he began to express his increasing sense of well-being through his body—through relaxed muscular tonus, improved coordination, a self-conscious grin, and much later, a real smile. As his non-verbal expressions progressed from clumsy bodily movements to more subtly differentiated alterations, his mouth in particular took on increasing importance. We were able to read his feelings in his frowns or pouts. Later, such facial changes became more or less deliberate means through which he revealed emotions and eventually communicated to us his inner thoughts and responses.

When Paul first came to live with us he was very meek. Most of all, he feared being beaten up by the older boys, as had happened to him in the orphanage. He was equally afraid of the staff members. But he soon realized that few demands would be made on him, and that we would protect him. On his first evening at the School, in self-instigated regression, he began sucking his thumb, although he had given this up while at the orphanage; from the third day on he did this almost continuously. For many months, if we wanted to understand what was going on in him, we had to watch closely the manner in which he sucked his thumb: desperately, or with pleasure; autistically, or because he was concentrating so hard on trying to relate. These were clues that told us how to proceed.

Similarly, the way he explosively shot out the single words from which he built up his brief communications became more revealing, in time, than what he actually said. For Paul delighted in using his whole oral apparatus aggressively. He belched, for example, frequently, loudly, and with an astonishing amount of expression. His favorite oral pleasure, second only to sucking, was making a smacking noise with his lips, which was immediately followed by a loud, clucking noise made with the tongue. This sound preceded and ended his every sentence and often accompanied every word. If other children mentioned his lip-smacking, or if we had to tell him that it interfered with understanding him, he would either fly into a rage, or withdraw into an angry and defiant isolation. This reaction he covered up by listening to the radio, scanning the comics, and violently and aggressively sucking his thumb. Often he smacked his lips when he seemed anxious to communicate but unable to do so in words. These noises, which often replaced speech, very much resembled the babbling of infants. Of course, as might be expected, he made deliberate and hostile use of his poor speaking ability to hold our attention through long pauses, to keep us on tenterhooks and tax our patience.

Although Paul was able to express many of his feelings and preoccupations in imaginative drawings, he immediately destroyed most of his art work as soon as it was finished. That it cannot be reproduced here is unfortunate, since it would add much to a report that, by relying largely on language, omits much of significance in Paul's life at the School. Among other things, what he revealed to us through his art must remain unrecorded. But since so many institutionalized children are tongue-tied in this fashion, any report on them will suffer from similar handicaps.[18]

On a visit preceding his enrollment at the School, Paul told us some tall stories about how powerful he was, how dangerous, and how influential, but he was totally uninterested when we, in turn, tried to tell him about the School—with one characteristic exception: whenever the conversation turned to the subject of meals he was all ears. Little as Paul talked, his brief and often incomprehensible statements nearly always concerned food. He worried that our meals might not be served at the same hours as they were at the orphanage, and that he might not be able to adjust to a change. In fact, the very idea made him feel absolutely helpless. Like an infant, he seemed to live only for mealtime; if that hour was changed, his whole life lost structure.[19]

18. Goldfarb's studies (W. Goldfarb, "Infant Rearing and Problem Behavior," *American Journal of Orthopsychiatry* 14, 1944; "Psychological Privation in Infancy and Subsequent Adjustment," *Ibid.* 15, 1945; and "Variations in Adolescent Adjustment of Institutionally Reared Children," *Ibid.* 17, 1947) have shown that such impediments of speech and other forms of communication are characteristic of all institutionalized children. His description of adolescents who spent the years from two to six in orphanages very well fits Paul as he was when he came to us. Goldfarb thinks that these persons never overcome their handicaps. Paul's development in the School permits a much more hopeful evaluation, provided that these children receive the proper help.

19. In this and many other ways Paul's behavior and reactions were similar to

On Paul's first day at the School he ate little; on the next, he asked for and devoured two servings of everything. After this, his demands for food kept on growing, and within two weeks he was eating at least four or five portions of everything. The amount of food he consumed was truly prodigal. Not only did he eat large quantities, but during these first weeks he ate virtually all day long.

This overeating certainly did not stem from hunger but, rather, from emotional starvation. All his life, Paul had been a healthy child, physically well developed and of normal weight. In School he immediately began putting on weight, and kept it up steadily. He ate very rapidly, as though he were fearful always that there might not be enough food, or that other children might take his portion. He would rush into the dining room, grab the food before sitting down at the table, continue to grab during the entire meal, and all the while accuse the other children of trying to take "his share." Actually, observation should have taught him that everybody in the School can have as much food as he wants, and there are no portions set aside for a particular child. As a result of his greediness, Paul gained two pounds in the first month; six in the second; and within his first half year at the School, a total of sixteen. In the next six months he gained at a less rapid rate but added another ten pounds. The second year he gained nineteen pounds and during the third, twenty-eight. Only then did his weight curve taper off. Later, under the anxiety of leaving, he once again began stuffing himself. In short, after the first few months, Paul was considerably overweight.

Coming to the School changed not only Paul's physical surroundings but his whole life. Primitively equating himself with the world at large, he seemed to feel that this radical change in his own life automatically altered everybody and everything else. By the end of his first week with us he wanted to go back to the orphanage for a visit, "since it had all changed." He insisted he did not want to see any individual there, but just "how the place had changed." It once had been a very big place, he said, where some five hundred children lived (a gross exaggeration), and even then there had not been enough space because "all the children wanted to get in." Now, since his departure, he fancied that everyone else was leaving the orphanage, and by this time, he felt sure, hardly anybody could be left.

These remarks introduced our first conversation about his life

---

the "protective mechanisms" shown, according to Goldstein, by patients who are living under "catastrophic conditions" (K. Goldstein, "The Effect of Brain Damage on the Personality," *Psychiatry* 15, 1952, pp. 257 ff).

at the orphanage. As was also brought out in Paul's later and more detailed recollections, it had been, for him, a place empty of human beings. He talked freely enough about "the kids," what they did, and how they fought each other. Significantly, he knew none of them by name. He referred to them only as "'big guys," shadowy figures with a terrible power to hurt and torture, to beat him up without reason. Equally anonymous were the adults with whom he had contact. Up to the end of his stay with us, he referred to all persons at the orphanage either as "big guys" (obviously adult male supervisors and older boys who enacted, or arrogated, the role of supervisor) or as "little guys" (all children who, like Paul, were pushed around by the more powerful). This anonymity he transferred to the children at the School. When speaking of them he would say, "the guys," or in addressing them, "youse guys." Years passed before he consistently used names in talking to or about the children at the School. Even then he would return to a shouted "youse guys!" when under stress.

There had been women workers at the orphanage, but at this time he had no recollection of any of them or of any other women in his life (with the exception of his mother, grandmother, and the one social worker who had been instrumental in placing him with us). Much later, he at last was able to recall some of his public school teachers as persons. Eventually, he remembered the names of these women and something about their personalities—at least the attitudes they expressed in handling him. But people in the orphanage, with the exception of the one non-resident social worker, remained anonymous to him until the very end. And even his memory of this worker hinged on the help she had given him in "getting out of it all."

In contrast, Paul remembered routines in greatest detail. During his first weeks with us he went on performing them conscientiously, mechanically, like an automaton, and quite obviously without interest in what he was doing. Any deviation from the routine he had known produced utter panic. For example, one morning, when he saw his counselor put out a clean shirt for him to wear, he began shaking and screaming. Throwing himself on the floor, he rolled and kicked wildly, until his counselor guessed that what he was screaming was the word "Wednesday!" She rightly surmised that he was accustomed to getting a clean shirt on Wednesdays. Only when she finally made him understand that he did not have to put on a clean shirt that day, since it was not a Wednesday, could Paul pull himself together again.

By and large, during those first days, Paul tried to be very well behaved and controlled. Actually, of course, he isolated himself from us and concentrated on anxiously observing what went on around him. The first time he came to life was when he went on a "kitchen raid." This activity, during which the children are taken by their counselor to the big kitchen to cook and eat whatever they want, is most popular. Although it is taken for granted by all children familiar with the School, Paul's first experience with it excited him enormously, and he acted as if he were doing something quite forbidden and daring. He seemed to think that, along with his counselor, he had put one over on the cooks, the School's staff, and most of all, on me. Afterward, he was fearful that the cooks might tattle on him and, despite the counselor's assurance, was sure that if the raid were discovered he would be thrashed. Paul obviously felt that everything done outside of what he thought was the School's routine justly deserved severe punishment.

Soon after this first adventure, Paul began acting out some of the dangerous and destructive tendencies that he had only talked about before. He directed his hostility against inanimate objects. Although at the orphanage he had threatened to destroy himself or others, with us he experimented with destroying articles of clothing worn next to the body. One day he set his pajamas on fire; he was stopped before much damage was done, but a few days later he made a heap of the other children's pajamas and again set a match to them. In the orphanage he had made his suicidal and homicidal attempts when adults were not around. At the School, he became destructive in the presence of his counselor, and experienced obvious relief when she extinguished the small fires. If these fires were not actually self-destructive acts, they certainly expressed self-destructive tendencies, for when we asked why he set them, he replied, "Don't want live; want die," and, in further explanation, he added that he was a "crazy killer."

Just why did Paul resort to fire-setting to express inner pressures? It is difficult to say. Perhaps the clothing, as a symbol of people, was a sufficient target for his destructive tendencies, just because at the School his impulses could find expression within some social context, i.e., the physical proximity of his counselors—although probably not yet within the context of a personal relation to them. If it is permissible at this stage to draw on the knowledge we acquired much later, another explanation suggests itself.

To Paul, our more subtle ways of setting limits and avoiding excesses may have seemed no control at all compared with what he knew at the orphanage. This sudden absence of control, as it seemed to him, was probably frightening. Later, he expressed this by complaining loudly that we allowed him, and the other children, to "get away" with too much. Just as he thought that he and his counselor had "gotten away" with something on the kitchen raid, so his present freedom to overeat may have given him the impression that in the School no holds were barred. This suggests that he used asocial conduct to test whether this notion, which he greatly feared, was true or not—since Paul was, with ample reason, terrified of what he might do if unchecked. That he stopped setting fires permanently after only two attempts implies that his real need was to test us out.

But this does not explain why he chose to test our controls by kindling fires rather than in some other way. It would be easy to speculate on the phallic and urethral implications of fire-setting. We knew nothing about Paul's toilet training, but it had probably been harsh, and certainly a matter of routine. There were bed-wetters among the boys whose pajamas he set on fire. That these boys freely wet their pajamas at night may have upset Paul by reviving old grudges and anxieties. And that the counselors did not punish them may have been, for him, one more threatening sign that at the School children "get away with everything."

Unfortunately, all this remains conjecture in the absence of confirmation from Paul's own remarks or from his behavior as we observed it in the context of the fire-setting incidents. There was, however, a striking parallel between his fire-setting behavior and his eating habits. He began, at the School, by eating moderately. Only because we did not stop him, did his appetite go out of bounds. His devouring of food was a self-stimulating process—an activity that, so to speak, fed on itself. Similarly, though he kindled only small blazes, if not checked, they could have grown into destructive conflagrations by devouring the substances fed to them. Paul was quite ready to provide the fuel, before we stopped him. Was he trying to find out, by setting fires, whether we would stop him from overeating if it, too, should become dangerous to him?

For his future healthy development, I think it was important that, instead of preventing him from setting fires altogether, we merely extinguished them without too much fuss or difficulty and afterward minimized their importance. Had we stopped him before-hand, he might have thought we shared his fear that, once the destructive processes were under way, they could not be halted. And if we had made a fuss, it could easily have inspired much the same feeling in him: he would have interpreted any sharp rebuke as an indication that we were afraid, or were only barely able to control the flames. Our lack of excitement and the ease with which we checked his destructive efforts seemed to convince Paul that we could control his negative tendencies. That this may correctly explain his experiments in fire-setting seems corroborated by the fact that, in the period immediately after, he burst out violently against both children and counselors, and announced that he was a wild creature—i.e., uncontrolled in his destructive tendencies.

Seen in this context, we can understand why Paul's self-destructive tendencies cropped up at the School in the form of fire-setting and attacks upon others, and never in suicidal form. In the orphanage, his acts of destruction had been mainly directed against the oppressive, outside world; only in final desperation were they turned against himself. But once with us, Paul sensed almost immediately that his world was now benign and permissive. Because he lacked inner controls—since he had lived all his life by external controls, which were alien to his own personality—this permissiveness appeared seductive; it tempted him to give vent to his destructiveness. Fortunately, his experience in setting fires, and our reaction, showed him that when necessary we could and would exercise control over him.

In retrospect, this is readily understood. The fact remains that we did not at first realize that we had allowed Paul to give up his old controls too quickly, and that he might have made better progress if, in those early weeks, we had fully understood the implications of his actions and the impact of our behavior on him. Even with this knowledge, however, it is hard to see what other course we could have taken. Although we try to tailor our actions as closely as possible to the needs of each child, the fact remains that ours is institutional living. We could have restricted Paul's overeating, but this, in turn, might have unfavorably affected other children, whose anxiety would be awakened by seeing us set such limits. While we do not hesitate to check potentially dangerous activities or those which create too great anxiety in the individual, it is difficult to carry this to the length of restricting eating, even though—as Paul's example shows—overeating can itself create anxiety. Aware of his craving for food, and the satisfactions it offered—satisfactions of which he had been sorely deprived in his previous life—Paul feared that he would eat so much that he would destroy himself, or "explode." He probably also sensed how destructive an act his devouring of food was, and this may have symbolized to him the destruction of those whom he hated. Thus, in order to be protected against destroying himself through overeating, or devouring others, he wished that we would set limits on his eating, and became anxious when we did not.

Since our actions must so often be based on scanty knowledge, we feel it is better to err in the direction of indulgence rather than over-restriction. Our philosophy entails offering the child as much gratification as possible, particularly at first, to help him form a more positive view of the world and relate to us. After he has experienced a great deal of satisfaction through the relations he forms to staff members, we feel that we can expect more social conformity from him. By that time, too, interpersonal rewards compensate for delays in gratification and for the frustration of asocial tendencies, and can be used in directing the child toward the sublimation of some drives. Unless we are quite sure it is wrong, therefore, we attempt not to limit satisfaction of the child's most basic needs, such as intake and elimination, rest and motility, self-regulation, privacy, and freedom to choose companions. While this seems preferable for most children, Paul's case demonstrated that it is not suitable for all.

In addition there were other difficulties, which inhere in our procedures rather than in our philosophy. To understand a child and help him, we must begin with at least some assumptions. This is particularly true in dealing with children who are so inarticulate that they cannot convey what is on their minds, and are apt to act irrationally. In order to make a wise decision about which child to admit, and then to determine in which group to place him so that he will benefit the most from association with other children, we need to gather as much information as possible about the child. It is inevitable that this background material influences our opinions. If, for example, we had approached Paul without any preconceived notions, we might have connected his fire-setting with his overeating, since these were his most characteristic kinds of behavior at the time. But what happened to impress us most in the information we received about Paul prior to his entry were his suicidal and homicidal tendencies. We were constantly on the watch for these, so that we could help and protect him. They had been the results of his desperation. To help him overcome this depressive view of the world, we tried to make him as comfortable as possible. We interpreted his fire-setting within this frame of reference, that is, as destructive acts consistent with his suicidal past, rather than as consequences of the overindulgence to which we had exposed him. Our mistake was to underestimate what the School's philosophy had already done for and to him, and to overestimate the importance of his previous suicidal tendencies.

Moreover, since Paul had only been with us briefly, it seemed reasonable to blame his actions on his orphanage experiences and to disclaim responsibility for them. It was not the first time that knowledge of a child's past had led us to indulge in a strange kind of narcissism, which makes us see ourselves as the creators of good experiences only, while we blame upsetting behavior on past events.[20] Actually, a deeper narcissism would lead us to view all that a child in the School does, good and bad, as being in part the consequence of our own actions. Knowledge derived from outside sources thus hindered us from spontaneously evaluating our own observations and using them in planning for Paul's future.

Let me return now from this digression about some of the problems of the institutional treatment of children to the narrative of Paul's life in the School. Once Paul was convinced that we were well able to forestall any far-reaching consequences of his destructive actions, he began to act out not only against inanimate objects but against persons, though the way he treated people often made us wonder whether he ever recognized them as human beings.

He hit the children and counselors; he threw things, though not always at anyone in particular. Whenever another child tried to retaliate, Paul did not fight back, but showed his excitement by laughing explosively and uncontrollably. He would fall to the floor, or hurl himself against a table, his body shaking wildly from head to foot, and his arms and legs thrashing about violently. His limbs, head, and body seemed to move entirely without central direction. While these movements were dangerous because of his physical strength (at a little more than ten years old, Paul was four feet, nine inches tall, weighed some ninety pounds, and was very muscular), they actually resembled nothing so much as the uncoordinated quivering of a mass of jelly. All this activity was accompanied by inarticulate screaming. Afterward, when the tantrums ceased, Paul played the clown or dumbbell. These temper tantrums were so frequent that they seemed to be continuous. True, they usually followed some frustration, but then everything was frustrating to Paul, particularly that we would not let him hit the other children.

---

20. The viewpoints of staff members are often distorted by what we are told about a child's past, usually for the same reason: to feed our narcissism. For example, knowing that a child has had unpleasant experiences with his parents may lead us to overlook the good experiences he enjoyed with them. His avowed dislike of his parents, or his liking for certain staff members, is accepted at face value, because of what we already know of the child's unsatisfactory relations with his relatives. But a child may make such statements in a particular situation to cover up his true feelings. Similarly, the improvement a child makes in therapy can easily be viewed solely as the result of staff efforts, and we may overlook the pleasant and positive experiences he enjoyed in the past with his relatives, which only later come to fruition.

Then, one day, he suddenly decided that he was a "wild critter." He got the other children to chase him, while he shouted that they must hold him down because he was so dangerous and vicious, and boasted that it would take three or four people to do this. In fact, it often required the efforts of two adults to restrain him. Again and again during subsequent months, he would interrupt the children's games by provoking them in many ways, insisting that he was "crazy," and acting like a "wild critter." He teased them into chasing him, and even into trying to beat him up, and when we prevented this, he stormed at us. Though it was he who continuously goaded them, he claimed it was the other children who were planning to "gang up" on him, beat him, or even kill him.

Within a month or so he was expanding his claims of being a "wild critter," or "crazy man." He became a "zombie," and again, a while later, the "Great Dictator." Although the other children were more upset by this than by his "wild critter" act (perhaps they sensed that one can be an animal or crazy man all by oneself, but a dictator must dictate to someone), actually these delusional statements suggested that Paul was progressing toward more human behavior. For a dictator is a human being, not an animal, and although he exercises control over others, he is at least aware of their existence.

The satisfaction Paul derived from just thinking that he could order us about may have helped him to behave less wildly. In any event, while his "wild critter" and "crazy man" episodes had been accompanied by a marked lack of control over his body, when he was the "Great Dictator," he exercised stringent control, marching about rigidly, Nazi style. He was still hitting out at the world, but he also ordered others to do his fighting and killing, which in turn meant that he had less need to be violent himself. This also represented some progress over the "wild critter." "I'm the Great Dictator," he would announce. "All kids do what I tell. They 've [to do] what I want."

As he strutted about, stiff as a robot or mechanical toy, he would laugh uproariously. But as the act wound up, he would relapse into making infantile sucking noises. Finally, when he calmed down, he would profess to be hungry and devour any food we offered him—quietly.

What lurked behind these delusions of being a dictator? Was it a desire to wield such great power that he need never again go hungry? His hunger reactions as his act subsided seemed to justify this interpretation. In any case, both the "wild critter" and the

"Great Dictator" characterized Paul at his least controlled. And as these episodes became less frequent, he at last embarked on the long, laborious process of acquiring mastery over himself.

The Beginning of, and the Fight Against, Self-Control

THE RELINQUISHMENT of external controls, and the process of becoming uncontrolled, constituted Paul's most obvious and dramatic emotional development during his first months with us—one that created great difficulties for everybody at the School. Still, this was not his only emotional transformation. Although experiences of a more directly positive nature were still too strange to him, too unexpected, to be "real," they did affect him at fleeting moments.

Our first intimation that Paul was accessible to positive experiences came on St. Valentine's Day, shortly after his arrival, when other children sent him valentines. "Didn't know [I] had any friends," he said in wonderment. The especially elaborate dinner and the favors the children received impressed him, too. "This school is more different," was the way he phrased it, without further elaboration.

Next day he went shopping with his counselor for new clothes, and was obviously pleased with the chance to pick out his own things. On the way home, he brought up the subject of death. He thought about it day and night, he told her; it was worrying him "crazy." The only time he worried less about dying was when he acted the "wild critter" and the "crazy man," that is, when he was provoking and attacking others.

Did Paul feel alive only while inflicting on other people the abuse he felt had been unfairly inflicted on him? Or could he only feel strong and vital while dominating others? Because he had been forced to live a life entirely regulated by others, he may have come to feel that his true self was "dead," and therefore he brooded about dying. Whatever his motives, the fact that he could begin to talk more freely about his "crazy man" behavior and could express his fears openly, once he had received tangible evidence of our good will (as in the Valentine presents and the new clothes), showed that he was not wholly insensitive to our efforts.

Every once in a while, thereafter, he showed some emotion toward the favorite counselor to whom he had confided his fears about death. But for Paul even this new friend was not a person with an independent existence. He had some use for her as a good and faithful servant, but the instant she did not gratify his every whim, this toleration vanished.

I spent quite a bit of time with Paul during these first months, but he had little use for me. This may have been caused partially by his general fear of men, which will be discussed later. More likely it was because my services could not always be of a positive nature, since I was often called upon to curb him. We try to free the persons who work immediately with the children—counselors, teachers, nurses—from having to exercise anything but the slightest restraint; at most they make an occasional critical comment. It seems impossible for children as disturbed as ours to form personal relations with anyone who must forcibly control them. Since our goal in Paul's case—as in others—was to guide him into at least one positive relation, we preferred that he have no negative experiences with the persons closest to him. On the other hand, it is sometimes necessary to restrain a child, particularly one who attacks others as violently as Paul did. I usually do this, or in my absence, some staff member who is not trying to relate most intimately to the child.

To Paul, I was just "another superintendent," a term no one else has ever used to describe my functions, although some of the children, before they grow roots at the School and relate to me, view me, to put it in one boy's words, as "a combination of janitor and policeman: he sees to it that everything we wreck gets fixed, and that nobody hurts anybody." But I did have my good points for Paul, too. "He don't walk around all [the] time checking," Paul said. "Don't carry [a] stick," and, "Don't beat you around here." Then he added with delight, "They're all scared of me." That was the only reason he could see for our not beating him for his bad behavior.

Within another three weeks Paul was telling his favorite counselor that he often deliberately shut his ears to the sound of other people and made noises with his mouth to drown out their talk— or else just pretended not to hear them.

This confidence showed that he had developed at least a minimal trust in this counselor, and he soon tried controlling his "wild critter" behavior in her presence. But even with her he could not feel like a human being. To express any of his positive feelings, which were as uncontrolled and asocial as his negative ones, he would shout, "I'm a laughing hyena!" And he would scream or laugh hysterically as he tried desperately to control his shaking body so that he could snuggle close to his counselor.

About the time he was showing this wish for human warmth

and contact, he began to worry aloud about the lack of externally imposed controls on his conduct. He may have sensed that while he was screaming or hitting out, he could not gain the satisfactions that come with emotional closeness to someone else. He felt quite unable to govern his asocial behavior himself, but realized it must be done if he wanted to be held and cuddled. Thus he may have wanted us to control him so that he could enjoy these pleasures.

As before, he complained at length about how we spoiled the children, and approvingly recalled the rigid discipline of the orphanage. In the same way, he asked us to curb the other children, but not himself. He claimed to have been a model child until he arrived at the School, and protested that now he was being pampered and spoiled just like everyone else.

During the months in which the "wild critter" and "crazy man" slowly lost ground to the "Great Dictator," Paul's screaming increased until it became almost continuous. He was now more articulate, however, as he found words to voice his grievances. Eventually, screaming became so habitual that he could not speak in a normal tone of voice.

Paul gradually seemed to be more aware, though still dimly, of the strength of his destructive drives, and of the way he turned them indiscriminately against himself and others. He asked to live with another dormitory group, with older and bigger boys who had frequently kept him from picking fights with the younger children. He seemed to crave the control of his aggressive impulses that they could provide, or perhaps he wanted them to inflict punishment on him and thus assuage his guilt.

It would be a mistake to consider these efforts solely as attempts to seek external controls or achieve self-control. Other motives, too, entered into his wish to re-create the situation he had known at the orphanage. For the newness of the School had by now worn off a bit. It was no longer just a change for the better. The impact and challenge of his new environment were slowly making themselves felt. To adjust to them meant developing a new set of intellectual and emotional attitudes and reconstructing his persoᵤality. While Paul may not yet have realized the implications of this challenge in full, he was well aware that, because of the lack of stringent controls, he would have to develop some of his own. This task simply seemed beyond him.

He asked no more from life than to vegetate in his present benign and pleasant environment without having to expend the emotional energy necessary in developing self-control. Never, at any time, did he wish to return to the orphanage. But he would have preferred to enjoy all the School's advantages without having to change his personality in order fully to do so. He thought he might be able to achieve this by transplanting the orphanage controls to the School. Additionally, he may have felt that, since his new environment was not oppressive and his needs were being so pleasantly met, the orphanage discipline, transferred to the School, would not seem as harsh as it had before.

Fears provoked by the lack of external controls were not Paul's only problem. Any kind of oral activity, as suggested before, was most perturbing. He continually tested us in the area of eating. Often he accused us of starving him. "I won't have no meat on my bones," he would cry wildly. It made no difference that, while he complained, we were bringing him more and more to eat, and even spoon-feeding him at his own request. On a conscious level his starvation anxiety seemed unrealistic, even to him, but he never ceased worrying about whether he would always have enough to eat.

It was not long before the focus of Paul's anxieties about eating shifted, and he developed fears and phantasies about being poisoned. For in spite of having food in abundance, deep within him his fear of being starved raged unabated. An insufficient quantity of food could not have caused this feeling, since there was always plenty, so he assumed it must be the unhealthy quality of the food that was to blame.

On other occasions he accused everyone of teasing him about his gargantuan appetite, and claimed that ridicule was our special tactic for keeping him from eating. Actually, none of us made fun of him, but he seemed to wish we would. Perhaps in this way he thought to cling to his starvation anxiety, or to provoke some kind of external controls, which would save him from the task he most dreaded: developing inner self-control. Even his poisoning phantasies may have served as a spurious kind of control, for if he could convince himself that the food was poisoned, he would not eat as much.

It was indeed an emotional predicament in which Paul found himself, and his anger about it was real enough. Most of the time he was so wrought up that he lashed out violently at everyone. It was dangerous to be near him at the dining table, as he pushed chairs and tables over, dashed plates heaped with food to the floor, and in the next moment demanded a fresh supply.

Threatening as this behavior was, it was somehow also comic. We could not help comparing this big, husky, ten-and-a-half-year-old boy with a baby in a high chair, who bangs his cup and spoon, tosses food overboard, and shrieks his anger and frustration. Even

Paul's appearance actually seemed babyish, as he smacked his lips and puckered them up.

Shortly after, he began vacillating between two demands: that we force him to eat and tell him when to stop. This seemed another expression of his battle against acquiring self-control. If we gave him both stop and go signals he would not have to make the decisions of which he still felt incapable. If he had to curb his own eating he might not get enough; yet he knew full well that by not checking himself, he over-ate. Thus we were thrown back into the quandary of whether to let him suffer because of his lack of self-control or to relieve him of the tough decisions at the risk that he might never develop the ability to regulate himself. Moreover, had we ordered him either to eat or to stop eating, he would probably have been just as angrily resentful of us as he was anxious when we did not interfere.

The same inability to control himself extended to the way Paul used his toys, bought his clothes, and so forth. Though he felt overindulged, he could not help asking for more in the same breath that he requested us to limit him. Here, too, he would have deeply resented any limits.

Half a year of such indulgence on our part at last had some effect. Paul openly conceded that the School had a few virtues. For example, in the light of his predominant anxiety, the head cook was the person of greatest importance for him. One day he volunteered, "She cooks good." More important, when we asked if he thought the meals had improved (for until then he had complained incessantly about them), he said, "Food didn't change; my taste did." This realization that he himself had changed, so that previously unpleasant experiences now seemed good, was a promising sign.

Paul was making true progress in other directions, also. Even within two months after his arrival, he was doing well in his classes. His clowning and outbursts of frustration made him a difficult pupil, but his genuine interest in learning made him a rewarding one, as well. Soon he was displaying an aptitude for drawing and painting. He derived great satisfaction from this interest, although he was mostly given to depicting graveyards and bizarre, even though gifted, elaborations on death. Was he expressing his own depressed feelings? Or was he trying to reach out for the father who had died? In any case, his artistic achievements won him his first recognition from children and adults.

With the coming of summer, gardening offered him a chance to deal with his pressing oral anxieties. While other children planted flowers, he planted only crops of radishes, onions, and corn. It was enormously important for Paul to raise his own food. The theme of his art work now changed to farming; but he still depicted rather autistic, self-centered activities, which excluded people. They were not yet present in his inner world.

Eventually, however, his isolation from other human beings began to yield. Perhaps his oral activities had proved satisfying, or his primitive needs had been better met—at any rate, Paul's deep longings did begin to come to light. One day he revealed to us his profound feelings of isolation. He said that he had never had any friends, and what is more, never would. Following one of his explosions, which occurred this time because the children had rejected him, he said, "I went up the Empire State Building and jumped down. After, everybody was my friend. I'd more friends than ever before."

Did this express his secret feeling that he must first be punished for his bad intentions before people could like him? Or that only a spectacular deed could win him recognition? The histrionics that colored even his most depressive remarks were quite evident here. Only the highest building in the world would do for expressing his suicidal phantasies, which arose from other motives than self-destruction. Just as his suicidal and homicidal explosions at the orphanage had been attempts to break out of his isolation, so now, when the children rejected his efforts to arouse their interest or sympathy through his "wild critter" act, he talked of jumping off the Empire State Building. Unfortunately, we could not be sure just what complex feelings had prompted Paul's erratic remarks, because he was either unwilling or unable to associate to them more elaborately. They were made more to himself than to anyone else in particular. Still, since he talked this way only when a relatively trusted counselor was present, they may have been early efforts at communication.

Such attempts to reach out toward contact with others happened only rarely. Mostly, Paul's emotional expressions, although explosive in their rage, were shallow in content. They were not directed at anyone in particular or connected with anything going on around him. Rather, they seemed to arise from inner motivations beyond his control and beyond our influence.

For months he entirely lacked orientation toward his life as a whole. For example, Paul could not visualize any future for himself beyond expecting that nothing good would ever happen to him. He lived only for the moment. Yet, for a long while he could not recall the names or characteristics of even the six children with whom he lived in the intimacy of his dormitory. Even after six months at the School he was able only occasionally to identify his playmates by name. He addressed everybody, child or adult, by shouting "Hey!" If the person whose attention he wanted to get did not answer, he would edge closer, tug at a sleeve or a coat tail, shove his face into theirs, and scream, "Hey, you!"

Most of the time, however, his expression remained dull and withdrawn. Although he screamed almost constantly, his voice was curiously devoid of emotional affect and modulation, so that it sounded flat.

When Paul was eating or drinking, any ephemeral interest he might have begun to take in what went on around him instantly vanished. At these times, nothing else in the world existed except the food before him. Even then, however, he was apparently torn by deep emotions, for he constantly shifted his position, so that his body was in continuous motion. Paul could not concentrate on anything, never felt relaxed, never did anything with ease. When he paused in his eating for a moment, he had to rise and walk about the dining room before sitting down to resume his meal.

Even casual observers were struck by how completely self-centered his life was. His sole motive for being interested in anything, it seemed, was what he could "get out of it." He had no concept of personal relations or of the normal give-and-take between people. "I" was his only concern; "you" did not exist in Paul's world. Imperiously, he made known his commands through single words. For example, wanting food, he would shout, "Milk!" or "Butter!"; for toys, he demanded, "Car!"; while gardening, when he was most content, he asked for "rake," or "shovel." If his requests were not instantly met, he flew into his usual rage.

His demanding manner, his violent anger at the least frustration, his need always to be the center of things, his total inability to share anything even for a moment, and his complete lack of interest in any person who did not concentrate on him exclusively—all revealed Paul's imperviousness to human contact. Even when he began to play with other children of his own volition, he barely tolerated them. It took him no less than four months after entering the School to be able to distinguish between the two counselors whom he saw daily and who cared for all his needs; and it was longer before he could ask any personal questions of his favorite counselor, the person he knew best. Once, having secured a physical hold on her by clinging hard to her arm—as though he would substitute this for the emotional closeness he still despaired of achieving—he brought himself to ask where she lived. The other

acking expressed obvious pleasure. But he was not yet able t
etter contact with those around him while eating, not even wit
es who fed him. The process of eating as such still so completel
ed Paul that he had little energy left over at mealtimes fo
ding to others.

this, his development did not parallel that of the infant, wh
lly begins to recognize his mother as a person while she feeds
aul's behavior may suggest that, while human relations are firs
ished at this time, if a baby has been fed with indifference and
ariety of people (as Paul had in the nursery) and if starvation
y is dominant (as it was in him), the eating situation becomes
f-centered that it is no longer suitable for establishing human
ons; other activities, such as dressing or bathing, must then re-
it. In this respect Paul also differed from other children in the
l, with whom we had been able to establish contact while feed-
em.

ut in many other ways, Paul was demonstrating that being the
was the most important thing now happening in his life. Playing
was his favorite game of all, and each time his turn came he
pose as a baby. He would lie on the ground, while he kicked and
med, and sucked his thumb. He could scarcely give up the pose
ume the game and would often remain on the ground, totally
are of the world around him.

is attachment to his favorite counselor took on other infantile
res. For instance, he had to know where she was and what she
doing, every minute of the day. If she only left the house on an
d, he asked when she would be back, checked the clock to see
she was on time, and grew desperate when she was late. He spent
of the time while she was away just waiting for her; sometimes
afed forlornly and aimlessly through a magazine. In his turn, he
ys told her in great detail where he was going, even for a moment.
n playing baseball, which later became one of his favorite games,
ept close track of his counselor and would interrupt the play
y few minutes (much to the annoyance of the other players) to
after her and ask, "Want me with you, or [should I] finish [the]
e?" On departing for class each morning, he told her what time
ould return (it was always the same) and made sure that she
d be there waiting for him.

This did not so much mean that he had established a true friend-
, as that he was anxiously clinging to the only person who meant
hing to him. He still felt very insecure about her feelings toward
especially about their permanency. The slightest frustration from
set off his violent rage. Often, however, the outburst was followed

children were aware that her room was only three doors from their dormitory, and Paul had been shown this time and again so that he could find her at any hour of the day or night. But his profound isolation had to lift a little before he could envisage her as a living, personal entity, who continued to exist away from him.

His only frame of reference during these first months, his only way of orienting himself, lay in contrasting the orphanage routines with those of the School. Even after six months with us he could evaluate anything in this way alone. He specifically weighed the School's advantages against those of the orphanage: our food was better, and he was not forced to eat it; he was busy and occupied and did not "always have [to take] everybody along." At this moment he saw our relaxed and permissive attitude toward eating in a favorable light, although at other times he still wanted to be forced to eat so that he would be sure of getting enough. His remark about not taking everybody along probably reflected his emerging realization that we respected his privacy and treated him as an individual, not just as a group member. Grown-ups, he felt, were still threatening, but you might occasionally find a friend among them, like his favorite counselor. Still, he summed up the comparison by saying that, best of all, at the School, "I can sleep as much as I want," which gave him freedom to withdraw from the world.

Next, Paul learned to distinguish grown-ups from children. Previously, adults to him had been simply children grown taller. Here, too, his only frame of reference was himself. This trait had been even more apparent when he first came; then he had been able to differentiate only "little ones," children like himself or smaller, and "big ones," everybody else. For the first time it dawned on him that there might be some drawbacks to being one of the powerful "big ones," who could beat up "kids" like himself. It might even be better to be a child, he decided, because grown-ups had to work hard to make a living. But then he instantly had to deny such a potentially dangerous differentiation, which took cognizance of an external world. He asserted that "it's all the same." Similarly, when he could not make up his mind whether he was "the good guy" or "the bad guy," it again made no difference, since everything was "all the same."

Once he tried to explain just how this was so: "Bad guy stabs good guy, good guy stabs back"—in revenge probably. Since everybody gets stabbed, it makes no real difference whether one is a good or a bad guy. In effect, Paul was denying any need for becoming more socialized; after all, he seemed to be saying, what is the use of trying when one always ends up by attacking other people? No direct solution was possible for the impasse in which he found himself. Like a small child, he needed to acquire self-control by assimilating the values of persons with whom he identified. But to identify with people he first had to relate to them.

Once more, it was a crisis that led to fresh developments in Paul's life, just as a crisis had been instrumental in bringing him to the School. Although we prefer not to have a new child enter a group until all the others are well settled, it sometimes takes a youngster like Paul such a long time to orient himself that we are forced to make an exception.

With the passing of a few months we could wait no longer to admit a new boy to Paul's group. His arrival in the dormitory was an immediate threat to Paul, but he did find ways of reassuring himself. For the first time, he asked his favorite counselor to come over to his bed, and kissed her good night.[21] Then he told her a story, which he called a "joke": two people started going somewhere, but soon found themselves back in the same place they had started from. Paul's fear that the new boy could set him back where he had started with his counselor, showed that he still did not trust the reliability of human ties. But he had learned to appreciate them, since he felt threatened at the possibility of their loss.

For the next few days, he once again relapsed into aloofness. The arrival of the newcomer revived all Paul's anxieties about being deserted, and rather than find himself forsaken, he gave up all human contact. But this time he began to discover that, in the School, a new child would not displace him, as his half sister had usurped whatever little place he had occupied in his mother's life. Once he realized that his fears of being abandoned were groundless, Paul let himself experiment with being more dependent than ever before. He requested his counselor to wash him in the bath, while he sang in a childish voice, "My mamma washes my hands for me," or "my face" or "my legs." As she dressed him, he would repeat in a sing-song voice, "My mamma puts on my clean socks," and so forth.

The satisfaction he derived from this infantile, tender care was of crucial importance for a long time. After a few weeks, another central emotional experience was added. Emotionally, this ten-and-a-half-year-old boy entered a period in which he seemed to be vacillating between an infantile (pre-oedipal) dependency, and an oedipal

---

21. We do not favor such adult ways of expressing emotions: we do not kiss children good night or let them kiss us. But in moments of great stress, such as this one, exceptions are made.

---

attachment. Like the oedipal phase in inf
many ups and downs.

Paul's first real phantasy, based somewh
he lived, was of an oedipal character. He mac
elaborated tale about marrying his favorite
for him played the role of a good mother. H
this in a situation in which a mother norma
small child—when he was being bathed. It w
for him to talk about his feelings for her. J
mised from the fact that he really tried to
softly, without raising his voice. It seemed
at all, and he spoke slowly, repeating almo
times.

The phantasy was roughly as follows: "
standing in the bathroom—I wonder if you
anyway, one day a young man came along a
in the bathroom, as I do. She was putting son
the man liked her because she did things
asked her to marry him. And so they got mar
celebration. Do you know who came to the c
halted. Then, with great hesitation and reluc
names of other boys in his dormitory group.
this girl and this fellow went to live in a hot
rooms there, and the littlest bathroom you ev
a true oedipal phantasy, in which he played t
his counselor, the wife (and mother), he a
while walking out of the bathroom with her.
leaned closely against her and said, "I'm goi
arm for the rest of my life." A few weeks late
and I'll wait until I'm twenty, then I'll marry

From then on, Paul slowly grew more cont
to laugh and smile, and often jokingly called
"mommy." The simplest services, of the sort
her child, led to the development of this, his
Frequently he remarked how nice it was to hav
clothes, buy him new ones, put his toys away f
bodily coordination was still poor and he per
ganized and dishevelled, but from this time on
to lose their characteristic rigidity or uncontrolle
ran, he now looked more like a very small ch
was less apt to play the crazy man, and reacte
three-year-old. His eating habits also changed,

by depressive feelings, and remarks that "nobody likes me." He interpreted the least, most unavoidable frustration as a complete rejection by the world. Another child had only to make the most innocent and slightly critical remark, and Paul's world fell apart. Dissolving into tears, he would cry that everyone was unfair to him; yet he never seemed able to point out the particular person who was rejecting him.

He felt quite strongly that counselors should not rotate duties or take time off, and complained, "Counselors are lazy." We encouraged Paul to talk more about this, and found that his complaints did not reflect any fresh desire for a close relation, but an older conviction that he was very dangerous. "You're scared [to] take care [of me]," he said. When we asked why he thought this, he could only repeat, "You're scared[to] take care [of me] all day, that's why you take turns." But at other times he was content to curl up in his favorite counselor's lap, saying he was her baby. He loved having her rock him and when she did so he would suck his thumb with great contentment. Hugging her ever closer, he would ask her to sing to him and stroke his head.

With the satisfaction of his infantile needs, Paul was able to view life more positively, particularly the eating situation. He frequently remarked that the food tasted fine. Before, he had chronically complained that he was not given enough to eat or was being poisoned, but now he could not praise the meals highly enough. To his continual amazement, they were always plentiful. He gloated, "Chicken at noon, and corn at night; it's just like getting everything you want," or, "I keep good and fat in this place."

He regularly inspected our pantries to check on supplies as they arrived and were used. He was afraid that we might exhaust the stores faster than they could be replenished. But he would also say, "You keep good food in this place." To anyone who would listen he reported such new items as, "They got in big box Krispies today, big box Corn Flakes." Out of the blue, when he had seemed to be watching other children or talking about something else, he would blurt out a remark revealing that this preoccupation had semi-consciously been preying on his mind: "They got lot pancake powder today; wonder when we're having pancakes." He was rather proud of keeping track of our supplies: "Just so anything happens, you know, I know what's here."

Another half year elapsed before Paul's newly found conviction that his basic needs would be cared for, and that he had the ability to care for at least a few of them himself, led him to achieve some self-control. Even this lasted only temporarily, and was dependent on the close contact existing at the moment between Paul and his favorite counselor. Together, they used to make fudge, and Paul was happy not only that he could mix as big a batch as he liked but that he could now make candy himself. Once, after a cooking session was over, in his excitement over this new achievement he started shooting water wildly around the room with his squirt gun. He had done this before and had enjoyed the play at first, but then he had become so reckless in his shooting that he had to be restricted. This time, he seemed to sense, himself, when he had gone far enough and was getting over-excited. He said to himself, "Just twice more." Then after shooting two times he put the gun down. It was the first time he had limited himself on anything; and the interesting thing was that this happened only after he had enjoyed to the full his new ability to make candy. This kind of self-restraint differed sharply from limiting his eating by claiming that the food was poisoned or tasted bad. It was open, direct, rational—but for a long time it remained the rare exception rather than the rule.

While Paul was forming a rudimentary friendship with his favorite counselor, his ability to do this did not extend to other people, children least of all. He still had to frighten them to make his own position safe. The "wild critter" and "crazy man" attempts to overawe them dissolved into more childlike ways of scaring. He would now jump out from corners, screeching, "I'm a ghost!" If this made the children angry he righteously protested, "I just said a couple of words, a couple of words, is there a law against that?"

His security rested on megalomanic notions about his own power. As the "wild critter" and "crazy man" he had remained outside the circle of mankind. As the great dictator, the ruler of the universe, he rejoined it. Customarily he called us "slaves," and ordered all of us around. "Get me this, slave," was a frequent order during this period. It was the way he expressed his underlying feeling about his relations to others, and it lasted until he became more socialized (about a year and a half later). Apparently, in order to impose some semblance of restraint upon himself, he had to assert control over everyone else. Only as master of a world of slaves could his security be assured.

Even this exaggerated method of acquiring self-control was hard to maintain. Again and again Paul went back to his old request that we control him so that he would not have to master the art of controlling himself. He protested, "All you do around here [is] give people candy bars, instead punishing them." This was again his frequent complaint—that we did not punish enough, though he never could explain why he felt so much punishment was necessary.

He may possibly have felt pangs of guilt about his misbehavior. But if so, his own explanation of his motives never revealed this. Whether he scared the children, or grabbed their toys and tossed them away, he always came up with the same excuse for his asocial acts: others might do these things to him, said Paul, and so it was best to do them to others first. When we tried to reason with him, he only became more unreachable, and complained, "What am I supposed to do? Just go around like a statue and never do anything? Stand around and let them hit me?" When we pointed out that no one had hit him, and that he knew we would not permit this, he maintained, "Yes, but at the orphanage they hit me, and so I've got to hit them first so they won't." To him, that was sufficient explanation.

An illustration of his inability to understand personal relations, especially with his age-mates, was his attitude toward another boy, whom we moved into his dormitory. The reason for making this move was that the two had seemed to be very friendly, and we hoped that the youngsters would benefit from each other's company. Paul was very pleased when we told him of our plan. This boy could now be his "servant," he said. Noting his counselor's raised eyebrows, he edited his remark by saying that he meant the boy would be his "secretary." When the counselor explained that we hoped they would be friends, Paul said this was exactly what he had intended. But he could not explain what "being friends" meant. So he returned to the notion that the boy would be his secretary, meaning that he would do things for Paul; in fact Paul would tell him exactly what to do and what not to. How little Paul was affected by our attempt to explain friendship could be seen when the boy arrived in the dormitory. In an effort to make him feel welcome, Paul said, "I'm glad you came live with me, because I read all your comics!"

While Paul was not yet relating to anybody except, possibly, his favorite counselor, after about a year with us, he did begin to "see" the world around him, and to perceive that it could offer worthwhile experiences. With this, his interests and activities changed. He gave up demanding frequent visits to the movies, which to him meant "mysteries" or Westerns, "exciting" or "murder" shows. He was able to tell us how they had increased his anxiety, so that he had to erect defenses against them; these defenses, while shutting out the movies, also blocked his contact with the world. Another boy happened to be talking about how upsetting motion pictures about murder were. Paul interjected, "Murder movies are fine; don't 've [to] hear what they say—that what I do."

As his life-experiences became less "murderous" for him, he could better endure hearing and seeing what went on around him. Life, for Paul, slowly took on new, fresh meaning. For example, though he had frequently visited the nearby Museum of Science and Industry, he realized for the first time how many interesting exhibits it housed. He remarked that he had never really seen them before; he had looked at them, but had been thinking about other things. His interest in handicrafts and art work also grew. From this time on, painting became his favorite means of expression, perhaps because his speech difficulties, though improving, continued to be a serious impediment to verbal communication.

This capacity for enjoying real experiences permitted him in some degree to relinquish his asocial ways of seeking status. Now he seldom acted the "zombie," and gave up playing the "wild critter" altogether; he now thought it "a crazy game," and was glad the counselors had stopped it. Grown-ups no longer seemed like giants, who might order children about or beat them up. In a playful way he began exploring a truer conception of life. In one of his phantasy games (these were also a new development), Paul called the manager of the Museum of Science and Industry on a toy telephone, and asked him to make sure that their new exhibits, in which he had only recently taken an interest, were better publicized. He wanted the manager to take particular pains to exhibit a Bikini goat, so that everybody could see it. (At the time, newspapers were carrying stories about the animals who were recuperating from radiation injuries suffered during the Bikini atomic bomb tests.) Paul said that he thought the goat was being cured "by loving it, taking good care of it." But he could only believe in the restorative power of affection when it was connected with security about having sufficient food. Pursuing his imaginary conversation, he suggested that the Museum stage a television show about a wheat machine, "so people see there 's enough bread for always." In a similar vein, he liked to draw cacti because "they save people's life: there's much water in them; people live if there 's water at least." When he was in good, friendly contact with his favorite counselor, his phantasies about food had reassuring qualities, beyond the confidence he felt in the amplitude of the School's food supply.

This more optimistic view of life, however, still was very short-lived, and a depressive, hostile mood generally prevailed. The more positive outlook hinged on whether Paul's favorite counselor could give him her undivided attention for long periods of time, without even a slight frustration interrupting their closeness. Moreover, he had to have tangible evidence of her good will before he could feel more optimistic—she had to do things for him, such as baking cookies, repairing his clothing, helping him make an airplane, handing him brushes as he painted, and so on.

For example, some time after Paul had become quite cheerful about the adequacy of the food supply, his counselor was very gently critical of him one day for pushing other children. His immediate reaction was to feel utterly desolate, and he lost contact with her for a while. In his isolation he drew pictures of a world without people. In a provocative fashion, as if proud of rejecting the world, he said, "My paintings have no people. All people left. Whole world blown up by time bomb. They installed [it] themselves, the last people. Nobody survived." Another time when he felt estranged from his counselor, he drew a train; as he sketched, he made the sounds of a train, and said, "Nobody's in train, nobody's living." In similar vein he had phantasies about accidents, about cars blowing up, or people drowning—always depersonalized "people"—never anyone with a name.

For protection, Paul still relied solely on himself; he could not yet trust another person. Significantly, the first object he used to protect him was a teddy bear that was given him shortly after he came to the School. He overpowered this toy animal so that it would "know who [is] master." For many months, he handled it aggressively, beat it, and totally mistreated it, just as he had attacked everyone at the School. After this treatment, it became his best friend, who watched out for him and protected him at night. Paul still preferred to trust an inanimate symbol of our good will, rather than the actual good will of any person.

Infantile Pleasures and
A Changing Outlook on Life

AT THE END of his first year with us, which brought Paul to his eleventh birthday, we noted signs of new developments in him. They first became visible during the holiday season, and may have been prompted by the festivities. As before, these new steps toward a higher achievement and a more positive outlook on life were linked to food. In gardening, Paul had always made sure that he planted enough for him, and no one else. Now he began worrying whether others were adequately fed. Thus his recognition of and interest in other people began with his inclusion of them in his main preoccupation.

Thanksgiving was Paul's first "real" holiday, and he thoroughly relished it.[22] In the orphanage, he complained, nothing special had ever happened. But this, he said, "is [my] first real Thanksgiving. [I] had first real Hallowe'en at School, now first real Thanksgiving." All day long he ate tremendous quantities (after his seventh serving of turkey, his counselor gave up keeping track), and seemed quite satisfied that there was an ample supply. Still he had to gorge himself to prove it.

A few days later I was talking to some of the children and asking them, as is my custom from time to time, what changes they thought should be made in School procedures, what improvements they could suggest, and what complaints they might have. These difficult problems disposed of, I asked the easier question about what features they liked best about the School. Paul's answer was, "Leola's cooking." (Leola was our head cook.) Good food was his bulwark against sickness and death, for a moment later he added that there was another good feature about the School: the sick room was so far away from the children's living quarters that the "germs [could] not get through" and hence sickness could not spread. This was the first indication that his eating had some relation to an anxiety about illness.

Shortly after Thanksgiving, Paul for the first time expressed a dislike of some foods, and even occasionally refused second helpings of his favorites. It seemed to us that he was rejecting the fare not so much because he disliked it or was reluctant to accept a second helping, as because he wanted to test whether or not he could limit himself and cut down on his eating without anything untoward happening. This was another entirely new development, for Paul had been eating everything compulsively, whether he liked it or not, and had asked for second, third, and fourth helpings no matter how full he was.

No longer did he claim we were trying to starve him; but he did feel most uncomfortable about his new, inexplicable restraint toward food. There must be some reason for it, he felt, and in the light of his deep oral anxiety, it could only be a bad one. He claimed, "I just know [you] put vitamins in food make us eat less." Yet vitamins are healthy, after all, so his remark suggested his ambivalence: our intentions were both bad (we made him eat less) and good (we gave him vitamins). These conflicting feelings toward us quite naturally augmented his confusion and discomfort.

22. Labor Day and the Fourth of July, which are also big holidays at the School, had made no impression on him; when they occurred, one day was still like another to him, empty and indistinguishable from any other, because it conveyed to him no positive emotional meaning.

Perhaps to find out exactly how we handled the food, in order to penetrate our true intentions, Paul now asked if he could help the cooks prepare some meals. We arranged for him to assist in preparing Sunday dinner, and soon he acted as though the major responsibility were his own. He quite believed that this meal was his exclusive creation, and boasted happily about it. His success in helping meant a great deal to him; it was additional proof that he could supply his own food. He also genuinely enjoyed preparing the meal for others. For the first time, he acquired a realistic notion of how much food went into a meal, and could convince himself that our supplies would suffice for any emergency.

In individual sessions with his counselor he had always loved to play tea party. At these times, he had only fed himself, though he and his counselor always prepared the party together. Now, Paul occasionally took over and fixed a treat for her, which demonstrated his new mastery in restraining himself when confronted with appetizing food and his new ability to do things for others.

This increased control of his oral cravings gave Paul the courage to extend his explorations of infantile behavior, perhaps because he felt that he would now be able to control this regression, too. Probably, the greater control he could exercise over his desires, the more primitive satisfactions he could permit himself. Also, cooking for his schoolmates may have reduced his guilt about his own voracious oral desires, and therefore he felt better able to give in to them. Having observed that feeding others did not give him overwhelming power over them, he felt fairly safe in letting himself become orally dependent.

In any case, in the wake of his success at controlling his craving for food and preparing meals for others, he reverted to the bottle. One day Paul was having fun at one of the tea parties he had arranged for himself and his counselor. While getting ready for the party, he noticed a little doll, which had a bottle and nipple. It had always been in full view during his play sessions, but for the first time he asked, "What about that bottle?" When his counselor countered, "What about it?" Paul said, "Thought might put some milk in," and did so. He began sucking on it, but soon put it aside with the remark that the rubber tasted "awful." Sucking through a nipple was not yet possible for Paul; more exploration of the dangers attached to oral regression had to come first.

He decided to try another way of getting the milk from the baby bottle into his mouth. First he poured milk from a big container into the tiny toy bottle, then, with his head tilted way back, he slowly shook the liquid into his wide-open mouth. When he had emptied the toy bottle, Paul checked the milk left in the big one and said in amazement, "Almost full as before." After drinking all the milk, a full pint, in this exceedingly slow way, he offered to wash the dishes and put things away. It was the first time he had ever volunteered to do this. The counselor told him she would be happy to clean up as usual, but he firmly rejected the idea. Shaking his head emphatically, he said, "I'm [the] mother." He had to be the mother feeding the baby and the baby who was fed, all at the same time.

During the next session, Paul sketched his favorite counselor as a baby sucking her thumb. Apparently, he wanted to reduce her to his own emotional level in order to bridge the gap between them. This seemed to make identification easier. Just as he had claimed to be both the feeding mother and the sucking baby, his counselor now had to be both. Only this double personification could make possible his identification with her.

Within a week after this identification was established, Paul began to suck milk through a straw—at first, only in the privacy of the session room, but soon, everywhere. Paul took his milk bottle even to class and to the playground, and from time to time would take vigorous swigs.

He also began to tell us about his dreams. In the first one he related, he was the king of the whole universe, a superman who had a million dollars and ruled everyone. Next morning he recounted another. In this dream, he had paid the orphanage a return visit, and now all the children liked him very much. As he splashed in the pool, everybody sat around watching and admiring him. Associating to this dream, he recalled that when he lived at the orphanage he just had not been able to learn to swim. Now he understood that his fear of the water was the consequence of his treatment by the older boys, who had pushed him into the pool, or had swung him by his legs and hands and thrown him into it. Recollections of past mistreatment always led him almost instantly to act the bully again. This time, too, he jumped up and began attacking the other children viciously, unable to control the violently aggressive feeling aroused by these memories. Such explosive responses made it difficult for us to help him master his past.

Yet, Paul's dreams suggested that at least on an unconscious level he was beginning to feel differently about himself, his past, and his future. His first dream revealed that he was attempting to compensate for his lack of personal status in the orphanage by imagining that he was omnipotent. In the second, his recent, real achievements in swimming and diving gave him prestige with people who used to look down on him. This new strength permitted him to develop a more assuring perspective on past and future. While the past had been unhappy, similar situations would not again find him helpless. As though testing the validity of such hopes, Paul had to demonstrate to himself immediately that he could now inflict upon others the torment inflicted on him, and this was another motive for attacking the children nearby.

For similar reasons, Paul still could not bear the least frustration. Each defeat implied the loss of all his gains and stirred up fears that he was right back in his old plight, with all power of self-determination lost, and himself again the helpless victim of all abuse. This may explain why the most trivial inconvenience assumed enormous proportions for him, and why his typical reaction to losing any game was, "I kill you!"

When he felt relatively secure and emotionally close to a trusted person, Paul could realize that he lacked control. Then he would invent stories to placate us, as he did one day while pretending to phone the School again on the toy telephone. This time he was a famous newspaper man, who knew "this boy, Paul, in School. He's a good fellow," he commented, "but gets [into] too many fights. You've got be patient with him!" Patience was indeed required of us all.

Such insights were rare, however. Most of the time Paul felt angry and he was beginning to feel guilty, too. Guilt was a relatively new development, which stemmed from his assimilation of some of the standards of behavior to which he had been exposed for some time. He could afford to adopt these now since he felt more certain that his basic physiological needs would be cared for. However, feeling guilty also made him angry, and he would violently accuse us of making him feel guilty by giving him too many things and taking care of him too well.

He even used his guilt about what the School did for him as an excuse for being aggressive against the children and counselors. When he had quieted down after one especially violent outburst of rage, he explained its cause by screaming, "[You] won't let me buy my things! Don't let me buy toys, ice skates, nothing! All I want, you buy [for me]. Won't let me buy [my] own things!" But when we suggested that he could spend his allowance on things he wanted, Paul became even more enraged, and accused us of trying to take advantage of him by putting pressure upon him to spend his own money instead of ours. This anger of his, Paul relished with a vengeance. To be just plain mad, and to vent it on others, were new luxuries for him. In the past, Paul had not been able to afford ordinary anger very often. His only resource had been to explode in acts of violence. Now he could be furious with us for days, if he wished. What a luxury this was, and what power over us! But when these orgies of anger were over he felt guilty, very meek, and enormously demanding of and in need of love.

There was another change in Paul, which became apparent about this time. His more hopeful outlook on life was reflected in his expectation that good things were in store for him at Christmas. But this hope evoked anticipatory guilt, which he felt the more severely because the pleasures he looked forward to were no longer shadowy wishes but expected reality. This reality was too good for him to enjoy. Its impact only evoked defensive reactions. He had wished so long for good things in life and had been so deeply disappointed, that when the good things came, they overpowered him, and he had to defend himself against their impact.

We have seen this kind of behavior again and again. If frustration has been too severe, then satisfaction becomes too threatening to be truly enjoyed. Moreover, it only evokes angry memories of all the past disappointments. To be reminded of these at the moment when, theoretically, it should be possible to enjoy oneself most, seems a dirty trick on one's emotions. Then the anger one feels in this situation, which had been expected to bring happiness, adds a new insult to old injuries. And the person who has provided these satisfactions that one has wished for years to enjoy, but now cannot, seems a torturer rather than a friend.

Still, in the long run, superabundant satisfactions will heal old wounds. On Christmas morning, Paul was the only boy who took pains to dress very carefully in his best clothes, which disclosed what a red-letter day this was for him. Most children run first to their pile of presents and leave the Christmas stockings for later. Paul first approached the fireplace where the stockings were hanging, and slowly took down his own. Then, instead of unwrapping his presents and becoming absorbed in them, he conversed with the other children about theirs. After that, he slowly repacked the presents in his stocking. When we finally reminded him that he had not even looked at his gifts, he harshly replied, "Let me in peace," and ran out of the room, shouting, "That's enough. I can't stand it. I can't stand it." After running wildly all over the house, as he used to do in his "wild critter" act (though this had been given up for some time), Paul at last returned to the living room where the Christmas celebration was in progress. But still he would not look at his presents. Only several hours later, when all the other children were through and most of them had left the living room, did he open his presents one by one, slowly and deliberately. He was content just to sit for a while, letting them sink in. Then he depreciated them all. "Oh, just got bunch of junk. Just got few junky things, [that's] all I got." Finally he picked up one very simple game, and began to complain steadily that he did not know how to play it. He was sure we had given it to him because we knew the other children could beat him at it.

It was a few days before Paul seemed to master his emotional shock and began to profit from this experience. He exclaimed to everyone that this was "the first real Christmas of my life." One night he was overheard to say in his sleep, "Yes, want work in orphan's home. No, don't take old pajamas away." When the boys in his dormitory told Paul about this next morning, he denied saying anything of the sort, and explained that he had only dreamt somebody was trying to steal his clothes. Could he really recall only unpleasant events in his life or in his dreams? Or did he not dare to admit his guilt and his wish, now that nice things were happening to him, to make amends by being pleasant to those who still suffered in the orphanage?

Paul was torn by other ambivalences. On the one hand, he wanted to be recognized as a mature, independent person; on the other, he reached out for infantile services and satisfactions, although by accepting them, he was made to feel even more immature. Another upsetting ambivalence centered in the conflict between his destructive tendencies, of which he now largely disapproved but which he could not yet integrate, and his budding constructive desires. This conflict was reflected in everything Paul did. Should he read, for example, or should he beat others in competitive games? Should he ask for something very childish, or for something very grown-up. Did he want to play with soldiers, whose guns could "shoot others," or to build houses with blocks, so that "people live happily" in them?

In a constructive mood, Paul would build villages of blocks and take pleasure in his achievement. But having played happily with the idea of living in the nice houses he made, he then invariably had to destroy them through "terrible earthquakes" or "crash-ups." Why? He usually explained that he destroyed these houses " 'cause it's home," or we might say, because they reminded him that he had never lived in such a home. Thus the construction of beautiful houses represented his desires, their destruction the reality he had known—and in his play he acted out the contradiction between reality and desires, a contradiction he could not yet solve. After the violently destructive mood passed, Paul usually became contrite and sought safety in some restitutive or truly constructive activity. On one occasion he looked desperately around the room until he finally hit on a solution: "Going make picture for wall." And in sketching one, he found relief.

Thus Paul opposed his destructive tendencies by creating an artistic object. This not only pacified his feeling of guilt by making restitution for his destructiveness, but, in a way, also showed that when he was closely related to a mother figure his destructive actions were only play (destroying the toy houses), while his constructive activities were real (beautifying the walls of his home). At peace with himself again, he once more called the School on the toy telephone. As a member of the School's "board of directors," he asked, "What [do] you need for [the] children? Candy? Paper? Paints? Crayons? You've all [they] need? That's good. Good-bye." The art materials he used in painting, which was his best way of sublimating, were now perhaps even more important to him than candy. Although candy, which represented Paul's need for oral gratification, was still mentioned first, Paul moved from it immediately to the art materials. When his counselor, food, and the means of self-realization through artistic creation—all three—were present, then, he felt, the School was complete.

This hardly means that Paul was always successful in sublimating his destructive tendencies. They still were far too strong, and his ability to integrate them far too weak. This inability was, in fact, one source of his guilt and rage. His sudden switches from aggression to guilty restitution, and then back to aggression, could be seen in the way he would change from one topic to another in the process of painting a picture. For example, one day when he was sketching a war scene in which big guns were firing, he suddenly painted it over, and created a peaceful garden scene in its stead. Had the idea of his garden, where he could grow his own food, evoked reassuring thoughts and allowed them to predominate? Or had he felt so much hostility while painting the war scene that he had to make amends by creating a more constructive and peaceful one? Perhaps sufficient tension had been discharged through his phantasies while he painted the first scene to give his integrative powers the upper hand. Whatever the reason, the battlefield was transformed into a vegetable garden, and the guns into harmless statues.

After he had expressed a peaceful state of mind, his mood changed again. "I'm the great dictator," he declared. When asked why he had returned to this ambition, he gave a new answer. We had first asked him this question a few months before, at which time he could only reply, "To dictate! To dictate! To dictate!" Thus he expressed his wish to enslave others so that he could feel more secure. But now he added, "So can make them all mad at me." Previously Paul had felt no need to justify his anger toward his environment. The anger persisted, but now, because of his new sense of guilt, he needed a reason for discharging anger against us; and this is why he craved the power to make us angry. It seemed to him that only if we were "mad," too, could he act out his hostile wishes against us.

Paul had become pretty much assured about his physical well-being, and with this most pressing anxiety out of the way, he could afford the luxury of satisfying other desires, such as taking revenge for all his past deprivations. Another explanation also suggests itself. As small children develop, they often go through a phase in which fear of the demands made by the superego overshadows their fear of reality. Now that Paul was developing a superego, his anxiety about its possible demands may have outstripped his anxiety about reality. This may explain why he no longer needed to be the dictator in order to insure that everyone would serve him as a slave and minister to his physical well-being. Rather, he needed assurance that he would be at peace with his superego. Paul's emotional well-being was not yet founded on being loved by others, and loving them in return, but on freedom from feeling guilty about his hostility. He wanted to rouse everyone's fury; he wanted to agitate the world in which he lived in order to justify his own aggressiveness. Then he need not fear his conscience's criticism of his hostility. Neither would there be any necessity for integrating his anger, or for undertaking the difficult task of changing and organizing his personality.

It also seemed probable that there was another mechanism, the oedipal, behind his wish to be the dictator once more. He craved the dictator's power to do away with all competitors for love and dependent care. Outraged that he had to share not only his favorite counselor, but also the other counselors, the teachers, cooks, and the rest of the staff, including myself, Paul often wished to do away with every single one of the other children. But as soon as he felt this impulse, he became so guilty that he had to act out his destruction rather than theirs.[23]

For example, Paul often played aggressive "games" with other

---

23. Or was he trying to control his own murderous wishes through a vivid enactment of retaliation by others? Yet after all, fear of retaliation is an important factor in the development of guilt and of the superego, so either explanation would be in line with the central task with which Paul was then struggling.

children, which had to be checked. He would then act out executions with the pounding board, blocks, or some simple play material. Usually he executed other people first, then himself; but this sequence was sometimes reversed. The play was invariably noisy, but only rarely were the noises articulate. Occasionally, however, Paul would say something like this: "Getting ready for execution. [There are] seven people [and] one child." (Paul was then living in a dormitory with seven others.) Suiting the action to the words, he would pick up eight wooden pegs, seven of the same length, and one shorter, which represented the child. The short peg would then proceed to dispose of the seven long pegs. Later, he sometimes changed the drama. Then the people were "getting ready for Paul's execution." In yet another version, the seven pegs became Paul's slaves.

Paul did not want to do away with siblings only. If he could have had his way, no one but he and his favorite counselor would be left. One day after she had finished telling him a story, he said, "Now I'll tell story. Once there was a terrible, lovely, lousy, beautiful school at Sixtieth and Dorchester [the School's address]. Everybody cried all time; kids got whipped with big whips. Finally girl named Gayle came. She said, 'I'm the law. You get out, you get out, you get out, you get out.' And she took all whips all away, [and then] only you and I were left in School."

In a way the essence of this story was true. While disregarding objective reality, it truly described Paul's emotional reality. It was not the physical move from the orphanage to the School that did away with the whips and the bullying "big ones." For his fear of them accompanied Paul to the School. He got rid of this anxiety as his emotional concentration on it was replaced by emotional concentration on his favorite counselor. For Paul, she had established a new law, a new way of life; it was their mutual attachment, and the services she rendered him, that banished the bullies from his mind. After that only he and she dwelt in the world of his emotions.

On the level of objective reality, he knew that it was not possible to have his favorite counselor all to himself; hence he wished to alter the world so that only the two of them existed. He wanted to destroy everyone else, as the small child (which emotionally Paul was) wants to banish daddy and the other children so that he can have mommy always to himself. But after all, Paul was not a three-year-old, and in line with his new sense of guilt—if not yet a new morality—he felt that he, himself, ought to be dealt with in the same way he wished to treat others. So from specific phantasies about destroying everyone in the School and living in splendid closeness to a mother figure, he would quite frequently return to more general phantasies about destroying the whole world, including himself.

As time passed, Paul became better able to talk about his hostile wishes, and no longer had to retire as often to his comics or to the murder dramas on the radio and in the movies. Other pursuits were more satisfying: his art work above all, and the painting to which he withdrew more and more. He was calm, to some degree content, and certainly very absorbed as he drew or painted. But the instant he stopped, he became aggressive.

His self-destructive drives—which so often carried overtones of seeking punishment because of guilt—were by no means displayed only in the play sessions. They showed up, for example, when he was skating or sledding and were often a means by which he tested our care of him. With very apparent anxiety, Paul tried to skate down an icy hill, though he knew we would not let him risk actual danger. He was angered when we checked him: "I can't do nothing. Don't let me do nothing. Just make me a privileged character." Being a "privileged character" meant that we were watching out for him and safeguarding his well-being, and also keeping him from potentially harmful acts.

In the play sessions, too, Paul craved the experience of being protected against his destructive tendencies. He liked to play with toy soldiers and invariably set them up with guns pointing at each other. But as soon as the two opposing armies were in position, he grew terrified. Paralyzed with fear, he dared not even touch them. "Turn them around," he begged. "Make guns point out. Don't [let them] point guns [at] each other."

Sometimes the toy soldiers seemed to prefer destroying themselves to shooting at one another. Some committed suicide by jumping off fortresses, others, by falling from the windows of buildings, as Paul had once tried to do. He always saw to it, however, that they were rescued in the nick of time.

The World Becomes Populated

WITH THE GROWTH of Paul's feeling that we were looking out for his welfare, he could sense that there was some security to his life. He felt encouraged to begin the struggle to find himself as a person. This goal had been unattainable as long as an insensitive environment had forced him into an externally imposed, depersonalized, and hence anonymous pattern of living. Within the responsive, personalized environment of the School, Paul was able to assimilate some values, and to forge from them a tenuous self-control. No longer was he helplessly driven and torn by his emotions. The process of acquiring additional values was strengthened by his increased self-control, and this led, in its turn, to the emergence of a more personal superego. Paul's behavior came to be marked by a developing inner consistency. Further, he found support for his ego in his success at influencing the world about him through reasonable actions, instead of irrational explosions. Most of all, his ego was bolstered by the social recognition accorded his artistic creations.

Having thus acquired at least the rudiments of a personality, Paul could conceive of himself as a human being, who was able to interact with others and to enjoy the satisfactions they could give him. However, the gap between being theoretically able to achieve this and actually doing so required long, hard effort to bridge. This posed the central problem of Paul's next two years, his second and third, with us. As he discovered himself as a person (not as a "wild critter" or a ruler of slaves), Paul began to regard other people as human beings. Insight into some of their emotions, motives, and ways of solving problems helped him to deal better with his own inner difficulties.

Much of this work of personalizing his world through the development of more intimate relations with others, took place while Paul was alone with his favorite counselor. Although he saw her in regular, scheduled play sessions, these meetings alone, as is the case with most of our children, did not prove sufficient, nor even most important. Paul's pressing emotional problems and difficulties in living had to be dealt with on the spot. Only when the same person was ready to listen to him, play with him, and do things for him at any hour of the day or night could he learn to appreciate how important someone else could become to him. This is usually the precondition for learning to recognize others as human beings.

Although this development is most difficult to recapture and describe, a striking parallel exists between what happened to Paul, and what happens in the development of a small child, who also begins to acquire the rudiments of personality (ego and superego) when he makes the discovery that his parents are not only providers of goods and services but personalities in their own right. In Paul's first year at School, we were chiefly providers—"slaves." In the next two years, the slaves slowly took shape as persons, at a rate of development that paralleled the change in Paul from tyrant to human being.

While this was his major "developmental task," Paul continued to work on the older ones, too. For example, during this period Paul's self-control, social adaptation, trust in the world and his own abilities, and most of all his likeableness, developed further and became more secure.

As one might expect, the first time Paul was startled by someone else's behavior and began wondering about its motivation, occurred in connection with two central issues—sharing food, and recognizing good will in another person.[24]

One day (as he had often done of late), Paul gave his favorite counselor some pieces of fudge they had made together. Quite naturally, she said, "Thank you." Paul looked up, startled, and asked, "[You] like [to] say 'thank you'?" His counseler asked why this surprised him; he replied that he had never heard her say it before. He was curious to know how she felt about saying thank you, and was quite astonished when she said that it came easily to her. After a characteristically long and thoughtful pause, during which he seemed to be struggling to overcome his inability to express himself, he exploded, "If I'm king, I'll have anyone [who] uses that word . . . prosecuted!" He was able to say this without difficulty until he came to the word "prosecuted." Then he began stuttering; failing again and again to say the right word, he finally asked the counselor to pronounce it. Only then could he repeat it correctly. With this help from her in expressing his aggression, he went on to say that he hated the whole world, and that most of all he hated "thank you."

A bit later, quite by chance and in a different context, his counselor said "please." Again Paul exploded. He hated both expressions! Perhaps his own wish to be fed without having to ask or give thanks (even as a child expects to receive food from his parents) was so great that he was astonished at her willingness to thank him. His reaction may also have stemmed from his resentment at having to accept things. He may have wished to deny that he had received certain things if accepting them either aroused the guilt he felt because of his underlying hostility, or reminded him of the fact that these gifts did not come from the person who was most important to him, his mother.

Paul's wish to abolish "thank you" and "please" suggests a further motivation for his megalomanic tendencies. If he were "king" of the universe, he could get along in the world without having to

---

24. In other children at the School, speculation about people's motives arises when they first realize that we do not mind if they dirty themselves, or when we trust their ability to understand and master the world, or when they realize how concerned we are with their physical well-being, etc.

use the words he hated. In short, he either had to change himself or rule the world. And he was by no means sure that he could bring his own wishes into line.

Nevertheless, Paul was changing, and was beginning to experience more varied and human emotions. These were revealed in his facial expressions. When he first came to the School, his face had seemed expressionless and nondescript. It mirrored, if anything, only his general emptiness, clumsiness, disjointedness, and lack of coordination. Then slowly, he took on a round and rosy appearance. While he had been gaining weight steadily, as described before, it was more than a year and a half before his face filled out and became very round and childlike. Sometimes it came alive with interest in the world. When Paul was very serious, he appeared mature beyond his age. His face then took on an expression of deep purpose, particularly when he was engrossed in his art work or his studies. But when something pleasant happened to him, although he never would admit that anything pleased him, he immediately looked babyish again. Occasionally he would smile with contentment. During this period, when Paul was angry, he was apt to pout and suck his thumb, rather than burst into one of his violent temper tantrums. In general, he was acquiring very childish mannerisms. The exaggerated, uncontrolled movement of his arms seemed now to be less aggressive than babyish.

On the other hand, little by little Paul was acquiring true prestige with the other children and the staff because of his achievements in learning, in baseball, and most of all in art; but he still could not accept this approval as genuine. When anyone said something complimentary about him, he could not enjoy it. He would immediately begin clowning, as if the praise were a joke played on him. Apparently, he could believe only the worst of other people's intentions and had learned to respond with appropriate feelings only to unpleasant experiences. So he reacted to pleasant episodes as if they, too, were depreciating. Yet, although previously he had expressed only emotional extremes—rage, or, rarely, self-centered happiness (as when he was eating voraciously)—now he slowly, on occasion, seemed to feel and express more moderate emotions, as well.

Paul was beginning to gain some real perception of how other children related to him. He continued to provoke them and discharge his hostility against them, but now he sensed that they disliked him; and this hurt. It was a first sign that he thought of others as human beings and wanted to be liked by them. But his ability to relate to the other boys in his dormitory, who were his closest companions, was impeded by their relation to the counselor he had to share with them. His jealousy complicated his feelings toward these youngsters, so that often he would refuse to admit their existence and retire into phantasies about living alone with his counselor for the rest of his life.

One day, when he was with her in play session, he painted a picture. He was in a good mood, and sketched the green grass, saying, "Spring's coming; winter almost gone." He sketched some figures, and said, "This [is] you, and [all the] little kids around you." When his counselor asked what she was supposed to be doing in the picture, he said, "You're telling kids nice fairy tale." Paul loved fairy tales and invariably asked her to read them to him. But the very thought of her reading to anyone else plunged him into deepest gloom, and so he revamped his painting to represent, not the reality he knew, but his desire for identification with his counselor. In this fresh picture, he depicted her life. "This's your farm house [in the] West," he said. "And there [is a] little lake near [your] house [and] here [are] your fields." He discussed the counselor's life history at some length with her, and probed into her childhood. He was trying to understand what someone else's life had been like and how people grow up to become successful persons. He was intrigued to learn that she had been reared on a farm. He decided that he must be a farmer, too, when he grew up, so that he could raise his own food. In this way, through drawings and phantasies about his future, he made his first true attempts to identify with his favorite counselor.

Paul's interest in her life reflected the change that was taking place in his attitude toward other people. Before, he had longed for his counselor to devote all her time to him and not be so "lazy" as to take time off for herself; now he wanted to partake of her life away from the School. This implied considerable progress in recognizing her as a human being in her own right. Where he had once wished that she belonged entirely to him, he now wished to participate more fully in her life.

In these phantasies, he also seemed to be trying to establish a common past with her, such as a child shares with his mother. As a result, he became even more outspoken about their common future. Another day, while again painting a farm scene, Paul explained, "You living on farm in West, and I [am going to] live on farm in West." Then, "Not far apart." He drew a little yard at the front of the house: "Here all children play." Having said enough about human relations, Paul then sketched a granary for storing food, "so that we'll 've enough to eat." Only this experience, which first ties mother and child together, could bring him to say "we." But at the same time the remark expressed his oral anxiety about having enough to eat, and the reassuring conviction that with one chosen person, at least, he was safe in this respect.

The wish that he could live with his counselor always lay just below the surface of these remarks. After sitting deep in thought for a while, Paul finally asked, "Did [any]one propose you?" She asked what he meant. "I mean, were you ever engaged?" When she replied, "No," he seemed very relieved. "Oh, I thought you [were] prob'ly." There he stopped without carrying his wishes any farther. Paul knew enough to realize that his desire for a married life with his counselor could not come true.

But this knowledge did not appease his anger and frustration, which soon after erupted in a burst of violence. He was playing ball, when for no visible reason, he picked quite a vicious fight with another child, and began pushing and kicking him; he might have gone farther had we not instantly stopped him.

When we questioned him about this behavior, Paul claimed that he was angry because we had forced him to play with other children. This, of course, was not true. The fact was simply that he wanted to be the only child, and he even asserted, "This [is a] school with only one child, Paul." His rage had exploded after he had expressed his desire to have no other children around.

Paul was probably angry at our wish, which he sensed, that he develop relations with others, while we denied him that most intimate and exclusive relation to his counselor, which he wanted so desperately. He could not discuss this openly, but he could talk about his fear of his own explosive anger. He did wish he could control it. But since he could not, he felt he was better off staying away from people, particularly in competitive situations like ball games, which had almost led, in this case, to his beating someone up. He sensed that only our interference had kept him from going too far. The mere thought of losing the game had made him unbearably angry. Of course when we agreed that he did not have to play these competitive games, he accused us of trying to keep him from his favorite activity, of not wanting him to win, and so on.

While talking these things over with his counselor, Paul picked up a piece of clay and shaped some figures, which he then knocked over angrily with a clay stick. He was blowing them all up with dynamite, he said. But this made him feel guilty, and he had to punish himself. Making another figure, representing himself, Paul said, "He's no good," and smashed it as he talked.

Thus far, Paul had not reacted with more than his usual rage and guilt. But new feelings cropped up at the end of this outburst.

He suddenly turned to his counselor, and said, "You're [a] baby."
Fashioning a little toy cradle, he remarked, "This [is] your cradle."
Then he took a hammer and smashed it. In this way, he projected
his own desire to be a baby onto his counselor, and then punished
her for not fulfilling his wish. Perhaps he made her a baby because
she was not better able to help him. Or perhaps he felt that she
babied him only because she, herself, was a baby. He also may have
thought that if he could only be a baby with her—or even better,
her baby—everything would come out all right; but since this could
not be, he became angry and destroyed her image.

The counselor suggested that he tell her why he was so angry,
but Paul would not do so immediately. "No," he replied. "Don't
want [to] talk about it. When I talk, [I] just get angrier." After
thinking it over a few minutes, however, he could clearly perceive
his reasons for not being able to discuss his anger. This, too, was a
new development. The fact that talking made him angry he now
traced to his miserable childhood. Once more he dredged up memories of the orphanage and his sense of isolation there. He claimed
that, not five hundred, but a thousand children had lived there. It
was a penitentiary, he said, because it was circled by a picket fence
with spikes on top.

Paul still resented the lost and hemmed-in feeling he had had
there, but he could also view other aspects of that life more realistically. For example, he had always complained that the orphanage
never fed him enough. Now he admitted that the "kids were fed a
lot, but still didn't get fat, 'cause [of] all [the] crying they did."
When we asked why the children had been so unhappy, Paul became
rather vague, and could only proffer the explanation that the older
boys pushed the smaller ones around on the playground. (This, incidentally, was just what he did in School.) He knew that his sadness
and depression could not be blamed solely on inadequate feedings;
someone could be adequately fed and still remain unhappy because
of faulty relations with others. Increasingly, in his mind, human
relations were taking the place of eating as the source of personal
well-being. This might have been because he felt more secure about
being well fed and hence was free to worry about other problems.
But this shift in emphasis from physiological to interpersonal gratification might also have been the result of his general personality
growth.

While on occasion Paul could talk about his anger and unhappiness, a great share yet remained unverbalized. He expressed it by
building and playing with destructive objects, for example, a gallows;
but he would not talk about the phantasies he harbored while play-

ing with such instruments of torture and destruction. Instead, he acted out the memories they provoked of his unhappiness and his suicidal attempts: he would move over to the window and lean far out, announcing that he was about to jump; or he would walk onto the fire escape, and shout that he was going to throw himself off. Assuring him that we were deeply concerned about his well-being, that we liked him, and sympathized with his feelings, always made him stop. These attempts were not really serious. They were a kind of play acting, through which Paul was trying to recapture some of the emotions motivating his former suicidal attempts and to find a way of mastering them. Here, too, then, he was reaching out for an understanding of human emotions—at least those that had driven him to his most desperate moments.

Paul also tried to understand the other kinds of asocial behavior that had pervaded his past life. He talked of how the orphanage children would eat at a restaurant and then walk out without paying. Paul blamed this on the orphanage rules, which specified that the children must be back by 8:00 P.M. sharp; otherwise, they were punished. Sometimes such a big crowd queued up to pay the restaurant cashier, Paul said, that he was afraid of being late, and so dashed out without paying. Thus he tried to blame his delinquency on the impersonal discipline. It was the first time we had heard of these incidents (either the orphanage had not known about them, or had failed to report them to us).

We asked Paul why he had not talked about this before, and why he always told us only about isolated incidents in his life, for we were interested in knowing everything possible about him. With this encouragement, he was able to explain that, throughout his years in the orphanage (and most of the time in School until recently), he had kept himself constantly occupied by becoming immersed in the radio and the comics, so that he could keep from thinking about his life. According to his recollection, he had never really played before coming to the School, and this was probably true, since he knew no games when we first met him. He mentioned the orphanage's playground, but could remember only two activities he had engaged in there: swinging by himself, or being in a free-for-all with the other children.

I might add that as he spoke of these memories he frequently said that the past bored him. Life at the orphanage or, earlier, in the nurseries, had been so empty and anxiety-evoking that he could remember it only as extremely boring; he recalled little but unhappiness and mistreatment. Everything else had been "all the same"—utterly boring. It is hard to say whether these feelings re-flected the actual emptiness and flatness of his past life or the anxiety he had once felt and was re-experiencing in recalling the past.

Probably Paul felt less anxiety about the things that had actu-ally happened to him than about what he feared might happen to him or he might do to others. This was suggested by his explanation of why he had been, and in lesser degree still was, an addict of the comics, radio, and movies: "I like murder mysteries best. Like [to] hear all I can, so if ever want [to] kill somebody, [I] know how [to] get away not getting caught."

Although Paul was speaking of his present feelings, it is likely that he could talk about them now only because they no longer seemed so threatening; to a large degree, he had overcome his wish to murder and get away with it. He now sought experiences in order to learn about the world and people, not to find ways of getting away with asocial conduct. A conversation about a puppet show he had seen at the Museum followed his remarks about murder movies. This was the best puppet show he had ever seen, he said, because "the man explained [it] all [afterward] how [the] puppets worked, how he did it. I understood it all. That's why it's better than [those movies] where they kill [people]."

To the disturbing memories of his past, which he could not understand, Paul reacted either with angry, "murderous" feelings, or with a denial of his very existence as a human being. From ab-sorption in the painful thoughts these memories evoked he could be brought back to reality only through his relatively new ability to express his feelings in sublimated form through his painting. In his creations, Paul could act out what was perturbing him, as the puppeteer did with his puppets, and thus "understand it all."

One example may illustrate: Paul had been ruminating again about how unappreciated he generally felt, how "no good" he was, how rejected by other children, and how he hated them in return. As usual, this evoked angry memories of his past. After a few violent words, he withdrew into an unhappy, bitter silence. Nothing could induce him to talk about these memories again for a while. Then he began finger painting.

Using blue alone, at first he sketched the sky. As he smeared the paint around, he began to talk slowly, to himself, in mono-syllables. He was painting, he said, an empty world. Then he added green: grass. His world was no longer totally empty, although still dehumanized. He played with the paint, as he rubbed it across the paper, by moving his fingers in the sticky mess. He seemed to find pleasure in the way it felt, which may have helped him to express himself more clearly. In any event, suddenly the words grew into sentences.

Quite clearly, Paul said, "He's on a hill walking down; goes away . . . no more Paul." Apparently he feared that by going downhill again into the anger and isolation of the past, he might lose contact with the world, disappear, and be destroyed as a human being, just as he had once tried to destroy himself. Thus he revealed how afraid he was of anything connected with his past, although, until he could overcome the shadow of the past on the present, he could not begin to build a good life.[25]

Paul's counselor reassured him that she would not let him disappear; we would watch out for him, and see that nothing bad happened to him at the School. But he repeated, "There's no more Paul," in a very human, sad voice. Then, more clearly, Paul drew a little hill with his fingers, and said once more, "He's on a hill walking down; goes away . . . there's no more Paul." But now it was not a soliloquy; it was definitely a communication. Recognizing it as such, his counselor asked Paul why he said this, and added that we wanted him to remain with us and would take good care of him. Paul replied, "O.K., tell you how it is. You and Paul, they're walkin' over the hill; [they] fall off a cliff; [are] dead. No, he's walkin' alone, to the end. [Then] Gayle comes, just in time when he's ready [to] go over [the] cliff, [and] pulls him back. [He] doesn't have good hold . . . slips down again. Gayle sees what's happenin', gets him quick, pulls him up."

As he told this story, he traced a path across the paint with his fingers to show how he was going down hill; then, just as he was about to fall off the cliff, he was pulled back by the other hand, representing his counselor. Several times he re-enacted this situa-

---

25. I have already mentioned that Paul dared to talk about the thoughts and emotions he was so afraid of recognizing only after he had demonstrated to himself both his ability to sublimate (through painting) and to enjoy primitive pleasures (through messing) in the presence of a mother figure. The appearance of both destructive and self-destructive phantasies (over which he could achieve some mastery while playing with a mushy substance) suggests the progress Paul was making from the more autistic, oral phase of development to the next higher, the anal phase. At this stage, the child more clearly recognizes, and responds to, environmental demands. Before, Paul's fear of destruction had cropped up mainly in the form of starvation and poisoning anxieties, while his angry and insatiable devouring of food had very destructive qualities in itself. Now, as he played with the finger paints, his fear of destruction appeared for the first time in the context of messing. He may have been expressing and trying to deal with not only the resentments and destructive phantasies that originally arose in the feeding situation but also those centering in his education for cleanliness. We can only conjecture, however, for this tongue-tied boy did not volunteer enough of his thoughts to make such speculations valid.

tion in which, lacking a sure foothold, he slipped and had to be rescued by her. In his first version of the story, Paul said that they were both going over the cliff to destruction, but he immediately changed the story so that he was rescued by her at the last moment. Thus, only her attachment to him, and her concern for his well-being, of which he convinced himself by acting it out again and again, kept him alive and going, and protected him from being dashed into the abyss.

What initially had been a doubtful hope (after all, at first they were both killed) was finally accepted as reality, as he came to believe her assurance that she wanted to protect him. But, once Paul gave this idea credence, he grew concerned about her ability to care for him. He wondered, "'Who takes care of you? How [are] you able [to] take care of me?" Eventually he answered this for himself: "Dr. B" (referring to me).

He seemed to be trying to grasp what the sources of real strength were. His counselor, through her relation to him, could save him from his destructive tendencies. But if strength is derived from such interrelations, how did his counselor get her strength? That she might derive some of it from her relation to him he could not yet credit; he thought too little of himself to believe that he could have such importance. Her power, like his new power to love, must be derived from some relation, and he concluded it must be her relation to me. Only in this way could she care for him despite his destructive tendencies. But what would happen if the destructive tendencies of other children were added to his? In that event, could she still look out for herself and him?

He made a new painting to deal with this new anxiety. Wiping out the previous picture and spreading the finger paint anew over the paper, he sketched out another story: "You're here in the middle; soldiers [are] comin' [to] capture you; you shoot gun, and all go away." However, shooting—i.e., destroying others—no longer seemed an acceptable solution. So he started all over again. Fingers deep in the paint, his brow furrowed in concentration, he pretended that enemies were closing in from all sides on the dot representing his counselor. As his fingers moved in on her from the four corners of the paper, he described how the enemy armies were threatening her, and how she managed to scare them away. Scaring is less asocial than killing, but still Paul was not satisfied. Once more he began. "From all sides they come, two men here, two men there." He moved two fingers across the paper from each corner to show how "they" were closing in again. Thus he made her repeat his own experience by showing how she progressed from shooting at people to scaring them (as in his "wild critter" act, and "I'm a ghost"), and finally made them her friends (in short, her children), a relation that he now recognized as the source of real strength. He explained the fact that in his painting the counselor remained safe from the aggression of others, and in command of the situation, by saying, "She's awfully strong." His real counselor asked, "Why is she so powerful?" and Paul's answer was, " 'Cause she has eight children."[26]

After he had thus dealt with his hostile wishes and phantasies, and had somehow concluded that only warm and close human relations could offer a solution to his unhappiness, Paul seemed to want to deal in a similar way with his megalomanic tendencies. He expressed these, too, by projecting them onto his counselor. Beginning again to finger paint, he said, "You're on a star. There 're lots [of] stars, but yours [is the] most beautiful, biggest; you're king of [the] University." He repeated this sentence several times; alternately, his counselor was king of the universe and king of the University—he could not make up his mind which. In his earlier dreams he had been king of the universe. Now the one from whom he tried to gain security, and with whom he tried to identify, was the king. The "University" probably was a concession to reality. It is, after all, the larger institution of which the School is a part, and indirectly had given him his new lease on life.

Paul continued, "There 're no people on other stars, first. They find out you're there, so these men [his fingers again moved in the paint] come up [to] the stars. Now they're friendly; there's no more chasin'!" Again he said, "There's no people on [the] stars till they find out you're there; then men come to be on other stars. They ain't chasin' nobody no more; they live happily with you." Turning to his counselor, he asked, "Wasn't that a nice story? Did you like it?"

Through his relation to her, Paul was able to overcome his loneliness and isolation. That she, who helped him, had to be seen as a person powerful enough not only to render the same service to everyone (for nobody lived on the other stars—they became populated only because of her), but actually to rule the universe, was in line with Paul's old megalomanic tendencies. These could be overcome by being projected onto the person with whom Paul most

---

26. This, incidentally, was an acute observation on a staff member's ability to put forth amazing strength, foresight, and energy once one of his or her "children" is deeply in need of it. These are qualities that staff members do not possess in this degree under normal circumstances. But their emotional involvement permits them, in moments of emotional or physical crises, to draw on sources of strength that are not available to them under normal circumstances.

closely identified. He could now do this safely, because while he was partly freeing himself of these tendencies, at the same time he could also retain them, vicariously, through identification with her.[27] In wanting her to like his story, Paul showed that the mainspring of his ability to express and admit his feelings was his relation to her.

Quite naturally, Paul's identification with his counselor did not prevent him from seeing her less positively at times. After all, the beginning of his story had her shooting at people. He frequently called her "crazy," or accused her of being "a kleptomaniac," or "stupid." He had often said these very things about himself in his early weeks with us, but had not done this now for some time. Projection of the "bad" part of himself onto his counselor also seemed necessary before he could fully identify with her; it almost seemed that if he narrowed the gap between them, it would be easier to become like her.

Much later Paul told us quite dramatically how his world had become personalized solely through his relation to her. Some two and a half years after he had come to live with us, a new boy entered the School. When Gayle, his counselor, introduced herself to the newcomer, Paul laughed happily and said, "That's the first name I ever knew." He said this with so much inner conviction that none of the other children questioned him or thought his remark strange.

Long before he consciously knew and could freely say where, when, and with whom personal relations had begun for him, Paul had begun to sense continuity and progress in the events of his life. As mentioned before, his first remarks at the School had been sprinkled with comments about how unpeopled his world at the orphanage had been, and how timeless and unending his life there had seemed. He had always thought he would live in the orphanage until the day he died. "I knew I'd stay there fifty years. Now I know better," he declared happily. His future was assuming new dimensions. Some hope lay ahead. But since this was the result of his

---

27. Similar ways of relinquishing megalomania have been observed in other children. They parallel the development in infants of a capacity to give up the belief in their own omnipotence as they learn to trust their parents and invest all power in them. Their "I can do it" and "I know" attitudes then change to "Mommy (or Daddy) can do it" and "knows it all." The infant, because of his vulnerability and dependency, feels protected only by viewing himself as all-powerful, at least until he has found an all-powerful protection in his parents. Under their protection, and often against their wishes, the young child then begins realistically to test his strengths and weaknesses. It is through the infant's relation to his parents that he learns to recognize and to relate to others—to populate his world, as Paul's world became populated through his relation to his counselor.

well-being at the School and his identification with his counselor, he could visualize his future, at first, only as an extension of his School life. He often spoke and daydreamed about one day becoming a counselor. Later, with increasing independence, he could imagine a future apart from the School. Then he considered becoming a teacher, because he felt that, since he did well in class and liked being taught, he might enjoy teaching others.

Paul's new sense of time—of present and future, and of the continuity of life—was in sharp contrast to the timelessness of his life in the past. While speaking in positive terms about the independent future he hoped to achieve, Paul suddenly recalled some of his pre-orphanage memories for the first time. He remembered that he had gone to kindergarten for two years and then to first and second grade classes, but had learned next to nothing there. To understand the nature of these experiences better, Paul wanted to have a visual image of them; and so he ordered his counselor to draw his whole life in a series of pictures. She was to depict his experiences in kindergarten and the primary grades. When she had finished, he looked the painting over very carefully. On finding that she had not quite accurately drawn something that he had learned in one grade, he said, "You almost flunked that grade."

Learning was terribly important to him; it was the only visible and trustworthy sign of his growing achievement. For months he was absorbed almost entirely in academic work. He made remarkable progress, and in less than three years reached an average academic level in line with his chronological age. But this statement does not tell the true story. He accomplished this gain by doing work far beyond his age level in subjects he had never studied before coming to the School, such as science and social studies. But he still lagged far behind in spelling, reading, and vocabulary. Although much had been learned, he still had not mastered the tools necessary for adequate communication.

Yet Paul harbored high hopes for himself, though he was not quite ready to admit this openly. At Easter, one year, he received a stuffed bunny to which he had become very attached. For a while the bunny accompanied him to class and studied what he did. Later, although Paul still carried the bunny to class, he often left it on the teacher's desk. Then one day, after he had been at the School some two years, Paul took the bunny back to his own desk and placed a pencil in its paws. He declared that the bunny had become an artist, and he made it draw a picture, which he held up high for everyone to admire. "My bunny is a great artist," he said. "Now let's visit the Art Institute. We'll see the paintings. He likes them. Everybody go to the Art Institute to see bunny's picture. Now bunny will draw another picture." This happened long before Paul began attending the Art Institute and developed his own considerable talent in painting. Encouraged by his unexpected and unhoped-for academic success, he could now seemingly recognize where his true talents lay, and through the bunny, unconsciously project them into the future.

Meanwhile, despite his cheerful hopes for the future and his excellent progress in the present, Paul had to make up for the experiences he had lacked at an earlier level of learning.

Outside of class, for example, he was most happy when exploring the world like a very little child. He would pick up everything he found on the street and examine it carefully. Rather than seek the companionship of other children, he would run back and forth to his counselor, as a small child does, showing her his finds; and having received encouragement or recognition, he would then go back to exploring the everyday wonders around him.

His reluctance to associate with other children may have stemmed partly from his language difficulties. His speech continued to be quite childish. He constantly misused words. When venturing a relatively new or difficult one, he faltered. In conversation, he slid over the words he could not quite pronounce. While these characteristics were in line with the level of his emotional development, or psychological age, they so little suited his chronological age that they made him very self-conscious, and this was another block to forming friendships.

Paul's embarrassment about his infantile traits was most marked when he was with other children. But with his favorite counselor he seemed willing to become progressively more babyish, so that the other children remarked about it. For example, one boy said, "You talk like a baby," to which Paul replied with conviction, "I'm a teensy-weensy baby." He was eager to have his counselor explain over and over the simplest facts about life and the world around him. He could listen endlessly to simple stories, and enjoyed connecting the illustrations in the story book with the text.

In many ways Paul indicated that he was now ready to learn "normal" ways of acting and reacting, which children brought up in a family learn as a matter of course. But such things, though easily, almost automatically, acquired in childhood, are very hard for a pre-adolescent to assimilate intellectually. Now, after more than two years in School, he wanted to know when to say "please," and "thank you." No longer did he "hate" these expressions. Rather, he hated not knowing when they should be used.

Similarly, activities and games had previously held little charm or meaning for him. He had not discovered that personal relations may be built through games between child and child, and child and adult. We had been aware for a long time that he did not know how to play even simple games, but he had hidden his ignorance behind an impenetrable mask of non-interest. This at last crumbled. He complained to his counselor about another child, but what he was actually saying was that he wished to speak and play with this boy but was unable to do so. He said, "How can I talk to him? Don't 've nuttin' talk [to] him about. Don't know nuttin'. What'll I do, start an argument?" Hostile discharge was apparently still the only way he knew of relating to people. Perhaps he felt that only by rejecting others, hurting their feelings, "starting an argument," could he stand up to them as a real person. That he, himself, had been hurt and rejected by others had, until lately, kept him from feeling like a person; and it was in an effort to master himself that he tried to inflict on others all that had been inflicted on him.

Paul Finds Himself as A Person

IT WAS A LONG, hard struggle for Paul to find his personal identity. After he had been with us for two years, this became his central problem. He battled to maintain and protect whatever little identity he had gained. This put him on guard against letting other children copy him, which, in turn, forced him to recognize them as independent beings who were neither slaves nor bullies. Now he watched the children like a hawk, and flew into the most terrible rage whenever he thought one of them was copying him. To be aped by somebody else was a threat to his very existence. He had gained some identity by imitating the few adults at the School who were important to him. Now he was afraid he would lose even this if he were copied.

Paul had always shoved the children aside because he could not recognize them as human beings in their own right. They were only a threat, and he had to intimidate them to feel secure himself. Now his bullying acquired a new meaning. The children had emerged as individuals in his sight; by showing that he was superior to them, he tried to become more of a person. His strengthened confidence expressed itself when he tried to hit the younger or smaller children, who he felt certain would not fight back. He upset their games because he wanted to be the center of all attention. When we interfered to protect the other children's interests, he felt that we were very unfair and were bullying him; he could not see that we were trying to protect others as we had once protected him.

He could not stand losing at games. Though he had finally learned to play checkers, Chinese checkers, and chess very well for his age, and his skill was recognized, this was not enough. As soon as somebody else seemed to be getting ahead during a game, he called him a cheat, a crook. Why? Paul's excuse was, " 'Cause you're winnin'."

This was not said in jest. He actually had to win to be able to feel that he was an autonomous person. He had been too long deprived and "cheated" out of this feeling. He had to win every game, every time. He would even go to the lengths of holding the hand of the person with whom he was playing to keep him from making a good move, while Paul made a bad move for him, instead. If his pawns or checkers were captured in the game, Paul would slap or kick his opponent. Of course, Paul cheated, sometimes openly and blatantly, at other times in the most clever way, and usually managed to win by hook or by crook.

In other ways, too, Paul defended his shaky identity. Change, as before, threatened him because he did not feel secure about being able to adapt to it, and any failure in mastering a new situation seemed to endanger his integration, which was yet so poorly established. The smallest deviation from the usual, from the routine that he had learned to follow—even to like and rely on—threw him into great anxiety. He would start to cry, but his crying had lost its angry, tantrum-like quality, and resembled more an infant's whining. He would wave his arms and whimper, "New, new, new. Change, change, change all the time. Don't like it. Don't like it at all." He seemed to fear he would disintegrate as a person if he had to master something unexpected, and the task of integration would have to be begun all over again, right from infancy on.

Even the improvements he requested himself made Paul uncomfortable. For example, we purchased a new hot plate because the old one was not working well and he had wanted to do some cooking. Yet on discovering it, he said with heavy anxiety in his voice, "Oh, now you bought a new hot plate. I suppose you're just goin' to keep on buyin' new things." This was not the old guilt about receiving too much, or becoming spoiled, but a new anxiety stemming from the possible consequences change might have upon his hold on himself and on reality.

Paul's desire to do everything very well, so that he would be "somebody" (but also a "show-off"), and his anxiety about not

doing very well and hence, in his terms, being a "nobody," permeated much of his thinking and behavior. He did "show off" much
of the time, and boasted about winning at games, about his importance to his counselor, to me, and so forth. That we could not help
but disapprove of some of this, did not make matters easier for
him. One day, for example, while doodling without apparent aim, he
drew the picture of a man. He called him "Mr. Show-off," adding,
"That's me." After some quiet deliberation, he said, "I could stop
it." But then there came to his mind, "Mr. Nobody," and he said,
"That's why I don't stop it." In short, he had to be a show-off,
because he was afraid that otherwise he would again be a nobody.
It seems significant that again (as with the bunny—see page 110)
he tried to express this idea when drawing, because through his art
work he actually did come to gain high status. It was as though he
were anticipating a future development in which he could become
a real "somebody," not by showing off in an unacceptable way but
through artistic achievement.

But this was in the future. At this time, Paul still had to learn
to bolster his security in more pedestrian ways, through actual and
social, rather than spurious or asocial, achievement (winning by
cheating). Thus real successes became ever more important in the
development of his personal autonomy and identity.

Paul's greatest success at this time—one that did not entail
cheating—was still his intellectual achievement. Though not free
of hostile and competitive characteristics, these were not its main
motivations. He genuinely enjoyed the results of intellectual endeavor, and knew that by concentrating on learning he could prevent
himself from bullying and fighting others. He still needed this tangible evidence of personal worth, as an antidote against his strong
desire to assert his superiority at all cost. He fully realized the value
of academic achievement for him. For example, he told me, "You
know, in class when I've a lot of work, I never get in trouble. Only
in free time I do."

Paul also tried to buttress his new-found identity by comparing
his way of life with that of other people, in the hope of finding a
way of life, an ego ideal, for himself. He read voraciously anything
he could lay his hands on, to learn how other people lived and
worked, and what their motives in life were.

As he projected a future life for himself, he became more realistic about his present strivings in relation to his favorite counselor.
After two years, Paul was slowly accepting his role as a twelve-
year-old boy with her. No longer did he plan to marry this mother
figure. Instead he began re-enacting in phantasy the normal family

situations he now knew about, but had never experienced in reality. In this play, he was the little boy, lovingly cared for by a good mother and father. Using dolls, he depicted all kinds of family scenes—parents humming to their baby boy, or singing nursery rhymes to him; taking him for walks; holding his hand. Whatever the situation, mother and father always concentrated on the child. For some time, when the parents slept, Paul placed the boy doll between them. Considerably later he assigned the boy a bed by himself, while father and mother slept in a big bed together.

The content of this play acting, in which Paul seemed to be capturing a past he had never known, eventually shifted to his future. Just as in his reading he was apparently trying to find models for his future vocational and social life, so in his play he explored possibilities for his private, or family life. He wondered whether he would be able to establish and care for a family. He spun phantasies about growing up, getting married, and having children. While engrossed in these daydreams, his expression revealed how pleasant they seemed to him; he actually was happy for a moment. But most of the time he was ridden by anxiety about whether he, who had never known family life (much less a happy one), would be able to provide a good life for his children.

Once, when he had been playing at taking care of a family, his expression suddenly changed from happiness to despair. As if instantly reacting to emotions welling up from quite a different area of his personality, he said, "You just come and see how I'll treat them." He was referring to the doll children with which he was playing father. "I'll just kill them, that's all." Depressed and unhappy, he pushed the dolls aside and stared vacantly into space. Paul still did not seem to trust in the likelihood that his more constructive tendencies would permanently win out over the pressure of his destructive desires.

His fears and doubts, his unhappiness and its origin in his past, he now discussed quite maturely; he had become familiar with these disturbing emotions. On the other hand, when he felt contented, he behaved very awkwardly. Positive emotions he could express only in childish fashion. When this was brought to his attention once, he agreed, saying, "Sometimes I'm a very little boy, ain't I?" and laughed happily, nodding his head for emphasis. We reminded him that in his school work, in sports, and in his art work, he acted maturely and perhaps seemed even unusually grown-up for his age, but he replied, "No, I'm a very little boy about three years old."

However, whether he would admit it or not, he was slowly relinquishing some of his more babyish types of behavior. The nature of his thumb-sucking changed; it became less intense and provocative. For over two years sucking his thumb had been an isolating activity, and a very aggressive one. Paul not only thrust his entire thumb deep into his mouth, but frequently poked a finger up each nostril. Now he abandoned this closing up of all bodily openings to the outside world. His thumb was no longer constantly in his mouth and when it was, it did not seem entirely swallowed up. Still, Paul continued to spend a great deal of his time in autistic withdrawal; while sucking his thumb, he embarked on grandiose daydreams in which he tried to forget the depressive events of his life and their impact on him. At other moments, however, he realized that only through positive success could he banish these shadows of the past. "I don't daydream about it [being a great dictator] when I'm roller-skating, or go around here, doing lots of things. It's when I'm quiet I think about it," he said, adding almost inaudibly, "and worry about me." He could more readily admit his delusions than his realistic anxieties. Later, Paul explained that this was why he always kept busy, and was so afraid of being left alone. It also accounted for the fact that he had not yet been able to give up completely the distractions offered by comics or movies.

Fear of being alone typically develops at a certain period in the rehabilitation of children who, on coming to the School, loudly assert their desire to be let strictly alone. Like Paul, during their first months with us they fight furiously against what, in the light of their past experiences, they consider intrusions on their privacy. Only after our actions have convinced them that we respect their privacy, and will not misuse their trust by imposing our will on them if they come out of their shells, can they give up their angry, anxious withdrawal. Paul, too, like many other severely disturbed children, had cut himself off from an unbearable reality and spent his time in angry and grandiose phantasies. These were his only solace, and he had to protect them against our interference as long as he could not believe that a good reality was within his grasp.

After such children begin to relate, they feel guilty about the old, hostile wishes that they still harbor, and fearful that they may lose the comfort offered by the new relations they have formed. If the person who by now has become useful to them (for love may not yet have developed) must leave them even for a short time, they feel a double fear: that they may permanently lose the only person for whom they care, and that they may fall back into the hostile isolation they once preferred but now dread. Part of their developing fear of loneliness is due to the realization that hostile phantasies no longer satisfy them, but on the contrary, create unmanageable guilt. While at first they hate our presence because it prevents them from thinking and acting aggressively, they eventually fear our absence because it permits them to indulge again in such thoughts or actions.

As soon as Paul had admitted that he worried about himself when he was not busy, he became very angry with his counselor. He pretended to telephone an insane asylum to request that they pick up "a girl who talks too much!"

We thought that occasionally Paul may have resented having to confess his shortcomings to a woman. We felt it might be preferable to offer him a closer relation to a man, to make masculine identification easier. And since his experiences with his mother had been so unhappy, he might be able to work through his difficulties more easily with a man. But Paul was not yet ready for such a step. We tried introducing male workers to him, at various times, but he could not accept them. (He could accept me, but only because I was a somewhat distant figure.) He was too afraid, and openly said that he hated men.[28] In short, our sustained efforts to encourage him to build up a positive relation to a man came to nothing. However, Paul was led to talk more fully about the fact that he had only known male supervisors in the orphanage. He finally realized that, for this very reason, he could not enjoy a satisfying relation with a man.

But there were other reasons, too, which were not so easily revealed by Paul. They came out on one occasion when the departure of a schoolmate made him once again fearful that he might have to leave School. Paul reverted to behavior that he had relinquished a good while back, which he described as acting "like a bum." Aware that this stemmed from his anxieties, I gave him ample assurance about the relative permanency of his stay in School. I reviewed the remarkable progress he had made, but also pointed out the deficiencies that would keep him with us for the next couple of years, at the very least. Encouraged by this, Paul said that he could not fathom why he responded to stress by acting like a "bum." Then once more he reflected upon his life in the orphanage. He was thinking this time less about his mistreatment at the hands of the supervisors and older boys, than about the temptation they presented to engage in homosexual activities. Older men tempted him to give in passively to them; younger boys tempted him to hostile attack. So it would appear that even the men who were nice to Paul, menaced him. They aroused his fears about

28. His anxiety about men also revealed itself in his reactions to the Rorschach Test, see p. 121.

what they might do to him, and an even greater anxiety about what he might do to them.

Although in the past he had complained mostly about his mistreatment by older men, he now told us that many boys in the orphanage, particularly the little ones, had been "pests." They had provoked him in many ways, mostly sexual; for example, they jumped provocatively on and over his bed, though he begged them to stop. Finally, when he could bear it no longer, he had kicked and shoved them, and on one occasion, had pushed a boy with such violence that his head was seriously cut. Paul was encouraged to tell us more about these experiences when we assured him that, while undesirable in itself, people did frequently react in hostile fashion to provocation and that he probably had not meant to hurt the boy so badly. This led Paul to admit that, while he had been greatly pushed around at the orphanage, he, himself, had injured several children. In plotting to get even with them, he had arranged matters so that he seemed blameless. On several occasions he succeeded in hurting other children badly in what, to the supervisors, appeared as accidents.

Paul projected onto the world at large his conviction that the weak could threaten and undo even the strong. Some boys were discussing the United Nations and suggested that if the great nations disarmed, the smaller countries would follow suit. Paul objected with vehemence. "If the big [nations] disarm first," he said, "the small ones [would] all gang up and jump on them."

The past, the anxiety it evoked that he might once again be taken advantage of and abused, continued to overshadow Paul's new achievements and growing security. But his progress in integration went on nonetheless. Frequently in an effort to reassure himself—a kind of whistling in the dark—he listed the things he had learned in School: "Learned ride a bike, learned baseball, learned roller-skate, learned to swim. Next thing I'll learn ice-skate." Enumeration of his past achievements inspired him to hope for even better things in the future. But on occasions when he tried something different, the threat of possible defeat, which was inherent in each new activity, led him to smack his lips again, in his babyish way, and to revert to babyish language. Only when the project was successfully launched, and he saw that all would go well, could he act more his age.

Despite this heritage of long-standing experience with defeat, Paul, now thirteen years old, dared to embark on many new ventures. He expanded in all directions. His reading horizons broadened beyond his former interest in life histories, and through rather indiscriminate reading he managed to collect an amazing amount of miscellaneous information. While not quite able to integrate it as yet, he worked hard and was continually striving to learn and know more. A whole new world was opening up for him and Paul was in a hurry to master it. The well-deserved and genuine recognition he received for his knowledge from the other children was of great importance to him. It provided satisfaction and at the same time served as added stimulus toward further achievement. Recognition from the children was more important to Paul than recognition from adults. In the orphanage, he had been depreciated by the older children, whom all the younger ones hated, so that now it meant a great deal to him to be an older child who was liked and respected by younger children.

The extent of Paul's intellectual growth is indicated by the fact that his performance on I.Q. tests (which in his first two years with us had remained stationary at 100) increased by twelve points within a period of a few months. Similarly, his academic progress, which had been slow at first, moved forward by leaps and bounds now that he was finding himself as a person. When he had first arrived at the School, his achievement lagged three years behind the grade expectation for his age. During his first two years with us he barely managed to master a year of academic work in twelve months' time. During his third year, however, he made such excellent progress that he completed the work of nearly three grades.

During the same third year in which he made such outstanding strides academically, the pace of his art work also suddenly quickened and his pictures assumed a completely different character. No longer were there doubts in his paintings, or wavering, or insecurity. There was no slavish copying, no looking for external models; he knew beforehand what he wanted to express, and with a fine sensitivity for color, form, and rendering of objects, he succeeded in doing exactly that. Spontaneously and on his own, Paul had found his true medium, his central talent.

His artistic achievement, and the well-deserved recognition it received, helped him to realize that he was a person who could make a real contribution and who had importance for others. Once, after he had presented me with another of his pictures, which I hung in my office because I truly liked it, he expressed pride that he could participate in relations in which he was the giver. He felt that he learned much about personal relations from such experiences. He told the psychiatrist that I liked his picture and added that he now felt so much more full of energy. "Before, I thought I could only get energy and strength from food. Now I know I get energy from children, counselors, baseball, swimming, and drawing. That is, if I make a picture for somebody."

He had arrived at an understanding of what is involved in relations of grown-ups to one another, of adults to children, and of children to each other. With pride, he stated that now he knew about grown-ups: "They act like ladies and gentlemen. They go to college, care for children, like children. I'll be grown-up, too—someday, but not for a long time."

THE SECOND RORSCHACH TEST

After Paul had been with us for some two and a half years, we felt that he had changed very much. Since this change was in line with our desires, we wished to check our impressions against evaluations made by an outsider. So we arranged for Paul to take a second Rorschach test.[29] The main findings were: "He is beginning to develop some intellectual defenses—few, to be sure. They take the form of occasional displacement; but there is effort at conscious self-control. But at a deeper level, he still turns to phantasy, especially when under the impact of anxiety.

"The ego continues to show its vulnerability. This is evident in perceptual disturbances; they can be very far from normal and very erratic. It also shows in his lapses of attention and in the limitations of his mental horizon. Most serious, there is still a dysfunction in the thinking—confusions, contaminations, and very immature concepts; these are seen also in language immaturities. The overt anxiety, and its effect on the personality structure, is of moderate degree; sometimes he binds it through conscious efforts, but just as frequently he fails to bind it. He does escape it at times by phantasy living.

"Occasional feelings of inferiority are emerging. They add to the anxious state of mind. But insofar as they project the need for self-appraisal they may be signs of some ego growth.

"A wish to be in contact has developed. In fact his principal growth since the preceding Rorschach test has been in the seeking for some emotional rapport with others. He shows some real assets here. Rich content is also stimulated by these figures. Color shock is found—evidence of a neurotic structure. While he still discloses an ego vulnerable to emotional stresses, it is evidence of progress insofar as it shows him developing out of his more infantile adjustment into a neurotic one. His mental life is much dominated by phantasy, which can be very painful—indicating critical personal

---

29. Test evaluation by S. J. Beck.

themes. This is in fact the outstanding finding at present. The phantasy is at times vigorous, strongly felt. More often it discloses the theme of the helpless, passive, or phobic. In its overbalancing of the externalized emotions, it shows him capable of introversive and autistic solutions of his problems. Thus he is still in danger of a schizophrenic adjustment.

"Total present adjustment: evidence of superior potential is present in some of the content and some of the language expression. However, conceptual thinking, as well as solution of difficult problems, is seriously low: he is not effectively using his intelligence. He does overadapt in respect to conventionality, and can attend to reality within the lower end of the normal range. The personal dynamics reflected in the content include scenes of isolation, insecurity, deterioration or damage, and the phobic.

"In summary: a deep, unconscious insecurity, related to hostility to the male, especially older males, with attendant phobic and anxious thinking, but with outward evidence of dysphoric mood. Immaturity is persisting, and the danger of fixation at an immature level of the ego, with autistic phantasy solution, is still present. Nevertheless treatment assets are now emerging. As compared with the earlier Rorschach test record, the intellectual dysfunctions are now less frequent and there remains only a remnant of the ego's former disabilities. Some real growth appears, especially in the affective sphere, together with a parallel advance in the ego. Continued treatment is imperative, especially in view of the danger of malignant introversive adjustment."

HIS SECOND TAT

About this time, Paul also took another Thematic Apperception Test. His reaction to the first picture[30] was: "This boy's studyin', thinkin' [he] doesn't like violin lessons—thinkin' how get out of it —studyin', thinkin'. And thinks might practice real fast so mother think he was interested and then he'd go out and play after short time. Or might think [of] learnin' play real well and be great man, play famous pieces and get rich and give money to family and help with money for college."

In comparison with the story Paul invented when he took the test for the first time, his sadness and anger seemed to be gone; no longer was anything broken, incomplete. His was now a populated world; there was a mother projected into his story, whom he tried to cheat. Once he had speculated about fooling her, he switched

30. For a description of this picture see footnote No. 7 on page 58.

to thoughts about his future. This he saw in positive terms; he could think of learning "real well" and becoming a success. He felt that he must succeed because he needed the money to help others (or himself) through school.

Paul's story about the second picture[31] ran: "This girl just got back from school, must 've had geography or history—thinkin' what it [farming] must look like, dreamin'. Dreamin' of past, where they used horses and plows instead of tractors. She's thinkin' how hard women used to work. She's thinkin' very hard about how increase easier livin' for these people with tractors and milking machines so kids can go to school and their kids will grow up [to be] good citizens."

Compared with the pessimism that permeated his previous stories, this one displayed healthy optimism, belief in progress, and in good citizenship.

At the time of his first test, Paul had invented a story about murder to picture five[32] (see p. 59). This time the story was: "Must be mother comin' into kitchen seein' how things going in there, or in dining room or around living room and seein' how that's going, checking up [on] things. She's going on tour around house and sees son reading and tells him go back to bed and [he] has [to] go to school tomorrow and won't get his lessons right. Then [she] goes up with son to his bed, opens door and sees that he gets into bed and tucks him in and goes out and closes door and then peeks back [to] see that he's asleep all right, and goes back to bed and goes to sleep."

The difference between the first and second stories about the same picture strikingly reflected the security Paul had acquired. Where he once had projected thoughts of murder, he now saw security and the experience of being cared for. The mother in the story, like the counselors in School, carefully saw that everything was in good order. From his counselors he had learned that caring for a child implied tucking him in and waiting to make sure that he was asleep before leaving him alone for the night. The same stimulus that some two and a half years before had evoked feelings of horror ("horrible sight") and violence ("the murder") now provoked phantasies about being well taken care of and protected. The "don't know" 's interlarding his first story, which reflected the indecision and insecurity of his own interpretations, now disappeared, and a straightforward account took their place.

---

31. This picture shows a country scene. In the foreground is a young woman with books in her hand; in the background a man is working in the fields and an older woman is looking on.
32. For a description of this picture see footnote No. 10 on page 59.

Equally characteristic of the change in Paul, though in quite another way, was the difference in his reactions to picture sixteen the blank card. The first time he had been able to invent nothing. Now his story was: "Could be just clear white day, no clouds, real bright, isn't blue, just plain white. Or [you] might be dreamin' going through space, seein' nothing but whiteness, nothing but whiteness, and you wonder [as you are] sleeping what might happen [to] make the world turn blank. Or might be real thick fog with sun shining down on top, making it white. Very dense fog." In the absence of a definite pictorial stimulus, his emotions found expression in phantasies about color and degrees of brightness. This reflected his best medium for self-realization, painting. No doubt he had turned to this particular means of sublimating in part because of his difficulty in expressing himself verbally. But his reaction to this card also showed that his talents for painting and aesthetic experiences permitted him to solve a problem that he could not tackle before.

About picture seventeen[33] he remarked: "I do this myself, not very good. The man's in a gym room, climbin' up a rope, showin' off how well he climbs. Showin' off [his] muscles, jerks them up and down. Or could be climbin' down rope [to] go to another part of gym where there's somethin' he wants, so he will get there first. Then [he] might go to [a] dance, maybe. Or could be wondering as he climbs up the rope if he's really great climber, if he could be world's champion climber." Paul began by honestly admitting that he was not very good at rope-climbing. Then his tendency to show off cropped up, as well as his desire to "get there first." But behind the adolescent showing off of physical strength lay feelings about adolescent heterosexual adjustment, about growing up, and going to a dance. At the end he admitted his desire to be a world champion, but also wondered whether he could really become as good as he longed to be. His old tendency to show off, to be always first and best, was still present, but was more controlled by doubt. His wish to be the kingpin had been mellowed by skepticism, and placed in juxtaposition to a more realistic evaluation of his present limited abilities.

In his story about the last picture[34] Paul seemed once more to project the battle between his old proclivity for getting things at any cost—even delinquency, or violence—and his new conviction that one gets things through personal ability and hard work. His

33. Picture seventeen (BM) shows a naked man clinging to a rope. He is in the act of climbing up or down.
34. Picture twenty shows the dimly illumined figure of a man (or woman) in the dead of night leaning against a lamp post.

story was: "This is night time. Guy leans up against lamp post. Man waiting for friends to come; they [are] taking him to club [to] have good time. Or be man waiting for someone who is rich-like to come rob him. It's dark all around and no one see, hiding in bushes so he make lot robberies at that spot so he [could] buy diamond rings for girl friend. Or [he] is part of gang waiting on corner see that no coppers come to get friends. Or [it could] be man going back from office after hard day's work. He thinks if [I] work hard [I may] get raise, get more things for family, buy nice house, maybe Washington State where lots trees and game [animals]. He thinking of this as he walks home. [He] is very happy man. He thinks he'll be president of the office." Thus the story ends on a more down-to-earth, optimistic tone.

From the majority of his stories in this second test, it appeared that Paul was strongly oriented toward his future. He expected things to get better in a realistic way, by and large, and through his own hard work. However, his former megalomanic hopes and delinquent wishes were not yet totally overcome. In comparing his performance on the two tests, the general impression was that he was moving from deep depression, which stemmed from lack of emotional security, toward a more positive, active, and realistic adjustment to the world. There were also indications that he was preparing himself for a normal adolescent and heterosexual adjustment. Measured and weighed against the first tests, the absence of deviate defenses and of elaborate defensive distortion in phantasy was impressive.

This, incidentally, was something that impressed all of us throughout Paul's development, and we can make the same kind of observations about other children who have come to us after having led a similar life. Although the general emotional vagueness of the institutional environment and the absence of human influences that can guide or force personality development in a definite direction, do not permit "institutionalized" children to develop definite personalities, neither are such youngsters pushed into developing well-structured defenses. Therefore, their latent abilities can be freed relatively soon, and their intellectual growth can proceed unhampered by strong, elaborately developed defenses. That is why Paul's rehabilitation, once we had overcome the pernicious consequences of his poverty-stricken emotional life, could get on rather quickly and without too many ups and downs, or detours. He could make realistic use of his inherent potentialities, such as his artistic talents and ability to progress academically, and both of these, having first been assayed cautiously, were soon developed with firm purpose.

As some of his stories suggest, Paul was increasingly engrossed in adolescent development. For him, this stage of growth was particularly complicated because he had never fully assimilated the parental images and values against which the normal adolescent revolts. He could not easily rebel against the adults from whom he still sought protection and gratification, often on an infantile level, and whose standards he was even then trying to make his own. For these reasons, his adolescent rebellion was unusually stormy and posed many difficult problems for our staff. But since it was only an aggravated and special modification of normal adolescent turmoil, it seems best to exclude his specifically adolescent difficulties from this account of his progress toward rehabilitation.

He Makes Peace with Himself and the World

THE THIRD ANNIVERSARY of Paul's arrival at the School was a very important landmark for him. He had been looking forward to it for months, speculating about what his fourth year might bring. The outcome was crucial, because at its close, Paul would become fourteen years old, which was then our age limit. Of this fact, he was only too well aware. Though we had promised we would let him stay longer, if desirable, and he knew that we had prolonged the residence of other children beyond fourteen, he also knew that these were exceptions.

His preoccupation with his future cropped up in his innocuous speculations about the number of presents he would receive on his anniversary. (On the anniversary of his coming, each child receives as many presents as the number of years he has spent in School. Paul was familiar with this custom.) He felt that in his case the number of presents was all wrong. Three presents would suffice this time, but on his fourth anniversary he should get not four, but four times as many gifts as on his third, and so on. "I'd end up probably getting big cars and things like that," he said in a loud, provocative voice. Then he was quiet for some time and in a thoughtful manner went on, "You know [what] I'd like, I'd like a big car and a big yard, but most of all I'd like them [to] tear down the Empire State Building." This was said very matter-of-factly as though it occurred to him on the spur of the moment, without conscious forethought. Why did he want the Empire State Building torn down? " 'Cause I don't like it. I wish some other building was bigger, more important than Empire State." Though he said this very seriously and with much feeling, he was unable to explain why he disliked the Empire State Building so intensely. Probably his exaggerated demands for a big car had reminded him of his megalomanic and destructive phantasies, which were again brought to the fore by his fear of having to leave the security of the School. He no longer wanted to jump off the Empire State Building, but so long as it existed, it represented his old anxieties about jumping out of windows, or leaping off the world's highest building, in order to achieve importance through self-destruction. In wishing this symbol destroyed, Paul seemed to want to rid himself of his suicidal and megalomanic tendencies once and for all.

In this connection, I might mention again that Paul's homicidal and suicidal acts did not represent destructive tendencies only. If that had been true, he might have been able to relinquish them much sooner. But after all, these were the tendencies that had led to his placement in School. For Paul, therefore, they had proved their merit. It was comprehensible that he should revive them when he feared an impending placement in another institution, where they might again prove necessary to improve his lot.

Paul's third anniversary must have churned up many of his old emotions. A few hours after having received his presents, he drew the legs and head of a man, with no body, nothing, in between. He explained, "Comic character. Saw him three years ago." When we asked him to tell us more about this "character," he said that he was "someone who had come from an island and was very odd." As if in free association, he added that he considered this drawing quite below his present abilities, and then elaborated on how much more he knew now. The drawing seemed to recall the person he had been three years before: a head full of phantasies, and legs to kick and run—no heart to feel, no "body" to support and unite his chaotic personality. Now he saw the old Paul simply as a comic character —not himself at all, but somebody he had chanced to see—somebody, perhaps, who had lived all his life on a strange island and so had become odd and ignorant of many things.

By and large, Paul's last months in School were characterized by further intellectual growth and ever greater academic achievement. Most important, he developed social sensitivity. In this area, there was a tentative improvement at first, which became steadier. As he grew in responsiveness and consideration for the feelings of others, he acquired some respect for their rights. He felt secure enough not to have to stress his own "superior rights" so much. Occasionally, now, he could play a game without cheating. And even when he lost, he did not fly into a rage and accuse his opponents of cheating.

More and more he developed a genuine gift for leadership and won recognition for it. This held particularly true for his three main areas of interest: sports, art, and stamp collecting, in which he became the accepted authority of the School. The children felt that if they asked his advice they would receive genuine help; and if they brought him their difficulties, he would find a solution.

Such quiet and rather uneventful progress went on for several months. Basically, Paul was now very content. This peaceful life gave him the leisure to attempt to find out more about how other people lived, and what their motives were. For example, he wondered why his favorite counselor, who disliked the movies, went to them with him. It was quite a revelation when he finally figured out that she might do it for his sake, and that for his pleasure she was ready to accept some inconvenience. Before this, he had dimly realized that counselors might act in such a fashion, but now he became fully aware of what this meant. And he proceeded to apply this fresh insight to everyone else. He now understood that a person —including himself—might do something to please someone he liked, even though he, himself, did not enjoy the activity. This was but one sample of the many efforts Paul made to fathom the motives of others, and to discover how other human beings function.

Paul realized that changes had been taking place within himself—that he had become more giving. No longer did he hoard things in miserly fashion, perhaps because he was now confident there would always be enough for him. When a generous selection of candy was offered him, he could select the pieces he wanted, and pass up the rest. He was amazed to find that for the first time he could say "no" to food rather than grab it all and save it until it spoiled.

But even though he no longer tried to protect himself against future exigencies by hoarding, he still worried deeply about his future. We tried to provide him with as many experiences as possible that would help him prove to himself that he could assume responsibilities and discharge them competently. This was not easy, because he was still afraid of failing at any new kind of enterprise, even those in which he excelled, such as art work or playing ball. To protect his self-love against the uncertain future, he had to depreciate the activity, his ability, the equipment, and the purpose. Only after he had tangible proof that he was doing well, could he overcome his feelings of inferiority and enjoy his success. For this reason, he long pondered each new responsibility before accepting it.

The activity he still enjoyed most was participating in the cooking of Sunday dinner. This helped greatly to satisfy his extreme oral anxieties about his future. To be able to cook well was crucially important to Paul, and he derived great pleasure from it. He put the extra money he thus earned to good use in bolstering his ego further by buying stamps for his collection. His became the best in School.

Again and again he disclosed how his early lack of a home, and his insecurity regarding his most basic physiological needs, continued to color his thoughts, feelings, and plans for his future. For example, he decided he would most like to study Egyptian history; the Egyptians had been the greatest of men because they built the most permanent buildings, the pyramids. They were wise to build such very strong homes, which could withstand all emergencies. For himself, he had only one goal for the future: to work "toward a better world."

Although he had avoided visits with his mother, in his last year at the School he grew indifferent about their meetings. As he said, "I take no offense." When asked to elaborate on this cryptic remark, he said the visits were "O.K.," but it would be more "O.K." with him if there were none. This did not conceal the fact that each one heightened his feelings of resentment at having been excluded from living with his parents at an early age. Just how deeply he felt about never having had a home was made evident following one visit. Some children were swapping jokes. Paul decided to tell one, too, but in doing so stuttered and stammered more than usual. The joke went: "Somebody lived in a room, the room had no windows, it also had no door." When the children protested that this did not make sense, he insisted it did, adding, "That's the room I had in my mother's house." He tried hard to pretend that he could joke about the fact that the only room available to him in his mother's home had neither light nor air, and was one he could neither enter nor leave. Or, if one wishes to speculate, this remark might be given a much deeper interpretation. He may have been telling us that he had once had a home, a place in his mother's life, but only before birth, in the womb—a room without windows or doors. And after he was born into the world, there was no longer any room for him in his mother's house.

In his doll play—in which he groped toward learning more about family living—he expressed similar feelings. He set up the doll house so that the mother was cooking in the kitchen and the father relaxing in the living room, while the children played in their room. Methodically, purposefully, he went about arranging the house, asking frequent questions to make sure that this was the way a family might live and behave. Suddenly his reasonable tone of voice changed and he said dramatically, "Many [is] the apartment I've lived in!" Then, catching himself, he went back to murmuring softly, in a reasonable fashion, "I mean, I've seen some apartments and houses; anyway, at least I know what they should look like, even if places I've lived in didn't, even if I haven't lived in any decent house." And he went on arranging the house and acting out family living. Next day he said, "Yesterday we talked a lot." On being reminded that, while he had done a lot of playing and had made some very meaningful remarks, he had actually said little, he was astonished. "I thought I talked a lot!"

This spontaneously led to free associations about his inability to talk when he first came to the School, and to more recollections about his early life. First he remembered that his mother had once dragged him into court, much against his will, when she was suing his father for money. He was thunderstruck to realize that this memory contradicted his former belief that his father had died when he was a baby. He recalled how unhappy he felt about his parents' hatred of each other, and how anxious and desperate he was as he sat and waited in court. This led to another memory of his mother's using him to get money. When he was either four or six years old (he was hazy about this), she had sent him to a camp. He had been hurt there—nothing serious, an injury he acknowledged to be his own fault—and he had fully recovered by his return from camp. "But my mother made a big fuss about it, tried to get a lot of money. She jerked me out of class. Had to stay in this office [at court] for six hours, just looking out the window. Wasn't my idea." After all these years, he was still angry and worried because she had embarked on an unjust lawsuit to collect money for damages, although he had been entirely to blame for the injury. Again and again he insisted that the suit had not been his idea. "The man said my mother was trying to get money from the camp for no good reason." With obvious relief, he ended, "She didn't get it." On various occasions thereafter he angrily dwelt on the times when his mother had attempted to use him as a tool, or a pawn, in getting money from his father or from other people.

These recollections made him even angrier about the untrue things she had told him about his father. All along, she had told him falsehoods to exculpate herself, first, for not having created a better life for Paul, and, later on, for not taking him into her home after her second marriage. When, at last, Paul had partially mastered these painful experiences, he summed up his feelings one day: "When somebody's fooled you, told things that weren't true, you know, fooled you all [your] life, you just feel fooled all the time.

And [if] you don't find out until you're grown up, it's all the harder."

When such realizations upset him, he tried to banish them from his memory, rather than master them. He wanted to forget his mother and the family who had let him down. He asked what a child's age limit might be for being adopted, and he wondered at what age a child "could change his name without feeling guilty." For some time he experimented with using different surnames. These attempts to escape from his past and his family by using a short cut were relatively short-lived, however. For the most part he realized that he had come to grips with his past, much as he was loath to do so.

Working out his past and present relations to his mother on a more conscious level, exploring his past—the how and why of what had happened to him—and tying his life together into a comprehensible whole, were some of the major emotional tasks Paul undertook during this last year with us. As he tried to piece his past life together, it became apparent that he was totally confused about its major events. I have already mentioned that he thought his father had died when he was a small baby, whereas actually the father had only left his mother about that time. Paul was amazed that he was six and a half years old when his father died. We had told him things like this repeatedly, but only now did he seem to comprehend and remember them. He was equally ignorant of nearly all the events of his life before he came to us.

In his new search for understanding, Paul wondered about many things he had not understood before or had unquestioningly taken for granted. For example, only now did he ask why he had been chosen from among all the other orphanage children to go to the Orthogenic School and to enjoy a better chance in life than they would have. This gave us an opportunity to explain the role the agency had played in his life. As he began to realize that he had indeed enjoyed good fortune, he felt quite guilty about it: "They picked me out and a lot of kids need to [come the School] and can't."

He may have tried combating this guilt by megalomanic assertions, or on the other hand, he may have had such inadequate mastery over his wish to feel superior that any stray fact that could be used to support his megalomania could kindle it again. In any event, the realization that he had been chosen to come to the School, immediately touched off phantasies about the important things he would some day do. For example, with great arrogance he dictated this story: "Take report down. Business increased one hundred per cent. We'll put up price ten per cent. Next year we'll make another billion dollars. We'll give it to government as present for keeping world in peace, [and to] feed everybody well. Signed Paul." He reread this manifesto; then signed it. At least he dreamed of using his power not just to show off or enslave others, but for the common good.

Beyond Paul's speculations about why he had been so wonderfully fortunate as to leave the orphanage, lay the problem of what had gone wrong there, of why things had been so miserable for him. For instance, Paul placed the blame for his unreasonable behavior when he first came to the School on his orphanage experiences. "See, there was no counselors there," he said, as if this accounted for it. Having counselors, he had learned from his School experience, meant having warm and satisfying contacts. Since he had had no such contacts to speak of in the orphanage, there must not have been any counselors. But he did not yet entirely understand that the lack of human relations was responsible for the ill effects, because when he was asked to explain his remark, he went on, "They did things without reason." Once he realized that reasonableness had also been lacking in the orphanage, this became his favorite excuse for acting unreasonably himself. For example, when his asocial behavior was pointed out to him, he no longer denied it or tried to justify it by accusing others, spuriously, of provoking him, but he readily enough acknowledged his unreasonableness. Yet, he did not feel responsible for it, because people in the orphanage had been unreasonable with him. He could not fully understand the connection between his conduct and theirs, but the fact that he remarked so clearly that they were related showed the growth in his insight.

Despite the fact that, at that time, Paul was not willing to assume full responsibility for his actions, we felt that he had made enough progress to be trusted on his own for short periods. We felt that he could handle himself well enough so that his behavior in public would not rouse too much open criticism, which, in turn, might have undermined his developing self-confidence. So we arranged for him to study once a week at the Art Institute of Chicago. He was successful from the very first class. At first, Paul mostly prized the prestige it gave him with the other children at the School, but soon his improved ability to express himself through painting acquired intrinsic value.

One unexpected, but very important, benefit was the chance he now had to observe and associate with boys and girls his age who were living a normal life with their families. For Paul, it was quite a revelation that they had quite a few of the same problems he did, that is, those typical of any adolescent. He had always thought all his difficulties were peculiar to him, or to living in the School. Another unforeseen consequence of his Art Institute experience was that he slowly gave up blaming any inadequacy in his work on his teacher or counselors, or on the fact that he was "no good" or "stupid." As he watched others making worse mistakes than he did in painting, he acquired the courage to stick with difficult tasks, despite initial set-backs. Applying this lesson to other activities, he soon could stay with a problem or project for as long as a week in order to finish it.

At the end of the academic year, some of his paintings were selected by the Art Institute for an exhibition of children's paintings that would tour the country, and he received an official congratulatory letter. To win a competition with normal children his age and older, enhanced his self-respect immensely. Reacting directly to his success, he launched on prolonged daydreams about selling his pictures for a million dollars. Then he spun a phantasy about an island, whose inhabitants were named only with letters of the alphabet. These islanders enjoyed unlimited power, with free access to diamond mines through which they controlled everything and everybody. They used electric switches and buttons to get everybody to do what they wanted. Each inhabitant had "one tremendous responsibility. One day a year he has to feed the whole island." Paul claimed to have heard this story from a professor, who had taken off in a balloon for a year's vacation. The balloon exploded just over the island, and the islanders saved him. Then one day a volcano erupted and the island itself exploded. The islanders now were rescued by the professor, but nobody knows what happened to them after that.

Was this story an allegory of his life—a phantasy through which he tried to find his way back to reality after his megalomanic daydreaming about earning millions of dollars through his artistic talents, and acquiring unlimited powers? Paul would not elaborate on his story, so we can only speculate. But seen as an allegory of his life, his story can be interpreted as follows: Paul was counteracting his delusions of grandeur, which had been provoked by his artistic success, by recollecting his degraded status in the emotionally isolated world (the island) of the nurseries and orphanages in which he had lived. There, people seemed not even to have names of their own, but were arranged in alphabetical order, as if they were not persons, but only letters. This degrading anonymity had led him to phantasies of having immense power—the power of controlling others through machinery, which was a reaction to his feeling of having been totally at the mercy of external and insensitive powers, of having led a life that was controlled by unchangeable routines, by push buttons, and electric switches. As these phantasies came to light in School, where he had acquired the ability to run his own life, they involved controlling others who were his slaves, the slaves of the great dictator. But these grandiose notions had been only flights of fancy, which were cruelly punctured by an unpleasant reality; and Paul feared that his high hopes for artistic success would prove equally empty. His oral anxieties were apparent in the remark about what a crushing responsibility it was to feed the islanders even for a single day—which was reminiscent of his plan to give the government his billions to feed people and foster peace.

But the ending was hopeful. The professor, who saved the islanders at the moment they were about to be destroyed by volcanic forces, may have symbolized the unexpected and fortunate turn in Paul's life, when he was rescued from the orphanage through the unforeseen arrival of strangers (who seem to have dropped from the sky). That this stranger was a "professor" may have had something to do with my profession; more important, in the story the professor's arrival on the island was simple chance. Paul still could not quite believe that his life, his removal from the orphanage, was planned and not just the result of a "balloon trip." This rescue happened just when he felt most threatened by the violent, "volcanic" eruption of his internal forces, which destroyed his island, i.e., whatever little security he may have felt in the orphanage before his suicidal attempts. Paul was still puzzled over this sudden change in his fortunes, which seemed to give him some hope that eventually things would turn out for the best, although he could not quite trust it yet: "Nobody knows what happened to the islanders since."

But Paul's feeling of security was reinforced as he met an unselected group of children in his art classes and shared important experiences with them. His classmates at the Art Institute now sought him out because of his artistic successes. He greatly enjoyed the respect with which normal children treated him. But it created a new problem. He became perturbed by his own misbehavior, and feared that it might affect the opinions others had of him. He was particularly conscious of his social awkwardness. Though slow to notice this, once he became aware of his deficiencies, all his energy seemed to be directed toward acquiring the necessary knowledges and skills.

As he later admitted, he concentrated on covertly studying grown-ups and their ways so that he could model himself in their image. He did not divulge anything about it at the time, he said, because he was afraid of being ridiculed or taken advantage of, if other people knew how important copying them was to him.

But as he moved out from the protection of the School and came more into contact with the outside world, it became increasingly apparent that he was ignorant of some of the simplest facts and procedures involved in social intercourse. It was not that we had neglected this aspect of his development, but he had been blind to our efforts until he came to recognize their value through outside criticism.

For example, he had not the least notion that the kind of remarks adolescent boys toss off to one another about girls or women in secret, among themselves, were not to be directed to the persons concerned. It had simply not occurred to him that he should take into account not only what he said, but to whom. The manners that other children pick up automatically in the process of normal family living Paul had to learn late in life, the hard way. And the fact that he was very big for his age made his adolescent awkwardness all the more obvious. Even we were astonished, to use only one example, when after more than three years with us it came out that he did not know the difference between Miss and Mrs. He had slurred his words so much, and we had become so adept at guessing what he meant, that we had not realized that he, himself, often did not know the meaning of the words he used. Motivated by his new desire to learn, he finally admitted his ignorance; until then he had deliberately pronounced these, and many other words, indistinctly so that people would not realize that he did not know their correct usage. This was another source of his speech difficulties of which we had had no inkling.

Paul's desire to make up for lost time was insatiable. About reading magazines, for example, he said, "Now that I've started [to] read magazines there's so much reading I'd catch up [on] and I need more and more and more and there'll never be enough for me." He dubbed himself a bookworm, and he certainly was. With equal intensity he branched out in all directions.

While his social behavior continued to improve, all too often he still blustered and pushed other people out of his way. He always wanted them to fall in with his wishes, but rarely responded to theirs. However, now that he realized this, he felt desolate, although before he had not given a hang. But much as he wanted to, it was so hard for him to change. Hypersensitive whenever his own feelings were hurt, he nevertheless never thought that his taunting, teasing, or blustering remarks might hurt somebody else. These, of course, were aggravated by his egocentricity and lack of respect for others, which characterize many adolescents as they grasp at independence from adults. Paul, too, wanted to assert himself against grown-ups, but at the same time, because of his past, he still needed a tremendous amount of dependent gratification from us. This conflict made the job of helping him during these years difficult indeed. While he wanted to acquire adult knowledge and behavior, he had also the normal adolescent's ambivalence about growing up. In his case, this was aggravated by the realization that growing up would also mean leaving the School. At times this interfered with his desire to learn, although he always returned to it. Given a new science book, he was at first reluctant to study it, because he was afraid he would be gone before he could finish it. Similarly, he was reluctant to begin any new courses of study for fear that, once they were completed, he might have to leave School.

Like any adolescent, he fussed and worried about his future. He feared it might prove as disappointing as his early life had been. He placed only a partial trust in our assurances, for his anxieties were too great to permit him to believe us completely. When something preyed on his mind, he had a difficult time discussing it, and this held true for his worries about the future. We asked him why he failed to talk about the things he was so greatly concerned about, and he said, "You're not around at the right time. You're not here in the middle of the night when I think and worry about it." We helped him to realize that he had to brood about his future at night because he staved off thinking about it, through frantic activity, during the day. As he so aptly explained his busyness, "I worry when I've nothing else to do." Again and again we went over his past with him, and explained how the agency had taken care of him before and would help him again. As he began to feel somewhat more secure about his future, Paul could say, "I know now that I won't have to go back to live with my mother. I hoped that, a year or two ago, but up to now I always thought I might, and worried a lot about it."

These conversations about his future eventually reassured Paul to some degree and freed him to plan with greater realism. But his plans were still mainly influenced by the nature of his past deprivations. For quite some time, he wanted to become a great chef—the most famous in the world, naturally—or to be major-domo of the world's greatest restaurant.

In our efforts to reassure him, we explained that he could put himself through college if he wished, citing as proof the fact that some of the counselors he knew best had done exactly this or were presently working their way through graduate school. Immediately he wanted more information about just how they supported themselves. As happened so frequently, only after feeling truly reassured could he admit that he had despaired of ever getting through high school, much less college, because no one would pay for it. Very often after these talks, Paul would say, "This was a very good discussion."

His increased security permitted him to free himself from the escapist techniques he had previously used to quiet or forget his anxieties and worries. On one occasion, during a visit to the dime store, he spent a long time skimming through various comic books, as he had habitually done in his first years at School. Now, having studied them carefully, he said, "They're not good any more." The kind of escape provided by comic books, and the phantasies about hostility and superhuman powers they provoked, were no longer palatable to Paul.

Paul's progress was by no means as simple and direct as my narrative at this point may suggest. He frequently resorted to his old behavior. But it was done much more consciously; he could openly state how much he longed to be an infant again, while at the same time he knew that this was not possible. Often the difference between then and now was that the things he had previously said out of desperate desire, were now said humorously.

The events of his School life were of great importance to Paul, and he kept careful track of them. They had to make up for the scarcity of emotionally meaningful events in his past. For instance, in marking his second anniversary of study under his present teacher, he said with an implied chuckle, "I'm teacher's two-year-old boy. Sometimes I think I might be three. But most time I'm still her two-year-old." Similarly, events that threatened his stability could still produce depressive or megalomanic reactions of the old type, but he, himself, no longer took these quite as seriously as before.

Nevertheless, when confronted with any new task in adjustment, Paul always seemed at first to return to these older forms of mastery. For example, at the end of the academic year, Paul was placed in another classroom with a male teacher. In part, the purpose behind this move was to help Paul master relations to men before he left us. Though Paul had been acquainted for some time with his new teacher (who had at one time been a counselor), to be put in his classroom was quite a radical change. Paul reacted to the loss of his old teacher with a real depression, and then turned to his megalomanic defenses to master the new situation.

On a single day in class these two incidents took place, which illustrated both reactions. The children were asked to write sentences incorporating the following phrases: "After a happy day," "In bed," and "With sweet dreams." Paul's sentences, written all in a row, were: "He die after a happy day. He die after a heart attack. He die with sweet dreams." Linguistically speaking, this performance ranked far below his present level of achievement; the urgent need to express his morbid feelings seemed to carry him away and, moreover, he made the mistake of neglecting to use the phrase "in bed." The loss of his old teacher and the necessity for making a new adjustment had immediately led him to fear that terrible events were lurking in the wake of the happy days he was just beginning to enjoy. Shortly after this, he picked up the globe and put it on his head; then, being consciously histrionic, he boomed out dramatically, "I'm the world!"

But such reversions to infantile desires ("I'm the teacher's two-year-old boy") and to depressive or megalomanic reactions, were now quite short-lived; Paul seemed to race through them, as if in a hurry to get back to more constructive work. No longer did he use exaggerated remarks to isolate himself from others, or to express his own isolation; rather, they were used to reach out for human comfort when he was in distress. Moreover, they did not express inner stimuli alone, but drew upon the outer world for their content (the phrases dictated by the teacher, the classroom globe), and this revealed how much more Paul was in contact with reality, even in his depressed moments.[35]

Any description of Paul's ups and downs should not blur the picture of what was now the main course of his life: the move toward an ever better integration, toward making peace with himself and accepting himself as the person he was, though he by no means came up to the high standards he set for himself. To accept himself and his life fully, he would have to accept his past in some degree, and he also worked on this task during the year. Repeatedly, he went over his life history until he understood its sequence of events. After at least the externals, the bad events, had been recaptured, placed in proper sequence, and considerably better understood, they no longer cast a pall on his whole life. As they fell into place, they left room for other memories. Pleasant recollections about his life at the orphanage began emerging for the first time. He remembered three games he had enjoyed and some children he liked to play with, as well as other people who had been kind to him. But most of these memories were depersonalized. For example, while he

---

35. This particular episode is also characteristic of Paul in that it shows the histrionic element involved in his depressive or megalomanic expressions—his clowning, and his desire to be noticed.

remembered a public playground where he had had some fine times, he could not remember ever having played there with another person.

Recollections of pleasant things, rare as they had been, went hand in hand with enjoyment of life in the present. As Paul, himself, said, "Life is good," though his ability to enjoy it was still limited. More important than such rare expressions of pleasure was his realization that happiness was not derived from autistic or physiological pleasures (such as sucking and eating), gratification of his overdeveloped narcissism (through winning in competitions), or inanimate play equipment (the public playground), but from personal relations. For after saying that life was good, he added, "It means you like me." Understanding the value of sound human relations, but also realizing how insecure he felt in this respect, Paul feared very much that on leaving us he might become "very stuck up." Why? " 'Cause I'm not sure about other people." So he fully understood that his well-being depended on feeling accepted. Fear that he would not be liked in his future life lay behind his great anxiety that we would have no further interest in him once he left us.

Paul's wish to establish and maintain meaningful relations with others besides his counselors and teachers often came to nothing because he still did not know how to behave, and hence unwittingly hurt other people's feelings. He recognized this blind spot and set out to remedy it by learning how other people felt. In the past he had been hurt so frequently, had been involved in so many emotional difficulties, that he could at least understand motives that were akin to his own. Frequently, he tried to interpret the children's behavior for them, in an attempt both to be helpful and to check the validity of his own understanding of their motives. A successful interpretation pleased him because then he could feel superior to the other person. So his efforts to come emotionally closer to others were, to a degree, a means of feeding his narcissism. But that he satisfied his narcissism in these ways meant that he was able to comprehend how others felt, and showed his increasingly real interest in them as persons.

One instance in which Paul interpreted another child's behavior involved a previously delinquent boy who still had a desperate need to run away from the School when anything upsetting happened to him. Once, when he was again planning to truant, Paul told him, "You want take a walk just like man who drinks. You know, there 're people [who] go get drunk when they've lots of trouble,

and think they'll forget. [But when] they wake up they've same
trouble, didn't get rid of it. It's just like that you want to take a
walk." The two talked for a while about why the boy was angry,
and why he wanted to run away. Paul ended the conversation
authoritatively by saying. "You're so darn mad 'cause you know darn
well that what I've said and [what the] counselor said was true,
and you're wrong."

While he thus tried to fathom others, and in this way come closer
to them, a discrepancy became more and more apparent between
Paul's wish to make friends and his persistent inability to express
himself. Very often he left us with the impression of sullenness, of
not wanting to communicate, while actually he was desperate about
not being able to express adequately what he felt. The forms of
intimate communication learned only in the closeness of family
living were beyond his ken. His intellectual exploring of family life
could not by itself make up for this deficiency. Only experience with
real family life would do, and so we tried to set the stage.

Whenever feasible, we arranged for Paul to visit families, particularly the homes of married staff members. These visits revealed
anew the degree to which he lacked knowledge of even the simplest
tools of social living. He told us how insecure he felt because, as he
put it, he did not know how or when to sit down in a chair, which
chair to take, where to leave his overshoes or hang up his wraps,
and so on. He had to learn all these simple but important things,
and once he was familiar with the rudiments of polite behavior, he
felt much more comfortable. Paul tried to convince himself that by
learning these externals, he had learned about family life. But we,
of course, provided these opportunities so that his experience in
family living, which was still to come, would not fail from the very
outset.

On his own, Paul continued to explore and fill in the experiences
he had missed.

For example, during the last months of his stay at the School,
he insisted on taking responsibility for our front lawn, although this
was the janitor's job. From this non-nutritive "gardening" he derived as much satisfaction as he had previously from raising vegetables for himself. One day, when I found him vigorously cleaning
the front yard of the School, he explained to me, "I wanted to see
what it'd be like to be a real child, have a real home, and do things
like that." In these and many other ways Paul was showing his
desire and need to experience family life.

. . . And Leaves Us

PAUL HAD NOW REACHED our age limit and was becoming ready for high school. We wished that he had come to us younger, so that his rehabilitation could be carried farther, if not finished. But only one more year with us would not suffice, and if the work had to be interrupted at all, the beginning of high school seemed the logical time to do it.

To help us decide whether this was a good time for the big change in his living conditions, Paul was given another Rorschach Test.

Some of the more significant findings were:[36] "The primary defensive strategy is a withdrawal into introversive living, as a result of the impact of anxiety. In coping with the anxiety, obsessive, compulsive defenses also occur in the mechanisms of isolation, displacement, and undoing. As part of the intellectual defense there has been an increase in verbosity and a tremendous increase in productivity. Along with this appears an over-adaptation to conventionality." Here we see in his test performance—as we saw in his behavior at School—the effects, good and bad, of his almost superhuman effort to adjust to the world around him. Throughout his early life he had never enjoyed the experiences that are usual in the world of a child, which make possible a smooth adaptation to the conventional demands of adult living. So Paul had to over-adapt, had to become overconventional, in order to act within the conventions at all.

The test findings continued: "The vulnerability of the ego is still apparent. A superior intellectual potential is revealed throughout the record. Compared with earlier tests, a more effective use of his intelligence is now apparent. Intellectual dysfunctions are still present—confusions, contaminations, and at times immature language usage; they are, however, much less pronounced than previously. Regard for reality is at the critical minimum for the healthy; however, conformity of thinking is considerably above average.

"Feelings of inferiority, noted as emerging in the previous test, are pronounced in the present. Together with passivity, they accentuate dysphoric mood trends. The phantasy is excessive and dominates his mental living. At times it is vigorously experienced. He frequently uses it as a means of releasing his hostile, aggressive impulses.

---

36. Rorschach evaluation by W. N. Thetford.

"The excess of inner living over outer affective expression carries the danger of autistic withdrawal, especially when stimulation from the external environment becomes too great. The danger of schizophrenic reaction is therefore still present. A tremendous amount of resistance is evident throughout. It is directed principally against his own unconscious wishes; and is indicative of the extreme struggle within him. Some release of affective energy is also found. The affect is predominantly labile, although the capacity for mature emotional rapport with the environment is now present. The ego is still vulnerable to emotional stresses; there is evidence of color shock indicative of a neurotic structure. Potential for paranoiac thinking is found both structurally and in the content.

"In summary: Insofar as the picture now assumes more of the structural aspects of a neurosis it may be said to represent some ego progress. The weak spots are: feelings of inferiority; sensitivity to the environment; some regressive thinking, confusions, and contaminations, which become overpowering under affective stimulation. The anxiety is deep, pervasive, and at times disruptive. But he does display the capacity to cope with it, primarily in phantasy. In the light of the large amount of hostility projected, it is imperative that his defenses continue to be strengthened. His use of obsessive-compulsive defenses is an asset that makes it possible for him to control the disruptive forces."

To a large degree the test corroborated our impression that, in the main, Paul's personality had changed. No longer was it predominantly unstructured, chaotic, or, one might say, schizophrenic, as had been the case when he came to the School. His difficulties were now more akin to a severe neurosis, which could be treated in ambulatory fashion. Institutional living no longer seemed necessary, and was perhaps undesirable. We could not fully complete the task of rehabilitating him: he had come to us too late in life for that. Moreover, the time was running short in which he must acquire certain kinds of experiences he would need in later life. Mainly, he needed to live with a family, and for this experience he would soon be too old.

One of our knottiest problems was to decide which was more important for him, to continue living in the School or to live with a family. If he stayed with us, with the people to whom he had related more closely than to anybody else in his life, he would continue to use these relations in integrating his personality. But this would require at least two or three more years, and by then, when he was seventeen, it would certainly be too late for him to live in a home, with a family, during what remained of his formative years.

If we waited that long, Paul would truly spend all his youth in institutions, and even in the best institution one must live a carefully arranged life. Paul's life had already been too much dominated by routine, and too little conditioned by his own spontaneous decisions.

For some time, we discussed with the agency various plans for Paul's leaving. We feared that an ordinary foster home placement, plus therapy (which would have been most desirable), would not work out. For despite Paul's efforts to acquire the skills of family living, and his emotional need to be part of a family, he was so deficient in the former that it was unreasonable to expect him to succeed in the latter. Moreover, defeat might have traumatic consequences for him, just because he longed so much to be a "real child" in a "real family."

In addition, we feared that if Paul were placed in a foster home he would be eager to establish himself, in relation to his foster parents, not as a foster child, but as an infant. This would entail tremendous emotional demands on them, which no foster family could be expected to meet, in view of Paul's awkward hostility and, perhaps even more, his awkward dependency.

For this huge, adolescent boy, by then nearly six feet tall, still acted occasionally with babyish dependency at one moment, and aggressive hostility the next. Both his aggressive and his dependent actions often seemed threatening, even to quite experienced persons. In either case, he was ambivalent about his behavior, and realized that it was not in line with his age. For this reason, he always feared rejection. For example, this young giant would try to plunk himself in the lap of his female counselor, and expect her to enjoy his show of affection. Or he would defensively assert his prerogatives as a young adult; still lacking manners, he would use all his 190 pounds to get his own way, to push others—children, men or women counselors—aside. Sometimes the pushing was figurative; other times, literal. True, he had every intention of "behaving himself" in a future home, and many of his present actions stemmed from his genuine effort to get as much out of the School as he could while he remained, since he realized full well his stay was drawing to a close. But he was quite likely to react to disappointment with either a temper outburst or a silent withdrawal. Both reactions were hard for any person to take and still remain giving, which was necessary for his progress.

So we had reached an impasse: though he needed intimate family living, it seemed impossible to find a foster family that could accept him with all his difficulties. On the other hand, if he were placed in another institution, he would not receive the family experiences he craved. Wise planning for his future was made even more difficult in view of his artistic talents and his wish to go on with his art training, which meant he should live where this could be continued. Finally and most important, in view of his still serious emotional disturbance, psychotherapy would be necessary.

The agency that had been concerned with Paul's care just about that time opened some special treatment homes, in which they tried to combine the suitable features of therapeutic institutional living with a family setting, if not family life. In these homes a small number of children—no more than would form a good-sized family —lived in a normal apartment setting. The foster parents were specially selected and trained, and worked under the close supervision of a child psychoanalyst. Each child in the home received casework help. Since the homes were located in Chicago, Paul could continue studying at the Art Institute and maintain contact with old friends in School, so that no total break with them would be necessary. For all these reasons, we jointly explored with the agency the desirability of Paul's entering such a treatment home at the end of the academic year. After a number of weeks spent in careful psychiatric evaluation of all the problems involved, it was decided that, although by no means ideal, under the circumstances this plan was the best the agency could develop for Paul's future.

During his last months with us, Paul was often fearful about having to leave. Whenever this anxiety took hold, he returned to some of his old symptoms. He would again stuff himself with food, perennially afraid that there might not be enough to eat in his new home. In those last months particularly, Paul's main worries revolved about the people with whom he would live, and whether he would leave with what he called "top honors." He was absorbed in the task of slowly preparing for the great separation.

Very carefully and realistically, he began painting everything that was important to him, as if compiling a record and impressing on his memory once and for all the various aspects of his School life. This was a sharp change from the highly imaginative and not very representational style of painting that had been characteristic for him until then. Interestingly enough, his first subject was his baby bottle, of which he made a very painstaking preliminary sketch, and then a painting. He then went on to sketch his dormitory, and finally the School building.

Having thus secured his past, Paul turned his thoughts toward the future. He worried about the obstacles within himself that might prove serious in getting along with others. He realized that he was "a kid who thinks a lot—too much—of himself." He also sensed it was a handicap always to have to be first, and he knew that his urge came from insecurity.

In his overnight visits to the homes of staff members, Paul carefully observed the adults; he tried to copy them, to develop nice manners, and to be more careful about his appearance. To some degree he really learned to master these social arts. Toward the end of his stay he became quite poised and charming in social situations, although he still retained considerable rigidity.

All this ground was temporarily lost when Paul was told about the definite program for his future. Although he had known he would be leaving very soon, the actual planning had been so difficult that we reached a final decision just a month before his departure, and could only then inform him of the details. As soon as he realized how imminent his departure was, he frantically tried to soak up everything we had to offer: knowledge, human relations, and most of all, food. Again he ate gargantuan amounts, and gained ten pounds this last month, so that by the time of his departure, he was forty-four pounds overweight.

At first Paul was disappointed that our plans called for him to live in the same city with his mother. In his worry about this and about the big change in general, he reverted for a short time to his old defense of denying an unpleasant reality by engaging in unrealistic hopes. He said that he expected to leave us for one of the most famous Eastern prep schools; next, he thought he would go to Europe to attend some famous school there. But fairly soon he accepted our assurance that he would not have to return to his mother, and reasonably tried to accept the plan as best he could.

Eagerly, Paul tried to become independent; he went out more on his own, and ventured by himself into areas of the city he had not dared approach before without a counselor. Also, he tried to make friends outside the School. Over and over he commented on how much he had changed during his years in School. Probably he did this to reassure himself, but also it was an effort to take stock of himself realistically.

Still, there were many symptoms of the great strain under which he labored. His speech became less clear; he engaged in rambling conversations, which actually were lengthy monologues, since they totally disregarded the person with whom he was talking. He also reverted to baby talk. But these regressions lasted only for short intervals; each time he checked himself, understanding that his anx-

iety had led him back to old ways of dealing with upsetting experiences.

His main fear was that his mother might get hold of him. He
had to be sure that she would not know where he would be living,
and that we would not give her his address. On the other hand, he
was afraid he might lose contact with us, although he seemed able
to accept our assurances that we would continue to be interested in
him, and available for help if he needed us.

From the moment he was notified about his leaving, he found
the preparation and waiting for the great change very difficult, but
he managed the actual transition quite well. In one way he was
relieved that a definite plan had been developed, which seemed to
shield him from his mother's interference, assured him of casework
help with his emotional difficulties, and most important, protected
his physical needs during his high school years until he could establish himself independently in life. On several occasions he visited
his future home, and he liked it. His first visit pleased him especially.
The foster parents "looked just like any other average American
family." His statement expressed more his need and desire to live
with an average American family, than a correct evaluation of the
foster home, since he was aware that this was a special home where
four other boys his age would live with him. But he was trying hard
to convince himself that from now on he would live the life of a
normal boy his age in an average family.

This tangible demonstration of sensible planning for him set
Paul's mind at rest about the value and good will of the agency,
which now took over. He established a fairly good relation to his
new case worker and could talk freely to him about how hard it
was to leave the School, and how afraid he was about the change.
Toward the end, he saw his move as "a real great adventure," and
he said, "I want it to go over real well."

In the days that were left Paul further tried to secure his past
and prepare himself for the future. He spent his last weeks going
over his possessions, packing and re-packing them. He repeatedly
asked for information about high school life and about the particular school he would attend. He tried, successfully, to understand
better the work of the agency, and its plans for his care. He felt
it was especially important that his friends at the School retain
contact with him. Through it all, he remained quite poised and
could talk freely about anything that troubled him.

When he finally set out for his new home, Paul summed up his
feelings about his life with us in words that seemed to show he

understood that, for some time, he had had to regress and regain infantile experiences—and also that he knew his rehabilitation was by no means ended. "When I first came to the School I was this small." He placed his palms facing each other in front of his face. Then, moving them even more closely together, he went on, "After that I got smaller and smaller." But his hands moved farther apart as he continued, "After that, I grew and grew and grew—and I'm still growing." This was said forcefully. His facial expression, until the last words, had been tense and preoccupied—almost anxious— but, having expressed his hopes for his continuing growth, his expression became pleased, relaxed, and even happy.

So Paul left us, as he had hoped and planned to do, with "top honors." While he was highly satisfied with his accomplishments during the years with us, we could not yet feel certain about our results. True, we had been able to change his personality in important ways, but by no means could we speak of a total "cure" of his initial disturbance. A great deal, though not all, of the damage to his personality had been repaired. But we could not predict whether the partial freeing of his vital energy that had been achieved would see him successfully through life—so much depended upon how fortunate or unfortunate the conditions of his future would be. Any prediction about the outcome of psychotherapeutic effort is hazardous, even for adults, who can use their newly freed energy to arrange their future lives in the light of the knowledge and insights gained in therapy. For youngsters, who depend so largely on others to arrange the circumstances of their lives, forecasts are virtually impossible.

This was particularly true for Paul. Not only was he without a family to provide "normal" living conditions for him, but inevitably his mother would remain an influence in his life. For the time being she was only a potential threat to his integration, but one could never be sure just how long she would remain in the background, once her influence on Paul was no longer subject to our control. The emotional impact of a mother so disturbed as to be unable to accept treatment might, at least temporarily, undo quite a bit of what had been accomplished, if she were permitted to pour out her feelings of persecution on Paul.

At least we could say that we felt Paul should be able to handle this difficult period of change with competence, and also his life during the immediate future; beyond that, we could only hope.

While this conservative evaluation of what had been achieved was the only objective way to look at what we had done for Paul during his four and a half years with us, our subjective viewpoint was quite different. It was full of pride and optimism. We felt that Paul had been a success. The boy had come to us in a desperate state of mind, haunted by delusions. He had not only been a delinquent, who violently attacked others, but he had also been suicidal. He had been correctly diagnosed as a schizophrenic, and this condition had been chronic for years. But now he had formed some very close, meaningful, personal attachments. He felt fairly at home in life and able to cope more realistically with the world, even in the difficult tasks ahead.

Our subjective feelings were substantiated by the objective data. When Paul came to us he had lagged more than two years behind in academic achievement. Now he was academically ahead of his age. His average achievement was such that he seemed ready for the tenth grade; actually we suggested placement in the ninth to make the new adjustment easier.

Paul's IQ had risen from 100 to 126, and was held at this level only by his persistent verbal handicap. According to non-verbal performance tests (for example, Cornell Coxe), his IQ was now 157.

For two consecutive years his paintings had been selected and shown all over the country as examples of outstanding art work for a child his age.

While such objective evidence permits some claim of success, Paul's story is not reported for that reason. Its main merit may be that it shows how the damage wreaked on children by some institutions can be rectified by yet other institutions. How much simpler it would be if the first type of institution could learn from the second, so that the second would no longer be required to help these "institutionalized" children!

Paul's Counselor

WORKING WITH PAUL was at times enormously difficult, and required special talents and emotional commitments from the people who were most intensively concerned with his care. I once asked the staff member who had done most for him how she had been able to achieve such success. Her reply was that Paul had made a very powerful emotional appeal to her from the beginning, an appeal that lost none of its strength through the years of hard labor and deep emotional involvement. Various factors entered into this, only some of which can be discussed here.

From the outset of her life, this staff member had been terrified by the possibility of losing her parents and having to live in an orphanage. Possessed by this worry, she felt guilty about enjoying a home, while poor, orphan children could not. Paul was the first child she had ever met who had actually grown up in an orphanage. He had been cheated out of a home. This counselor, who felt so guilty before all homeless children, now saw a chance to do something about her guilt. At the time, of course, these thought processes were not conscious.

She had other motivations, as well. When Paul came to us she felt that he was too far gone, too entrenched in his disturbance and infantile in his reactions, ever to grow up to be a normal person. Although she knew how schizophrenic a number of other children had been when they entered, Paul seemed even worse, and his way of acting out aroused great anxiety in her. She was convinced that I had made a mistake in admitting him, and we had a number of discussions about this issue. Our consulting psychiatrist had joined her in thinking that Paul was too far gone to be treatable, and agreed that it would be virtually impossible to find anyone who could meet Paul's excessive needs.

This seems to have been just the challenge she needed. While on a conscious level she went on trying to convince me that Paul was beyond help, unconsciously she only wished more strongly to prove me right and herself wrong. So she was caught in another conflict, which it was necessary to resolve through helping Paul. The conflict lay between her conscious opposition to me and her unconscious wish to be loyal to me and to the School's efforts. She also felt ambivalent, if not guilty, about her attempts to prevent this child's admittance, because of the general sense of guilt aroused in her by children reared in orphanages. In a way, by opposing Paul's admission she was also testing me and the School to see whether or not we would withhold our help from an orphan. Had we failed him, we should have failed her, and she might have come to feel that her work in the School could not offer her the chance, which she so much desired, to expiate her guilt.

This feeling probably would not have become conscious. On a conscious level, working with us might no longer have seemed attractive, or might have become "too difficult," which is the reason some workers give for leaving after a relatively short training period. Since we measured up to the test, this meant that, contrary to her childhood fears, orphans can be helped, and are not necessarily "tainted" for life. Once, contrary to her opinion, we admitted Paul, it became vitally important to her that we succeed. For, among other things, success meant that even if she had been placed in an orphanage she need not have been a lost soul. In her determination to succeed, therefore, she generously gave her all in helping Paul. Later, as he began to improve and she realized that he could be helped, she felt he was "the most thrilling child to work with."

At a still later period, it became possible for her to identify with Paul in many ways. His deep-rooted desire to be a good, respectable citizen, and his struggle against his fear that middle-class values could never be achieved by him, were akin to her own experience. It became even easier for her to identify with him when he began reaching out frantically for education, for knowledge and learning, for she herself had handled similar anxieties. She, too, had acquired her education by fighting against unfavorable circumstances, just as Paul had. In helping him in his struggle, she resolved many of the misgivings she still harbored. She had successfully crowned her struggle for education by acquiring a higher degree at the University of Chicago—the same University that helped Paul to acquire his education, both academic and in learning to live. Small wonder that some four years later Paul's greatest wish was to enter the College of the University of Chicago.

The narcissistic gratification and ego-supporting experiences always inherent in helping our children, need hardly be mentioned. This, incidentally, holds true not only for the person working most intimately with a child, but for the rest of the staff and myself, depending on how directly we are involved with the youngster.

Out in Life

PAUL PHONED US repeatedly during the first weeks in his new home, partly under the pretext of asking for things he had deliberately left behind, in order to maintain his ties with us, and partly to learn how things were going without him. But as time passed, he called less and less often. At first he was a frequent visitor. Later, these visits also tapered off, and now, four years after his departure, are rare.

The move itself went smoothly, and initially Paul made a good adjustment to his new situation. During the first year, he did very well academically in high school, and after some great anxiety at first, his social adjustment slowly improved, too. He pursued his art interest, and seemed on the way to achieving what he most craved: learning how to live the life of an average boy in an average American family.

Then, toward the end of the first year, there came a time when things were not so smooth for Paul. The honeymoon with his foster parents ended. The foster mother, who at first had been very fond of this big baby who was so anxious to be loved by her, after several months felt emotionally exhausted, despite her best intentions. This huge adolescent was literally hanging onto her apron strings, and would not permit her a moment's privacy. It was unfortunate, too, that among the other boys living in this home, and also in the high school to which he went, he met some of the same "big ones," older boys, who had made life so miserable for him at the orphanage. Thus his new home was tainted by old, unpleasant memories.

Disappointed in his foster mother, Paul became disappointed in himself, and his school work, which had been very good at first, fell off in quality. The foster parents, wishing to encourage him, paid little attention to the fact that he was getting only average grades. This attitude was most disconcerting to him, for he had set high standards for himself and knew he could live up to them. Their ready acceptance of his mediocre achievement was interpreted by him as expressing a low opinion of his ability, instead of the effort at encouragement it really was.

Disappointed with himself, he tried to achieve status by associating with a rather tough group of high school students to whom artistic endeavors were sissy. His case worker, unfortunately, in an effort to help Paul toward male identification and masculinity, also agreed that painting was not boyish. Discouraged in his artistic leanings by foster parents, peers, and therapist, he gave it up, thus losing the activity that had been most meaningful in his life. On each visit with us he looked wistfully at one of the oil paintings he had given to the School before his departure. It made him happy to see it on our wall, but this was not enough to give him strength to go against his present environment. Having done so well in art during his first year after leaving us, he dropped his art lessons in the second.

In his discontentment with the foster mother who could not live up to his extreme demands for mothering, he began asking to see his mother, and by the end of the first year he visited her for a time every Sunday. He also did this partly because he felt the Sunday program in his new home was not particularly attractive. In her usual fashion, his mother carped about the agency and his foster parents. This tallied with Paul's own disappointment, but realizing that his mother's criticisms were exaggerated beyond reason, he felt guilty. Disappointed in his own mother, who could not give him what he craved, he returned from each visit even more demanding of his foster mother, who found it more impossible than ever to satisfy him. By the end of the week, this cycle led Paul to seek his mother's company afresh, although by the close of each visit with

her he felt so let down he vowed he would never repeat them. That
his own mother kept trying to arouse his hopes about what she or
the family would do for him one day, in order to maintain her
hold over him, was evident to all.

Although the agency was well aware of how pernicious these
visits were for Paul, they felt that, since he would have to master
his disappointment in his mother in reality after having thought it
through with us emotionally, he might as well do this now.

Needless to say, some of these developments were disappointing
to us. Paul could have accomplished excellent work in high school
and in art and accrued a great deal of strength from it. The realistic
adjustment to his mother and his father's relatives could have been
postponed until his overwhelming need for dependency was no
longer so pressing and he had gained sufficient intellectual and
emotional maturity to make this experience less painful.

Still, even under these difficult circumstances, Paul was maintaining himself, making average grades in high school and progressing somewhat in his relations with his schoolmates.

Things took a turn for the better during Paul's third year in
high school. As he gained confidence that he would succeed in
graduating and in becoming independent, he was able to deal more
realistically with his mother and her demands, and with his foster
parents. He requested a move from the specialized treatment home
to a normal foster home, and this took place. Though the new foster
parents had some emotional difficulties of their own, he could deal
with them realistically. He held jobs during his last two years in
high school, and performed conscientiously and successfully. In the
summer he worked as a lifeguard on the city beaches. During his
last year in high school, by working as a salesman in a shoe store,
he earned over a thousand dollars, and saved most of it.

Because of its intrinsic interest, Paul's case was chosen by the
agency as one of several to be evaluated by an out-of-state committee
of experts, who had been asked to judge the effectiveness of the
agency's program for disturbed youngsters. This study, completed
a few months before this history was finished, said of Paul:[37] "This
child's improvement is tremendous, as reflected in his social adjustment, in his expression of feeling, and in repeated Rorschach
tests. At the point of admission to the specialized foster home, he
had progressed within the Orthogenic School to a point where he
could maintain good social adjustment within a completely con-

---

37. I am indebted to the agency, the Jewish Children's Bureau of Chicago, and
particularly to its director, Mrs. Mary Lawrence, for permission to quote from this
report.

trolled environment. Within the foster home, progressively, he has shown ability to take quite marked changes in routine without evidence of upset: move to the country for vacation; move of the home to new premises; changes of job; ultimately change to foster home living.

"He has progressed from a child who, at eleven, wanted to be carried when he was emotionally upset, to a youngster who, at fifteen and sixteen, could work, accept the limitations of his allowance when he earned enough, take responsibility for his own job changes, not asking the agency to fill in immediately by reinstituting allowance. While carrying job responsibilities he could continue to go to school, doing adequately there, and to carry an active social program. From needing to save everything and have money for its own sake, he could spend it on himself, and (even more progress) on a girl, to a point of considerable extravagance at times.

"He shows improved heterosexual identification and adjustment: from a major interest in cooking and a barely concealed anxiety about his acceptance by other youngsters as male to easy acceptance in boy's groups, socializing with boys and girls appropriately, and dating relationships. He is able to give a party in his foster home even when he is having difficulties there, which seems to show an acceptance of his own identity and place. He can hold his own in difficulties with the foster parents, and advance to behavior and attitudes reflecting normal adolescent rebellion and difficulties, at the same time showing an ability to tolerate frustrations in his relationship with the foster parents.

"In his relationship with the case worker, he is able to use words and to verbalize, bringing problems as well as acting them out; which is particularly notable in a child who has had difficulties in speech and in communication as part of his pattern of illness.

"For this youngster, the behavioral improvement noted reflects major personality growth, with movement from the choice of autistic solution to his difficulties to consistently increasing reality-connection solutions, and developing object-relationships.

"His improvement is probably grounded on the great advances from his most acute regression and illness which he made in the Orthogenic School. Of basic importance in his continuing improvement is the fact that he has a relationship with one consistent male figure in the case worker, with the possibility of positive male identification; and for the first time in his life, has simultaneously a continuing living relationship over a period of time with an adult couple, acting as foster parents."

Not quite four years after he left us, Paul graduated from high school, 73rd in a class of 305 in a school with high academic standing. He had applied for admission to the College of the University and hoped very much that he would be able to enter it in the Fall. At this time, he paid us a visit, and I asked his permission to publish an account of his life with us, to which he freely agreed. We took this opportunity to review his life with us in the perspective of the four years that had elapsed since he left the School.

Paul remembered that on leaving us he had been "pretty terrified going out in the world; let's put it that way. Meeting people who didn't understand my condition, situation, past life—wouldn't be able to understand some of the actions. I would bore them with things I would say, so I was scared and frightened about how I'd do in school." He continued, "I had a bad first quarter [in high school] because of being terrified and watching every step and being so careful. I had a lot of pressure on me, so I made lots of mistakes, you know; tried to avoid mistakes, so I got out of that a little and came out of that very nicely, and I've gone through the four years pretty well."

I told him how much I regretted that he had stopped painting, and asked him why. "I really don't know," he answered. "I don't know how to say it but [at the School] I was reading, painting, and trying to be pretty independent, you might say. But when I got out, you know, you meet new people and people don't understand, and [you] try to conform to their ways, and all the sudden I got extremely lazy; and as time went on I didn't get back to it and just got lazy—just like your memory, you know; if you don't keep working at remembering things you actually forget how to remember."

He seemed to be saying that the task of adjusting to the outside world was so difficult it drained him of all energy—so much so that he was unable to do anything else, which he called laziness. The adjustment to lower middle-class respectability and conformity, which the foster home expected of him, forced him to give up his originality, which was most clearly centered in his painting. He, himself, made the connection that his adjustment to conformity could be bought only at the price of repression. Giving up his art was only part of the larger process of giving up "remembering things," which he had to do to the extent that he even forgot "how to remember." What a price to pay for becoming a real child in an average family.

Of course, though the cost was high, he reaped some of the

rewards society confers on those who conscientiously conform. With pride, Paul told me that he graduated in the upper twenty-five per cent of his class. He had even given up his speech difficulties in order to conform. I complimented Paul on how well he talked, and reminded him of the strange, clucking sounds that had still accompanied his speech when he left us. How had he gotten rid of them, I asked. It was due to a conscious effort to divorce himself from his past, he told me. "I went for a physical examination about three or four months after I left here, and I was in a room and there was this girl about sixteen years of age talking, and she heard me making that sound, and she says, 'Where have I heard that before? I know. I've heard it at the orphanage.' She remembered that. And then I was amazed that she remembered me through that and was a little ashamed, so I tried to get rid of it. And then, [you remember] what I had is, when I'd eat I also used to go [Paul made his smacking noise]. And she made some remark about that and then I had to go like this [Paul made his clucking noise], and so I decided to stop it. I got a good will power, you know."

Finally our remembrance of things past led to the question of what he thought about the changes that had taken place in him during his stay at the School, and why he thought his life had become better. "Well, I think the first thing and the most important is understanding and being very patient with us. [At first] I didn't like any of your methods, I remember—discipline. I'd been used to the rod —let's put it that way—so I always used to complain, I remember, about not having any strict discipline." "That's right," I replied, "You always used to complain that we would make a privileged character out of you, that we would spoil you." Paul agreed, and then went on, "I think that's where I first learned—maybe about nine months or a year after I finally stopped complaining about let's have a strict way. I guess that's about the first step."

I asked Paul whether he remembered anything else that was important to him; we wanted to know what helped him so that we could help other children better. He thought for a while, and then said, "Well, I'd say that it's a lot of little things that do it. It's nothing big—and of course as it shows in the records, the biggest factor is time. Nothing changes overnight. It's just the little things —you know—that change a person." I was very struck with these remarks, and since he already knew that I planned to publish his history, I said, "You know, as I listened to you, it seemed to me that what you have just said makes an ideal title for your life history: *Little Things and Time*." Paul replied, "Good title, and add *understanding and patience*."

PART III

EMOTIONAL DEATH AND REBIRTH:

Mary, A Schizophrenic Girl

Mary's Childhood

MARY was eight and a half years old when she entered the School. The referring agency described the immediate causes for her placement as follows: "She has shown increasingly difficult behavior, and at this point the situation is acute. During the last few weeks, Mary has been stealing from stores in the neighborhood and from porches of various neighbors. She fights constantly with other children, and recently struck another child over the face with a rope. She also tried to attack a child with a knife." But even long before this, Mary had been of serious concern to several social agencies in the city.

Mary's father was born in Chicago in 1900, her mother in Eastern Europe in 1905. They were married in the late 1920's and were said to have been closely attached to each other. The father had been previously married and divorced. He worked at various occupations, such as installing gas ranges and driving a cab. During the depression, when Mary was three and a half months old, he died of a heart attack. His wife was left without resources.

Mary's mother had been brought to the United States when she was two years old. She grew up in poverty, attended school through the eighth grade, and worked in factories from the age of fourteen until her marriage. After three years of marriage, the couple had their first child, a daughter whom we shall call Frances; nine years later the girl here named Mary was born.

Mary's earliest life seems to have been normal. She was a full term baby, and weighed five pounds at birth. Her physical condition was good. She was bottle fed, spoke simple words at nine months, and walked at the age of thirteen months.

Her troubles seem to have begun after her father died. The mother suffered a severe emotional shock upon the death of her husband. Relatives stated that after his sudden death, she lost all will to live.

We learned later from Mary's recollections, and also from Frances, that the mother became melancholic upon her husband's death, and physically ill shortly thereafter. She withdrew from the world, and never left the two small rooms—kitchen and bedroom—that she shared with the girls. Growing extremely fat, she eventually developed gall bladder trouble, but she would not or could not be operated on. Thus Frances, who was ten or eleven at the time, became more or less wholly responsible for Mary. Most of the time, however, Mary was alone with a deeply depressed mother who left her bed only infrequently. Occasionally, but irregularly, a neighbor came in to cook for them. Otherwise the two girls were thrown entirely on their own resources.

Before Mary was three, she was sent to a nursery school, and travelled there alone on the bus. People commented about the tiny child who sat on the bus and talked and sang to herself. At nursery school she stayed entirely aloof from the other children. She would lie alone in the middle of the play yard and masturbate continuously.

When Mary was three and a half, her mother died. She and her sister (Frances was then twelve) were placed by the Aid to Dependent Children in the home of a maternal aunt who did not want them, but whose husband convinced her that it was her duty to take them in. These relatives had two children of their own, whose "good" behavior was continually held up to the foster children for comparison. The aunt was appalled by Mary's masturbation and thumbsucking, her wetting and otherwise completely asocial behavior, and handled it with severe threats.

Although nominally the girls were under the care of the Aid to Dependent Children, they were actually shifted about among their relatives without the agency's knowledge. Soon this agency requested that a private children's agency investigate the aunt's home, since grave doubts had arisen about its suitability. Psychiatric evaluation of the home (and of Mary) was such that an immediate effort was made to secure psychiatric help for her, but the aunt and other relatives first resisted and then refused point blank to cooperate.

Before Mary was five, or perhaps earlier, she showed a preoccupation with animals, and displayed great cruelty toward them. Once, for example, she tried to kill a cat and burn it. She played with dead animals, which she may have killed herself, such as a rat she painted green. Although she pretended to love animals, she invariably almost squeezed them to death, and on occasion actually did so. She was also very aggressive in her play with children. By the age of six, she often attacked them viciously, and once, in a disagreement with another child, she picked up an iron rod and hit her so violently that the skull was exposed and several stitches had to be taken in the child's forehead.

There is reason to believe that Mary had already undergone a number of sexual experiences. One of these, when she was seven, was established as fact. She was accosted by a man who offered her money, which she accepted, to go with him to a nearby building, where he exposed himself to her.

That year a second psychiatric evaluation showed that Mary was "almost psychotic, completely affectless and unrelated, with a complete suppression of fears and other emotions." The aunt with whom the sisters lived was evaluated at the same time and was found to be extremely rejecting of Mary. The plight of the two girls was so unhappy that Frances tried at least twice to commit suicide by taking aspirin in quantity.

Despite all this, every effort by the agency to remove Mary from the home was frustrated by the aunt and the other relatives until, finally, matters became too threatening to their social status. The aunt suddenly asked to have Mary removed from the home without delay. This ensued after Mary's neighborhood thefts and aggressiveness toward other children had mounted in intensity, and eventually culminated in the attack with a knife on another child.[1]

1. Special credit is due the Jewish Children's Bureau of Chicago, which not only placed Mary in the School and then helped to maintain her there, but also gave us splendid cooperation throughout her stay and carried on the occasionally quite difficult work with her relatives. This agency also arranged for a special placement when Mary left us, which made her re-entry into a less protected life workable.

She Comes to the School

WHEN WE FIRST SAW Mary she was small for her age, but she had the face and stance of a very old woman. She looked extremely tired and totally withdrawn. She talked with some facility, but seemed to use speech as a means of avoiding contact, of quickly getting rid of the person she was talking to. She displayed no emotion whatsoever.

During her preliminary visit to the School, Mary said that she could not recall her parents because her father had died before she was born and her mother shortly after. Without visible emotion she went on to say that her five-year-old cousin was preferred by her aunt and uncle. She knew of no difficulties in her life, past or present. When we asked what we could do for her, she expressed only one wish—to own a dog—though she could not decide on a particular kind. She vacillated between wanting a big, black, ferocious one—a he-dog; or a she-dog, a puppy, preferably white. When we asked about her dreams, she said she never had any, but added, "I dream all day—about having a dog." She did say that once, as a baby, she had experienced a nightmare, but even then she had known it was not true. In it, she had killed Frances by sticking a knife in her back: "I was a murderer." Mary thought the reason for her dream was that she and Frances had to share a bed and Frances had kicked her. In speaking of her wish to own a pet, she said spontaneously that she had made a horse stand on its hind legs by hitting it "real hard."

We offered to show Mary the School, but she did not want to see either it or the children. She was only interested in pets. We told her that we had some and she agreed to look at them. After handling fish, turtles, etc., though still reluctant, she let us show her more of the School itself. As we walked around, Mary's expression indicated that she was overwhelmed by all the toys and play equipment. Yet, while taking it in with wide eyes, she kept saying, "Is that all you've got? Haven't you got any more room—haven't you got anything else?" Having inspected the boys' and girls' dormitories—which are similarly equipped, the girls' rather more elaborately—she commented only, "Why don't the girls have any of these things—why don't they have anything?"

She was very fearful about meeting other children. Her anxiety seemed to hinge on their ability to retaliate, since over and over she asked how old they were, how big and strong. Our assurance that we would amply protect her did not noticeably abate her fears.

While we toured the School, she seemed observant but uncommunicative. Still, when I asked if she would be willing to live here, and to come on the very next day,[2] she agreed. She tried, however, to put me in the position of forcing her, by insisting, "My aunt will put me away in this School, anyway." My assertion that her aunt had no influence over me seemed to interest her vaguely; after she realized that it was probably true I had never seen or spoken to her aunt (the social worker had brought her to the School) she sighed, possibly with relief, and agreed to try living with us.

The next day, Mary arrived. Again she was most reluctant to meet the children, but she asked a few questions about them—anxious questions, such as, "Do the kids ever talk in school? Even in class? What happens if they do?" Other queries expressed curiosity: "What time do you go to bed at night?"

Coupled with this was some exploring of human relations. As her counselor took her around on that first day, some children called out as they went by. "They're calling you," Mary said, "Does that mean that they like you?" Immediately after wondering aloud if counselors were liked by the children, she evinced a wish to be the only one to receive love and attention. Some of the girls mentioned a trip they were going to take with the counselor that afternoon, and in response to a questioning look from Mary the counselor assured her that she would be included in their plans. Immediately Mary said, "You're going with me alone. I'll have you to myself all alone." The counselor replied that she had promised to go with the group, but they would be happy to have Mary come along; also, there would be many times when the counselor would take Mary out alone. She explained that she was available whenever Mary wanted her, but that she could not be with Mary alone all the time. Disregarding this explanation, Mary merely repeated, "You're just going with me. Maybe the other girls will be there, but you'll just be with me."

At the same time, in a roundabout way, Mary revealed her confusion about sex. As they were passing a picture, she pointed to it and said, "Look, he's having kittens." The counselor said, "She's having kittens," at which Mary looked up and with a little laugh said, "Oh, I always get the he's and she's mixed up."

Mary was then introduced to the seven girls with whom she was to share a dormitory. One of them, Grace, did her best to make the newcomer feel at home. But her questions met with no response.

2. In view of Mary's history, the severity of her symptoms, and the seriousness of the diagnosis, we had decided to dispense with the usual introductory examinations in order that she might be removed from her old environment as soon as possible.

Although she seemed to sense Mary's reluctance to relate, Grace continued to take the initiative, and soon volunteered the most important fact about herself—namely, that her parents were dead. This broke the ice momentarily, and Mary replied that she had been living with an aunt. Making another effort, Grace went on to say that things were not bad in School—as a matter of fact, the School was much better than the foster homes in which she had lived and been kicked around. With a nasty grin, Mary countered that she had once hit a girl over the head with a pipe, which hurt her so badly, she had to have stitches taken in her head. Mary wound up by warning Grace that the children had better watch out and not cross her. Although the security of the School kept the children from becoming really frightened, Mary's behavior was threatening enough to make them steer clear of her, and leave her strictly alone.

In spite of Mary's aloofness, we were able to demonstrate our attitudes to her in more or less practical fashion. While she and her counselor were still touring the School, she showed an interest in some paints in one of the playrooms. With some encouragement from the counselor, Mary remarked that she would like to paint; she explained that she had never used real paint, but had once helped out the painters when they had come to the house, which had been fun. When they were not looking she had painted a little, but had gotten a "real licking" for getting paint all over herself. The counselor made no attempt to assure her that such behavior was acceptable in the School; for one thing, she felt Mary might sense it as an attempt to sell her on the School rather than letting her accept it autonomously; or Mary might have thought the counselor was lying, or even trying to play up to her because she (Mary) was so dangerous. So the counselor merely remarked that Mary could use the paints right now if she wished.

Mary approached them hesitantly, but soon, gathering courage, she asked what would happen if she smeared paint on herself. The counselor told her "nothing"—she would just wipe it off; and she demonstrated how easily this can be done with turpentine. As a test, Mary dipped her fingers deep into the paint jar and put paint blotches all over her arm. Then she held out her arm to be wiped. When the counselor obliged, Mary asked, "What do you do to girls who stink like turpentine?" The counselor just laughed. Reassured, Mary began pouring out a long stream of questions: who took care of the children? what did they do together? and when? Winding up with some queries about playing with clay, she commented, "I've never played with clay, but I want to." However, in spite of being encouraged, she could not nerve herself to try it that first day.

This same room and equipment had been shown Mary, by the same counselor, on her preliminary visit the day before. Mary had also been encouraged at that time to ask questions, but had not done so. Only after concrete experience had shown her something of our attitude toward children, did she begin to ask questions and listen to what we had to say. Perhaps she had been loath to talk to strangers; perhaps she did not trust us to tell her the truth; or she may simply have been showing her extremely negativistic attitude toward adults. At any rate, as she listened now to what the counselor told her about life at the School, what impressed her most was the assurance that she could rest or go to sleep whenever she wanted to. This very tired child tested this immediately by retiring to her bed, where she remained during most of her first days in School.

DISCUSSION

As we reviewed our impressions of Mary on that first day, we saw her as an extremely deprived, sullen child who appeared—on the surface—to be physically and intellectually adequate. Superficially, she seemed able to relate, though mainly in hostile ways. She expressed herself well, but with long pauses and only in very short sentences. She talked to adults mainly by answering questions; her responses were to the point but did not lead to conversation. We noted that whenever tenuous contact was established it disappeared the instant any emotional difficulty arose. When certain subjects came up, such as her aunt, her parents, or her dreams, or at any time that it was necessary for her to share activities with other children, she immediately became aloof. In brief, when her feigned relation with a person was put to the test, it vanished, immediately and completely. We had expected her to distrust others, but had not anticipated such a skilled ability to render them nonexistent.

Mary's ambivalence in wanting both to be dependent (the pets, the white puppy) and to destroy others (the ferocious dog) was clear from our first interview with her; it was also evident that her hostile wishes won out, and were even directed against those she claimed to love most (killing the sister, hitting the horse). This hostility was without reason (hitting the horse) or justified only by the most threadbare rationalization (the crowded bed). Her predominant ambivalence also showed up in her confusion about the sexes; and again hostile or jealous features were uppermost (the boys have more and better toys).

Very apparent, as well, was her great anxiety about control ("Do the children talk in class?" "What do you do to girls who stink?") and her jealousy and hostility toward other children. Another striking feature was the way Mary asked questions and seemingly accepted answers, with apparent objectivity, on matters of no emotional concern to her, and then suddenly switched to emotionally loaded material unrelated to what had just occurred. She seemed to be following a stream of inner motivation that remained untouched by the immediate situation.

Mary's demands for exclusive attention were also obvious, as was her inability to be satisfied with things that were offered her ("Is that all you've got?"). Apparently, she could enjoy only the most primitive satisfactions (messing, resting on her bed), but she also had relatively strong defenses against at least one of these— her desire to smear.

By and large, during these first days Mary impressed us more as a severely deprived and repressed child than as an unusually disturbed one—at least when compared with the rest of our children. We had the feeling, at the time, that it should be relatively easy to help her. It seemed to us that she had reacted to an unbearable life situation with asocial behavior, and we hoped that pleasant and protective living conditions, good human relations, and other gratifying experiences, would largely suffice to help her toward a better integration.

The perturbing features of this picture were the rather indifferent ease with which she took to adults, the flatness of the more positive feelings she professed, and her unusually intense hostility toward children. Her inability to relate to children was sharply etched by their "instinctive" reluctance to have anything to do with her.

Mary, however, seemed not to care. She kept very much to herself, and stayed indoors most of the time, preferably on her bed. Even when the children arranged little eating parties, she approached the table only to collect food or pop, which she then took back to bed with her.

Anger and Hope

ON THE FIRST nights after her arrival, Mary fell asleep easily, although she always claimed she had been wakeful till long after midnight. One night, for example, after the evening story had been read, Mary called her counselor and asked how long she would be there. When the counselor replied that she would stay until Mary fell asleep, Mary said, "Oh, that'll be a long time," but she turned over and went to sleep almost instantly.

It took quite a bit of persuading to get Mary to leave her bed and go outdoors. She seemed to be afraid of activities that even quite anxious children of her age dared to explore. It was most difficult, for example, to induce her to use our enclosed playground. After much encouragement, she said she would like to play on the jungle gym, but when she approached it she was afraid to climb up even as far as the first rung. Looking at the seesaw, she said quite definitely that she was afraid of it. Surveying the rest of the play equipment and the large sand pile where several children were playing and obviously enjoying themselves, she said forcefully, "Well, there's nothing else to do, let's go back."

Despite her anxiety about learning new things, by the end of the first week Mary began to explore simple activities, such as painting and working with paper dolls or clay—but only when sitting with her counselor on her bed. She began to experiment further with messiness, but kept it within a socially acceptable context—painting. One day she got paint in her hair; when she realized this, a sudden look of terror seized her face and she began to stammer incoherently. After her counselor assured her that it would wash off, she seemed quite relieved and ventured a frightened little smile. Another time, after spilling some paint on her blouse, she stopped painting immediately and clung anxiously to her counselor's hand. "Would my aunt get mad if she saw that!" Nevertheless, by her tenth day in School, Mary had become so free about smearing with paint that she completely daubed her hands and fingers while pretending she was making gloves, and also smeared her skirt and blouse without signs of anxiety.

More characteristic of her first days with us, however, were her compulsive attempts to keep things in order. "I'm going to have everything all nice and clean here." She scrubbed the drawers of her cabinet, and insisted on washing some of her socks and underwear, although we assured her that such things were sent to the laundry and that no child needed to wash his own.

Mary's unusual sensitivity to smells soon amazed us. She repeatedly commented on various odors that neither we nor the children particularly noticed—the scent of soap, smells about the house, the odor of the chlorine in the swimming pool, which clung to the skin.

By the end of the first week she was talking repeatedly about writing to her relatives; but she never did. Only in the case of her sister did her correspondence get beyond the talking stage. But even then she never got further than "Dear Sister," though the counselor was most willing to write the letter for her as she dictated it. After three or four efforts Mary tired of the task and began drawing pictures instead.

Within the first week, too, Mary began getting bossy with the children, and they resented it. She reacted by threatening to hurt them, and actually began hitting them if things did not go entirely her way. But if she became more aggressive she also seemed livelier and her face had more expression. With adults, she was very compliant, and tried to fit as best she could into the School routine.

This picture soon changed. With the passage of some ten days, Mary's self-imposed isolation on her bed came to be interrupted more and more often, and for longer and longer periods, by outbursts of violent hostility, which for the most part took the form of screaming. Screaming remained Mary's characteristic reaction to the least frustration for more than two years. "I'm going to kill you!" she would shout at the other children whenever she was afraid things might not go as she wished. In the midst of these angry, nerve-wracking outbursts, however, Mary insisted on absolute quiet. If another girl so much as talked, she would threaten to hit her over the head with an iron pipe, as she had done once before coming to the School. The police, she announced, would never do anything. That time they had not; they had let her go with a mere admonition to be good from now on. When the counselor said that she would stop Mary if she tried to hurt another child, Mary threatened, "Well, I'll kill her when you aren't around." Then, as if remembering that one counselor or another was almost always about, she added, "I'll kill her when you think I'm asleep." That her threats to kill stemmed from mortal anxiety was suggested by the fact that, while she would shriek and hit out at the slightest provocation, her cries were most piercing when she was concerned about her health. The tiniest scratch, which even the most anxious children in School could more or less ignore, set her screaming for hours on end.

By the end of her first month she dared to threaten to kill adults, too. Her parting shot at her counselor before falling asleep was, "You better not wake me up tomorrow or you'll be sorry," or "You better not, or you'll be killed." But by then Mary was also saying, "I'm going to kill myself sometime," though the counselor assured Mary that she would never let her harm herself.

This repeated assurance, and our letting her scream it out, may have been the factors that made it possible for Mary to have moments of softness, and to bring out her desires for dependent satisfactions.

Having thus discharged her negativism, Mary could see that "one thing is good at the School, the food. There is always enough." We asked her again about her dreams, and Mary once more maintained that she never dreamed. As before, her sister appeared in free association with this question, but in a quite different emotional context. Mary now said, "I miss my sister," but added, "I sleep well all through the night."

With the two counselors who had become her favorites, she could now relax, although still rarely,[3] for short intervals. By the end of the first month, Mary was able to spend a full five hours with one of her counselors without once growing impatient or angry or abusive. But this was exceptional. Meantime, the security she had acquired with this counselor permitted her, while in her presence, to refrain occasionally from counteraggression when she felt frustrated. She began looking to her counselor for protection, instead of seeking it in defensive hostility. When a smaller child annoyed her she did not always lash out now and scream that she was going to kill him, but sometimes ran to her counselor for comfort. In her presence, Mary's threats about killing were also occasionally replaced by less murderous desires. No longer did she have to annihilate all competitors for attention; it was sufficient to have them permanently out of the way.

---

3. Several staff members worked with Mary. The personal relation she was able to form with two of them, in particular, led her to change her opinions about herself and the world around her, her emotions, and, in short, her personality. Most of the credit for Mary's progress should go first to Joan Little Treiman and then to Gayle Shulenberger Janowitz, both of whom devoted themselves—often pressing the limits of their endurance—to helping this child. Each of these counselors worked directly with Mary throughout her entire stay at the School and at one time or another either of them, or both, were her favorites. One of them is usually meant, therefore, when throughout the history I refer to a counselor. (If it is necessary to distinguish either of them from other counselors, these two are specifically referred to as "favorite" counselors.)

But to give Mary the opportunity for such emotional concentration upon one or two people, other staff members had to render her many services. Despite the fact that she denied their very existence, totally disregarded them, or used them for unloading her displeasure, they made it possible for her to relate positively to the staff member who was her sole favorite at the time. These important figures in Mary's school life included Anna Lukes and Katherine Howard, two of her teachers. Other counselors involved were Esther Blustein, Lisa Cohen, Dorothy Flapan, Jean Leer, and several others. The suggestions of the consulting psychiatrists, Drs. Emmy Sylvester and George L. Perkins were also most helpful. I had direct contacts of importance to Mary only on relatively few occasions, although I saw and spoke to her almost daily. Without the understanding and devoted help of all our staff, including secretaries, maids, cooks, and janitors, we could not have created that microcosm which eventually helped Mary trust life as a whole for the first time.

As Mary's desire to kill waned, she grew more demanding. At first she had asked for little and seemed satisfied with whatever was given her, even the most modest presents of toys or other objects. Though she would not use them, she hung them all up on the wall beside her bed. Even a necklace and a little note, which had been given her as a welcome present, and similar trifles that almost no other child would cherish, were hung on her wall space. "I'm going to put lots of things there," she said, "everything I get at the School." Now, however, she became greedy; nothing we gave her was good enough. Moreover, she expected us to divine all her wishes and fulfill them immediately; just having to convey them to us seemed to Mary an outrageous imposition—perhaps because she would then have to recognize us as human beings, a recognition of which she was not yet capable. She could not brook the slightest frustration in having her needs met—even when it was unavoidable. Particularly, delay was insufferable where food was concerned. But neither could she be satisfied when her needs were met; at least, what she received never seemed either right or adequate. She was convinced that her interests would never be protected, despite our efforts to supply experiences that would persuade her to the contrary.

Mary's inability to accept satisfying experiences, her jealousy, and her need to refuse dependent satisfactions, all cropped up on a shopping trip that she made with her counselor toward the end of her first month at the School. They had been buying clothes and toys, but nothing had gone right so far as Mary was concerned. She complained that the counselor was deliberately taking her to stores that did not carry what she wanted and that the salespeople, too, were showing her only things she did not want.

While shopping, and later at dinner, Mary tried to force her counselor into saying that she never took any other children on such trips, and then to promise that she never would, in the future, take anyone but Mary. When the counselor refused, and made it clear she also served other children, Mary repeated point-blank that no other School child had ever been taken on such outings.

Yet on the return trip, Mary reversed her attitude, possibly in anticipation of again having to share the counselor with others. Now she protested that only she was deprived, that the other children got everything they wanted and more, and that nobody ever did anything for her. Despite the load of parcels the counselor was carrying for her, Mary insisted (and not in jest) that she had no idea what they contained. Although the counselor reviewed their purchases, Mary insisted, "No, you didn't buy me a coat; you didn't buy me boots." She seemed to be trying to drown out the voice of reason with her screams, as she got more and more worked up. Her accusations mounted from, "You didn't buy me anything," to "Nobody ever buys me anything," and ended up, "I have to do all sorts of things for you. It's me who gets everything for others, but nobody ever buys me anything"—all said in dead earnest. We understood that she may have been feeling overstimulated and guilty about all the presents she had received.

At the same time, with her favorite counselor—who served her so intimately by waking her in the morning, offering her food, buying her things, and tucking her into bed—Mary at rare moments was less callous, and began to resemble a sad and deprived little girl. Toward the end of the first month at the School, Mary revealed to this counselor her first, though quite distorted, memory of her life before her mother died. She mentioned how little she had then been: "so small that I wet myself all the time." Then she followed this up by saying she wished she were a baby again.

In contrast to such infantile desires, as Mary became more secure in her new environment, her competence grew and she waxed bold in approaching the world. For example, her initial fear of the playground was overcome, and she began using the seesaw and climbing up on the jungle gym. She also learned to swim, and even dared to jump into the pool. It was apparent, by the end of the first month, that Mary was feeling more secure in the School.

It also seemed that Mary was beginning to progress toward some rudiments of a relation with one (and possibly two) preferred adults—though otherwise, her world was depersonalized. In one instance, when Mary met with the psychiatrist toward the month's end, she began a conversation easily enough, and even put her arm around her. Yet this was experienced by the psychiatrist as an empty gesture. Mary claimed that she was making friends with everybody and playing with all the children. But she could not name or say with whom she had played. Her world was still empty.

But with one difference: Mary's hostility and negativism had been veiled at the first interview, or projected onto dogs; now she had the courage to display these feelings more openly. About the School personnel she had only one comment. "I don't like them. They say no to anything I want. I don't like anything here." Her one wish was "to be sent back to my aunt," because now she could get along with her, although she could not say what her troubles had been or why she thought matters would improve. This wish did not seem genuine; it was, rather, a defiant way of indicating that we could not possibly please her.

Our main problem was to help Mary form at least one close

friendship. The early age at which she had first lost the essential services of her mother, and then the mother herself, suggested that she would probably be best able to relate to someone who was near her most of the time and who served her most infantile and immediate needs—in short, a mother figure. Unfortunately, in our setting, this person—her counselor—also had to serve a few other children in the same capacity. Afraid that this might rouse her unmanageable jealousy, we decided to offer Mary an opportunity to form another close relation to someone who, while near most of the time, did not serve the other children in Mary's group. This person would spend a great deal of time alone with Mary. In some respects this plan worked out well. But there were also disadvantages, we later learned, when Mary began groping for an ego ideal and found it difficult to merge the two figures who meant so much to her into a consistent pattern.

One day toward the month's end, Mary painted the face of "an unhappy little girl." (Plate 1) She made it clear that this was a picture of herself, but then said that it was the picture of "just any girl, a girl without any name," which seemed to reflect her feeling that she had no personal identity. Immediately after giving expression to this deep feeling of isolation and depersonalization, Mary began eating some food in a solitary, completely withdrawn manner. And food, "the only thing good at the School," saved the day. After eating for a while in the company of the person who was trying so hard to relate to her, Mary was able to re-establish some contact. She asked the counselor to read a story with which she was quite familiar. It was about a caterpillar (in Mary's words, "an ugly worm") who after many adventures turned into a beautiful, gay butterfly. In listening to the happy ending, she showed some positive emotion; it was as if she had begun to hope that one day she might change from a nameless, just-any-girl, into a particular person.

Her belief, even for a moment, that she could become a distinct individual, and that satisfaction and happiness might be attainable, was part of her first positive response to the School. It may have been this belief that permitted her to face up to some of her deep dissatisfactions about her past. Thus far she had talked easily but without emotion about the death of her parents, and about the way the various families and relatives with whom she had lived had rejected her. By the end of the month, however, the first feelings about her infancy came out; what these were was made evident one evening when she asked her favorite counselor never to sing to her the lullaby beginning, "When I was a little girl upon my mammy's knee."

DISCUSSION

Because it was a most immediate and aggravating problem, we pondered most, during Mary's first month with us, about her violent outbursts of anger, in the hope that a better understanding of what they were all about might make it easier for us to help her. Since it was such a pressing and dominant symptom we felt it was important to handle it correctly, and this, in turn, hinged on our being able to formulate some hypothesis about it.

We wondered whether in her screaming Mary might be imitating her aunt, while in her angry insistence that everyone else be quiet it seemed she might be trying to enforce on us an obedience that in the past had been exacted from her. Such a simple reversal of roles —she as the aunt, we as the sufferers—did not do justice, we realized, to the complexity of the symptom, but it was the best theory we could devise at the moment. Mary might also be testing how far she could go in discharging aggression, what the limits of our endurance were. In any case we felt that we should neither check her outbursts—which we could not have done anyway short of using brute force—nor disregard them.

What we did not realize at this time (because we learned about her early life only later) was that in her disorganized and aimless screaming she might have been re-experiencing the earliest trauma of her life, when her crying went unnoticed by a melancholic mother. We did not fathom that her angry insistence that everyone else be quiet as she screamed might have been a re-creation of the earliest setting she had known, when everyone around her (her depressive mother) had been silent and she alone had cried in the wilderness. Neither did we know that her insistence on not being awakened ("I'll kill you if you wake me up") was an effort to protect the only satisfying experience she had known: that of escaping it all by sleeping.

There were signs of all this, at the time, but we did not understand their meaning. And even if we had understood them, I doubt if we could have acted much differently.[4]

---

4. Since the ability of both the children and adults to accept Mary's screaming without too much counteraction was so critically important, I might mention how they were able to do so. As often happens, it was the group that first helped in enduring and finally resolving this difficulty. Whenever Mary began venting her frustration or hostility, the counselors did their best to satisfy her demands and make her more comfortable, and some of the children joined them in these efforts. If this did not seem to help, or aggravated Mary the more, as frequently happened, the counselors resumed their activities with the other children, but from time to time would renew their efforts to establish contact with Mary and assure her of their interest and desire to be helpful. Meantime, the attentions of neither coun-

She "Adjusts"

BECAUSE WE REFUSED to act in ways that would contribute to Mary's sense of isolation and withdrawal, she was able to occupy herself, during the next half year, with tentative efforts to form relations with adults, and eventually with children. The wish for human contact seemed to emerge only after she began to think that her stay might be somewhat permanent, although she was still most doubtful about this. At the end of the second month, she began showing concern with this question.

One morning, she found her counselor pushing a boy on the swing. Mary wanted to be pushed, too, and while swinging asked, "Will you keep on spending time with me even when I'm a big girl?" Not waiting for an answer, she pressed again, "You're going to see me for a long time, aren't you?" After the counselor had given her

---

selors nor children were entirely concentrated on Mary or her screaming. Thus there was rarely a time when they were experiencing nothing but her rejection.

For the counselors, the situation was also somewhat relieved by the constructive services they were rendering other children, which kept them from feeling completely useless and frustrated. And the same services helped the children to overlook Mary's outbursts. There was always somebody present on whom Mary could discharge her hostility, which was what she wanted. She was never left to cry in isolation. Yet these people were not so upset that they lost contact with her or, even worse, tried to retaliate or put an end to her tantrums, in self-preservation.

However, it would be erroneous to give the impression that Mary's behavior did not drain her counselors' emotional resources to the limit. To withstand the ordeal, they had to be able to unload their discomfort, often immediately and repeatedly, after their hours of working with Mary, and receive replenishment of their libido through contact with others and through narcissistic satisfactions. Here, working within the microcosm of an institution was of great help. To be able to talk about their suffering and how they "could not take it any longer," to find a congenial and often admiring audience for their complaints, to be told in return how important it was for Mary's rehabilitation that they continue to "stand it," helped the counselors bear up. Assurance from others that they could not have withstood a particular onslaught of hostility provided Mary's counselors with the comforting thought that they were not falling down in their task, and challenged them further to show that they could stand it.

Occasionally her counselors even told Mary that they could bear her violent and aggressive outbursts no longer and would be unable to serve her well if she continued them so unabatedly. While the rational part of this argument was probably lost on Mary at first, the fact that she could now wield such power over important adults (whereas before she had always found it necessary to submit to their wishes) may even have provided her with narcissistic satisfaction and strengthened her feeling of importance, and in this sense may have been therapeutic.

If the counselors had lost contact with Mary during her screaming, her isolation could not have been penetrated; if they had become desperate or retaliative, Mary would have been correct in assuming that her tantrums were an effective way of controlling us; and if they had tried to stop the tantrums out of self-interest or for the sake of the other children, Mary would have been convinced that even in our School, the momentary comfort of others was more important than her own despair.

this assurance, and Mary had repeated her questions and been reassured again, she fell silent. Several minutes passed, and then Mary turned to the children and said, oddly enough, "I'm going to leave here when I'm five years old." At the time, we supposed that this figure might have had something to do with our age limit of fourteen. Mary, then almost nine, may have been expressing her desire to remain in School as long as possible, i.e., five years. In any case, her remark was not a slip of the tongue, because on the same day she spontaneously told the children that she was going to remain in School a long time. When asked how long, she repeated, "Until I'm five years old." Though the deeper significance of this remark was seen only later, it was nevertheless evident that Mary was not now as insecure about the permanence of human relations as she had been a month previously. At that time, when her counselor told her that she would be seeing her next on Thursday, Mary replied, "There won't *be* a next time."

Mary's greater feeling of permanency at the School—or at least her desire to stay—combined with the liberty given her to discharge hostility, may have permitted her, after two months, to let herself become more and more dependent. In the dormitory she took to sitting on the counselor's lap, while she watched quietly and in a detached way what went on around her. Although she did not seem happy, she did drop her defiant independence, and now liked her couselors to dress her, tie her shoes for her, and so forth.

In spite of this tentative reaching out toward the adults around her, basically Mary remained insensitive to human relations. A counselor who had been taking care of Mary's group was about to leave. Since this counselor had known that she would soon be leaving, she had deliberately kept away from Mary so that no ties would be formed between them, only to be broken. At a farewell party for the departing counselor, some of the girls who were very attached to her became quite moved and began crying. When Mary saw this, she began crying, too. It may be that she felt empathy for the group, or perhaps any leave-taking was upsetting to her. Perhaps her own misery was so deep that she welcomed any occasion for expressing it. Whatever the reason, Mary denied that her crying had any connection with the leave-taking. Her favorite counselor, in trying to comfort her, asked what was wrong. Mary replied that she wept because she had mislaid one of her prized possessions, but quite contrary to her usual behavior, she was easily comforted and asked the counselor to help her find it. Then a few minutes later Mary went up to the departing counselor and said, "Well, we cried for you. Now won't you take us out for sodas?" The shocked reac-

tion of the other children to her lack of feeling left her mystified.
Positive attachments were obviously beyond Mary as yet, perhaps for reasons apparent in the following incident. A few days
after the party, Mary played aggressively with some kittens. Next
day she told her counselor, "I saw some kittens 'that little' yesterday—they were just born. I picked one up, and I held the mother
away from it, and I kept the mother away. They were so little you
couldn't even count them, and after I put back the one I took, the
mother had to count them again to be sure they were all there."
Mary looked triumphant as she talked about how she had separated
the one little kitten from its mother.

While she seemed to understand negative emotions well enough,
the only positive one she could show was an aggressive holding on.
For instance, she was unexpectedly given a baby doll, which she
immediately clutched very tightly. But when she first glimpsed the
present, and even as she held on to it for dear life, her face expressed absolutely no emotion.

On the other hand, though she did not let us in on her positive
feelings about people or objects, she did seem to be trying to behave
more acceptably about things she imagined we disapproved of, such
as masturbation. When Mary first came she masturbated freely and
often, perhaps with defiance, and certainly with intent to provoke.
She would lie on her back and masturbate openly, staring vacantly
or aggressively at whoever was near. After two and a half months
in School, when she must certainly have observed that masturbation
is taken as a matter of course, she began to be more "modest" about
it. She would cover herself with her blanket before masturbating,
and for some time afterward would be in quite a bad humor, seemingly as a result of feeling guilty. She seemed particularly angry
that we neither stopped nor interfered with her, but showed no
reaction.

Why Mary should have tried at all to control her masturbation
was difficult to understand at the time. (Her masturbatory phantasies were revealed only much later; see p. 198 and p. 201.)
Perhaps the feeling that we were not controlling her created overwhelming anxieties, which had originated in the definite threats of
punishment that had been made to her in the past; and she may
have been trying to reduce these fears by controlling herself. That
this may have been a partial cause was suggested when, shortly
thereafter, she began to show her tremendous anxiety more openly.
So great had this become that it was almost impossible for her to
undertake any activity without deep agitation. Anything out of the
ordinary, the slightest noise, created unmanageable dread. If an

airplane flew overhead (which happened rather frequently, since the School lies on the route to the airport), she insisted it was a bomber and that a bomb was going to drop on the School and destroy us all. She stated flatly that she could hear the bomb doors opening and the bomb falling. (And this was at the School, where she felt relatively secure!)

A trip downtown provoked countless anxieties. Mary was sure she would fall out of the streetcar; or, riding the suburban railroad line, that she would fall between the platform and car and be run over. The train would jump the tracks, there would be a crash, or some other railroad accident. Yet she had lived in Chicago all her life and was perfectly familiar with streetcars and with the train we took downtown. In these situations Mary's anxiety resulted from her fear of utter destruction.

Within the security of her individual play sessions with one of her favorite counselors, she acted out her anxiety about being deserted. Toward the end of the third month, Mary began to play with the doll house and pipe cleaner dolls. The two main figures were "a lady" (depersonalized, any lady) and "a dog." As she moved the dolls she said, "She's a bad lady. The dog is bad. The lady teases him with food. It isn't really his fault—she made him bad." Then Mary introduced a little clay figure, "the little girl." The dog scratched the girl's face all over, after which dog and girl pushed each other about. The bad lady was then hung up by one foot on the dollhouse chimney, as Mary said, "Since the bad lady could do it, the little girl thought she could, and tries it. But she tries it and falls off." Yet contrary to this remark, it was the girl who pushed the lady violently and repeatedly off the roof. Mary acted out how the dog and the girl mistreated the lady, but emphasized in what she said how the lady had made the dog bad and the reason why the dog scratched the girl—and, one might add, why the girl wreaked revenge on the lady.

Her next doll play began with doll figures that represented adults being pushed very aggressively off the roof and thrown out of windows. Then the action changed. Mary set a small dog beside the doll house. "The dog lives here with his master." Then she picked up the toy "For Rent" sign and put it in front of the dog, saying, "He's for sale." Next, she brought over a cow and, placing the "For Rent" sign in front of it, she said, "The cow bunted them all with her horns and that's why she's for sale now." She performed the same act for a horse, and a pig. After a violent scene in which each animal pushed and trampled the others, they all wound up for sale.

This kind of aggressive play went on for weeks; it was interrupted, however, by long periods of emotional respite when Mary would drop the doll play for safer activities, such as eating quietly, or listening distantly to a story.

Not only her favorite counselors, but other staff members, too, noticed a slow change taking place in Mary. Without appearing less unhappy and withdrawn, she nevertheless, for short periods, was acquiring greater freedom. Occasionally she smiled; and her anger and anxiety were more freely expressed. She sometimes went up to people spontaneously and talked about things that really seemed to interest her.

And she began playing with children. At that time, this mostly took the form of a mother and child game, which often became rowdy. Mary always looked for an older child to play this game with her. The older girl had to pretend to be a mother (or counselor) and the game consisted in the mother-figure shaking the daughter, played by Mary. "Shake me harder," Mary would insist. "Shake me till I cry," and so the game invariably ended when Mary pretended to fall or get hurt in some way.

As she began to play these self-punitive games, her many physical complaints became less incessant. She continued to worry daily, particularly in the morning, about being sick, and to complain that we did not do enough to assuage her many aches and pains. She hated to meet the day. "Don't ever wake me," she asked every evening. But her laments slowly became less insistent.

This marked the beginning of a long period in which Mary oscillated between discharging hostility in play and actuality, on the one hand, and, on the other, directing it against herself by falling, cutting, or otherwise hurting herself. Mary also made efforts to suppress her hostile tendencies, which led again to inner tensions that were experienced as physical ailments. Although the direct discharge of tension in overt hostility led to the easing of these physical symptoms, the problem was not really this simple. For if Mary went too far in her aggressive actions she felt guilty, and took it out on herself in physical discomfort. Still, the more she learned to integrate her hostility the more secure she seemed to feel. She was then able, for certain periods, to give up clinging to her physical ailments. One morning after five months with us, she told the nurse that she had "no sores" that day, and she looked pleased as she said this. Now, for the first time, she could occasionally meet the day feeling "well."

Although for a long time the dominant theme of her games with the children remained that of being punished and otherwise mistreated, by the fourth month, Mary began adding to her repertoire of imaginative play. Instead of forever, in a sort of frenzy, asking maternal figures to shake the children because they were bad, she now occasionally played a quieter game in which she copied her classroom experiences in detail. Once she even said to the children, "You've been good, and I'm going to give you all a present," upon which she turned to her counselor and smiled self-consciously. It was obvious that she was trying to please the counselor and not the children. But this happened rarely.

Most often she fell back on the aggressive-submissive type of game. One evening when she was playing house with the children, Mary took the role of the adult and pretended to spank some of her playmates. The counselor remarked that we do not spank children in the School, to which Mary replied, "I'm not a counselor now— I'm a mother." So when she wanted to, Mary could differentiate between what belonged to the past and what was really of the present.

Slowly, too, she began to differentiate between people. This was seen first in her recognition of those who might prove most reliable in filling her needs. "You'll take care of me," she frequently said now to her favorite counselors, though more with challenging belligerence than assurance. Her threats to kill the other children and her own counselors waned, and such vehement outbursts as "I'll kill her!" were directed more at the cooks and maids. With these "outsiders," she lived in constant warfare. Simultaneously, as Mary continued to persecute others, she also began to feel persecuted by them. Now she complained that people were stealing her things, but at the same time she could occasionally admit that she stole, too, although this was something she had thus far denied.

With her apparent progress in socialization, some fear of retaliation began appearing, as a brake on her misbehavior. Such fear of retaliation is an initial step in the eventual development of conscious feelings of guilt. For example, after Mary had been at the School for about six months, she was fooling with another child's toys one evening. As she handled them and almost destroyed them in the process, she said under her breath, "She's going to kill me if she finds out."

Up to this time, Mary had had only bad things to say about her aunt and seemed quite free of conscious guilt about her own actions, either before or after she came to the School. Now Mary began to accuse herself of misbehaving; when her counselor remarked that, after all, Mary's relatives had not been very nice to her, Mary said, "Yes, they were; I was just mean." The counselor tried to suggest that if the relatives had known better how to take care of a little girl, Mary could have gotten along with them. But Mary just enumerated the bad things she had done. She repeated the story about hitting the girl with the pipe, except that this time she showed some emotion as she told it and almost shuddered at the recollection. This remorse, incidentally, was closely connected with an incident during which Mary lost control of herself. Her admission that she had been mean in the past was made immediately after she had hit a girl at the School with a broom, because this girl had been slow about doing something Mary wanted done. Thus, in a way, her self-accusations about the past took the place of guilt about present misbehavior, which she was not yet ready to acknowledge.

Mary's fleeting insight into the way she, herself, had contributed toward the unhappiness of her life with her aunt was followed immediately by extravagant demands to "buy me this toy and that and that." She seemed to need an immediate reward for trying to see her own role in creating her difficulties; perhaps she wanted instant, tangible evidence that she was still loved even though she had done such bad things. She might also have been trying to distract her budding conscience with new toys.

That Mary could now face up to her emotions to some extent, and differentiate between them—although before she had denied their very existence—was apparent one day in a talk she had with her counselor. As she sat in her counselor's lap, she took one of her keys, held it against the counselor's head, and pretended to turn it, while she said, "I'm a counselor now, I'm going to open your brain." Another girl who was present asked what she found inside. So Mary pretended to open one side of the head and said that the counselor was a dumb-bell. Then she said, "Now let's look at the other side—there she's not a dumb-bell. Now let's look at her heart." Turning the key around, Mary said, "This side says she's in love—the other side says she isn't." In this way, Mary first expressed awareness of the ambivalence of her emotions, although she seemed able to face her own feelings of inadequacy (being a dumb-bell) and ambivalence only by projecting them onto a relatively trusted person. At the same time, Mary recognized that the counselor could understand other people's feelings, while she could not. Only by pretending to be a counselor could she look into another person's brain and recognize emotional ambivalence.

As she became more aware of her own emotions, memories of her mother appeared, although she did not recognize them as such. One day in her doll play, Mary commented, "They're all sad, aren't they—except him," pointing to the father. (Actually the dolls were quite expressionless.) Then she looked them all over carefully and

PLATE NO. 1. *Self-portrait: "Just any girl, a girl without any name"*

PLATE NO. 2. *Attempt at cheerfulness*

PLATE NO. 3. *Self-portrait*

PLATE NO. 4. *Mother panda providing food for her baby*

PLATE NO. 5. *The School becomes a home— fencing the world out*

PLATE No. 6. *Self-portrait*

PLATE No. 7. *Attempt to overcome the trauma of mother's death*

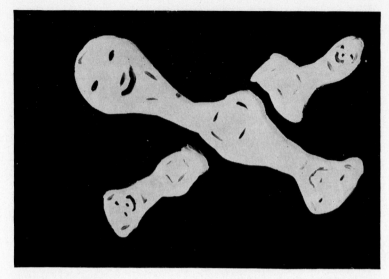

PLATE NO. 8. *Mastering death through morbid humor*

PLATE NO. 9. *Mother and baby*

PLATE No. 10. *Incorporating the mother*

PLATE No. 11. *Her mother, independent of herself*

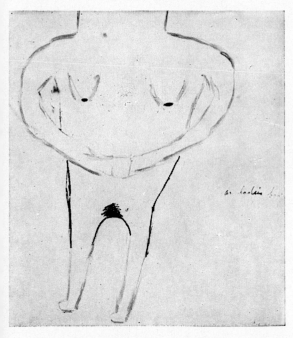

PLATE No. 12. *How the baby experiences her mother*

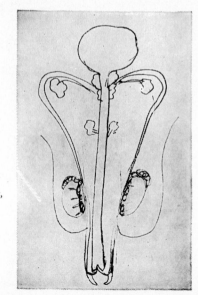

PLATE No. 13. *The father's penis, with damaging claws*

A Delivery Room

PLATE No. 14. *Her rebirth*

PLATE No. 15. *Self-portrait*

A BALLET DANCER

PLATE No. 16. *She thinks of becoming a dancer*

PLATE No. 17. *A happy girl with her dog*

PLATE No. 18. *"Fun on the beach"*

Fun on the Beach

repeated, "The father's happy, but the mother's the saddest." But she could not elaborate further. This continued for several play sessions, with Mary commenting, "The mother's sad, but the father's the only happy one." When asked why, she could only reiterate, "I just think they are—the mother looks so sad."

After this, she began to remember specific unpleasant events. One hectic day Mary had a particularly unhappy time with some of the children. That evening at the supper table she turned to the counselor and said, "Once my aunt had a pan of grievance." Asked what she meant, she repeated the word "grievance" several times; then she said that when she was very little and lived in her aunt's house, her aunt had a pan of grievance on the stove. Only after much encouragement did she elaborate: "My aunt asked me to turn off the fire and I was only half as high as the stove. So when I reached up to turn it off, the pan spilled and hot grievance spilled all over my leg and burned me. I cried and cried."[5] Having gotten that out, Mary was able to answer another child's question about the word "grievance": "It's that hot stuff they have in pans." Then she grudgingly conceded that hot grease had scalded her. Emotionally, however, for her the pan was still full of scalding "grievances."

Memories of her past unhappiness may have had something to do with the efforts she now made to cut herself off from her old life. At the end of her sixth month with us, she spontaneously decided to pack up all the possessions she had brought to School and get rid of them by sending them back to her aunt. She packed them in the box in which they had come and carefully sealed it herself. Then a few days later, Mary showed concern about her family name. We first realized this when she could not leave the name tapes on her clothes alone. On a hunch, her counselor suggested she might want to have just "Mary" instead of "Mary Blank" printed on her name tapes. With a sigh of relief, Mary said she would like that very much.

With this wish to break away from her life with her aunt, Mary made efforts to return to even earlier experiences. She developed a passion for onions, which she explained, had been her father's favorite food. Mary ate them in all shapes and varieties, and at all times of day. At about the same time, Mary began to be absorbed with food in general. Two months previously, there had been some presage of this in one of her dreams. Mary had called out in her sleep to her counselor, "Why are you the only one who has it?"

---

5. What Mary probably meant was the Jewish dish *grieveness*.

When her counselor asked what she meant, Mary again questioned, "Why are you the only one who has all the food?" Saying nothing further, she seemed to have been sleeping soundly through it all. It was in the next few months that she expressed an intense desire for onions, which was soon followed by incessant cravings for all kinds of food.

However, Mary was not satisfied even when offered an abundance of food. It was impossible to provide her with enough. As soon as anything was given her—food, toys, or attention—she tested the limits of our giving by making the most unreasonable and extravagant requests. When candy was offered her, she took it in handfuls and threw it on the floor; she would then ask for more, only to toss the new supply after the first. When we finally refused her any more she became violently angry, fearful always that her reasonable demands would be denied because her unreasonable ones were rejected.

Yet, along with being unreasonable, Mary was redoubling her efforts to deal with what she considered unacceptable behavior, that is, her masturbation. This time, she went beyond merely trying to be more modest and sought a constructive solution. Often during the day, and regularly in the evening, she began to bounce violently on her bed. Eventually she asked for a rocking horse so that she could play cowgirl, and ride and bounce on the horse instead of her bed.

Mary had been with us just six months as Christmas drew near. It was a very difficult time for her. Her feelings of having been deprived and neglected made it most painful for her to see other children receiving presents. Although she liked her own gifts, in a way she was too jealous of others to enjoy them. She deliberately caused the Christmas tree to fall on a girl she was particularly jealous of, and who more than any other child represented her sister. Then immediately afterward, Mary insisted on playing with a metal toy belonging to this girl, and cut her finger on it. Although not serious, the cut was bad enough to hurt quite a bit and prevent Mary from playing freely with her own new toys.

During the holidays, Mary surrounded herself with all her presents. At night she kept them beside her in bed. One was her especial favorite, a fuzzy dog; this she tied securely to her bedpost. Her ninth birthday came less than a month after Christmas, and she was given an additional, ample number of gifts from the School. All this may have had something to do with her new ability to stop acting out when her favorite counselor spoke firmly to her. At any rate this control was important to Mary, although she raged at her counselor, "You force people. You force them to do things."

The fact that Mary had learned to be more controlled with one person did not make her less unreasonable with others. Her aggressive outbursts continued and were particularly violent when another child received what she interpreted as special attention. Then Mary still reacted by screaming, by destroying her own toys as well as those belonging to others, and even by attacking children or adults. But these actions were more or less controllable when she was with the one favorite counselor, and her outbursts toward others seemed less severe, which showed that it was no longer entirely impossible for Mary to achieve restraint.

Mary's new realization that coming out with her true emotions was no longer dangerous, and her recognition that her life could have rewarding moments, such as at her birthday and Christmas, seemed to permit her to open up about feelings she had previously kept to herself. Perhaps she had been quiet about them, also, because she feared that some of her preoccupations would repel us, or that she could not deal with them while she still lacked minimum self-control. Whatever the roots of this new freedom, Mary began to re-create family settings in her doll play and to act out sexual topics.

This began with a discussion between two dolls, representing parents, about whether the children needed to go to the bathroom and whether the mother or the father should take them there. Mary, playing the mother, took the little girl to the bathroom first, and then the boy. She made the girl sit on the toilet, but when it was the boy's turn she said, "Oh, I was going to make him sit down." Then she had him stand up beside the toilet while she made the sounds of urinating. With this "mistake" she seemed to revert to her earlier confusion about "he's" and "she's."

Perhaps to cover up her own involvement, Mary now had the boy act out her aggressions, though in a devious way. Walking about the room, he accidentally knocked over the table; she said he was sorry and hadn't meant to. But he continued to upset the furniture, after which Mary became afraid and abruptly changed the topic. She returned, as it were, to the safety of non-aggressive, non-sexual security, before awareness of sex differences had begun to disturb her peace. Taking up a baby doll, previously unheeded, she put it in the mother's arms. She said emphatically that the mother was holding the baby very tightly, and at the same time, Mary made crooning sounds. Obviously she was identifying with the baby and enjoying it.

After a while Mary dropped this play as abruptly as she had begun it, and asked that a school be set up. Returning to her actual role as a school girl, she insisted that the father doll be identified with me. In other ways, too, Mary definitely showed her desire to combine the family setting with that of the School. For example, she arranged the family living room to look like the School's; and the father was placed in an office arranged to resemble mine. Having created a setting that as easily represented her past as her present, Mary returned to the sex motive, with violent, acting-out play.

The boy and girl dolls began fighting each other, in the course of which Mary let the boy jump up and down on top of the girl. "They're fighting, and she's crying." Actually, her doll-children were enacting intercourse, and for this they were immediately punished. The mother complained to the father about the children's misbehavior, without referring to their fight (sex play); the mother said only that the children were wrecking the house and that something should be done about it. To her excited complaints, the father answered indifferently that nothing need be done.

The "wrecking of the house" and the parental arguments went on for several days, as the children persisted in their sex play and destructiveness, and the mother pressed the uninterested father ever harder for some drastic solution. Finally he gave in, and agreed that nobody could bear this state of affairs any longer. The children were sent to the Orthogenic School, and it was the mother, significantly, who took them there. At this juncture Mary introduced me into the play by having me ask the mother what she wanted. I should keep the children, the mother instructed, because they "just tear the house to pieces."

In this doll play Mary re-enacted the events in her aunt's home at the time when the aunt wished to place her elsewhere, and kept arguing about it with her uncle, who resisted for quite a while before finally yielding. Mary also seemed to be trying to master the most recent drastic change in her life, her placement in the School. This was now a reality that she tried to accept—perhaps because her recent experiences had been pleasant; she felt a little more hopeful that we would not "put her up for sale" as punishment for her bad behavior (a fear she had acted out in the play in which animals were put on sale). Apparently Mary had decided that she had been shifted about among her relatives as punishment for being too aggressive, but she was now somewhat hopeful that this lack of concern for her feelings in arranging her life might be over.

Mary's reactions during these months suggested that, for her, her favorite counselors were more and more assuming the meaning and aspects of good mothers. From her conduct it was also obvious that other adults had become her punitive relatives, and she made the most of her opportunity to fight the hated relatives vicariously by waging total war against the staff members she disliked. Similarly, the other children at one moment represented her sister, and at another, her hated cousins.

To the child who for the time represented her sister, Mary became ambivalently attached. She expected more than this girl could possibly give, and was constantly disappointed because she had interests of her own in which Mary was not involved. Also, Mary was jealous because she was sure that this child's lot was better than hers. Perhaps Mary's sister actually had had an easier time. Since Frances was older, and had lived for several years within an intact family, she may have been better able to look out for herself by the time they had to live with the aunt.

With the children who represented her hated cousins, Mary was merciless, since she no longer had to fear retaliation from her aunt. We felt that it would be best not to attempt to control her acting out against children and adults unless it became necessary to safeguard everybody's physical welfare and the children's right to ignore her if they wished. In our opinion, Mary was not yet strong enough to integrate her hostility, and would have to discharge it against others before she could build up any positive relations to her favorite counselors. With the help of these counselors, we hoped she would later view the world more positively.

DISCUSSION

In evaluating Mary's progress at this time, we felt encouraged. Both her anger and frustration seemed reasonable when viewed in the light of past deprivations. She appeared to be finding more satisfaction in life, and to be functioning more adequately. Apparently, also, she was forming positive personal relations. In conference with the placing agency and the consulting psychiatrist it was thought that after another year, or perhaps even sooner, Mary might be ready for foster home placement, or even adoption. This seemed particularly desirable since then she would not have to share things with other children, which was still too difficult a task for her. The plan of having her adopted was suggested by the psychiatrist, who saw Mary at her best, when no other children were around to be jealous of and no frustrating demands were being imposed by the outside world. In this situation, he was struck by her apparent ability to relate and to become more and more a person.

Mary's new freedom and actual mastery in certain areas was

best demonstrated by her excellent academic progress. This was possible, perhaps, because her previous school experiences, though they may have been empty and devoid of meaning, had at least not been negative. There had been no traumatic experiences in her classes to scare her away from all efforts at mastering this situation. Mary was able to function as a student and to attempt to participate in a student-teacher relation. Helped by good intellectual endowment (her I.Q. was then 107), she could even appease her jealousy by succeeding in competitions she herself created, although we tried to eliminate this element from the classroom.

But we realized that, in spite of these achievements, Mary was never relaxed. She could be cheerful only by borrowing from others, not in her own right. In the classroom, one day, with the help of her teacher, she cut out some pretty birds and pasted them on a tree she had copied. (Plate 2) This picture she insisted on presenting to me. It was a token of good will, and showed that she realized we wanted her to see life more positively. But such efforts to please us did not seem to be genuine results of her personal experiences. These she expressed in many drawings of girls with very sad faces, an example of which is reproduced in Plate 3.

There were other danger signals, too, though at the time they seemed overshadowed by her steady improvement. Much of the time, for example, she still did not live in this world, but was preoccupied with her own thoughts and oblivious to what went on about her. Nightmares, too, occasionally cropped up; one was particularly persistent, in which she was sinking in quicksand and there was "something about a mother and a baby." We were not overly concerned, because since her fourth month she had seemed better able at night to let go of her counselor, who previously had often sat on her bed for hours before Mary could go to sleep. We took this for another sign of increased well-being.

What we overlooked was the fact that in offering and giving Mary so much, compared with the emotional and material deprivation she had known, we had created too great a temptation for her. She could not afford to reject what we offered; it was too good. Of course she accepted it—not autonomously, or on her own terms, but uncritically. Just as unpleasant experiences had overpowered her in the past and prevented her from integrating her personality, so now she was overwhelmed by pleasant experiences, with similarly undesirable results. Our good will had provoked in her a tremendous anxiety that a wrong move might jeopardize what she had gained. She strove frantically for a surface adjustment that would satisfy us and so insure the permanence of her present living conditions.

It was a desperate attempt to acquire a new life, a new personality, on short order—to find a substitute for mastering past experiences and integrating them by means of an ego strength she did not yet possess.

But try as she might, freeing herself from her emotional past was not yet possible to her. She could deal with some of the externals, for example, by not using her last name; but the inner flexibility required for a true adjustment to a new living situation was way beyond her. Therefore, it was necessary for her to move the emotional essentials of her old living conditions (the giving and undemanding mother, the punitive aunt, the ambivalent sister, the hated cousins) lock, stock and barrel into her new environment. Such a transference is possible in an institutional setting. But it should be nothing more than the framework for a later working-through of the past, which should subsequently lead to a realistic adaptation to the present, the development of new personality features, and their final integration.

In hindsight, of course, it is quite easy to understand Mary's anxious desire to please those who seemed most powerful to her. Our attempts to discourage these efforts, which we partially recognized as spurious, could not penetrate her anxiety about the danger of displeasing us. We did not see clearly enough how her concentration of all positive emotions on her two favorite persons, and her discharge of hostility against all others, made her even more helplessly dependent on the good will of her favorite counselors. The angrier she made others, the more vital became the protection of these two. The less we curbed her nastiness to others, which caused her to become alienated from them, the more willing she became to pay a high price for the continued good will and protection of her favorites.

Yet one cannot say that Mary really identified with these two counselors; so much anxiety to please made it impossible for her to risk the slow process of identification. She did not even try to take them as her ego ideal. Mary just plainly behaved as she thought they expected her to. She was overly in a hurry, and in line with the primitive stage of her ego development, used the most primitive way of incorporating what she wished to acquire: since she had neither the time, tools, nor energy to plumb beneath the surface, she simply copied the externals of their two personalities, without integrating their values. In addition, while her counselors shared similar values, they of course expressed these in line with their own personalities. Their mannerisms—the only features Mary could then recognize and hence try to acquire—were quite different. Since this gave her two models to follow, neither of which tallied with her own emotions, her efforts to acquire a ready-made personality through imitation inevitably broke down.[6] A true integration of her own personality became the only solution open to her, but she was not ready to try this.

Therefore, in the next months, we witnessed the slow falling to pieces of most of Mary's superficial adjustment and the emergence of a much more chaotic and primitive personality. It was much sicker than we had ever expected. Slowly, as we learned how disparate its elements were, how "schizoid," we realized how difficult it was for Mary to take even the first steps toward integration. No wonder she was so eager to settle for a borrowed personality rather than to develop her own.

Breakdown and First Efforts at Integration

MARY BEGAN to make remarks suggesting that, dimly, she had become aware that hers was only a surface adjustment—although at the time we did not quite grasp this. She said she was trying to keep from screaming and out of fights. She wanted her teacher, counselors, and those less intimate with her to be more strict, so that she would "keep out of trouble." When they refused to serve as "policemen," Mary warned them, "You'd better take me to Dr. B. to settle me down."[7] Completely unable to deal with the tremendous problem that faced her, Mary kept searching for external controls.

After Christmas and her ninth birthday, when she received so many presents, Mary occasionally brightened up and sometimes said that she hoped to remain at the School for a long time. But by the end of February she was asking to be controlled so that she could leave the School. From inviting external controls so that she would "stay out of trouble" and get along better with people, she now regressed to the point of seeking external controls because she wanted to leave. She could not say why she wanted to leave or where she wanted to go. She did not want to return to her sister and aunt, or to other relatives. She just wanted to get away from the School. Obviously we had disappointed her. Her moments of appearing more cheerful, her occasional smiles, vanished, and were replaced by an ever more disorganized and unhappy mien.

These were straws in the wind. We became certain that things

---

6. I have dealt at some length with our error in accepting Mary's rapid progress, because we learned to recognize it only through our experience with her and in a few similar cases. (See remarks on pp. 260-264.)

7. "Dr. B." serves as my nickname.

had changed for the worse when Mary's screaming increased in frequency and intensity. At first it duplicated the tantrums of her early
months in School; then it grew more severe. Her destructiveness,
also, returned in full force and became even worse, as did her isolation from children and adults. Each time Mary had to meet reality,
even when we tried to make it as attractive as possible, was a
traumatic experience for her, which brought on a total breakdown
of whatever integration she had so far exhibited.[8] Getting up in the
morning, for example, or going to school—though neither activity
was ever forced upon her—evoked violent outbursts of desperation.
It was impossible to suggest anything to her, even that she need do
nothing.

Tantrums of despair occurred several times daily—sometimes
so frequently that they seemed continuous. When we asked what
she would like to do, or wanted us to do for her, Mary could make
no suggestion. *"You* tell *me,"* she would scream. The tension was
so great that if a suggestion were not immediately offered she began
throwing things and herself around. On the other hand, no sooner
had we submitted ideas for helping her than she rejected them with
equal violence.

The outbursts often began with Mary's shouting, "I'm going to
be bad! I'm going to scream! I'm going to make noise! Take me
somewhere! Do something for me! You never do anything for me!
I hate you!" With the first words, her head and then her whole body
would begin to shake. At other times, she might suddenly freeze up
physically while continuing to scream at the top of her lungs. Or, in
other ways she would keep up a racket that made hearing impossible
and taxed one's patience more than her outright shrieking, for example through continuous opening and slamming of doors, or
drawers. Sometimes she would shriek, "Take me somewhere!" for
as long as twenty to thirty minutes straight, though she remained
deaf to all offers of relief made by the counselors. She was equally
impervious to their quiet listening. Perhaps she knew that the
"somewhere" to which she wanted to be taken, the good mother she
had known only in earliest infancy, no longer existed.

Mary's frantic cries became particularly intense as she moved
from one experience to the next, probably because of her fantastic
hopes about what the new event might bring and her certain disap-

---

8. It occurred to us only years later on rethinking Mary's development with
us that this was about the time of the year that her father had died and her relatively
happy infancy suddenly ended. The anniversary of this event may have had some
thing to do with Mary's "falling apart." But since we did not receive from her
material supporting this theory it has to be viewed with caution.

pointment that it could not possibly satisfy her. If this held true for
a change of activity, her feelings were even more intense on meeting
a new person. Whenever a new teacher, counselor, child, or even a
visitor arrived at the School, Mary threw herself against them with
a devouring expectation. If they reacted at all favorably, she poured
forth a stream of wants. Usually she was unable to express her real
desire, and even if she could say what she wanted and it was given
her, it was never what she actually craved. So all her efforts to form
relations with other people or obtain satisfaction from them provoked only fresh disappointment and ended in ever deeper despair.

The depth of Mary's frustration, and the primitive nature of her
anxieties, was evident in her fear of utter destruction, which sometimes came out in her screaming. "I'm dying, *do* something," she
would shout or whine for hours at a time.[9] She remained deaf to
any efforts to reach her, no matter how we tried.

Mary's complete distress lifted so slowly and imperceptibly that
we could only begin to recognize the improvement after several
months. Her screaming changed slowly from a deadly repetition of
"I'm dying" or "I hate all of you" to more specific complaints. She
would begin by crying, "You hate me," shift to "I hate you," or
"I hate the School," and then repeat the cycle over and over again.

At length, over a period of months, the shrieking fits did subside.
They now occurred only a few times daily, and finally not even that
often. In their place ensued a quiet, but equally devastating isolation.

As this phase (which lasted even longer than the violent outbursts) began, Mary, worn out from a screaming fit, would isolate
herself on or near her bed. Complaining under her breath, she would
putter with her toys and other belongings, which she compulsively
arranged and rearranged. She seemed to be all hunched over, almost
as though she were rolled up in a ball. From time to time she interrupted her puttering to lie quietly on her bed or kick her feet—
preferably against the wall but also just in the air. Again she was
unreachable, however we tried to make contact.

She may have been reliving experiences of her infancy. Like an
infant, she had first screamed to draw attention to her desperation.
Then, since our best efforts could not relieve her intense distress,
she withdrew into isolation, which was interrupted only by the aimless kicking. Efforts to draw her out led to fresh fits of screaming,
and increased physical activity, such as slamming doors, which she
could keep up for a half-hour at a time. Then she would return to

9. Had she "died as a human being" nine years ago when, at about this time
of year, her father had suddenly died and her mother had withdrawn her emotions?

her quieter isolation, and the compulsive arranging and rearranging of little objects.

Mary's depression, at its deepest, lasted for almost three months (her eighth through tenth months in School). Emotionally, Mary re-entered the world through a reawakened interest in animals. Although our efforts may have helped to give her strength to emerge from her shell, we cannot directly link the kindling of her feeling for animals with our attempts to serve her needs.

Mary's interest in pets had been obvious from the start. Now, however, to attract her attention they had to meet one cardinal requirement: that they be unwanted and uncared for. She surrounded herself with animals she claimed nobody wanted—everything from goldfish and newts to turtles and mice and rabbits. (Unfortunately, we could not let her keep larger animals.)

Usually she took good care of them for a while, only to torture them or let them die of neglect in the end. As soon as they began to seem well cared for, she lost interest. More than a year later, when she was much better able to relate and express her feelings, she still clung to this behavior pattern, but then she was able to wonder "How come all my people die?" On her own, she corrected her question to "How come all my people-animals die?" but it never became "How come my animals die?" With her pets she acted out being unwanted and neglected, but she lacked strength to go beyond that negative experience.

Never did the lives of those with whom Mary identified have a happy ending. The animals whom she picked out to protect and rescue from desolation wound up as she feared she would herself. So long as she doubted her own happy ending, her animals could not enjoy a better fate. Mary acted this out not only with her live pets, but also with toys. Though she played with the stuffed animals that had been given her and even loved them for a few days (as she had the fuzzy dog she received her first Christmas at the School), they soon lost meaning. But when another child neglected his stuffed animal, Mary immediately claimed it as her own. She would wash and patch it up, and then lose interest when it was respectably repaired.

Once she found a stuffed dog in the room of the seamstress, one we had not deemed nice enough to be used as a present.[10] This "unwanted" toy met an additional requirement—it had not been

10. It has become a Christmas custom that each child receives a homemade, stuffed animal in addition to his other presents. These animals are made in a cooperative effort by all staff members and have special meaning for the children because they know we make them ourselves and do not just buy them.

given to Mary but had been adopted spontaneously—and it became
her lasting favorite. She called him "Onions," after her and her
father's favorite food. Once again she revealed on how primitive a
level human relations had become fixated for her.

Just as she had to eat onions daily, her dog, Onions, had to accompany her wherever she went, day and night. The intentions of
children and adults were now gauged by the way they treated Onions.
When Mary could interest herself in others enough to be concerned
about their relations to Onions (if not to her) she was slowly
emerging from her deep depression; soon she was also showing
other small signs of reaching out for human contact.

Mary also began to draw again, which was another token of
her fresh interest in the world. At that time she mostly drew her
stuffed animals. The relations between the animals differed from
those she had acted out before in parting a mother cat from its
kittens. One day she sketched an animal that looked very much
like the panda she was holding in her arms. When this resemblance
was drawn to her attention, Mary snapped angrily and disparagingly,
"What do you know." But a moment later she added a baby panda
to the drawing and wrote on it that his mother had gone to the
store to buy candy, ice cream, cake, and meat for the baby, who
was three years old. (Plate 4) When asked the reason for the baby's
age, she remarked that when she herself was three she had lived
with her aunt, since her mother was dead. In such rare moments
and roundabout ways, she told us what preyed on her mind. But
most of our efforts to talk to her met with a sullen muteness or an
angry "Let me alone" or "I don't know," which were like slaps in
the face to those who tried to penetrate her isolation.

As her depression continued to lift, Mary at first seemed to
cling to it rather than to let it go. Although there was less screaming
or retiring into melancholic isolation, she was just as gloomy, for
the most part. Yet now some of this gloom seemed affected rather
than genuine, and often had a tinge of exhibitionism. At the same
time Mary became even more deliberately hostile, and seemed to
want to see others suffer.

In this mood she kept aloof from her two favorite counselors.
She remarked again and again that she only liked counselors who
were in charge of other groups. When we asked about the two who
had been her favorites, she acted as though she hardly knew whom
we meant. The people she now claimed to like were those who had
almost nothing to do with her and whom, actually, she avoided.
She also shunned the children she lived with in the dormitory and
those who were in her classroom. Much of the time during this

period of trying to remain aloof she roamed from group to group, but would leave as soon as a child or counselor tried to draw her into a game, read to her, or make any other effort to establish contact.

We were not quite sure how best to deal with this situation. We could only follow Mary's own leads. For example, when she expressed a wish to live with her sister, we arranged for more frequent visits between them. But while these meetings seemed to have little meaning for Mary at the time, they evidently threatened her feeling of security about how long she could remain in the School. For instance, after a visit with her sister she would say, "I want to leave here before I'm fourteen; maybe when I'm thirteen; no, when I'm eighteen. Then I'll be able to take care of myself. No, I'd better stay till I'm twenty and then I'll leave." In short, such visits made Mary cling anxiously to the School despite her protestations about wanting to live elsewhere.

As she became less depressive, Mary took to sleeping with her thumb in her mouth. Evidently her pleasure in living had to begin (or re-begin) on the most primitive level. Although we asked no questions, she volunteered that she did not know how her thumb got there, it just seemed to pop into her mouth. She wondered why we did not mind this, and made derogatory comments about other children who sucked their thumbs. Righteously, she announced that she never did it when others were present; she only sucked her thumb in bed at night.

This was the first time Mary had related the behavior of other children to her own. Before, her only reactions to them had been to object, or be jealous, or feel persecuted. But now it became apparent that her return to thumbsucking resulted from watching other children. Her wondering why they did this, and why we let them, was a first step toward comparing herself with others, and this time she was not out to convince herself that what they could do and have was denied her. Rather, she was trying to see if she, too, might not enjoy the things other children did.

Adopting thumbsucking, and trying to understand our attitude toward it, were among the most important steps Mary took toward rejoining human company. Sucking her thumb, of course, was understandably in line with Mary's early experiences. This was borne out by her most deep-rooted and lasting complaint against her aunt: that she had taken away her baby bottle. For Mary, this had abruptly ended oral pleasure, the only positive thing her mother had given her (though inadequately) and the only interpersonal gratification she had ever really known. She could never forgive or forget its loss. Long after she came to understand her own part in her diffi-

culties with her aunt, and to realize why the aunt might have preferred her own children, Mary always angrily returned to the same
complaint: "Why did she throw away my bottle?" (Incidentally, in
her last year with us Mary needed to be repeatedly assured that
when she left she could take her baby bottle with her. It was the
same bottle she had used for some time but had by then given up,
though she kept careful watch over it on her shelf. When Mary
finally left us, we reminded her of the bottle, but she left it where
it was; by that time she was really done with it.)

After we frankly encouraged Mary to enjoy sucking her thumb,
she began to believe that we really had no objections. In this confidence, she was able to talk about how her uncle and aunt had
slapped her or put bitter-tasting things on her hands to prevent her
from sucking.

There were other recollections of cruel treatment. She remembered (possibly exaggerating) how she had been beaten with a
belt and buckle; and even had been slapped across the face with it.
If Mary asked for food when she was hungry, her aunt used to
strike her across the face with a knife handle.

These memories were accompanied by strong emotions, quite
different from Mary's former, stolid way of talking about the past.
She angrily mulled over each anecdote, day after day, for weeks;
and more and more of her "grievances" kept coming to light.

Then suddenly Mary checked herself; although we encouraged
her to unburden herself, she was unable to talk any further about
the past. A few weeks later she tried to go on, but again had to stop.
Finally she was able to explain why. "I'm scared," she said. "I want
to talk to you about my aunt but I'm scared. I don't understand it.
Why didn't she hit her own children? Why did she only hit me
and Frances?"

What had blocked her was taking the difficult step from complaining about her fate to trying to understand it. Not that Mary
was interested in grasping her aunt's motives; such an interest in
others was still far beyond her. But she did want to fathom why
these things had happened to her. The wall separating her from the
world was crumbling. No longer was she entirely convinced that a
merciless fate had singled her out. She had begun to wonder about
the reason for her misfortunes, as she compared her aunt's behavior
toward her with the way she treated her own children. Mary described in detail how she was hit if she annoyed her cousins, while
her aunt never struck her own children. Why had she been so unjust?

This new ability to open up about her own miseries, to wonder about their origins, and to recognize others as human beings, also changed Mary's attitude toward other children. She stopped threatening to kill them, and no longer wished them dead. But she began to provoke them in the areas it hurt most. She could find the most subtle ways to make other children angry or anxious. To one girl she said that her only relative, a brother, had died. She "wondered" whether another child's parents had been in an auto smashup. Then she stood back and watched the child's agony of anxiety. When we confronted Mary with this, she claimed, "I didn't do anything. I only asked if her parents were in an accident."

Human beings seemed to become real to her largely to the extent that she could unload her aggressions on them, and make them as unhappy as she. The fact that she used illness or the death of a close relative to upset them also suggests that Mary was trying to find out how others (particularly children) reacted to such events. Perhaps through watching their anger and anxiety she could understand her own. Or by creating her own emotions in others, she may have hoped to feel closer to them.

As her aggressions became more goal-directed, Mary's attempts to control herself became more consistent. She could not yet do this on her own; outside help was needed. But now when she was upset, or too anxious, her demands for control ("you'd better settle me down," "take me to Dr. B.") became frequent rather than exceptional.

In attempting to learn control, she began playing counselor to the other children. Besides being a small token of her greater interest in them, this was an effort to test her influence realistically. Although before, Mary had placed her playmate in the bad mother's role while she herself was the suffering child, she was now the counselor who told children what to do.

After acting out this play, Mary transferred it to reality. Whenever she felt that another child had misbehaved, she ran to the counselor and told her about it, or she came to me or the teacher— anyone in authority. Apparently she was trying to develop a conscience in much the same way a small child does, first by playing parent, then by recognizing unacceptable behavior in others, criticizing it, and wishing to see it punished.

Groping for a superego drew Mary closer to the person who more or less represents superego functions at the School. Mary dreamt and wished that she were my child, a desire, incidentally, that is by no means common among the children at the School. She daydreamed about living with me when she left the School. One day she claimed to be my daughter. These phantasies, in a minor way, suggested that she was achieving a somewhat more hopeful, if unrealistic, outlook on the future.

Generally, however, in spite of these daydreams, Mary became less immersed in phantasies and more in contact with reality, which did not necessarily make matters easier for those who lived with her. For now she was able to act out on the basis of her bad experiences. Although she sometimes tried to justify her violent attacks on children and adults by blaming them for the mistreatment she had suffered from her aunt, usually she could differentiate between those who had let her down in the past and those she now mistreated.

As she remembered more and more of her past, she made efforts to bring order into the chaos of recalled emotional experiences. Thumbsucking had led to memories of how her relatives had tried to stop it. Now, as she began differentiating further between past and present, and hence feeling moderately secure, castration threats and separation anxieties that once had been used to control her came to her mind. When she sucked her thumb, for instance, her uncle had forcibly removed it from her mouth and placed it on the table; then, taking out his pocket knife, he had threatened to cut it off. "I knew he wouldn't do it," Mary said, "but I wish he wouldn't have said so, because I was dead scared anyway."

Just as thumbsucking led to memories of these threats, her freedom to get as dirty as she pleased evoked others. Once, after rolling in the mud, she remembered how her aunt and uncle had been furious at her for getting so dirty. Saying that they were going to place her in an orphan's home, they drove her in the car quite a distance, to show her an orphan asylum, and then brought her home again. "They were always telling me they were going to do terrible things to me," she said, "and then they didn't do it."

Shortly after this conversation, Mary found the courage to tackle her fears about masturbation, an old source of satisfaction that she was afraid we disapproved of. One day as she and her group were walking to the Museum, a stray dog jumped up at one of the girls, and rubbed his genitals against her. Mary remarked to her counselor that dogs had done the same thing to her. She said this rather provocatively, as if she expected the counselor to do something drastic to the girl, but the counselor did not reply. Then in an even more provocative tone, Mary asked what the dog was doing. When neither of her efforts to provoke met with response, her tone changed, and in a normal and perhaps slightly frightened voice she said that sometimes she played with herself, and was that what the dog was doing? Now the counselor responded by reminding Mary that she knew we did not mind if the children masturbated. Mary, herself, had seen that no one hurt himself by doing so. There was nothing "bad" about playing with oneself, the counselor added, and most people did it at one time or another.

After learning what she seemed to want to know, namely that we mind masturbation no more than we do thumbsucking, Mary suddenly switched back to her aunt. "Why did my aunt just come up and hit me when she saw me doing it," she asked, "Why didn't she talk, but just come up and swat me?" She repeated still other stories of being mistreated. The conversation ended with Mary asking that the term "masturbation" once more be explained. Now she laughed easily at the big word and asked if she had to use it in talking. Certainly not, replied the counselor. Mary's expression "playing with myself" was perfectly all right. At this, Mary confided how for a long time she had no word for it, and how pleased she had been on discovering the expression "to play with myself."

About this time, Mary began talking about "monsters" and babies. It started with a nightmare. In the middle of the night she called her counselor and told her that she had dreamt about people being killed. In the morning, she either tried to discharge the anxious tension created by her dream, or wanted to test how another child would react. At any rate, she claimed that the bad dream had been about a floor with a big hole, and that the other child had fallen into it and been killed.

This led to talk about such monstrosities as two-headed babies. First Mary wanted to know why mothers sometimes died after giving birth to deformed babies. Then she talked anxiously about other deformities, and wondered whether she had any. The counselor suggested that by observing other girls in the dormitory she could see that they were perfectly all right, and that she was, too; moreover, the girls' mothers had been in good health both before and after their birth. But Mary shrugged her shoulders as if to say she knew that her mother had not been all right. Eventually she came out with the idea that her mother's illness and death had some connection with her birth, which perhaps made her a "monster." She still felt this way even though she claimed that she knew her mother had died of a "gall bladder." Then, with another of her sudden transitions, Mary switched to questions about lactation, how babies are fed, why they eat more often than older children, and how they are nourished before birth.

Thereafter, and until she left (but with many significant interruptions and variations), the topic of mother-and-baby was one of her major preoccupations. Phantasies about it began appearing in her violent play with a rubber baby doll. At first she pushed the doll around abruptly in the buggy, so that it spilled out several times; carefully replacing it, she would again rock the buggy so violently that the doll fell out. Again, she promptly put it back into the buggy, only to spill it out once more. Later, when Mary was making the doll baby walk, she first picked it up very tenderly and then let it crash to the floor. In this way, Mary treated the doll much as she had treated her animals. Then for a while she dropped this play.

Resuming it about a month later, Mary announced that on the next day she would wash her baby doll. She proceeded to carry out this plan, which apparently she had made well in advance. As she played, she grew thoughtful, and asked, "Is it fun to have babies?" A bit later she folded the doll into the blanket and said crossly, "Now she'll start to wet right away." This led to conversation about how babies are a lot of work but most mothers like it, or at least don't mind the work because they are fond of their babies. A few minutes later, as she walked across the play yard with the baby doll wrapped snugly in her arms, she glanced down at it and said, "I wish I was in that blanket—it looks so warm and comfortable." It was the first time in months that Mary had wished to be a baby again.

With the ability to express this wish, the world seemed to appear more benign to her. Or it may have been the other way around: because the world seemed less threatening, she could afford to wish she were a baby again, and to relish the idea—or the hope.

She may have been expressing such feelings in telling her counselor that just a few days ago a man had sold her a thirty-five cent pineapple for only twenty-five cents, when he found out that that was all the money she had. With a broad smile, this time genuine, Mary asked, "How come people are so nice to me?" It was the first time, to our knowledge, that Mary had ever said people were nice to her.

As she came to live more and more in the present, we slowly assumed a meaning for her on our own. It was no longer her aunt whom she wanted to punish by being angry at us; she could now become angry with us in our own right. Ingeniously, she found excuses for doing so. For example, she would ask for round squares of candy, although she knew perfectly well there could be no such thing.[11] The absurdity of her requests made it possible for her to

---

11. Of course, on a deeper level this demand made good sense. It was her way of telling us that only the impossible would satisfy her: to have her mother brought back to life and to re-experience with her a happy infancy. The nasty provocativeness with which Mary made such statements and, through them, derided

go on making demands without our ever being able to fulfill them. As a matter of fact, after a year in School she became conscious of this herself. Her counselor once observed that Mary almost seemed not to want people to give her what she asked for, so that she could feel they were being mean to her. Mary laughed and said, "How did you guess?"

As Mary became more capable of directing her aggressiveness against a particular person, she seemed to be in closer contact with reality. But when attempts were made to discuss her provocative actions, she would barricade herself behind her old attitude that people were persecuting her. Cupping her hands over her ears, she would say, "I won't listen to you."

The better her contact with reality, the more she needed to bolster her waning conviction that she would be persecuted or deprived no matter what she did. So she made sure of providing herself with the requisite experiences. On a very chilly day, she tried to go out wearing nothing but the flimsiest sunsuit. When we prevented this, she screamed and lashed out. But even if we had permitted her to dress that way she would have thrown a tantrum, since then we would have been exposing her to a chill, which would have proved that we wanted her to get sick and die.

That Mary had to make conscious efforts to create grievances indicated the progress she was making. This was also obvious from the way she counteracted our efforts to please her by saying, "I want to be sad." On being asked to explain why she misbehaved, she said, "I want to be locked up, like the teacher at the old school threatened me." She also deliberately wore clothes that did not fit or match. "I want to be a ragamuffin so I can feel bad."

As Mary grew more deliberately provocative with adults, she began to play more easily with children, whom she now annoyed and ignored less frequently. Either through a process of physiological maturation, or because of her developing superego and better contact with reality, Mary, who was now almost ten, seemed to enter a tardy latency period. There were marked efforts to develop self-control, which proceeded at first on the most primitive level of the *lex talionis*: she punished the part of her body that had sinned. One day, for example, Mary grew very angry and upset about the unjustified attention she felt was being paid another child. When her unreasonableness and the mainsprings of her actions were brought to her attention, Mary said, "I did it because I'm jealous." Then a

our sincere desire to give her whatever she wanted, frustrated us. And this, in turn, kept us from understanding how genuine and deeply felt her desires for the impossible, which she expressed symbolically by asking for round squares, were.

few minutes later she bit her tongue. After a couple of hours, she was again in a rage, this time about the fact that another child had left the School several weeks earlier. Mary violently accused the counselor of having deliberately forced this child out. And again, after quieting down from her outburst, she bit her tongue quite badly.

Mary was also consciously trying to masturbate less. She stopped, or at least checked, conspicuous masturbation in the daytime, and in the evening waited until the lights were turned off. One evening, after witnessing a minor accident in which a boy had chipped a tooth, Mary did not masturbate at all. She was wakeful, and seemed particularly crabby and anxious. She asked to be told once more just how the accident had happened. The counselor had a hunch that there might be a connection between the accident and Mary's failure to masturbate, and gave her renewed assurance. As the counselor showed her understanding of Mary's unvoiced anxiety, Mary suddenly put the finger with which she usually masturbated into her mouth and bit hard. The counselor took advantage of this incident to reassure her that there was nothing wrong with masturbation and that she need not punish herself for it, or be afraid that anything bad would happen to her on this account. Relieved, Mary began masturbating and soon fell asleep.

Eventually actual acts of violence gave way to imaginary deeds. Mary strung out phantasies about how she would get a dog and train him to bite people. But she also went on hurting herself when she was angry or distressed. After her favorite counselor left on a short vacation, Mary cut the inside of her mouth with a pen point on which she was chewing; on the day I left for a short trip, she managed to bruise her hand quite badly—and so on. Perhaps she was trying to control herself through the use of self-inflicted pain, or perhaps she was simply trying to handle these ordeals by acquiring some physical ailment, in order to make sure of being comforted although people of key importance to her were gone.

Shortly after, two opposing tendencies in Mary's behavior gained prominence. On the one hand, she began again to deny her past and try to convince herself (and others) that she had always lived at the School with us. For example, by the end of her first year she would ask, "What did we do *two* years ago?" or, "What did we get for Christmas *three* years ago?"—an attempt to imply that she had never known any other home. She also drew pictures of the School that emphasized the fence that kept people away. (Plate 5) On the other hand, her doll play began reflecting her earliest experiences, those that reached farther back into her past than she had ever gone before. She kept re-enacting, with variations, this basic situation: A mother seems to exert herself a great deal, or claims to, but actually cares very little for a small child (sometimes a puppy). Then right away the mother goes to bed. The pattern of the mother's behavior is always the same: she does something for a little child but she does too little, too late. And then immediately she must rest for a long time. Yet, even while acting out in her doll play these experiences she had known with her mother, Mary was elsewhere consciously denying them. Curled up in her counselor's lap, she would say, "I want some parents; I never had any," and she emphasized the "never."

During a hot summer, Mary's nightmares multiplied. At first we attributed her restlessness at night and her frequent seeking out of her counselor to the hot weather. But with a cooler September, her nightmares became even more severe. A few remarks made while sleeping, which we overheard, suggested that the anxiety haunting her stemmed from her intense hostility—but this was speculation.

Her counselor's room was immediately below Mary's dormitory.[12] As frequently as ten times nightly, Mary would go to it and wake her up. Night after night, Mary got out of bed to make sure that the counselor was in the house and willing to be with her, no matter what the hour. Mary also checked on the whereabouts of other people who had acquired some importance to her; she wanted to assure herself that they, too, were in the house and available. Often, on her nightly rounds, she visited me in my office. My presence helped to reassure her, but it was not of central importance. Her favorite counselor's was.

Only later, during her sixteenth and seventeenth months with us, when her night wandering had somewhat subsided (probably because we submitted to it), did we get some inkling of its relation to her old fear of being separated from her sister. Mary talked about the anxiety, which had always plagued her, that her sister would die. They had had to share the same bed in the old days, and when Frances was ill (which happened on a number of occasions, including the attempts at suicide), Mary would lie awake at night gripped by unbearable anxiety. In her present nightmares, she relived these experiences. That was why she sought out her favorite counselor in the middle of the night: she was afraid the counselor might have died since she last saw her.

Yet, even Mary's obvious anxiety was mixed with a feeling of triumph at submitting us to such an ordeal. She had managed to

---

12. The new dormitory wing is arranged differently.

inconvenience us at night, just as the nightmares inconvenienced her. The counselor also represented her sister, and Mary wakened her at night both to make sure that she was still alive and to inflict on her the discomfort that her anxiety about Frances had inflicted on Mary.

During one of the repeated talks Mary had with her counselor about her nightmares, Mary suddenly switched the topic from her sister to her mother. She had been talking about how she feared her sister might die in bed beside her and leave her all alone. Then she continued, "My mother was sick all the time, too. She had awful stomach aches." When asked what else she remembered, Mary replied, "Most of all, I remember that. And then I remember when she died, and then I thought my sister would die, too." She recalled learning of her mother's death. "When my sister told me about my mother I was in nursery school. She came and told me that she was taking my mother to the hospital, and then she came back and said she was dead, and I cried." Mary had not understood the implications of this at the time. "I didn't know," she said, "I just cried because my sister cried and my teacher seemed so upset."

Mary's ability to recall the circumstances of her mother's death apparently seemed to encourage her in wanting to understand other experiences of the past. She tried not only to remember events but also to grasp their emotional meaning. For example, although she had discussed thumbsucking without ever (on her own) entering into the emotions behind it, she did make efforts to understand the reasons why she masturbated. Secure in our relaxed attitude about it, she asked us to explain why she did it, what it meant, and what other people's reactions to it were. Why did she do it mainly when she was trying to fall asleep? Why did it make her sleepy and tired? She pondered the details, and said that "something sticks up in me when I play with myself." She even began talking about her attendant phantasies. She said that when she masturbated she also talked to herself, so quietly that no one could hear, because she did not want anyone to know what she was saying. Her main phantasy was that she was the husband, her doll the wife, and that they were having sex relations.

Soon after, the nature of her nightmares changed. They no longer revolved about her sister's death, or Mary's own destruction, but about her being left all alone. She woke her counselor in the middle of the night to talk about one nightmare in which she was deserted. "There weren't any other people in the world. I didn't have any parents and there weren't even any counselors around." Then she whimpered, "Why do I have to dream like this? I had a good time

today. Why do I have to have a bad dream when I had a good
time during the day?" It seemed that only the actual experience of
enjoying life and being able to master it, in some small degree, gave
her the strength to let such upsetting dreams occur. But her bad
dreams also probably stemmed from her feelings of guilt. Nice things
happened to her, though she felt she was bad; we treated her well
although she mistreated us—so she was punished in her dreams.

In many of her dreams she was being given away. "I don't want
to be given away," she protested. "I don't want to be sold. Why do
they want to sell me?" The material she had enacted much earlier
in her play with animals thus began appearing in her dreams, and
was remembered and reported. In her play, she could still find
reassurance in the fact that it was "only pretend," or that only animals were gotten rid of. But in her dreams, these things happened
to herself.

Mary's anxiety about being deserted, "sold," entered into her
play with children. One afternoon, when playing with dolls, Mary
kidnapped a doll from the girl who was pretending to be her mother.
Mary told the mother that she would not give her daughter back,
because she had been mean to her. The mother said she had not
done anything very bad, but Mary kept insisting that the mother had
never liked her child and that therefore her daughter need not return
to her.

She dared the pretend-mother to call the police or do anything
else she wished, but said again that her daughter would never return
because she had mistreated her. The game went on with the arrival
of the police, etc., but by now Mary was so wrought up that her
counselor felt it was best to stop what clearly was no longer a game.
The counselor explained that if parents mistreat a child not just
anyone can take the child away, as Mary seemed to fear. A social
agency would be called in to study the situation, and if the mother
had really mistreated her child the agency would be entrusted with
the task of finding a good home for her.

This led to a number of conversations about the functions of
social agencies, and the ways in which society protects children. For
the first time, Mary began to comprehend the role of the agency that
had played such an important part in her life. Before this, the
agency's social worker (or even the one who had placed Mary in
the School) had aroused no interest in her whatsoever. She was
just another adult who pushed her around. When Mary began understanding that the agency and the worker were genuinely interested in her, and in taking care of children in general, she was very
much impressed. She brightened up on perceiving that life held

greater security for her than she had realized. She could appreciate the advantages of being under the agency's guardianship, and came to understand why and how she had been placed in the School. With this increased sense of security, Mary could again enjoy babyish pleasures. She liked to crawl into another child's buggy, for example, and insist that she was a baby. She habitually acted the baby's role when playing with other children. No longer was she the child who must be spanked, reprimanded, or pushed around; rather, she was the baby who must be well cared for. She continually made sucking motions with her mouth, particularly when she was isolating herself. This mannerism was so persistent that, most of the time, her mouth looked quite like a snout. Nevertheless, she would not use the baby bottle herself, though she fed her baby doll with a play bottle and she knew that other children used the real baby bottle whenever they wished.

Mary now was better able to accept presents and articles of clothing, although her feelings about receiving things remained ambivalent. To any major gift she reacted with aches and pains, particularly stomach aches, which represented her main way of storing tensions. This may be explained through material that came to light much later, which showed her strong incorporative tendencies, and was in line with her mother's major ailment (gall bladder trouble), which had been located in what Mary called the "stomach." Mary's identification with her mother through these pains shed new light on her attempts to punish herself by bruising and skinning her knees and legs. She said that her mother, during her illness, often fell to the floor or down the stairs and bruised herself quite badly.

Mary's efforts to be like her mother were part of her relatively new strivings to integrate her contradictory emotions and acquire more adequate mastery of them. Efforts to achieve inner control were mingled with testing to see how far she could safely go in relaxing her controls. For example, while cleaning her cabinet one day, Mary asked if her counselor would like her even if she were a very messy girl. The counselor assured her that liking a person had relatively little to do with how messy or clean they might be at any one moment, but Mary persisted, "Would you like me even if I were very, very messy?" The counselor replied that their feelings about each other were so well established by now that Mary's messiness or cleanliness could make little difference. With this reassurance Mary stopped arranging her possessions so rigidly, although after some hesitation, she did go on straightening things up.

Similarly, her defenses against her sex fears and desires continued to diminish. Her masturbation phantasies, in which she was a man, and her doll (or the pillow) the woman, had already been revealed. Now she asked why she liked to imagine herself in the male role. Assured that most girls have strong feelings about the fact that they are girls and not boys, and that this is a consequence of their physical differences, she went on to admit that her masturbation was accompanied by aggressive phantasies, also. Every night, while masturbating, she also imagined herself kicking her doll in the rear, at which time the doll represented her aunt.

After she had divulged some of her feelings about being a girl and had begun to understand their cause, Mary mentioned some additional themes in her nightmares, such as being chased by a man, or by persons who were trying to take away a part of her body. In her play, she asked her counselor to make clay penises for her dolls, and began to say such things as, "I have three noses." She became keenly observant of the size and shape of the noses of all male staff members and evaluated their personalities on the basis of how she felt about their noses.[13] But at the same time she also became better able to accept her femininity.

Mary was now questioning her old conviction that nothing nice would ever happen to her. When she was given a new doll, she asked if it was "for keeps." Her counselor told her "of course," and Mary wondered, "How come I'm always afraid it won't be true when something nice happens to me?"

More than ever before, Mary was able to accept the nice things that happened to her during her second Christmas with us, which rounded out the first year and a half of her stay. Although she seemed very anxious and tense before opening her presents, she later wondered, "Why was I scared?" But at the time, her excitement was so great that just before receiving her presents she wet her panties—an accident that had never happened before in School and never did again.

On Christmas Eve Mary once again recapitulated the unhappy events of her life, including her sister's illness, her mother's death, and her own resulting night fears. But then spontaneously she said that she thought she would be happy the next day, Christmas Day; and this really seemed to be the case. It was the first occasion on which we felt that she was truly accepting of her presents and able to enjoy them. What's more, she did not even object to the fact that the other children got presents, too.

---

13. So much so that, among ourselves, we jokingly referred to this period when Mary was making so many remarks about noses as her "Tristram Shandy" period. (Such an allusion, when talking of a child whose behavior is somewhat upsetting to the staff, often helps them to remain fully accepting of the child despite remarks that hurt the staff members' narcissism.)

After Christmas, in her play with other children, Mary continued to re-enact the events of her life more realistically, especially her behavior with her aunt. Again she was the "daughter" who passively suffered the blows and hard work forced upon her by a mean, driving mother. But on the sly, she took a toy animal away from the girl who was playing the mother and cut off its head. Such play was almost lifelike, considering the way she had actually discharged aggression at her aunt's home by killing and torturing animals.

Yet despite her new grasp on reality, Mary's efforts to integrate her conflicts were still tenuous and rather devious. If her tension or discomfort reached any magnitude, she soon fell back on angry defiance or stolid isolation. The conflict between her aggressive and isolating tendencies, on the one hand, and her desires for dependent, infantile attachment, on the other, was nicely demonstrated when one of her favorite counselors was about to leave for a two-weeks' vacation.

At first, Mary tried to deal with the separation quite realistically. She asked repeatedly how long the counselor would be gone, where exactly she was going, and when she would be back. But then she seemed to collapse, and began whimpering, "Mama, mama," while she puckered up her mouth, and made sucking motions. We tried to comfort her, but she stopped herself short, and at once began shouting how much she hated the counselor. Then, as suddenly, her mood shifted again, and without any display of emotion whatever, she said flatly, "So you're going on vacation. So what. I don't care."

When her counselor returned from her trip, however, Mary was able to regain contact quite well. Like a much smaller child, she sought protection at night by clinging to some possession her counselor had given her, as though this reassured her in a symbolic way, if not of her friend's physical presence, then at least of her good will. She would cling to a toy, or to some little thing, such as a ribbon, that her favorites had given her; this she would finger as she tried to fall asleep, and hold it close to her throughout the night.

DISCUSSION

Nearly a year had passed since the complete disintegration of Mary's surface adjustment. Now that she was able once again to achieve satisfactions, though on an infantile level, and to look to her counselors for comfort and support, we renewed our efforts to understand the reasons for her breakdown. Mary could not evade indefinitely the continual challenge to form true personal relations, which originated mainly with her two favorite counselors but was also implicit in the general atmosphere of the School. But in order to relate, Mary had to meet us with a personality of her own, and here her defensive system broke down.

She was thus confronted with an emotional impasse: as her wish to relate became stronger, she felt ever more keenly her inability to do so with any permanence. So, she tried the easy way out: to avoid having to face up to the task, she denied the relevance of the School environment by trying to convince herself that she would leave the School soon.

We did not recognize at the time that her efforts to deny the validity of her present living conditions might be symptoms of a central conflict, although we probably could not have acted much differently if we had. We knew that in all external matters, including physical comfort, she enjoyed greater well-being than ever before. Hence, on that level, she did long for permanence, and behind her requests to leave lay a wish to hear us say she could not. On that level, too, we felt that our promise of a prolonged stay in School would be reassuring, and we promised exactly that.

But on a deeper level, for Mary to integrate her personality implied the necessity of giving up a total allegiance to her dead mother and transferring some of her emotions from this attachment to her counselors. It meant separating herself from the earliest mother, and beginning a new life, independent of her. All this Mary felt was beyond her ability. For these reasons her wish to leave—and the sooner the better—was genuine.

The challenge to change her personality seemed clear to Mary in at least three situations: our desire that she should relate to her counselors, their disapproval of her unwarranted hostility toward other children, and their positive emotional attachment to her. For example, the counselors had to disapprove (though with the greatest concern for Mary's feelings) of her demands that other children like her and be forced to play with her, even though she had just abused them violently. Similarly the counselors' positive attachment to Mary could not help but be affected by her lightning changes of mood: from pleased acceptance to sullen isolation; from positive response to their affection, to violent outbursts of hate.

Her counselors tried to remain giving, and certainly remained understanding and accepting. But the changes necessarily produced in the counselors' emotions by her actions became ever more important to Mary, particularly as her favorites grew more meaningful to her as persons. Eventually she had to re-evaluate her behavior in line with her interest in retaining their affection.

That her actions could be of such emotional importance to us startled Mary. In the past it had made no difference to others how she acted or felt. Warm or hostile, her aunt always rejected her. At the School Mary was confronted with the completely new experience of seeing her feelings change significant aspects of reality. Her ability to believe that her emotions had such importance for others was not helped any by her feeling that we had let her down, as indeed we had. For we had tantalized her by offering a physical and emotional comfort she was more than anxious to grasp, only to provoke an even deeper inner discomfort, which jeopardized it all, by challenging her to restructure her personality.

For quite different reasons, too, Mary was disappointed in the School and anxious to leave it. This became clear to us from her attitude toward newcomers, from her frantic expectation that each new person was the one who would magically supply her with everything she wanted, all she had missed. Emotionally, Mary seemed forever in search of the all-giving mother. Even the School, which had raised so much hope in this respect, had let her down terribly, and she wanted to be on the move again. Our insistence on the permanence of her stay not only shattered this hope, but put us in a punitive, inhibiting position. She may therefore have reacted against us so violently because we were preventing her from finding the ideal mother. Also, she may have hoped to force us into letting her go on with her search. Perhaps she thought, in view of her past experience, that if she just behaved badly enough there would be another new placement, so that eventually she would find the dream-mother, the all-giving mother, who would supply every need without requiring her to restructure her personality.

I need hardly mention that it was Mary's new security in School that enabled her to give up the defense of pseudo-adequacy and reveal how intense her hostility really was. Mary felt pretty certain, for example, that we would not resort to physical punishment or the withdrawal of necessities, no matter what she did. While she was most insecure about her relations to people, she did feel certain, in this respect, about the staff and what the School stood for. The fact that the physical comfort, and as much emotional solace as she could accept, continued without interruption during her depressive phase, may have helped her in emerging eventually from her worst depression. It may have given her the courage to think that if she tried even more to be herself there would at least be no negative consequences.

As a matter of fact, Mary's reawakened interest in animals, which was the first sign that her depression was lifting, may, on some level, have resulted from her identifying with our actions. We had taken her in when she was unhappy and deprived, and we went on caring for her, though she gave no more signs of response than her dumb animals did. Thus, identification may have marked the beginning of Mary's efforts to integrate her personality.

But the concentration of all her emotions on one person, as a baby concentrates only on the mother, and the relatively easy identification this permits, was no longer possible to her, both because of her age and her past experiences, and for this reason her integration had to be helped along by observing other children. Her efforts to understand their motives and reactions, as well as her own actions ("why did I hit the girl?") had to proceed at the same time that she was forming relations to adults. As the children's opinion of her acquired importance, she tried to assess the impact of her actions on them. Simultaneously, she became more openly provocative and nasty to adults. It appeared, then, that Mary's initial aggressiveness toward children may have been a double displacement.

By this I mean that Mary's hatred may originally have been directed against the only person who competed with her for her mother's attention: her sister (whom she killed in her dreams). After the mother's death this sister became the only positive factor in her life, and her hatred was then displaced from her sister to her aunt and her cousins, who, by their actions, made the shift seem more than justified. But Mary could not discharge this hatred, because it led to overly severe punishment. If they threatened to cut off her thumb for sucking, what might they not do if she hit them over the head? So she struck her playmates instead. Once Mary was convinced that discharging aggression against adults at the School was not quite so dangerous, she proceeded to do just that in her outbursts (screaming at the counselors, slamming doors, throwing things). At the same time it became less necessary for Mary to discharge her hostility against children and so she got along with them better.

Of course, most of her actions were determined on many levels; each one was the result of a variety of past and recent experiences. This was certainly true for her violent outbursts. When she asked for the impossible and used our inability to provide it as an excuse for being angry, she was reversing what had happened to her before she came to the School. Her aunt's demands had seemed impossible, and because she could not meet them, she had been punished, as now she punished us. Again, since no matter what she did, she had always been in the wrong, so must we always be in the wrong, however much we tried to please her. Such a reversal of roles satisfied her longing for revenge and increased her feelings of mastery. But otherwise the effort was sterile. Counteracting the topsy-turvy world she had known at her aunt's house (where she was always wrong) by creating an equally topsy-turvy world at the School (where she was always right and everybody else always wrong) still left her with a topsy-turvy world. And because the last one made no more sense than the first, she could not master it.

In other ways, too, Mary tried to create a situation that was a reversal of one she had known before. For example, Mary did her best to play one child against another. In doing so, she created situations of jealousy and competition, which paralleled those that had existed between herself and her sister (and between herself and the preferred cousins); but this time, Mary was the one in control, and not the victim. Similarly, she later tried to play one adult against the other, experimenting with and enjoying her power of controlling and depriving others as she had been controlled and deprived.

The return of the nightmares, their heightened intensity and frequency, may have sprung from Mary's efforts to repress her hostility and guilt rather than integrate them. The change in the content of her nightmares was the first sign of the breakdown of these efforts. She tried controlling her hostility during the day, so it came out at night. In her dreams she feared that her counselor, or her sister, had died or been killed (by her hostility). Later she dreamed that she had been deserted (as punishment for her hostility). Thus we may assume there was progress from the discharge of hostility to the fear of its consequences, which provided the motive for further efforts at integrating hostility.

Two more items round out the discussion of Mary during this crucial year: information received from her sister, and the summary of a Rorschach test.

Conversations with Frances on the occasions of her visits augmented our understanding of Mary. It became apparent that Frances felt a heavy burden of guilt for not having protected her while they lived with their aunt—a conviction that must have increased Mary's feeling that her sister had willfully neglected her. For her part, Frances could not accept the fact that she, too, had been only a child, unable to assume such a heavy burden. (Frances also had been quite a disturbed child and now, in late adolescence, was still poorly integrated. Unfortunately, she was unable to avail herself of psychiatric treatment or casework help, although the agency repeatedly offered her both.) Frances said, for example, that a night never went by that she did not dream about her sister—a sign of her close tie to Mary. It was, of course, an ambivalent attachment. Frances admitted that, being herself a little girl and not quite sure about what was right, she had often sided with her aunt against

Mary. When Frances came home from school, she would hear her
aunt complain about Mary's misdeeds and threaten to get rid of
them both. Anxious for herself, and eager to remain in favor with
her aunt, Frances sometimes turned against her sister and punished
her; but she was always devoured by guilt immediately afterward.

If more evidence of their ambivalent relation was needed, merely
seeing the two sisters together was a convincing demonstration.
Frances, in particular, clung desperately and seductively to Mary, as
if expecting the love and security from her that neither child could
provide for herself or the other.

During the end of this period, a Rorschach test was given to
Mary. Since the earlier evaluations of Mary's progress, which had
been influenced by her skillful surface adjustment, had been optimistic, the agency hoped to arrange an early adoption in line with
the psychiatrist's suggestion. Disappointed when subsequent developments shattered this hope, and wondering whether this change for
the worse (certainly worse so far as surface conformity was concerned) had been brought on by the institutional environment, the
agency decided to look to Rorschach test findings as another means
of assessing the nature and severity of Mary's disturbance. These
were the test's most significant findings:[14]

"The child suffers from an inhibition affecting all spheres of
the mental life. Her productivity is very low; the intellectual horizon is limited; the interest range is narrow. The procedure is immature, and perseveration is also found. The constriction is very
damaging to her inner life. Not a single affect-dictated association
is produced; the spontaneity, the sparkle expected in a child are
entirely absent. Nor is she capable of emotional rapport.

"The fantasy life is poor; only one such association emerges and
it uncovers a passive submissive attitude. In numerous other instances
she has associations which normally would lead to fantasy, but in
her they do not materialize as such—the repression is too severe.

"A deep set anxiety is projected in the structure. It is, of course,
the force explaining the inhibition. Color shock is also found, pointing to the neurotic reaction pattern. There is a failure of growth in
respect to conventional percepts, representing a possible rebellion.
The ego is not adequately organized to stand up against anxieties and
conflicting needs, and she defends herself by circumscribing her
psychic life. The performance as a whole is too restricted to project the personal dynamics, but there is evidence of a hostile attitude.

"In all: an anxious, conflicted child, too badly reduced at present

---

14. Rorschach evaluation by S. J. Beck.

for any therapy other than supportive and encouraging. The Rorschach Test findings point to the need for a benign psychological climate, one calculated to thaw out the frozen affects."

And Mary was like this after having been given, for more than a year, just such supportive and encouraging experiences in as psychologically benign a climate as was within our power to provide for her.

Between Two Traumas

UNFORTUNATELY, the sheltering and constructive environment that we had created for Mary was not impervious to disruptions from without. We could not shield Mary from the impact of the marriage of her sister, which took place a month later. This was a severe trauma, in the face of which Mary could not maintain the little integration she had so far achieved.

Superficially, Mary seemed to take the preparations for the wedding quite well, and was even able to play a prominent part in the ceremony itself. But in a matter of days, she completely lost contact with counselors and children. She could not speak of what troubled her; her old hostile and frozen personality returned in full force. She developed a blinking tic and in addition, avoided looking directly at people, either counselors or children, as though she wished to shut the world from sight. Intense night terrors reappeared. Her general behavior and inability to talk indicated severe emotional blocking; but serious as this reaction was, it at least brought no return of the violent outbursts of prolonged screaming and physical aggression, which had taken so long to control.

Although the shock of Frances' marriage rendered Mary incapable of interest in individual human beings, it did strongly stimulate her sex curiosity—so much so, that most of her energy may have been exhausted by this revival of the intense emotional (sexual?) experiences she had once shared with her sister. She was able, however, in the midst of her deep depression, to communicate her fears and curiosity about sex.

Previously, Mary had seemed to be relatively indifferent when other children talked of sexual matters. For example, when two children were telling some story about a man who, presumably, dropped his razor while shaving and thus cut off his penis, Mary acted as if she had not heard. But now, three months later, the curiosity and anxiety roused by her sister's wedding suddenly gave this story a personal meaning. One night, waiting until the lights were turned off at bedtime, she recalled it and asked questions about it.

She did not bring this up with one of her favorite counselors, but chose a relatively new counselor with whom she had had little contact before, and whom she afterward ignored. Perhaps this counselor was selected because she was married. The story seemed to serve mainly as an introduction, since Mary went on to query the counselor about her sexual relations with her husband. In roundabout fashion she asked whether the counselor enjoyed intercourse. The counselor told her that she did. Mary then wondered: having had intercourse on the preceding night, would her counselor be on duty the following morning? Again, she was assured on this score. But Mary wondered if the counselor might not then have a baby and cease helping to care for her. On being told that the counselor did not plan to have a child for some time, Mary was reassured. Obviously Mary was interested not in this particular counselor but in the implications of her sister's marriage for herself. She was afraid that sex relations might keep her counselor away, just as she feared that the marital relation might undermine her sister's interest in her.

Six days later, again at bedtime, Mary resumed the conversation. This time it revolved about sex relations as such, rather than the fear of separation. But this was Mary's last try at doing something about her depression; it had been settling over her for days, and now isolated her completely.

During this period Mary scarcely spoke to anyone. She never approached or looked at people directly; she sidled up to them, slowly and imperceptibly. Her voice lost the timbre and modulation it had acquired and became as harsh as when we first knew her. While her behavior had always been characterized by sudden changes of emotion, she now evinced absolutely no sign of feelings for long stretches, and when they did appear, they were inappropriate to a degree that was unusual even for Mary. Her bizarre actions, such as suddenly coming up to another girl and biting her on the nipple, completed the general picture, which supported the psychiatrist's conclusion that Mary was in the midst of a schizophrenic episode. It lasted in full force for two months.

Then, gradually, during the next few months, Mary showed rare, small signs of breaking through the wall of depression that she had erected between herself and the world. Mary told us how, during her isolation, she had felt that nobody else existed; and she spoke of her compensatory feeling that she was all-important. She could most easily open up about these megalomanic phantasies; it was more difficult to tell us about the way her fear of being deserted had been rekindled when her sister separated herself from both Mary and their common past (which was the meaning she attached to Frances' marriage). In her unhappiness, Mary had apparently returned to archaic and self-centered phantasies, which she could reveal only as her sense of isolation lessened.

At first she spoke about her megalomanic conception of her relation to other human beings. For example, one day her counselor was teaching some of the children how to tell time by linking the hours of the day with the degree of daylight, and the revolution of the earth with the turning hands of the clock. At this Mary said, "No, everything revolves around me!" A bit later in the same day, Mary angrily and with deep inner conviction declared to those present, her counselor and several other children, that she was the only one in the room.

She had similar delusions about objects. The more important an object was, the more it was exclusively hers. This attitude was illustrated when she remarked to some children who were looking for the Mississippi River on a map, "I know all about the Mississippi. It's very important, and that's why it belongs to me and nobody else."

This overevaluation of her importance may have resulted in part from her efforts to compensate for her feelings of loneliness and desertion, because a few days later Mary consciously tried to emerge from her depression by attempting to understand why she had been deserted by her parents. She came to me, whom she regarded as the highest authority available, to find out exactly when and why her father and mother had died, how old she had been then, and other facts about the past. I used this occasion to review the length of time she had been with us, and to stress the heartening progress she had made until her latest difficulties. Then I asked her if she would talk to us again so that we might know how to help her. All this must have encouraged her, especially since her coming to me for help in tying together the facts of her life was done on her own initiative. That evening she unearthed an old piece of blue satin ribbon, which had once been given to her by her favorite counselor and to which she used to cling at night, and tied it to her bed, so that this symbol of her relation to her best friend would always be visible.

At breakfast, next morning, having asked to sit beside this counselor, Mary let her put an arm about her, and finally cuddled up to her. That afternoon she cut a piece off an old pair of discarded blue

jeans, saying that it felt nice (for the first time since her sister's
marriage something was "nice"), and that she would suck it along
with her thumb at night. Thumbsucking again was a pleasant experience rather than the act of desperation it had seemed during the
preceding weeks. In the evening, Mary asked for all the stuffed
animals that she had put away several months before, and set them
up carefully at the foot of her bed. Then, turning to the counselor,
she asked whether she (Mary) had been following my suggestion
that she talk to us again. The counselor said that she certainly
seemed to be trying, which was all that counted, and that we were
most happy to see her attempting to make life pleasant again for
herself. Next morning Mary said that she now would like to keep
her animals on her bed. She arranged them carefully, and then
covered them so that they could sleep comfortably while she went
off to class. Thus, parts of herself—the animals with whom she identified—were well cared for and could now enjoy life.

Obviously things looked better to Mary, and this well-being also
seemed to pervade her dreams. At breakfast she said, "I dreamt
that my sister is divorced." She went on to complain about her sister's negligence in not having sent her a birthday present; obviously
she blamed the marriage for the oversight. But then, partly to cover
up her wish to have her sister entirely to herself, Mary added that
she hoped Frances really would not get a divorce. Mary's motive
for this was selfish. She hated the marriage but she liked Frances'
husband.

While yet suffering from her sister's desertion, Mary reacted
violently one morning to the arrival of a new maid. "Always new
maids," she complained. Then she laughed in a frightened way and
said loudly enough for the new maid to hear, "The maids are afraid
of me." (Laughing was something relatively new for Mary. She had
never laughed when she first came; now she did so only when anxious, and her laugh sounded as if she had not yet quite learned
how.) As though explaining why she felt the maids were afraid of
her, Mary continued, "Because I'm afraid of the maids."

Another month and Mary could approach life with more courage. As she voiced her anxiety about others and recognized its roots
in her own hostility, she became able to relate again and to feel
somewhat assured that she had not been totally abandoned. This,
along with continued reassurance from her favorite counselors,
helped Mary to realize that not everything had been taken from
her with her sister's marriage.

Unconsciously what Mary seemed to want was to partake in her
sister's sex life, i.e., share her husband. At bedtime when, as is the

case with so many children, Mary's sex fears and desires were strongest, she questioned her married counselor in great detail about whether brothers (brothers-in-law) and sisters could marry, enjoy intercourse, have babies, and so forth. She began by talking about King Solomon and his many wives, and wondered how he could have had intercourse with all of them. The suggestion that he might have taken turns satisfied her, perhaps because she felt that she could also take turns with her sister and not be wholly deprived.

From such relatively mature sex interests Mary soon reverted to more primitive desires. She wondered about her counselor's breasts, asked to be cuddled and carried, and then became more boldly direct. Pointing to a little pin, shaped like a bird, that the counselor was wearing, she said that the bird was drinking from her breast. Mary leaned up against the counselor. "I'm leaning against your breast," she said, making sucking noises. In every way possible she wanted to be babied and indulged.

But this married counselor with whom she had relatively little contact was not the most suitable person for satisfying her primitive needs. So she turned to her favorite counselor with a frantic request for the baby bottle. She could not suck the milk fast enough, so deep was her greed. The nipple had to be adjusted again and again, and the holes enlarged so that she could drink the milk faster. But after this one attempt, she did not go back to the bottle for several months.

Her bedtime talks now turned once more to her feelings about being a girl, and for help with this topic she chose the other of her favorite counselors. Mary wondered what would happen if she made a doll and put a penis on it: would anybody be angry? On being assured that no one in School would be, she asked more specifically if I would be angry. The counselor said that she was sure I would not and why did Mary think so? Mary replied, "He has a penis, doesn't he?" Her counselor said that every man has, upon which Mary said, "Well, then he knows about them," and with this, went on to make some observations about men.

She remarked that the swimming coach, whom she had carefully watched in the pool that afternoon, had large sex organs. It was explained to her that sex organs develop like any other part of the body, and are larger in the adult than in the small boy. Mary asked if boys ever have emissions at night, and being told that they did, she next wanted to know how this differed from bedwetting.

On the next evening, just before going to bed, she went ahead and did the things she had only talked about doing the previous night. Using clay, she fashioned male genitals for one of her dolls. A bit later, when already in bed, she told her counselor that once she had cut herself with a razor, and held up her finger to show the mark. The counselor helped her examine it, and pointed out how well the cut had healed, which led Mary to talk about how some time previously she had tried cutting her hair with a razor. When asked why she had done this, Mary indicated that the story she had overheard about the man who cut off his penis with a razor had given her the idea of trying to cut her pubic hair. Further conversation revealed more about the nature of her sex anxieties—her misinformation about sex, her belief that she had once had a penis, which had been cut off, etc.—which permitted her counselor to give her correct information.

Her sex anxieties came to light in her relations with the favorite counselor whose function was maternal, rather than with her other favorite whose function, traditionally speaking, was more that of a therapist, since she saw Mary regularly in individual play sessions. On the whole, throughout this period the counselor who conducted the play sessions seemed to represent Mary's sister. By maintaining a stable rapport with this person who took Frances' place, she could counteract somewhat her acute separation fears. She could also assure herself that realizing or talking about her wish to usurp her sister's husband would not interfere with this rapport, since the things she told the maternal counselor at night (the dream about her sister's divorce, her thoughts about intercourse and babies) were independent of her relations with the sister-figure whom she met chiefly in individual sessions.

This separation of roles and feelings paralleled the split in Mary's "day" and "night" views of herself, and the split between her dependent desires and hostile feelings. By day she tried to appear as a relatively well-functioning girl, who was indifferent to everyone, untouched by emotions, and content in at least one relation—that with her "sister." But by night she was her sister's rival, if not her enemy.

But Mary's most pressing concern was still about babies. Could she have a baby? And if not, why not? Could her sister have a baby? How did intercourse feel? Was it like masturbation? And then back again to babies.

What was going on in Mary's mind was revealed, long before she could talk about it, by the marked change that was taking place in her physical appearance. This once fairly agile girl grew very heavy. She combined, strangely, the stance and attitude of a very old woman with the general appearance of a pregnant one. Curiously, her face alone did not quite follow suit, but more and more took on the helpless look of a baby. Her cheeks hung flaccidly, like a newborn infant's (or perhaps an old woman's), and her lip movements become progressively more infantile. Her aggressiveness was no longer expressed so much in shrieking and attacking others as in infantile spluttering and spitting. Her bodily movements, too, seemed to reveal a deep regression. Sometimes they impressed one as being close to the characteristic motions made by very young and inhibited infants; at other times they were like those of a pregnant woman.

This behavior seemed to incorporate, simultaneously, two contradictory tendencies: those of mother and infant. As the mother she wished to satisfy the infantile needs that she, as the baby, felt so deeply.

At the same time Mary began worrying that her sister might become pregnant. As this anxiety grew, her own stance changed even more perceptibly. Her stomach protruded and she walked and stood very much like a woman in the last months of pregnancy. Simultaneously, her hostile anal tendencies were revealed as her rear began to protrude farther and farther, as if she were pushing it into everybody's face. At such times her characteristic expression, "Huh!"[15] sometimes sounded like flatus; at other times it was like the grunting noise that small children make when defecating.

As Mary's body was becoming frozen in this unnatural posture, her conversational inhibitions continued to thaw. Her sex interests reverted from her sister and her sister's husband, to her own body. She invariably opened her conversations with her counselor by wondering if her sister could or would have a baby. Then she would ask for more information about her own body, particularly its various apertures and their functions, and usually wound up by wondering if she herself could have a baby, how old girls must be before they can have babies, whether she might begin menstruating at eleven, and if she could then have a baby immediately.

Perhaps her changing appearance provoked additional worries

---

15. Her "Huh!" connoted angry defiance and was not meant to be a communication. (Much later Mary told us that she used to say "Huh!" at her aunt's when she did not understand what was expected of her or what was going on, and that this so enraged her aunt that she slapped Mary's face each time she said it, no matter how many times it was repeated. But her aunt had expected her to have toilet habits that Mary, in view of her preceding life, could not understand as being demanded of her.) I might at least mention here another frequent exclamation that Mary repeated many times daily. It was an angry "So what!", interspersed with an occasional "So what are you going to do about it?" or "So what are you going to do about me?" Eventually we came to understand that these exclamations expressed Mary's various emotional attitudes, which ranged from malicious defiance, triumph over our inability to help her, and emotional indifference, to utter desperation about the fact that neither she, herself, nor anybody else could do anything to help her.

about whether she was healthy or not, though it was undoubtedly
the nature of her anxieties that originally accounted for the change.
In any case Mary's earlier fears and complaints about specific ailments (pimples, bruises) were now supplanted by the fear that she
might have inherited a sick body. Why did both her parents die so
young? Might her sister die if she had a baby? Was it probable? Did
she (Mary) have a bad heart, a "gall bladder" like her mother, that
could prove fatal? In these fears more than anything else, Mary
showed that she was at least beginning to see herself as part of a
family, and not as a totally isolated person or one related only to
a dead mother.

Her anxieties about herself seemed to herald an ability to view
herself (and her life) within the framework of a family. This was
again in line with Mary's over-all pattern of seeing the bad in life
long before she could recognize its more positive aspects, for her
family, as a unit, first appeared in her mind as a possible source of
disease. Her fears of bodily injury were revived acutely, and this
time were often specifically related to the illnesses of her father
and mother. She claimed that she was dying of a heart attack or of
gall bladder trouble. With every little scratch she screamed, "Help!
Help!" in great despair, just as she had screamed on first coming
to the School.

Without ever revealing it directly, she quite clearly indicated her
belief that she was pregnant. She speculated for hours on whether
she would die of pregnancy, a heart attack, or from "having a gall
bladder." Mary never mentioned her fear that she was actually
pregnant at this time, but she spoke openly and often about being
afraid of menstruation. She neatly combined this with her fear of
masturbation, and, amalgamating the two, said that she was afraid
she would die of "mensturbation."

Whatever Mary experienced was distorted in line with these
dominant fears. Once, in a motion picture, she saw a horse rear up,
and later she claimed that the horse had kicked the girl actress in her
penis, vagina, and breasts. Male and female sex characteristics were
thus combined in one girl, who was injured in all sexual regions.
Mary insisted that she and every other girl had penises. She evinced
considerable anxiety about the danger of falling apart. In play, her
dolls invariably lost their arms and legs. She herself took them
apart, as she explained with anxious glee, "Now the legs come off!
Now the arms come off! Now the body comes off, and now even the
head comes off!" Each exclamation was punctuated by a very
frightened little laugh.

On the streets she kept a sharp lookout for people who had

lost an arm or leg, and spoke at length about how this frightened her. She wanted to know if people were ever born crippled, whether she had been born a cripple, whether doctors can sew limbs back on that have been lost, and so on.

Again and again, she came out with questions about gall bladders. Did everybody have one? How many people die of gall bladder trouble? What had been wrong with her mother's gall bladder? What was wrong with her own? Would she die from it? When?

Her fears that she or the School would be bombed were now connected more closely with infantile experiences. She dreamt about the war. In this dream there was an old lady who threw bombs at people when she got angry, an old lady who resembled her mother at the time when she had been sad and no longer went out. Mary could now openly say that she had been angry that her parents died when she was so young. Either she should have been older, she said, or her parents should have lived longer.

Her phantasies and feelings about her mother's death became more intensive and at the same time more infantile. She asked if her mother would ever come back to life again. She was angry at the doctors who had not helped her parents to get well, and had made them die.

What happens to a corpse? she wondered. What happens to people in hospitals? And to their limbs, if these must be sawed off? Could one find corpses, arms and legs in hospital garbage? How does human meat taste, and does it make people sick? Do doctors ever eat it, and would she herself become ill if she ate human meat? Thus were her cannibalistic phantasies related to her mother's illness.

But if Mary's phantasies were wild, her interest in these subjects was not entirely unrealistic and became a useful means for re-exploring the past. Nearly half a year had passed since her sister's marriage. But this time Mary was not only more willing to express her phantasies, but also to accept realistic explanations in their stead. While still claiming that doctors had killed her father, she asked for the first time for real information about him: what his occupation had been, what he had done on his job. She wanted to understand the connection between the deaths of her father and mother, for she believed that the father's death, which she thought had occurred at her birth, had caused the other.

Her craving for a family of her own increased. Mary was very resentful that Frances had not established a home for her when their mother died and was not caring for her now. But just as she gradually, at least in part, accepted the fact that no one had deliberately killed her father, she began realizing that Frances had been barely eleven years old when their mother died. Mary had given lip service to this fact, but now with a shock she realized that she herself was just about Frances' age at the time of their mother's death. For the first time she was struck by the irrationality of her expectation, during all these years, that Frances would take care of her, when Frances had been just a child. She recalled that Frances had then seemed to her grown-up—very tall, powerful, and experienced.

In her search for knowledge about her early life, Mary derived a great deal of comfort from being told that she had been a healthy baby. She was particularly pleased when we showed her from our records that she had started to talk at nine months and had walked at thirteen. She understood that this was rather early, and became very excited. With a true and appropriate emotion, she exclaimed, "Did I really?"

Yet despite this absorbing interest in piecing her past life together, Mary was still ridden by anxieties. In speaking of her past she talked slowly and carefully. When asked why, she said, "Because sometimes when I talk I say too much." At other times she varied this with, "Because sometimes I ask too much." This was said with a rush, almost as though she did not want it to come out. "I was bad for telling even that," she said.

To counteract her wish to become a baby again and her fear of pregnancy, Mary began acting like a tomboy. For a few weeks she wore only blue jeans, and played only with boys. She learned to ride a bicycle rather quickly, something she had been afraid of even trying before. She also became quite skillful in shop work. And in line with these new efforts to act her age, if not her sex, her class-room learning improved. But just as in the past she had sought quick or easy solutions for intricate difficulties, she again seemed to be pushing herself too hard in trying to convince herself and others of an adequacy she did not possess.

At about that time she had a visit with her sister and brother-in-law. As soon as she read the letter announcing that they would come to see her, her blinking tic reappeared, though it had not been evident for more than two months. Faced with any unmanageable experience, Mary seemed to have to restrict her contact with the world by partially excluding visual experiences. She did not really want to see what her world or family were like.

The visit itself was uneventful and Mary said that her sister did not mean as much to her as she once had, or as much as Mary thought she would. But within a few days there was a strong reaction. Severe night terrors recurred. Mary dreamt of "murder and my sister," with the aggressive elements of the nightmare most impor- tant. At last she could see how she had put herself in her sister's place, how jealous she had been, and how she had wanted the hus- band for herself. She then admitted wondering if Frances would die in childbirth and speculating about whether she might then marry Frances' husband.

Mary could freely admit that she hated the idea that her sister might have a baby, mostly because she wanted to be a baby her- self—Frances' baby. Opening up about these feelings led to an intensification of Mary's babyish ways. She increased her sucking motions until her mouth more than ever resembled a snout. "As you get older you've got to be more of a baby around here," she would say with exaggerated despair, or, "As you get bigger you shrink."

The realization that she would never find in Frances the all- giving mother she longed for was a hard blow to Mary. It was a long time before she could really face up to this disappointment. The dent in her hopes made by the visit led her immediately to despair of being taken care of by anyone. "One of these days you're going to sell me," she would say, or, "You're going to sell me when I leave the School." To all assurances to the contrary, she responded with a knowing smile, "Oh yes, you're going to put an ad in the paper for me when you want to get rid of me." Yet these remarks were not altogether serious. True, they con- veyed her deep and still dominant anxiety, but they also had a quality of playfulness, as though she were teasing her counselor. To this extent, they showed that progress had been made in spite of the upsetting events of the past few months.

When the effects of the visit wore off, Mary seemed to be devel- oping some hope of being able to look out for herself. In June, she planted a garden. She made me guess what she had planted, and I correctly guessed onions. Such understanding evoked a wide and genuine smile from her. She was pleased, and told her counselor about it. For a minute she was thoughtful and quiet, and then finally said, "I just wish I could raise bread and butter, too, in the garden; then I'd have everything I like." She discarded our assur- ance that she would always have enough bread and butter to eat as beside the point. What she really wanted was to be able to take care of herself. That was the issue. Obviously, planting onions was her first step in that direction.

By chance it was in this garden, too, that Mary later showed us how far she had gone in freeing herself from her sister, although she could do this only at the cost of identifying Frances with every- thing bad from her past, as symbolized by her aunt. Several weeks after their disappointing visit together, Frances came by the gardens with her husband, obviously trying to see Mary. Frances stood for some time at the fence, watching, and though Mary saw her she said nothing. Then turning to her counselor she remarked that her aunt was there, watching her. She seemed quite surprised when she had to realize that it was her sister. Strangely enough, or perhaps not so strangely in view of the fact that in the past her sister had often taken the aunt's side against Mary, on this visit Frances acted in a way that fitted the role of the aunt. She disapproved of Mary's pot belly and kept telling her how dirty she was. When Mary excitedly tried to show the visitors her plants, Frances was completely uninterested.

Disappointment in her sister led Mary to become more realistic about the relation to her aunt: she no longer heaped all the blame for her difficulties on her. She was more realistic, too, in understanding the reasons why she had been placed in the School, and why she could not get along with others.

There ensued a period in which Mary intensively worked on her old and new problems. She seemed to prefer seeking help with each problem area from a different person. Still keeping questions about sex independent of all others, she reserved them for nightly discussions with the married counselor who otherwise did not mean much to her. With one of her favorite counselors she wanted only to be babied. With the other she continued talking about her separation from mother and sister. She acted out the unhappy experiences in her aunt's home by discharging massive hostility against still other adults. And finally there were some people, her teacher and the children mostly, with whom she tried to behave more in line with her chronological age. In the classroom, she continued to function adequately and took great pride in her achievement and intellectual progress.

All this extended through the summer and well into the fall. Mary continued her outspoken accusations against the School and against particular counselors, but she also was enjoying infantile pleasures much more. Like many of our children, it took her quite some time before she dared to suck milk consistently from the baby bottle. Some children at first drink carbonated beverages from the bottle; others, like Mary, begin with water, although milk is always offered. At first Mary pressed the water from the nursing bottle into a cup before drinking it (or sucking it through a straw). Later she sucked water directly from the bottle and then, at last, milk. By fall she drank from the bottle with great abandonment and genuine pleasure for ten to fifteen minutes at a time.

Mary's relief at being able to turn to these pleasures in the company of one of her favorite counselors seemed to enable her to tackle her deep anxiety about death and destruction with the other counselor. With this favorite, she expressed her intense fear of dying, and also insisted that we had killed her mother. At the same time, she did not cease trying to fill in the actual events of her past. She asked a great many questions about her relatives and tried to recall important experiences of her infancy. As her outlook on the future grew somewhat less pessimistic, it became possible for Mary to realize that she had once had a family, even if her parents were now dead. For the first time she requested, and was willing to accept, information about the other members of her family circle, her uncles and aunts and their children. She also seemed to feel less need for blocking out the traumatic past with her mother, although she remained tremendously fearful of death, separation, and isolation. These anxieties she not only displayed more openly, but discussed much more freely.

In her play, Mary made it evident that she was dimly realizing how, for her, the whole world had vanished when her mother died, and that ever since she had felt she had nothing to live for. Slowly and very hesitantly she gave voice to the feeling that she, herself, was responsible for her mother's death and that her masturbation might lead to more destruction of herself and perhaps of her whole world.

From these remarks and her various play activities it became increasingly clear that Mary had actually been living under the impression that she had killed her mother. In general, she believed that mothers die of childbirth, and in this way she thought she had provoked her mother's death. In particular, she imagined that while in the womb she had kicked her mother in the gall bladder, which hurt her so badly that the gall bladder ailments developed of which her mother later died.

The tremendous relief Mary experienced in revealing these anxieties reduced the disturbing effect of her dreams, and made falling asleep easier. "I'm sleeping better at night," she said, and gave us her own explanation: "It's because I don't try to forget what I dream about. I wake up and remember it, and then I go back to sleep." Her crabbiness, ill humor, and depressed attitude in the morning also changed. For the first time she talked positively about wanting to grow up and have her body develop. She became interested in wearing feminine clothes and made remarks showing her greater acceptance of being a girl. But, "On Hallowe'en," she said, "I'm going to dress up and act like a boy." In a realistic way, Mary was taking advantage of the outlets that society provides children for acting out their less acceptable tendencies.

Roughly then, she was more hopeful about her future. She talked about eventually finding a family with which she could live —a family that would accept her and raise her as their child. She made up a little story about this:

"Once upon a time there was a dog named Chips and he was lost. He wanted some food so he went to an alley and got a bone and some meat from a garbage can. After that he was cold and tired and wanted a nice bed to sleep in. So he went across the street and scratched on the door. A little old lady opened the door and said, 'How did you get here?' She told her husband and he said, 'Let's put an ad in the paper.' So they did. But no one claimed him, so Chips lived with them for a long time."

Her new feeling was also expressed in her drawings. One day, after trying, first, to make a mask, and then a dog, Mary finally decided that she would like to paint a little girl with curly hair like her own. In drawing the face, she sketched in little marks that resembled tears. Mary had been in the habit of making tears on the faces she drew, but this time when the counselor asked what they were, Mary said that they were freckles. The counselor, reminding her that she used to paint tears, asked if these might not be, too. To which Mary answered, "Yes, I'll make tears on her." Then, "No, I won't. I want a happy girl."

Later she drew another face; sketching the mouth first, she remarked that its corners were turned up "because it's a boy." When questioned about this, Mary said that if she were drawing a girl it would be different. She said that whenever she drew faces the girls' mouths always "sort of turned down" and the boys' "turned up at the corner." Suddenly she seemed to become aware of what she had been saying. She looked up and, as if it were a real revelation to her, said, "But there really isn't any reason, because girls can be happy and smile, too."[16]

Mary became increasingly aware of the connection between her unhappiness and the abrupt way her infantile pleasures had been interrupted. When Mary went to live with her aunt, she had suddenly had to relinquish sucking and messing (she had never given up wetting while her mother lived). The new and lasting unhappiness that began at this time was reflected in her dreams, in which

16. In her self-portraits made during this period, the eyes were wide open, and looked at the world with an empty, devouring stare. The mouth still rested on the bottom outline of the face, with no space left for a chin, and the neck was quite "choked." (Plate 6) Basically the faces were all mouth and eyes; there were never bodies to go with them.

the whole world was on the verge of collapsing and coming to an end. She had told us about this before, but now when we asked her why she dreamt these things she linked them with one particular event. Her association was, "Why did my aunt take my baby bottle away when I came to live with her?"

A few months later Mary chanced to have another visit from Frances and her husband. Though we advised otherwise, the young couple always came to see Mary together, and on this visit Mary immediately threw herself into her brother-in-law's lap, put her arms about his neck, and buried her head on his breast. She took absolutely no heed of her sister, who witnessed the situation helplessly, without knowing what to do and incapable of acting because of her own emotional difficulties. After the visit, Mary asked whether a ten or eleven-year-old girl could marry a man of twenty (her brother-in-law's age), what kind of marriage it might turn out to be, and could they have babies? In other ways, as well, she speculated about taking her sister's place. But this kind of reaction to these visits was short-lived by now and did not seriously hamper Mary's over-all progress.

Interestingly enough, and perhaps tallying with her new ability to enjoy infantile experiences, Mary's next recapture of things past was evoked by a particular smell. Her sensitivity to olfactory sensations has already been mentioned; most odors perturbed her and none pleased her. This time she noticed the disinfectant used in mopping corridors, an odor with which she should have been thoroughly familiar and about which she had repeatedly remarked before. Yet now, sniffing it carefully, she said it reminded her of the bus that had taken her to nursery school when her mother was still alive. Mary remembered how lost she had felt, riding alone to and from the school. Frances would put her on the bus and then call for her after school, because her mother was too sick to leave the house. That an association was also made to the disinfectants used during her mother's illness is suggested by the fact that specific memories of her mother's illness and death were brought out, which had formerly been blurred in Mary's mind. She recalled details of the funeral—how she had cried in the car riding to the cemetery, and the efforts made to comfort her. These were her first positive memories of her relatives.

Mary told us that occasionally, when things got very bad, a neighbor woman from across the hall came over and cooked for them. Mary thought she was very nice. She had even occasionally invited Mary into her apartment to look at her turtles and goldfish. Now, after being with us nearly two and a half years, Mary's fascination with turtles and goldfish was explained. In her inarticulate observation of them, if not in the way she treated them, Mary may have been re-enacting her only benign human contacts outside the home during her first years of life.

Mary remembered that her sister had been the only person who cared for her and their mother, and that whenever Frances went out, either to school or to play, Mary was shut in with her mother. On rare occasions her mother would get up and cook a little. Most of the time she stayed in bed and lay with her face to the wall. Some days there was a little food to be eaten and some days they just went without. It was when they had gone hungry for a day or two, or more, that the lady from across the hall came over and cooked. Mary also remembered, "When I was little I talked to myself. You probably think that's funny, but there was nobody else to talk to. It's true, I talked to myself all the time. I played with myself all the time. There was nothing else to do."

These were not distorted memories, and reviewing these happenings in true perspective helped Mary to understand how unreasonable it was, under these circumstances, to have expected anything more of her sister.

The holiday season preceding Mary's third Christmas in School was particularly difficult for her. She had grown increasingly aware of her desire to be part of a family and was openly jealous of children who were visiting their parents on Christmas. In previous years she had been too hostile and withdrawn to care what other children did or how they lived. Now for the first time she saw quite realistically how much better off children were who had families, and she was most irritable and jealous on that score. Once the children went off on their vacations, however, she enjoyed the holidays quite thoroughly.

Comparing the three Christmases she had spent with us: the first (after six months) found her completely miserable; the second (after eighteen months) showed that she was quite content with her presents but still indifferent to what happened around her. This year, she was keenly aware of events, and although she felt unhappy about her lack of family, she still could enjoy what we offered her.

Although Mary was in relatively good contact through most of the holidays, her moments of being closest to others still occurred in connection with activities associated with primitive pleasures. She was most comfortable and in contact while she sat in the tub or was being dried afterward; to this, she reacted in a very cuddlesome, babyish manner. One day, as Mary sat in the tub, she saw her counselor's keys dangling from a cord around her neck. Mary put them in her mouth and began sucking on them. Then she batted them with her face and caught them with her mouth, very much like a baby in a crib playing with a rattle his mother is holding.

At the end of the holiday season, Mary felt more than ever that she might have a chance at a different life, and a better one. "Why can't we start the whole world over again?" she asked. She had a real wish now to begin afresh and lead a more satisfactory life.

The following month, January, was a quiet one for Mary, but in February she again made serious efforts to come to grips with her central difficulty, her need to have a mother. She declared, "My mother is real," and went on to explain without being questioned, "Just because she's dead doesn't mean she isn't real. It doesn't mean that she doesn't mean anything to me." She seemed ready to relinquish a palpable reality that was impossible for an emotional reality that was possible.

With that, she tried, successfully, to divorce herself somewhat from her mother, to accept her death as a fact of the past and view it less desperately. One day, in talking about her mother's death, she painted a grave. As if to indicate that this was something that happened long ago, she sketched cobwebs in the corners of the painting, and by adding several crosses, transformed it into a picture of a cemetery. Then she pondered the gloominess of her painting, decided to alter it, and heavily painted over the crosses with white, so that only the borders of the cobwebs remained visible; then she added a red flower at the center of each cross, and dedicated the picture to one of her favorite counselors—perhaps in appreciation of the way the counselor, through the years, had helped her overcome her depression step by step (just as Mary had changed the mood of this painting) and had helped her master the loss of her mother. (Plate 7)

Mary could even poke fun at her thoughts of death and destruction if memories of her mother were not directly involved, but only after her depression had been expressed. She sketched two bones crossing each other against a very dark background. Then she painted faces on them, and declared that these were funny "dancing bones." (Plate 8) The ambivalence expressed in such paintings came to Mary's awareness in other contexts and she began to be amazed by some of her behavior. "I get lots of things but I'm still not satisfied!"

These changes in Mary's attitude were reflected in our behavior toward her, and she soon recognized this. She wondered why, when she was nasty to other children or misbehaved in some way, her counselors spoke to her about it. When she had first arrived at the

School, she had behaved much worse and we had barely reacted.
Why the change in our behavior? Mary was trying to understand
not only her own actions and attitudes, but ours, too. More important, she no longer felt that our behavior, and the changes in it,
were arbitrary or devised chiefly to make life miserable for her.
She was beginning to sense that our actions had purpose. While we
had always tried to make the reasons for our actions clear, now
at least she understood us.

Mary's anger was no longer without a goal or unrelated to what
went on around her. She could now point out the provocation readily.
Often her anger was the result of real frustrations and discomforts,
which could be relieved by us.

One day she was playing aimlessly with the typewriter, when
all at once she became purposeful and typed out the following story.

"The Lonely Cactus"

"Once upon a time there lived a little cactus plant and his name was
Prickeley. One day he said to his friend who was very old: I want a
friend to play with. And the old cactus said, why can't you play with me?
Because you are too old. If that is the reason it is very silly said the big
cactus I will find you a friend, and he found him a cactus just like
himself."

In her story, Mary seemed to say that she herself was so prickly
because her only friend, her mother, had been too old and sick. Now,
however, it seemed silly to remain prickly and without play companions for the rest of her life just out of loyalty to her mother.
More important, she also seemed to feel—as in the story—that her
old friend (her mother) was not only permitting but helping her to
enjoy more pleasant things. Memories of the nice times she had
had with her mother—real or imagined—had been recaptured, which
gave her a more positive attitude toward life.

All this while Mary continued to be engrossed with intercourse,
pregnancy, and the process of childbirth. Her body was still con-
torted into the outline of a pregnant woman, but at the same time
Mary often acted like a baby. The use to which she put her body
suggested that she was both the baby and the woman who carried
the baby within her.

Then, suddenly her interest in babies grew until it came to be a
monomaniacal preoccupation. Though never directly expressed, it
seemed to center around the earliest experiences of a baby with his
mother. This interest first showed up quite innocuously in Mary's
apparent attempts to prepare herself for her future role as a mother.
Again, she tried to acquire on short order an adjustment to, and

acceptance of, her present female and future maternal role. This effort to gain a surface adequacy preceded by some time the appearance and mastery of much deeper problems.

As Mary became increasingly concerned about whether or not she would be a good mother, she wondered whether she could care for a baby of her own, since no one had ever adequately cared for her. She began playing with dolls, in the fashion of normal girls her age. She dressed the baby doll, fed it from a bottle, bathed and changed it. Frequently and with anxiety, she asked, "How would a real mother take care of a baby?"

This intense enactment of the care of an infant apparently made it easier for her to relinquish the desire to have a baby right away. One day, as she talked about the pain of childbirth, she said, "Some day I'd like to be married and probably I'd like to have a baby some day, too. But I'd certainly want to wait quite a while, even after I was married, to really get to know my husband. Because you don't want to have a baby and then get a divorce." For Mary, having a baby still meant losing a husband, just as she felt that her own birth had deprived her mother of a husband.

Out of a strange combination of needs, Mary approached the mother-baby theme in every way possible. She rivaled her sister in wanting to be pregnant; she acted out her own deprivation as an infant and her efforts to compensate for it; and perhaps, to some small degree, she was also trying to prepare herself realistically for a future that had now acquired meaning and importance.

She drew a woman lying in bed nursing a baby (supposedly in a maternity ward), and labeled everything to make it very clear that it was she who was nursing the baby. (Plate 9) Mary's insistence on labeling the mother in her pictures with her own name, and her accompanying remarks that suggested she was also the baby in this painting, corroborated what we had suspected from the way she used her body: Mary was expressing a desire to be mother and baby all at once. This painting indicated the impasse in which she found herself. After having stated it, she seemed to try to separate herself, as the baby, from herself, as the mother, or, in other words, to resolve her double personality resulting from being mother and baby at the same time.

Her next picture seemed to be a statement of how she had incorporated her mother, and thus begun her double role of mother and infant. While speaking about her jealousy of children who had parents and of babies who nursed at their mother's breasts, Mary created a pictorial world consisting solely of breast and infant, or one might better say, she drew an infant whose whole world is the nursing breast he is incorporating into himself. (Plate 10) Mary very carefully labeled the composition: "A baby drinking the mother's milk from the breast."

During the rest of her time with us Mary drew and painted a good deal. After having pictured her identity with the mother and shown how this introjection had come about through incorporation, she tried to separate herself from her mother, to see the mother independent from herself. One of the pictures illustrating this was of a woman's body without a head; lines indicated a neck, at the top of the page. The neck was very broad and the upper half of the body was proportionally huge, so that it took up almost the entire page. Most noticeable were the large, pendulous breasts and the relative lack of space for the lower parts of the body; least room was given the legs. Two openings were indicated for vagina and rectum, both in front. Mary retraced these body openings until they stood out very sharply. Finally she drew over the woman's breasts again until they, too, dominated the drawing. (Plate 11)

Mary seemed to be portraying only what the nursling sees of his mother—the breasts turgid and enlarged, the suggestion of a neck—and what the small child would be most interested in exploring, the body openings.

On another sheet of paper she drew a man's body. Here Mary could be more objective and hence the portrait was somewhat more complete. There was a head, all the facial features were indicated, and the proportions were better. Then she drew a male and a female dog, and put eight nipples on the female.[17] As before, she heavily outlined the nipples and penis on the dogs. These drawings (as well as her remarks) showed her tendency to identify the nipples of the female dog with the penis of the male. Then she said, "They go outdoors like that, don't they? They don't have to wear clothes." This indicated another possible reason for her fascination with animals, namely, their freedom to satisfy instinctual desires.

Then Mary dropped this type of painting for some time. Eventually, after making elaborate preparations, she took a new set of paints and paper and announced, "This one I'm going to paint good." She thumbed through various books as if looking for a subject to copy, but found no pictures that suited her. Discarding that idea, she set to work on her own with great intensity, and spontaneously re-created the world as it appears to the baby: breasts, and directly over them, the mother's mouth and eyes—nothing else. She must

17. Perhaps she gave the she dog eight nipples because her counselor had to serve eight children.

have delved this from the depths of her unconscious for no later experience could be drawn upon to explain this picture of a face seen so immediately above the breasts. And as if to emphasize other primitive sensations belonging to the earliest period of life, she put finger marks all around the border of the picture, which suggested her fascination with touch as her fingers groped for her mother's breasts and face. (Plate 12) In her earlier picture of the female body she had left off the head, probably because she was still unable to remember her mother's face. Here it seemed she had recaptured her memory of it.

A few days later Mary again broached the question of lactation. First she asked about the various functions of the glands, and then announced that she would draw a baby smiling because it was drinking from the mother's breast. But all she drew was the breast, and in spite of her reference to a smiling baby she did not draw it. When the picture was finished, she pondered a while about what to label it, and finally decided on: "A woman's breast getting ready for nursing." Then, reflecting on her new knowledge, she said that this was not really quite right, because not only was the breast getting ready to care for the baby but the mother's whole body. And she wound up by drawing a baby in the uterus.

As Mary drew, she talked about her future. Lately, she said, she had thought a lot about what she wanted to do when she grew up. She thought that being a stenographer might be a good profession. We told her that these were pleasant and perfectly reasonable thoughts, but that she had plenty of time, and it might be more important to decide what kind of person she wanted to be than the particular kind of job she would hold. "Well," she said, "all I want is to be just a plain person." When asked what a "plain person" was, she said, "Well, no. I guess I'd rather be a nice person."

Conversations about childbirth, having a baby, how babies grow up, and so on, continued for weeks. Then Mary's interest shifted to ailments and deformities again, but with a new emphasis on how they could be overcome. She wondered why, since she had been a healthy baby, she had still undergone very unpleasant experiences as an infant. Once, after deep thought, she blurted out, "Which things are more important, the physical things that happen to you or the things that happen to your feelings?" With further talk, Mary herself arrived at the conclusion that both are important, but although we can do relatively little about permanent physical damage, there is a lot we can do about our emotions.

Early in April, Mary determined to write "a book about my life." Bringing pencil and paper to a little table, she said, "I'm going to call the story 'My Life.' " And she wrote at the top of the paper, "My Life, by Mary." She next decided, "My life is different at different times; it better be in chapters. The first chapter will be 'When I am Little.' " Thereafter, during a number of sessions, Mary dictated her life to her counselor. The following are excerpts:[18]

CHAPTER I. *When I am Little*

When I was little (I was bad, wasn't I?), about three years old, my mother died. Before my mother died and when I was a little baby about nine months old my daddy died. Then I went to live with my aunt and she had two children. She had my mother's dresser, and me and my sister Frances had my mother's bed.

After about three or two years when I was with her I wanted a dog, but my aunt didn't care for dogs very much so we didn't get one. So there was this little dog sitting on the back porch of two little colored girls and they were not very nice to him (this is all true). So I stole him. Then they were looking for him for a couple of days. They came to my house and they asked if we had seen their little dog and I told my aunt when I first found the dog that I found him. But I really didn't. So when they came, my aunt said, 'Is this your dog?' and they said, 'Yes.' And then my aunt knew that I stole him, because after they took it I told her why. (Do you believe me that this is really true?)

CHAPTER II. *When I am Older*

I lived with my aunt for about five and a half years. Then a case worker took me to visit a school before I went to the Orthogenic School that I will talk about later. My sister went with lots of boys that she liked but most of them my aunt didn't like. One day my sister was with Joe who is now her husband and when my sister came home from seeing Joe my aunt kicked her out of the house and told her not to come back. Then when she was gone I was very sad because my sister told me that she would come back and get me but she didn't.

CHAPTER III. *The School I am Now At*

After the case worker took me to visit the School I came the next day to live there. When I was at the School for about a month you took me wading and I caught a turtle. It was a mud turtle (do you remember this?). Then we had a party and there was puzzles for all of us.

CHAPTER IV. *The Orthogenic School—All About It*

In the girls' dorm there is one room which I and Charlotte sleep in. Then there is six other beds for other people because the house used to

---

18. Her asides to the counselor are indicated in parentheses.

be . . . (what did it used to be?) oh, yes, a minister's home, and the School used to be part of the church. There are only eight girls in the entire School (that's right, you're a woman) and there are twenty-six boys.

She gave a detailed listing of all the rooms, the groups, equipment, etc.

The fifth chapter Mary dictated was entitled *The School Rooms,* and the sixth *The People in the School;* both were concerned largely with enumerations. She became somewhat more personal in the seventh chapter: *Counselors of the Orthogenic School.* It seemed that she needed to enumerate these facts and names more or less mechanically in order to separate the unpleasant past from the more satisfying present. After the seventh chapter Mary requested that the whole history be read back to her, and then she went on dictating:

CHAPTER VIII.   *Counselors That I Like Best*

The counselor that I like best in the girls' dormitory is Joan. (I'll go get my bottle, OK? I'll be right back.)

At this juncture, Mary went to fill her baby bottle; returning, she asked, "Will this bottle last as long as I live? If I broke it could you get a new one?" By this action Mary established the connection between two facets of her School life: her real attachment to her favorite counselors and the infantile pleasures she had rediscovered and was still enjoying. But apparently she was not sure that either (or both) of these satisfactions would last a lifetime, or that response to her physical and emotional needs was permanently assured. Going on with her dictation, she referred to Joan. "I like her best because I know her better than any of my other counselors." And then, not wanting to hurt anyone's feelings, she mentioned the names of two new staff members and explained that she did not know them well, yet.

Mary was now ready to stop dictating because she had nothing more to add to her story. With some hesitation, as if she felt obliged to, she remarked that she liked most of the other children, but now she was finished; and then she sat sucking quietly on the bottle for some time.

The writing of her life history seemed to be another effort to bring order into her life, to understand its sequence. But Mary still had difficulty in establishing a continuity; her life had been divided into separate parts, which had forced her, as it were, to divide the story into disconnected chapters.

By the end of this period, Mary was still occasionally losing her temper and screaming, but she explained to her counselor that she never screamed at people she trusted and knew well, and with whom she felt secure. This was true. It was when her anxiety was aroused by her fear of new people, and what they might do to her, that she reverted to fits of screaming. She also said, "Sometimes I just have to. I feel like screaming and I can't help it." At first she would not elaborate beyond saying that this happened when she was very angry. When asked at whom she was angry, she replied, "At everybody." Then she corrected this to, "No, maybe not everybody. I just don't know who I'm angry at."

Part of Mary's concern about losing her temper was motivated by her thoughts of the future. She hoped to live with a family when she left the School, and feared that she might scream at them and arouse their dislike. She was afraid that maintaining control might prove especially difficult in the first week, before she got to know them; once she knew and trusted them, she would no longer have to lose her temper. On the other hand, she felt we would select the right family for her, and that once she got to know them, things would go fairly well. In this way Mary was slowly making ready to leave the School and live in a more natural environment, which was, incidentally, in line with the agency's desires.

Despite the rather empty statements Mary made about other children in her autobiography, they, too, had become more important to her. She was now not only getting along with them better, but really enjoying their company. At the same time she was more aware that some of the children disliked her, and that she had done things to provoke them. She no longer screamed at the children because of this, though she still reacted angrily by saying that she was glad nobody liked her. Such remarks were less frequent, however, than her genuine feelings of misery at not being appreciated. Bursting into tears, she sometimes said how unhappy she was because other children did not like her as much as she wanted them to.

In this period of growing interest in human relations, Mary suddenly noticed that she had never decorated the walls of her room with anything but objects, animal pictures, or maps. She now replaced most of these with pictures of people, particularly mothers and babies.

Mary's habitual, "Give me something. Buy me toys," was too ingrained to cease at once, but one day she did suddenly stop herself in the middle of such a request, and looking about the room, said, "Well, I really wouldn't know where to put it if you'd give me something. I've so many things, I really don't need anything more."

Her frightening dreams were now populated by protective figures —those to whom Mary was most closely attached. She actually re-dreamt some of her nightmares, and gave them reassuring endings. For example, she again dreamt that bombs were falling on the School, but this time she was wearing a gas mask that had been supplied by her favorite counselors and myself. We saw to it that nothing happened to her, in spite of the war. Mary's understanding of the changing nature of her dreams led to conversations about other matters that still roused fear. "I know I'm afraid of being sick and dying, and I'm afraid about my body being hurt. But I know you'll take care of me." When we asked why she still harbored these misgivings when she had not once been ill in the nearly three years' time she had spent with us, she said, "Well, it's because my mother and daddy died. I might get sick too."

This is not to say, of course, that all her anxieties about herself or misgivings about her past disappeared. But Mary could occasionally joke about them and find the joke funny. One morning, for example, she asked her counselor if anything on a man's penis ever had to be cut off. She was referring to circumcision, which was explained to her. Except for this, the counselor added that she had never known of anyone's having anything cut off his penis, at which Mary giggled and said, "Yes, me." This was not an anxious laughter, but an effort to gain mastery over her castration anxiety through joking about it. A bit later she returned to this conversation, apparently to reassure herself that she need not feel too bad about not having a penis. "Never mind," she said. "As soon as I grow up I'm going to get married and have a baby."

It was most untimely that just now the fear Mary had so often conjured up was about to come true: Frances became pregnant. It seemed that nothing could ever go smoothly in the life of this child. Her early life had been split into isolated fragments that prevented her from reaching integration, and her rehabilitation at the School was twice set back by outside events. The first serious setback came with Frances' marriage and the things it reactivated. Now her life was to be once more unsettled by her sister's pregnancy. To avoid any unnecessary anxiety we delayed telling Mary about it until the end of April, when the pregnancy was in its fourth month and there was little likelihood that it would not be completed.

DISCUSSION

It was only after Mary had lived with us for nearly two and a half years, that we were able to fit our observations—particularly the material which had recently come to light—into a tentative explanation for her baffling behavior, its possible origin and meaning. Two different sets of factors, each of them complex, seemed to have contributed to the central features of her disturbance.

The first had to do with the death of her parents, and particularly her mother. With this, Mary felt that her life had become totally empty and hopeless, and could never yield any satisfactions for her. Worst of all, she was convinced that she, herself, had brought about her misery by killing her mother through her uncontrolled hostility (kicking her mother in the gall bladder). This burden of guilt she felt she had to carry for the rest of her life. In retaliation, she expected to be equally destroyed. She should suffer as she had made her mother suffer—hence her terrific fear that one of her little real or imagined ailments would utterly destroy her. This was also a clue to her melancholic withdrawal from the world and retirement to her bed. She deserved nothing but to be sick in bed and uncared for, as she, through her imaginary kicking, had caused her mother to be sick in bed and uncared for. Moreover, only by staying quietly in bed, or remaining inactive, could Mary make sure that she would not add further to her guilt by destroying other persons through her hostile actions. Such stern repression of her hostility was necessary to prevent her from being put up for sale, kicked, or otherwise hurt, in retaliation for her having kicked her mother. After all, it had been her own act of hostility, so Mary imagined, that had led to her mother's dying and therefore to Mary's being put out of the home.

This guilt and anxiety, which had originally been unconscious but eventually became conscious or semi-conscious, was the underlying dynamic of Mary's disturbance. Superimposed on it was the second set of equally complex factors. They seemed to originate less in unconscious feelings of guilt, worthlessness, and the impulse to destroy (with its resulting fear that she would be destroyed in retaliation), than in the actual experiences of her disjointed life.

For quite some time we had been aware that it was very characteristic of Mary to keep her relations with various staff members separate and distinct, and to seem like a different person in each relation. Equally characteristic was the way the nature of her relation to one and the same person could so abruptly change. This may have been a function of her efforts to live out again the various phases of her past. Children appeared as sister figures, cousins, and the like. A counselor might be cast in the role of the sister who at one moment provides satisfactions, in the next, competes for the mother's attention, and at still another time is the sexual seducer. A second counselor might sometimes be the giving mother, and, on other occasions, the melancholic, neglecting mother. A third adult might represent the hoped-for lady from across the hall, who brought Mary food or invited her in to play, only to rouse a fear that this new, helpful person might leave just as unpredictably as that other lady had appeared and disappeared in Mary's infancy. By becoming suitable targets for the discharge of Mary's hatred of her aunt, other adults helped Mary to master the rejection she had experienced from her.

Most, if not all, of these real people in Mary's life had been utterly inconsistent in their relations with her. The mother was at one moment giving and at another indifferent, if not openly depriving. The sister would care for Mary and then neglect her for play companions, boy friends, and finally a husband; sometimes she sided with Mary against the aunt and sometimes she reversed her support.

Even Mary's aunt was not solely rejecting and punitive. In reality, she did provide food and lodging, if only at a price; but still, Mary might have had to dread starvation without it. The uncle, likewise, was at one moment ready to leave Mary in peace (nothing needs to be done about the child's misbehavior), and at another to castrate her (threaten to cut her thumb off).

To make matters worse, the various episodes in Mary's life had been so radically disconnected from one another that she had never been able to see them in any intelligible sequence, without which she could not develop an integrated attitude toward life—much less an integrated personality.[19] Hence her schizoid behavior, with its baffling shifts from one mood to another, without any visible reason for the change or any sensible transition from one form of behavior to the next, paralleled the way her life had been fragmented, and its events isolated from one another. At last, however, we began to understand, from what we had learned directly from her and from her reactions to us, that Mary's life had been divided, mainly, into four distinct, emotional phases of development and experience, which seemed to her to be wholly disconnected (unless, as mentioned before, these strokes of fate were seen as punishment for a terrific misdeed).

The first was the short, rather benign period of early infancy, before her father's death, when the family was still relatively happy and well integrated. During this period she probably received ample gratification from her mother.

A period followed that may have been slow in evolving but was

---

19. This, incidentally, was an added reason for Mary's clinging to the idea that she was guilty of having killed her mother. Only as punishment for such a misdeed could these inconsistent experiences make sense to her.

probably fully developed when Mary was one, or one and a half, years old. This was the time when her mother became progressively more melancholic and withdrawn from the world and failed to provide any regularity for her baby; at odd moments she would pick her up and feed her, but for the most part she remained unresponsive to her crying or whining. While Mary's needs were barely met, at least no demands were made on her for emotional maturation or socialization. Thus, on the one hand, there were moments of gratification in Mary's life, which were followed by long and irregular periods of deprivation; on the other hand, virtually no demands were made on her at all. Both sets of experiences may have characterized her second phase.

This period of isolation was fully recovered later, though at the time we could recognize it only in dim outline. It was the period when Mary's mother turned away from her, not only figuratively, but literally. Most of the time she faced the wall, with her back to her baby and the world, as Mary was so often to turn her back on us. Mary had relived this later by never looking at us—even when addressing someone she averted her eyes and buried her head in her counselor's lap or arms. The tremendous anxiety with which Mary started each day, her wish not to wake up, her morning complaints of various hurts, all may have been the consequence of her anguish when, as a baby, she was not taken care of in the morning, was not fed by the melancholic mother who remained indifferent to her wailing.

The third phase of Mary's life began with the trauma of her mother's death. Suddenly she was confronted with an extremely demanding environment in which a great deal of regularity was expected of her, the kind of regularity and proper behavior for which nothing had prepared her. The fact that her emotional needs were going virtually unsatisfied, when coupled with the severe, punitive attitudes of her aunt, awoke in Mary, who had been so little socialized, an infantile rage. This, in turn, provoked more punitive action by her relatives. But, on the other hand, she was now regularly and adequately fed, housed, and clothed, which made her not only hate her aunt but also fear her displeasure.

The fourth and, so far, last period of Mary's life began with her arrival at the School.

Only one person appeared in all four phases of Mary's life. Frances was the only visible link, so to speak, that tied the periods together or could even prove to Mary that they had ever really existed and were not just figments of her imagination. This explains the tremendous importance of Frances for Mary over and above the *bona fide,* though ambivalent, relation existing between them. It also suggests why any change in Frances' life (marriage, and her subsequent pregnancy) was so shattering to Mary. Since her sister was the only contact that in any way bound her life together, any radical change in Frances' life put Mary's very existence on the verge of falling apart again.

In their common desperation the two children had been constantly thrown together, even in the same bed. There they may have tried to find comfort in one another, although only at the price of overwhelming guilt-feelings, particularly on Frances' part. As the elder of the two she had, after all, enjoyed a more sheltered and pleasant childhood and was, therefore, more socialized. It was in bed, too, that Mary witnessed Frances' suicidal attempts, which may well have reinforced her guilty memories about her melancholic, dying mother.

Here, then, was the clue to why, in one of her first statements to us about herself, she had called herself a murderer. In the first dream she had told us about, she had killed Frances because Frances had kicked her in her sleep, as (she thought) she had kicked her mother—this aroused such anger in Mary that she wished to kill Frances, not because Frances kicked her, but because through so doing, she reminded Mary of her belief that she had destroyed her mother. That Frances kicked her may have meant to Mary that Frances knew Mary had killed their mother and wanted to punish Mary in kind. That Frances thus seemed to give truth to Mary's delusion, was the unforgivable sin for which Mary wished to murder her.

Mary was fully convinced that whoever kicks is killed in punishment; whoever gets kicked dies. Therefore Mary had no hope for herself, since she had deprived herself of her mother by kicking her and eventually would be punished for this misdeed by being killed. One of the proofs that her reasoning was correct lay in her aunt's punitive attitude, which Mary understood as punishment for having killed her mother.

It probably took a strange combination of real experiences to force Mary to hold on to her mother so desperately. Loyalty, she may have felt, required that she make no new friends in life, and that she reject the world as her mother had. The way Mary had so abundantly enjoyed certain infantile satisfactions (such as masturbation, wetting) and the relatively few demands made on her while her mother was still alive, also kept Mary hopelessly bound to her mother as the sole person who had ever supplied her with at least some pleasures, though never in sufficient quantity to quench her all-pervasive desire for more. Throughout most of Mary's life, therefore, her mother had seemed to be the only person who could provide satisfactions; as proof, all pleasures had been withdrawn when her mother died (for example, her aunt had taken away the baby bottle). Mary's hopes that other people—her sister or aunt—might offer her satisfactions always ended in disappointment. Mary's susceptibility to sexual experiences with men probably arose from the same wish: that they might fulfill her needs. But this had only led to further disappointment and severe punishment, as well.

With this reconstruction we can understand how and why the dead mother's hold on Mary could at last begin to loosen. Once Mary could accept the infantile pleasures we offered, her mother ceased to be the only possible source of these satisfactions. The less indispensable her mother became, the less extreme loyalty to her seemed required of Mary. As she was well cared for at the School, and nothing untoward happened to her, Mary began to think that perhaps she would not be destroyed for having killed her mother, and even began to doubt that she had killed her. By the same token, her mother seemed less powerful, and therefore less threatening, now that other people, apparently, could offer Mary the same gratifications, more consistently. Hence, in her story about the prickly cactus, Mary was able to picture her mother as approving her search for friends of her own age, including even the counselors, who, compared with her mother, seemed to be Mary's contemporaries.

No child could have mastered without special help the inconsistencies and ambivalent relations that filled Mary's life. She had never enjoyed adequate periods of peace and quiet, and she had experienced so much deprivation, that she had never been able to accumulate enough emotional energy for integrating her experiences. Events had been far too unpleasant to offer her sufficient incentives for trying to master a life that seemed to promise no rewards for coming to terms with it.

Any one of these factors, any one of these inconsistent relations with significant persons, would probably have produced a neurotic or delinquent child. Their bewildering combination led to the chaotic, schizophrenic-like personality and behavior that characterized Mary for the greater length of her stay at the School. No matter what the occasion, all her reactions to reality were dictated by the pressures originating in her previous life experiences. At the same time, to make matters even more confusing to us, and to her (because she could not explain her actions either), restitutive efforts of her ego were also at work. These restitutive efforts again had little connection with the external reality of the moment, but went back to any one of the various phases of her past experience or, rather, to her distorted view of them.

These factors led to a complete lack of consistency in Mary's relations with adults or children at the School. To every contact, she responded with a different pattern, depending on which phase of her past was being reactivated at the moment. Since this was unpredictable, and since there was little connection between what we did and how she reacted, our behavior toward her, despite our best efforts, was tinged with a certain feeling of not being to the point. Hence, working with her was frustrating and emotionally exhausting. Mary, who would never commit herself, always required a total commitment from us. A minor example of this was the way she asked questions, where other children would express themselves. She forced us to make statements or seek response from her, which we would have preferred deferring until she could speak on her own.

Only after Mary had been two and a half years at the School, and had, herself, begun to integrate her past experiences, understand them, and develop appropriate reactions to them, did she become somewhat oriented in the present, so that she reacted appropriately to the adults around her and made it possible for us to form really strong emotional ties to her. In attempting to socialize herself, Mary at last permitted us to invest our own emotions more deeply in her. We could finally drop our deliberate and conscious efforts to help her and could begin to establish a freer, two-way relation that had a consistency and uniqueness of its own.

At about that time a second projective test was given to Mary, this time a TAT. Her first reactions to many of the pictures characteristically expressed deep anxiety and helplessness. Some of the stories she made up, particularly those covering topics that were not immediately related to her past life but were conditioned by the pictures themselves, were fairly realistic and pervaded by a somewhat optimistic outlook on the future. Other stories that expressed an initially gloomy reaction to the pictures, were followed by inventions showing how much Mary now remembered of her early life, and how much it preoccupied her. If a story revolved about themes of the past, however, it was nearly always gloomy.

There was an interesting sequence in the stories Mary spun. The tales she made up to the first pictures shown her were more realistic; they dealt more literally with the content of the pictures and they contained associations arising from her current experiences. Later on in the test, as Mary became swamped by material and feelings originating in her past (apparently induced by the process, similar to free association, of inventing the stories), the pictures' content became less important for her imaginative production. The phantasy-material that emerged related ever more closely to her earliest history; at the same time, her outlook on life became progressively more pessimistic insofar as could be judged from the stories.

Mary's new achievements, therefore, such as her ability to master tasks (learning in school, understanding her feelings) and to view life more optimistically, still seemed restricted to the rather thin layer of her current life. This layer seemed to give way under serious emotional pressure, particularly from emotions originating in the past; these could still engulf her in deep depression and hopeless anxiety, though she often tried her best to break through with more positive hopes for the future.

The following excerpts from Mary's stories may illustrate these impressions.

About the first picture[20] Mary said, "He got this for his birthday or something and didn't know how to play it, and he's going to take lessons. He's puzzled because he didn't know what it was. Then he was happy; he's going to learn how to play real good."

There was an indication here of an initial inability to do or enjoy things, but there was also conviction that she would be able to learn how. The ending was optimistic about the future.

The relative security with which Mary attacked the first story wavered a bit with the second picture.[21] But after a question expressing momentary uncertainty, Mary recovered her poise and invented a story appropriate to the picture's content: "What's all this? She's coming home from school and she sees some people working on their garden. She wants to know what they're going to plant. And they said they were going to plant corn and when some of it was grown they gave it to her and her family and then she ate it and came back and gave them some cookies she baked. That's all; all right?"

This story related to Mary's wish to be able to supply her own necessities, particularly food. Since the girl in the story succeeded in doing this, the story might be classified as rather cheerful in outlook, although only on the level of bare necessities and the most primitive (oral) satisfactions.

Mary reacted to the third picture[22] with feelings of deep helplessness, anxiety, and inability to comprehend. Perhaps these emotions were evoked by the picture's subject, or by the primitive associations with food prompted by the previous picture. It may

---

20. For a description of this picture see footnote No. 7 on page 58.
21. For a description of this picture see footnote No. 31 on page 122.
22. Picture three (GF) shows a young woman standing with downcast head, her face covered with her hand. Her left arm is stretched forward against a wooden door.

also have been possible that Mary's ability to connect the content of the pictures with the present had been exhausted. At any rate, Mary's story seemed conditioned by recollections of her mother. All Mary said was, "Oh, help, help! How come she's doing that, do you know? She's been working real hard and is all exhausted and tired and she is so tired she can hardly walk. She's going to the house and lay down to sleep. Then she gets up and makes supper and then she feels better. And that's all about this one."

In the light of Mary's desire to be a boy, which was still quite marked at the time of the test, we decided to supplement the cards with some that were originally devised for boys. We therefore presented her next with picture three (male).[23] The figure was easily recognized as a boy, but although Mary seemed to realize this, she changed it to a woman, perhaps so that she could continue with recollections of her mother. Her story: "She's crying. Is it a man? A lady, and she was real tired, fell against the bench and her keys dropped. And a man picked them up, carried her in the room and put her in bed and when she woke up she said, 'Where am I?' And he said, 'In your room.' And she said, 'How did I get there?' And he said, 'I carried you, because you fell.' And then he left her alone and she went to sleep again and then she woke up and made supper for her husband and children. Because her children were in school. And then they came home and she told them the story and they said they were very sorry. And so she took them to the movie. It was 'Connecticut Yankee' and 'Ichabod and Mr. Toad.' "

This ending seemed to reveal an effort to deny the validity of her past, to connect or counteract unpleasant recollections with pleasant experiences of the present, and to seek, if not a happy ending, at least one that implied a family life (Mary had seen these movies recently).

Mary's response to the fourth picture[24] was: "What is this lady doing? She likes this man and he wants to go away to work and she's trying to tell him not to go but he has to. And he's trying to get away and she doesn't want him to go. He has to go to work and if he doesn't get there on time he'll lose his job and not get any money. And he comes home and says that he's going to try the job for about two months and see how it is. And she says no. And he says he has to go get money. And she agrees and then they get married and get children and live happy ever after."

In her story, Mary was moving farther away from the actual memories that prompted her preceding stories (the mother who was

---

23. For a description of this picture see footnote No. 8 on page 58.
24. For a description of this picture see footnote No. 9 on page 58.

tired, fell down, and was carried to her room while the children were in school). Instead, she drew on what must have been hearsay to her, namely, her mother's reluctance to let her father go to work and his difficulties in finding and holding a job.

Following these recollections of life with her mother, the fifth picture[25] seemed to inspire material relating to her sister's marriage, at least insofar as sexual relations between Mary and a brother (brother-in-law) were projected into it. Her story went: "Oh, this one's going to be hard! She's come into her house. She's looking into the room and sees somebody in there and then she's real puzzled and she walks in and the light is turned on and it's her brother. And he hugs and kisses her. Don't write that! [Laughs] And then they go to bed and in the morning he tells her he had to go back to the war and he goes. And he says the reason he came when the lights were turned off was because I was tired from driving on the bus and the train. And then he says I'll come back again some time. And then that's all." At this juncture Mary got up and got herself some candy.

That Mary was dealing here with phantasies she herself could not accept was suggested by her request that some of her remarks not be written down (the stories were being taken in shorthand) and by her anxious laugh. Perhaps because these phantasies were unacceptable to her, the story had no happy ending. The brother-lover leaves; he may come back and he may not.

The topics of Mary's stories now became increasingly gloomy and hopeless. Her first association to one of the next pictures was, "This is a man—he's talking to his old grandfather because he's going to die pretty soon." About another picture: "Oh, help! This man's going away to the war and he kisses his wife good-bye. And she doesn't want him to go and she's real sad." Again about another picture: "What's this? She's thinking that this is how she's going to look when she gets old and then her grandmother comes and says she probably will." And still another story: "What's this? This lady, she's going to Riverview [an amusement park] and she goes on the roller coaster and she's afraid. Oh, have I got a headache!" Thus the thought of a trip to Riverview, which most children enjoyed, in Mary created anxiety and a physical symptom.

Mary's story about the blank card (picture sixteen) involved fighting (boxing) with a parent figure, being lost, married, having children, and then being sold because she was mean; however, Mary projected a more hopeful outlook about the future at the end.

---

25. For a description of this picture see footnote No. 10 on page 59.

Her story: "Oh, scare, scare! [Throughout the telling of this story Mary was agitated and squirmed about.] Once upon a time there was a dog. And his name was Boxer. And he was a boxer. I don't want to look at this. [She put aside the blank card.] And he knew how to box with his master real good. [Mary began chewing her gum frantically and blowing big bubbles.] So they named him Boxer. And one day he got lost and he couldn't find his way home. And he went up to a policeman and howled. And the policeman looked at his collar and saw his address and took Boxer home. And every day he saw the policeman he ran up to him, and the policeman always gave him some candy or something. [Mary reached for some candy.] And then Boxer had puppies with the other boxer in the house. One was a boy and the other was a girl. And the puppies were real cute. And then the boxers' master and the mistress didn't want to see the puppies, so they bought some kennels. And then they got more and more doggies and pups and then after a while some of the pups were mean and didn't want to live in kennels. And so they were sold. And the boxer was happy that he had some of his children to play with, and he lived happily ever after."

To picture seventeen (boys)[26] her reaction was, "Oh! He's naked, isn't he? Help, help! I can't think of anything. He's a burglar. Is that all right? He's a burglar and somebody stole his clothes and he was escaping out of the house so that nobody would see him without his clothes. So he ran and the police caught him and they put him in jail and gave him some jail clothes. And that's all."

To picture eighteen (girls)[27] Mary's story was: "What's this woman doing? Help, help! Is she strangling her? Will Dr. B. get mad if I say that she's strangling her? [She was assured that lots of people see that picture the same way she did.] This woman's mad at her daughter because she went out with a man that the lady didn't like. So she strangled her. When the man found out, he took that mother to the police and they put her in the electric chair. And that's the end."

And so it was: for reasons that can be understood from this last story, Mary was unwilling to go on with the test.

Emotional Rebirth

IN VIEW OF Mary's considerable progress and her genuine desire to live with a family, the agency and the consulting psychiatrist felt

26. For a description of this picture see footnote No. 33 on page 123.
27. This picture shows a woman with her hands squeezed around the throat of another woman whom she appears to be pushing backwards across the banister of a stairway.

that Mary should leave the School in order to experience family
life while she was still young. We at the School should have preferred to have Mary stay with us at least another year or two, since
we felt that her ego was by no means sufficiently strong yet to cope
adequately with life. The agency, however, had started a program
of special treatment homes, and believed that in one of these Mary
would find sufficient protection and adequate treatment to meet her
still unfilled needs. At the same time, she would be in a more family-
like setting. A compromise was reached, according to which Mary
was to leave the School in June, at the end of both the academic
year and her third year with us.

When we learned of Frances' pregnancy, however, these plans
had to be changed. We felt strongly that Mary should remain with
us until the baby was born so that we could help her with her reactions.

From the moment Mary learned that her sister was going to
have a baby her concern about pregnancy and pregnant women
reappeared in much intensified form. Her fears of desertion and
utter deprivation returned in full force, but this time they did not
lead to severe depression and isolation. Mary did go back to screaming, but only rarely. She again said that she wanted to be a baby,
and even insisted that she was one. But most characteristic of the
ensuing months was her feeling that she could not cope with the
tasks confronting her. This was expressed in her recurrent cry of
"help, help" and "scare, scare," which had been frequent in the
past but had been virtually dropped from her vocabulary in recent
months. Confronted with an overwhelming emotional experience that
she could not master, her ego again lost its power to exercise control.

Once more, Mary was afraid that no one would ever care for
her and that she would never be able to look after herself. As she
went to bed one night, she called out to her counselor, in real
misery, that she wanted her mother, and someone to cook for her
and feed her. "If I had a mother she'd cook for me, but I don't
have a mother." When we offered to cook with her or to give her
food at these times, she usually refused. On the few occasions when
she did accept food, it seemed to afford but little relief to her feelings of deprivation. In this time of stress her longing for her mother
came back in strength and again the mother was identified with the
chief service she either had rendered Mary or Mary had wished for,
that is, giving food.

While during the preceding months Mary's posture had become
somewhat straightened out, she now reassumed, even more than
before, the look of a pregnant woman. Indeed, as her unconscious
preoccupations expressed themselves mainly through changes in her

body, she insisted that she really was carrying a baby in her stomach. Sometimes she thought that she was carrying her sister's baby. Unable to master the impact of the new event realistically or through higher forms of defense, and motivated by her deep oral fixation, she tried to master it through incorporation. But incorporating the baby, and perhaps her sister as well, made the ego boundaries she had only recently established again become fluid.

Restitutive efforts were not absent. Consciously, for much of this time, she tried dealing with the new situation realistically. She asked frequent questions about what it is like to be an aunt. But these conscious efforts only led to another deep anxiety, as her fears about being an aunt revived her fears about whether she would be a good mother. The two anxieties now merged, and acquired a new and dreaded meaning. She was about to become the aunt of a child of whom she was intensely jealous and whom she hated, even as she felt her aunt had hated her. In the old days, she had hated her aunt in return and had wished to kill her. But now that Mary, herself, was to become an aunt who hated her niece, her old wish to destroy the aunt meant now that she had to wish to destroy herself.

The somatic changes Mary observed in herself, as well as the emotional turmoil she was experiencing, re-evoked additional anxieties about her physical well-being. But here again, as in her realistic questions about being an aunt, Mary was able to question us intensively about how she could remain healthy.

Probably because the news of the coming baby had heightened Mary's jealousy and hence her feelings of hostility, she grew more worried about whether she would be able to restrain these emotions. She seemed most afraid of reverting to her violent attacks upon other people, which might have made her fear she would lose control when confronted with the baby. One day, as she watched a television program (which children do only rarely at the School) Mary remarked to her counselor that the purpose of looking at television was "to learn how to kill people." Since she got no reply to this provocative remark, Mary altered it to, "Well, maybe really *not* to kill people." She, herself, seemed to be wondering whether her ambivalent desires would lead her toward discharge or integration.

Mary was very curious now about why people might want or not want to take care of babies and children. Again she began by uttering recriminations against her aunt, although, by and large, this kind of accusation had now become an old stand-by, a more or less empty rationalization for not mastering her difficulties. Then she said, "Cruel people hurt other people," and wanted to know if this was correct. When told that it was, she asked, "Was I cruel when I hit other children?" The counselor asked Mary what she thought about it. Mary slowly admitted that she thought her actions could be called cruel and that at the time people had probably considered her very mean.

After this flash of insight she needed immediate reassurance about how much she had changed since coming to us. She was somewhat comforted by her own statement, which we gladly corroborated, that it had been a long time since she had attacked anyone physically. She vehemently avowed that she would never hurt anyone again. If she had once done these things, she added, it was because she had been unhappy and did not care what she did, but now she was not unhappy and she did care. True, Mary was in part pretending to feel confident about her ability to contain her aggressions in order to cover up the insecurity she actually felt. But while her insistence that her behavior was good was more wish than fact, it showed how strong her wish was, and this was a good portent. It also gave us the chance to reassure her that she had really improved a great deal, which further reinforced her good intentions.

After several weeks of worrying about whether she would be able to curb her hostility, Mary seemed to grow more sure about it; at least she was comfortable enough to go back to learning about how to be a good mother (or aunt). She spent much of her time washing doll clothes, bathing her doll, and learning how to take care of children—babies, in particular.

With the great emotional difficulties aroused by her sister's pregnancy, Mary seemed to need to retrace and relive most of her old problems again in order to find assurance that she was now better integrated than when she had come to the School. This permitted her to grasp them once more with still greater understanding.

The first problem to reappear, with which she vigorously tried to come to grips, was her jealousy. This had probably originated in Mary's early relations to her sister. Now she tried to master it realistically, not only by talking about it with her counselor, but also by seeking her counselor's help in the presence of other children. She no longer withdrew from the children, or provoked them by yelling nasty remarks, but, instead, approached her counselor quietly and confessed to feeling jealous. She could explain why she felt that way, ask what remedy there might be, and by and large follow the counselor's advice.

As these actions brought home to her how much she had really changed, Mary's curiosity about her father and mother was renewed. She showed her concern about her father's death, when she suddenly blurted out, "What happened? What hurt him? How come I can't remember when my father died and I can remember when my mother died?" With her newly acquired ability to see the world realistically, Mary went on to remember that after he died, "nobody worked." "How did we live?" she wondered.

At first she tried to revive the idea she used to have that Frances had been earning the money and supporting them at that time, but this no longer made sense. Then how on earth had her mother managed? There came to her mind shadowy memories of a lady who had come to their home and helped them. It was now possible to tie this memory in with the social agency, which had taken care of her even before her mother's death, and Mary began to understand not only more about the functions of social agencies in general, but about that particular agency's role in her life. She found reassurance in the agency's interest in her, and her understanding of why and how she had been placed in School deepened. All this bolstered her hope that the agency would continue caring for her until she grew up and could look out for herself.

Perhaps her growing security enabled Mary to seek further help in mastering her still immediate and pressing concern with pregnancy. Although she had not talked much about this recently, her desire to be pregnant, coupled with her anxiety that she might be, still preyed on her mind. Despite the fact that she had frequently talked with her favorite counselors about both pregnancy and sex, she selected, as she had for her talks about intercourse, a relatively new staff member for discussing her fear of being pregnant. It is hard to say why she did this—she may have been ashamed to admit her unrealistic phantasies to the person who had so successfully helped her face other problems realistically. Whatever Mary's reasons, she approached the new counselor late in May, and with the greatest urgency said that there was something she had to know right away. "When a man and a woman have intercourse," she asked, "can two seeds get in? Can one get in a baby girl's vagina?" The counselor, uncertain what Mary wished to know, asked her to be more explicit. So Mary asked: if her mother had had intercourse with her father during the time that she was pregnant with Mary, could a seed have entered her [Mary's] vagina as well as her mother's?

The counselor explained that this was not possible, that the baby is protected in the uterus from anything that might enter from the outside, and that the umbilical cord is the only link between baby and mother. She added that before a girl's sexual organs are fully matured and she begins to menstruate, she cannot conceive a child anyway. Mary, tremendously relieved by this answer, lay back on her bed and said, "Whew! And I thought I was pregnant all the time. That's why I'm so fat." A great burden had been lifted from her mind and she went to sleep relieved and satisfied.[28]

This conversation, like so many important ones, took place just before Mary fell asleep. She had learned that she slept better when freed from anxieties, and hence sought help in the evening. As a matter of fact, the process of falling asleep, with its reduced control over the unconscious, makes it easier for all our children to bring up their preoccupations at bedtime, rather than at other times.

Next day Mary exclaimed to one of her favorite counselors, "Baby me, because I'm a baby." It was to be her last remark of this kind during her stay with us. Soon afterward she began to lose weight. She lost the look of a pregnant woman, and during the following three months (her last in School) she acquired the appearance of a normal girl her age. But there was still a final step to be gone through before she would be completely rid of the incorporated baby.

A week after her talk about being impregnated, Mary fashioned a figure from clay, scooped out a hole in the stomach, and placed a tiny baby inside. This was the introduction to returning to the question of whether she, as a baby, might not have been impregnated while inside her mother. But now she was quite sure that this had not happened. She was still afraid, however, that as a baby she might have been damaged or hurt by the father's penis during intercourse. This idea seemed in line with her conception of a penis, which she depicted as having claws. (Plate 13) This drawing gave us an opportunity to correct another misapprehension.

Just as Mary had learned to link her crabbiness in the morning with her nightmares, and to understand that talking about her dreams brought relief, so now, having voiced her most basic fear about the possibility that her body had been damaged, she could realize the connection between her physical symptoms and her emotions. She wondered why she no longer suffered from so many aches and pains, and finally said, "I used to have aches after I had a good time." And then, after some thought, "I had headaches so I wouldn't have a good time."

Under stress, Mary often turned to finger painting, and mostly chose to mess with brown paint. A few days following the above

---

28. This throws additional light on why it may have been difficult for her to talk to her favorite counselors about this. As has been mentioned, these favorites represented mother and sister to her. Her reluctance to talk frankly to a mother figure about her fear of being impregnated by her father is quite understandable. On the other hand, her belief in her pregnancy had its immediate origin in her rivalry with Frances, which may have barred her from taking this problem to the counselor who most represented her sister.

conversation, after contemplating one of her paintings quietly for a while, Mary remarked that it looked like a vagina. Then she said it looked just like the pictures in a test she had taken nearly two years before (the Rorschach test). She said she had not liked the test, and wanted to know what its purpose was. Explaining that it was a test of imagination, we showed her how different people saw different things in the ink spots.

Mary went on to say that to her the cards "all looked like parts of the body. Mostly it looked like vaginas, but I didn't say so." We asked her why. "Because I'd have to tell a story about these vaginas, and I didn't want to." When we queried her about what she had actually said, she replied, "I'd just say that it looked like a wolf." And pointing to parts of her finger painting, she said, "See, it does. There's the head." Then Mary asked why it was that she had seen only parts of the body, particularly vaginas, in the test. With some help, she came to understand that if a girl broods about her health and worries about certain parts of her body, such as her sex organs, she may be very apt to see them in the ink spots and in this way reveal her preoccupations.

Mary went on playing quietly with the finger paints and then asked, "Do people ever kill themselves?" and, after a while, "Did you ever know anyone who did?" The counselor said she had never known anyone really well who had attempted suicide, but that she had heard about such happenings. The counselor then asked Mary whether she knew of anyone who had committed suicide. Mary was unable to answer at first, although she was probably thinking of her sister's suicidal attempts. She continued playing with the finger paints and wrote "yes, no" with them very rapidly, but aloud she maintained that she had never known a person who had committed suicide. Nevertheless, in roundabout fashion she pursued her train of thought by remarking that if somebody thought about suicide, or actually did kill herself, "that would mean she was very unhappy. That means that she should really come to the Orthogenic School. But if she can't come to the Orthogenic School, where could she go?" She may have felt guilty at having had an opportunity for help that was not open to Frances. But Mary was also concerned about receiving help if she should ever be unhappy after leaving the School.

Mary continued her attempts to deal realistically with her anxiety about health. She asked to visit again with some of her elderly relatives because, as she phrased it, she was afraid they might die. When we asked how long a visit she preferred, she said an hour, and so this was arranged. But when we told Mary that she would be visiting with them from two to three o'clock, she said, "Oh, a half hour only. That's good." On actually meeting them, she remained quite distant and cut the visit short. In other ways, too, Mary evidenced reluctance to meet her relatives, or for that matter anyone connected with her past.

However, Mary still needed to recapture and master, both intellectually and emotionally, more real events of the past. This process was resumed when she again voiced an aversion to going outdoors, into the sunshine. She preferred sitting quietly and passively inside. On being questioned, Mary linked this to her anxieties about falling, or having other accidents happen. When we asked if she had ever known anyone who disliked going outdoors, she was able to trace her present feelings to her mother, who never ventured outside, and who was always fearful of what might happen to her if she left her room. With this, Mary again launched into long talks about her early experiences with her mother.

Speaking about this and about her sister's pregnancy, again brought Mary's feelings of loneliness and desertion to the fore. These were expressed in a phantasy, in which she was "a cave lady and all my people had been cave men." To some degree, Mary realized that this idea represented deep regression, coupled with cannibalistic tendencies. She said, "I was born in my mother's cave. All my ancestors are cave people and they live in caves." After a while, she added, "I write letters on stone, and they aren't answered. I wrote my sister two letters and she didn't answer me, and my aunt promised me a camera and she hasn't sent it yet." There followed a long list of complaints, which indicated how deeply Mary felt about her relatives' neglect of her. These "cave people" who did not answer her "stone letters," and thereby showed their rejection of her, she feared she might destroy in a cannibalistic rage produced by their neglect.

The phantasy about ancient and extinct cave people led to phantasies about similarly ancient and extinct animals. "A dinosaur is going to come and eat my sister and eat my sister's baby." Mary probably had harbored such cannibalistic phantasies for many years; however, now that she could recognize and express them, she found sufficient strength to view them as very ancient and more or less extinct wishes. Actually she had quite a good hold on herself. "I don't really want to be a cuckoo girl," she said. "I don't really want to stay all my life in this School. I'm not really crazy. I just act this way." And, climbing into the counselor's lap, she curled up like a very sleepy, tired baby.

Apart from such phantasies, all during Frances' pregnancy Mary worked at mastering her feelings about the event. She kept careful track of how far along in her pregnancy her sister was and followed the baby's development in the uterus month by month by making diagrams of it.

Mary had learned to understand that feelings must not be repressed—all that is required is restraint over asocial actions. No longer did she deny her anger about her sister's baby; she even acted it out in play. She would lift one of her baby dolls up in the air, manipulate it aggressively, and then shouting, "Kill the baby!" she would drop it to the floor. Mary explained quite realistically that no harm was done because the "baby" was only a doll.

She spoke openly of her feelings. "I wish Frances wouldn't have a baby," she said. "I don't like it." But she also tried to deal with her own involvement in the matter. "I don't know if she can take care of it, but it's her business and her baby, not mine." With that she settled down and contentedly played with her toys as if she were convinced at last that there were some real pleasures proper to her age and readily available to her, which she could enjoy as soon as her mind was at rest about Frances, the baby, and her own past.

With renewed vigor, Mary continued to deal with her past. Increasingly, she remembered more of it—how, for example, her mother and sister had slept in one bed, while she occupied a baby crib at their side. She also recalled in considerable detail how greatly upset she had been when she went to live with her aunt because she could not bring along any of her clothes or belongings. She felt she had lost everything. As she concluded this account, she asked, "How come I can remember such a lot now?"

Following up these recollections a few days later, she unearthed the reason why she had gotten off to such a bad start with her aunt. "I can't remember any of these aunts coming to see Mommy and me," she said. "That's why I always thought my aunt didn't like my mommy, and that's why I didn't want to have anything to do with her."

In recapturing what she could of her past, Mary also realized that there were long gaps in her memory of those periods when nothing of great emotional impact had happened. She wondered why she could remember so much of her life with her mother and her first experiences at her aunt's house, while she could scarcely recall anything of the following years up to the time she came to the School.

As soon as Frances' baby was born, Mary was told about it.

Her immediate response was to complain about pains in her stomach. A few hours later, while she was watching the children playing games on the Midway in front of the School (she had not joined the games because of her cramps), Mary suddenly threw herself on the grass and began to moan and cry. Re-enacting childbirth, she lay on her back and moved as though she were in labor; all the while she was screaming, "Oh! the baby's coming out of me!"

This marked the culmination of Mary's efforts to cast out all the objects incorporated within her. Like the ancestors of folk lore, who may become the evil demons of today, these objects had become Mary's evil demons, who fed on her vital strength and prevented her from living a life of her own. All these she now exorcised. The mother, herself as a baby, the baby she thought she carried because of being impregnated by the father while she was still in the womb—she finally got rid of them all. Soon it became evident that her re-enactment of giving birth had a double symbolism. She drew a picture of a mother in labor (Plate 14), which made it clear that she, as a mother, had given birth to herself. It was just as though Mary had been born, at last, as a real person.

In mastering this last trauma, Mary also seemed to master many additional aspects of the preceding ones. Mary could speak candidly not only about how angry she felt toward the baby, but also about how worried she was that it might not be adequately cared for, since her sister had never been treated right and hence might not know how to take care of a baby. All the time Frances remained in the hospital, Mary worried that it might possibly burn down, and that Frances and the baby would be killed. Or else she feared that the nurses might kill the baby. She kept ejaculating disconnectedly, "I'll die. I'm going to die now. The baby was born and now I'll die." But with help, she overcame both her anxiety about the bad effects the birth might have on her, and her worry about what she might do to the baby.

Within another few days she could regard the birth quite calmly. She was wholly relaxed and the pictures she now drew reflected this, despite her deep concern with motherhood and childbirth. Mary had become—perhaps for the first time in her life, certainly more than ever before—truly herself.

Her ego boundaries were fairly secure. The separation of imagination or play, and reality—of past and present—was well established. Less and less did she transfer the past to the present. Her ego, while still relatively weak, was strong enough to maintain some inner balance between superego demands and instinctual strivings, and to deal realistically with the outside world, though often this could only be managed by restricting somewhat the areas of her life and experience.

With this great change in her inner existence, Mary once more wished to take stock in order to find a personal consistency that would unite the various phases of her life. This she accomplished. Her father's death, her mother's illness, her life with her relatives, her permanent separation from her sister, all were accepted quite realistically. Again admitting to herself how angry she had been about the baby, she nevertheless realized more strongly than ever that over the preceding years she and her sister had grown apart, that they had different lives of their own, and hence the birth of this baby in reality did not have too great a bearing on her own life.

Less preoccupied by the past than ever before, Mary turned her interest to the present, and the shape of the future. Viewed from the vantage point of a satisfying present, the past, too, seemed more benign. She recalled pleasant experiences at the School, and before —even some that had occurred during her life with her aunt. She could even accept her new nephew, once she had worked through the trauma of his birth, because he gave her the feeling that she had some family of her own.

DISCUSSION

Only during this last half year of Mary's stay at the School did we arrive at a sufficiently comprehensive understanding of the dynamics underlying her behavior to guess the meaning of her actions as they occurred. The major achievement of this final period was that, for the first time in her life, Mary tried to integrate a traumatic experience rather than avoid facing its relevance, as she had in the past, either by withdrawing into depression or by discharging tension in acting out. In addition, while mastering the experience of the sister's pregnancy and the birth of the baby, Mary simultaneously integrated many, early psychological traumata, which up to then had split her life and personality asunder.

In the way she handled herself this time, Mary demonstrated that she had become quite a different person, with a new and relatively well-structured personality. Now when she met an upsetting experience, she could deal with it adequately. The precipitating fact of the sister's pregnancy and the birth of the child challenged her once and for all to establish clear ego boundaries and define herself as the person she was. This implied that she must relinquish her hope of someday being somebody's baby again, preferably her mother's, or, if this were not possible, her sister's. This "baby" that she had carried within herself, which represented her all-consuming desire for infantile life-conditions and gratifications, she ejected from herself by symbolically giving birth to it on the Midway in front of the School. She could henceforth be herself and nothing but herself. In this way, she at the same time gave birth to herself as a person.

That this was possible, was the result of the infantile, and, later, the age-correct satisfactions, as well as the interpersonal gratifications, she had received at the School; they permitted her to give up her wish to be a baby because, to some degree, they satisfied this wish. These infantile and interpersonal satisfactions improved and buttressed the previously deficient substructure of her personality to the point where it was possible for her, with our help, to master even such difficult traumata as the sister's marriage and pregnancy. In turn, the experiences she gained in mastering reality served to build up her ego so that she was strong enough to get rid of the old introjects—herself as the mother, herself as the kicking baby in the mother's womb, herself as the baby impregnated in the uterus by the father.

When Mary discovered that her destructive wishes and violent attacks did not damage us, the other children, or even her sister and her baby, she began doubting whether she was as destructive as she feared, and hence whether she actually was the cause of her mother's death. Our consistently accepting attitudes in the face of her hostility had led her to hope that she would not be destroyed in retaliation for her angry wishes and misdeeds. All this served to strengthen her ego and help her to view the world as no longer all bad.

As the time drew near when Mary would leave us she was not a perfectly well balanced child emotionally; that would be expecting too much in view of her past history. But she was a neurotic child whose further treatment could well be ambulatory psychotherapy. Therefore, we believed that the School had achieved its purpose by helping Mary change from a schizoid child, in need of institutional treatment to a neurotic one, who could get the assistance she still needed while living in society.

Mary's Leaving

THE AGENCY HAD PLANNED that Mary should leave the School at the beginning of an academic year, so that she could start her new classes at the same time the other children did. But this plan was made before we knew of Frances' pregnancy, and if it were carried through now, Mary would have to leave us very soon after the baby was born, and would not have sufficient time to adjust fully to this event. Thus the question arose whether Mary should remain with us for another year. This, we would have preferred. The agency felt it would be best to make its decision on the basis of the results of a psychiatric evaluation.

To the examining psychiatrist, Mary appeared at that time to be an alert child who still had some depressive features. By and large, she seemed relatively well integrated and in good contact with the world. In response to his questions, she gave a reasonably complete and well organized account of her past life, present desires, and her wishes for the future, all of which seemed quite adequate and normal for a girl her age. This evaluation, seen in the context of her good academic achievement and her desire for family life, suggested to him that she was ready for placement in a more homelike setting, and he felt that her departure from the School should not be postponed.

On the other hand, he agreed with us that Mary was not yet ready for a normal foster home. Particularly it was to be feared that if the foster home did not work out satisfactorily, a further change might prove very damaging to Mary in view of her past history of being shifted around. Therefore, it was felt that it would be best to place her in one of the specialized treatment homes maintained by the agency at that time. There she would live in a family-like setting, but under close psychiatric supervision, and she would also receive casework help. As it had been decided beforehand that the agency would proceed on the psychiatrist's recommendations, Mary was placed in one of these special foster homes.

When this plan was first presented to her, it pleased Mary very much. The preplacement visits in the foster home, and the preparations for the move went very well. After all, Mary was still hoping against hope to find an all-giving mother, a mother figure who would not, as her counselors did at the School, try to guide her toward age-correct personality integration and the permanent discarding of her unrealistic desires. A foster mother seemed to offer another chance to find fulfillment of the wishes she had only reluctantly given up. With high hopes, therefore, to counteract her understandable anxiety, Mary re-entered society.

Her Counselors

I SHOULD NOT CONCLUDE Mary's story with us without remarking on what made it possible for the School staff to "take" Mary, relate to her, and carry out her rehabilitation despite the great strain involved.

Mary managed to create a feeling of tremendous urgency in all of us—more so than did most of the other children at the School, although they certainly needed help as desperately. Life in her vicinity was always turbulent, tempestuous, noisy. Her behavior had an extraordinary emotional impact not only on the people who worked intimately with her, but on the entire staff. The urgency was communicated even to those of us who were not exposed to her direct impact. Repeatedly, in both staff meetings and casual bull sessions, someone would plead that something be done "right away" for Mary. Many hours of many days were invested in trying to figure out how we could help her "right this moment."

This urgency evoked a feeling of deep and immediate personal involvement from all of us. Occasionally, I deem it necessary to ask staff members who are not working directly with a particular child to concentrate on and think about his problems, for the purpose of promoting stronger empathy and concern with the child's difficulties. (This is, of course, a precondition for successful treatment in an institution like ours.) But with Mary there was no such necessity. Her symptomatic behavior automatically aroused everyone's deepest concern, and this, in turn, increased our ability to help Mary in important, though intangible, ways. Of course, this held particularly true for the two counselors who worked most intimately with her.

One of her counselors, from the very outset, made a considerable identification with Mary because she, too, had been brought up in an aunt's home. Shortly after birth, this counselor's mother had died, and her father thereafter took little interest in her. She could suffer Mary's negativism because once she had wanted her aunt and uncle to suffer her negativism at being forced to live with them; but she had never dared to vent these feelings. In a way, Mary's daring, in subjecting us to such violent outbursts, pleased her.

Like Mary, this counselor needed an outlet for her feelings of deprivation, which had originated in her own motherless childhood. Like Mary, she had been very resentful of having to share her aunt's attention with her cousin, who had always seemed the favored child. This gave her an unusual empathy for Mary's inordinate jealousy. For this reason, she participated vicariously in the gratification and comfort she could offer a child who had undergone an experience that paralleled her own. In addition, this counselor planned to make up for her deprivation by one day taking good care of her own child; in the interim, Mary filled that child's role. In one sense, this attitude speaks well for Mary's future. For just as the counselor found vicarious, if belated, gratification in caring for Mary, so Mary may one day be able to repeat a similar experience herself.

The attitude of Mary's other favorite counselor was quite different. She was soon deriving gratification from the fact that she was one of the very few staff members who could "take" Mary's acting-out behavior relatively well. In her own childhood she had suffered from her family's characteristic "niceness," and their repression of all aggressive behavior. For this reason she enjoyed Mary's ability to "let it all out," which was the kind of behavior she had never dared attempt. Moreover, the only gratification her family allowed was eating, and oral desires were always amply satisfied. Therefore, Mary's oral demands, her extreme greediness and unending demands of "give me," did not threaten this counselor, nor seem unpleasant to her; rather, they seemed quite familiar. For these and other reasons, she could enjoy the conviction that she neither rejected nor deprived Mary, and that Mary's alienating ways did not affect her.

With most of the staff members, Mary's chief weapon was to make them feel guilty because they could not "take" her, or do enough for her, which quashed their ability to really gratify her. Whenever anything was done for Mary, when efforts were made to make her feel more comfortable, to give her reasonable explanations, or to help her view situations more realistically, her inevitable reaction was, "So what?"—meaning to the adult: "What's the use of trying to please Mary or make her more comfortable? She never lets me comfort her, and neither she nor I derives any satisfaction from my effort." That her favorite counselor was able to take all this without losing patience, afforded her a great deal of narcissistic gratification, which she then used to help Mary.

SUMMARY

Extensive reports on the treatment of schizophrenic children are quite rare. To my knowledge, the literature contains not more than a few case histories that are relatively complete. One of the reasons for this, to quote the author of an authoritative textbook on child psychiatry (who is particularly interested in schizophrenic disturbances of children), is that "schizophrenic children have not been treated until recently."[29] He adds that "efforts made of late to do something about and with the patients have brought a few rays of light to a hitherto dark situation."[30]

The case of Mary does not offer any definitive answer to the baffling problems of the genesis and treatment of childhood schizo-

29. L. Kanner, *Child Psychiatry* (Springfield: Charles C. Thomas, 1948), p. 727.
30. *Loc. cit.*

phrenia, but I hope even the "few rays of light" it may shed on them will be welcome in a "hitherto dark situation." Moreover, since one of the best known investigations of childhood schizophrenia as recently as 1941 summed up the prevailing attitude by stating, "The prognosis of childhood schizophrenia appears to be uniformly bad,"[31] an opinion still widely held, a report that contradicts this uniform hopelessness may help to create a more optimistic view of the success of prolonged treatment efforts. Mary's history, perhaps more than the three others presented in this book, also seems to illustrate the fact that in some cases, at least, the rehabilitation of schizophrenic children requires concentrated efforts by a number of persons, who work preferably within an institutional setting—an environment that is therapeutic in its totality. In a sense, this remark seems to contradict Kanner's findings that "by far the best results were obtained when a child was taken over by one or two good-natured, warm-hearted, unsophisticated persons."[32] This apparent contradiction might stem from the fact that Kanner was thinking largely of one special type of schizophrenic withdrawal, infantile autism, in very young children; also, Kanner had no experience with children who had been placed for a period of years in a setting so designed as to create a total, therapeutic milieu.

Our experience at the Orthogenic School seems to suggest that Dr. Kanner's prescription would not hold good for children of grade school age. We have found that the kind of people he describes do not possess the emotional resources necessary to meet, fully and instantly, the physical and emotional needs of these children—a requirement that makes heavy demands on the adults' endurance. The rehabilitation of these children requires skills and inner resources that one cannot expect to find in unsophisticated persons. Even experienced therapists seem to need the support of a comprehensive institutional setting in order to meet the extraordinary demands involved in treating such children.

That the schizophrenic child needs more for his rehabilitation than any one human being can offer, is not new. This realization, for example, forced itself on Sterba, who in 1933 published the first extensive report on the treatment, based on psychoanalytic principles, of a schizophrenic five-year-old boy. Starting out to treat the boy by means of classical child analysis, she soon had to call on the help of various "adjunct" therapists, such as nursery school teachers, camp counselors, etc. Similarly, she had to arrange—at least for

31. C. Bradley, *Schizophrenia in Childhood* (New York: Macmillan, 1941), as quoted by Kanner, *loc. cit.*, p. 727.
32. Kanner, *op. cit.*, p. 728.

certain periods—to place the child outside his home in special settings, such as camps. To progress at all, his education had to proceed
in a very special school conducted along psychoanalytic principles,
in which all teaching was done by psychoanalytically trained teachers.[33] Kanner, too, stressed the importance of "change of environment," which "means a change of people," as essential for "weaning
the schizophrenic child away from the temptation of schizophrenic
withdrawal."[34] Our own experience suggests that the treatment of
schizophrenic children proceeds best within a total therapeutic environment and through the cooperative effort of several people. But
this assertion needs much more critical evaluation, and our methods
should be tested against the experiences of other workers in the field.
It is hoped that the histories published in this volume may serve as
a starting point for such a critical discussion.

The use of a therapeutic team, of course, creates special difficulties, especially during periods when the child needs to concentrate all or most of his emotions on one person alone, in order to
achieve the identifications necessary for building up his personality.
Similarly, difficulties arise when the child needs to direct all his
positive emotions toward one staff member and to concentrate his
negative feelings on others. Often these periods last for months, or
even years. At these times, as in many other short-lived situations,
the hated, neglected, or abused therapists must be able to remain
positively attached to the child, or else their efforts will become
empty gestures. To get well, the child needs to continue receiving
their services, in the same quantity and quality as if he were relating
to them positively. Thus the neglected or hated staff member must
take all the child "dishes out," yet be content to remain in the background.

It is difficult to accept this. It is even harder to become, as it
were, merely a "handmaiden" to one's colleagues (as, for example,
when a staff member who is being physically and mentally abused
by a child must help him make an intricate love gift for another
staff member). After all, a staff member selects his profession because he wishes and is ready to serve children. He may not feel
equally ready or willing to become an object of displeasure while a
fellow worker enjoys the double pleasure of being loved and carrying forward the therapeutic work, for all to see. True, the person
who is the target of negative feelings contributes significantly to

---

33. E. Sterba, "An Abnormal Child," *The Pyschoanalytic Quarterly*, V, (1936),
pp. 375-414, 560-600. This report appeared first in German in 1933 in the *Zeitschrift
für psychoanalytische Paedagogik.*
34. Kanner, *op. cit.*, p. 728.

the child's progress by his very acceptance of this role, but it is
much harder to accept this role for oneself and for others to recognize it. At the moment, it may seem to the worker that he must suffer
so that his colleague may succeed. Therefore, to cooperate not only
fully but willingly with the person on whom the child concentrates
all his interests and positive emotions, is no easy task.

Unavoidably, such situations create inter-staff difficulties. And
for the child's well-being, the staff members involved must be able
to master them. Thus a process of integrating these difficulties often
must proceed simultaneously with the child's integration. The continual resolution of these, and many other staff difficulties, presents
a major problem in a therapeutic institution.[35]

Mary's progress in treatment sheds some further light, directly
or by implication, on some of the particular deficiencies in personality development that seem to lead to schizophrenic disturbances.
Fenichel says: "From a psychoanalytic point of view, it can be generally said that infantile psychoses represent less 'regressions' than,
rather, severe disturbances in the development of the ego, which
thus retains more or less archaic characteristics."[36] This still leaves
unanswered the question of exactly what the ego disturbances are,
and which archaic characteristics are retained.

Mary's history may contribute to a better understanding of
dynamic and structural configurations in the personality, which
account for the schizophrenic symptomatology, at least as much as
any single case ever can help our understanding of such a complex
phenomenon. In the literature the criteria for diagnosing childhood
schizophrenia are not too sharply defined. Because symptomatic
behavior changes with such fluidity in childhood, for example, from
schizophrenic to delinquent symptomatology, on the basis of manifest behavior one cannot say with any conviction whether a particular child should be diagnosed as delinquent or schizophrenic. Eventually, it is to be hoped, such diagnoses will not be made on the
basis of symptomatic behavior, but on structural considerations. Just
now, we often must be satisfied to arrive at a differential diagnosis
after the mechanisms and the personality structure underlying the
overt behavior have been discovered. Only after our therapeutic
efforts permit the child to reveal more of his conflicts and uncon-

---

35. It would take us too far afield to discuss here the procedures we have
found most useful for achieving this purpose. It is one of the important questions
that the future volume on the School's staff will discuss.

36. O. Fenichel, *The Psychoanalytic Theory of Neurosis* (New York: W. W.
Norton and Co., 1945), p. 443.

scious motivations can we be certain about the nature of the disturbance.

In Mary's case, too, there was a question about whether she did not suffer from delinquent rather than schizophrenic manifestations. Her asocial symptoms were certainly more marked; they ranged from sexual delinquency and stealing to violent physical attacks on others. However, we eventually came to consider her a schizophrenic rather than a delinquent child because the types of behavior that are roughly characteristic of schizophrenics, though at first less obvious, in the long run were much more persistent and prevailing in Mary, as her development at the School revealed. Her delinquency, on the other hand, disappeared within a few weeks after she entered. Her inability to relate, the inappropriateness of her emotions, her awkward body posture, the oddity of her movements, and above all, her disregard for her physical and human surroundings and her constant fear that she would "explode," and be utterly destroyed at any moment, as well as her delusions, were much more resistant to change than her delinquency. All this suggests that her disturbance should have been categorized as schizophrenic; this, in fact, was the diagnosis that one very experienced psychiatrist made before she came to us. But another child psychiatrist had been taken in by her apparent adequacy in mastering life in a delinquent way; he had considered her relatively little disturbed and saw no need for institutional treatment.

Along with others we have observed, Mary's case suggests that the schizophrenic child is never able to form any satisfying object-relations, not even to his mother during his first years of life. In an emotional sense, he never feels confronted with a "thou," certainly not with a "thou" who seems important enough to be recognized by the child as such. Nor do schizophrenic children ever meet, emotionally, any person who possesses sufficient inner consistency to permit the child to experience what a well-structured personality is like, not to speak of evoking in the child a desire to form his own personality in that image. This, incidentally, may explain why so many of the schizophrenic children we have observed had very disturbed mothers, though their mothers' disturbances often remained unrecognized as such for years. Whatever the reason, these children never developed a true self—never established even relatively definite or permanent ego boundaries. What belonged to the external and internal worlds remained unclear to them. The more sick they were, the more this held true. Their external experiences and their inner strivings were never reconciled through the mediation of a reasonable ego. What in other children takes the form of organized

personality, in these children was an ectoplasm-like response to
inner and outer irritations, which never developed a definite and
permanent form, or structured personality.

Sometimes these children fool the casual observer. Since they
have no personality of their own, it is easy for them to copy, to
"borrow," a personality. In a deeper sense, we have found that it
does not make much difference whether a child seems to have given
up contact with reality by withdrawing into a stupor or an automaton-
like rigidity, or whether he has discovered that he can remain even
less disturbed by and more aloof from the world if he pretends to
possess a "personality." Such borrowed personalities are empty
shells. Because they find acceptance in the environment, the children need not develop their own structured personalities; moreover,
these substitutes can protect the children from the challenge to form
their own, to which they might otherwise be exposed.

We have especially observed that among children who have lived
in settings that starved them emotionally and that were bereft of
any material comfort—in short, among children whose lives have
been underprivileged or submarginal in all respects—the temptation
to borrow a personality can be overwhelming. For them, the comfort
of the institutional setting or of the new and better foster home,
creates a tremendous temptation to hold on to it at all costs, even
to the extent of suddenly changing one's colors, and adopting a personality suited to the demands of the environment. All this happens
at the expense of the child's emotional energy, which is severely
drained in the effort to make the artificial adjustment. There is very
little energy left to expend on building up a truly integrated personality. In fact, psychic economy, under such circumstances, almost
seems to require that the individual make use of the advantageous
conditions at the institution for storing emotional energy, since he
feels that he will need all the energy he can muster in handling each
new impending placement in turn—the institution, the foster home,
and so on. He may think: Why develop a personality that may not
be acceptable to the next set of important persons? Why not wait
until I know what they will want? The notion that an integrated personality is a source of strength whatever the new situation may be,
is not grasped by severely disturbed children, if indeed it ever can
be by an age group so dependent on others. Only because we convinced Mary that her stay at the School was permanent, could we
induce her to venture beyond such surface adjustment.

For Mary, too, had the ability to borrow a personality, and the
consequences of this for her and us made the reporting of this case
an inner need. Mary's pseudo-adequacy fooled some staff members,

even some psychiatrists, into believing that she was ready to leave the School long before she had developed an adequate personality. Much to our regret these errors in judgment shortened her stay with us. Since then we have learned to be much more careful not to take what on cursory observation seems like mastery for signs of true integration. I have seen since then, in other settings, how frequently failure to recognize deep disturbances because of seemingly adequate functioning leads to premature placement of children in foster homes, or non-therapeutic institutions. These children are thus punished by not being sufficiently treated for their desperate feelings of nothingness, which they try to combat or deny by the pretense of adequacy.

Mary's history at the School illustrates this particular pitfall in the institutional treatment of severe behavior disorders in children. For some time, until we finally got to know her intimately, we, too, accepted her rapid progress at face value; we then thought that we had originally underestimated her emotional resources, her ego strength. (Our narcissism as therapists facilitated our making such errors. We wished to believe that we could produce such remarkable improvement in short order and to take pride in our accomplishment. This helped us overlook how empty her seeming mastery actually was.) Only much later, when there could no longer be any hope that we had "cured" her in a few months' time, did we realize that our initial evaluation of the severity of her disturbance had been correct. Hers was not the only case that provided a similar experience.

This suggests that some of the speedy improvements recently reported in the literature by other therapists or treatment institutions may well be due to factors similar to those we later learned were at work in Mary. Since the ephemeral nature of such relatively rapid recoveries may escape attention, the intensive therapeutic efforts to develop a genuine personality are discontinued and the child is returned to his parents, or placed, for example, in a foster home, on the basis of his superficial adjustment. These children appear to get along fairly well with the borrowed personality they have acquired on short order. But the eventual breakdown is only postponed until they are up against serious stress; then their totally inadequate personality structure suddenly falls to pieces like a house of cards. The never-integrated, the hidden, the genuine—though schizophrenic —processes, break through. Since the old, deficient personality may by then have become ossified rather than kept in flux during the delinquent, acting-out period, we have actually rendered such a child a disservice. We have done this by not helping him develop a genuinely integrated personality; by settling (and permitting him to settle) for acquiring the props of a superficial adjustment; and by allowing him to borrow a personality, which can never truly be his own, in line with the expectations of his new environment.

One more factor should not be overlooked. From observation, we know that in state institutions for the insane, for example, when a new administration suddenly takes over and radical changes are instituted, some patients seem suddenly to improve. Such gains later turn out to be illusory. Sudden changes in environment seem to activate whatever emotional energy may be dormant in the individual. In this respect it is immaterial whether or not the radical change is for the better. But any such improvement soon disappears if it does not lead to integration of the personality and to satisfying personal relations, which alone offer the steady supply of emotional energy needed for a continuous mastery of life.

A change in administration that leads to a suddenly benign change in the handling of the patients by the staff, can temporarily have far-reaching consequences. In some patients it will lead to violent outbursts, in many others to an "improvement" in symptomatology. In line with our observations on borrowed personality, it can be understood why these patients so readily adjust to the more favorable climate—why their symptoms become more "benign." This change is easily mistaken for improvement. Actually it has little meaning for their real recovery.

I had such an experience when I took over the Orthogenic School from my predecessor. The institution of a much more "benign" regime led to a violent acting-out by some children whose aggressions had previously been checked by restrictions. Other children's symptoms improved miraculously, much to everyone's delight. Unfortunately, within the next year or two I learned that those who had reacted with violence to the lifting of restraint later made much more progress in rehabilitation. I came to understand that they had reacted to change not by copying the significant features of the change, but by responding in terms of their own inner needs, and their own personalities. Those without personality borrowed the new attitudes represented by the staff; on the surface, they readily changed their symptoms, supposedly for the better. However, in the long run their rehabilitation proceeded much more slowly than that of the children who had reacted with violence, and the final results of their treatment were in some cases less successful.

Since here, as in other instances, I have cited the advantages of institutional treatment for severely disturbed children, a word of warning also seems in order against possible misuses of its treatment potentials. Even though the severely disturbed child may show a rapid surface improvement and seems to be ready for foster home placement, it is a serious mistake to use institutions for short-term placements. This is not meant as a criticism of receiving or diagnostic homes, where less disturbed children are studied and evaluated preceding their final placement. The purpose of these homes is quite different, and they are outside the scope of this discussion. But severely disturbed children need to undergo an extended process of rehabilitation—extensive with regard to both time and effort. In Mary's case, we have seen how easy it is to settle for what seems to be fast improvement, and how cheated a child is when that mistake is made. Therefore, whatever we can learn from her story about the potential mistakes that can readily be made in the institutional treatment of children constitutes an additional reason for the discussion of this summary.

During the last months that Mary was at the School, other processes, moving parallel to and interrelatedly with the process of integration, were taking place, which from a theoretical viewpoint, may be of interest. We assume that the neurotic personality develops as the consequence of an unresolved oedipal conflict. We also assume that the schizophrenic processes have their origin in developmental periods preceding the oedipal phase. If these assumptions are correct, we may be justified in further assuming that, in the process of rehabilitating a schizophrenic child, the oedipal period must be regained in the transition from a schizoid to a neurotic, if not integrated, personality.

It was one of Mary's difficulties that she had never known a father, and had never discarded a most primitive, oral, incorporative attachment to her mother. She had not felt ambivalent about this attachment, since she had never seen her mother as a rival for the father. As a matter of fact, the only person she recognized as a rival for the mother was her sister, which in part explains why she saw this sister in a parental rather than a sisterly role for much of the time. For this reason, and many others, her development had been fixated at a preoedipal level.

The degree of this fixation on an early, mostly oral level, can be readily seen from Mary's behavior during her first years with us. Only at a fairly late age, in her reaction to her brother-in-law, did Mary experience something resembling the oedipal situation, with her sister playing the role of the mother whom Mary wished to retain as a mother and yet do away with as a rival. But because this constellation was so very different from that which the child normally experiences in the average home, the conflicts Mary transferred to brother-in-law and sister were not quite suitable for permitting the development of a full oedipal situation, or its resolution. Mary's efforts to re-create in phantasy the father she had never known were themselves insufficient for recapturing the oedipal development. Therefore she created within herself, in phantasy, the fruit of her oedipal desires: she felt impregnated by the father. In this way, without ever having experienced a personal relation with a father, she created an oedipal situation for herself, and by giving up the idea of having a baby by him, she was able to resolve it.[37]

The radical change that took place within her after she had freed herself of her introjects, integrated the disparate pieces of her life, and resolved this self-created and acted-out oedipal development, can best be seen by comparing the wide difference in her drawings. At the end of Mary's stay at the School, and despite the stresses provoked by the pending birth of Frances' child, her rendering of human figures, especially of girls' heads, was suddenly and newly free. A comparison of Plates 15 and 1, 3, and 6 illustrates this sharp change. I wish to stress the fact that not only did the face of the girl in the drawings become well organized in its constituent parts, but also the overemphasis of the mouth, which had always characterized Mary's drawings, was radically changed. Previously the faces she drew never had chins, even as a desperate, wailing baby seems to have none. But the faces of the girls she now drew had well-formed chins and pretty features, and seemed even gay. The preoedipal baby disappeared as Mary acquired a "chin" with which to face the world.

That her outlook on life had changed is further illustrated by the appearance of entirely new topics in her drawings: a happy child at play, gay flowers, and other pleasant themes. The settings no longer expressed her emotional turmoil, but illustrated present reality: children riding horseback on the Midway in front of the School, or playing on the beach at Lake Michigan. (Plates 16, 17, and 18)

---

37. How much does a nine- or ten-year-old child "know" about the oedipal development? Does he "know" that it should be solved at about five or six years of age, and that only after its resolution can a child develop an integrated personality? Mary's early insistence that she would remain at the School until she was five (see p. 171) seemed to express some dim awareness that she had not yet developed further than a five-year-old, emotionally speaking—that she still had to enter, go through, and resolve the oedipal difficulties before she would be ready to leave us. At the time she made these cryptic remarks, could she then have compared herself with other five-year-old children and realized that, although she was already nearly ten, in order to master life she would first have to acquire what they already possessed?

The Next Three Years

MARY'S LIFE after she left us was not as smooth as all of us had hoped. In spite of the efforts that were made to find the best possible placement for her, the special foster home turned out to have unexpected shortcomings. Some of these, but by no means all, were the results of Mary's own behavior, the nature of her neurosis, and the foster mother's reactions to it. At first Mary seemed to adjust to her new home with relative ease; she also did particularly well in school. But within a few months difficulties arose in the home, clashes in personalities, which even the psychiatric supervision of the home could not prevent. The foster mother, in particular, was considerably more rigid and less accepting of Mary than had been expected. She occasionally was even compulsive in her demands on Mary, who, it is true, was not a very conforming girl. Mary's defense against what she felt were unjustifiably high demands was to avoid relating intimately to the foster parents or to the other children in the home. Not without reason, she felt that these children were preferred to her, were held up to her as good children, while she was the bad one.

Although Mary had always wished to live in a normal home and go to a normal school, and although she had tried to come to terms with her new environment, within a year she demanded to be moved out of this home because it had become unbearable to her. On each of her visits with us she complained about how unhappy it made her to be viewed as a bad girl. She felt exploited, partly because she felt that the foster mother kept her only for the money the agency paid for her keep, and partly because the demands made on her to behave herself and help with the chores around the house were imposed, not in order that she might learn socialized behavior, but to make life easier for the foster family. Thus, in a way, fate again brought Mary into a situation that seemed similar to her experience with her aunt.

Fortunately, Mary was no longer helpless; she could defend herself, and her defense was to understand and see through the foster mother's motivations and recognize her rigidity as weakness of character. She shrewdly assessed the personality deficiencies and unmet needs motivating the foster mother and the other persons living in the home. She could understand what was going on in herself in reaction to all this. While she was deprived of the emotional closeness she had hoped for, her understanding of others served as a defense, which protected her own inner integration.

The casework help she received, valuable as it was, could not offer her the intimate relation she craved and needed at this time. It was wanting for a very different reason than was the foster home. Mary soon took a liking to the worker who had arranged for her placement in the home; she saw this worker in weekly sessions. But before this relation could become very helpful to Mary, some eight months after the placement, the worker left the agency. Then the person who continued with Mary married soon afterward and left for a vacation. This, together with the previous worker's departure, created acute separation fears in Mary; she again became quite depressive, and wished to die so that she could be reunited with her mother, since in this world there seemed to be no permanently satisfying relations available to her.

Approximately half a year after Mary had begun seeing the second worker, and again just when this relation was becoming meaningful to her, the worker became pregnant. As was to be expected, all the experiences Mary had undergone during her sister's pregnancy were revived. Because of the approaching birth of her baby, the worker left the agency approximately a year after she had begun her work with Mary. In reaction to the severance of this new and budding relation, Mary expressed strong wishes that the baby should die. To our horror, exactly this happened. It seemed that nothing in Mary's life could go right. That her death wish against the baby had come true created extreme guilt in Mary and revived her equally haunting megalomanic ideas about how dangerous her destructive wishes were.

Finally, after this bad experience, matters took a turn for the better. The third case worker, who is still working with Mary at the present writing, was able to establish a good relation. Within a few months, this seemed to give Mary the courage to become more active in fighting against her unpleasant situation in the foster home and particularly the exaggerated demands of her foster mother. Three years after she left us, this fight led to a running-away episode. Mary was picked up by the police, and to the police officers she gave such a vivid account of what the foster home expected of her, and how unreasonable these demands were, that the officers expressed quite outspokenly their opinion that this was no suitable home for her. This experience, as well as others, convinced the foster mother and the agency that Mary ought to be moved to a new home.

Mary is in this new home at the time of this writing. After six months there, she feels happy, well-liked and understood, and what seems most important, convinced that finally she has found a good home. The fact is that, while too many restrictions were placed on her in the previous home, in this new one she was a little fearful at first because she was given so much freedom. Because of this good placement, she could relate better to her worker and take advantage of what this relation could offer.

At this writing Mary is fifteen and a half years old, and in the throes of typical adolescent difficulties. She is beset by the usual adolescent anxieties about sex, and is both attracted to and afraid of the behavior of the fast-living boys and girls among her high school mates. She still feels not fully accepted by the most desirable children in school and rationalizes this on the basis that she has no family. She tends to identify with youngsters from broken homes, while at the same time she is aware that they might not be the ones who can offer her the best companionship.

She still relies for mastery on a somewhat passive understanding of the psychological motivations of others, and is extremely perceptive in doing this; but she is rather afraid to relate intimately to people. She has been disappointed too often and too much by having people leave her. As a protection against similar disappointments, she does not let others come close to her at the moment.

Mary is doing well along academic lines. She meets life with somewhat greater maturity and disillusionment than might be expected from other children her age. But in her present permissive environment she is slowly developing greater enjoyment of life. There are some difficulties, but all in all she manages her life in society better than anybody, at the time she came to live with us, would ever have expected. That she was able to manage quite well the very difficult experiences in the first foster home, the loss of two workers in short succession, and the particularly traumatic circumstances of the second loss, seems proof of the gains she made while with us and augurs well for her future.

Mary Looks Back

ON THE OCCASION of Mary's most recent visit to the School, I asked permission to publish her history. She was thrilled by the idea that she was important enough to have her history published, and gladly gave me permission to do so.

As we looked back over the many years we had known each other, I asked her what she felt were the most important experiences during her stay at the School—the experiences that made her change while she was with us. Her first response was to mention two people —one of her favorite counselors, Joan, and me. (I must admit that this astonished me, because I had not known that I had been so important to her.) Then she mentioned some of the other counselors and her teachers; but she completely forgot her other favorite counselor, Gayle. I believe that the reason she had forgotten how significant a role this counselor had played in her life was simple enough. Gayle had married and had recently given birth to a baby girl. That this mother-sister figure was having a baby of her own (rather than adopting Mary, which may have been her secret wish) was too much for Mary, and she dealt with this painful event by forgetting, for the moment, about this counselor. Later, when we happened to talk about Gayle, Mary readily remembered her as being important to her.

Talking about her first foster home placement, Mary said again that everything had been wrong with it, that she had been pushed around nearly as much as when she was with her aunt. In defending herself against this experience, she said that she had got "hard; if it had gone on, I might have gotten mean." But in the new foster home, she felt things were as good as they possibly could be. "Not everything is perfect, but it mostly is. If I had been moved from here [the School] to where I am living now, life would have been easy for me."

I asked her to tell me more about why she had felt able to change while with us. What experiences, in addition to the persons she had mentioned, had helped her to develop, from the way she was when she came to us, into the person she was when she left. In answer, Mary said that when she came to us she had felt that the whole world was against her, that everybody was convinced she was mean; she probably thought she was, too. But she began to change her mind about how bad the world was when she was never punished for getting herself dirty or for masturbating. She reminded me how she had been threatened with having her finger cut off for masturbating and how her hands had been taped when she sucked her thumb.

Next in importance in inducing her to change was: "I wanted to be like other people, probably—like Joan, Gayle, my sister, anybody." Also, "Miss Lukes [her teacher] helped me a lot. She made me interested in learning. It made me feel that I was as good as other children." Thus, according to Mary, freedom to enjoy herself and suitable images for identification—who through their behavior created the wish to identify with them—were the most significant curative factors and experiences.

I asked her what we did wrong. The only thing that came to her mind was that when she had her long screaming spells the counselors ignored her and would not speak to her. This she did not like. But she could not think of anything that she had wanted the counselors to do at such times. Although I encouraged her and told her how much I wanted to know what we did wrong, she could not think of any other mistakes we had made in handling her. But she spontaneously remembered some good things that we did for her— "mostly the animals." That we let her have them, and were interested in them, had been very important to her. She added that she still had all her stuffed animals, particularly "Onions—he's doing fine; I still like him a lot." This, and the toys we gave her, made her feel that perhaps this was not such a bad world to live in.

At the end of our conversation, I asked her whether in looking back there was anything we could do differently in running the School, or whether we should continue to conduct it along the same lines as when she was with us. She answered with great conviction, "Sure!" and added that she thought we did the right thing for children like her. Then, in retrospect, she said of her life, "It was both good and bad." The bad was that "with my mother and my aunt, I didn't grow up the right way." The good was found at the School: "I got my way and I wasn't scared any more."

Mary, as of now, is on her way, still no longer scared.

PART IV

"ICE CREAM IS BETTER THAN GOD"

John, Phantasy Life and Rehabilitation of a Boy with Anorexia[1]

John's Oral Trauma

JOHN'S SEVERE DIFFICULTIES in eating began on the seventh day of his life, when he developed a thrush mouth infection, which persisted uninterruptedly until his rehabilitation at the School was well under way. According to the hospital records (see p. 280)) the affliction was much better within two days, and mother and child left the hospital on the tenth day after his birth. Nevertheless, John was fed by eye dropper for the following six months and his mouth was painted with gentian violet for the first eight months of his life. Eating was very difficult, even painful, for him, which placed great strain on those who took care of him. From the very beginning he experienced neither the pleasure of sucking nor the feeling of satiation, since the small amount of food he could take at a time was not sufficient really to quell his hunger.

---

1. An extensive and illuminating discussion of three Rorschach findings on this boy is to be found in S. J. Beck, *Rorschach's Test, III. Advances in Interpretation* (New York: Grune and Stratton, 1952). It forms the sixth chapter, which is entitled, "A Boy in the Orthogenic School."

The mother's pregnancy was normal, and John was born at full term, with the use of instruments. In describing the birth some seven years later when we were seeking some explanation for John's behavior from the parents, the mother recalled that the back of his head had been marked by instruments. When we asked if he had been injured by the instruments, the mother said that he had not, but added instantly that he had borne a red mark in the area of the third or fourth vertebra. We were never able to determine just when his parents conceived the idea that their son was physically and mentally damaged rather than emotionally disturbed. But whenever it was, they cannot be blamed for accepting the notion, since it was suggested to them by many experts and was seemingly corroborated by the child's erratic behavior and lack of development.

When John's parents first told us about his life, John was seven years old.[2] We learned more about him during our frequent and regular contacts with his parents over the next few years. But by then, his parents' recollections of past attitudes and events had been colored by what had happened since in their relations to John and, because of John, in their reactions to each other and to life.

Parental involvement in an early and persistent emotional disturbance of a child—even where the origin is a physiological trauma, as in this case of thrush mouth—is likely to be very strong and to increase with the passing of time. This makes it difficult, if not impossible, to determine later which phases of the parents' emotional involvement and the child's difficulties originated in the personalities of the parents, which stemmed from interactions between child and parents, and which were new emotional impasses brought on chiefly by the child's own difficulties. John's lack of development—which was due to the early, severe, oral traumatization; the impact of parental emotions; or the interplay of these factors—was reflected in his extreme negativism. Such total withdrawal from and rejection of the whole world might have provoked severe reactions even in otherwise perfectly "normal" parents. In any case, the more severe the emotional disturbance of any member of such a threesome, the more intricately interwoven the strands of its causation and aggravation become. After this situation has existed for several years, it is almost impossible to establish the sequence of cause and effect with any accuracy. This seems to have been the case with John's family.

Still, I must begin John's story somewhere and so, simply because

---

2. John came to the School when he was five and a half, but we began to compile his complete history only after I joined the School's staff, nearly two years later.

his parents' lives antedate his, a brief sketch of the factors in their life histories that seemed significant to John's disturbance precedes here the boy's own history. But it should be remembered that, as soon as John was born, and possibly as early as the mother realized she was pregnant, John began to influence his parents. From this point on, to separate their life histories (or the histories of their emotional involvement with each other) no longer makes much sense, and can be justified only as a means of permitting orderly presentation.

The Father

JOHN'S FATHER had a very hard life. His parents were divorced when he was thirteen, but even before that they never got along. "There were constant battles and arguments," he told us. "I remember all through my childhood the sound of breaking dishes. They would not only throw them at each other, but to emphasize a point, they would break a dish." Even before his parents separated, and certainly afterward, he knew little happiness. Following the divorce, he lived part-time with his mother, and the rest of the time with his father. He was shifted about so much that in one year he moved thirteen times. Consequently he became quite dependent on his mother, since she alone loved him. His father seemed to have no interest in him and the two drifted apart. But he never failed to see his mother daily, and this was still his habit at the time he told us the history of his life.

John's father had been a rather sickly and nervous child, although he was quite active in high school sports. During his last three years in high school, he worked to support himself. His mother, too, was a sickly person who, after the divorce, had scant time to devote to her children since she had to work—and work hard.

The unhappier he was about his boyhood, the more utopian his dreams became about what his own family should one day be like. He was anxious for it to be extremely close and free of all discord. After his marriage, he was loath to give up his mother, and wanted her to continue to live with him. But since she was opposed to his marrying, he had to abandon that plan. He later came to realize that he had always been a perfectionist, and that this had added to the strain under which he lived. Although successful in the business he owned, he remarked that he only enjoyed the economic results of his work; the work, itself, he felt, was not rewarding.

John's parents, a very handsome couple, married young. Soon after, the mother became pregnant. They were very happy about this event. A first son was born, but he died at the age of eight months after a three-day illness. According to the parents, he had been a beautiful child, well formed and alert. After his death, they seemed to go to pieces. They left town immediately and went on a long trip, but this proved no solace. Nothing seemed to ease their pain. Finally they returned to their home town, but they could not face the memories there. They literally never set foot in their home again; friends moved all their belongings to a new residence. Then, to forget their grief, they plunged into working long and arduous hours at their business. Their whole life came to revolve about the shop, and the parents came to depend on each other more and more.

For a long time they were fearful of having another child, and almost five years elapsed before the mother became pregnant again. Though she had cared for her first child at home, this time her husband insisted that she hire nurses to care for John so that she could go on working in the shop. As it happened, John's subsequent illness was yet another reason for both parents to seek forgetfulness in work, and to lean ever more heavily on one another. This mutual dependency grew even stronger during John's stay at the School. In interviews held some five years later, when we were preparing them for John's return home, the father described how his marital life had changed in the meantime: "It's different. I would say that we're more preoccupied. All we do now is work. We talk about our business and work at it almost all the time we're not asleep. We're together constantly, every minute of every hour. Even on a business trip, we go together. Since we're together all of the time we don't spend much time at home. We don't give thought to our home. We don't fix it up like most people do. Home to us is a place to sleep and sometimes a place to watch television for a while. We're not proud of our home the way most people are, and have lost the desire to build a home."

That the father's marked dependence, first on his mother and then on his wife, may have been due to unsatisfied oral needs is suggested by his reaction to his sons. At the birth of the first boy, he developed a number of food allergies. When the second arrived, he became afflicted with "'terrible abdominal pains, and they persisted for a few years although it was finally proven to me at the Mayo clinic that I really didn't have any illness. They said it was because of my emotions." Later the pains returned, with the same diagnosis. Nevertheless, and possibly for good reasons, the father felt that he showed signs of "neurotic instability only in regard to

John. I become terribly alarmed when he's not feeling well. I immediately demand that a doctor be called in."

One might surmise that his anxiety reflected an unconscious
hostility against the son who, by his illness, was making such heavy
demands on the father's wife and business partner. But we know
that in later years John's vomiting, his extreme messiness with food,
or even his generally dishevelled and dirty appearance regularly
made the father so sick to his stomach that he was barely able to
keep his food down when he and John sat at the table together.
Did this result from an understandable disgust with John's eating
habits, or was it the expression of a much deeper hostility quite
divorced from John's behavior? It is hard to be sure which was the
case. That the father was at least an unconscious rival of his son
for dependent care seems evident from his wife's report that he
became ill whenever John was ill, that whenever John had to go
to bed the father soon did, too.

The Mother

JOHN'S MOTHER told us that her family had been small and very
closely knit. On the whole, she felt she had enjoyed a happy childhood. The entire family, particularly her mother, were very protective toward the father and the children were taught to control
their emotions to spare him. So she felt that she had never been
permitted to express her feelings. Even when her first son died she
kept her grief under control after her mother warned her that crying
might upset her father. On the other hand, John's mother described
both sides of her family as an "emotional bunch." Her father had
ulcers, and her mother and brother suffered from various allergies.

Even after her marriage, John's mother remained very close to
her family. Like her husband, she felt that her marriage was a pronounced success, and that marital differences arose only over John.

The mother thought of herself as a rather secure person, though
"too submissive." While this may have been true of her relation
to her parents, seeing her with husband and son gave the impression
that, if anything, they were too submissive to her. She apparently
managed them with a firm hand. With the exception of what she
called her submissiveness, she felt quite adequate and secure outside her relation to John.

Her strong attachment to her first-born son was very obvious
throughout our contacts with her. Even when John was on the verge
of leaving the School, and eighteen years had elapsed since the death

of her first child, the least mention of John's brother upset her greatly. Comparing her two children, she said, "I think if we had had a child soon after the first died, it might have been a replacement. But by the time John came along it was just nothing. I didn't care one way or another about having a child. And John was a sick, apathetic baby, excruciatingly homely." Another time she recalled that the first child had been "very easy to handle. I had confidence in myself where he was concerned." But as for John, "I didn't have any confidence with him. He frightened me because he was so thin and sickly, and I was really afraid to handle him."

It seems reasonable to assume that this lack of self-confidence characterized her relation to John from the beginning. Just why she lost her original assurance is difficult to say; we also could not learn much about the specific nature of her deep involvement with her first son, which caused such a total break in her life when he died. But there is reason to think that both parents considered his illness and death not wholly a matter of chance. They felt guilty about it, and this guilt may have influenced their feelings about their second child even before his birth.

The only direct statements his parents made to us about John were recorded long after his conception and birth. But the feelings his mother expressed then (when he was seven) seem characteristic of their attitude from the outset. She said, "I worry about him and watch him too closely. When he's around I'm never sure of myself. I'm trying very hard to have a normal relation to him, but I'm too nervous in handling him. By the end of the day I find myself overprotective, or not using good judgment otherwise."

How much these attitudes stemmed from John's lack of development, we did not know. But in rudimentary form, they must have appeared very soon after his birth, since she let a nurse take over his total care right after he left the hospital.

It would be fascinating to speculate about the parents' involvement with each other, which had become so deep by the time John was born that there seemed little place for him in their lives—so little, that he may have seemed an intruder. Matters were aggravated, of course, by the parents' oppressive feelings of guilt, for they clearly saw the inadequacy of their relation to him, and valiantly tried to remedy the situation. But this only made them feel more "all thumbs." There seems some truth in the statement each made independently that they were neurotic only in regard to John, and that otherwise they were both perfectly normal. John evidently furnished a focus for whatever neurotic tendencies existed; by directing these onto their son, they kept the rest of their lives fairly free of

JOHN   [277]

disturbing factors. To the casual observer, this couple would have
appeared quite normal, except that they lived such withdrawn and
intensely hard-working lives.

When I had become thoroughly acquainted with John's parents
and they had gained confidence in me, I suggested that they should
seek psychiatric help. The father could never accept this idea. But
after much hesitancy, the mother finally agreed to see the School's
psychiatric social worker regularly. Within three months, after
having skipped several appointments for no apparent reason, she
broke off the relation. While it lasted, she revealed her great sense
of guilt at what she considered her desertion of John, that is, the
way she handed him over to nurses so that she could continue helping her husband in his business. Sending him later to the hospital
and then to the School seemed additional acts of desertion.

It was also impossible for her to admit to herself or to others
that she could not handle John and his problems. She blamed her
mistakes on the misguided psychological principles and techniques
she had used with him. Once, as an example, she cited her desire
to spare his feelings when he got hurt. To that end, she always
laughed when he fell and bruised himself; of all the various and
contradictory advice she had read and heard, she chose to carry
out such Spartan suggestions. As she reported this incident, her
desire for self-castigation seemed quite obvious. She felt excruciatingly guilty about her failure as a mother, and compensated for
it by blaming everyone else who had contact with John—her husband, the nurses, doctors, then the staff of the School. This, in general, characterized her attitude; but the guilt always predominated.

Both parents frequently complained about how passive John
was; when he once failed to stand up to a younger child who bullied
him, they openly called him foolish. Yet in her first conversation
with the social worker the mother spoke with evident anxiety about
an attempt of John's to hurt her. She feared the growing aggressiveness she thought she could observe in him, much as if she were
anticipating that he would try to punish her for her failures. She
realized that it was probably healthy for John to become more
assertive, but admitted that this was very difficult for her to take.
When John began using mildly abusive terms, nowadays accepted
by most parents without much fuss, the mother asked whether she
was supposed to "take everything" from him.

But these were minor worries compared with her greatest anxiety: that our work with John might undo even the slight progress
he had made. Since John was so severely retarded in all kinds of
achievement, including the academic, the parents kept trying to

push him toward greater accomplishment. His mother, especially, was afraid that at the School, instead of being pushed forward, John "might even be led back to the bottle." She voiced this fear long before John actually did return to the bottle. How early the pressure for achievement had interfered with John's well-being is illustrated by the fact that this sickly child was toilet trained when he was but six weeks old.

Squaring up to these, her true feelings, must have seemed impossible to the mother, and this alone may have been sufficient reason for breaking off treatment. But there were other motivations, too. In her first interview with the social worker, the mother spontaneously remarked that she had been happy with her husband until then, and feared that therapy might complicate her marriage. In the past she had mastered her difficulties without help, and she planned to do so in the future. She saw no reason for further meetings with the worker.

Our feeling was that she was not so much unable to face her guilt about John's troubles or to explore her relations with her husband and others, as she was unable to face her anxiety about yielding to a suppressed desire for dependent gratification. In her marital life, she had furnished dependent gratification for her husband while her needs went unsatisfied. She had ignored her deep wishes to be cared for, just as she had suppressed her own feelings as a child to please her parents; as a consequence, on the surface, at least, the marital relation seemed satisfactory. Her desire to be taken care of must have been very great when her first child died. She may have begun to repress her need at that time so that she could provide her husband with the emotional satisfactions he required. Then along came John with new dependent demands.

All this began to come to light during our abortive effort to help the mother. Unable to satisfy both son and husband, she had decided in her husband's favor. Perhaps she did so because he had at least remained with her, whereas her first son had not. It was our impression that, having repressed her own dependent needs to satisfy her husband (and feeling guilty about her failure to meet John's needs), she came to the very first interview wanting just such gratification for herself, but also defending herself against it. As her defenses began to crumble during the three months' period when a relation to the worker was developing, the mother became panic-stricken at what might happen if she were to give them up. After all, they had enabled her to get along in life. This, therefore, was probably why she discontinued therapy.

The parents' emotional inability to cope with John continued

throughout his stay at the School. From time to time, when particularly knotty problems came up after home visits or when the
parents seemed temporarily more susceptible to the idea, we suggested treatment to one or both of them. Once the mother actually
followed through again, and for a time saw a psychoanalyst weekly.
But she dropped this treatment, too, within three months, again
after several broken appointments. Both she and the analyst agreed
that, given the mother's resistance, there was no purpose in trying
to continue treatment. The analyst felt that the mother did not
really wish to change; the mother was sure that he was unable to
help her.

Finally, when John was about to leave us, we once more urged
treatment for the mother to prepare her for his homecoming and to
help her with any problems that might subsequently arise. She too,
she said, was anxious to prepare herself in this way, but no psychoanalyst we named was acceptable to her, and she could not select one
on her own. At long last, she decided to consult the psychoanalyst
she had seen previously, but he had moved out of town. She lost
his new address, which I had given her. Next she planned to see
him on a visit to the city where he was practicing, but once there she
could not find the time to consult him. Finally she wrote him, only
to fail to follow his recommendations.

In our last contacts with her before John left the School, we felt
that she had achieved a precarious integration, which she was unwilling to risk through treatment; and we could not help feeling that
perhaps she knew best. There was a chance that with John home,
she could see for herself that she was not as damaging to him as
she may have feared, and she might become less timid about facing
her unconscious. She was, therefore, urged to consider psychotherapy at a later date if she felt the need or desire for it.

John's First Years

IT WAS DIFFICULT for us to find out what John's earliest life had
been like. When the parents told us about it, despite sincere efforts
at objectivity, they could no longer sort out the facts from their distorted recollections, or distinguish between their actual motives and
feelings and what they now thought those feelings had been. Driven
by anxiety, they had talked over every detail of John's life with so
many people, including physicians and advisers, and had received
so many, often contradictory reactions, that assessing what was fact
and what was fiction seemed impossible.

The center of their feeling about John was that things had gone wrong from the very beginning. Since they put such emphasis on his having been, at birth, a sickly and fragile infant who developed thrush mouth on the third day of his life and consequently had to be fed with an eye dropper for many months, we checked the hospital record. It contained the following report:

"Mother did not bear down well, outlet forceps necessary. Normal baby boy delivered. Did not cry readily and seemed somewhat narcotized. However he responded after tracheal catheterization and cutaneous stimulation. Mother and baby left delivery room in good condition. Birth weight: 2897 gms. The baby was fed on glucose for three days, then went to breast and was nursed the seven following days and was also given supplementary bottle feedings. On seventh day mouth lesions noted, picture of thrush; smear taken for *moniliasis albicans*. Rx: gentian violet. The eighth day, clinical thrush. On the ninth day, better. Discharged on tenth day: Weight: 2750 gms. on discharge."

Aside from the thrush infection, the infant's record was perfectly normal. The nursery notes mention no feeding problems. John lost weight for the first five days, but only ten or fifteen grams daily, and then gained on the last two days. He was discharged with the mother, which indicated that the doctors did not deem the thrush infection serious.

The father remembered things differently: "At the time he was born, on the second day, he developed thrush mouth, which according to the pediatrician was the fault of the hospital. With constant care that was eliminated. But he was fed with an eye dropper right from the start. Never breast fed at all. He vomited constantly and we'd always attempt to refeed him. Regurgitated almost from the moment he first began to eat. I wouldn't know so much about the hospital as I do from the home. He went home after two weeks. The dropper was used exclusively for six months. Then he began to have a bottle. There was great difficulty in changing to the bottle. He didn't know how, or couldn't draw the milk from the bottle. We made the hole large enough in the nipple so that it could drop out —that was at the beginning. But there was constant regurgitation. We would give him a little more and then wait a few hours—he would get fed about every two hours—sometimes in less time than that. He had a slight case of rickets because of lack of nourishment— I don't know. The pediatrician gave us the inference it was that, but not the full diagnosis."

The mother's memory tallied more closely with the record. She recalled breast feedings and also that his feeding problems did not begin in the hospital but only after John had left it. She added that he was unable to suck. (The records show that this was not true during his stay in the hospital.) He was "apathetic as an infant. He had thrush mouth, and feeding problems started when he left the hospital. He vomited from the beginning. Milk was pumped from my breasts for two or three weeks. He had supplementary feedings with that, but he was unable to suck. He was fed with an eye dropper for from six to eight months. He had thrush mouth and his mouth was sore. It lasted for a long time—his mouth was painted for eight months—although it is supposed to be a forty-eight hour disease. We just had trouble clearing it up. John was completely on a formula after the third week. He could never hold the normal amount of food a baby his age would take. He vomited a great deal of the time—I wouldn't say after every feeding, but nearly so. This vomiting has persisted. Sudden noises bothered him much more than the average infant. He was slow in physical development. He seemed to have that feeling of insecurity from the beginning. He 'wasn't a happy baby."

I have quoted what both parents said about John's early feeding experiences, since eating was the crux of his problem. As for the rest of his life before coming to the School, the following is a composite account of both parents' stories.

From the first, they were afraid of handling John because he was such a fragile baby; it was anxiety, not indifference, that kept them from caring for their son. The same anxiety prevented them from letting the nurses take proper care of him. The parents made the nursing job, which in itself was none too easy, impossible. The mother described how her husband, on arriving home, would immediately interfere with John's care, in excitement or anger. "He, too, was nervous about what John was getting, and as soon as he would come home he would take the bottle from the nurse and test it to see if it was the right temperature for John." Only the "he, too" suggests that this pattern was characteristic of both parents. Some nurses left, because whatever they did, they were severely criticized. Others proved so incompetent that the pediatrician asked for their immediate removal. There were at least four nurses during the first six months of John's life, not counting those who stayed but a few days. This ever-changing regime went on until he was two and a half. So John was cared for by a bewildering succession of people, which made it impossible for him to adapt to any one person's ways.

How rigidly some of these nurses trained John with parental consent can be surmised from the previously mentioned fact that toilet training of this ailing child began when he was only six weeks old. Further overconcern about it must have been present, since according to the parents, John had been constipated from babyhood, and was given regular doses of mineral oil for some time. His constipation, if it was real and not just imagined by the parents, seemed connected with his tenseness around feedings rather than with the premature toilet training, for during the brief periods when he could keep food down, his bowel movements were normal. The moment he began regurgitating his food, he became constipated again.

His eating difficulties were handled with deep anxiety, if not outright punitiveness. First his nurses and then his parents reacted to his resistance by literally forcing food down his throat. When he rebelled and fought back, one parent would hold him while a nurse —or the other parent—crammed the food into him. Meals he threw up were often forced back down his throat. These protracted fights filled many of his waking hours. Later, when he occasionally ate by himself, he did so with excruciating slowness and messiness.

Otherwise, the parents could recall little about his early life, since nurses had taken full care of him during most of his infancy. Nevertheless they felt sure that in comparison with their first baby, who developed rapidly, and whom they now idolized beyond reason, John's growth had lagged from the very beginning. Even when reminded that, according to their own recollections, he went through each stage of development at the average time—for example, he learned to walk and talk at a normal age—they still insisted that he had been abnormally slow from birth. He never played actively, as did other children, was forever catching cold, and always looked very sad and unhappy. When he responded to the world at all, it was by whining. He gagged frequently, especially when he saw food. But even when confronted with something that had been torn— bits of paper, pieces of clothing, or lengths of string with which other children enjoyed playing—John gagged violently.

After two and a half years of this life, a good nurse finally was found to take care of him. She did not respond with anger when he vomited and the vomiting cleared up to some extent. In many other ways, too, she handled John gently and with positive feeling for his difficulties. Within six months the good experiences she provided led to improved relations between John and his parents. By the age of three his emotional development at last began catching up with his physical and intellectual growth. He wanted to be around his mother and tried in all kinds of ways to catch her attention. Unfortunately, for reasons not made clear to us, the good nurse left when he was three and a half. She was replaced by a maid who "would yank John around and be very impatient with him." The plan had been that the maid would take care of all the housework so that the mother, who was to stay home when the nurse left, could devote herself more to John. But despite this plan, for reasons that, as likely as not, included the father's demands on the mother's time, John's care was still left pretty much to the inadequate maid.

A few weeks later John had a very upsetting accident. It is hard to say whether this in itself had a traumatic effect, or whether it raised the parents' anxiety to a traumatic pitch. The mother told us the story: "My family was coming to visit; I was busy preparing dinner for them and I needed something at the store. I asked the maid to take John with her to the store, but I warned her to be cautious about holding his hand going up and down the stairs. I never had any degree of calmness when it came to John. I couldn't even delegate authority to anyone with calmness. I worried about every little thing and I would give explicit directions whenever anyone took him out. Well, anyway, they had been to the store and John was carrying a clothespin in his hand. He fell and the clothespin penetrated through his lip and up into the roof of his mouth, lancing the gum. That was a terrible thing. John was just again showing signs of being a little happier when this happened. The vomiting had decreased from several times to just once or twice a day. I didn't realize how severely John was hurt at the time. Finally I carried him to a drug store. John had to be hospitalized. For a while we didn't think he would pull through."

After this trauma, John reverted to the worst type of feeding difficulties. There were nausea, gagging, and vomiting at every meal, and the parents, in their anxiety, once more relied on forced feedings. Each meal again became an excruciating and exhausting battle, which ended with parents and child both totally defeated by one another's emotions. It was almost impossible, later on, to pinpoint this traumatic experience as the particular cause of any one of John's difficulties. For example, John developed a phobia about walking on stairs, which persisted well into his second year at the School. But we do not know whether this phobia came from the accident itself or the parents' subsequent anxiety about letting John go up and down stairs.

For years after this, John was a very sickly child, although none of his various ailments, except the anorexia, was serious. In time, he began to vomit not only when he was supposed to eat, but also in all other frustrating situations—and just about any experience seemed to frustrate the boy. Yet even after this last shocking mishap, there remained one person with whom he could enjoy eating, or at least with whom the vomiting seldom occurred: his maternal grandmother. "I think she (the grandmother) accepts John exactly as he is," his mother told us. "My mother never worries about how dirty John gets. It just doesn't bother her. She doesn't care how long he takes eating and how much he messes with his food."

In view of the way John's mother had been brought up to inhibit her emotions, to be overly neat, orderly, and hard working (the same characteristics that, incidentally, also applied to John's father), one might speculate about how she must have felt on observing that her own mother could enjoy John's dirtiness. It may have been destructive to her pride as a mother to realize that John's grand-mother was able to feed him so pleasantly, when this very issue damaged her own relation to her son. Yet whatever the mother's feelings, she never showed them; her training in not expressing emotions held fast.

John's oral apparatus seemed never to be at peace. As if his inability to eat, his gagging, spitting, and vomiting were not enough, he had frequent colds and a heavy secretion of mucus made breath-ing and eating difficult. He did not learn to blow his nose volun-tarily until he had been at the School for many years; his face was always covered with grime. When he was four and a half years old, before he had time to overcome the emotional consequences of the trauma to his mouth, his tonsils and adenoids were removed. This surgery did not improve his health, and the frequent colds continued.

Since all his sucking and eating experiences were so painful, it is not surprising that for years we never once saw John suck his fingers or put objects exploringly into his mouth. We do not know whether he ever tried these things while under the nurses' care, or whether they prohibited them. On the other hand, food was an obses-sion with John, even though ingestion was so frustrating for him. His favorite pastime was naming varieties of food. Talking about food, as a matter of fact, was one of the few ways his parents could elicit a response from him. For example, the father said, "Sometimes I don't know whether or not he's hearing. I spoke to him five times this morning and he paid no attention. But mention chocolate, banana, or almost anything sweet and he'll respond. Otherwise he just doesn't bother to answer—unless he's in the mood. And he's more that way with us than with anyone else."

When John was five, an attempt was made to send him to kinder-garten, an experiment that was repeated six months later. Both attempts came to nothing since he reacted to the strange environ-ment with such great anxiety and frequent vomiting that he could not continue.

His inability to attend kindergarten was part of his general pat-tern of being unable to form a relation to more than one person—

if his anxious, hostile, clinging could be called a relation. John, said his mother, had always "been overly attached to one individual at a time. He is a police dog type of individual. As long as he's attached to one person he has no use for any others. He's been so attached to the nurses and me. When he was in the hospital he attached himself to a small colored boy. This attachment was so violent that he refused to eat, sleep, or see me without this boy being present."

It seems strange that the mother chose the analogy of a "police dog" to describe John's attachment to a single person. It is usual to think of police dogs as vicious toward opponents and protective of the persons to whom they belong. The mother's observation that John, like a baby, had use for only one person at a time and could not bear divided attention, either on his part or his mother's, was probably correct. This being so, however, one might conclude that John needed a "police dog" kind of person to care for him, rather than infer that he was such a person himself. That the mother possibly rejected his great need for her, and was annoyed that he wanted her to be his "police dog," seems further suggested by her complaint that John had a "mother complex" and needed to become more independent.

The attachment to the Negro boy, of which she spoke, was formed during John's last hospitalization, before he entered the School. Just why he was hospitalized was not clear. His physical symptom was a light upper respiratory and middle ear infection, which was by no means serious enough in itself to warrant hospitalization. The pediatrician recommended it because he felt that the parents were not able to handle John adequately at home, because of their emotional involvement. While he lived at home, the physicians had been very dubious about the outlook for John's future.

But in contrast to his behavior at home, John made a fairly good adjustment to the hospital, and this suggested to the doctors that contrary to their previous opinions the prognosis in the long run might be fair if he were permanently removed from the home. After careful pediatric and psychiatric study the parents were advised to place John in the School for a prolonged period. Even after his infection had cleared up, John was kept on at the hospital, so that he could enter the School directly without having to return home first. The following observations were made while he was in the hospital.

Physical examination revealed "a nervous, high strung, alert child." The psychiatric examination prompted the following remarks: "There appears to be a significant discrepancy between the child's apparent intellectual development and the apparent retardation in walking and talking. There is clear evidence of strong attachment to the mother with emphasis on exclusiveness of the relationship." The final diagnosis was that John suffered from "excessive infantile dependency. (Vomiting is a frequent part of such situations.) Primary behavior disorder with neurotic traits and fears."

Soon after his arrival at the School, John was examined at the University of Chicago Clinics. Although the neurological findings were negative ("All fundi normal, all cranial nerves normal in action, all reflexes normal"), because of the choreiform position of both hands, continuous athetoid movements of both hands and both arms, and the given history, the prognosis was very dim. It was assumed that "the mental retardation and the athetosis are presumably the result of a prenatal failure in complete development of the cortex." The final diagnosis was: "Cerebral agenesis, congenital athetosis, and mental retardation."[3]

He Comes to the School

JOHN CAME to the School when he was five and a half. I would like to say right here that his story is not so much an example of what we feel we can now achieve in the institutional treatment of such a disturbed child, under favorable conditions, but rather a report on what we learned about his disturbance and achieved in his rehabilitation under difficult circumstances. To a large extent, John's specific difficulties seemed to be the consequence of his early oral traumatization and fixation. During his years with us he apparently had to recapture all later phases of development. In a way, his story suggests to what degree early stages of psycho-physiological development can be recaptured once they have been by-passed. It also throws light upon the nature of very early oral fixations and shows how they interfere with later emotions and life experiences.

Our greatest handicap was the fact that treatment was not begun in the proper and necessary way for this boy when he first entered the School. He came to the School before it was reorganized as a total therapeutic setting based on psychoanalytic thinking about primary behavior disorders of children. When John entered, some of the children with whom he lived were mentally retarded, others were epileptic, etc. Only with the School's reorganization, which was begun more than a year later, were better conditions for his rehabili-

---

3. See footnote No. 14, p. 302.

tation created. But it took nearly two more years to complete the reorganization, so during John's first years with us he did not benefit fully from it.

Since none of the present staff, with the exception of one teacher (who had only little contact with John), worked at the School when he first came, we can only speculate, from early reports that we could not check, and from later observations, about what he was like at that time. We doubt that before our work began to bear fruit he had ever learned to recognize himself as a person, or his parents as separate from himself. While he had lived in physical proximity to the others, he never related to anybody, with the possible exception of the one good nurse. So, at a time when it would have been crucially important for John to feel immediately that things were different at the School, that it was a new setting in which positive human attachments were not only offered but possible, the School must have seemed only a worse version of the home.

Breaking the Anaclitic Ties

JOHN'S DIFFICULTIES were in the nature of a triangular problem; in addition to his own primary behavior disorder, there also had to be considered the emotional difficulties and interactions between his parents, and their intense involvement with him. For these reasons, during John's stay at the School, parental contacts proved a major factor in his life, and later, after the School's reorganization, became the worst impediment to our efforts. The tribulations occasioned by John's visits home, while very important, cannot be covered in detail, although his specific reactions to some of them will be mentioned. I shall here sketch in a few remarks about them, however, since they had such grave influence on our work.

When John came to the School, the policy was to have the children visit their homes every week-end. On nearly every one of these visits, John developed a cold; therefore, he spent more days at home than at the School. Years passed before we could reduce these visits to Sunday only, and later, under the repeated threat of dismissing John, to those few visits we deemed advisable. In order to achieve this, we worked unceasingly at building a good relation between parents and School. Our efforts were successful so long as we made no real demands on the parents. But when we found it necessary to gain for John a reduction in the number of home visits, we had to risk our good relation in order to achieve this.

We could have sent John home and temporarily abandoned our attempts to help him, in the hope that the situation would then become so intolerable that the parents might be forced to seek psychiatric help or to accept our restrictions upon the visits. But this seemed unfair to John and unpromising. After all, treatment had already been suggested to them before John had been placed in School. They had not been able to accept it then and there was scant reason for believing they would now. And even if they did, and were benefited, we could not be sure just what this would mean for John. It was conceivable that the mother's treatment process might even prove so stormy that, if John were home, his disturbance would be irreparably aggravated.

In the light of this evaluation of the situation, into which many more factors entered than are mentioned here, we strove to keep mother and son apart as much as was safe and feasible, so that John could become a person in his own right. Separation, we hoped, would sufficiently weaken the disturbing elements in their ties to each other, at least as far as John was concerned, so that he could form a close and constructive relation with someone else. With such support he might be able to master later the neurotic aspects of his relation to his mother.

We also hoped that, after their symbiotic relation had been loosened, the mother might feel readier to accept psychiatric aid, since some of the secondary advantages she received from her attachment to John, which were detrimental to him, would no longer be available to her. For a long time we strove to have her seek treatment, because for the mother to give up her neurotic involvement in John seemed to offer the best chance for his improvement. But failing in this, we had to attempt the difficult task of separating John emotionally from his parents and strengthening him sufficiently so that he would not succumb to neurotic involvement with his mother when he eventually returned home. This separation, mother and son (and often also the father) resisted most strongly.

It would really have been best to part the two for a couple of years, and thus make it easier for John to form a relation with some staff member. We would have preferred this "traumatic" solution to the long, drawn out process of weaning John away from his mother, which only meant that more time was lost before he could establish a healthier relation with someone else. But, unfortunately, the parents could not accept this. For years nothing could shake their insistence that he come home every week. Yet, the more we saw how he reacted to these visits, the more obvious it became that unless the parents' attitude to the boy changed, and probably their personalities as well, the reunions could only influence John adversely. At home, he clung to his mother, but this closeness gave him neither comfort nor strength for independence. Rather, he tried to exact even greater services from her by developing sundry ailments (mainly upper respiratory afflictions, such as colds) and anorexia, with its accompaniment of gagging and vomiting. Unfortunately, these illnesses, which were really pleas for dependent gratification, only set off the old, vicious circle. For they increased the anxiety and guilt of his parents so much that he actually received less instead of more gratification. And so he became worse. Each time he returned to the School, his terrible unhappiness and increased vomiting showed clearly how he reacted to being with his parents.

On these visits John sensed his parents' deep dissatisfaction with him. He could neither fully enjoy infantile pleasures at the School, nor find satisfaction in his small gains, since they never sufficed for his parents. Actually, on each home visit, his parents were anxiously evaluating the progress he had made in the interim. This pressure for "progress" was reflected in his School life in diverse ways. The most obvious was John's ceaseless worry about whether he was getting anywhere. He could never quite define what he meant by this, since he did not really know what his parents expected of him. He could only sadly remark one week that he had to "learn to fight," the next that he had to "learn not to fight and make friends," or "learn to play games." To complicate matters, John worried about whether his parents would still accept him if he did change. He fought to keep the hostile control he could exert over his mother through his symptoms, because he could not feel sure of receiving any satisfactory or lasting rewards in its place. We could see that as long as John was caught in the meshes of this family situation he would not learn new ways of mastering his problems.

For two or three days after each visit he lived under the impact of his parents and the pattern he had evolved for dealing with them, particularly his mother. During the second half of the week, his energies were concentrated upon imagining how he would press his family to serve him every moment; he planned in minutest detail and with fantastic elaboration just what he would do with and to his parents. These plans and phantasies he revealed only much later, after we had succeeded in reducing the frequency of his visits.

More than two and a half years passed before our efforts to persuade the parents to relinquish his weekly visits were successful. Thereafter, visiting was limited to about four or five times a year —at Christmas, John's birthday, the summer vacation, Thanksgiving, and perhaps the Fourth of July week-end. Such long-term periods of separation were needed before John, little by little, could form close ties to people at the School. Only, too, when he felt fairly free of the pressure for achievement put upon him by his parents each week, was he able to regress and enjoy the infantile satisfactions he craved so much. Thus, in many ways, faster progress began only when the weekly visits ceased. Until then, we had to be content with reducing the intensity of the traumatic experiences that occurred when he was home, and with slowly weaning John and his parents from each other.

John and the Staff

JOHN'S EVENTUAL IMPROVEMENT, more than in the case of some other children, came about only through the coordinated efforts of several staff members. While the other three histories show how much individual workers have been able to accept and tolerate, no one person could afford the emotional expenditure John required. So primitive and unstructured was John's oral hostility that no one could endure his symptoms without feeling an enormous displeasure. Only several people working cooperatively could supply him at all times with the amount of satisfaction for his needs that he could permit himself to accept at any particular moment.

Unique among our children was John's resistance to genuine emotional contact with staff members for, not months, but years, despite their best efforts to serve and help him. He thwarted them in the most ingenious ways. It was a full four years before this significant aspect of his behavior—and of his personality—began to change.

To be accurate, for months on end he made almost no progress at all, which could not help but disrupt the workers' inner security. When he persistently met even their most genuine and loving efforts with hostile indifference, it was most difficult not to counter by overlooking or ignoring him; this, in turn, was the very attitude John wished to provoke because he yearned to give up living. He was so unhappily entrenched in his hostile isolation, that any halfway normal response from him marked a red-letter day for the staff.

Much later, when working with John had become considerably easier, several staff members remarked independently of each other that, like everybody else, they had sensed the danger of finding him repulsive. He was so homely and dishevelled, so repellently smeared with spittle, mucus, and dirt, and wore so hostile an expression, that even those most devoted to him had to exert special efforts in order to accept him. One of his counselors told us that when he seemed least likable she concentrated on his eyes, which were appealing. "At such moments I used to seize on that aesthetic gratification in lieu of dwelling on the rest of his face or body, which always looked so crummy. I guess I just like dark eyes. I am speaking of the physical conformation—that sad or burning hostile expression was more disturbing than pretty."

Straining to find appealing qualities in John despite his behavior continued to drain the people working with him of their resources; to be able to suffer his really unpleasant symptoms and still maintain positive attitudes toward him, they had to rely on identifying with his inadequacy and helplessness.

Yet this, in a way, was helpful because it fostered their efforts to give him the kind of emotional care that is normally received only by a baby. Through such services, John was eventually able to recapture to some degree the developmental stages he had never (or inadequately) experienced as an infant, and for a long time, the only possible way for him to form any kind of attachment was on the basis of receiving infantile care. On the other hand, because this was so deeply satisfying to John, it later became difficult to guide him to higher stages of human interaction; such guidance he resisted stubbornly and effectively, though passively, for years. Eventually this impasse was overcome by introducing new workers to him when he finally became able to relate on a somewhat higher level; thus, new associations were formed on quite a different emotional basis, a more and more truly interpersonal one.

His First Experience in the School

AS MENTIONED BEFORE, when John came to the School it was conducted neither along psychoanalytic lines nor as a therapeutic milieu. Later, when its reorganization was sufficiently under way so that we could devote our thinking and planning to each individual child, only two staff members—teachers—stayed on; the rest left because they could not agree with the new, psychoanalytic approach. One of those who remained (although she unfortunately also left relatively soon afterward) had been John's teacher.

From her, from the School records, and from what other staff members told us before they left, we learned that John had been extremely withdrawn and repressed when he came to the School. He was painfully slow, particularly about dressing and eating. His table manners were abominable. He played dreamily with his food —spilling it, handling it, only occasionally putting a bite in his mouth. Milk gave him the most trouble. He threw up during every meal, and was particularly prone to do so repeatedly and violently after each home visit. His vomiting seemed an effort to avoid eating altogether—a rejection of life itself.

His motor coordination was so poor that everybody thought he was spastic. He lived in terror of the more aggressive boys, who used him as a scapegoat in their games. Since it was impossible for him to show anger or disagreement, he camouflaged all feelings behind an artificial smile. Months later, on the rare occasions when he dared to act as if he were ready to strike another child—an empty motion at best—he did not use his fist or the flat of his hand. Instead, he formed a sort of claw, very much as a baby might do, who cannot yet grip an object or make a fist. In this and other movements, his arms, hands, and fingers seemed spastic in their lack of articulation, and very much resembled the motions of an infant. Most of the time, and whenever left to his own devices, he lay on his back in his bed and made random movements of his arms and legs, like a tiny baby—all the while staring at "nothing." Any effort to establish contact with him, he warded off as an unpleasant intrusion.

With his sad, hangdog look he could make almost any staff member feel guilty. He masturbated openly and often. He seemed lost in daydreams all the time. If spoken to, he quickly went through the pretense of doing what he thought was expected of him, and put on a great though purposeless show of being busy. After a minute or two, during which nothing was accomplished, he again relapsed into daydreaming. Unfortunately, during his early months in the School, pressure was exerted on him to learn, to play, and to improve his eating habits. All this only aggravated his vomiting and induced further emotional withdrawal.

Nevertheless, some progress of a sort seems to have been made with him during that first year and a half, but this progress was in the nature of automatic conditioning. The pressure exercised on him to eat in more orderly fashion, to keep himself clean, and so forth, met with some success, that is, he acquired some conditioned responses. One might speculate why the School succeeded in this respect, although the parents' similar efforts had failed. The reason was probably that at the School, such pressure was exercised by people who did not feel anxious or guilty toward John. Because they were less involved, John could respond more readily to their efforts. But he did so at the price of further repressing his true desires. Externally he conformed a little more to the outer world, but inwardly he paid even less attention to it. Later, this made him even more resistant to the efforts we made to satisfy his needs and stimulate personal growth.

When we started to approach John on the basis of quite different principles about the rehabilitation of emotionally disturbed children, he deeply resented this change. We felt that before John could make any real progress he would have to be given far more leeway to live in line with his desires, including his aggressive and regressive wishes, and that any step forward should be taken in his own good time. This seemed to us the only way he might eventually be able to develop some self-regulation—no easy task, because he had already been pushed in too many, and often in opposite, directions, such as into both premature independence, and dependence imposed through overprotection. Therefore he could not immediately react to our efforts to let him have his own way, because that, too, seemed externally imposed and not a challenge to self-regulation or mastery. For quite some time, he remained indifferent to a new regime that let him play with his food as much as he wanted, be as slow as he wished, get as dirty as he pleased, etc. The vomiting, for example, first kept on unchanged and then later became more deliberately aggressive. As if by design, he began throwing up on those people who cared for him most intimately.

Still, after a few months, at fleeting moments, John began to show more openly both his desire for infantile pleasures, and his hostility. He did this first with his teacher, perhaps because he had known her longest or because, as a teacher, she had less to do with the areas in which his strongest conflicts about conforming had arisen, that is, feeding, dressing, and cleanliness. Once he asked spontaneously: how could she expect him to butter his bread? Had she ever seen a month-old baby do so? He was using the removal of the old pressures to show his hostility, to make fun of anyone who expected that John (who felt like a baby a month old) could possibly care for himself.

As were so many of the remarks he made later, this one was motivated by his wish to be treated like a baby. It accused us of expecting too much of him, and of being stupid and full of bad intentions, since we did not understand his needs and abilities or make sufficient allowance for them. A few days later he told the teacher that some day he would visit her home and wet the carpet. How would he do it? "I'll make a stream of water," he said. This statement of revolt against imposed cleanliness was another demonstration of the infantile way in which he wished to assert himself and punish others.

Shortly after, he made another effort to be babied by this teacher. As he was eating one day, he began sliding closer and closer to her. She encouraged him, by remarking that if he continued he would soon land in her lap. John shot back quickly, "Would you like that?" Unfortunately, instead of showing pleasure, for she had not acquired the new spirit of the School, she replied, "Would you?" For months, this checked John's efforts to reach out for physical closeness. That John's dependent and hostile desires were inter-related was implicit in his reply: "You better not, because I would shove you to the wall, and I would hurt you and hurt you, and you would be so badly hurt that you would have to put forty hundred bandages on you to make you well again."

For a long time this mixture of wishing for utter dependence and cuddling, yet feeling that physical contact was tantamount to extreme hostility, made it most difficult to come closer to John. He purposely made it hard because he feared what might happen, as a consequence of his intense anger, to any person he permitted to come close to him. So his hostility was effective in frustrating any attempt at relating. In addition, the teacher was reluctant to hold him on her lap while he ate because of his eating habits: emesis might occur at any time, particularly when John was excited. Her revulsion to this unpleasantness might then more than negate the good of taking him on her lap. John could be helped only by a person who could fully accept him even when he spat and vomited on her; and this teacher's personality did not permit her to do this.

His eating habits, at very best, were described by her at about this time: "When John eats—peas for example—he takes them off the plate with his left hand, then transfers them to the palm of his right hand, then rubs them between the palms of both hands; then if they have not previously landed on the floor he will open his mouth with the fingers of one hand and with the fingers of the other hand shove the peas into his mouth. But my impression is that he would really like the food to land on the floor rather than into his mouth." Thus John used his new freedom to eat as he pleased. He did not chew his food, but mashed it, mainly with his hands, and then put it deep into his mouth, so that he could swallow it without using his mouth. He appeared to be re-creating the old situation at home, when he was fed with an eye dropper, or later, when he was force fed by cramming the food down his throat. In this first possible step toward freer self-expression he seemed to revive a familiar situation; the difference was that now he inflicted force feeding and suffering on himself.

With other children John was not just passive, but went out of his way to be extremely submissive. He was obviously very afraid of the more aggressive boys. Occasionally he participated in games in which he made himself the weak subject of the other boys' play. He preferred games of war, in which he could become a prisoner right away. He was content to have his hands tied to a fence, or to be physically restrained in other ways.[4] The counselor's attempts to protect him from such abuse met with stolid resistance. He insisted that he wanted to play this way.

Again it seemed that in this play he was re-creating on his own initiative the only kind of human interaction he had known, that is, in which he was the passive subject whose "hands were tied." We suspected that he derived a secondary advantage from this role in that it prevented him from explosively discharging his aggressions, which was something he might well fear. Yet his facial expression showed none of these emotions; it never revealed anger or disagreement, but just a general feeling of disgust with the world, which he showed all the time. Several staff members described his forced, artificial, sickly smile as one that made them feel that here was a most unhappy child, who was trying to cover up.

What John could not stand, apparently, was the threat of being overpowered; to ease his anxiety, to "get it over with," he immediately made himself the willing victim of aggression rather then endure his conviction that he would be overpowered anyway. Better right now and of his own volition than later at some unknown moment. Thus he showed a minimal desire for mastery, in submitting himself to being overpowered rather than run the risk that others might overpower him against his will. Yet he was ambivalent in his submission. He was greatly interested, for example, in quietly watching the aggressive play of older boys—a seemingly indifferent but actually very much involved observer. His real fear of others, children and adults, did not show up so much in his eager and submissive participation in such games, but rather in the way he drew away when anybody touched him or even came near.

In many ways John behaved more like a three- or four-year-old than a boy nearly eight; and even this infantile behavior seemed empty and false—actually the only thing he liked was to do nothing. For instance, when we were planning an activity he pretended to like he would jump up and down in fake excitement, clap his hands feebly and say, "Goody, goody." It gave the impression that he was copying something he had seen small children do, perhaps because he felt that he was expected to show a pleasure he really did not feel or know how to express.

---

4. All this was during the early period of the School's reorganization. Since then such games have been out of the question.

The movements of his body, even more than the emotions he simulated, were like those of a small child. His walk, for example, was more insecure than that of the average two- or three-year-old. All his movements were jerky. While for a long time his fear of stairs did not permit him to go up and down them without holding on frantically to both an adult and the bannister, later, when the phobia had lifted, he still could only take one step at a time, and had to hold tightly to the railing. When boarding a suburban train from the platform, or entering a bus or streetcar, he was never certain which foot to move where, and needed to be helped up and down.

Slowly, as John began to realize that adults were always present, willing, and able to take care of him and to protect him against the aggressions of others, he became more openly hostile. For the next two years, his rancor took the form of tickling. To "tickle" somebody became his main threat. We first heard him use it when another boy accidentally hit him with a ball. John said softly, but in furious anger, "I'll tickle you." After a few more months of feeling protected against retaliation, he dared to tickle a counselor or child, even without provocation. He did this tentatively but with a great deal of suppressed hostility, which was evident in the way he gritted his teeth and distorted his face. Tickling others now took the place of fearing and avoiding all touch. Possibly his early experiences with being touched, that is, being held anxiously or angrily when force fed, had been so unpleasant that merely touching another child, "tickling" him, was the worst expression of hatred he could imagine. Tickling also may have connoted the sensation he felt in his throat just before vomiting, or when food was forced down him. This would further explain why tickling was for John the consummation of hostility. In addition, it probably had significance on many more levels than we knew. Certainly there were sexual connotations, since he "tickled" both himself and others in the genital region. In the latter case, although John usually started out as the aggressor, he soon turned into the victim.

John's Phantasies

ONCE JOHN HAD DEVELOPED at least a minimal trust in his favorite counselor, we hoped that he might feel sufficiently free to tell her about some of his phantasies. So a Thematic Apperception Test, which he had rejected a few months previously, was given him again toward the end of his second year in School, after he had been exposed for some four months to the new regime of greater freedom. His immediate, and almost his only reaction to the first picture[5] was, "This is a baby."

He more or less rejected the second picture. His reaction to the third[6] was, "This is a picture of a baby. A man who has to be in a hospital for a long time, and then he wanted to sit on the sofa, but he couldn't because he had a hard sore, and he started crying, crying, and then he said to his mama that he wanted an orange."

His preoccupation with the baby theme, which characterized his responses to the first picture, was combined here with desperate crying, hospitalization, and a "hard sore"; possibly these were memories of the time when stitches had been taken in his mouth. (Incidentally, orange juice and milk comprised his first diet.) Similarly, John's stories about almost all the other pictures had little to do with their content, although he often started out with an isolated detail that was actually there. In interpreting reality, John was entirely moved by overwhelming pressure from within; this inner stimulus was so great that the outer world meant virtually nothing to him.

His story about the third picture also disclosed another of his confusions: "baby" with "man." Here, his neglect of reality embraced time, which for him, as for a baby, was non-existent. No growing up took place in his world; the grown man, like the baby, cried to his mama for liquid food.

John's inability to organize life in time was further suggested by his story about the fourth picture, where he showed confusion about how long it takes a baby to grow inside the mother. That lack of knowledge did not cause the error was suggested by his seemingly deliberate disregard of the meaning of time in speaking of a baby two months old being born after only two weeks of pregnancy. John's story:[7] "This is a picture of a woman and a man who got married just yesterday, and the wife is getting a baby in two weeks —a two months' old baby. Here's a picture of a lady sitting down in back of some writing. And here's a picture of a window; and then at night they went to bed, and in the morning they had some nice oranges and cornflakes, and then they went out, and the lady went home and prepared breakfast." The muddled mealtimes—first they ate breakfast, then they went out, and only later, they prepared the meal—again reflected confusion about the organization of life in time. It was a life centered only on eating, but otherwise amorphous, inarticulate.

---

5. For a description of this picture see footnote No. 7 on p. 58.
6. For a description of this picture see footnote No. 8 on p. 58.
7. For a description of this picture see footnote No. 9 on p. 58.

As John went on, his grandiose disregard of the topics presented by the pictures continued. His imagination more and more revealed his preoccupation with food, and in his stories, as in the life of a baby, this interest was interrupted only by sleep. His story about the fifth picture was:[8] "This is a picture of a lady in a bathroom going into the living room to read a book, and then she went to the breakfast table to eat and she had bacon and eggs, and then she had lunch and she had potatoes and a glass of milk and jello for dessert, and then she wanted to lie down in her room, and that was all she wanted to do."

The story to picture six[9] introduced memories of John's life at home: parents going off to work and then returning home. But these activities seemed shadowy and insignificant when compared with eating and sleeping. His story was: "This is a man and this is a woman, and this is a picture. And now the man is eating breakfast and the woman's eaten breakfast already, and then the woman is going to clean and then she's getting lunch later. And then pretty soon it's dinner time and they eat their breakfast, and the man goes to work and the woman does the dishes. And this time the woman went to work and she didn't wash the breakfast dishes, and she laid down and she was sleepy and she forgot to wash the dishes, and the man had to do it all alone, and he said, 'Oh, dear, oh dear, what can my old woman be doing.' And he woke her up and she said, 'Oh, yes, I forgot to wash the breakfast dishes,' and she said, 'I went to bed.' And then she said, 'Oh, dear, oh dear, what can I do?' "

Here again John projects in his story his total disregard of or confusion about time: "it's dinner time and they eat breakfast." Not even the most important event in both his real and his phantasy life, mealtime, could help him organize his existence into an orderly or logical sequence of events. In this story a new element was introduced, which was previously suggested only by the crying in his story about picture three. This element was a feeling of incompetence and desperation, and it may have been a reflection of not only his own desperation but also that of his parents, who never knew what to do for him.

This sense of being unable to cope with any situation, particularly those requiring an emotional attachment to another person, such as love, was also expressed in the next story (picture seven).[10] "Once a long, long time ago, far away, there were two people

---

8. For a description of this picture see footnote No. 10 on p. 59.

9. For a description of this picture see footnote No. 11 on p. 59.

10. For a description of picture seven see footnote No. 12 on p. 59.

named Noah and Noah, that loved God; and they said, 'God, God, we love you.' And then they said, 'No, no, I don't, I don't love you.' And then they said, 'Why, how do you do?' And then they said, 'Oh, we must get some ice cream. Come, that's the best thing in the world. That's better than God.' And God said, 'Oh, dear, oh, dear, what can I do? What can the matter be? I don't know what to do.' And then they said, 'You must go out and tell God that the earth is falling.' And they went back to that house and then after all they didn't love God, they liked ice cream instead. They loved everything else better than God who is such a nice man. And then they said, 'Oh, oh, what can the matter be.' "

At the beginning of this story, John was apparently groping for reality, since he temporarily took in the picture and observed correctly that there were two people in it, possibly a father and son. But that was as far as he could go in comprehending the manifest content; at this point the pressure of his emotions overpowered his imagination. God was introduced, as if to provide an excuse for stating, more outrageously than he had so far permitted himself to do, that food (in this case ice cream) was the most important thing in the world, even more important than God. But to love food exclusively, while rejecting its provider, whether it be parents or God, leads to desperation. The world, everything, was "falling" apart.

It is hard to say why two Noahs were introduced. Perhaps John meant the biblical Noah and himself, whom he thought of as Noah in this story because he, too, feared that he would be swallowed up and destroyed by his desire for food, as everything was destroyed by the great flood. Again John expressed desperation about not being able to love, and about life in general, and ended with, "What can the matter be?" But there was also a megalomanic, hostile irony in his remark ("Why, how do you do?") to the super-father, God, who is so ridiculously helpless when confronted with John's exclusive interest in food—one might add, just as his own parents also felt stymied by their son's absorption in food to the extent of rejecting them.

John's question, "What can the matter be?" in which several of his stories culminated, seemed to find some answer in his story about picture eight,[11] in which violence appeared, as a possible explanation for his hostile, devouring preoccupation with food. "This is a picture in the old-fashioned when they stab a knife in someone. This is a story about a long, long, far, far, away that was a man stabbing a knife in a woman and he (*sic!*) didn't like it and the other man

---

11. For a description of this picture see footnote No. 13 on p. 60.

said, 'Ha, ha, ha, what can we do? I don't know what you should say, but we must go out some place and then they could say the other two. And then they could stick a knife in them.' And they said, 'What can we do but help them play along?' and they said, 'We can play a trick,' and they would play a trick and it was to stab a knife in him, and he fell dead. And then she said, 'Ha, ha, ha, we stabbed a knife in you,' and then they said, 'You must stay here until the right moment and then we will let you go.' And he said, 'Well, I will, but I can't.' Then they all went back home. Then they ate. Then they had a nap, and then they read their story book. Then they said, 'Hurrah, let's eat our supper,' then they went to bed. After they ate their breakfast they went out for a walk and then they said, 'Oh, oh, what can we do?' They said that, because they wanted to know what they could do with the man because the man had thrown a stone at them, and that's what they said, 'Oh, oh, what can we do.' "

John's story, although motivated realistically enough by the scalpel in the picture, showed the unstructured, primitive nature of his hostility, which seemed to be directed equally against men and women, as the change in the sex of the victim suggested. It was a story of the long ago and far away, a time, perhaps, before any object relations had been established. Just as a very small child might imagine things with no respect for reality, at one moment both parental figures were being knifed as a "trick," and at the next were expected to read him his story book after his nap and feed him his supper. But the recurrent theme was not the violence, but the desperation shown by the cry, "What can we do?"

It was noteworthy that in this story, where murderous hostility was projected, John could organize correctly the sequence of events in time: after supper they sleep and sleep is followed by breakfast. Here seemed an indication that the total lack of organization in John's life was the consequence of his total inhibition of violent phantasies.

The same topic of desperate bewilderment appeared in the next story (about picture nine[12]), which in part carried on the ideas of the previous one. It began with a statement that seemed to declare that in John's thoughts, as in those of an infant, parents appeared as giants. "This is a picture about all giants. All the men don't like to go on ships and they said, 'Oh, oh, what can we do? We don't like to go on ships and the Americans do, so we must fight them and throw them in the lake.' And they said, 'Oh, oh, we fight the

---

12. This picture shows four men wearing overalls, lying on the grass and taking it easy.

ships and we don't know what to do.' And the next morning they
woke up, and then they ate their breakfast, and then they went to
work in their secret hide-out. And then they said, 'Oh, oh, let's dig
out our hole and get a knife and stab that man again,' and they
said, 'Okay, let's do it.' So they did it and they did it, and then they
stopped. And when they were done they threw the man in this hole,
and they said, 'You are just like the other man,' and they said, 'Oh,
what a good story.' And they went home and went to sleep, and
next morning they woke up and ate their breakfast and went to
the same place, and then they were almost done with their work.
That's the end of the story."

John's preoccupation with food, violent hostility, and desperation, threaded its way through all the rest of his tales. His story
about the blank card (sixteen) may round out this account of the
content of his phantasy. "This is a picture of a little boy and his
mother and his father and his little baby. The baby didn't like to
be the little baby. He wanted to grow, and pretty soon he was grown
up and then all of them went for a walk, and they started walking
and walking and walking. They're walking on the picture. Then
pretty soon when they are done walking they said, 'Well, how do I
think? I think I shall go out to eat dinner.' And they went out to
eat dinner, and the next morning they had a good, good, good
breakfast. Then they had their lunch, and then they said, 'Well, I
think this is the end of the story.' " Although John expressed a wish
to grow up and leave babyhood behind, he could envisage only one
gratification even for the more mature person—eating. That was
"the end" of John's story.

If additional evidence were needed beyond that we had already
observed, John's reaction to the test further showed the depth of
his fixation at the oral, incorporative level, the earliest stage of
psycho-biological development. His phantasies were in opposition
to his total rejection of food in reality. Infatuation with eating was
restricted to his imagination, where it excluded all other topics with
the exception of violence against paternal figures and desperation.
And even these latter two seemed to fit into the dominant theme:
the father interfered with John's total concentration on eating by
taking the mother to work. John's desperation may also have been
closely connected with the eating problem; although in his phantasies
food is the greatest good, better than God, in reality it was his worst,
most painful experience—hence his inability to find a solution to
this conflict, and his cry, "What shall we do?"

About half a year after John took the TAT, we felt that he
trusted our intentions sufficiently to cooperate with us in taking

a test that could not be administered by his counselor. With much encouragement from her, he took a Rorschach test.[13] The over-all impression given by the test was rather unfavorable. Disturbance of functioning was so great that it suggested brain damage, and the process appeared irreversible.[14] The conclusion drawn was: "All in all this record is most suggestive of those uneven conditions in which the failure to develop is partly due to damage to the brain tissue. The outlook toward psychotherapy is therefore unfavorable, depending, however, on the extent of any damage. There is evidence that intellectual potential may be latent, adequate for self-support at a modest level. Personality development is likely to remain retarded; but periodic examinations, especially with a view to checking interim growth, appear advisable."

Some details from the findings were: "A thinking disorder, in the form of arbitrary, far-fetched associations. They include recurrence of geometrical forms and alphabetical symbols, a class of percepts which are rare in the healthy child or adult. On the other hand, they are frequent in regressed conditions." Thus John's interpretations of the ink blots showed the same regressive features that characterized his attitude toward eating, his inability to relate, and his generally infantile behavior.

The report went on: "The child's undeveloped condition is further projected in the affective sphere. There is much capacity for feeling contact with his world, but it is all of a very primitive variety. That modulation which normally sets in by reason of a child's introjection of his environment, and which is owing to his regard for persons around him, is absent. This child has not yet acquired it." This again was entirely in line with our observations: the inability to form or sustain human relations, the failure to recognize the environment, and the lack of effort to come to terms with it.

"He is capable of absorbing some of these feeling trends in a phantasy activity; but only to a small extent, which is not adequate

---

13. This and the two other Rorschach Tests mentioned later were administered and interpreted by A. G. Beck and S. J. Beck. The quotations are from their reports. (See also footnote on p. 271.)

14. Here again, as was true in the previous clinic examination (see p. 286), the seriousness of John's presenting symptoms prompted a diagnosis of such severity that it discouraged efforts at treatment. At the School we have been able to rehabilitate a number of children despite such diagnoses, which later turned out to be based on insufficient evidence. In some cases, scepticism about its outcome prevented efforts at rehabilitation which, if instituted early enough, might well have succeeded. Thus, in a social sense, one might say that the unfavorable diagnosis itself may sometimes make the process of the disturbance irreversible by discouraging treatment. We can hope that case reports such as these may help reduce the frequency with which severe symptoms are accepted as conclusive evidence that nothing can be done.

for all the feeling pressures. The phantasy, too, is such as is found at a very young child's level. In some instances he is entirely animistic. There is not reflected that critical psychic equipment whereby the individual builds his imagination into mature, and useful, construction. The cause for this is seen in another psychic sphere: his level of regard for accuracy. It is definitely below that found in the healthy. This boy is not learning to correct his phantasy living by referral to reality. Many of his inaccuracies are impersonal, i.e., such as are due to faulty attention. He has not learned to discipline the intellectual equipment which he does have so as to use it most appropriately. Here, too, he is displaying the immature ego, retarded in its development. Qualitatively this is confirmed by the infantile language and expressions; it is confirmed further structurally in the excessive distraction of his interest by the irrelevant and unimportant. Adaptive thinking is at a low level, and conformity at zero. This is a serious finding, since it reveals the failure of intellectual adaptivity—just as he fails also in the affective adaptivity.

"An occasional sign of intellectual potential does crop up, which is discrepant with the unpromising picture as a whole. Also, the capacity for phantasy living is not only unexpectedly high for the rest of this record, but above that of the average child of this age. Thus there is some equipment for functioning above the present actual level.

"The content included also certain themes reflecting possible consciousness in this child of his own debility, and it also brought out apparently serious, apprehension-laden preoccupation. There is evidence here of reactive factors aggravating the probably impaired structural psychological equipment."

Despite these unpromising findings, we felt that because John presented such interesting problems and was making some definite progress in responding to his counselor's efforts we were justified in continuing our work with him.

First Achievements

IF JOHN WERE TO BE HELPED to come out of his depressed isolation and to relate to other human beings, we had to start at the very beginning. As much as possible, within the setting of the School, he had to learn to concentrate on only one person. One of his counselors volunteered to spend at least an hour alone with him every day, doing whatever might please him, so that eventually he might relate to her. This hour was spent with him in addition to the time she devoted to his group as a whole, which included four (sometimes five) other children. Yet despite her best efforts, for a long time John did not emerge, during the period he spent alone with her, from his characteristic, angry and defiant isolation.

The counselor[15] who chose to devote herself to John so intensively thus explained her decision: "I was attracted to John by the feeling that help for him was somewhat within my ability. His extreme insecurity and fear seemed to be things that my concern and feeling for him could alleviate." Several months later, when John had indeed formed a slight attachment to her, which was to grow as time passed, she reflected on what she thought might have helped John to relate to her. She felt then that it was less the hour spent alone with him daily than the many menial services she rendered him all day long. Unfailingly and untiringly, she kept putting on his clothes, which always managed to fall off, and tying his shoes, which came untied a hundred times a day; again and again she protected him from critical remarks made by other children; she rescued the toys they tried to take from him and found those he dropped or kept losing. Most of all, she continuously functioned as his protector.

Any physical closeness was impossible for a very long time. Even having someone hold his hand was unpleasant to John. But, with the security her protection provided, John slowly began allowing some of his hostility to come out. He became more aggressive and more negative. This was his way of relating, or testing out a person before daring to trust her. Repeated experiences with her assured him that whatever he did she would not turn against him in action or feelings, that she was a relatively reliable support, at least in regard to his most pressing anxieties.

This security with a woman permitted him to become aggressive, in playing with dolls, toward the figure that represented the father; he often threw this doll around and piled furniture on it. When weeks of such play produced no adverse reactions in his counselor, he arranged a tea party for the dolls. It was a peaceful, hour-long party, during which the counselor fed him cookies and candy. As it ended, John abruptly said, "I'm going to make you all chocolate and cut you up in little pieces and eat you." Having destroyed or done away with the father, in his play, he now tried to have this mother figure all to himself by ingesting her. Just as all personal relations begin in infancy with the child's taking part of the mother, her breast, into his mouth and thus feeding on and from her, so John tried to eat this mother figure as a first step in forming a closer bond between them.

---

15. Betty Lou Pingree (now Mrs. Rallahan), to whom much credit is due for our first successes in helping John to relate.

Once he had dared to show openly his oral hostility and his desire to make her all his own, and had been convinced that she would not only not punish him, but, instead, that she understood, accepted, and in a way was pleased at his aggressiveness toward her, John began to permit himself ever more elaborate cannibalistic phantasies.

Despite these rich, imaginative outlets for oral hostility, eating did not become easier or more pleasant for John. The refusal of food remained his central symptom, his central defense for fighting back against an overpowering world, although time and again we tried to make the eating experience pleasant enough for him to establish personal relations around it, as normally happens in early infancy. (If any such ties had existed previously for John, they had long since broken down.) We made no headway for a long time. John went on gagging and vomiting as usual, though we left him completely free to eat or not, as he chose.

Automatic vomiting and gagging were the weapons he developed, in his fight against a hostile world, after more deliberate efforts, such as pushing away the food or spitting it out, had proved insufficient as a defense against being fed and as a way of getting even with his parents by rejecting what they most wanted him to accept. In other words, emesis was the latest form into which his hostility had become frozen. Now, however, with his counselor first, and then with others, too, John began what seemed to be a retracing of his life experiences. As he became more secure with his favorite person, he began recapturing some previously lost freedom, and he used this liberty to become more daring not only in his phantasies but also in his actions. In a process of unfreezing, or reversing the former trend, the impersonal symptom through which he had been discharging hostility, although still an automatic, physiological reaction, was now aimed at a particular person, his counselor. He no longer vomited just anywhere, but rather, directed his vomit against her. In short, the oral discharge of his hostility became goal-directed and acquired a personal meaning.

As time went on, and his favorite counselor—slave is a more apt word—continued to become more of a person to him, John added to his vomiting a new form of oral aggression: he began to spit at her. Thus, with his recognition of at least one person as a distinct and unique human being of some importance to him, John progressed from a more or less involuntary physiological reaction (vomiting) to an autonomous, deliberately hostile action (spitting), but one that still used for its aggressive purpose the physiological equipment of the oral apparatus. For a while, he spat at her only when eating, but later he did so in all other situations. After he again found that nothing untoward happened when he did this to her, he began to spit at others also—first at the counselors, teachers, all adults at the School, and then at the other children. When the latter would not stand for this, and we had to stop him for his and their sake, he accepted this limitation, only to spit and dribble more intensely and frequently at the adults who took care of him.

Eventually, after years of this kind of self-assertion, John was able to give up the symptoms of both vomiting and spitting. But their decline was a long, drawn-out process. During this period, at the table, particularly, John evolved new ways of discharging hostility and controlling people around him. One of these new techniques was quiet procrastination. It literally took him hours to begin eating, and he usually would do so only when convinced that the adult accompanying him was becoming exasperated after an hour or two of patient waiting, and was about to leave. Then, in a few minutes, he would gulp down his food so fast that it brought on another fit of vomiting.

Thus John chose, first, immobility (not eating) and then procrastination as his favorite ways of punishing or controlling others. Both these traits—as in other children like John—pervaded not only his eating habits but all his other life activities, though less intensely.

Just as his parents had once forcibly kept him at the table for hours until he submitted to their will by eating, so John now subjected his counselors to the ordeal of passive waiting. During this waiting, he ignored them. He became conscious of them as human beings only when he finally began to eat, at which time he reverted to vomiting and gagging, or spitting. Apparently he was inflicting on his counselors another phase of his earlier existence when his life had been hardly more than an anxious or empty, passive waiting for the trial of being fed.

Much later, after he progressed from passive attempts at overpowering his counselor to these more active methods, there came a period of dependency, in which he permitted and even desired her to feed him by hand. At that point, John began to grow attached to her to the degree that she acquired meaning for him beyond being the safest and most conveniently available object against which to discharge his hostility. Then he slowly formed a true relation with her, at precisely the point where human relations, for him, had always broken down: at mealtime. But before meals could become fairly pleasant experiences for him, John had to go through yet one more stage.

While still clinging to his habit of spitting, John now took to messing with his food, and getting it all over himself, the table, and the counselor at his side. Somehow, it seemed, he had to deface the appetizing look of what he ate until it resembled the vomit he had once been forced to swallow. This possibly was another effort to master, actively, what he had had to suffer passively before. Revulsion against being force fed had left him no way out but to vomit. Now he could reproduce it deliberately, out of his own free will.

In a still further development, later on his messiness with food led to an astonishing ability to dirty and mess not only himself but everything around him. We cannot tell whether this may have been, at least to some extent, a recapturing of the anal phase of development, a stage he had not fully mastered because he had never been able to free himself of his deep oral involvement. All other bodily functions and life experiences, including the anal functions, remained so closely tied up with his oral fixation that I doubt if they had acquired any independent psychological meaning for John. That he messed mainly with food, and always started by dirtying the area of his mouth, suggested that his oral fixation was so great that he had to take recourse to messing in this area even when he was trying to master not only oral but anal conflicts. Thus kneading food with his hands and smearing it over himself may also have been his way of belatedly fighting back against his early and rigid toilet training.

Other observations, too, indicated that the usual relation between messiness and toilet training was not as marked in John's case, but was overshadowed by oral experiences. For one thing, he became constipated only after periods of severe vomiting. When his eating improved, so did his elimination; when his eating became more difficult and unpleasant, such as after prolonged home visits, he also became seriously constipated. Thus his sphincteral functioning seemed to be closely linked to the emotional constellations that conditioned or centered around his oral experiences; in short, his anal behavior was subservient to his orality.[16]

John's vomiting, also, may have been a symptom that served anal as well as oral conflicts. He may have wished to retain the stool

16. Much of John's behavior, its causation in infancy, and the stages of oral fixation through which he passed during the years he was with us, could now be much better explained by means of the theoretical models on infantile sexuality and the modalities developed by Erikson (E. H. Erikson, *Childhood and Society*, New York: W. W. Norton & Co., 1950). The reason I have chosen not to do so is that when we worked with John from 1944 to 1950 we were not familiar with Erikson's models, and our thinking, planning, and acting were based on those psychoanalytic concepts with which we were then familiar. It would be distorting this account if I now used different theoretical models for explaining John than those guiding us while we worked with him.

(as shown by his consistent constipation), but had found this impossible because oil was given to him. So he had given in to his mother's (or the nurse's) demands to "give up" or let go of bodily contents, not only by eliminating, but also by orally rejecting the contents of his stomach. So whenever he aggressively asserted his wishes over those of his parents through vomiting, he also victoriously asserted his defiance of them by retaining feces, by being constipated.

The deep irony, if not ridicule, with which he met parental wishes seemed here apparent, too. He kept the feces his mother wanted him to eliminate, and threw up the food she wanted him to retain. On the other hand, if things went well, and John did not need to battle the world by vomiting, he also did not need to fight back by becoming constipated. Or, to put it differently, since we have suggested that his anality never attained independence but remained closely linked with the dominant orality, mouth and anus, even more than in physiological reality, remained tied together as a psychological unit. Only one end of this tube could give out and only one end could retain at any particular time. If the mouth retained, the anus could give out; if the mouth rejected, the anus had to remain closed. Since the two functions had not been truly separated, each conditioned the other.

Independent behavior of mouth and anus came only a great deal later. Returning to the beginning of this digression, I might repeat that John's spitting and messing with food was finally replaced by what should have been his first life experience, the acceptance of being fed as a pleasant occurrence. This stage was eventually reached, but only on rare occasions, when he let his favorite counselor feed him by hand. Until the very last, eating was never wholly free of some unpleasantness for John.

The close contacts with his counselor, her acceptance of his spitting and vomiting, and the daily play sessions set the stage for John to tell her about his dreams. The very first dream he related was "about chocolate pudding." As in his more conscious phantasies, John's dreams revolved about one all-absorbing topic: food. Neither his early traumatic feeding experiences nor his distrust of food as being poisonous (which came to light only much later) alone seemed responsible for the anorexia: matters were greatly complicated by the conflict between his more or less conscious feeling that food was hateful, and his unconscious, voracious, overwhelming, desire for food ("ice cream is better than God"). It was this longing, so severely frustrated in reality, that came into conflict with his oral trauma each time he was confronted with food.

Probably no actual feeding experience could ever have satisfied so great an appetite, even if there had been no traumatization. But as eating and the experiences around it became less traumatic for John, his desire for food—which was so great that anything, to be experienced at all, had to be conceived of as edible—became ever more apparent. He was now absorbed in equating people and events with food. He no longer called his favorite counselor by name, but dubbed her "candy bar" or "chocolate pudding." As she became more identified with nourishment, he could become freer in expressing his aggression, perhaps because all his feelings could exist only in connection with food. Sure that she would not retaliate, he said, "Chocolate pudding, I'm going to hurt you. I'm going to push you, candy bar. I'm going to kick you right out of the room."

Viewing his favorite counselor as food was not the only way in which John showed the primitiveness of his attachment to her. For example, as the infant does not want to share his mother with any other person, so John was most jealous of his counselor's roommate, who was her close friend. He imagined that he would take this roommate away from her. Then his counselor would be very lonesome and he would put her in her room, up on the ceiling, where she would have to stay. If her friend (and here John meant himself more than the other girl) wanted to see her she would have to look at her up on the ceiling. Thus John placed himself not only in the place of his counselor's best friend, but more significantly, put his counselor in the position in which a baby in a crib sees his mother hovering over him, as if she were projected onto the ceiling.

This phantasy was evidence of intense jealousy and possessiveness, but not yet of a true relation. It expressed less an acceptance of this counselor as a mother substitute, than his need to see her not only as omnipresent (fixed to the ceiling) but also unable to act on her own. Disappointed in his parents, he was unable to relate to them, as a child normally would, by trying to be like them. So he used the opposite approach with his counselor: he wanted to make her always available, but in a way that implied no challenge to growth or action on his part. However, on such a basis, no relation is actually possible: a baby alone in the crib and a mother affixed to the ceiling just cannot relate to each other. So this phantasy, too, while it revealed his tremendous need to have a mother hover over him all the time also showed his wish to accomplish this in such a way that he would remain unrelated to this person.

At the time he was having these phantasies about his counselor, John, sure that she would not retaliate, was becoming still more aggressive with her. He incited other children to "beat her up" and to call her dirty names. He walked or stopped directly in front of her, so that it was practically impossible for her to move. But neither his own inarticulate and seemingly passive hostility, nor his attempts to provoke others to be aggressive toward her, seemed to offer the satisfactions he sought.

He turned similarly aggressive feelings against his father. Planning his next visit home, he talked about some of the things he meant to do. "I can't wait until my father comes," he said. "When he comes I'm going to give him a big bear hug." What did he mean by bear hug? That he would hug his father so hard it would hurt him badly. "I'm going to squeeze him like a bear. I'm going to squeeze him so hard that I can't see his face for a few minutes. I just don't want to see his face."

This remark certainly expressed John's hostility, his wish to do away with his father so that he could have his mother all to himself. But in consequence of his effort to hurt his father, he did not want to see his face. John, too, may have been afraid of being forced to recognize that he really was not strong enough to hurt his father, and so avoided testing his megalomanic ideas about being powerful and dangerous. When he actually met his father two days later, there was no touching, much less hugging on his part. On the contrary, as was customary on such occasions, he avoided, in possible resentment, his father's hug. Only in phantasy, then, could John inflict on his father the hurt that he, himself, had had to endure.

As John denied his hostility by calling a supposedly painful squeeze a hug, so he also tried to deny his anxiety by insisting that threatening experiences were funny.[17] A typical incident may illustrate how he tried to master horrible experiences by reacting as though they were jokes. In a magazine, he saw a picture of Mussolini, executed by the partisans, and lying on the ground with his head bashed in and his face bloodied. Studying this photograph, John said, "That's something very funny. Ha, ha, isn't that funny." To the counselor's astonished remark that she could not understand why he called such a gruesome event funny, he countered with a stolid assertion that he thought it was.

Perhaps the picture of Mussolini's execution appealed to him so much not merely because it depicted violence, but because it showed a father figure who was "stabbed" by his subjects—his sons, as it were. Next day, apropos of nothing at all, and speaking in precisely the same tone of voice he had used on the preceding day,

---

17. See John's TAT story about picture eight (pp. 299-300) and the frequent laughter there when a person was stabbed.

so that he seemed to be continuing what he had said then, John told his counselor, "Something's funny. One day my father was coming to visit me here at the School, and said hello to me, and when I met him in the living room, he stepped on my foot, and it hurt badly. Wasn't that funny." Only after being greatly encouraged could he admit that perhaps he was "a tiny bit angry" because it hurt so much.

So with his parents, John could still only imagine that he might be aggressive. But at School he continued to be more and more out-spoken in his negativism, although in very infantile ways. His actions resembled those of an enraged baby, who discharges his anger and frustration at random. For example, in the morning, on awakening, John would pound his pillow or covers ineffectually but furiously. Although previously he had gone through the motions of comply-ing with any request, while actually doing nothing, he could now say, "I won't." After a while, he added expressions that gave vent to his inability to stand frustration or delay: "I can't wait" was added to "I don't want to." Messing with food, spilling it over his counselor and on himself, which he at first had done casually, as though he did not know what he was doing or was helpless to stop himself, became an ever more purposeful, goal-directed activity. John smeared the food on his hands and arms all the way up to the elbows, and eventually all over his body. In another assertion of negativism he refused to be cleaned up at all. In between home visits, a span of five or six days, he would not permit us to wash him, and objected to any other effort we made to get him clean. At the same time, he finally began to eat his food rather than to mash it with his hands and then push it deep into his mouth, so that all he had to do was swallow it. He now mashed it in his mouth as a baby would, without using his teeth in the biting and chewing proc-ess. But while his actions were spontaneously becoming more nega-tive and babyish, his pronunciation became clearer, and his sentence structure more complete, understandable, and mature.

Then, after a few months of greater self-assertion (which to the outside world seemed only greater negativism) and our acceptance of it, John gave further signs of wanting affection, though he re-mained unable to use it. Interestingly enough, the first time he defi-nitely reached out for human warmth was closely connected with a real achievement on his part, which was due both to his own efforts and his counselor's help. After great anxiety and avoidance even of trying, with his counselor's untiring help, John finally learned how to row. Previously, the oars had always slipped from his hands into the water; then he had been unable to manipulate either the oars or the boat; but now he managed to row, if not well, at least so that he moved the craft in the general direction he wanted to go. And this was accomplished at a time when he had not yet acquired the ability to walk up and down stairs safely by himself.[18]

Right after he managed to row successfully, on leaving the boat, he dared to be aggressive with a boy who was smaller than he. Much to everybody's amazement, since John had never before even ventured to touch the boy, he grabbed him, and dug his nails into his arm. After this double achievement in self-assertion, John drew very close, physically and emotionally, to his counselor. He turned his face to her and addressed her directly, although before he had always talked only into a void. He snuggled against her while they walked away from the dock. Having dealt adequately with a difficult task and having discharged aggression against another child with no bad aftereffects, John seemed at last to dare to come close to another person. But when his counselor, very pleased with his overture, lightly placed her arm across his shoulders, he withdrew. As long as the initiative was with him, he felt safe. But physical contact initiated by any other person still overpowered him, and hence created anxiety. Therefore, as soon as one of us moved as though to touch him, depending on his feelings about the person he either angrily or anxiously withdrew.

The same kind of reaction marked John's response in situations even where no direct contact was involved and which to most children were non-threatening. For example, when his counselor tucked the other children into bed in the evening, John would sit halfway up in bed, and look sharply, accusingly, and probably enviously, at what was going on. Yet when she tried to tuck him in or straighten his sheets, all without touching his body, he angrily shied away, as though he feared possible physical contact.

---

18. This was one of many examples we have seen that such severely disturbed children learn even complicated tasks more readily if no previous attempts have been made to teach them before the children come to the School; easier achievements remain beyond their ability to master if parents have pushed them toward mastery. That John's parents had exercised pressure upon him to learn so many things made it more difficult for us to help him succeed, because to his lack of skill and anxiety was added spiteful resistance. Or to put it differently: when we taught John to row, what he wished most was to manage the task in order to please us, and to prove to himself and others that he was adequate. Given this emotional situation, he could overcome to some small degree his great handicaps: lack of muscle tonus and bodily coordination. But as far as walking up and down stairs was concerned, it was not only the trauma of his fall that stood in the way. What he wanted most in this situation was to spite his parents' wish that he should master it. As long as he wanted to assert his independence against them more than he wanted to go up or down stairs by himself, he could not do it, despite the inconvenience this caused him.

As time passed, and John became a little more secure, it seemed to us that he became more daring in expressing his aggressive wishes, and that they became more elaborate. One of his favorite daydreams was of torturing those who had annoyed him by making them eat unpleasant substances, as he had once been forced to do. This was the most severe punishment he knew, and he enjoyed imagining how he would inflict it on others. For example, when another boy made some critical remarks to him, John said, with a face distorted by violent anger and with venom in his otherwise soft voice, "If you don't stop I'm going to get so mad I'll make you eat ten thousand pounds of sugar. No, sugar and salt. That's sweet and sour." His first response to aggression was to invoke the memory of what remained the most basic hostility he had experienced: being forced to ingest overwhelming quantities of food. It seemed that, at this time, he could experience all types of violence only in this form. Functioning on a primitive level, he knew only one kind of retribution, the *lex talionis*. Since any critical remark, for example, about his inability to play games, was emotionally comparable to having overlarge quantities of food stuffed down his throat, that is what he wanted to do to the aggressor in retaliation.

It was the quantity of food and the fact of being forced to eat it that constituted the punishment. Only as an afterthought did he add the bad taste. Perhaps in his infancy the painfulness of the eating experience had come from the quantity given him and the forcefulness of those who fed him; the unpleasant taste may have been only a concomitant. The "sweet and sour" also may have had roots in his early experiences. After all, his parents had begun feeding him out of concern and with a fairly reasonable, if not always loving, attitude. Only as the struggle against his resistance to eating progressed did the parents become sour and the sugar of their good intentions turn into the salt of their rock-like determination to have him eat. That this may have been the case is further suggested by the fact that John made such statements with a sugary voice but, as mentioned before, furious intentions.

As he became able to talk about his hostile phantasies, of which possibly he, himself, had not been aware before, he also acquired freedom to enjoy himself and have fun—although only at moments, and usually only when he could also discharge hostility at the same time. On Hallowe'en, for example, when he had been living under the new regime for some fourteen months, John showed for the first time some real enthusiasm for an activity in which he and other children participated: carving out pumpkins.

Contrary to his usual, listless behavior, he was quite alert when he went to buy the pumpkins, and actively selected the one he wanted. The counselor asked the children what kind of faces they preferred, so that she could draw them on the pumpkins before the cutting began. Despite his interest, John, as always, could not speak up on his own as the other children did, but had to be prompted. By then he had heard all the other children request happy faces or laughing mouths, but when asked what face he wanted on his pumpkin, after a long period of resistant silence, he said, "I want a sad mouth." Although the counselor did not ask why, he went on to explain, "Do you know why I want my pumpkin to have a sad face? This pumpkin is sad because he is home and his mother isn't. His mother has left him home alone when she went downtown and he feels very sad. The pumpkin's father is home, but he wants his mother."

Usually John was afraid of even touching a knife, or if he did, was completely unable to use it, but now for the first time he insisted upon doing the carving himself. At this task, John displayed a great deal of hostility. He jabbed the knife into the pumpkin, and said again and again, "I just love to do this cutting. This is fun, cutting into the pumpkin's face. I could do that all day long." The face was quite well done, although messy, like all of John's handiwork. But after he had managed to form the eyes, nose, and mouth adequately, he continued, despite warnings, to enlarge the mouth opening until this portion of the pumpkin face completely collapsed. Instead of a face, he wound up with a huge, gaping hole. He was well aware of this "mistake," as he called it, and was proud to point it out to adults and children.

The longing for his mother that John expressed when he explained why his pumpkin was sad, might suggest that he should have been allowed to spend more time with her. But when they were together nothing she did ever satisfied him, his demands were so insatiable. His "gaping hole" could no longer be filled by her, perhaps because he blamed her, if not for the original oral traumatization, then for the last one, when the clothespin cut a "gaping hole" into his mouth. After all, this had happened at a time when the mother had turned away from him and entrusted him to a maid, although the mother herself had been doubtful about the wisdom of letting John go out with the maid. To make matters worse and add insult to injury, the reason the mother had turned him over to the maid at that moment was that she was busy cooking, not for John, but for her relatives. The accident happened when John was sent along on an errand to buy food, not for himself, although he desired it so much, but for others.

When with his mother he continuously wished to be fed, but whatever she offered never satisfied him. On home visits he thought and talked only about food, and discussed interminably what his parents should cook for him, where they should take him to eat, what he wanted on the menus. But once this food he so hungrily desired appeared, he could not eat it. He gagged and finally vomited, after having messed so much with the meal that his parents could not help becoming disgusted and angry.

Each week when he came back to School from his visit, John had only one topic of conversation. All day Monday and sometimes part of Tuesday he would review in minute detail what he had eaten during the week-end. Eventually he could tell us why the visits were so unsatisfactory and kept him so furious all the time he was with us. "I am angry. I am being angry. I am very angry," he said. "I don't get a chance to be angry at home. That's why I have to be angry here." Why was he so angry at home and yet helpless to do anything about it. "I never get a chance to do what I want at home." Why? we asked. "You know, I want to make her into a kind of dough." It was not food John wanted to devour, but his mother. Thus, perhaps, she would always be with him. Or, as he was nourished in the womb without having to eat, he might have hoped that if he could incorporate her, she would then feed him internally, so that he could receive food from her without the hated eating experience. Whatever the reason for his desire to make his mother into dough and eat her, since this was, in fact, the wish stimulated in him by his mother's presence, it is clear why his week-ends at home always turned out so unsatisfactorily.

While John's dissatisfaction with whatever his mother fed him was connected with his feelings about her, his wish to eat was linked up with his hostility toward his father. Eating was particularly painful in his father's presence. At about the time he told us of his wish to make his mother into dough, John said that he wished to eat a great deal in order to become as strong as his father—"so that I could beat up on him." Here, then, was an additional conflict with no escape for John. He wanted to eat the mother so that he would be strong enough to do away with the father. But this would leave him a helpless infant without any protection.

The mother he wanted to incorporate; the father he wished to eliminate. The latter wish, however, was not so much prompted by the fact that John viewed his father as a sexual rival. Rather, John wanted to do away with him because he was John's rival for dependent gratification from the mother; if the father were not around she would feed only the son. A few days later John remarked,

"I want my mother to get real strong." When asked why, he answered, "So that she can beat up on my father," and thereafter devote herself entirely to feeding John. Thus it seemed that his oedipal conflicts and phantasies, too, proceeded within the framework of his oral involvement. Oedipal feelings, which normally herald the development of independence from the parents, in John's case, remained tied to his oral dependency.

We could not help John to solve in short order his oral ambivalence in regard to his parents. But we could support him in giving vent to his hostility. In general, we try to prevent all acts of physical violence again persons; yet with John, whenever possible we let hostility take its course. For example, when one of the boys invited John to hit him on the back with a teddy bear, we did not interfere. Thus tempted, after great initial hesitation, John succeeded in swatting the boy. He could permit himself to do this because it was "teddy who did it." He laughed and laughed, as he hit out ever more spontaneously and heartily, and wanted to go on with this hostile "game" indefinitely; but the other boy had had enough and we had to stop John.

It was the first time we had seen him laugh with his whole face, with his mouth and eyes. Before, he had sometimes pretended to laugh, and had distorted his mouth into what he thought was a laughing expression, but what was actually an angry, anxious, frustrated grimace. Even this time, the more he laughed with his mouth, the more the expression on the rest of his face changed to fright, but nevertheless the laugh was much more a true laugh than ever before.

All this was small, slow progress. Things began moving a little faster only when, after nearly two years, we were able to persuade John's parents to cut the week-end visits to Sunday alone. Now that he no longer slept at home on his weekly visits, John let down some of his defenses against regressive behavior of which they disapproved, but on which they could no longer check so easily: he began to wet his bed at School. The first time he dared to be enuretic he told his counselor about it the next morning with happy excitement, as if it were some remarkable achievement; and so indeed it was, considering the barriers he had erected within himself against enjoying such primitive pleasures. So great was his pride, as a matter of fact, that he did not want the sheet changed. Two nights later, when he repeated the performance, he proudly remembered that only two days had elapsed since the last time he wet. Quite openly, he moved his hand back and forth over the damp spot, almost in a caressing manner. When he was not criticized for this breaking down of toilet training, he went further and wet his pants occasionally.

After John had been wetting for a while, and later also soiling, he permitted himself to wet and mess in more normal fashion, in appropriate places. In time, smearing especially with paint and clay, he did this with abandon. His favorite site was the bathroom wash bowl, where he embarked on activities he called "experimenting." So occupied, he truly showed independence and enjoyment. During his "experimenting" he became thoroughly dirty, which he had permitted himself to do before only in what either was, or was camouflaged as, a consequence of his physiological inability to retain food (supposedly he did not wish to vomit) or control his movements. Now he got dirty deliberately, and recognized this fact as such. These actions, and his facial expression while messing, made him resemble a two- or three-year-old youngster.

Once John had begun to enjoy these self-initiated activities— which were out of line with his chronological age but not with his infantile desires—he gave up the pretense of being interested in more mature enterprises. Shortly before, he had more or less feigned a wish to play games with children his own age. Though he had claimed that he wanted to play ball, he actually never could throw or catch a ball; it inevitably dropped from his hand. Now that he was messing, he gave up all such pretenses.

By any ordinary standards, John's eating habits still were revolting, but after a few months of playing with paint, water, and clay, his messiness in eating decreased noticeably. This improvement did not extend to the area around his mouth, however. Even when he condescended to let himself be washed, his lips and chin never remained clean for long. Within a few minutes his whole face was smudged and his mouth again crusted with food and dirt, regardless of what he was doing. Though his table manners did improve slowly, he still made more random movements when he ate than at any other time, although his other movements, too, were often out of control. But while eating, his entire body, hands and feet included, shook so badly that it was difficult to sit beside him. Yet, compared with what his eating habits had once been—vomiting over his counselor and himself, gagging, dirtying the entire table— there was great improvement, and eventually John became slightly less messy at the table and got his face less dirty. It seemed that, as his ties to his parents were loosened and he asserted himself more, his anal functions slowly came into their own, so that his oral apparatus no longer had to pinch hit for them. About then, John also tried to stop vomiting.

Now that his mouth was becoming more a mouth and less an

instrument for aggressively eliminating ingested food, John occasionally gave us a glimpse of the variety of purposes his vomiting served. Once when he had again vomited, which by now he was doing only rarely at the School, he said, "That's what I do when I am upset. Other people scream when they are angry." As some people weep and scream with their urethra or their bowels, so, too, did John use the process of elimination—not through the bowels, but through his mouth. His vomiting, which he had directed as other boys direct a stream of urine, had always given us the impression of also being a sexually aggressive act against those who were most closely related to him. Now he told us that it had been in the nature of angry screaming. Had his mouth also served the function of discharging phallic aggressiveness? If so, John's oral fixation had forced him to discharge and satisfy through his mouth all the emotions and experiences that in the normal course of development are connected with other organs.

In any case, so intimately were his various symptoms linked to one another and to the intensity of his relation to his parents that it was impossible to distinguish cause from effect. Assertion of anal urges to wet and soil, improved functioning of the oral apparatus, and greater emotional independence from his parents proceeded simultaneously in John. Only in the last case did we have to help him along by insisting that the time spent with his parents be curtailed even against John's and their will. All the other changes were autonomously wrought by John himself—though he was helped in these achievements by our efforts—after and perhaps because his home visits had been shortened.

In considering how these results came about, our ability to exercise restraint over the parents' authority to regulate John's life should not be underestimated. This was probably even more important to him than spending less time with them or no longer sleeping regularly at home. Here, too, as is so often the case, the psychological meaning of an event seemed greater than what really took place. The fact that his parents had to accede to our request against their wishes demonstrated to John that they were not as all-powerful as he thought and feared, and that the School, which encouraged him to act more freely, also wielded an important influence over his life. He had to become convinced of this before he dared to soil in contradiction to parental commands; as the parents became less able to stuff food down his throat, it became less necessary to fight against eating by using a physical symptom (vomiting).

That this close relation existed between his throwing up and his fear of the mother (or her tenseness) was revealed by John after

the reduction in the time spent with her, and again it came to light
immediately after a new achievement in self-control. One Sunday
evening, just after he had returned from a visit (when he usually
vomited profusely), he began coughing in the way that usually
meant an attack of emesis was coming on, but this time he did not
become sick. This was repeated the following morning. But again
he did not gag or vomit after each cough; instead, he looked carefully and expectantly at his counselor. When he had done this three
separate times, she finally became aware of what was going on. As
he coughed a fourth time, she looked at him and said, "No, John,
you are not going to vomit this morning." He coughed once more,
but no emesis ensued, and then the coughing ceased. A few minutes
later he made a connection: he said that every time he rode in the
car when his mother was driving, he got sick—her driving made him
vomit. And in his final remark he indicated that what made him
throw up was less the way she drove the car, than the way she
drove him.

Despite this progress, John's development toward higher integration was excruciatingly slow. As a consequence of the shortened
home visits, the parents—less able to exercise pressure on John—
pressed us even more to try every way of speeding up his progress.
And they certainly were right in insisting that nothing should be
neglected that offered any ray of hope. So it was arranged for John
to have extramural psychoanalytic treatment, in addition to the
work at the School. While the parents could not accept psychoanalysis for themselves, they wanted it for their son, so John began
seeing a child analyst regularly.[19]

The central focus of his sessions with the analyst for a long
time was the way he permitted himself to regress by sucking out of
a baby bottle. He had to concentrate on that for months before he
would let the analyst touch him; only much later did he occasionally
and briefly seek bodily contact with her. But even when he was with
the analyst, John was very conscious that his parents did not want
him to regress. Having used the baby bottle for more than six
months, he said he did not want it any more. "I had one after all
when I was little, then later from you; now I am through with it."

Even such a temporary and ambivalent return to the bottle resulted in slightly improved bodily coordination. After two years of
exposure to the School's new approach, John, who had previously
not been able to hold a ball in his hand, learned to catch and throw

19. John was treated by Dr. Emmy Sylvester, who for some time previously
had helped us as consultant in planning our work with John. Credit is due her both
as his therapist and our consultant.

one. Before, when a soft ball was tossed or rolled in his direction, he ducked or avoided it, but now he tried to catch it, although it took many months to learn to do this successfully. Then he dared to enter our swimming pool with an inner tube. Here at last he found a setting in which he could move his limbs freely. His motions were freest, though still totally uncoordinated, when he was kicking in the water. Finally, during the summer he ventured into the lake, and began kicking with his feet and touching bottom with his hands. Moving about in the water in the form of dog paddling, which his parents had never tried to teach him, again came easier than other tasks, which a child normally learns much sooner. He even learned to tie his shoes, a real accomplishment for him, although he tied them so loosely and clumsily that they usually came undone within a few minutes.

With each new step in mastery, John made progress in self-assertion; mainly this took the form of more open criticism of his relation to his parents. He particularly objected to the way they let him control them. For example, he told our nurse that he had once been called "Bamby." She, thinking this might be an invitation to call him some endearing name, asked him what he preferred being called. John countered, "Oh, no, I don't want to be called anything but John at the School. When I am home my mother and father call me 'kitten' or 'puss.' I told them I wanted them to call me that. I did that to try out. They always do what I tell them." With this opening, he went on about how completely he controlled his parents. "When I go home on Sunday I tell my parents what to do and they always do what I tell them." He said this, not in praise, but in depreciation.

As he reflected further on his visits, John decided that it was his mother's anxiety and immaturity that spoiled his enjoyment of them. Pondering what he might ask his parents to do with him next Sunday, he considered going on some rides in an amusement park. Then he changed his mind: "I guess I better have somebody else take me on these rides. My mother would be afraid. She's too young to go on these fast rides." He felt that he had to take care of his parents, at least to the extent of protecting them against experiences with him that they would find too emotionally threatening. Thus their emotional dependency on John made them appear less able to handle life than he, with the consequence that he felt totally unprotected in their presence, yet constrained to take care of them —a frightening task for such an inadequate child.

The same day, as the School's nurse read to him, he picked up

the book, *When We Were Very Young*.[20] He said that it contained
his favorite poem, which he wanted to show her. The poem was the
familiar one about the three-year-old boy who was supposed to look
after his mother, and who warned her not to go to the other end of
town because something bad might happen to her. John talked
about the poem at great length, and then questioned the nurse about
whether she liked it. She replied noncommittally and asked what he
found interesting in it. John said, quite forcefully, "That's like me.
The boy in the poem took care of his mother, and he was only three
years old. That's just like me." If we take his statements literally we
might say that by now John had grown from a one-month-old baby
(see p. 293) to a boy three years old.

At about the time John was gaining such understanding of the
difficulties of his parents, two years had passed, as mentioned before, since we had begun the reorganization of the School. By now
it had pretty well taken the shape we had in mind when we started
out. The mentally retarded, epileptic, and post encephalitic children who were living at the School had left, one by one, in line
with the new policy of caring only for youngsters who were free
of organic involvement. A full new staff had been assembled and
had gone through the initial training experiences. A new program
based on our theoretical convictions had been tried out, adjusted
to the children's needs and the reality of the setting. The combination of individual and group therapy, of programming and therapeutic living, which was basic to our philosophy, had become integrated into a total milieu, a therapeutic community. We were not
yet ready to sail full steam ahead, but the shakedown cruises were
over, the necessary adjustments had been made, and the ship and
crew found seaworthy.

While we felt that all the changes we had made were for the
better, John did not necessarily think so. His world was so empty
of human beings that he took hardly any interest in staff changes,
or in the coming and going of the children—with two exceptions,
one good, one bad. The good exception was his favorite counselor.
The bad one was the change in population. As far as their functioning was concerned, many of the mentally deficient children who had
been at the School when he entered it were more inadequate than
John. He remembered this and complained about their leaving.
Despite his lack of interest in his human surroundings, he liked
having children around who were even less able than he; in com-

20. Author, A. A. Milne, published in New York by E. P. Dutton & Co., 1924.

parison with some of them, he seemed relatively competent. He resented that they were replaced by youngsters who actually or potentially were more adequate. Most of all, he resented me, because I had been instrumental in changing the School's population; or as he put it, I had "ruined the School."

As was typical for John, he did not respond actively to the challenge presented by the new children but dealt with his resentment by daydreaming about the day when we would all leave. He planned to outlast my stay at the School—then the old children would return and he would again be top dog. He felt that passive waiting on his part would eventually right everything. As a baby reverts to total passivity when his crying fails to bring relief,[21] John hoped through passive waiting to achieve his desires.

John's Progress Evaluated

THE END of these two years of change seemed a good time to reassess John's progress so far—an endeavor that has since become a regular feature of our work. Every other month, the whole staff, including the psychiatrists, discuss and evaluate our work with a particular child and plan the steps to be taken in the future, and this is in addition to the daily planning and our continuous discussions. But at that time we were still so busy getting the work under way that such review and planning did not take place as frequently as now.

This evaluation of John, made during his fourth year at the School, and at the end of the second year of our work, disclosed that his fixation at the oral stage was basically unaltered. Eating remained an obsession, and a most painful one. Progress in meeting the world in any way had been and still was terribly slow. Every activity remained fettered to the oral area. When the boys in his group were given new toy guns[22] and pretended to shoot wildly at one another and at the counselor, John could shoot his only if he aimed it directly at the counselor's mouth. Otherwise he could barely hold the gun, it seemed so heavy. But when he shot directly at someone's mouth, he could do so with an astonishing display of skill and aggressiveness. John also had made some progress in permitting himself to regress, and to enjoy it, but he had not seemed to gain commensurate strength for striving toward more normal intel-

---

21. See R. A. Spitz, "Hospitalism," *The Psychoanalytic Study of the Child* 1, 1945; and "Anaclitic Depression," *ibid.,* 2, 1946.

22. Again something we would hardly do today. While the children may have toy guns, we do not encourage this by giving them to all children.

lectual or motor achievements. His very limited progress in personal integration, too, was not in line with our hopes. A comparison of his performance on another Thematic Apperception Test with the one given earlier may illustrate the development that had taken place in his phantasy life during the past two years.

THE SECOND TAT

John's story about the first picture[23] now began: "This boy is playing with a train." Two years ago, when he had taken the test, his only reaction was that this was the picture of a baby. Now his interpretation hewed closer to reality, and the normal interests of a boy his age. Still, reality is misinterpreted in line with childish preoccupations, for the violin in the picture is seen as a train.

The first time John took the test he had seen a baby in the third picture,[24] and associated it with a man who was hospitalized and crying because of a bad sore. Now his story was: "A boy is sad. He is lying his head down on the sofa." (Again, this is a much more adequate response to the stimuli contained in the picture, when compared with his previous performance.) John continued: "He left his knife down by his leg. He was playing with his knife. Then he put his knife away. And then he ate his supper and then he played a little bit after supper and then he went to bed and dreamed that he was playing with his knife. He dreamed he was throwing it against a target. Then he woke up and had his breakfast."

That he perceived the pistol in the picture, which he interpreted as a knife, again revealed John's greater respect for reality, for the picture's actual content. During the first test his associations to a knife (specifically, in reaction to picture eight) had been within the context of a story about parental figures. This time, however, the knife was thrown only against a target. This restraint was not simply due to a more rigid censorship, since in the meantime he had become more openly and consciously critical of his parents. Perhaps this very fact explains why he could be more restrained in his phantasies.

John's greater respect for reality may also be seen in the fact that he relegated the knife-throwing to a dream. Throwing a knife at a target, like the train in the story to picture one, seemed more in line with the normal interests of a boy his age. Still, the old preoccupation breaks through in the parts of his story that might be likened to free associations (i.e., stimulated by nothing repre-

---

23. For a description of this picture see footnote No. 7 on p. 58.
24. For a description of this picture see footnote No. 8 on p. 58.

sented in the picture): the boy is sleeping and eating, which are the life activities of an infant. John's efforts to deal with reality were again and again interfered with by his preoccupation with sleeping and eating. Also it seemed that he needed to seize on aggressive topics to keep his hold on reality, as though his only way of escaping a passive giving in to the wish to vegetate (eat and sleep) was to call on his hostility to keep him alive and in contact with the world.[25]

On the first TAT, the topic of John's story about picture four[26] had been centered on a baby and his mother; now he viewed a little boy as the main figure. But once again, his preoccupation with eating was dominant. "This is a mother and father. They are happy and they are downtown at a department store shopping to get something for their little boy. Then the mother and the father and the little boy went to bed. Yes, before that the boy ate his lunch at school." As in the first series of tests, John seemed to have more or less exhausted his ability to remain in contact with reality by the time he came to this story. From then on his infantile, oral preoccupation asserted itself even more.

His story for picture six[27] was: "This is a man and lady looking in a window of a store. They want to buy some clothes. Then they ate their lunch and then they went home. Then they went to bed."

The highlight of John's reactions to picture seven[28] the first time he took the test was his statement that ice cream was better than God. Now he said, "This picture is about two men. They are selfish. I can tell by the looks. They want to get married and they want a little boy—two little boys. Then they went to bed. And then before they ate their breakfast and read some books about history, which I know little about. And they feel very sad." There is greater respect for reality here, but at the price of relinquishing phantasy. For example, after his remark about men wanting to marry and have a little boy, he corrects himself realistically by saying (since they are two men and each has a wish) "two little boys." Men still appeared selfish to him—shall we assume because they want to have their wives to themselves rather than hand them over, as mothers, to

---

25. If one wishes to speculate about John's psyche along the lines of Freud's theoretical structures, one might say that a strange reversal of drives could often be observed in him. While normally Eros has to restrain Thanatos, in his case Eros, the life drive, could assert itself only if awakened by Thanatos, that is, if Eros could attach itself to his destructive wishes. If hostility did not motivate him, all John wished was to eat and sleep.

26. For a description of this picture see footnote No. 9 on p. 58.

27. For a description of this picture see footnote No. 11 on p. 59.

28. For a description of this picture see footnote No. 12 on p. 59.

their little boys? Or because fathers want little boys only in order
to overcome their own sadness? He had to rationalize his feeling
about this by saying that he could see it in their faces. The desperate
"what can we do?" and the grandiose "ice cream is better than
God," so characteristic of the first test, now gave way to sadness
and a realistic admission of his inadequacy and lack of knowledge
("I know little about [it]").

This story could also be interpreted on a much deeper level.
John said that the men wanted a little boy, then two little boys—
and that there was a history about which John knew very little, but
which made the parents feel very sad. Might it not be that the story
about which he knew very little, and which made them feel sad, was
the story of the other boy, the brother who had died? This interpretation would seem reasonable, if John knew about this brother.
The parents insisted that he did not. But material he brought to us
years later suggested that he felt as though he were a replacement
for something or somebody and therefore could never be really acceptable to his parents, could never quite be a person in himself.
At that time we felt that he could be told about his dead brother,
and that the parents should be the ones to tell him. After much
hesitation and delay the mother finally dared to do this. Thereafter,
and in various contexts, we helped him to adapt himself to this information and to see what it meant to him. But up to the end he
insisted that before that time, he had never known about the brother.
So we cannot be sure that this story reflects the dead brother and
the parents' feelings about him.

To return from such speculations to observations about John's
performance on this second TAT that can be made with some certainty, it may be said that the same improved respect for reality
mentioned previously also showed up in his reaction to picture
eight,[29] which John now recognized as portraying a surgical operation. "There are two men, operating. There was another man looking out of the window. After that he went to bed, but before he had
eaten."

As in the first test, picture nine[30] reminded John of fighting, but
his present story was less imaginative. "This picture is about some
men fighting. They fought because they did not like each other.
Then after the fight they made friends and went home. Then they
went to bed and then they got up and had their breakfast."

One sentence of his story about picture ten should be included

29. For a description of this picture see footnote No. 13 on p. 60.
30. For a description of this picture see footnote No. 12 on p. 300.

in this summary. John said, "This picture is about two men. They looked as though they did not have any mouths." But this did not prevent him from returning to his preoccupation with eating, for he continued, "They decided to go downtown, eat, and then went to bed."

His reaction to picture thirteen[31] was: "This is a boy on the window-sill of a house. He does not know how to get down because he is sitting on the third floor window. And if he jumps he would get hurt very badly or maybe killed. And then he thought of a way to get down. He asked a man for a ladder and the man gave him a ladder and finally he got down. That's all." When asked what the boy had been doing before he perched on the window-sill, John said, "I think that the boy was down eating his breakfast." Why did the boy want to get down? "He wanted to get home and then he ate his supper and went to bed." This interpretation of the picture was somewhat in line with its content, but John exaggerated the difficulty of the situation. The doorstep became a third floor window-sill—high enough for a boy to get hurt if he jumped from it. We do not know whether this was a reflection of the accident in which John fell on the stairs, but the story showed that John despaired of the hero's ability to solve the difficulty in which he found himself. John was somewhat hopeful that somebody would furnish the means (the ladder) for getting out of his predicament. But the only reason for solving his difficulty at all remained the same: so that he could eat, go to bed, and sleep. Life seemed to hold nothing else for him.

John's comments about picture fifteen[32] were: "This is a church. With a lot of wooden chairs. A man is standing by one of them praying to God. Before that the preacher came in; he ate his breakfast on Sunday morning. And then he got ready to go to church. After that the preacher went home, ate his lunch, and went to the ball game. Then after that he went home, ate his supper, read the papers, and went to bed." The figure of the preacher was appropriate to the graveyard, the topic of the picture; the tombstones were too threatening a subject, however, and hence were seen as wooden chairs. The hero again was absorbed in eating and sleeping. But the ball game at least constituted a normal interest for a boy John's age.

Comparing the two tests, the absence of daring or deep desperation in the second performance was striking. John did not completely

---

31. For a description of this picture see footnote No. 14 on p. 60.
32. This picture shows a gaunt man with clenched hands standing among gravestones.

ignore the content of the pictures, neither were there any phantasies of direct aggression against paternal figures. No longer did he grandiosely flaunt his ridicule of God. His totally frustrated cry, "What can we do? What shall we do?" was gone. So was the revolt against the Lord, or shall we more aptly say, his Fate. Now there were visible efforts to come to grips with reality. John's mood was less desperate, but also less original. When the knife appeared, it was as a plaything, which was only thrown against a target. And even this happened not in reality but in a dream.

Thus, at a time when John did not dare to act out his hostility against children or counselors, his phantasies were quite violent. But as he became more aggressive in his actions, he restricted his hostile phantasies, perhaps because he could now, in some small degree, discharge them in reality.

In fact there was a general reduction in the use of imagination in his stories. His reactions were more stereotyped, and the whole tone was more restrained and restricted. There was more conformity; no one was killed, and ice cream was no longer preferred to God. The revolt, in short, had subsided. Although John showed some concern with normal activities for a boy his age (the ball game), there was still but one topic of importance: to eat, sleep, and eat again. If there was little concern about the future, there was also less obvious recollection of the past—where the past did appear it was much more hidden. Perhaps John was now trying to get rid of it. Eating was no longer as painful, so the need for hostile phantasies was reduced, but eating was still the central problem. Since his hostility had been mitigated, and nothing new had been added to take its place, there was even less content to his inner life than before. Or perhaps John had finally become ready to start life anew where it should have begun long ago: with eating and sleeping.

The Third Year

IN THIS THIRD YEAR of our concentrated efforts to help John within the context of a total therapeutic milieu, his attitude toward the world around him slowly, slowly began to change. Before, when children had teased or taken advantage of him, or when something was not to his liking, he never complained openly, but looked at his counselor or teacher in the most devastating and accusing way because she was not better able to protect him against his self-provoked misfortunes, or to divine his wishes and guess the real meaning of his cryptic remarks. Now, his accusing look—which had been similar to that of a baby who expects the adult to know what he wants, as if by magic—changed to the demanding, more aggressive attitude of the small child. John no longer always took his inadequacies for granted, as inevitable, but he could not yet accept responsibility for them. Making mistakes, being unable to play, dropping things, were much more painful to him now because he was more in contact with reality, and less able to distort it delusionally. Previously, when these things had happened he claimed he had done them deliberately or as a joke. Now he realized, but could not admit, his own responsibility—he preferred to reproach the counselor for his shortcomings. This, again, was like the behavior of a three- or four-year-old, and quite out of line with John's age, which was then nearly ten.

His interest in the world about him was awakening, yet to a large degree this still depended on whether an event lent itself to elaboration in line with his oral preoccupations. For example, John could not keep his attention on anything going on around him for more than a few minutes; after that his mind would wander off into phantasies or empty waiting, during which he would often masturbate. One day an exception occurred when he became absolutely fascinated with watching a steam shovel cutting a ditch in front of the School. Nothing we suggested could divert his attention. For hours, without moving or talking, he watched as if hypnotized. On the surface this seemed a normal boy's interest in machinery. But what actually so engrossed him was seeing "the teeth of the shovel digging deep into the earth, biting into it, eating out a lot of mud."

Meeting his parents was becoming more and more of an ordeal, which John consciously resisted. One Sunday morning when a few children were talking about visits with parents, a boy who until recently had had home visits on Sundays remarked that this week he would be staying at the School. He noted, "This is the first day that I won't go home for a long time."

On overhearing this, John said, mostly to himself, "I wish I'd have a first day for not going home." The conversation then turned to the frequency and length of visits. John spoke up and said that his visits once had been longer, but now the School limited them to Sundays only. With no little satisfaction in his voice, he observed that his parents did not relish this change, but that these decisions were the prerogative of the School, not the parents.[33]

---

33. Such reactions on the part of children, and even more our observations that uniformly faster progress in the rehabilitation of these severely disturbed children is achieved under a program such as ours if there are no weekly or monthly home visits, led about this time to a change in our thinking about them. We concluded that it would be better for the children to have one, two, or at the most three home visits a year, each of relatively longer duration, so that child and parent could re-experience real living together, which they could not do in a

Still, even with the relatively greater freedom from family control implied in our ability to overrule parental wishes and insist on shorter visits, any contact with his parents made John less able to meet the world actively. Though in some learning or play situations he no longer passively resisted by lagging behind or becoming immobile, on Sunday mornings, as if protesting against the impending visit, he did revert to such behavior and to other forms of procrastination, including vomiting. He would not get dressed; then he would not get to breakfast. When at last he arrived at the table, he ate more slowly than ever; it literally took hours for him to finish the bowl of cereal, which he insisted on eating as soon as he was told that his parents were waiting for him. Then he began to gag and to vomit so that he had to be cleaned up again. When he was finally ready to meet them, sometimes he walked toward the living room where his parents were waiting, and sometimes in the opposite direction. Either way, he seemed quite lost, as if in a dream.

With the more conscious realization that he did not wish to meet his parents—not because he did not love them, for on the contrary, if he had not loved them, their impact on him would not have been so great—John also became more aware of what was wrong in their relation to him. For example, one day he was talking about his great liking for his maternal grandparents. The reason for this was that with them his mother was also a child; hence he knew that the mother's desire that he should eat and be clean would not win out—instead, the grandparents' indulgence of his infantile desires would carry the day. While we had known all along how much John enjoyed being with these grandparents, never before had he stated so clearly what it meant to him to have his parents' desires and values subject to superior control by persons who were willing to pamper him. John had totally given up living his own life, had lost hope of doing anything but vegetate, because the most, indeed the only, powerful figures in his world did not permit him to live as he wished. Now that he was slowly becoming ready to strive for independence, it was terribly important to ascertain that his parents were not the supreme authority, but mere "children"; hence it would seem more possible to live his own life against what he surmised were their desires for him.

Such thoughts and motives led John to make the first applications of his developing reasoning power to the emotional difficulties

---

meeting of only a few hours' or a weekend's duration. Frequent and regularly spaced visits, we found, made it difficult for the child to feel at home anywhere. The eight years that have passed since we began this policy have supported our opinion that this is a preferable procedure.

confronting him. In order to become more mature, to grow not only physically but also as a person, one must have some grasp of what is involved in being a child and what in being an adult. If there is no difference between the two, one need not worry about one's integration. That John began to speculate about whether there was a difference between adults and children showed that he had begun to approach this problem.

This task of growing up, of maturing, of reaching higher integration, John still wished to avoid. Characteristic of many conversations he had on this topic with his psychoanalyst, counselors, and teachers was one in which John asserted to his analyst that the only difference between adults and children was that the former smoke and work, "otherwise they are all the same." When the analyst wondered whether grown-ups did anything for children, John answered, "They give them plenty of fresh air and play games with them." What games? "Who can do it faster, who can get dressed, and eat fast." Did John believe things were like that at the School? "At School there are counselors; they don't play the game 'who's faster,' " he replied. When asked what he did at the School, then, John replied, "I am slow."

Parental pressure upon him to do things faster—and better—than he was able, continuously overpowered John. It confronted him with the gap between their expectations and his ability to perform, an abyss so deep that it seemed hopeless to try to bridge it; and this led to a feeling of total defeatism. At School, John's slowness, with which we did not interfere, permitted him some personal autonomy. At least he could be as laggard as he wanted, which thus restored his hope that he could somewhat manipulate his own life. Moreover, since we did not confront him with his inability to do things fast, new blows to his self-esteem were prevented. Although we occasionally encouraged him to learn new things, we took great care that he should do so only slowly and in his own good time. Sometimes this yielded results. Where once he had frantically tried to join in a basketball game, impossible though this was for him, he now practised throwing the ball through the baskets for hours at a time, all by himself. He rarely succeeded, but since nothing was expected of him, with our help he could keep on trying, and instead of being discouraged about his poor shots he kept a tally of how close they were when compared with previous efforts.

Unfortunately, his parents had not only exercised pressure upon him in the past, but they also continued to do so, though consciously they fully agreed that this was bad for John and they sincerely wished to avoid pushing him. The things they wished John to do

and their feelings about him gave him the impression that they
were still making him play the old games of who-can-do-it-faster,
and who-can-do-grown-up-things. In fairness to them it should be
said that their anxiety about John's future, and the severe damage
to their narcissism caused by his inadequacy, made their actions
quite understandable.

On one special occasion, which lent great meaning to the gift
he was expecting from his parents, they gave him quite a valuable
present: a pair of skis. On other such occasions the parents had
asked us what they should buy for John, but this time they did not
inquire whether this present was advisable. The parents seemed to
divine quite well that we should have objected—so much so that
John did not bring the skis with him when he returned to the School,
nor did his parents tell us about them. The first we heard about the
skis was when John made some seemingly casual, but actually quite
deliberate, remarks. He was full of praise for this wonderful gift.
John, who could barely stand straight when he walked, said that
with these skis he really could go skiing on the highest mountains
and steepest hills; they were skis with which one could run very,
very fast.

Yet, while describing their superb qualities, he became quite agitated and anxious; his articulation became so poor it was hardly
possible to understand him; and his gestures were progressively exaggerated until finally he seemed to have no control whatever over
his movements.

After this flight of fancy, John began pondering whether he
should bring the skis to the School, and use them around the Midway
(where the highest hill is some twelve feet). Finally he said, "Well,
I won't use the skis around the School, I won't use them around
Chicago, and I won't use them in Illinois. I might use them sometime, in many, many years." He added that, after all, there was no
hurry about using the skis because they would fit him when he was
sixteen, or twenty, or forty. After he had thus indefinitely postponed
coming to grips with the problem presented by the parents, in his
usual fashion, with more encouragement from us, he dared to assert
his negativism and say that he probably would never use the skis.
As he reached this decision to flout the parental request, implied by
the gift of the skis, for an achievement that was impossible for him,
he became able to settle down, his hyperactivity disappeared, he
grinned, and his enunciation again became fairly clear.

A few months later, while pursuing with the psychoanalyst the
subject of the difference between grown-ups and children, John was
able to recognize a real distinction between them. In his mind,

grown-ups began to emerge as more capable than children; therefore it might be desirable to grow up. There was one task that adults alone could do: "Grown-ups should breast feed children." Thus John was still either denying the difference between men and women, or perhaps holding on to the notion that he, a boy, did not need to grow up, since growing up made a difference only in the case of women. At any rate, he again stated that the sole important function of adults, so far as he was concerned, was dispensing food. Asked how he knew about breast feeding, he said, "I read it in mother's cook book. It's good for them. In the cook book is a picture of it, the baby—but I don't remember." Spontaneously he added, "My mother doesn't make cakes so good," and, after a pause, "You know, we cook at School. We make fudge and pancakes. My counselor's done it often with me."

John's life still revolved solely about food. For him, therefore, the storehouse of the most important knowledge, including information about child rearing, was the cook book. His mother had one but did not know how to use it well, just as she did not know how to treat him well or what to expect of him. But his favorite counselor knew these things: the cakes she baked were good, in contrast to his mother's.

The security John derived from feeling more accepted at the School, and perhaps even indulged (the cake here was good) permitted him from time to time to achieve insight into some of the ways in which he denied his true situation. Once, for example, he inadvertently dropped a toy, as happened many times daily. His first reaction was, "I wanted to drop it." But after a short pause he softly, almost inaudibly, said to his favorite counselor, "That's what I always said before."

However, such isolated moments of understanding the empty rationalizations he used to explain his actions away or deny their emotional impact on him, could not be coalesced as yet into a true picture of himself. Parental pressure for achievement, which was re-enforced on each weekly visit, was too powerful to permit John a realistic view of his inadequacies. This he could not gain as long as he did not feel certain of having sufficient time and leisure to overcome his shortcomings slowly, step by step. Since the urgency with which the parents wanted him to change did not permit him to take things easy, the only way out was to hide behind the claim that he did not want to do what actually he did desire to do but could not.[34] The yawning gap between what his parents expected

---

34. In many ways John's behavior showed the characteristics of what, some

and what was possible for him was too great, so John just gave up trying. Once again everything at the School seemed distasteful. We had begun to help him achieve mastery step by step. He had taken heart and tried. But what he achieved seemed so little, compared with what his parents looked for; moreover, as soon as he made some progress they at once seemed to want much more (e.g., performance on the skis). Thus, for John, following the leads given by the School seemed only to increase his troubles.

His defense against the difficulties he encountered was the old one: he began withdrawing from any effort. He complained again about how much worse the School had become since its reorganization. It had been a better School before because he "did not have to do so many things." This was true, in a sense. John had been forced to conform, but no one had expected him to do anything on his own, nor was any challenge given him to form personal relations, to master his hostility and the world. All he had to do was submit passively. He could thus retain his hostility and remain out of contact with the world; he did not have to test his deficiencies against reality, and his inadequacies remained restricted to the field of physical accomplishment—nobody challenged him to relate, hence his biggest difficulty in living did not become apparent.

Thus in the most crucial sense the old School had been "better" because it had not challenged John to form human relations. As a matter of fact, he had not known what they were. Now, as he was beginning to find out, he was evaluating his parents in the light of his new knowledge, and this only increased his conflicts with them.

ten years later, Erikson described as negative identity (E. H. Erikson, "Identity and Totality," *Human Development Bulletin, Fifth Annual Symposium,* University of Chicago, 1954). As if speaking about John, he writes: "A mother whose first-born son died and who (maybe because of complicated guilt feelings and phantasies) has never been able to attach to her later surviving children the same amount of religious devotion that she bestows on the memory of her dead child may well arouse in one of her sons (because of special inner and outer circumstances) the conviction that to be sick or dead and buried is a better assurance of being 'recognized' than to be healthy and about." Applying Erikson's concept of negative identity, which he developed mainly by means of adolescent examples, to a child such as John, one might say that since he could not become a distinct person in himself by performing well, he sought an individual identity by being more inadequate than anybody else. His behavior here was similar to that of the young man whom Erikson quotes as saying, "I would rather be quite insecure than a little secure." Since Erikson's statement on negative identity is so applicable to John, I would like to quote Erikson once more: "The negative identities chosen are desperate attempts at finding a basis for a new beginning. I have, on another occasion, expressed this by saying that the late adolescent would rather be nobody or somebody bad, or indeed, dead—and this totally, and by free choice—than be not quite somebody." John's example, and that of quite a few other children whom we have observed, suggests that this phenomenon is not restricted to adolescents, but occurs in children, too, though it takes on different external forms.

He tried to find out what "parents" were. The most pleasant thing they did was play with him—but then, he added, so did children. On the Sunday visits, his parents seemed to create a delusional world in which he could always do just as he pleased. This made the School a hateful place because it encouraged him to face his difficulties and try to master them. The result was still the old impasse: John withdrew from all human contacts into an angry and desperate isolation. Nothing made any difference; everything was "all the same—counselors and parents." He insisted that the children and everyone on the staff—not only those he scarcely knew but also those closest to him—were all the same. This applied to parents, too. There was no difference between his father and his mother, his grandparents and the School staff.

Given this situation, we felt that continuing as before would create more conflicts than it would solve. It would be better for John to return home and live there, testing out what parents were, and whether they would really always let him do as he pleased. After such an experience we hoped he might again become accessible to treatment.

When we suggested this idea to the parents, they at first were overjoyed. But soon they began stalling—a suitable school could not be found, maid service was not available, it was financially impossible for the mother to give up working with her husband. In short, it became obvious that as much as they liked the idea of having John with them, both were scared by the reality of it, an anxiety well justified by John's difficulties. No parents could successfully handle a child who was so destructive to their narcissism. So the plan was discarded as unfeasible.

But before this plan fell through, the psychoanalyst encouraged John to take the initiative in asking his parents if he could return home, since he was so dissatisfied; she assured him that she would continue his treatment in any case. We, too, encouraged him to speak to his parents about this matter. But after each visit he had to admit, week after week, that he had forgotten to talk with them about it. Finally he thought it best to wait a bit before making a move toward returning home. This insecurity about whether he wanted to leave the School, coupled with the parents' reluctance, seemed reason enough for letting him stay with us.

As soon as we told John that, since he was unable to make up his mind, we had decided that he would definitely remain at School for the next few years, he began complaining about this decision because it "would be more fun at home." There he could make the kind of "experiments" not permitted in School, such as the one he had made last Sunday. He had mixed zwieback crumbs and salt and persuaded his mother, although she at first refused, to cook this concoction in soapy water. Not only that, despite her revulsion, he had not only forced her to admit that she would like to eat it but had actually made her do so! Grinning widely, he noted that in School he could never have forced anybody to do such a thing. The way he said this left little doubt that he was glad that, by remaining at the School, he would be protected most of the time from carrying out such experiments in reality.

With the security that came with knowing that he would be in School for some years and hence unable to carry out his hostile plans in reality, John could tell his psychoanalyst how he spent all his time thinking up unpleasant concoctions. For example, he had been thinking about forming a club. Its main function would be the initiation; new members would have to drink a mixture of pepper, ink, and salt. This mixture would be cooked, spread on bread, covered up with butter, and then fed the initiates, who would be fooled by its innocuous appearance, only to discover, too late, its evil taste. On Sunday at home he had wanted to try this on a cousin, but had not dared. In these "poisoning" phantasies, he apparently wished to do unto others what he felt had been done to him, when the good nourishment he had been so painfully fed tasted somehow like "pepper, ink, and salt, mixed together."

Speaking about these phantasies released afresh his resentment of his parents. Once more he made angry and degrading comments about them, beginning with seemingly positive remarks, which only made the biting asides that followed even more deprecatory. For example, he began by telling about the wonderful Sunday he had had. It was so wonderful because he and his parents had played a game in which they fought for a toy, his mother and John on one side of the bed, his father on the other. He and his mother had won every time. It was great fun. Toward the end the mother left and he fought alone with his father. Just as the father was winning, John had to return to School.

One might say that in their play, mother and son acted out an oedipal victory over the father. But as soon as there was danger that reality might assert itself in the father's victory, John was able to avoid coming to grips with it by going back to School. So John always played his home against the School, and the School against the home. Neither of the two environments acquired enough meaning for him to be able to relinquish his retaliatory, oral phantasy world, by which he compensated for past wrongs and present short-comings so well that he did not need to strive for higher integration, for success in the real world.

For weeks he talked about nothing but these phantasies at School and in his psychoanalysis. In speaking of his "experiments" with food and his phantasies about initiation ceremonies, his face would light up brightly and eagerly. Finally he dared to act some of them out. At home he had talked his mother into acting out his phantasies, but it was the freedom gained at the School that permitted him to make this "experiment" himself. Interestingly enough it was done with a milk bottle, and its purpose was to make the drinking of milk from a bottle unpleasant for another child. John put pepper into a milk bottle, then capped it again and left it casually on the table in his dormitory, in hopes that another child would drink it. A big step toward self-assertion, toward making his deepest wish become a reality, was finally taken. It consisted in making good food taste bad.

Such experimentation, a response to our challenge that he assert himself, and come out with his hostility instead of repressing it, was and remained the exception rather than the rule. Most of the time he resisted the School's efforts to free his personality. He did not want to leave his passive, dream-existence. Therefore he remained dissatisfied with the School. One day, in response to his complaint, John's analyst asked him to describe what a good school should be like. So stimulated, John embarked on phantasies about "the Orthogenic School when I am principal." Uppermost in importance in this imaginary school was, "When someone is sleeping, then the others should not make noise," and, "Everyone should share toys; that would make it more equal." Desire for undisturbed sleep came first —next, protection for his weakness. Actually both his sleep and his toys were protected, but despite our efforts he all too often suggested to other children that they use his toys; because of his weakness he did not dare state his wish not to share them. Only one other change did he desire: the chance to satisfy his hostility by passively watching violence. "If anyone starts to fight, a big, strong boy should box with him"—then, with great relish, "and I'll watch!" Otherwise, "everything should be exactly as it is."

This was how the ideal School would be if John were its director. But things would be different in the ideal school, he said, "when I am the student." In that case, the first requirement would be, "Drink milk from the bottle," and the second, "Have hard work." Thus he neatly expressed his ambivalence about regressing to the bottle and being able to achieve, which to him meant having to work hard.

Following this statement, he drank from the baby bottle with pleasure and abandon, thus showing which of the ambivalent wishes he could at this time translate into reality.

In his next session, John would not continue with how the ideal school should operate because "you were too interested in it." But after sucking from the bottle a while, and eating candy, he went on. "Reasons for staying at the School and not wanting to go to another school. I like gym and swimming so much." As mentioned before, at this time he could only dog paddle, since he was still too frightened to attempt to swim; and he never took part in gym activities. He continued, "Reasons for wanting to live at home. There aren't any reasons."

One might speculate just why John selected as reasons for wanting to stay in School only activities he feared or did not engage in. Perhaps he "liked" them at the School because there he was neither forced nor encouraged to participate in them beyond his capacity, as happened at home. Or possibly, because he was not forced to take part in them at School, he could retain his delusion that he could do well at them but avoided them because he was just not interested. In any case, once John came to the conclusion on his own that there were no reasons for living at home, he remarked that it was unfair that he should have to visit home more frequently than other children at the School.[35] When we took up this clue and asked him how he would feel about visiting his parents only occasionally, he answered quite realistically that he might be sad the first two or three Sundays but that he would get used to it. Then he went on to talk about our Sunday activities, which he would not have to miss if he could remain at the School.

Meanwhile, our conversations with the parents continued, in which they came to realize, as mentioned before, that they were not prepared for John's return. By now this salient fact had really sunk in. Therefore, in view of the feelings John expressed about his weekly visits, and most of all because we felt that as long as they continued John could not make much progress, we requested that the visits be restricted to two, three, or four times a year, two of a couple of weeks' duration (at Christmas and in August), and the others just for a day or two, on his birthday, Thanksgiving, or a similar occasion. Such visiting arrangements had by then become more or less our preferred pattern. This led at first to fresh objections by the parents, but when they were confronted with the choice

---

35. By this time he was the only child at School who had weekly visits with his parents.

of withdrawing John from the School or acceding to our request, they compromised by giving up the regular weekend visits and agreeing to our plan, with the addition of a day-long Sunday visit once a month. Once this matter was settled, they seemed to be as relieved as John was when he learned of the new arrangement on the next day.

One of the ways the parents reacted to the plan was to repeat their account of how terribly disappointed they had been in John from the very beginning. In conversations following their acceptance of the new visiting arrangement they freely commented on John's extreme ugliness at birth; the father had dared to visit the hospital nursery only after all the other parents had left, because he had been loath to become known as the father of such an ugly baby. They remembered how their pride had been hurt, for many years, whenever people commented on John's appearance. The visits with him every Sunday had been an ordeal, they could now admit to themselves and us, because John continuously made them feel guilty, and dominated their actions by his "sad looks." His treatment of them, they felt, had been "merciless," and he had successfully used his power to keep them so busy and emotionally exhausted that they had no time left for themselves. Even so, they had not been able to accept our original plan for irregular visits a few times a year. They wanted the regularity that permitted them, and John, to hold on to each other emotionally in the interim between the visits by planning and thinking about the next one.

Almost immediately after John knew that he would have a visit only one day a month, his relations with the other children improved. He began participating more actively in their play. Within the first month following this new arrangement he learned, with great effort, to roller skate, an activity that up to then he had rejected as much too strenuous and beyond his capacities. This immediately brought him into closer contact with the other youngsters in his group, for whom skating was a favorite pastime at this season.

Much more important, within a month of this new restriction of his visits, John embarked on his first real friendship with another child, a friendship that lasted many years and continued even after he had left the School. In general, John seemed happier and livelier now, and more adequate in his accomplishments, limited though they still remained. These new achievements, or perhaps the cutting down of the visits, which demonstrated the School's power to diminish the impact of his parents' demands, seemed to permit John to try out more infantile behavior. Certainly the connection between higher achievement and giving in to regressive desires was dramatically demonstrated when, a few weeks later, shortly after John had managed to learn to ride a bicycle for a few yards without falling off, he began to smear his feces over the toilet seat, and when we did not criticize him, also on the bathroom floor.

After a short period of messing with feces, John easily moved on to mess with paint. But the world he painted was still gloomy and devoid of human beings. His pictures were always of houses, usually black, sometimes surrounded by grass or a tree. By the time he had finished working on it, the whole painting inevitably wound up one dark mess of paint.

John also became freer in enjoying oral satisfactions. He cooed, sucked, and chewed throughout most of the day, regardless of any other activities he might engage in. But food was still too unpleasant to be enjoyed. So he chewed rather vigorously on anything else handy. It was not unusual for him to gnaw up two or three pencils in the course of a day. Saliva dripped from his mouth constantly. After a few months of this he finally, for the first time, sucked on his food instead of pushing it deep into his mouth by hand. And rather than play with the food in his hands, he now toyed with it in his mouth. This happened for the very first time during a meal when he was eating canned apricots. John first tore off a part of the fruit with his hand, then cut it with a spoon. He put a piece of apricot in his mouth, then sucked on it for quite some time until it dropped from his mouth onto his shirt. He replaced it on his plate and began again the whole process of tearing off small pieces with his hand and putting them into his mouth to suck.

It was a few minutes later during this same meal that John for the very first time sucked his thumb. He did not seem to dare to do it all the way, or even to enjoy it. But his thumb kept inching up to his mouth and he sucked on it just ever so slightly. Then he took it out. He did not look at anybody all the while, but seemed totally lost in his own phantasies. As was always the case at the dinner table, he did not speak at all and he acted as if no one else were present. Other children might talk heatedly, or be quiet; to John it made no difference. He was completely absorbed in sucking. For a long time to come, John ate in this detached manner, sucking with apparent lack of emotion, in great contrast to his day-long, enthusiastic talk about food.

With his new self-indulgence in sucking freely, which followed his first tentative experiments by only a few days, and with his freedom to mess with paint, John's physical coordination improved. Now he could really run, and run fast, though in doing so he swung his arms about wildly and disjointedly, and threw his legs in all directions, like a young colt. John often looked like the clown in the circus who makes a joke of running. He would grin broadly, as if deliberately trying to be funny, while he was actually trying to cover how deficient his coordination still was despite his much improved mobility.

Greater freedom to mess, to suck, and to move about seemed to enable John to become freer, too, in releasing his phantasies. In his psychoanalytic sessions he began inventing stories. The first of them was about a dog who had "a mother and a father; and a few years after he was born, his mother and father died of sickness—of pneumonia—and then a man heard about this dog and took care of him. When he was about three years old this happened." When John was three he had fallen on the stairs and experienced his second oral trauma. Did his parents then "die" for him?

A couple of weeks later, John wrote a story in which his heroes no longer needed to be disguised as animals. He dared to phantasy about human beings.

"Chapter one. Once upon a time there was a man named Mr. Jones. One day when he was working someone very strange came in and stole his typewriter. And then the very same man stole his adding machine.[36] This time Mr. Jones was so furious that even before the man left he went straight to the police station. And then the police went out to look for the robber and found him the very same day and put him in jail. The kind of a person the robber was: at the beginning he was very nasty when the parents taught him about robbery and then after he had had his jail punishment he did not rob any more." In his story it was the parents who had taught him bad things, made him be nasty, and had been responsible for his landing in jail.[37]

"Chapter two. He got to see movies in the jail and had meetings with some other friends of his. He could play cards and games. He was allowed to write letters and he had to sleep on a hard bed, that is a bed harder than his at home. He got good food and good care. But he liked it not very much, but he liked it. He liked the things he was allowed to do. He was allowed to visit his parents every month. But his parents had to stay in the jail with him while they were visiting. He did not like the hard bed, that was the only thing. His bed at home was much softer." The pleasant jail where he saw movies, met his friends and played games is like the School. Even

---

36. The adding machine and typewriters are office equipment with which the children frequently play when they come to my office.

37. At this time when children were dissatisfied with the School, they frequently called it the Orthogenic jail.

more important, in view of his severe rejection of all food at home, he liked the "good food and good care" he received in "jail." His only dislike was the harder bed at the School. In his story he "was allowed to visit" his parents once a month, but he made one important change: he did not visit with them at home; they had to visit him in the "jail." John did not know that when the once-a-month visits were arranged, we had suggested that the parents visit with him at the School, which we would have much preferred, but to this they could not agree.

"Chapter three. Why his parents taught him robbery. Because they thought he could learn it. They were robbers because their parents taught them that, and so forth."

"Chapter four. Guilty conscience. The mother—his parents, I mean—had to stay—no, visit—with him in jail because of guilty conscience, because they might take him away from jail and stay away." John made two important corrections in this part of the story. First it was only the mother who had a guilty conscience; then he changed it to both parents. Actually, the mother did feel much more guilty than the father about what had happened to John. Secondly, he had the parents stay in jail because of their guilty consciences; then he quickly corrected this so that they only visited him there. Why had he first said that they should be in jail? He correctly assessed his parents' feelings of guilt—he, the robber, obviously felt no guilt, because it was all their fault. The parents, already guilty about having taught him bad things, felt worse now that he was in jail; because of their guilty feelings, they might try to take him away, and thus interfere with his rehabilitation. He repeated once more that his parents should visit him at the "jail." This, too—that visits "had to" take place in jail only—he blamed on the parents' guilty consciences. Another interpretation might also be valid. As much as he himself needed to be rehabilitated in this jail, so did his parents. The impact of their guilty consciences upon their handling of John was not permitting him to get well. They must be freed of guilt for John to be able to live well with them.

"Chapter five. The chief of police. The chief of police knew Mr. Jones very well and sometimes [they] even saw each other practically each day in the week. The chief of police was nice. He wore a black cap, a black jacket, and black pants, and white shirt, and brown socks, and black shoes. He talked in American but he still had a Jewish accent. He had some black hair. He let some of the people get out of the jail early." If I did not see a "Mr. Jones" daily, I certainly saw John. I usually wear dark suits and white shirts, and have a German accent, which, combined with the fact that I am

Jewish, might very well have seemed a Jewish accent to John. And at the time of his story I still had some black hairs left on my head.

Other phantasies expressed John's deep oral hostility. He returned to his daydreams about what he would inflict on others in initiation ceremonies, which he now set up in a hierarchy:

"The first initiation: If somebody likes cakes, give somebody a nice cake, only put some salt and pepper on it; then they would not like the taste, then they will never again want to eat that piece of cake." To enter John's secret society, in short, one first had to lose interest in eating, as he had done in his infancy.

"The next initiation: Give somebody a nice peanut butter and jam sandwich, and put some paprika on it."

"Next initiation: Have someone drink some coffee even if they don't like it. Pour it in their mouth when they are not looking. Open their mouth, like they did it to me."

In this initiation the victim moved from solids to liquids, from eating to drinking, a reverse procedure from that of the infant, who begins with liquids and progresses to solid food. The final initiation represented John's initial trauma, when liquids were forced into his mouth, and the parents (or his nurse) tried to achieve their goal against his resistance by taking advantage of the moments when he was not looking. It is remarkable that John should weave these hostile oral phantasies around initiation. Literally, an initiation is the act of beginning. It was his initiation into life, his first experiences with it, that John wanted to re-enact. As is so often true of our children, John tried to master what was done to him by inflicting it on us. As his life of passive suffering had begun with his being orally overpowered, so he wished to begin his active life of mastery by overpowering others and forcing them to ingest food that tasted unpleasant.

While dictating these initiation ceremonies, John became more and more animated; his expression was particularly dramatic when he demonstrated how the victim's mouth should be forcefully pried open. Later while giggling excitedly he denied that he had ever been coerced in this way, though he had at first admitted it. But he spontaneously remarked during this conversation that "no forcing to eat" was one good rule that had been instituted with the reorganization of the School.

Next, John's initiation phantasies became more specific. He no longer wished to overpower one and all. He seemed satisfied to inflict initiation only on children whom he disliked.

In one of these phantasies, John said that he would put the other child "in a real hot bath, in real hot water. Then he would get mad, and after about ten minutes I would take him out—I mean, turn off the hot water and turn on cold water until he began to freeze." In the second initiation: "I would make him eat something that he does not want to. I would ask one of my friends to open his mouth and then I would throw the stuff in. I mean, I would pour the stuff in." As if covering up or justifying such mistreatment, John ended by specifying a rather innocuous initiation for children whom he did not dislike, but who misbehaved: "Give them a piece of cake with salt and pepper and paprika in it."

In these fancies, remnants of early experiences with painful eating dominate. What was new were the hints that there had been also agonizing experiences of a tactile and kinaesthetic nature, which he now mingled with his oral frustrations. Such physically painful experiences may have been just as far-reaching in their consequences as his oral deprivations. In general, we know less about them because they are not so apt to be expressed verbally.

John's fear of touch and his lack of motor coordination and control (the athetoid movements, his spastic appearance), suggest other fixations, as deep-rooted as the oral ones. To attribute them to traumatizations that took place in what is called the oral phase of development is, in a way, misleading. We have been able to observe quite a few children who, due to very bad experiences early in life, are terrified by touch and do not develop mastery over their movements. Although their traumatization took place in what, psychoanalytically speaking, is called the oral stage, they actually suffered tactile or kinaesthetic traumatizations. Much further study into the nature and consequences of such early experiences is needed. The concept of oral predominance in the first months of life requires elaboration in view of the great importance of tactile and kinaesthetic experiences during this period.

In any event, in these phantasies John seemed to be reacting to extremely unpleasant experiences, which possibly happened when he was bathed or handled in infancy. This would further explain his bodily incoordination and great resistance to, and fear of, touch or physical closeness. His loathing of proximity made it difficult for us to approach and make him comfortable by offering him the primitive, non-verbal, tactile and kinaesthetic experiences that he should have enjoyed from the beginning, and which now could have provided relief for at least some of his emotional needs.

After a while, John continued with his analyst to spin stories about robbers; this time his subject was a child who first got into trouble, and then reformed. "Once there was a robber named Jack. He was a robber only when he was little, and stopped it when he was big. One of his experiences was that he started a bank robbery; and they put him in jail until he got older and knew enough not to start a bank robbery and not to listen to his mother and father talk about them.

"After that, he became a man—several years after—so when he grew up he became chief of police. Now the chief of police was very wise. He knew a lot about how to stop robberies. A few years after, one day, he went home to see his mother and father. His mother and father said, 'Did you start the bank robbery?' and he said, 'Yes, but I got put in jail for it, so I decided to stop this funny business.' "

In his story John seemed to be trying to come to grips with his feeling that he could become rehabilitated only by not heeding his parents' demands. These, he seemed to feel, could be met in no honest way, but only through antisocial maneuvers like robbery. True, he was not a delinquent, and perhaps this was one of the reasons that he accused the parents in his story of teaching their son to rob: he could do this since he knew his own parents had never done any such thing. But John did recognize the inherent dishonesty in the devious devices he used in order to live up to his parents' demands for achievement. Covering up his ineptness by claiming "I wanted to drop it," "I want to run funny"; making megalomanic assertions about his abilities ("I have to look out for my parents"); or trying to please his parents by voicing desires contrary to his true feelings ("I want to ski")—all these maneuvers, because of the School's insistence on genuine emotions and expressions, appeared to him as dishonest as robbery.

John expressed the hope that once he grew up he would be able to resist distasteful parental demands, not only by not listening, but by taking positive action to prevent future "robberies," that is, by becoming chief of police (almost as though he were aware of the psychological ties that exist between criminals and law enforcement agents). The jail may again have been the Orthogenic "jail," but why did he speak of a bank robbery? And what did he steal? Had he been robbed, was he the thief, or both? Possibly he felt deprived of those infantile pleasures that are the birthright of any child, of those satisfying relations to which every human being is entitled. Perhaps his hostility drove him to attempt to gain by violence what he had not received in the normal way; thus he became both the one who was robbed and the robber.

Whatever the meaning of these stories, greater leeway in expressing his phantasies, greater oral and kinaesthetic satisfactions, plus some real achievement, led John to want to "stop this funny business." He no longer needed, for example, to run in such a "funny" way, because he was actually making substantial strides forward in motor coordination. At the same time he also began to achieve academically.

As John tried, through his stories, to extricate himself from parental influence, so also he began seeking a solution to his oedipal conflicts. Here again he used a recent achievement for dealing symbolically with an old conflict that he had not felt able to tackle before. He finally learned to play Chinese checkers rather well. Previously, because of his poor coordination, the marbles had fallen from his hand or landed in the wrong places; now he could manage them quite well. After he had played this newly mastered game over and over again all by himself, he succeeded in beating many of his age mates.

From his behavior when he played by himself one could deduce that a battle was in progress between the black and the white marbles. Unfortunately, only occasionally could we overhear remarks he made when engrossed in the game. He would say, for example, "The black ones are the father and the son, and the white ones are the mother," or "The mother and son are against the father." Meantime he maneuvered the marbles back and forth, while he muttered to himself, deeply lost in thought and emotion.

When he played with his parents at home, he and his mother always triumphed over the father. But when he played by himself at School, father and son often won battles against the mother. In imagination, he seemed to explore the oedipal situation—one time siding with the mother, next with the father; at times he even sought its solution through identification with the father. In reality, and particularly when at home, he clung in preoedipal fashion to his mother, while ignoring or hating his father. His relation to them was always symbiotic—John siding with one or the other of the parents —never independent—never John in his own right. This tallied with the fact that he still could not form a genuine relation with any adult. Even the one friendship he had formed with another boy was symbiotic, a *folie à deux,* rather than a truly helpful and salutary association. Although we had gone far toward unfreezing John's emotions and relieving his symptomatic behavior (particularly his anorexia), we had not yet made any real progress in helping him with his greatest need—for establishing a close, sustaining bond with another human being.

The Fourth Year:

A New Friendship Takes Root

UNFORTUNATELY, THE COUNSELOR who had most intensively devoted herself to John since the School's reorganization, now planned to leave. To what degree this decision was motivated by the fact that for three years John had been heavily draining her emotional resources, cannot be said. Be that as it may, in making new arrangements for John, we had to take cognizance of the fact that within a few months he would lose the person who had been most important to him until then, and with whose help he had made his greatest strides.

By this time his psychoanalyst, as well as we at the School, had reluctantly come to the conclusion that John could not establish away from the School the very type of relation he needed most for further improvement. It had become obvious that, for example, even the trip downtown to the psychiatrist's office too greatly drained his energy to permit these sessions to be very profitable for him. For his greatest benefit, we felt he needed to be able to establish another relation close to the center of his living.[38]

That John spontaneously voiced his resentment of having to go downtown for his psychotherapy, and his wish to have sessions with a person who would always be around the School, also influenced our decision. In addition, we had to face the fact frankly that John exhausted the emotional resources of those who were closest to him. So, we concluded, it might be best if he could form an intimate association with someone other than his counselors, with a person who, while available to him every day, would not have to live with him all the time—protecting him, planning for him, constantly being with him—and who would, therefore, be less likely to be worn down by his symptoms, his negativism and lack of response. For anyone who accepted more of this burden than could be carried without an adverse reaction, would be handicapped in creating the type of relation John needed most.

Because of her warm, motherly personality, the School's social worker seemed ideally suited to offering John such a relation and

---

38. Important as was the help John received from Dr. Emmy Sylvester on a higher professional level—whether directly, in sessions with her, or indirectly through her advice to the staff—the actual mothering John experienced all these years from Betty Lou Pingree Rallahan was the true basis for his emotional development. In her work she helped, of course, by various co-counselors, teachers, nurses—in short, by the staff, in a degree that varied from person to person.

helping him through it. The decision that she should see him in individual sessions was strongly influenced by the spontaneous interest she had taken in him, and by the fact that he had sought her out from time to time on his own. From then on until he left the School he met the social worker at least three times weekly in regular, scheduled sessions, and in addition had many short, casual contacts with her every day.[39] At the same time, psychotherapy with the analyst was continued, because we dared not risk terminating John's relation with her before a relatively stable attachment to a new person had taken root. So for another year John saw his psychoanalyst once a week.

In the first conversations with his analyst touching on the topic of his new friendship with the social worker, John was completely noncommittal. He could talk about human relations only negatively, and in a way that avoided emotional commitment. But after two months had passed, during which John was convinced that no positive statement was expected of him, he expressed his feelings about the social worker in typical fashion. He said emphatically, "If someone would say *not* to see her, I would say 'no.' "

One day, in an early session with the social worker, John decided to color. Looking over the crayons, he was surprised to find one labeled rose pink. This seemed contradictory to John. After being told that it was a delicate shade, he remarked that, of all colors, he liked best a "delicate black"—meaning gray. After evincing interest in a warm color (pink), he thus backtracked immediately from this implied expression of positive emotions by indicating preference for a color lacking definite hue. Apparently John wished to let his new friend know very early in their relation that strong or definite colors (emotions?) were inaccessible to him. But in a very tentative and no doubt unconscious way, by contrasting his interest in pink with his preference for gray, he may have been expressing his hope that this new relation might help him to like and use pink—the color of flesh and, therefore, of life—instead of gray, which perhaps stood for his current depression and shunning of emotional ties.

Soon John was bringing most of his old problems and preoccupations to this new friend. When he got around to telling her of his phantasies about initiations they reflected a higher level of integration. No longer were they daydreams about forcing others to eat ill-tasting or nasty concoctions. Now he wanted to become a chemist and experiment with various substances. He asked for a chem-

---

39. Florence White was the social worker who became the most important person for John. Most of the credit for his progress from this point on is due to her.

istry set in order to "change water into blood, blood into something solid, this into ink, and ink into water." In short he wanted to change water into blood, a life substance. Yet, in harmony with his general depression, the experiment he described came to naught: he wound up where he began, with water—or nothing.

John had been having three sessions a week with the social worker for a period of three months, when his favorite counselor left the School. Losing her was a great blow to him and caused a substantial setback. On learning of her impending departure, he had immediately withdrawn from all human contacts. It took some time and a great deal of encouragement—not only from this counselor but also from his new ones, his social worker, and the analyst— before he could admit how angry he was. He finally summed up his feeling by saying, "I'll never forget it; maybe sometime I'll forgive." As yet, he did not think he could ever truly forget an emotional hurt, but he did hope that some day he might forgive her for leaving him. If he could learn this, he might then be ready to forgive his parents for his early traumatization, which he blamed on them.

With this progress in adjusting to the separation from his former favorite counselor, the psychotherapy with his psychoanalyst continued to become less significant to him. John's relation to the social worker, on the other hand, was acquiring greater import. This growing intimacy seemed to consume all his capability for sustaining intensive contacts with adults, though some sessions with the analyst were still valuable to him. In any event, the new relation was John's most important emotional experience and remained so until he left the School. Though the beginning of this friendship was shadowed by his depression about the loss of his favorite counselor, this in itself was something new. For the first time in his life, the focus of John's relation with another person was something else than his frustrations in regard to eating. The loss of a friend was now a more pressing problem to him than the old oral preoccupation.

After his counselor finally left him, John withdrew into such complete isolation that it took no less than five months before John could again show any spark of feeling toward anybody. It returned for the first time after he managed to release some of his hostility, not only in phantasy, but in action while with his new friend, the social worker. One day he picked up a hammer and peg toy. He was afraid at first to use the mallet, but after much hesitation on his part and encouragement from her, he hammered for nearly a half hour without stopping, and with an ever increasing ferocity. He attacked the pegs in every possible way, as he sought to smash them harder and harder. All the while his facial expression evinced greater and greater satisfaction. Despite the fact that his motor coordination was poor, he managed to hammer so heavily that several wooden pegs splintered. Apparently happy, he then halted—exhausted both physically and emotionally. He became very limp, very infantile and cuddly—rare in this child—and asked to be read to for the rest of this session.

From then on John continued again to make progress in learning how to master life. During the summer he began to play in the sand box, to finger paint, and to enjoy other pleasures of childhood. Still, his most contented moments came when he was sitting alone in a lukewarm bath, playing with water toys, to the exclusion of the rest of the world. Largely through what his new counselors did for him while he sat in the tub, he slowly began to accept them. His ability to relate to them no longer hinged so much on the discharge of hostile oral aggressions (spitting, vomiting) as on pleasurable experiences centered upon touch, a form of contact which, till then, John had shunned.[40]

That John was able to continue to take new steps forward—such as being forcefully aggressive in manipulating a tool—comparatively soon after the setback of his counselor's leaving, was due chiefly to the fact that the intervening months had not been entirely devoid of human contacts. His friendship with one particular boy had continued, and was cemented by the fact that this child had also been closely attached to the departed counselor. Previously, because their attachment had been partially based on their fondness for the same person, the two boys had often been rivals. Now they were drawn more closely together, and their rivalry was temporarily overshadowed by their common loss.

Once John had overcome his depression about the loss of his old counselor, he began to take advantage of this friendship with the other boy to assert himself more and more with all the children. John's friend was just as inadequate in games and sports as John, had equally poor motor coordination, and also had to rely heavily on the support and help of his counselors. Together they formed a twosome, which no longer needed always to be the longsuffering butt of other children's criticisms.

John never did become very good at "taking it," but he could now "dish it out" as well as some of the other boys—not through physical mastery but through teasing or taunting remarks. He was

40. The new counselors who took Betty Lou Pingree Rallahan's place (by doing the same kinds of things for John at first and then also by slowly becoming important in his emotional life) were Calvin Axford and, a short time later, Josette Dermody Wingo.

more free to employ his intelligence, and he used both his greater knowledge and a biting irony to fight back more aggressively. One situation alone remained consistently unimproved: to the end, his behavior at the dinner table was most aggravating to the other children. He managed to make each meal unpleasant for them by his procrastination, messiness, and unpleasant handling of food, all of which were outstanding even within the free and easy manners customary at the School. Friends he acquired among the children in the following two years could not help but be annoyed at his manners, and they voiced their displeasure. Against their more threatening expressions, the counselors had to protect him.

But in other situations, he tried to participate in activities that were normal for boys his age. He could not join in baseball games, of course, or any other games requiring a high degree of coordination, but during the winter months particularly he chalked up new successes. He took up stamp collecting, for example, and though his collection was never orderly, for he tore his stamps and made them messy by handling them, nevertheless he enjoyed hoarding stamps, and occasionally traded them. He took part in playing with trains, joined table games, and even made some feeble attempts to put simple airplane models together; but he soon gave this up in frustration, since he realized that the work was really being done by the adult while he was merely the onlooker who, in trying to help out, inevitably destroyed the model.

During this year, John's progress in holding his own with the children always went to pieces under the impact of any lengthy visit home. At one time, with our encouragement, he worked up enough courage to plan on buying a wind-up train; by combining this equipment with what other children had, he could have developed a larger project. But as soon as he learned that a visit with his parents had been planned, which was to last a week, John decided not to buy the kind of train that could be used in playing with other children, but got a wind-up car for himself alone. He took it home with him and then left it there, because, he said, it was too difficult for him to wind up, and he feared that the children would ridicule him for not being able to do so. On returning to the School, he isolated himself; again "nothing made any difference." In contrast to the languid, detached way in which he talked about his lack of interest in playing with the children, and his general, depressive state, he described the exploits of the visit itself with animation and assertiveness. He spoke with pleasure and irony of how he had tyrannically controlled his parents. To him the whole visit was a string of dictatorially stated wishes, which his parents had obeyed in every detail.

The interval between seeing his parents at Thanksgiving and at Christmas was only a time of empty waiting, which he covered up with ruminations about whether he had made any progress, and in what areas. Eventually he came to connect these speculations with the fact that his parents were prone to test his achievements. He felt that the only area in which he was really growing was in relating to his social worker; this, he said with some glee, his parents could not test. But he could not say more specifically why he thought that this was the area of growth, or in what the "progress" consisted. Yet, in making these remarks he appeared quite convinced, and convincing.

In contrast, his other claims about the steps he had supposedly taken forward seemed empty. For example, he started out by asserting that he had gone far in athletics. But as he went into this in more detail, he became ever more dubious, and finally said how deficient he was. Once this was realized, he talked about the time his parents had taken him to a public playground and tried to examine him there by asking him to show how well he could climb, or slide down the slides, though such feats were still scarcely within his reach. When we tried to console him, and show him that it was more important for him to learn how to enjoy himself and communicate with others, he became very irritable and returned to his initial thesis that he was making headway with his social worker.

In another conversation, which had also begun with the subject of the "progress" he had made in athletics, after John again came up against the emptiness of his claims, he went on to discuss his lack of academic achievement. True, during the fall—perhaps because he was mourning the loss of his favorite counselor—he had only marked time in class. He saw this not as his fault, but as the School's. It was our duty to see that he improved; we were cheating him of what was his due, because he was not learning. Such feelings, unreasonable on the surface, made sense emotionally. The School had prompted him to reach out more actively toward the world by throwing him into an enforced intimacy with his favorite counselor; accepting this challenge and encouraged by it, he had let himself become very attached to her. Now she was gone, for which he naturally blamed the School. Therefore, in a way, he was correct in saying that the School was hindering his progress, by depriving him of the friendship whose growth we previously had fostered.

When the time of his two weeks' Christmas visit drew near, John multiplied his delusional statements about his importance in the life of his parents. He planned to "help them with their lives." He intended to "put salt on dough when my mother makes pancakes, hold the egg beater for her, and help my father in driving the car."

How would he do the last? "By holding the steering wheel." At such moments, when he was making a pretense of "helping," though his actions were most likely to hinder, John felt especially close to his parents. One might wonder to what degree his feelings were in line with the emotional reality of his situation. When he tried to do anything by himself, his efforts inevitably ended in failure, which disappointed all three of them. By offering token help, he and they could overlook or deny his shortcomings (and still avoid blank intervals of time); in a way, his activities helped them all by permitting them to ignore the reality of his inadequacies. But John was probably not unaware that his "help" was actually a nuisance; very likely, he enjoyed the irony of having his parents fall in with his pretense of helping while in reality he was interfering with what they tried to accomplish. Playing at being helpful, which makes good sense in a four-year-old, was turned by John into a parody of good child-parent interaction.

As on previous occasions, waiting for the visit stimulated John to invent a story about robbers. In class he had been reading about Lincoln, and John's story began innocuously enough with a jumbled account of the Civil War, which ended, "Lincoln got shot by John Booth, a crazy actress, at the Lincoln Theatre.[41] Three days later they decided to call this place the Lincoln Memorial." John continued talking about the frequency of robberies: "Practically every bank in Springfield, Illinois, was robbed. Finally the robber got caught and became chief of police." Thus the topic of the reformed villain who becomes the mainstay of law and order cropped up again during the period that he was waiting for the visit. Then immediately before he left for the Christmas holidays, John returned to memories of being force fed. "A long time ago my mother forced me to eat. She forced me to eat what I did not want. But she gave that up. Now I eat what I want and stop when I want." But this last statement was one of hope rather than fact.

When John returned from his visit, he dwelt again on how he had controlled his parents while he was with them. He also recovered some distorted memories of the hospitalization that had preceded his coming to the School. He maintained that he had gone to the hospital "for a little cold," but then he also completely denied

---

41. We do not know why he changed Booth into a woman. Was it because, in his mind, only a woman could commit great crimes? Or there may have been another reason for the change. By this time John was struggling to identify with males, and with fathers, and Lincoln certainly is a superfather figure. In John's experience, women invariably won out in fighting against fathers. But such victories no longer seemed desirable to him—on the contrary, they were bad—therefore, an actress would have to be crazy to kill a father.

that he had had any eating difficulties in the past, or that he ever vomited, though he admitted to being slow in eating. As if matching these denials of the past with a similar distortion of the present, he went on to make exaggerated statements about his athletic prowess. When we deflated them, he replied, "But I planned to do all these things." Why? "Because my parents want me to." It was parental pressure that kept him from separating reality from phantasy.

It took about two months for John to recover from the after-effects of this visit, but all along, quietly and unobtrusively, his relation to his social worker was developing. By the beginning of March, some eight months after he had begun seeing her in regular sessions (and five months after his favorite counselor had left) John started to permit himself some infantile satisfactions during his sessions with her. He began by playing with a wetting doll and a tiny baby bottle, toys that had been handy all the time, but that he had ignored. He asked to be told in detail how other children used these dolls, although he had seen this done in his dormitory. When we replied that most children liked to pretend that the doll was wetting, he said that he did not want to do that, but would make an experiment instead. He proceeded to fill the doll with water from the toy nursing bottle, and then squeezed the doll's cheeks or body, so that it regurgitated. He did this again and again, for many whole sessions, while he watched with intense concentration. Then he re-turned to experimenting with the chemistry set, as if he wanted to convey the connection between his initiation phantasies (so closely related to his chemical experiments) and his oral traumatization, which he had re-enacted by making the doll regurgitate.

For weeks, he remained oblivious to anything except such doll play and the experiments with the chemistry set, which consisted mostly in messing with various substances. After some time, this freedom in acting out his oral preoccupations seemed to lead to a greater ability to achieve academically, to play games with children and, most important of all, to better recognize his real feelings. Their ambivalent and depressive nature became evident when at Easter he wished his social worker "a happy unhappy Easter." Not sure she had heard him correctly, she queried: had he wished her a happy unhappy Easter? John smiled wanly and said, "Yes, I said I wish you an unhappy happy Easter," and added in an even lower voice, "Isn't that what most people have?"

About a month later, again at first within the protection of this intimate relation, John dared to launch an investigation of the real world. He began by using elementary instruments through which one looks at objects, particularly the kind of kaleidoscope with which

designs can be made by putting various objects into the apparatus
and then turning it.[42] Whatever the reason, John enjoyed playing
with this kaleidoscope; then, in a short time, he graduated to a
magnifying glass and eventually to a telescope.

After his daring in viewing the outer world had proved so successful, John came back to coping with the inner world of infantile
pressures and unsatisfied hungers, but on a higher level, because he
could be more true to his emotional needs. No longer did he have
to play with toys, like the wetting doll or the nursing bottle. He now
used a real baby bottle and nipple. With an air of whistling in the
dark, he said, "I'm not going to suck it—I'm going to make an
experiment," as though he were afraid of the regression that sucking
from a bottle implied. He filled the bottle with water, but not bold
enough to put on the nipple himself, requested that it be put on for
him; then he began dribbling the liquid into a cup under various
pretexts—he wanted to find out how many drops would fill the cup,
or were in the bottle, or would leak out per second.

This play, too, went on for weeks without much variation. John
was trying, it seemed, to re-create his earliest experiences of being
fed with the eye dropper, so that he could master actively the excruciatingly slow feeding that as an infant he had had to endure
passively. Eventually he was persuaded to give up repeating the oral
frustrations of the past and to try to suck from the bottle. But he
could be induced to do so only by using the pretext of wanting to
find out how much water or milk could be sucked out of the bottle
in a given time. Even then, he could not suck freely, as many of
our children do once they are ready to "return to the bottle"; though
he put the nipple in his mouth, he did not seem to know how to use
it. He rather expected the water to seep from the bottle by itself—
perhaps because, in infancy, the milk had been trickled from the
eye dropper into his mouth and he had done almost no sucking.
Only after he had been patiently taught and greatly encouraged, did

42. Several of our children begin expressing their interest in the external world
and their readiness to investigate it first by playing with kaleidoscopes. Comparing
the actual objects inserted with the various designs that form when the kaleidoscope
is turned, affords unending pleasure and astonishment to these children who have
been too ridden by anxiety to "look at the world." The fact that objects can be so
transformed, and the assurance that one is safe in just looking, seem to account,
in part, for the toy's fascination, at this stage of exploration. The viewer may also
make an easy check, back and forth, between the objects and their transformed
appearance. Perhaps learning that these objects, though they form so many changing
and complex designs, actually remain simple and unchanged, is reassuring to the
children. In a vague way, they may thus have a first inkling that their anxieties, for
example, which appear in ever-changing and overwhelmingly complex forms, may
actually have arisen from simple and understandable experiences, just as the elaborate
designs seen in a kaleidoscope are created from well-known, simple objects.

he try to suck, but it was a tentative and hesitant attempt and he did
not seem to enjoy it.

Nevertheless, once he had learned how to suck, he used the
bottle all during his session time. For months, any other activity
offered to him was rejected. Once when he seemed to have his fill
of the bottle the suggestion was made that he play with the doll
house and figures. John rejected the idea with great anxiety: "I'm
not yet ready to play with it." Apparently he did not yet feel ready
to deal with the feelings aroused by the problems of family living,
which children usually express in playing with these toys. Within
the security of his relation to the social worker, he was too preoccupied with making up for the infantile pleasures that he had
missed to be able to concentrate on his relation to his parents, which
he was not yet prepared to master, even in play. So, in addition to
sucking from the bottle, he would rather spend his time measuring
the liquid it contained by ounces, drops, or tablespoonfuls; or the
amount of milk or water that leaked out in a given interval, ad in-
finitum—anything to keep his mind on sucking liquids and nothing
else.

Eventually there came a day when John added to this play some
simple games, which he played with his social worker, and also
with his counselors. These were uncomplicated games of chance,
where the throwing of dice determined the winner. But we wished
to give him the experience of winning where some skill was required,
so that success might encourage him to strive for better bodily
coordination. If he could only score in some simple competitive
games, we felt that he would no longer need to make delusional
claims about his superior abilities in athletics or deny the true cause
of the children's reluctance to play with him. It became our problem, then, to give him the courage to expand his activities until he
could take part in more difficult games. This could be accomplished
only by convincing him that despite his handicaps he could succeed
in at least one.

Obviously it would have to be a game in which coordination
could be practiced without great physical exertion, since he was
incapable of it. We felt that the game should also force him into some
personal contact, which he usually dodged, if he could, in order to
avoid having to face up to his inadequacy in such situations. Another
requirement was that failure had to be an accepted part of the game.
For given John's lack of motor skills, frequent fiascos would be
unavoidable and might lead him to abandon the effort and return
to delusional denials.

This was what happened, for example, when he was confronted

with even very simple puzzles. He rarely could fit the pieces into place, and always ended up totally blocked. When using crayons or paints he was content with the worst scribbles, which, he explained in great detail, were the planned expression of his artistic talents. In coloring pictures, he could never manage to stay within the lines. We did not like having him embark on unstructured activities, like painting or drawing, because this left him free to withdraw again into angry and frustrated isolation when he could not fill in the spaces properly or draw the way he wished. Usually he rejected cutting with scissors as too much trouble, and since he lacked the necessary skills anyway, it soon resulted in another defeat, from which again he would retreat into his impenetrable shell.

John was particularly inept at any game that involved a rhythmic shift in the tide of fortune. For example, he would have liked to play with toy soldiers, but this eleven-year-old simply did not know how to begin. He could set the soldiers up, but was unable to go on and simulate the ebb and flow of battle. At least he no longer wanted the person he was playing with to kill or capture his soldiers, but maneuvering the toys back and forth was impossible for him.

John finally became able to play competitive games through learning how to play jackstraws. In this game, the coordinated use of only one hand is required, and but two fingers at that. No exertion is necessary, since lifting the sticks hardly uses up energy. Temporary defeat is a part of the game, else the two partners could not take turns. There need be no loss of face, because both partners inevitably make mistakes. This was a visible demonstration to John that his defeats, too, were only temporary.

John played at picking up sticks regularly for more than a year and a half. He had begun learning the game with the psychoanalyst and continued with his social worker. For many months he was not capable of this higher motor achievement if others were watching— especially children whose superiority he both envied and denied. He could not take the risk of their challenging and defeating him. Only after he had learned to play jackstraws quite well with adults in whose company he felt secure, did he venture to play it with other children. Later he resumed the game whenever he was defeated at sports that demanded more coordination than he could muster.

It was during this period of his development that John was able to take his first steps in learning how to swim. Until the spring of his third School year, he had avoided the pool and beach under such pretexts as having colds, coughs, and other imaginary ailments. Only then, did he begin to feel sure that we would not push him beyond his capacity. This enabled him to give up his imaginary

aches and pains, with the protection they offered against defeat, and
to begin splashing in the shallow end of the pool. After two years
of playing and occasionally paddling in the water, becoming acquainted with it, and shedding his fears (and after the radical reduction in the number of home visits had taken place), John
expressed a wish to learn how to swim. In the safety of his session
room and, more important, protected by his relation to his social
worker, he one day casually asked how it was done, and then gladly
accepted her offer to teach him privately, step by step. Unobserved
by others, and with her patient help, he learned the movements involved in swimming, first separately, then in coordination; and
finally he transferred this skill to the pool. During the ensuing months
he also learned to pitch and bat a ball, while alone with her, secure
from being watched by other children. Having thus privately mastered the rudiments of the game, he ventured to play ball on the field.

Though he had made substantial strides in motor coordination,
his over-all progress in this and other respects was still so slow
that we felt we should, if possible, further intensify our efforts in
his behalf. But this we had to do while remaining relatively uncon-
cerned. These two statements are only seemingly antithetic, and their
very contradictoriness, illustrates best the complex emotional attitudes required to help children like John. His spontaneity had been
destroyed, or probably I should better say, had never had a chance
to develop, because from the beginning he had been forced to submit to an externally imposed regime. Later the parental attitude
vacillated between forcing him to do what they wanted, and demanding, whether directly or by implication, that he do things on
his own. Both attitudes had a paralyzing effect on him. Therefore,
a very special point of view was required in order to help John
overcome his inertia. It may be best described in the words of one
of his counselors:[43]

"For example, in getting John up in the morning, and having
him at least partly dress himself, I found that a friendly non-
committalness worked best. It was rather difficult, because it would
not do to be too cold about it, but any anxiety or great desire about
getting him to do things just made him worse. I found myself thinking, 'I don't care how long he takes to do it.' This was best if I
could get a 'proper' tone to my voice in talking to him. I felt bad
that, because of this, working for John so often became such a
calculated thing. I always felt myself wondering whether just a
slight touch of urgency might work, or perhaps a supporting hand

---

43. I owe this statement to Josette Dermody Wingo, who was John's counselor
during this very important period and until the end of his stay at the School.

might now be accepted. Fortunately, after a while it became less conscious. But while it then became less thought out, I never could feel completely natural with John. I never could really let my emotions come out, because even a normal amount of emotional attachment was too hard for him to take. I liked the kid very much, I felt sorry for him, later I also admired his guts, because it took a lot of guts for John to even try occasionally, and that he did around that time. I wanted to help him, he had such a hard time just living. Still, I never could be very fond of him for a prolonged time, because soon things went wrong just because of my emotional attachment for him and I had to return to think out my every action, which, of course, interfered with the naturalness of my emotions.

"That does not mean that I cared for John out of a sense of duty—there was much more to it than that—but it never could remain for a long time from the heart only. If I would make in my mind a list of the children in my group, whatever was the activity I planned in my mind for them, or whatever services the kids needed, John was never forgotten or listed last, but as warm as I felt for him he hardly ever came first to my mind, either. If I should put it down in the most simple words, I might say I cared for him not so much, or not so often, out of an immediate feeling of love, and most often out of a broader sense of charity."

While such an attitude on the part of staff members working most directly with John might not have been ideally suited to his rehabilitation, it was the best they could offer and hence the best the School could provide. And, in fact, it did prove sufficient for helping John to make progress toward integration.

But so much of his energy was drained by the monthly home visits, he regressed so much in preparing for and recovering from them, that continuing at the School did not make much sense for John even under the present restricted visiting arrangements. We explained this to his parents, and suggested that they forego the monthly visits. This they could not accept. We did not want to get involved again in a long series of arguments, which in stretching over months, would lose time for John, so we suggested that if they did not wish to abide by our decision as to what was best for John, we should like them to make other arrangements for him, that is, withdraw him from the School. Confronted with this alternative, they reluctantly agreed to terminate the monthly visits in the fall.

It was during this period that John's psychoanalyst had become convinced that her therapeutic efforts had served their purpose and outlived their usefulness for John, while his relation to his social worker was becoming ever more important. John, on his own, had remarked that, rather than continue seeing his psychoanalyst, he wished and desired to concentrate all his life's activities at the School. Before his relations with the analyst came to an end, however, after a series of rather sterile sessions, it acquired a new importance for a short time. Although John had not yet been told of our intentions, he began to talk about his past life at home and to compare it with his life at the School, as though he wanted to tie things together before these sessions ended.

His comparison revolved around "making decisions." At School, "when someone doesn't want to go (on a trip), then he can't go."[44] At School, apparently, decisions were made in line with his real wishes. John claimed that when he was home he could make more decisions, but he cited a revealing example: "Nobody decides; if we don't go (on a trip), it is because of the weather." Was he thus conveying that no one had any personal power at home?

Warming up to his subject, he revealed what had been pressing on his mind. "When I was little, there were more things I could not decide." Here he began to cough and gag, and finally retched quite badly. "When I didn't want to eat, they used to make me." This led to thoughts about his infancy. Correctly he noted that he was born in a hospital. "I was very little then. After a few weeks in the hospital they took me home. Then I did what all babies do." What do all babies do? "Stay in bed and cry." Why? "They cry because they aren't used to the place yet. When they get stronger, then they don't cry." When asked how babies get stronger, John replied, "Through fresh air and getting older." It was suggested that parents might help, and he agreed, "They help, too," but when asked how, he knew only one way, through "talking to the baby." To make sure, the analyst asked him again whether parents could not do more to help a little baby grow, but he insisted, "They just wait until the baby is strong." What happens then? "They send him away to get strong." At no time would he say, on his own, that parents

---

44. This statement might need some elaboration. That a child does not have to go on a trip if he does not want to is well understood. But John was referring to something else, namely, that we protect children against their feeling that they must conform to certain expectations, or social canons, even if they do not wish to do so. Many children, for example, are afraid of some rides in amusement parks, but are either expected to like them, or are afraid of being considered sissies if they show their fear. So they claim that they want to go on these rides, but if we are aware of their fears we do not let them. So John meant to say: if I don't want to go on a trip, even if I should claim that I want to go for some reason, such as to safeguard my status, the School will prevent me from doing so. Perhaps he particularly wished to express the dilemma in which he found himself at home: in order to cover up his inadequacies or anxieties, or to please his parents, he had to pretend to like certain activities, but this meant that he had to do things he did not want to do, because he had asked to do them.

feed and otherwise care for babies. He felt at that time that parents just talk and wait, for the most part, and if the child does not thus grow strong, they send him away.

Given these emotions, it is small wonder that John felt that he had been robbed of that care to which any infant is entitled and that he had to steal what had not been spontaneously given him. For the same reasons, he may have felt that it was up to him to "reform" his parents, and teach them a better way of life. That these ideas contained a considerable measure of anger and megalomania can be deduced from the following excerpts from John's last story about robbers:

"*The Robber.* Once upon a time there lived a man. One day he was captured. He was out of prison and became the detective and helped find out the others and won all the fights. His picture was known all over the U.S. After that he decided to tell his parents that he gave up robbing. So his parents said, 'Why?' and he said, 'I'm a detective!'

"After a while his parents decided that they would give up robbing, too. After that they became known as the only parents who stopped robbing after their son did."

He ended the story on an optimistic, much less megalomanic, and more realistic note. The emphasis shifted from the man who was famous all over the United States for reforming his parents, to the fun the family had playing games. "The next year they had found out a great many more things to do, so they did those things. They had fun doing those things. Then they started to have more games that they made up. It was fun to play those games."

THE SECOND RORSCHACH TEST

Our plans both to curtail further John's home visits and to discontinue his psychotherapy (though the psychiatrist would continue seeing John occasionally at School and therapy could again be resumed on his initiative whenever he so desired) involved risks, so we decided to test our opinions about his current personality structure by means of another Rorschach test. The following material from the findings seemed especially significant:

"John's test performance shows that there is serious arrest of the intellectual functioning: the thinking is erratic, immature, and organized in odd relationships. Perseverations are frequent and center around a constantly recurring topic in a very stereotyped fashion. It is perseveration amounting to aboulia. His uncritical fluctuating of productivity and limitation of his mental horizon, and the extraordinarily high stereotypy, all fit into the picture.

"In the affective sphere a moderate amount of contact with others is indicated and while under control, it tends toward the immature. Not a single phantasy association is produced. Thus the inner life is extremely narrow and impoverished. This supports the restricted picture projected in the intellectual living. So far as dynamics are concerned, there is no evidence of color shock, i.e., the structure is not a neurosis. A mild anxiety shock does appear— not enough to account for the impoverished mental life.

"As compared with the earlier Rorschach of three years ago, the changes are critical in the inner life. In regard to affectivity they are in fact dramatic: the former primitive, infantile, instant response to feelings is now lacking. He has given up this very immature reaction pattern. Equally decisive is the change in respect to phantasy: he has given up this activity, which was animistic or regressive. Thus, inner richness has been lost. Since so much of his earlier thinking was farfetched and arbitrary, we see here an improvement in giving up sick thinking, without, however, acquiring the more mature variety. Respect for reality is almost exactly at the same level: the ego has not grown. A single conformity of association at present emerges, which was formerly altogether absent—a possible vestige of growth. Growth, too, may possibly be detected in the absence of negativism which formerly marked him.

"The conclusion is, therefore, that his functioning is chronically immature. He had adjusted at an infantile state for so long that it is now habitual. The effective functioning is in fact at the level of mental deficiency. Treatable assets are essentially lacking. The ability to relate himself emotionally to his environment is however indicated, and some supportive treatment looking toward his developing this rapport is all that can be hoped for from this second test record."

Comparing our own observations of John's progress in the interim between the two Rorschach tests, we could only agree, by and large, with these findings. We had succeeded in making John as comfortable as we could, and as a consequence, the "serious, apprehension-laden preoccupation," for example, which was so marked in the first test, had disappeared. He had also given up his infantile, instantaneous response to feelings, and his other immature reaction patterns. No longer did he harbor animistic and regressive phantasies, perhaps because there was no longer any urgent need to escape an unbearable reality. He may also have given up some of his infantile phantasies because he was no longer concentrating solely on infantile feeding experiences. Yet, yielding up these immature patterns of reaction had not led so far to greater intellectual adequacy or richness in phantasy production; John's use of his intelligence, as well as the content of his phantasy, had become stereotyped—which suggested an effort to seek a solution to his inability to cope with life in neurotic, if not compulsive, defenses.

We could not quite agree, however, with the pessimistic over-all evaluation and prognosis, nor with the finding that the ego had not grown. True, when confronted with the task of interpreting ink-blots, the ego might appear as inadequate as before. We had not concentrated on helping John to master these or any other abstract tasks. All our efforts had been invested in helping him to take advantage of what the School stands for (to become oneself; to achieve control over one's own life, emotions and body; to enjoy instinctual satisfactions as far as possible within the existing society; to relate to and identify with significant persons and to accept and enjoy their services; and to become companionable with other children), and this he was slowly doing. We had succeeded in freeing him of some anxiety, and had helped him draw closer to reality so that he could give up his farfetched and arbitrary responses. But the test results suggested that in order to achieve along these lines he had to restrict himself in other areas of living.

He could now deal with reality in a way that had been impossible for him previously, though such mastery was still most inadequate when gauged by "normal" standards. He could also meet the world —though doing it was still most frustrating for him—without a total collapse of ego-function, as was previously the case. To our mind it seemed probable that he could now test his experiences against a backdrop of introjections, a frame of reference derived from the School, which would permit him to judge reality more cor-rectly than ever before. But this framework did not tally with the point of view of his parents. And his ego was far too weak to manipulate two different frames of reference successfully. That was one of the reasons he still could not manage tasks that faced him outside the safety of the School. Therefore, so long as he saw his parents regularly, and their attitudes remained basically unchanged, John could not fully appropriate, in his own personal way, what the School offered to him, nor acquire the ability to apply the School's lessons outside of its immediate environment. While we had suc-ceeded in alleviating some of his worst sufferings and inadequacies, and while healthier responses had indeed taken root, these signs of real progress were still limited to a restricted area of living. In this sense, then, the test corroborated our feeling that unless John ceased living in two disparate worlds he might not progress much farther. The only way we had of providing him with just one world to live in was to prevent him from seeing so much of his parents, while we at the same time intensified our efforts to offer him satisfying personal contacts at the School. Therefore we went ahead with our plans.

His Last Years in School

WHEN WE TOLD JOHN that his monthly visits home would cease, he showed little concern. As his birthday drew near, we learned why our decision troubled him so much less than we had expected. We discovered that, for John, giving up the visits did not mean that he was ready to relinquish his delusions about exercising magical control over his environment. Since he no longer could use his own inadequacies to manipulate his parents, the most important persons in his life, he now transferred these efforts to us. In a way, we had hoped that this would happen. As long as John continued to hold on to this destructive way of achieving mastery at home, he could not relinquish it altogether; and giving up old defenses was a prerequisite for becoming an adequate person. He had been able to disregard our implied suggestions and outright requests that he should move in this direction as long as his experiences at home provided him with tangible proof that control through inadequacy still worked. Because of the new and drastic reduction in the number of home visits, they no longer served to renew, over and over again, his conviction that, contrary to what we tried to show him, this was an effective way of mastery. Stopping the visits deprived him of any further chance of proving this to himself, and by the same token made our encouragement of efforts to achieve at a higher level more meaningful. John was compelled to use the School as a new (or I should say an old, but for quite some time not used) testing place for his old method of control through inadequacy. This gave us a chance to help John decide how well such a method really worked, when employed against those who would not give in to his claim of personal incapacity and inability whenever they knew he could do better.

What actually happened was that he began to apply again at the School, in fullest force, those patterns of behavior that he had previously nearly abandoned there. He again refused to let us know what troubled him, for example, or what he wanted. Again he continuously gazed at us with accusing eyes. In short, all his old techniques for making us feel guilty about his own shortcomings, and their consequences, reappeared in new strength.

John also returned to his old denial of the significance of the external world, which was characteristic of his early days at the

School but had become increasingly infrequent in recent years. Everything once again was "all the same." Yet he never stated what he wanted; he expected us to know it intuitively, and was most resentful if we did not guess his wishes and guess them correctly. This attempt to transfer to the School environment his central and hence most distorted methods of mastering personal relations made them accessible to us. We could show him again and again that his magic efforts to manipulate his life and environment to his liking were ineffective, and that he could reach his goals only through dealing realistically with his problems, through recognizing other people as persons, and assessing what they were humanly able to do for him.

In speculating about John's behavior, one might consider that, in trying to achieve a purpose, the first important step from magical thinking to verbal communication is made by the baby when he somehow dimly becomes aware that his demanding cry does not produce the desired result (nourishment, for example) by some magic, but, rather, because it is a communication that is received, understood, and acted upon by another person. Next, the infant comes to realize that this person is able to withhold what he wants, but is most of the time willing and able to gratify his demands.

John may have missed these experiences to a significant degree. He was fed, although he did not seek it. He cried to avoid being fed, for it had become so unpleasant to him, but this communication seemed to have the opposite effect. The more he cried, spat, and fought back, the more tense the parent (or nurse) became, and the more determined to feed him: any action on his part only resulted in his being forced more strongly to do what was unpleasant. Thus, stating his desires had rather the opposite effect from what he intended. After all it had been his experience that the quiet times, in between forced feedings, when he was apathetic, were, if not the more pleasant moments in his life, then the least unpleasant; so what was more natural for him than to expect that good things occurred, or at least displeasure was avoided, when he did nothing, and remained, in fact, unobserved. If this is a correct reconstruction of what had happened, and of its present consequences, one can understand John's reluctance to state what he wanted, to take any action in his own interest, and to rely instead on a hope that his unspoken wishes would materialize. But to live at all successfully in the world, he had to learn to act differently. This was the major learning experience we had to provide. For John to master it took more than two years.

One example, typical of John's expectation that he could obtain

JOHN [365]

what he wanted by magic, was mentioned previously: he expected to learn without any effort or cooperation on his part, and believed that his teacher withheld from him the academic progress he felt was his due, out of deliberate spite. Although lately he had been learning in class, now that he no longer could exercise control through passivity at home, he tried to do this again in school. Any suggestion that he might have to study to make academic progress made him indignant.

It was not possible to change his attitude in the classroom; a very special occasion was needed to achieve this. We decided to make such an occasion of a visit with his parents, which was to take place on John's eleventh birthday. Despite the restrictions we had placed on John's home visits, he had been expecting to see his parents on this day, for whenever possible, birthday visits then, as now, were regular events for the children at the School. Children who wished to see their parents on this occasion could do so, and John knew this quite well.

But as his birthday approached, he became more and more depressed, inert, and negative, even in his relations with those few staff members toward whom he had up to then shown some positive feelings. For example, he gave up talking or playing with his social worker, and was sullen and silent. The birthday seemed to prey forcefully on his mind. As for our part, we had decided to "sit this one out"; he would have to make the first move toward securing a visit. Any token action on his part would suffice, as long as it permitted us to show him that things happen, in consequence of goal-directed efforts, that would otherwise not take place.

Finally, the tension became too great for John to remain silent, but still he would not ask directly for a visit. Instead, he made the enigmatic statement to his social worker, "It's just six more days." When she asked what he expected or hoped would happen in six days, he said, "It will be just like any other day," implying not only that she should guess that he meant his birthday, but also that he feared nothing special would take place on that day.

After a long silence, and with considerable help from the social worker, he finally admitted that he expected to be disappointed, as usual, even on his birthday. Then, after further prodding, he said that he was thinking about whether he would see his parents. Since this bothered him so much, the social worker advised him to ask me about it and settle the matter. He declined. She reminded him that other children told me when they wanted a birthday visit, and suggested that it would be better to follow suit than wonder and worry, but John replied, "No, I will wait to find out." Going one step further, the social worker emphasized that we liked having the children tell us what they wanted so that we could make arrangements accordingly, if possible, for we had no other way of knowing their wishes. John's reply was, "I know it, but I won't ask. I'll wait."

Now we had reached a real impasse. We knew that he would be terribly disappointed if he did not see his parents. But we also felt that it was particularly important for him to communicate his wishes, so that he could learn that communication has beneficial consequences. It was necessary for John to make some move before he could begin to realize that his life was not arranged either by people who did not consult him, or by his hidden desires, which, through some magic, were turned into reality. We wanted to make a dent in his total reliance upon his hope that others would guess his wishes and make them come true without his taking a positive step; he had to stop letting his life be arranged for him, as the life of a baby is arranged. Therefore, we told John that the decision was his to make. If he would not take at least a token step toward securing what he wanted, he would not get it. Magic did not work at the School or in the world; desired ends were gained only through realistic handling of real problems.

The next day his social worker again brought our policy about birthday visits to his attention, and said that if he wanted one, he should request it. Again he said no. In the following session John tried to prevent her, and himself, from talking about what was on both their minds by occupying himself with empty play; he strictly avoided looking at her, and tried to move and sit so that she could not see his face. Since we wished to force the issue, she asked once more why he did not request the visit. Now John began making excuses: "I forgot." When asked why he had forgotten, since his birthday weighed so heavily on his mind, he answered angrily, "I can't remember why not."

The worker decided to prod him a little to help him clarify things in his own mind, and also to suggest that unless he told us what he wanted, we might misinterpret his wishes. Therefore she said that perhaps he did not want a visit, that in fact this seemed to be the case, since he would not even go to the trouble of asking for one. John merely replied, "I don't care." But "I don't care," the worker told him, did not tell us what he really desired, and therefore we were still at sea about making arrangements for the kind of birthday he would like best. At that, John only became more negative and to any further efforts to make him take action he sometimes sullenly, sometimes angrily, repeated, "I don't care." But he did begin to play quite aggressively: picking up a toy bus, he pushed it around on the floor so violently that all the people in it fell out. That scared him and he tried to explain his action away by saying that the bus "skidded," which made the people fall out, but no one was hurt. His emphasis was again on things "just happening." No one was responsible, no one did things purposely; and since that was the way of the world, why should he act instead of waiting for things to happen?

Nothing more was said until the day before his birthday. Now there was no time to be lost if we wished to gain our goal. When the social worker confronted him again with the possibility that he might be ambivalent about having a visit, John for the first time said what he wanted, but at the same time insisted emphatically that he would not ask for it. For a person who wanted a visit, she pointed out, he was acting quite strangely. But when he was thus brought up against the fact that he had stated what he wanted, he immediately denied having done so and returned to saying that he did not care; this time, however, his tone of voice and mien did not preclude further conversation. It was possible to go on and show him that because he had not indicated to us or others what he wanted on previous occasions, he had built up a great deal of resentment before every special event, since he was convinced that he would not be pleased; then later, he had always felt disappointed and cheated. While agreeing that this was true, John still did not want to take any steps about his birthday. Time was running out, so at the end of the session the social worker told him as casually as possible that this was our last chance to make arrangements for a birthday visit on the next day. John then said that he would go and request the visit from me right away after leaving the session room. But an hour later, at lunch, when she asked whether he had seen me, he said, "I've decided not to. I've decided to wait and find out. That's what I've decided I'm going to do."

At this juncture we decided to tell John point-blank that if other children, some of them mentally less alert than he, were able to ask for a visit if they wanted one, he could, too; there was no reason "to wait and find out," because we had repeatedly told him that there would be no visit unless he requested it. He would have to ask for one now; and if he did not want one, he should say that, too.

At long last John was confronted with the necessity of taking his fate in his own hands—especially his life at the School, about which he had never up to then taken decisive action. He became very angry, but finally realized that we meant business. Then, as if rationalizing his reluctance to ask for a visit, he said he had feared the answer would be no. But he also admitted that all his observations at School contradicted this anticipation. Asked why he thought the reply would be negative, he could only say, "I don't know, but I always expect the worst to happen."

Since John was actually well aware that this was contrary to what happened when other children asked for birthday visits, he finally decided to come to me. All he could bring himself to mutter was an extremely angry, "I want a birthday visit." I said I was very glad that he had told me what he wanted, but that I also needed to know more details, such as how long a visit he desired. Even more angry, he replied curtly, "From 1:00 to 7:00." Then he wheeled around and walked away. And so it was arranged.

This was a turning point in John's life. Though he had to undergo many similar experiences, with each new one he became more prepared to take a hand in events that concerned him. Slowly, step by step, he moved toward greater self-reliance. Never again, after this birthday, did we have to push him as hard to make decisions on his own; but it took, for example, more than six months before he would ask for visits when he wanted them, and another two years before he became fully convinced that in most other respects, too, things just do not happen by silently wishing for them.

Nearly every new achievement in making autonomous arrangements for his life brought progress in other areas of living as well. A discussion of how angry he had been when we forced him to take steps to obtain the birthday visit led John to the spontaneous realization that in taking this action he had departed from his previous mode of life, in which he had always let things happen to him without doing anything about them. This initiated conversations about his inability to ask for what he wanted in all areas of life, or to show his true feelings, particularly anger. We now felt that we could push things a little further by bringing to his attention the fact that when he was angry, he did not show it, but expressed it in devious ways, such as in accusing looks; and that perhaps in the past he had done so by throwing up. He was quite startled at that, and asked, "How could I throw up the food?" When we replied that he probably knew this best, he pinched his own cheeks in precisely the same way he had pinched those of the wetting doll to make it regurgitate. With conviction he said, "Yes, that's how I did it."

This initial progress in understanding his own actions was, of course, short-lived and within a few days he reverted to trying to get things without effort. Once again, in discussing his birthday, he was quite angry that he had had to ask for the visit. But he denied his feelings. "I'm not angry," he said, at the same time kicking toys viciously and throwing them on the floor. In defiance of our efforts, he kept trying to prove to himself that his magic control still worked and he often returned to the phantasy-planning for the future that had kept him from living in the reality of the present. "There are visits you don't have to ask for," he insisted, "like Christmas. All children get Christmas visits—there you don't have to ask." Yet this time when we emphatically told him that this was not so, he believed us, and before Christmas requested a visit, which was arranged as he wished.

From then on, whenever he wanted to see his parents, he asked us and we always tried to arrange it, so that he could convince himself that taking autonomous action brought results. After three or four requests for visits had been made and were duly granted, he came to believe that doing something about his life really produced the outcome he desired. By then he must have realized that a visit was his for the asking. Still, he took advantage of this situation only sparingly—living in the School, where he had reasonable control over his life, had become more attractive to him than exercising the total control he still had over his parents. Sensing his own inadequate ability to master life, he felt threatened and unprotected when with his parents, for the very reason that he could regulate their actions toward him beyond the limits of reason.

During ensuing months, John also began to use his new ability to look out for himself and arrange his life more as he wished in his relations with other children. He stated what he wanted more openly and hence got his way much more often than before. This in turn helped him to give up some of his infantile behavior. His messiness and procrastination at the dinner table decreased until the children no longer fought to avoid sitting next to him. Occasionally he also could participate in table talk. Eating became more pleasant for him, more of a social occasion, as he no longer concentrated entirely on playing with, or ingesting, the food.

Slowly, further improvement in bodily coordination took place. In this area too, John seemed to be growing up. The way he cried when he became upset or angry was now different. Previously, when he wept his whole body shook, and he gagged, coughed, and even vomited, the way an infant does. Now, his crying involved his face —eyes and mouth—alone. No longer did he react to an emotion with his total organism; his bodily responses were more specific. This progress paralleled a general increase in muscular coordination.

While John had not wholly given up the old tendency to seek satisfaction in phantasy rather than in reality, a new element was added, which seemed to be an outgrowth and elaboration of his new experience in improving his lot by asking for visits. For example, he made up a string of long, involved stories; some of these were based on actual events that had taken place in School and some utilized an entirely different setting. But the plot was always the same: big, powerful, boys were cruelly torturing a passive little boy; then the aggressors were severely punished for their misdeeds. When the locale of his story was the School, I did the punishing; otherwise, this was done by another powerful father figure, but never by John's real father. The essence of these stories seemed always the same: a weak, totally passive, small boy is successful in controlling and striking back at even a vicious environment, under most threatening circumstances, by reporting the misdeeds to a powerful father figure. As he told the story, John was always very tense, but he seemed to experience great emotional relief the moment he had reported his tribulations to a figure in authority; this relief seemed even more important than the imagined punishment of the evildoers.

Perhaps here again was a parallel to what happens in the infancy of normal children. Because of his inability to care for himself and the anxiety this creates, the small child invests his parents with nearly supernatural powers; only thus can he feel that they can protect him, come what may. An example of this exaggerated idea about paternal power is the way the child relies on it in times of stress. If another child threatens him, long before he is able to protect himself or to retaliate in kind, he will appeal to the superior power of his parent (or big brother) in trying to restrain his adversary. Telling the father, or threatening to do so, exerts control on the opponent. This is often a child's first experience in asserting, if not his mastery of the world, at least his ability to call upon a protective and friendly influence in an inimical situation. So, in his stories, John revealed some of the typical phantasies of these much younger children, who also daydream about the terrible punishment with which their father will avenge them on their adversaries. Independent action seems to be the last step in a development that has three stages: wishing that the parent would protect and revenge, requesting him to do so, and doing something oneself in self-protection.

John's phantasies now suggested that he was getting ready to make the step from only wishing to be revenged to requesting it— an important step in the unfolding of the art of communication, since receiving help alone proves the value of communicating and fosters its further growth. Spinning stories in which John was vindicated by telling on his opponents was still a long way from actually assuming control over his own life, but it represented an important move in the right direction.

A meaningful part of the new development was that he turned to a father figure to achieve his goals. So far it had always been women—first the nurse and his mother, later his female counselors and therapists—who had been significant to him. But for John's growth toward masculinity it was necessary that men should become increasingly important to him. His self-realization, first as a boy and later as a man, could be achieved only if he were convinced that males were at least as powerful as females, a conviction that his life experiences up to this time had not supported. His new confidence that telling me (or another male in authority) his wishes would bring desirable results was helped, as we learned only at that time, by a preceding experience, that of my restricting his visiting, which demonstrated my superior power not only over his magic wishes but also over his mother—or so it seemed to John. At least as far as John knew, his father had never been able to impose his wishes upon John's mother. The change in visiting arrangements had made the first dent in his belief in the utter superiority of women. Since the mother's power, so he thought, had proved inferior to mine in determining whether a visit should take place, John's trust in gaining his goals just by wishing, and his belief that males were hopelessly inferior, both broke down. Reliance on me, as a man who was more powerful than his old tormentors, the female caretakers, gave him courage to believe that there was a chance for him to come into his own as a boy.

Still, in consequence of his great negativism, John never used the power of his male protector for positive ends in his stories, for gaining desirable things, but only for fulfilling negative wishes, by having his enemies punished. He was able to believe that superior powers could inflict bad things—as had been inflicted on him during infancy—and hence could punish his enemies. Unfortunately, his past had not prepared him to trust superior influence to achieve good things for him.

Because he had no such hope, the development of more positive attitudes to life remained painfully slow. Occasionally he made progress in learning to wash himself, for example, or play a game, or in permitting himself new infantile pleasures, such as free play in mud. But only very rarely and momentarily was he able to recognize his emotions, particularly toward people. It seemed that John had to learn, as a baby does, to manipulate his body well before he could move on to better interpersonal achievement. To some degree, he had now overcome the worst symptomatic consequences of his oral traumatization, but he had not really mastered the feelings from which they had sprung, much less freed himself from them altogether.

After he was able to give up to some degree his continual re-enactment of this trauma through rejecting food and making meal-times painful for us, John began to progress along the developmental line that normally comes after the infant has had his fill of pleasant oral experiences, namely, mastery of the body. It was this problem on which John now worked with purpose and persistence. But it is very difficult to acquire at eleven the coordination that is ordinarily learned, almost without conscious effort, at two. Hour after hour John practised hopping on one leg, so that he could play hopscotch. Hour after hour, he threw a small, light ball against a wall, trying to catch it on the rebound. With his social worker, in session after session, he practiced playing jacks with dogged persistence, or had her pitch a ball to him as he learned to catch it well. What he was really trying to do during these final two years at the School, he could sum up only shortly before he left. With a big, wide grin he said, "You know, Miss White, once my muscles had control over me. Now I have control over my muscles."

How painfully slow this learning was could be seen in his efforts to master swimming. It has been mentioned before that he could learn the necessary movements only within the security of the session room, from which he eventually transferred his achievement to our pool. But this meant only that he was able to hold himself on the water's surface for a stroke or two at the pool's shallow end. Later he wanted to go beyond this and learn to swim really well. It took John more than a year after making this decision to graduate from swimming a few strokes to passing the deep water test and swimming the length of the pool, a feat that children his age usually master in a few weeks. He was very happy when this was finally accomplished, and described his feat by using the same expressions with which he had described his new skill in playing jacks: "Before, the water controlled me. Now I can control the water."

Then, as happened so frequently now, a new achievement provided the fresh courage necessary to attack another of the many, long-standing deficiencies that up to that moment he had resisted tackling. The day after he swam the length of the pool and told us so proudly about it, he blew his nose for the first time, and did it well. Till then his constantly running nose and drooling mouth were among the more disagreeable features of his appearance, and were partially responsible for his slurred speech, which was so difficult to understand.

John himself connected his progress in motor achievement with the steps he had taken in overcoming his central disability, his anorexia. This came out in a conversation two weeks later, after he had just played a game of baseball in which he had made a two-base hit. He was bursting with pride. When we asked him how he accounted for his great improvement over the previous year, he said, "My muscles are stronger." Granting that this was true, we were somewhat afraid that he again might think that this had happened by magic, and wished him to recognize that this achievement was the result of his own efforts. Therefore we added that his improvement might also have had something to do with the fact that he now dared to exercise his body. Rather than reply to this, he answered, "And I eat more." Thus he directly related his new success in motor coordination with his progress in overcoming his very first and central difficulty.

During his last year at School, John finally began to enjoy many of the things that normally give pleasure to children, such as holidays. There were no longer any "happy unhappy" Easters. He said very definitely, "I have had a very good Easter this year." Each new pleasure in life was put to use in encouraging more complicated feats of skill. He returned to playing jackstraws, by means of which he had first acquired some finer motor coordination. But very soon he tired of this simple game and instead set up an empty tin can and tried throwing the jackstraws into it; then as he succeeded, he widened the distance between himself and the can, and set ever higher goals for himself. These were goals to be reached in reality, not fantastic statements about supposed abilities. Improvising further on the game, he aimed at other targets—always using these very light sticks so that he would not have to manipulate heavy weights while he was still developing higher, more difficult skills in bodily coordination.

Of course, even now John's development was not without setbacks. Efforts to fall back on his old delusional ways of mastery always cropped up. Each new achievement, while it led to new and greater efforts in reality, was also used for megalomanic elaboration. As soon as he could hit a ball occasionally, he dreamed of becoming a professional ball player, one of the most famous in the whole United States. Each such flight of fancy had to be punctured, because as soon as he gave in to it he gave up trying in real life. Although pointing this out to John made him terribly angry, it became more and more easy to bring him back to reality.

John still could not talk about his anger; indeed, revealing any of his feelings remained extremely difficult for him up to the end.

Just how completely his deep preoccupation with eating had filled his unconscious life, and crowded out all other emotions from the place they normally hold, is suggested by the fact that only at the beginning of his last year in School did he start dreaming about his parents, and his feelings toward them. I might also mention here that during the year when family visits were first curtailed he often spoke about how empty his future seemed. He could never fancy himself living with his parents, or within a family setting. Since everything was "always the same," he could never envisage a way of life any different from what it was at the moment. He expected to spend the rest of his days in some institution similar to the School.

Only long after he had become more divorced from his parents could he slowly accept the idea of leading a life in which he would have to make many more decisions than an institutional setting required. As he did so, dreams and daydreams occurred, which dealt with his relation to his parents. He was becoming ready to tackle this problem now: giving up being the eternal infant and becoming a person who expected one day to have a life of his own. The timeless existence ("all the same," "no different in the future") in which the infant lives gave way to thoughts about the future and his own independence—an independence he sought in dreams about leaving the School. In one such dream, he told us, "I was visiting my parents. Nearby was a stable of horses trained for racing. But one of the little horses was lame." In another part of this dream two other children from the School were sneaking out with John to the stables. Once there, they found that they were really going to visit their parents. They turned around and went back to the School, "but I went out on my own and visited my parents." This—leaving the School at the time he himself chose—was in the end the supreme way in which he asserted his newly acquired rights as a person.

John's interest in sex was also awakening. For the first time he became curious about sex differences. He had been masturbating all along, and there had been that prolonged, mutual play with other boys of a most immature kind, which he called "tickling"— a sufficiently correct name for it. While it was more or less sexual to the other boys, and therefore engaged in by them, for John it had been, up to then, mere skin stimulation of a pleasantly exciting nature. This tickling, despite its seemingly interpersonal nature, for John was basically self-centered. It had been an isolating experience, not one of reaching out for contact with others. This now began to change.

His new interest in sex became apparent when he finally dared to investigate and then play with dolls that had some sex characteristics. They had been there, in the session room, all the while; the other children had talked about them, and he had occasionally glanced at them, but never touched them. Now he dressed and undressed these dolls, and showed a marked interest in their sex characteristics. But when we asked if there were something he might wish to learn about sex, he immediately became hesitant and awkward in handling the dolls, denied that there was anything he did not know, or wished to know, and dropped the game entirely.

In the next session, however, John spoke about the "funny ideas" he claimed he had harbored as a small child—he had thought pushing a pedal, for example, made a car run. After lengthily listing his other "funny ideas" he got around to his thoughts about sex and his parents. "I used to think my parents were giants, and I thought, when they went out, that they went out to play baseball together." Saying this, he began giggling violently.

After some discussion of this notion, which was probably one of the reasons he wanted to become a famous baseball player at the time he began to be interested in sex, John could finally admit that he wanted to know what parents "do with one another." This led to the first conversation in which he seemed interested in, or permitted himself to talk about, intercourse, pregnancy, and birth.

Now that he could discuss sex more freely he was able to explain why he had always planned in advance, in the greatest detail, every meeting with his psychoanalyst, and later with the social worker. We had known this for a long time and realized that his progress in treatment had been seriously handicapped by his need to remain in control of the sessions. We had seen this as a counterphobic measure against the total control he had experienced in infancy, and indeed it was. As such, it had to be accepted, because when any deviation from his plans was forced on him during these years, he either became so panicky or retreated into such angry isolation that he was totally unreachable. Another reason why he had to plan his every move was that he wanted to talk about sex but was so afraid to that he was forced to decide carefully in advance all he would say. The result was that he could hardly disclose anything that was really on his mind.

Now, however, after talking about sex had provided him with the information he had craved but feared, he became relatively spontaneous during the sessions, and later in other situations as well. Many occasions, such as holidays, had already become pleasant for him; to his appreciation of these he now added an optimistic attitude toward his future. The seventh anniversary of his arrival at School was celebrated, as is customary, by our giving him a present for every year he had been with us. Pleased, he began talking about the past. He tried to remember what his first years at School had been like, but soon gave up thinking about the details and instead, beamed while he said, "I couldn't do anything, and now I can do a lot of things; and I'm going to learn a lot more." Having reassured himself about the present, he could recall all that he had been unable to do in the past. "It was terrible. I could hardly move. Now I can run, play ball, jump, and swim. I even can learn in school." Yet the old desperation was still present, though with a realistic tinge. He switched to talking about things he had not yet learned, such as typing, which we were trying to teach him both because his poor coordination made his handwriting illegible and because we thought it might be easier for him than writing. John, however, feared that it would take him "about ten years to learn."

Three months later (six months before leaving) John was speaking freely about his problems with eating in an effort to understand them and to comprehend why he had come to the School in the first place. Again and again, as he retraced his history of eating difficulties, he elaborated on whatever he told us with further details and brought out new associations that added to his understanding. Then, having acquired an adequate insight into the origin of his difficulties with eating and motility, he wanted to find out why he had not been able to get along with other children.

Here, too, John seemed to follow the steps of development that are characteristic of the young child. The oral phase is followed by the development of bodily movement and the control of muscles, at which stage the coordination necessary for walking, or for sphincter control, is achieved. Along with this development comes a recognition of the parents as independent persons, and later, mastery of the difficulties arising from just that realization. Resolution of these oedipal difficulties usually takes its course parallel to interest in one's age mates and efforts to get along with them. So John, in trying to understand his various problems, first attempted to fathom his eating difficulties, then his motor inadequacies, and finally his hardships in forming personal relations with other children. He figured out the origin of the last problem by himself: "It's because I didn't have any self-confidence. The other kids could always do more than I could. It made me feel mad and jealous, but I didn't show it—I covered up. Then I felt like blowing my lid off."

A few days later, John wanted to talk more about the past. Specifically, he said, "I would like to talk about some of the foolish thoughts I had. I thought all men were my fathers. Then I thought my father owned everything—all the cars. I thought that streetcars run all by themselves. I know of another funny idea I had—I thought my mother and father were the parents of all my relatives and friends." He dimly recognized that his overevaluation of his parents stemmed from the total power they wielded over him in the eating situation.

Such insights did not mean that John entirely relinquished his old ways of mastery. He no longer needed to prepare a careful agenda for each session, or for future events. But he deliberately tried our patience by refusing to cooperate, keeping us waiting, or by other expressions of his pervasive negativism. He openly said that he enjoyed doing these things. About his slowness, particularly in eating, he said, "I think I did it to make the others angry."

By this time John had gotten rid of his anorexia and constant regurgitation. He had not yet fully mastered them, however, but dealt with them partly neurotically by repressing them and developing a counter-reaction. This became apparent one day when he picked up the wetting doll while he was talking about his past. Another child had filled the doll with milk; when John touched it, a drop leaked from the doll's mouth. His reaction was to go into a stupor. Then panic-like anxiety set in, from which he needed quite some time to recover. Even after he had gotten hold of himself it took ten minutes more of quiet fighting against his revulsion and anxiety before he could explain that his experience had been so terrifying and utterly disgusting because it reminded him of what he "used to do." He did not want to think about those things; he wished to banish such memories entirely; and that was why he had become so upset.

This prompted John to wonder why, in the old days, he had not reacted against being forcibly fed. Why had he suffered it all those years without fighting back? He first tried to deny the validity of these thoughts by using sarcasm. What could a mere baby do? After all, a baby could not talk. But shortly he realized that he had continued to suffer passively even after he had learned to talk. As he put it: "I think about two things most of the time. I wonder why I didn't (fight back) in the first place, and why I kept it up (vomiting and suffering the forced feedings)." He now felt that previously, when something unpleasant happened, he "just walked away, or pretended it didn't exist." After some thought, he concluded that he had changed greatly. "Once, Miss White, I said 'yes' to everything, even here at the School; and then there was a time when I said 'no' to everything; and now it is 'yes' or 'no' because I know what I like to do and what I don't like to do."

Toward the end of this year John thoughtfully remarked one day that he was tiring of the School. "Seven years are awfully long." He added that he would like to try living at home. He realized that it would be quite difficult and that he was fearful about it, but soon reiterated his feeling that seven years was a "very long time."

We felt that his point was well taken. During the last years our efforts to help him had been based on the assumption that he would have to learn to do something about his own life, and that he could do this only if we demonstrated to him that such activities have positive consequences. Since he now expressed a wish to live with his parents, we felt that we should accede. A change in living conditions might prove a new challenge, which would further stimulate him to grow. Yet, until the very end, he was quite ambivalent about leaving.

As the time of separation approached, John felt most apprehensive about managing the relation to his parents. Again, the parents were advised to seek treatment for themselves, but were psychologically unable to do so. However, they agreed that a child analyst should help John during the difficult transitional period. The analyst first began working with John during his last month in School, in order to tide him over the period of adjustment to his home and to help him when difficulties arose later. This treatment continued for not quite two years. It was also planned that John would attend a small, special school for a year or two, where his handicaps could receive all possible consideration and he could continue his academic training under maximum protection.

In Conclusion

ALL THROUGH HIS HISTORY, the nature of John's phantasy life has been stressed, because it seemed to permit unusual insight into the nature and consequences of early oral traumatization; that is also why the name given this history was derived from one of these phantasies. Therefore, let us conclude the story of his stay with us with examples of how this inner life of John's had changed.

Its growth may once again be illustrated by his response to the Thematic Apperception and Rorschach tests. They were administered nearly at the end of his stay to provide a check on his progress, so that we could assess how well John was prepared for this major move in his life.

The examples that follow may suffice to show the differences in his various TAT performances.

JOHN'S THIRD TAT

John's story about the first picture was:[45] "This is a boy think-ing about music—about musical instruments. He wants to become a great musician and become very famous. He wants to be known throughout the world. Later he plays and his mother comes home. She is really anxious to see him become a great musician. She doubts it. He says, 'I don't know about that. I think I will. I am positive. Let's hear the story. I was dreaming when I was practicing until I became good. I still have a long way to go.' The mother said, 'I know you have a long way to go but if you try hard you will make it.' Later he does become a great musician and plays in all the great symphony orchestras. He says, 'It is not easy, but I did it. I am very glad about it, too.' He likes the instrument a real lot.

"He gets a child and the child does the same thing. He dreams a lot and becomes a great musician. This happens generation after generation until at last they make up a new instrument. The father doesn't like it, but the son does like it and bought it after the father died."

The greater closeness to, and regard for, reality, which John had acquired step by step can be seen by comparing this with the other two stories about the first card (pages 297 and 323). The first time, all he had seen was a baby. On the second test, he had at least recognized the main figure as that of a boy, but childishly misinter-preted the violin as a train. Only at the end of his stay could he interpret the picture correctly as that of a boy contemplating a musical instrument.

The wish to become world-famous, while in a way megalomanic, was a phantasy quite in line with what is normal in children his age. His remarks about the hero who first dreams, then practices, but still has a long way to go, admirably summed up his develop-ment up to that time. And his further elaborations divulged a rather good understanding of his relations to his parents. He recognized his mother's anxious desire to see him do well, although she had mis-givings about his ability to achieve. Her doubts at first made him doubtful, too, but soon he felt more positive about what he could do. Here we find reflected John's experience that only after he had gained some confidence in himself could his mother's doubts about him be displaced by his own more positive hopes for his future.

It is more difficult to interpret his last remarks about "future generations." They might suggest that John was pondering being a

---

45. For a description, see footnote No. 7 on p. 58.

father himself. They certainly reflect his feelings of being independent of his father, and the realization that a son may prefer different things than his father did, and even be looking forward to coming into his own, after the father's death.

John had rejected the second card[46] the first two times he had taken the test. This time when he saw it he exclaimed, "These pictures at least have real people in them. I don't like those other pictures where you have to make up what they are." Now he liked this down-to-earth country scene. His story went:

"A pioneer lady is going to the house. Her father is plowing the field. Her mother is standing by a big tree. She doesn't want to be a farmer. She wants to be a teacher. The mother says, 'Oh, no, you must be a farmer just like it happened to us for generations.' The girl says, 'No, I am bound I will become a teacher.' The mother tries to stop her but she can't. She reads and practices until when she is twenty-five years old she becomes a teacher. She teaches at a little red brick school house near the farm. The mother doesn't like it. That shouldn't happen. The farmer thought it was a good idea. The wife gets angry and yells and screams. In fact she leaves the farmhouse for a couple of days. Then she returns and does everything to make up."

The main topic here, too, was the child's fight to gain independence from the parents, to live according to his own wishes. The father took the child's side and the mother was forced to give in. Fighting for independence, against parental demands, occupied John's mind so strongly that it not only formed the essence of this story, but carried over to the next inventions in response to card three.[47]

"This boy is dreaming. He wants to become a great musician. His mother comes in and says, 'You don't want to be a musician. You want to be a businessman and make lots of money.' 'No, no, I refuse. I am going to become a great musician if it takes all my life to play one symphony. I'll play the harpsichord.' His mother says, 'The piano would be easier. So would the violin. Almost anything would be easier than the harpsichord.' The boy says, 'Oh, no. The harpsichord is for me—nothing else.' The mother says, 'You should become a businessman.' The boy says, 'Oh, no. I want to play the harpsichord.' They argue and argue, and finally the father comes in and says the boy should become a musician. The boy said, 'O.K. I will study music after I have studied business.' In the

---

46. For a description of this picture see footnote No. 31 on p. 122.
47. For a description of this picture see footnote No. 8 on p. 58.

end he became a musician for about a year but he didn't make enough money. He decided to become a businessman and make enough money for a good living. He said, 'I guess mother was right. I should have become a businessman in the first place.' "

Again the child was fighting for his own choice of a profession against maternal pressure. After a successful revolt, in which he was once more supported by his father, and a period of self-assertion, he ended by making his peace with his mother's desires, which turned out to be more practical. By finally choosing the occupation of his father, he also seemed to identify with him to some extent. The difference in tone and content between this story and that invented on the second TAT is striking (see page 323). There a sad boy dared to vent his anger only by dreaming of throwing a knife against a target, while in actuality he concentrated on eating. Now, in his third version, a boy was realistically fighting to achieve his own wishes against parental desires, and was succeeding in finding his place in the world.

Equally revealing is a comparison of the stories about card eight,[48] which John told on his second (see page 325) and third TAT's. The most recent one follows:

"It is a boy dreaming about becoming a doctor. He dreams so much he doesn't do much work. He is lazy. He dreams until he is fifteen. All of a sudden he gets down to brass tacks. He works and works. But he gets too tired too fast, so he has to work easier. At last when he is twenty years old he becomes an apprentice at doctoring. He helps the doctors so much it isn't funny. So he becomes a good doctor, but if he hadn't stalled he could have become famous. He never became famous. He keeps clinging to his work and it is very satisfying. Most people are so amazed that news spreads around and finally it reaches the president. He is very startled and he calls the doctor. He says, 'Is it true that you are satisfied with your little business?' 'Yes, yes,' says the doctor. 'You are the kind of doctor that we need in the government,' the president said. 'All people need a doctor like you to help them. You could earn lots of money and become well known.' So the doctor said, 'That suits me fine. That is the life for me.' "

John seemed to recognize that early in his life he dreamt too much to achieve anything. Then he tried working hard, only to find that he tired easily. He now seemed to accept a moderate position in life and to relinquish the idea of being famous; he was satisfied to do a good job. Still he hoped that, magically, this would bring him

---

48. For a description of this picture see footnote No. 13 on p. 60.

fame. But this is more of an afterthought, as if he were clinging to
his megalomanic hopes in the face of a more realistic evaluation of
his abilities. The emphasis is on an average but successful way of
life.

The rest of John's stories dealt with the same theme in many
variations: finding one's place in society and making a living. Great
concern with adolescent revolt against the parents, and with his
future adjustment in life, also pervaded John's third TAT. The
stories were mainly directed toward the tasks of the future—quite
a difference from the other two TAT's, which were characterized
by fixation to the most distant past.

JOHN'S THIRD RORSCHACH

While the third TAT disclosed John's concern about the future, the results of the third Rorschach test indicated a growing
ability to master it. In particular, his Rorschach test performance
suggested that John was now seeking adequate solutions to the
problems confronting him. The number and quality of accurate responses were much higher than before; though the underlying inadequacies were still present, they were reduced to a lesser intensity.
As for his emotional life and reactions, the test findings supported
our impression that these, too, were more than ever in line with
his age. His previously frozen feelings now had become more fluid,
and hence more amenable to change in line with reality. The most
encouraging finding was that his interest in, and grasp of, reality
had reached the normal range. Some specific results were:

"Growth in important spheres of the personality is indicated,
as compared with the findings in the second Rorschach test, and
therefore significant growth as compared with the findings in the
first test. But there is also, still, a drag on the personality's development. This drag shows up chiefly in immature thinking, some perseverations, and suggestibility. A logical solution of his problems is
noted. Some of the associations are tangential, suggested by previous percepts. Departures from accuracy still have the flavor of
the impersonal. But the percentage of accuracy is now notably
higher than on either of the first two Rorschachs. Thus perception
is more realistic. He did much card turning, without aim or plan;
showing the ego's inadequate control over motor trends. The improvement shows up in language and grammar forms, which are now
becoming mature; in some instances these are at superior level.
Most notable, structurally, is the emergence of conceptual thinking,
and of more difficult intellectual activity, such as is involved in

problem solving. A latent ability has thus emerged. There has been real progress, although uneven.

"The anxiety appears bound in the two parental figures, and more especially in the mother. This imagery definitely agitates, but does not now disintegrate him. It activates the feelings of inferiority, which are general throughout the test. In all, he does not show acute anxiety shock, and appears to bind this emotion as a matter of defense.

"A passive, resigned mood is noted. It is infrequent, but can be intense; and painful emotional experiences are here projected. He shows a much better balance in his affects than he did on either of the first two Rorschachs: distribution of the emotional reaction nuances is more nearly at expectancy for a child of his age. To be sure, he still shows impulsivity, as well as instability and irritability; but the struggle for self-mastery also appears. In all, it is a much more fluid condition, even if still accenting the immature or ego-centric. At the same time he persistently rejects color, i.e., is defending himself against the opportunity for healthy emotional contact and reaching out to others. The language in this rejection can be very positive: 'not a single bit did color help.' He is thus showing neurotic shock, which is paradoxically a good finding as compared with the earlier, undeveloped, affective conditions. He is now sensitive to his world, even if he does remain 'offish' about it. Structurally his most disintegrative reaction is in one of the color shock cards. Thus, the ego insufficiency persists; nevertheless it is an ego conscious of its relations to the outside world. He maintains his integration, but he shows that under enough trauma he is not far from slipping back. One may say that the psychologic homeostasis is inadequate.

"In the sphere of phantasy he is again showing some of the ability appearing in the first Rorschach, which was absent in the second. In fact, in the second Rorschach the condition was in several respects more unpromising than in either of the other two—a finding frequently noted as a concomitant to treatment, both in children and in adults. The therapy appears to effect a temporary contraction in the personality and its wishful living, or affective response. He is, therefore, now regaining some of the lost ground. But the phantasies are immature and autistic in quality. Insecurity is present in them, and the inner experience projected is thus a painful one. The total phantasy is not enough now to contain all the externalizing emotional pressure, and outer symptomatic behavior must therefore be expected. But the total balance of the inner living, both as introverted wishes (phantasy) and outer emotional response, is fluid, and within a range such that it can be healthfully directed.

"He is again showing resistiveness, at about the normal range—something which he had lost at the time of the second Rorschach as compared with the first, when it was higher than at present. In view of the extra-tensive total inner balance, the likelihood is that this resistiveness will display itself as against the outer world.

"The ego's total reaction to the world: In conceptual thinking and higher intellectual activity, he is now showing an overcompensatory intellectual reaching—an effort to extend the ego. But he overdoes this, and the unbalance in the reaction pattern may make for an inferior adaptation. Interest in the object world is within normal range, and so also is grip on reality. In this latter respect he has made the most notable progress as compared with findings in the first two Rorschach tests. Also, conventional thinking is now significantly above the very inadequate findings the first two times, but it has not yet quite reached normal expectancy. The growth in this respect is, however, very important, showing a learning of social canons, even if only at the surface level. He has affective assets, but they are now operating as general unrest, impulsivity, instability, with very little emotional warmth. Aggressive behavior is still likely to be maladaptive.

"In summary: The present findings show important and encouraging growth. Most important, this is found in the ego's conscious grip on reality. Emotionally he is warding off the outside world but responding to it, even if egocentrically. A bound anxiety is found, bound around the parental imagery, especially the mother. The mood can be discomforting. The sense of insecurity, and possibly of being incomplete, is the most critical psycho-dynamic. Treatment logic from these findings is therefore: the sense of self-assurance and of security need to be fostered. He is now showing assets which to this time have been latent. These consist not only in the ego's comparative strength, but also in fluidity of the inner life, and in intelligence potential."

John's Worker

AT THE END of the story of John's life with us I might mention that working with him was more difficult, because interpersonally less rewarding, than was true for the other three children whose histories form this volume. Therefore I would like to conclude my account of our experience with John by letting a staff member speak for herself about what made it possible to carry on the difficult work day after day. His counselors have been quoted before (see pages 291, 304, and 357-8). The person of prime importance to John during his last years with us was Florence White. She said about her feelings:

"John's helplessness and inadequacy made a strong appeal to me, and this was all the more marked because I came in at the point when his relations with others had worn down, or not developed at all. I was very accepting of him in a situation that did not lend itself at first, nor to such an extent, to John's old ways of getting along, and soon both of us more or less relaxed. Then when he began to have some feeling for me and I for him, he was able to use me in areas that were not so emotionally charged and in which he had already acquired some limited success, as for instance, in throwing and catching a ball and then going on to the use of the finer muscular coordination required in playing jacks. His evident pleasure in freely experimenting with me in order to gain confidence, and then his use of it in reaching out to play with children, was rewarding and induced my most positive feelings for John. However, when it was necessary to show John what his part was in shaping some of his life experiences, particularly at the School, this brought out extreme negativism in him. He had great endurance in this respect and could sit the entire time of session without saying a word. The depth of his hostility made me feel he was 'sitting on me' and so he could frustrate me. I, too, was vulnerable to his sad and reproachful look and felt in some way that I had contributed to his not being able to enjoy life.

"Perhaps one of the most difficult periods I went through with John was when I knew he wanted some privilege or treat that other children felt free to ask for and enjoy while he could not. Even if he did ask with my encouragement and it was given, he would then use it hostilely against me, by turning it down disdainfully as soon as he got it. At these times I am sure that I revealed my own feelings about this in spite of not putting them into words: a resentment that he would not take what I offered him.

"But these were only moments. Over and above all, John appeared as such a desperately helpless child that any slight overtures he made in a healthy direction were magnified by me, which made it possible to feel warmly toward him throughout the time I knew him."

The feelings of other staff members were quite similar. John's terrible unhappiness was so obvious that his openly hostile acts (vomiting and spitting on us, for example) were relatively easy to take; at least they showed some recognition of the outer world. Much harder to bear was the reproachful sadness with which he responded to our most sincere efforts to do nice things for him. His extremely slow rate of improvement until the very end taxed the narcissistic desires of those working with him, and they felt cheated out of their own reward: to feel that they had been of some help to John.

After Leaving Us

SETTLING DOWN to living at home with his parents was difficult for John, particularly at first, but as the years rolled by, his adjustment became better, and is now, considering the circumstances, a relatively good one. During the first two years after his leaving, he occasionally visited with us. He appeared not only to be retaining all that he had gained here, but to be making further progress beyond the level he had achieved up to the time he left. This was confirmed by his psychiatrist during the time that he saw John.

The parents, and possibly John also, have wished to forget that he was ever at the School, and as much as we regret that he has not visited with us during the past two years, we have to respect such desires. Perhaps the circumstance that he was the only child who had been at the School before its reorganization accounts for the fact that he is one of the very few children in whose case we feel we achieved our task but with whom we have subsequently lost contact. Other children tend to come back from time to time and so we can tell from direct observation how they are getting along in life. In John's case we have had to rely on reports from his school and his psychoanalyst in order to discover how he fared after he left us and how he is doing today.

As was to be expected, John's relations with parents, school, and psychiatrist were fraught with difficulties, although he made good progress both socially and academically in school and in therapy. After two years in a special day school, his teachers felt that he was ready to move on to a less protective setting. This was arranged, and during the last two years John has been attending a well-known private school, which serves normal children and maintains very high academic standards. At about the time of this transfer to a school for normal children the parents discontinued psychotherapy.

At this writing John is getting along well in tenth grade work, which is not more than one year behind his age group. His teachers feel that he is improving all along, academically and socially. Without being a leader, he is well liked by his age mates and is little different from the rest of this unselected group of private school students of high academic achievement.

When John left us after seven years of our efforts, we did not feel that he was fully "cured"—this might never have been possible —but it could be truthfully said that he had vastly improved. We believed that he had a very good chance of succeeding in life. His satisfactory history out in the world so far has borne out this conclusion. We all feel happy that by now, for John, ice cream is no longer better than God—that, in fact, it is truly enjoyable only when eaten in the company of a good friend, boy or girl.

PART V

"I NEVER KNEW YOU CARED SO MUCH"

Harry, A Delinquent Boy[1]

Harry and His Family

WHEN WE FIRST MET HARRY, he was a healthy, seven-year-old delinquent of normal intelligence, who gave the impression, despite a tensely maintained overneatness, of confusion and disorganization. His parents, feeling totally unable to deal with him, had asked for help at first one, then another social agency, until the last one recommended that he be placed with us.[2] Up to that time, the family unit had been at least physically intact.

The outstanding symptom of Harry's delinquency was a virtually constant truancy from home and school. This was combined with

---

1. The case of Harry appeared in a short version in *The Journal of Abnormal and Social Psychology* in April, 1949 (Vol. 44, pp. 231-265). I had compiled that report early in 1948, when Harry had been with us only two years. Thus it was based on what we then knew about the psychological phenomena underlying his behavior. A comparison of that study with the following account, it is hoped, will reveal some growth in our understanding of Harry, due to our association with him over an additional three-year period and to our improved understanding of his psychology, as well as that of other children. Much of the difference may be explained by the fact that in 1948 we had hardly three years' experience with the type of institutional treatment we try to apply, whereas now we can draw upon nearly ten years of such experience. Suffice it to say, that in rewriting Harry's case on the basis of our present knowledge I found it hard to stomach some of the things I said in '48. I am grateful for this chance to correct some of the errors I made then without, I hope, adding new ones to the old.

2. This agency, the Chicago Child Care Society, and the case workers assigned to Harry's parents, gave us the most understanding and far-reaching cooperation.

breaking-in and stealing and aggravated by various other types of deviate conduct.

Harry began running away from home before he was four years old. This behavior was never traceable to any immediate or specific provocation; he would run away at any time of the day or night. Sometimes he came back spontaneously, but more often he was picked up by the police. Usually he was absent until two or three o'clock in the morning, and occasionally he did not return until the next day, or later. His parents made various efforts to restrain him —using corporal punishment, locking him in, or taking his clothes away; all of these proved ineffective. When, in despair, they gave up punishing him and tried to humor him instead, they were equally unsuccessful.

Harry spent most of his days and nights riding streetcars and "El" trains, roaming the streets, or sitting in movies. He got money for these activities by stealing or begging. Sometimes he visited taverns at night and gave "performances" for drunken patrons, who enjoyed his antics and rewarded him with gifts or drinks. Later, with the help of older boys, he broke into and pilfered from cars.

Equally serious, though his parents did not realize it, were Harry's self-destructive tendencies. He rode the last coach of elevated trains, where a guard chain hung aross the opening in place of a door, and leaned far over the chain in defiance of the conductor's request that he find a safer place. He deliberately crossed busy streets against red lights, played on railroad tracks in front of oncoming trains, and crossed and recrossed the charged third rail of the "El" tracks.

Harry's aggressive tendencies were also directed against others. This, it seems, was quite in line with his mother's expectations: she considered him the "meanest child in the world" because he had already bitten people while he was still in the play pen. Between the ages of three and seven, when he came to live with us, he chalked up an impressive record of delinquent acts. He threw pots and pans or the washboard out of the third-floor window, narrowly missing pedestrians. He tried to set his younger sister's hair on fire and hurt his other sister severely on several occasions. He often threatened to kill his mother by stabbing her in the heart with a butcher knife, and made the attempt at least once.

Harry was not the only one in his family to have an unhappy childhood. His mother also had known little pleasure as a child. Her father drank heavily[3] and she reacted to the disorganization of

---

3. Although her marriage to Harry's father failed supposedly because of his alcoholism, she selected for her second husband a tavern keeper, only to have him later change his occupation to insurance agent.

her own parental home by becoming compulsively neat and orderly. When Harry frustrated her desire to have a "model" son, she punished him severely. At the same time, she remained totally unemotional toward his violence and showed only a very detached interest even when it was directed against her. Harry, himself, was often ashamed of the things he did, but his mother would prod him to tell visitors all about his exploits and fill in the gory details if he did not mention them. The more reluctant he was to re-enact these scenes coolly for a spectator, the more she insisted that he do so. He had to show how he had threatened her, and tried to stab her with a knife. The end result was that Harry lost his reluctance to reveal his misdeeds and learned to enjoy the attention he received for them. It can be assumed that he felt behind the mother's surface detachment a deep pride in the violence of her son.

As soon as Harry's first sister was born, she was immediately accepted by his mother as the "good" child; and the same held true for the second sister. They were praised and held up as examples, and this all the more as Harry, possibly in reaction, fitted himself into the role of the "bad" boy, which was the only one left to him. By that time it was already difficult to say whether the mother rejected Harry and favored the sisters because of his behavior, or whether Harry's conduct was the result of her rejection. In any case, all along she took great pride in his daring, whether it was socially acceptable or delinquent, and encouraged his megalomanic ideas of his own powers and indestructibility, although, to Harry, they were more counterphobic than real. "Nothing ever happens (or can happen) to Harry," his mother would say. She was sure that exploits that would hurt or even kill other children his age would leave Harry totally unscathed. She made a special point of telling him that he was the "smartest boy," much "smarter than all the other children on the block."

Harry's father, too, had encountered many difficulties long before his marriage. At seventeen, in an effort either to get away from home or escape further trouble with the police, he joined the Navy. Perhaps he had hoped the Navy could reform him; but he could not get along there either, and eventually was dishonorably discharged for drunkenness and being absent without leave. Shortly after he married, he gave up drinking, and seemed to "reform" for a time, in passive submission to his domineering wife. But after a few years of this he again sought relief in alcohol.

During his recurrent periods of intoxication he boasted of his strength and misdeeds, much as Harry's mother boasted about her son. He threatened and abused his wife and children, destroyed the furniture in their home, and occasionally broke into stores to steal. When he sobered up after such explosive outbursts he was again submissive and remorseful.[4]

He wanted his son to be a strong "he-man" and he interpreted Harry's running away as a commendable effort to gain independence from women. Most of the time he, too, was proud of his son's daring. At other times he was irritated by Harry's bid for independence and by what he termed his lack of respect, and on such occasions beat Harry unmercifully.

Thus, even on the most casual inspection, it became clear how inconsistent both parents were in their attitudes to Harry; they punished him for misdeeds in which they secretly took pride and subtly encouraged him. While Harry was openly rejected by the mother in favor of the sisters, at the same time both parents encouraged his megalomanic tendencies. Of the two parents, the father was the one who, in a way, loved the boy, and though his behavior was much more unacceptable socially, his actions therefore served as the example to be followed. Finally, the often violent and always smoldering discord between the parents may also have had an impact on Harry that penetrated much deeper than the trauma of their open fights.

When we met the parents, the enmity between them was so great that a divorce seemed imminent. I feared that if they separated soon after placing Harry with us he would interpret this as a result of his leaving home. Such a demonstration of power over his parents, namely, that his staying with them kept them together while his leaving caused them to break up their marriage, would tend to re-enforce his ideas about his own powers and, in particular, his notion that he could control the lives of his parents. Therefore, we accepted Harry only on condition that his parents would not separate for at least six months after his enrollment. This promise they made, only to break it as soon as Harry came to live with us. They separated within a few weeks, and sued each other for divorce. After a protracted fight in court, the mother received custody of the girls and the father of the boy, but Harry was put under the guardianship of the court, which ordered that he should remain at the School. Within two years after the divorce became final both parents remarried.

---

4. In his second marriage he chose a domineering woman who was considerably older than he, reformed permanently, and became a stalwart church member. But this socially acceptable behavior was acquired at the price of debilitating allergies, which got progressively worse until he could hardly work. He became entirely dependent on the care of his wife, who became the main breadwinner, and whom he treated as his mother.

Initial Evaluation

AFTER WE HAD OBSERVED HARRY for a few days (in this, we were handicapped, since much of the time he was truanting), we tried to understand the meaning of what we had learned and observed as a first basis for future planning. Psychological and medical examinations disclosed no additional factors that might account for Harry's behavior other than those inherent in his past history. We assumed that his main motive for running away was his wish to escape situations that created severe anxiety in him, which he was totally unable either to suffer or master. He was desperately trying to find security somewhere, and this had to be a place away from his home: typically the street, or the movie theater. He often spent all day or night at the movies, and frequently was found asleep in his seat when the ushers closed the house. It was not the show that provided the attraction, since he failed to understand what he saw on the screen. Any place seemed desirable so long as it gave him security from his parents.

His dangerous and provocative behavior, on the other hand, seemed to spring from efforts to overcome his feelings of guilt about his misdeeds. He may have reasoned that, if oncoming cars or trains did not kill him, or if he did not fall off the "El" trains, he was obviously not so terribly bad. But in direct contradiction to these efforts to relieve guilt, were other motives for his conduct, which made it impossible for Harry to overcome his anxieties by acting out, since the very behavior that alleviated anxieties originating in one set of motives, aggravated other fears. This was the vicious circle that forced him to increase the intensity and dangerousness of his acting out. One of these other motives was the positive wish to get hurt. The mother saw him as indestructible, but also as something very bad, "out of this world," a monster. On the other hand, humans are destructible and get hurt when they expose themselves again and again to danger. Therefore, if Harry alone did not get hurt under such circumstances, that proved he was indeed an inhuman monster. Finally, the more he wished to get hurt in order to prove himself human, the more he feared it, because he could not be certain that, as a hurt child, he would receive the dependent care he needed, and which his mother lavished only on his sisters.

Harry's aggressive acts were also motivated by the deep insecurity of his relation to his parents. On the one hand, he was trying to get back at his mother and the preferred sisters because they had contributed most to his unhappiness. On the other hand, he was trying to satisfy his father, who took his side against the mother, by being a "tough guy" or a "big shot," who could frighten others and beat them up. Like many anxious children, he tried to copy the anxiety-creating parent; sometimes he tried to show his father how much anxiety he created by mimicking him in an exaggerated way. But when he attempted to treat his mother in line with the example set by his drunken father, the father punished him for this —which was utterly bewildering. In his daring, Harry was also trying to live up to his mother's expectation of him, as any good child should. Finally, in line with his oedipal desires, he may have wished to separate his parents through his actions—as indeed he succeeded in doing by being sent to the School.

On still another level, Harry tried to alleviate specific fears by endangering other people; as long as they were afraid of him, he felt secure. But at the same time his aggressive behavior increased his anxieties. For example, his violence made people so angry that they actually became dangerous to him. Harry's way out of this situation was again to run away. But running away, in its turn, created more anxiety, for then he often went hungry, or was chased by older boys and men and beaten up.

Based on this tentative analysis of Harry's symptomatic behavior, we began our planning for his care. We wished to guide him toward realizing that in the School he was liked, he was safe and appreciated, not as a "big shot," but as a little boy. We intended not to make any immediate efforts to combat his running away, since it seemed to be a counterphobic outlet that provided a chance for motor discharge, which was very much needed at this stage in his development. We feared that any interference with his ability to relieve tension through motility, by removing himself geographically from anxiety-evoking situations, might increase his anxiety beyond measure. On the contrary, we wished to concentrate all our efforts on reducing his anxiety in the area of open aggression. Therefore, rather than curb his asocial behavior altogether (which would have necessitated overpowering and anxiety-provoking physical restraint), we simply tried to prevent him from hurting anyone. In this way, we hoped no additional fear or guilt-feelings would be created and the probability of Harry's being exposed to anxiety-provoking counter-aggression would also be diminished. This was the extent of our initial planning for Harry.

It should not be supposed that our original treatment plans were based on a full understanding of the etiology of Harry's disturbance; on the contrary, only his progress in rehabilitation made possible the slow revelation of his emotional attitudes, which, in turn, shed light on the probable origin of his difficulties. A fuller understanding of the genesis of his behavior was the consequence, rather than the basis, of our procedures. While our first efforts were based on the initial analysis summarized above, each subsequent step was the result of continuous re-evaluation of Harry's total situation, of our reactions to him and his behavior, and of our increased understanding of his needs and problems. Our growing insight helped Harry in developing the personal relations that finally led to his rehabilitation.

Nevertheless, it may be possible to follow Harry's progress in socialization and personality integration while he was with us more easily if some further remarks are made at this time on the probable background of his disturbed behavior.

Impulsive running away is often due to efforts to escape both from an inner state of tension and an external danger; but frequently, too, it involves the hope of improving one's situation, for example, by finding a better home.

The external reality from whose pressure Harry sought to escape was, first of all, the punitive and rejecting attitude of his mother, who took pride in his asocial exploits and showed much more interest in his "badness" than his "goodness"; and, second, the equally inconsistent behavior of his father, who was dependent when sober, and aggressive when intoxicated. In order to retain the image of at least one good parent, an accepting father, Harry had to avoid, if at all possible, encountering the bad, the intoxicated father. This he tried to achieve by returning home so late that he could be reasonably certain his father would be safely asleep.

The nature of the inner conflicts from which Harry tried to escape was made more complex because of the age at which he encountered his greatest difficulties with his parents. At about four, when he began to run away, Harry was ready to give up the initial attachment to his mother in favor of identification with his father. This process, although complicated by the fact that the mother had until then been the more powerful figure, was supported by her punitive attitude and by the birth of a sister at that time. While his mother did not gratify Harry's emotional needs, and rejected him, he had not known that she could act otherwise. In many ways she was a hard working and conscientious mother and he had been well taken care of in a physical sense. But when his sister was born, and he saw the tender care and emotional acceptance she received from the mother, he was suddenly forced to realize that his mother could be very different. This created intense rage in Harry and forced him to attach himself even more to his father, who preferred him rather than the sister.

The disparity between the mother's attitude toward Harry and her tenderness toward and acceptance of his sister, created not only rage, but also a deep fear that something in him accounted for this difference. Had he not been told that he was "the meanest child"? Perhaps this was true, and it was his own fault that he was rejected by his mother, who, he now saw, was capable of giving love. So to his rage at mother and sister was added deep discouragement about himself; and this was aggravated by still another factor. Up to the time of his sister's birth, whatever care he had received from his mother he had accepted unquestioningly. On this basis, it was evident that, while he now rejected the mother and identified with the father, he was still strongly identified with her at a deeper layer of his personality, and as a result, had incorporated her stringent values. His misdeeds, therefore, created severe guilt-feelings, which were in line with his mother's compulsive personality, and made even more painful his sense of total worthlessness as a person.

To escape his misery, Harry tried more and more (in line with his age and sex) to lean on his father and identify with him. Compared with the mother, the father offered relative warmth, when he was not under the influence of alcohol, but even less security than the mother. His submissiveness to his wife was most upsetting to his son. Harry, rejected by the mother, looked forward to the father's return in the evening. But as soon as he came home, the mother would report that Harry had been naughty and would ask that the boy be punished. The father at first would object, thus raising Harry's hopes, only to shatter them by finally complying. He would spank Harry much more severely than was warranted, or than he or the mother had intended; and then, furious at his own weakness in giving in to his wife, he would turn to her and say, "Are you satisfied now?" This irresolute behavior, which again and again raised hopes for security only to destroy them utterly, made it clear that the father, in his weakness, was sacrificing Harry to his wife. Such actions led Harry to despair. Nevertheless, goaded by his mother's rejection of him, and pressed by the emotional needs of his age, he was seeking to free himself of the oedipal ties to the mother and to turn to the father for satisfaction of his emotional needs. But the father's attitudes, as well as Harry's own anger and frustration, led Harry to identify with his father's pseudo-masculinity, which was based not on inner strength, but on drunken violence.

To make matters worse, at this crucial point in Harry's life, the father's conduct became worse. It was a period when he ever more frequently turned to alcohol. From being an occasional protector, however inadequate, against the punitiveness of the mother, the father became, more and more, a threatening figure himself. In addition, when intoxicated, his violence was often climaxed by the sexual subduing of his wife, which added fears about sex to Harry's anxieties. Moreover, it was at this time that the father added destruction of the furniture to his aggression toward the mother. This made Harry wish to protect, if not the mother, at least his home, while he, himself, longed desperately for protection against the hostility of both parents.

The frustrations and deprivations Harry experienced made him shy away from all human contact. Unable to resolve his conflicts, he remained fixated on a non-relational, phallic, and aggressive level. This became obvious from certain overt elements of his sexual behavior, which we observed, while the intensity and depth of his fixation was suggested by the violence of his aggressive acts. For months after coming to the School he would provokingly display his genitals; pointing his erect penis aggressively at others, he would shout at the top of his voice, "Look at my beautiful p----!"

At the same time, he often would anxiously and aggressively ask women to show him their penises. Convinced that he would find their penises hidden under their underwear, he made many efforts to crawl under and forcefully lift the skirts of women in order to inspect their genitals. His confusion, not only about the roles played by his parents, but about their physiology as well, could be traced back to his feelings about his mother, which he revealed in such statements as, "My mother has no tits; she's a man."

After Harry had been with us for some time, he revealed how closely his truancy was related to his fear of being castrated. He built a snow man and threatened to punish it by tearing off its genitals because the snow man had supposedly run away. This, then, was the punishment he feared for his truancy, and it explained his reluctance to return home even when he was suffering serious discomfort. Harry's castration anxieties were so great that he made self-destructive efforts at mastery by inflicting on himself what he feared others would do to him. He stated, for example, that he was going to eat his own genitals—thus combining castration fears with even more primitive tendencies toward oral incorporation—in order to make his genitals secure from external dangers.

His fear and hatred of mother figures and his desire to knife them were illustrated by his actual attempt to kill his mother, and later by similar attacks against his female counselors. It was evident that he sought to inflict on them with a knife the punishment with which he felt so threatened. He had been with us nearly a year before he could state symbolically, by means of the snow man, what this punishment was that he feared and expected for his truancy; it took twice as long before he could tell us directly who he feared would mete it out. One day, while taking a bath, he suddenly grabbed his penis with one hand and made sawing gestures at its base with the other. In extreme agitation, he asked his counselor, "Do you think any mother would do this to her little boy?"

There had never been any quiet, secure person in Harry's life with whom he could identify, never any time to develop a personality of his own. Desperation had forced him to seek security with one parent, to try to accept his values and form himself according to what he considered this parent's desires. But this had brought him only disappointment and mortal anxiety, so that he was forced to turn to the other parent; and this see-saw went on eternally. Thus all he ever achieved was identification with isolated and often contradictory aspects of the personalities of both parents, which made the formation of any consistent personality of his own, not to speak of a scheme of values, impossible.

One example may illustrate: Harry, out of an unconscious desire to please his mother, occasionally was compulsively clean and neat. Also, since his mother preferred his sisters, to receive her love he wanted very much to be a girl. This went so far that, even much later, he now and then would claim half seriously to be a girl, and would dress up in girls' clothes, which he carefully arranged so that they hid his otherwise chronically displayed genitals. Shortly afterward, he would have to overstress his masculinity by loudly asserting that he hated all females, and by committing aggressive acts against them. Denial of his passive and feminine strivings through violence was in line with his father's overt personality, and possibly was the result of his uneasy effort to identify with him. By the same token, the father's passive, feminine tendencies may also have contributed to Harry's deep wish to be a girl. In this context, it might be mentioned again that it was the birth of Harry's sister that deprived him of his mother's attention, if not love; also, his sister's birth coincided roughly with the father's return to drinking and violence, and as likely as not may have provoked this change in his behavior.

These contradictory tendencies in Harry's personality made it most difficult to handle him. He would suddenly and unpredictably switch from a feminine, passive or submissive attitude, with its attendant desire for dependent gratification, to uncontrolled, aggressive and destructive behavior, which readily reminded one of an intoxicated person.

How closely interwoven these opposite predispositions were is illustrated by the fact that nearly every one of his running away episodes showed two types of behavior—one pertaining to his father, the other to his mother. It was characteristic of Harry that, in either case, his identification was only with the destructive aspects of his parents' personalities.

His delinquent acts during truancy (stealing and breaking in), were derived to some degree from his father's destructive acting out. Visiting bars and taverns, and ingratiating himself with the men drinking there, were also efforts to come close to his father. The strong, self-destructive actions that Harry indulged in when he ran away were derived from his mother's self-punitive attitude, which was in accordance with her rigid standards, and were thus a consequence of Harry's original identification with her. While his father could act out without becoming self-destructive,[5] and his mother could be self-punitive without acting out, Harry combined the destructive tendencies of both parents in his conduct. And these tendencies were not tempered in Harry, as they were in his parents, by any constructive attributes, such as his mother's meticulous performance of the tasks set for her by society.

Of course, as mentioned before, Harry's self-destructive actions were motivated on many levels, such as his efforts to test his indestructability. They were also meant to propitiate his mother, and to make a forceful appeal for her protection, which he so obviously needed. It was only after he had been with us for quite some time and had made considerable progress in integration that we could more fully understand this from his behavior and from what he said. After a year had passed, for example, he revealed that he had been having frequent nightmares in which he, in the form of a giant, knocked his father unconscious. At another time, while playing with a doll house, he pretended that the mother doll put his crib on the roof of the home because she did not like him. But he explained her action by saying that he did not like his mother. Thus, in effect, he was indicating that being put out of his home, i.e., running away, had conflicting meanings. It protected him from his desire to assault the father, it was a protection against the threat he felt from both parents, and it was also his punishment for hating them.

Only after Harry had been with us for more than two years did he tell us about another aspect of his running away: that he was also

---

5. Later, in his second marriage, the father became self-destructively ill, but by then he had given up acting out.

trying to prevent the recurrence of certain nightmares and his consequent fear of what they might cause him to do. On the day and evening preceding this revelation he had been very preoccupied with memories of home because he had learned that a promised visit from his parents would not take place.[6] That night he woke up, screaming, "I see a man at the window! His face is all bloody! Take him away!" When his counselor had reassured him, he told her that when he lived at home he had had frequent nightmares, and that was why he had not wanted to sleep there. He continued by saying that when he had such dreams he had gotten out of bed and walked in his sleep until he killed someone. The counselor voiced her doubts that this had ever happened and continued to reassure him, but Harry steadfastly asserted that he had actually committed such an act, at least once. He had walked in his sleep, he told her, and nearly strangled his little sister; only after her screaming had roused his mother, did he awake.

While Harry's truancy can be explained as an attempt to avoid actual and psychological dangers, usually the impulse to run away, as mentioned before, is also motivated by the hope of finding "good" parents. This was true for Harry. He tried to find in the taverns he visited a "good" father, a father who would be masculine only, a father who would never turn against his son to placate a demanding and rejecting mother. And in a way, in these taverns Harry temporarily found such good fathers: the men, amused by this "big shot" little boy, encouraged him to show off in "masculine" ways; they petted him, fed him, joked with him, devoted all their attention to this play-thing. So, until they tired of him and kicked him out, he found there something resembling a good father. The "good" mother, whom he might have experienced in earliest infancy, was by now accessible to him solely in phantasy. She could be found only in the dream world provided by the modern dream factories, the movies. There he could enjoy the warmth of the dark room, the softness of the chair in which he curled up; he could eat—if he had something to eat—or suck his thumb, and feel relatively happy and secure. But, unfortunately, even these havens were full of anxiety-creating experiences. In the taverns it was the fighting and boisterousness of the men, that frightened him; in the movies, the threatening and

---

6. According to the terms of the agreement with the court, occasional visits with either parent had to be arranged. These took place at intervals of six months or longer. On these visits, because of their feelings of guilt about neglecting their child, both parents made promises to the boy that were not kept. On this day, reassurance that the hoped-for, yet feared visit would not take place revived memories of past home experiences and led Harry to realize that his present anxieties were closely connected with his past.

incomprehensible events on the screen. In the end, all his efforts to
escape his anxieties and find a good home only increased his anxieties and thus forced him to additional acts of discharge, of delinquency.

These remarks may serve as a background for the story of
Harry's stay with us. They should by no means be accepted as a
complete explanation of his behavior.

Disintegration of Delinquent Symptoms

IN RETELLING HARRY'S HISTORY at the School, in describing the
disintegration of his delinquent behavior and his simultaneous progress toward personality integration, the main phenomena of each
process are discussed separately. However, it cannot be emphasized
too strongly that this is a mechanical measure, which is useful only
for purposes of presentation. In reality, the various symptoms of
both his delinquency and his striving for integration, as well as all
other psychological phenomena, were strongly interrelated and in-
tegrant parts of his total individuality. Therefore, as Harry's personality slowly evolved, the improvement of one symptom affected
the others and the disappearance of all delinquent symptoms was
the result of a continuous process of over-all personality integration,
and not the result of our dealing with specific and isolated types of
behavior.

As with all our children, the initial efforts were directed mainly
toward helping Harry establish at least a rudimentary relation to one
other person.[7] While the nature of our children's disturbances always makes this most difficult to achieve, Harry's symptomatic behavior created unique hurdles, which had to be overcome before
such a relation could be established. Whenever he was with us, he
tried to master his anxiety by intimidating others. Practically as soon
as he saw one of us, out of guilt and fear of retaliation for his last
misdeeds, he felt he must protect himself by some violent, aggressive
act. Afterward, certain of our intention to punish him, he would
run away so quickly and skillfully that it was almost impossible to
catch up with him. Even the best-intentioned staff member was
rarely able to follow an escape that led over roofs and fire escapes,

---

7. Credit for most of the work with Harry, particularly during the most difficult
initial phase of his rehabilitation, is due to Gayle Shulenberger Janowitz. His adjustment to the schoolroom was achieved through the untiring efforts of Anna J. Lukes.
In addition, the help of several other staff members was significant in Harry's
rehabilitation, of whom at least Calvin Axford, Iris Friedman Leviton, Betsy
Schroeder, and Josette Dermody Wingo should be mentioned. Dr. Emmy Sylvester's
advice was of great value in our planning for Harry.

through the windows of private dwellings, across busy streets against the lights, between and even under cars.

Our plan had been that one of his counselors should accompany him when he ran away, so that she might be at hand to protect him, and thus establish some relation to him. In practice, however, this task proved not only very difficult but psychologically unsound. Harry used the protective presence of an adult only to strengthen his bravado. When he ran away by himself, he stole on the sly, begged money by playing the sad and subdued little boy, ingratiated himself with the patrons of the taverns he visited, and destroyed property after making sure he was unobserved. But he interpreted the presence of his counselor, who did not forcibly restrain him from asocial behavior and who did not threaten him with punishment, as an indication that she approved of his actions and that he had succeeded in intimidating her. He probably viewed her as secretly enjoying his misbehavior, and proud of his daring, in line with his mother's pride in his exploits.

But, unlike the mother, he soon realized that his counselor would protect him. And he took advantage of this by defying the mores of society even more drastically than before. He swore at passersby, hit them, and threw stones at them. He walked down the aisles in streetcars lifting women's skirts. He broke store windows, and stole openly. This type of reality-testing could not continue unchecked, since, not to mention many other valid considerations, the counselors would sooner or later have been unable to protect him from the punishment of outraged adults. This, in turn, would have destroyed Harry's trust in our ability to protect him from the dangers of the outside world.

Thus we had to abandon our original plan of establishing a relation around his truancies. It was decided that our next best chance was during the relatively few and usually stormy hours Harry spent with us. At the beginning of his rehabilitation, these periods were equally traumatic for Harry and the staff, for we frequently had to protect the other children from the consequences of his aggression. If he were to be reached, he had to be with us and unrestrained. Therefore, we concentrated our efforts on mitigating his aggressive behavior so that he would not always be running away from new misdeeds and could eventually learn to trust at least one person.

AGGRESSION—INITIAL PHASE

In Harry's aggressiveness there was little differentiation between destruction of property and violence against persons. The sequence

of events was usually something like this: He first committed some
act for which he feared severe retaliation, such as stealing money,
destroying other children's toys, breaking up furniture, flooding
bathrooms, or throwing things at people. When this was done, he
became panic-stricken and tried to ward off punishment by intimidating others and hampering efforts to catch up with him. His anxiety
in such situations gave him extraordinary strength and agility. Indoors, he threw chairs about and tipped over beds, chests, and
heavy steel cabinets in order to block the path of possible pursuit.
Outdoors, he hurled heavy stones at us, steel bars, or whatever other
implements he could find on the street.[8]

Often it was difficult to know which actions Harry expected
punishment for, and this impeded our efforts to diminish his anxieties. Once when he was taking a bath he seemed in an agreeable
mood and things were unusually peaceful. He was having a very
good time splashing water over the sides of the tub. Then he went
further and urinated on the floor. His counselor, seeing a perturbed
expression appearing on his face, told him not to worry, and said
that she would get a mop and pail to clean the floor. But his guilt
and, as likely as not, his past experiences made it impossible for
Harry to accept her statement. As soon as she left the bathroom, he
became panicky; he stuffed up the drains and turned on all the
faucets, so that part of the house was flooded. Afraid of meeting his
counselor in the corridor, and by then in a state of irrational panic,
he did not even wait to open a window to escape, but broke through
several window panes and fled over the roof.

Another time he threw three chairs down the stair well from
the third floor and then ran away.[9] Only much later, in the early
morning hours, when he returned to the School totally exhausted,
did we learn to our astonishment that he had done this in an attempt
to ward off some children whose toys he had taken and whose pursuit he feared. Still another day Harry overturned all seven heavy,

---

8. His behavior was similar to that of his father, who, when intoxicated,
threatened to beat his wife or destroy the pieces of furniture she liked best unless
she stopped berating him and gave in to his wishes. When there was no immediate
submission, he carried out his threats, setting an example for Harry of how to
achieve one's ends through violence.

9. This was in our old building before it was remodeled and the new dormitory
wing was added. Experiences such as this taught us to do away with open stair wells
and to incorporate other features into our buildings that make it unnecessary to
worry about safety or having to restrain the children for security reasons. For
example, our safety screens make escapes over roofs impossible, and play near the
windows harmless. These screens do not give the children the fear of being locked
in, since none of our doors can be locked from the inside. See also footnote No. 17
on p. 30.

metal beds in the dormitory, as well as several chests of drawers, and battered down a closed door, too panicky to notice that it was unlocked, because he was afraid of being punished or ridiculed for wetting his bed—although neither we nor the children pay any attention to bed-wetting.

Such situations arose so frequently that it was impossible for us to anticipate when Harry would feel that he had done something wrong and was ready to go on a rampage—he felt guilty all the time; but what specific misdeed he feared usually could be discovered only if his behavior made it obvious, or if he told us after his return. This he did quite readily as soon as he began to believe tentatively our promise that he would not be punished and to hope—though with doubt—that we would meet him with friendliness on his return. From then on he spoke more freely about his misdeeds, and about the fears behind his acting out, but still only after the act.

Harry's hostility was so great that he expected retaliation commensurate with it; and against this he protected himself, first, by further aggression in order to forestall the expected punishment, and then by running away. At such times he could not recognize or trust our friendly intentions. But once his fury was spent during his truancy, he could return and talk about it.

Our hope was that things would get better if he could learn to trust us even while he was acting up. But it seemed obvious that he could not master his hostility as long as it remained in full force; it first had to be decreased. Therefore, we concentrated on alleviating Harry's fear of punishment so that he could be sure that his violence would neither be dangerous to himself nor have consequences that would create new guilt-feelings. Equally important were our efforts to prevent frustration by gratifying his needs whenever possible, and, further, by making real or symbolic restitution for his past deprivation and anxiety, at least as far as lay within our power. We hoped that our efforts would slowly reduce the intensity of Harry's hostility to the point where he could manage it.

In order to achieve the first of these goals, we emphatically and repeatedly explained to Harry that children at the School were not punished. We might have to interfere with their actions for their own or others' safety, but this was not done as a punishment. Perhaps our genuine astonishment that he expected us to punish him severely for such things as wetting his bed or taking another child's toy to play with made a dent in his conviction about our threatening nature. It took many a sincere, "My God, Harry, you really thought we'd punish you for that!" or, "What do you think I am, a monster, that I'd beat you because you had to urinate and didn't have time to go to the toilet?" or, "What kind of School do you think this is —that we hate boys like you?" before he so much as heard what we said. But eventually he did listen and did begin, if not to believe our intentions, at least to wonder about them.

As is the case with many children, at first Harry was much too anxious about himself and our intentions toward him to be able to evaluate our actions correctly where he was involved. Gradually, however, he began to observe our attitudes to other children more objectively, and no longer used them only as further ammunition to convince himself that his siblings—here the other children, at home the sisters—were always preferred. It was to our advantage that he lived with a group of boys. At the School, the mother figure, his female counselor, even though he believed she treated the others better than him, was at least nice to boys. This was one unmistakable advantage he could see in the School. Though he, himself, did not yet feel liked, boys were liked here by both male and female parental figures. And he could also see that we did not punish boys for their difficulties and misbehavior, but tried to help them, instead. Whether the same might also be true for him, as we told him, he began to test by behaving in an aggravating way against every member of our staff. This violent testing-out continued for about a year, before it gradually decreased in intensity and frequency.

A crucial event in this period of exploring our attitudes was a step we took to assure that Harry's destructive acts would not endanger himself or others and thus create new anxiety and guilt. With the exception of the chairs, all movable furniture in his dormitory—tables, beds, and chests—were firmly attached to the walls or floor.

Our decision to do this was due as much to our desperation about Harry's violence, and our wish not to have the room always in a shambles, as to the hope that, if he were unable to destroy the room in which he lived, he might feel more secure in it. We had the furniture bolted down immediately after Harry had once again totally upset the room and then run away. The other children were told of our action, but not Harry. This was done deliberately. For one thing, we hoped it would be another demonstration to him that there are disadvantages to running away, for if he were not around, he could not know about events that concerned him. Another reason we gave him no forewarning of the change was that we wanted him to learn, in a way that would startle him, and thus perhaps be better remembered, that although we would not retaliate neither would we suffer his aggressions without some counter measure.

Sure enough, in the course of his next tantrum, Harry again

tried to throw the furniture about. But this time, to his amazement he found that it was impossible. He was infuriated; but this very frustrating experience turned out to be also quite constructive. For the first time Harry found himself prevented from committing a misdeed without having been physically restrained, threatened by punishment, or actually punished. Despite his anger, he realized that at the School people were so concerned with his and the other children's well-being that they were ready to go to some length in safeguarding it, while at the same time they made special arrangements to avoid the use of restraint. This provoked a first realization that brute force does not always succeed against an effective use of wits. From such experiences he learned that quiet nonviolence can be stronger than blind fury, that preplanning can achieve one's ends more effectively than immediate discharge.

It may also have dawned on Harry that he was just a small child who could not overpower his environment, and that it might be preferable, therefore, to come to terms with at least a few of its aspects. Some inroads were thus established in his delusions of grandeur and his belief that he was the best and the strongest of children, to whom nothing untoward could happen.

Finally, as we learned much later, our ability to protect other children against the consequences of his violence gave Harry hope that we might protect him, too, against the dangers to himself inherent in his destructive desires.

But such deliberate frustration by us of Harry's wishes was a very rare exception. On the contrary, we made great efforts to fulfill them wherever possible. He was fed whatever and whenever he desired and was given enough money and candy to discourage stealing and thus avoid additional guilt and anxiety. This made it easier for him to support himself without resorting to pilferage during his truancies, so that these episodes were less asocial and anxiety-evoking. Whenever he gave us a chance, we gave him explicit permission to leave the School, so that running away would be more an adult-approved activity. Such leave was always accompanied by our telling him that we would greatly prefer to have him with us, but that when he felt he had to get away he had our permission to do so. He was continually assured that the School was a safe place, where everyone was desirous of helping him and making friends with him. But because of his past, it took a long time before he stopped seeing everyone as an enemy.

One evening, at the end of his first month with us, he went to the kitchen with his group for a so-called kitchen raid. There he picked up a carving knife and threw it at his counselor—narrowly missing her head. At this, the other boys turned on him in fury, and he grew paralyzed for a moment. But before he had time to turn and run, his counselor went up to him, took his hand and held it firmly; then she told Harry and the other boys that no one was to blame but herself. She said she knew Harry could not control his temper and so she should not have taken him to a place where there were knives lying around, or have let him out of her sight for even a minute. This calmed the other boys to some degree; nevertheless, though the crisis was over, Harry still wanted to run away. But his counselor continued to hold his hand and insist that he participate in the group activity. If he could not share in the preparation of the food, he was at least to help eat it. This he agreed to do after everybody had quieted down, and he finally enjoyed the party a great deal.

Harry was not blamed for his violence; it was rather his victim who assumed responsibility. That she was a mother figure was particularly important, since it contradicted Harry's past experience with his mother. He had hurled a kitchen knife against a woman, but the reaction was the opposite of what had happened when he had attacked his mother the same way. This experience became an important step in his realization that the world picture he had formed was not wholly valid, particularly for the School setting in which he was now living. He also learned again that restraint may have advantages. If his counselor had not controlled the other boys, he would probably have been beaten up by them. If she had not also restrained him, he would have run away and missed a treat.

In line with Harry's strong sense of guilt, his self-punitive actions were as intense as his aggressions. During his first weeks at the School, while his violence sometimes bordered on the homicidal, his self-destructive behavior was similarly injurious and near-suicidal. Almost daily he engaged in "games" in which he tried to kill or injure himself. He made loops, which he pulled tight around his neck or asked others to do so; he played on railroad tracks in front of oncoming trains; he pretended to stab himself with knives or drown himself in the swimming pool. Frequently, he maneuvered himself into very dangerous situations. For example, he crawled into a big garbage can and rolled down an incline into the path of oncoming cars.[10] As late as four months after coming to us he broke a bottle, spread the splinters over the floor, and walked barefoot over them until his feet were cut. Other self-injurious actions were more directly connected with what he considered specific threats

---

10. For some time after this, the School had to get along without this type of garbage can.

to his body made by his mother. He stole or otherwise managed to get hold of mousetraps and affixed them to his penis. This particular behavior was meaningful to him on many different levels. He gained some pleasurable physical sensation. More important, in this way he punished himself for some of his misdeeds in the preceding days. But what was perhaps most important to him was that in spite of the heavy punishment nothing bad happened, either to him or his body. Even the mousetrap could not sever part of his body from the rest of it. This reassurance he needed against the threats he imputed to the attitudes of the adults around him.

In terms of his mother's pride in his exploits, as well as his own, it could be thought that some of this suicidal or otherwise self-injurious behavior was mainly exhibitionistic in nature, or that it had some masochistic, sexual connotations. But children who engage in such deeds for the first reason tend to make sure that others will be present to watch and protect them. Not so with Harry. His self-destructive efforts were literally meant as such. He wanted to punish himself, to test out his indestructibility. Therefore, he was careful to arrange matters so that his counselor would be unaware of what he was doing, at least at the outset.

These actions were, in part, meant to expiate for his misdeeds, so that he would be protected against the otherwise greater damage he feared if he were not justly punished. Once, when quite depressed because of a recent act of aggression, he remarked sadly, "I'm no good." Reassurance was of no avail. He insisted he was "no good." Encouraged to tell us why he thought so, he replied, "I have lots of germs in my ass." He added that there was only one solution: "if the police kicked me in the ass really bad so I'd get rid of them."

Such fears of sickness, which served him as a form of punishment or deterred him from further misdeeds, appeared for the first time after Harry had been with us for about three months. Much later it became clear that this marked the beginning of the development of psychosomatic symptoms. Anticipating what happened years later, it may be mentioned here that much of the energy Harry had expended in acting out, during the earlier period of his rehabilitation, was later stored in his body, which became rigid with this concentration of restrained power. Toward the end of his second year with us, this energy was no longer being stored in the parts of the body that are moved voluntarily, particularly the extremities, but seemed to find an outlet in specific, physical symptoms. For some time thereafter this channeling of tension into psychosomatic symptoms became Harry's principal means of combating his tendencies

to act out.[11] But his continuous progress in integration protected him
from permanently exchanging his acting out, particularly his self-
destructive behavior, for a psychosomatic ailment. Much of the
spontaneity that was temporarily lost was gradually regained, and
rigidity was again replaced by smooth, well-coordinated mobility.
Harry once more needed a great deal of motor discharge, but this
discharge then took place only in socially approved forms, such as
sports.

RUNNING AWAY

Efforts to lessen the violence of Harry's destructive behavior
were made simultaneously with attempts to decrease the frequency
of his truancies. But the latter could not become effective before
the first had been achieved, since his own aggressive acts kept him
in constant flight.

Harry gained an initial understanding of the counterphobic nature of his truancy in connection with his visits to the movies. This
was probably so because, for Harry, running away was the major
issue, not running toward something. It was the home situation and
what he experienced there that drove him to run away. That, for
reasons mentioned below, he found the movies the best place to
run to was not sufficient in itself to motivate his truancies. Never once
did Harry play truant specifically in order to go to the movies,
though many times he ended up there after he had run away from
us in order to get away from his own anxiety and unmanageable
emotional conflicts. Since the prime motive was the running away,
he could become rational about the place he ran to much sooner
than he could about the act of running away itself.[12]

In addition, Harry's addiction to the movies was a symptom one
step removed from his central conflict, that is, his anxiety about
the terrifying scenes he might have to watch at home, his deep de-

---

11. It is interesting that after Harry had begun this process, it also became
true for his father.
12. In other cases the situation may be reversed. For example a schizophrenic
girl who was deserted shortly after birth by her parents, ran away not to remove
herself from her present environment (the foster home, orphanage, and finally
the School), but to find her mother. Each place she ran to disappointed her, since
she never found the mother. Therefore she never ran twice to the same place. Her
rehabilitation was much more difficult than Harry's. Since she did not run away
because she was uncomfortable at the place she lived, making her more comfortable there was less of an incentive to stay; since she did not run to any specific
place, we could not use this place to bind her to us, as we tried to use the movies
in Harry's case.

sire for his parent's love, his hostility toward them because this longing was frustrated, and his consequent feelings of guilt. The unfortunate price he had to pay for enjoying the relative peace of the
movie house was an additional anxiety created by the threatening
and incomprehensible pictures he saw there. But as "scary" and
confusing as the screen pictures were, they were still less so than
events at home. And once he had experienced the relative security
of the School, once he had learned that the School offered him a
better peace than the movie house, he began to wonder why he
felt so driven to run from a place in which he felt safe to a place
that made him anxious. His visits to the movies now taught him
that this method of combating his anxiety was not only ineffectual,
but actually increased the conflicts and fears he was trying to evade.

Harry would ask to see the same screen plays, preferably Westerns, over and over again, and would always sit through several
showings of each film. He hoped that he would eventually understand the picture, or at least grow sufficiently familiar with it to
overcome the dread and tension it aroused. That this was the case
became clear from the anxious questions he asked about the films
while he and his counselor were at the movies together, questions
that showed his total lack of comprehension of the story, his exaggeration of the violence, his projection of destructive hostility into
even the most peaceful scenes, and his fear of what he imagined
was taking place on the screen. Harry, himself, said quite frankly
that his desire to see the films over and over again was due to the
hope that he might eventually find them less threatening, a hope
that never came true.

All this suggested that it should be easy to wean Harry from the
movies, since they did not really offer him any peace. But our first
efforts to do so came to nothing. We had taken too simple a view
of the meaning that going to the movies had for him. We had based
our efforts on what we knew of his reactions to the films themselves,
as if viewing the film were the only or most important meaning the
movie houses had for him. Only as we were defeated in our initial
attempts to wean him away from them, did we begin to observe
more carefully what else he did there. Then it became clear, as was
mentioned previously, that going to the movies was also an effort
on his part to find the security of an archetypic, "good" mother, to
rest in a place where it was dark and warm, where nothing was
expected of him, where dim sensations were only vaguely experienced.

Once we understood this, we could utilize the visits to the movies
in helping Harry to establish a better relation to a mother figure.
From this point on, his favorite counselor took him to the movies

—trying, whenever possible, to do so without having the visit preceded by asocial or self-destructive acts, and selecting the most innocuous films we could find, though the nature of the film at first made little difference. There she would sit with Harry and feed him, for hours. After this had gone on for many weeks, Harry permitted her for the first time to hold him affectionately, and finally would curl up in her lap while he sucked on some candy. Only when this point was reached was he able to turn from the screen and talk to her or just seem content to be with her for short intervals.

Such contacts were used to reassure Harry about the movies and to make him understand why they confused and frightened him. The relation to his counselor permitted Harry to have confidence, for example, that the actors were not actually being killed, and helped us to understand a little more about the nature of some of his fears, as well as to see how his repeated visits to the movies tended to increase them.

From then on, Harry asked to go to the movies less frequently, although he continued to assert vehemently that he enjoyed them. After a year, however, these visits became quite rare. He was able to reduce his need for pseudo-gratification of his hostile wishes through the film scenes to the degree that he learned to avail himself of real satisfaction of positive desires through his relation to his counselor. How Harry's attitude toward the movies had changed after ten months at the School, was revealed in incidents such as the one following.

He asked to go to a movie and was denied permission by his counselor, who suggested other activities instead. As usual when crossed, he attempted to browbeat her, but in this he got nowhere. When he was sure she was firm in her refusal, his mood quickly changed from one of angry pestering and defiant threatening to one of near elation. He asked for his allowance, not, as before, to pay his way to see a movie, but so that he could buy her something "for not letting me go to a movie." He was assured that buying presents for counselors was out of the question, and that the only purpose of having a weekly allowance was to spend it on himself. So he took his money to the store and bought candy and pop. Returning with this purchase, he said, "I'm going to have a party. Now we can sit together in the dorm and have a really good time. I've spent all my money and now I don't have to worry about going to the show."

Two months later Harry was ready to state openly his disgust with movies and even to devise means of preventing himself from seeing them. When he heard that some of his friends were planning to go to a show one Sunday with the allowances they received on

Friday, he spent all his money on Friday. Then when the time came
to go, he gleefully announced that he had spent his allowance already and could not join them; then he added, "There are a few
good movies but they're usually scary."

Just as the movies had counterphobic meanings for Harry on
various levels, so also had his truancies. Besides protecting him from
dangers originating in the uncontrolled actions of an intoxicated
father and a rejecting mother, running away also protected him
from the possible consequences of his own hostility. Playing truant
from home was not a leisurely or enjoyable activity. If not in a
movie house, he was continually on the run. When he finally returned home, he was utterly worn out and fell asleep immediately.
He only returned after extreme exhaustion made it impossible for
him to endanger those persons against whom he felt such hostility.

His fear of his own anger and its consequences had been intensified by the frequent comments his parents made about his toughness
and strength. Even after he came to live with us, his mother and
father continued to re-enforce his ideas about his power over them,[13]
and his dangerousness.

As long as Harry remained confident about his sway over adults
he had to run away when he was angry so that he would not destroy
them. Therefore his truancy could be decreased only by convincing
him by experience that his might was limited and that his aggressive
acts did not seriously hurt others.[14]

A factor that contributed to Harry's continual state of excite-

---

13. An example of how his parents fostered the idea that he was able to control them was provided on a visit with his father. Harry made his father promise
that he would stay away from drinking, and when this reasonable promise was
exacted, he used the superiority thus gained to reverse their roles; he began asking
the father to do certain things that parents usually require of their children. First
the father had to promise that he would brush his teeth every day. With this
victory, Harry went further. He asked his father whether he did not want some
of his toys to play with, and when the father said he did, Harry went to his dormitory to get some toys he had recently discarded as too childish. While in the
dormitory picking up the toys, he boasted that he had gotten the father to make
these promises to him, and said that the toys he had discarded were still good
enough for his father. I was told of this and felt that things had gone much too
far. So, contrary to our usual practice of not entering into a parent's visit with
his child, I decided in this case to find out whether or not Harry's boasts had
been empty. When I entered our living room I found Harry's father delightedly
pretending to enjoy the toys and assuring Harry that he would play with them at
home. As soon as I entered, Harry told me in a superior and spiteful way how he
had made his father make these promises. It was obvious that he was testing to
see how far he could lord it over his father and make him look ridiculous. Therefore,
I felt it best to interrupt the visit at that point.

14. The crucial experiences in convincing him of this were, among others,
finding the furniture fixed to the walls and realizing that the knife-throwing incident did not intimidate his counselor.

ment or angry exhaustion was his inability to enjoy an undisturbed night's rest. During his first weeks with us he dared not undress at bedtime because he had to be ready for immediate flight from the threatening events that he feared might occur during the night.[15] Much later he revealed how frequently he had had threatening experiences while asleep. He told us of his "night visits with my parents," which made him want to be ready to flee at any moment. During his first nights at the School he feared that, to prevent flight, his clothes might be taken away while he was asleep, as had happened at home. So he slept not only fully dressed, but with as many pieces of clothing on his body as possible. He often wore four sweaters on top of each other so as to be ready for any emergency. Letting him do this permitted him to feel greater security at night, and in this way he at least got some sleep, though little comfort.

Three weeks' experience at the School taught Harry that his night rest would not be disturbed by fights between parents, that he need not be prepared to run away, and that his clothes would not be taken away from him while he slept. Harry then permitted his counselor to undress him. This was not yet an acceptance of dependent care but rather of manual help in divesting himself of the cumbersome, though protective, layers of clothing. He would not yet let go of them on his own, but he could now permit one favored person to take them off. In this way some contact was established, though it was still largely of an external nature. Harry permitted it only because of its convenience for him, not because it symbolized an existing relation.

At about the same time, Harry began to enjoy some of our other attempts to make him feel at home. From the very first day he came to stay with us, sandwiches, candy, and a bottle of milk were placed by his bed every evening so that he would find something to eat on his nightly return. These he ate and drank either as soon as he came home or in the early morning before running away again. However, at first he was incapable of recognizing our efforts to take good care of him on his terms as deliberate and friendly actions. They acquired this meaning only after he had been able to establish rudimentary personal relations.

After more than two months his intense efforts to exhaust himself on his nightly trips decreased so that he did not always return in a state of near collapse. This gave his counselor, who always waited for him, an opportunity to do more than just put him to bed

---

15. This fear probably originated in his experiences at home. The intoxicated father often came in after Harry had fallen asleep and wakened him rudely while abusing the family.

while he ate, too sleepy to know what was going on; now she could take him into the kitchen, prepare him a warm meal, and stay with him while he ate. His counselor was neither demanding nor reproachful, but only helpful, as she prepared the food and fed him. Although he was too tired to talk, they would sit together quietly.

These occasions served to re-enforce, at the School, the contacts with this counselor that were already being formed in the movie theaters, which were also centered around feeding. It always had to be she—nobody else. From others, he would accept nothing—but simply grabbed or "stole." With anyone but his favorite counselor he always had to be entirely in control; he could never permit himself to be passive.

Slowly this one person transformed the School into a familiar place, while the repeated experience of being neither punished nor restrained made it also seem a safe place to Harry. His sense of security still depended on his ability to flee, so he derived some assurance from the fact that the doors were always unlocked from the inside. Once he was satisfied on that score, he no longer needed to escape through windows and over roofs.

When Harry first came to us, we told him that we did not want him to run away since we could not then protect him, feed him, and help him have a good time. We repeated how much we preferred to have him with us, but that, if he had to run away, he would always be welcomed back and never be punished. For quite some time Harry had no faith in our promises; that adults could accept his behavior without retaliation was too contrary to all his past experience. But when we pointed out the dangers involved in running away, this, together with our assurance that we wanted to have him with us, found a more receptive mind. We stressed how he might run into trouble, be picked up by the police, be cold and hungry. We emphasized our desire to protect him, but pointed out that we could do so only while he was with us.

Harry repeatedly tested the truth of these statements, and as a result was slowly convinced that the School was a fairly good place to be, although he still felt safer roaming the streets or sitting in a movie than being in any house. As time passed, we placed more emphasis on the protection and outright satisfactions his counselor could offer, if Harry would only stay with her. How much his ability to control his impulse to flee depended on his relation to this one person was dramatically illustrated one day. While running away at top speed, he stopped dead in his tracks when his favorite counselor appeared by chance. After standing absolutely still for a second or two he wheeled around and with equal speed ran back to the

School. There he comfortably parked himself on our front steps and waited for the counselor to arrive. When she joined him on the steps, he readily cuddled up to her, and let her know how he had planned to run away, but had given up the idea when he saw her.

Experiences such as this encouraged us to make special efforts to induce him to stay with us and, if possible, to set an hour, himself, at which he would return at night. Eventually he decided that he would be back by midnight. We then made an agreement with him that we would protect him up to that time, i.e., if he were arrested before midnight (as he frequently was when begging in taverns or stealing), we would make arrangements to call for him immediately and see to it that no hardship would ensue for him. But if he were found by the police between midnight and morning, we would offer no assistance and Harry would have to accept the consequences of a broken agreement.

As usual, he had to test the veracity of our promise. Previously, being picked up by the police had been a rather pleasant experience. The policemen were amused by the fantastic stories he told, by his childish appeal, and by the "big shot" attitudes that in so small and winsome a child unfortunately charmed many adults. Therefore, Harry was usually fed and entertained at the police station and, when he lived at home, often returned to his parents in the grand style—riding in a police car with the siren sounding. All this added luster to the exciting adventure and contributed to his megalomania.

Now things were to be different. One night shortly after our new agreement was made, Harry was picked up at 3:00 A.M. When the police called us to come and get him, we suggested the following procedure. Explaining our reasons, we asked the officer to send Harry to the juvenile detention home, with the understanding that we would call for him there on the next day.[16] This we did, and Harry informed us angrily that he had not had a very pleasant time; that he had been bored at the detention home; that the bed was uncomfortable and by no means as good as his bed at the School; and that as far as the food was concerned, "there was not much and it was lousy." We told him that we regretted his unpleasant experience, but that we could not offer him protection against the police if he

---

16. We had made arrangements for this event with the detention home's social worker. She understood that the hope for Harry's final adjustment depended on cooperation among police, detention home, and School. The social worker made it possible for Harry to be kept from all contact with other inmates so as to avoid any unnecessary traumatic experiences, but arranged for him to be treated otherwise strictly in line with the normal routine, as well as the regulations permitted, but with no special favors. Thanks to her cooperation, the worst part of Harry's experience there was that he was bored.

failed to stick to his bargain and return on time. He had to understand that the police and the detention home were there not to give
him a good time, but to prevent him from misbehaving. We very
definitely forewarned him that, next time, he would remain at the
detention home not only for the night but for two full days.

For the next few nights, Harry returned to the School well before
midnight. But the experience wore off and he again took to staying
out until the early hours of the morning. After he had done so several times without being detected, he was once again found by the
police and taken to the detention home.

As we had warned him, he remained there for two full days. On
his return to the School, he wanted to make much of how we had
let him down, but we dismissed his recriminations in a matter-of-
fact way. At the same time he was strongly warned that his stay at
the detention home might be even longer next time. Although he
pressed us to say how long it would be—two or three days, a week,
or a month—we did not commit ourselves, and told him that we
deliberately did not want him to know what to expect in this regard.
He obviously had learned his lesson. Harry was never again picked
up by the police.

Perhaps even more important than the avoidance of any further
run-in with the law, was an experience Harry had shortly after his
second stay at the detention home. He had run away again and had
not returned by midnight. At that we became quite concerned.
Having him stay once more at the detention home would make little
sense. The last time he had remained there for two days. If we let
him stay there again for two days, he would know that this was the
maximum consequence we planned for his escapades, and we feared
that this might not be a sufficient deterrent in the future. On the other
hand, to let him remain there for several days would be a real punishment, and we wanted to avoid giving him the idea that we wanted
to punish him because he went against our desires rather than to
teach him a warning lesson. We had hoped that two days at the
detention home would make a sufficient impression on him without
giving him the idea that we were trying to get even with him for
causing us trouble. Now it seemed that this plan had not worked
out and we did not know what to do next. For hours we discussed
whether or not we should let him stay in the detention home for
several days, but we decided against it.

As it got later and later, we also began to fear that something
had happened to Harry, since we thought we knew he wished to
return on time. By four o'clock his counselor and I, who were
waiting for him, were tired, worried, and exasperated. Then he

finally appeared meekly at the door. As I opened it, I felt carried away by a feeling of desperation about what I would have done if he had been found by the police again, and of utter relief that he was safely back with us. I gave him a good talking to, which obviously conveyed to him how worried we had been about his well-being, how concerned we had been about what to do if he had been picked up by the police, how upset we had been while waiting for him (this was said in not a few words) and how relieved we were to have him back hale, if not hearty. When I was through, he straightened himself up and the worried expression left his face, to be replaced by a happy smile. He said, "I never knew you cared so much."

Then and there he was convinced that our concern for him was great and sincere. This and the warning experience of his stay at the detention home led Harry from then on to make spontaneous efforts to keep from running away. Our hope that he would do this was behind the plan of having him stay at the detention home. We did not realize that he interpreted both this plan and our worry about him as sufficient proof of our true concern for him, a proof that each of the two alone had not offered. We had felt it would be unwise to exercise a restraining influence before Harry himself felt a desire for it, and we expected that he would feel no such a desire until he was confronted with the harsh realities of the existing social order. This alone had not been enough, but when our worries about him were added, the result we hoped for was achieved.

Had we tried to prevent Harry from running away—which, short of locking him in or taking away his clothes, would have been impossible—he would either have come to hate us, because of the punitive connotations of physical restraint, or to feel superior, because of his ability to circumvent our efforts—or both. Moreover, he would have felt he was being prevented, without good reason, from using a defense mechanism that had served him well in the past. Therefore, it was only after Harry himself began to feel some desire to reduce his running away that we could be more forceful in our attempts to encourage him to remain with us.

Such encouragement, and, if necessary or desirable, even some occasional verbal restraint, had to originate with me. By then, Harry had accepted me to some small degree as a father figure. He needed to see me as such, since I was the person who regulated his contacts with his parents, and, consequently, their influence on his life. He could feel safe only if they no longer had important powers over him. And not only in regard to his parents, but within the School, too, I represented authority, and was the mediator with the outside world (the placing agency, the police). In short, I represented that "law and order" with which Harry was in continuous conflict, but without which he was totally unprotected. So in order to feel safe, he had to come to some terms with me.

In this and many other ways I represented to him, as to many of our children, an external superego. Therefore restraint, or tendencies toward control, could and should originate in me. In Harry's case in particular it was important that consistent control over his actions, to keep them within the bounds of socially acceptable behavior, should originate in a man who, though in sympathy with Harry's needs, would not permit him to seek their satisfaction in destructive ways because he was concerned with the undesirable consequences this would have for Harry, himself. Thus far, most of Harry's control, including his guilt-feelings for his asocial actions, had originated in the mother's strict demands, that is, they were the consequence of rejection rather than of concern with his well-being. The behavior of Harry's father, on the other hand, had given him the idea that men do not have strong, restraining controls, and do not care about conforming to society, but simply follow their impulses, even when they are destructive. Therefore, it seemed important for Harry to learn both that males, also, comply with standards of social behavior and that not all females are harsh and punitive.

Harry's rehabilitation required that he develop inner controls, which would direct his actions and replace his diffuse and irrational sense of guilt. His ability to develop a strong ego and a reasonable superego depended on his being convinced that self-control could not only be consistent with adequate id gratification, but could produce lasting well-being. Therefore, in line with a division of function that is rather typical in our work, his female counselor, who was much closer to him than I, functioned as a benevolent and protective *alter ego,* satisfying whenever feasible, all instinctual demands that could be satisfied without outright destructive consequences. She tried to make no demands on Harry and to gratify all his instinctual needs as far as possible. She tried not to be annoyed with his behavior and, what was of crucial importance, for reasons originating both in her personality and in her relation to Harry, was hardly ever annoyed by it in fact. She truly regretted that, by running away, he made it impossible for her to be with him, play with him, feed him; and she let him know this. While I encouraged and accepted such promises to improve his behavior as seemed possible for him to keep (such as to return each night at a certain time), and did not accept any that were beyond his ability (such as never to run away again), his counselor told him that she was neither interested in hearing nor willing to accept any promises. She wanted him to arrange his life strictly as he liked best—he was not here to please her—but she hoped very much that he would arrange his activities so that they would be safe and pleasurable, and she would like it best if they could have a lot of time together.

When Harry began to feel that he should cut down on his truancy, he asked that the doors of the dormitory building be locked from the inside, so that he could not leave if he wanted to. Submitting to externally imposed control seemed easier at this point than restraining himself. This demand reflected some of his old desperation that he could never learn to control himself, and also his megalomania in thinking that living arrangements for the whole institution should be changed for his benefit alone. In response I stressed that we would never lock our doors from the inside since we felt that only a personal decision—never locks—should prevent anyone from leaving the School.

Since the School would not provide physical restraint, Harry next tried to create it for himself. He had strongly identified with a stuffed dog that he had brought to the School. During the initial phase of his violently self-destructive behavior, he would spank this little animal, throw it around, fling it at people, and hang it by its neck. Now he tied it to the post of his bed "so that it wouldn't run away." A short time later, we gave him a teddy bear. Each evening, he tied his arm to the bear and fastened it to the bed to prevent himself from truanting. Still, giving up his old pattern of running away from difficulties instead of dealing with them was a slow and tedious process, a constant see-saw of many relapses and many new efforts. And since "teddy" was supposed not to let him run away, "teddy" could be blamed when Harry truanted; it was the bear's fault for not keeping him here, and not Harry's own doing.

Eventually the relatively great security offered by the School, and the satisfaction it gave his bodily and emotional needs, combined to allay Harry's irrational anxieties. They no longer drove him irresistibly toward a mirage of happiness, which eluded him the more he ran after it. Instead, a new pattern of truancy slowly began to replace the old. Harry no longer ran away primarily because he was impelled by unconscious inner pressures, by fear that something unexpected and terrible would happen to him. More and more frequently now, he ran away only from real events, which he recognized as the reasons for his truancy. Unless there were some tangible motive, he no longer ran.

Of course, what Harry considered real and sufficient reasons,

such as fear of retaliation or frustration, would not have been sufficient to terrify other children. Any frustration of any desire, even the
most unreasonable, if not immediately removed, was unbearable to
him. And he feared as much retaliation for destroying some small
thing of no importance as for hurting somebody seriously. Nevertheless, that he now knew what drove him to flight, and could tell
us about it, was a significant step forward, because the closer Harry's
truancy became connected with reality, the more accessible it became to modification and control.

The next development occurred after approximately another two
months. Up to that time Harry had always run away after, rather
than before, an aggressive act. He now absconded in order to prevent himself from discharging his anger in aggressive actions. And
after some time, here, too, he became able to indicate, upon his
return, why he had run away, by pointing to the source of his
annoyance. It was a red-letter day when he revealed that he had
run away to prevent himself from breaking a chair that he had
stumbled over while playing. Another time he said that he had run
away so as not to hit a boy who had been calling him a name.

As his tensions became reduced and, with this, as his ability
to integrate them grew, it became possible for Harry to put a time
interval between impulse and action. He complained that the boys
were teasing him: "I'm not going to like that. If it doesn't stop,
something's going to happen. I'm going to run away—you better
stop it." He often made threats of this sort, but once he began announcing his intentions, it became easier to dissuade him from
carrying them out. When he was frustrated, he would dart out-of-
doors, come back, and then run out again, thus indicating all too
clearly the conflict he felt. At other times he would leave, but hang
around the house, rather than try to get away as fast and as far as
possible, as he used to. An offer of additional gratification, such as
a sweet or a new toy, and eventually simple attention, became sufficient to compensate for his tension so that he could refrain from
running away. The most successful means of getting Harry to stay
with us showed his growth in responding to true affection. At first
only material things, such as money or toys, were effective persuaders. Later, the candy bars reassured him less than the spirit in
which they were offered. While at first he sought only a bribe, he
finally found anything assuring that he could recognize as a token
of good will and affection.

When Harry's truancies had been reduced from daily to merely
occasional events, he began to experiment with symbols of control,

and to act out some of the anxieties connected with running away. For example, as alluded to before, he made a snow man and called it by his own name. In talking to it, or perhaps I should rather say, to his own self, he said, "You're a bad boy, running away all the time. I'm going to sock you and hit you." At that, he spanked the snow man furiously. Then he continued, "Now I'm going to pull off your p----," and in pantomime he carried out his threat.

Harry's efforts to master his urge to run away did not always take such aggressive forms. Once he brought me his favored teddy bear and asked me to keep it for him. I played with it for a moment to show my interest, but then handing it back to Harry, I said that it was his toy and he should keep it. A few hours later he admitted he had been on the verge of running away, but added, "How can I, if nobody takes care of teddy while I'm away?" Thus gratification (in this case, having toys) was again the deciding factor.

One evening, at about this time, a picture-story was read to him. It concerned a little chick who was accidentally hatched out with some ducks. It told of the chick's return to his own yard and his own kind. The chick had many adventures and frights on the way over the hill to the barnyard, but the last picture showed him in the presence of a whole group of chicks exactly like himself. When the counselor got to this point, Harry looked at the picture and exclaimed with delight, "He's home! There they are, all those others are just like him. He's with them now."

Harry asked to have this story read to him over and over again. It was his favorite for a long time, and he stopped requesting it only after he had virtually stopped running away. To him, it obviously meant that, like the little chick, his long series of fearful adventures were over and he was safely at home, among people to whom he belonged.

After a year's time Harry ran away only when he had good reason—causes for anxiety or anger that would be upsetting even to normal children. For example, an anticipated visit to the dentist proved to be more than he could bear, though he had not run away for two months previously. He left, but returned an hour after the time of his appointment with the dentist. On these occasions, which were now rare, he tried to make up for his misbehavior on his return. If he missed a class, he asked for extra assignments to make up for lost time; when he absented himself after school hours, he asked for extra work on his return, such as tidying his dormitory. Of course we did not fall in with such simple ways of getting rid of the guilty feeling we wished him to develop, since it was the only guarantee that he would curb himself in the future. We told him "nothing doing"—if he wanted to do his school work, he should be present in class—there would be no after-hours work for him or anyone else. As for the dormitories, they were taken care of by the maids. The purpose of cleaning up was to have a nice place to live in, not to buy off punishment, or reduce guilt.

Stealing, while it most often got him into trouble with the police, was really of minor importance to Harry. There were no unconscious or otherwise complex emotions at work here. Although he stole rather regularly while on the loose, he did this mostly to support himself, to get the price of admission to the movie theaters, if he could not sneak in. True, before he came to stay with us he had participated in robberies that involved breaking in, but he had done so only to maintain status with the gang. He had not belonged to a particular group; his life had been much too disorganized for that. His robberies were the consequence of the fact that he had by chance joined other delinquents who, more often than not, used him, because of his small size, to crawl through skylights or other small openings. Therefore, it was comparatively simple to deal with this symptom, which not only did not originate in psychologically complex motives, but also had no symbolic meaning for Harry, as did, for example, his daring of fate through self-destructive action. He pilfered only because it seemed the simplest and most direct way of getting what he wanted. If his needs were supplied, he had no wish to steal. Therefore, Harry's thefts decreased with his growing conviction that we would give him, as a matter of course, things that he had previously had to acquire through stealing—food, particularly candy, and the small amount of money he needed to satisfy his desires.

To convince him of the advantages of "domestication," as well as to establish a personal relation, we overindulged him for a considerable length of time. This overindulgence, this giving of more than he asked for, did not lead to any abuse on his part, as it often does in other children. Harry never played us for suckers. On the contrary, it very gradually decreased his need to steal. After approximately nine months of this regime Harry habitually returned any lost property he found, including money and keys, whose "value" often far exceeded that of his reward.

But although giving up stealing was relatively simple, giving up as complex and deeply anchored a symptom as running away was a long, difficult process. As a regular symptom, it disappeared almost entirely after approximately a year and a half, but its causes remained with him much longer and he was still tempted to fall back on it in times of stress. Harry ran away occasionally throughout the second year, but by the middle of his third year with us, he had stopped doing so permanently.[17]

Long after Harry had given up truanting, he still had to fight within himself against using this easy way out of meeting emotional difficulties. Combating this tendency remained the recurrent and central topic of his life for more than a year after he actually stopped running away, and was an important concern even longer. In play sessions he continuously acted out both the temptation to run away and his defenses against it. He steered many conversations so as to receive ample approval for remaining with us. Later he became concerned about why others wanted to truant, and this led Harry to come to grips with his father's drinking bouts and his own sibling rivalry, which, as it turned out, had been another contributing factor that made him run away. A few examples may illustrate Harry's spontaneous and effective efforts to resist the temptation to truant.

A child had left the School. This aggravated Harry's fear that some day he, too, would leave, and his uncertainty about what might happen to him then. Rather than suffer the tension of waiting until we sent him out into the world, it seemed simpler to run away right now. But he fortified himself against this by inventing a story that vividly brought to his mind the great dangers that he might meet outside the School. His story was:

Once upon a time there was a little mule who ran away all the time. Finally he became the property of a little boy named Harry. The mule had been beaten up a lot and was glad to have found a good home. Harry's father said he could keep the mule if the mule wouldn't run away. But one night the mule ran away and Harry ran after it to find it. He didn't come back and his father went out for them and finally found them sitting at the foot of a cliff, with the mule in Harry's lap. (Harry added here, as an aside, "It was a very little mule, and they were both fast asleep.") Things went all right for a while, and then the mule ran away again and Harry followed it. This time it was a very cold night and the searching party looked and looked for them, but couldn't find them, and finally they told the police and the police looked for them, and then they found them at the foot of the cliff and the mule and Harry were dead.

When he reached this end to his story he sadly explained, "You know, Harry, that's really me."[18] It seemed that nothing short of

_____

17. Up to the time of this writing Harry had never again run away, though life was not easy for him after he left us.

18. For curiosity's sake I may mention that Harry invented this story shortly

death was a sufficient deterrent to keep Harry from leaving us at that moment.

Imagining the dangers of running away was one way of combating his tendency to truant. Putting real impediments in his way was another. When Harry was told that I was leaving for a short trip, the first thing he did was to wreck both his shoes. In explanation, he claimed that there was a nail in one of them, so he could not wear them anyway. When his counselor, not realizing what he was trying to do, pointed out that there was no nail in either shoe, he began to destroy them even more furiously. As the imagined death in the story served to prevent him from running, so now an imagined nail in the shoes might have sufficed. But since the effectiveness of this imaginary prevention was destroyed by the counselor's insistence on objective reality even in the face of pressing emotional needs, Harry had to resort to still more drastic indications of his feeling of abandonment and his fear that in the absence of a protecting and controlling figure there would be no one to provide him with the satisfactions he needed so much. He lay down and bent his head as far as he could toward his chest, while making sucking movements with his mouth. The counselor asked him what he was doing, and he answered that he was sucking his nipple. Now she realized his desperation, and the fact that both types of behavior were expressions of his anxiety about the departure of a person of importance to him: the destruction of his shoes was an effort to shield himself from embarking on asocial ventures, while his attempt at self-feeding was an effort to find reassurance that he would be very well fed even in my absence. Discussion of the whole matter with him in the most friendly and reassuring way permitted him to express his fear that the train in which I was traveling might be wrecked, and other similar anxieties.

Harry's actions revealed that he was now able—though still in a very primitive way—to exercise some control over himself so that he would not leave, even in a crisis. More important, he could realize that two different psychological experiences were necessary to keep him from running away from difficulties: first, both external and inner controls, and second, assurance that satisfaction of all his central needs would be forthcoming despite any crisis.

---

after I had completed a first draft of this manuscript in which I used the pseudonym "Harry" in place of his real name. He had no way of knowing that I had chosen this name; moreover there was no person by that name who was in any way connected with the School, or with his previous life.

CONTROL OVER AGGRESSION

At the same time that Harry was learning to control his truancy, he was acquiring mastery over his aggression. As he ran away less frequently, and was absent for shorter periods, he was less exposed to anxiety-provoking experiences and felt less guilty. In addition, we had more opportunity of providing him with pleasant experiences. It was possible to satisfy his physiological needs for food, warmth, and rest more regularly and abundantly, and he gained the security that is derived from feeling certain about what will happen at a particular time and knowing that it will be satisfying. All this helped to decrease further his tension and hostility.[19]

When Harry's rehabilitation had proceeded to a certain point, it seemed advisable to change his group placement.[20] He had been living with a group of boys who were more or less his own age and he had begun systematically to terrorize them. He might have succeeded in establishing an absolute ascendancy over this group, which could have been maintained even after his violent outbursts were reduced to a manageable level. Therefore, we decided to place him in a group where some boys were two and a half years older than he. These boys he could not overpower. Originally, we had thought that it would be undesirable to place Harry in this group because, during the initial stages of his violent acting out, he was able to overpower boys of any age, since no child can successfully defend himself, for example, against chairs sent flying through the room. If Harry had been placed in an older group we feared his megalomanic feelings of power would only have been reinforced by his success in terrorizing boys twice his size.[21] Now that he was no longer explosively violent, however, these older boys exercised a beneficial influence and helped Harry to control his outbursts of

---

19. This, too, was a slow process and the mitigation of his aggression, as of his truancy, was simultaneous with, and a consequence of, the establishment of personal relations. More about this later.

20. Or so we thought at the time. While the reasons for moving Harry from one group to another were valid, we have since learned that in the last analysis, the immediate advantages of a change in grouping are paid for by insecurity about the permanency of human association, on which the forming of personal relations rests. This is far too high a price to pay for the benefits derived from regroupings. But to keep our groups relatively permanent, as we now do, requires much greater care in admitting new children to insure that each newcomer will truly fit into his group. On the basis of what we learned from Harry and others, we now tend to place a violently acting-out child right away into a group where there are some older and physically stronger children than he.

21. The preceding footnote explains that we no longer think along these lines.

aggression. Such outer control became useful only because it coincided with his own efforts at inner control and thus could support
them.

At about the same time, Harry's counselor changed her attitude
toward him from all-permissiveness to active support of his attempts
to decrease his violent behavior. He could now accept her help in
restraining himself because of the great services she had rendered
him in the past, and which were continuing in the present, and because of the security he was beginning to derive from this relation.
She now tried to show Harry that he could discharge his hostility
without creating situations that would be dangerous to him or about
which he would have to feel guilty. How this was possible, he was
taught, for example, in connection with his tendency to throw
things when in a rage. When Harry became tense—usually the only
sign he gave us that he was experiencing frustration—while out
walking on the street or in the park, his counselor encouraged him
to throw stones at trees, rather than to wait until his frustration had
reached such an unmanageable pitch that, in fury, he would throw
stones at passersby, merely because they resembled some feared
individual. His counselor also played stone-throwing games with
him almost daily. Eventually there came a time when Harry, who
had formerly tried deliberately to hit people, began as deliberately
to miss them.

At first, this was possible only when he was with his favorite
counselor and in good contact with her. This was rather dramatically
demonstrated one day. He had been throwing rocks at a strange
child and was just winding up to hurl the next, when he suddenly
recognized his favorite counselor coming toward him. The throwing
movement, which involved his whole body—a difficult motion to
interrupt midway—was immediately stopped dead. His body became
rigidly arrested, but his hand grew limp and the stone dropped out
of it.

It was a long way yet to the point where he could also stop
throwing stones at others when his counselor was not phyically with
him and only her mental image restrained his actions. But eventually this point of control was tentatively reached. Then stones were
replaced by balls—again, at first, only when he was with the one
person to whom he was closely attached, but later, also, with
others. After that, Harry was ready to participate in organized ball
games or in semi-aggressive games like "kick-the-can."

Previously, such games had always been avoided because Harry,
who could neither stand to lose nor bear the frustration of waiting
for his turn, would become violently aggressive toward the rest of

the players. That he became able to participate in such games was an important step because it went beyond mere socialization of his aggressive drives. He had become a person who was willing to abide by rules in order to enjoy the companionship of others.

The gradual socialization of Harry's aggressiveness revealed it-self in other types of behavior, too. For example, his transition to a higher integration resulted in the giving-up of such infantile behavior as bed-wetting. At first, Harry wet his bed regularly, and while this may have been due mainly to a combination of passive, feminine tendencies, with only a small degree of aggressive tendencies enter-ing in, there can be little doubt about the phallic, hostile character of his urinating during the day. When Harry became angry, he urinated on the floor with a great display of his penis and loud attention-calling to the stream of urine. If annoyed at a particular child, he urinated on the child's bed. This was eventually stopped after he had been at the School about four months, but not until an intermediary step had been passed, during which Harry managed to wet the floor or furniture with some fluid, when he was angry, but did not urinate on them. For example, he would deliberately flood the bathroom—a behavior that, while socially more acceptable, often did more damage and entailed much harder work for the staff than urinating. Thus Harry showed that he had acquired the ability to delay immediate response to frustration, though not yet to react to it in socially acceptable ways or to master it without acting out. He had also learned that he had to remove himself from the presence of the person who annoyed him because otherwise he would soon violently attack him; this he now tried to forestall, not because he did not wish to hurt another person, but because he wanted to avoid being criticized for his violence by those few persons who had acquired meaning for him, that is, his counselors, or myself.

An example may illustrate. One day a boy annoyed him while they were eating in the dining room. A few weeks before in such a situation, Harry would have thrown the dishes around, or might even have tried to turn over the dining room table; and then would have run away, not to return for many hours. This time, however, he ran out of the dining room and went to his dormitory. There he got hold of a sprinkling can and, filling it repeatedly, poured the water on the bathroom floor. Then he trickled water across the corridors and through the dormitory up to the bed of the child who had made him angry. Finally, he put a puddle of water in the middle of this bed.

In line with the primitive character (again similar to the *lex talionis*) of his guilt-feelings and self-destructive concepts, Harry now sometimes sprinkled water on his own bed when he felt guilty or angry at himself, although he did not carry this self-punishment so far as to make his bed uncomfortable—he had his counselor change the wet sheets for dry ones before he went to sleep.

Only after Harry had added to his involuntary bed-wetting, first, deliberate, aggressive urinating during the day and then wetting with water in place of urination, did his enuresis at night decline in frequency. After he had been with us for six months he began to have occasional dry nights. At the end of a year, bed-wetting became quite rare, and during his third year it disappeared entirely.

Punishing himself by wetting his bed was a great step toward moderation when compared with the initial suicidal attempts to which his guilt had driven him. Harry was now trying to pacify the pangs of his conscience in less serious ways, another example of which was his destruction of favorite toys.

These we replaced immediately. Breaking toys as a means of self-punishment was so much more desirable than destructive acts against his own person that we wished to avoid any possible return to the latter. This he might have done if he had run out of toys, or if his anger about their loss had aggravated his existing frustration. Moreover, if Harry had found that he could pay for his aggressions by losing toys, he might have felt free of all guilt, while our intention was, if possible, to create a situation that would make him feel sufficiently guilty to want to control his behavior, but not so much that he would suffer inordinately. Therefore, he was prevented from using self-pity over the loss of his possessions as a belated justification of his hostility. Replacing his toys served both to increase his guilt-feelings mildly, and to demonstrate once more our good will and our desire to see him enjoy himself in normal ways for a child his age.

It also seemed to us that if Harry were left without toys after an outbreak of violence, it would prove to him that he was a "bad" boy, a boy without anything to play with. That we gave him new toys to replace the ones he destroyed, he interpreted to mean that, contrary to his own fears, we viewed him as basically a "good" boy. Words to this effect he had learned to distrust; deeds he was more ready to consider as genuine expressions of our true feelings. If we considered him a potentially worthwhile person, one deserving of new toys even when he had been "bad," he wished, if at all possible, to preserve this image of himself, and this was another incentive for him to try to behave.

Harry's last serious effort to injure himself occurred after he had been with us for approximately nine months. Then his new conscience was already functioning, although with difficulty. One day, on an excursion, Harry and another boy, Dick, were throwing stones. A third boy was accidentally hit and hurt—not at all seriously. The "fatal" stone was thrown by Dick. Nevertheless, Harry knew that he was the one who had introduced the stone-throwing game. After Dick had injured the boy, Harry came to his counselor and told her that it was his fault, because he had started the game. The counselor assured him that it was by no means his fault, but on the trolley trip home Harry deliberately cut his finger on a window that happened to be broken and proceeded to smear his face with blood from the cut. When asked why he had done this, he merely said, "I cut myself, too." It was clear that Harry had acquired a conscience, which criticized him and forced him to seek punishment when he behaved aggressively.

This, however, was not the sort of conscience we wanted him to have. It was unreasonably strict, and more interested in securing punishment for any misdeed, irrespective of the motives behind it, than in permitting satisfactions that would make misbehavior less likely. Also, it was a conscience bent more on preventing misbehavior than on reaching, step by step, long range goals of socially acceptable and successful conduct. Nevertheless, an overstrict conscience is often an undesirable but unavoidable step in the rehabilitation of delinquents; it is closely related to the temporary neurosis that has been mentioned as a necessary, transitory development in their socialization. In Harry's case, too, its emergence indicated that he had started on his way, not yet toward true integration of his personality, but toward giving up delinquent acting out.

And at this particular stage Harry needed an overstrict conscience. Particularly in times of stress, he was still shaken by violently hostile tendencies. For example, after he had been with us more than a year, a short absence of his favorite counselor was still a traumatic event. (This, in a way, was a good sign, because it showed how important at least one person had become to him.) Such deprivation immediately evoked strong aggressive impulses. On one occasion, when he was told that she would be away for a week, despite all explanations about the necessity of the trip, reassurances about the day of her return, and the promise of a gift at that time, he violently and viciously attacked a watermelon that his other counselor had brought him as a special treat. As he cut it to pieces with a knife, he exclaimed, "This is Gayle!" (his favorite counselor's name). But after a while he calmed down somewhat and said in a low, subdued voice, "No, it's a watermelon and this is a knife. This isn't Gayle at all." This voice of reason was still weak, and could make itself heard only after some hostility had been discharged, but it was already strong enough to reduce physical aggression (such as on a former occasion when he actually threw a knife at her) to a symbolic form.

These two incidents in which he used a knife aggressively against the same person, the first time in reality, the second symbolically, show the distance Harry had travelled. This time, despite mistreatment by an adult (his counselor's leaving him), which still evoked strong hostility, he could control himself, as a consequence of the many satisfactions she had given him in the past. But his ability to enjoy gratifying experiences depended on a corresponding ability to recognize her as a human being of importance to him. Even the best food, or the most expensive toy, given without the personal touch, is not truly enjoyed, and often satisfies nothing, not even physical hunger. Therefore, whatever Harry had experienced at the School at best added only to his physical comfort, until the moment his counselor became important to him as a person.

However, as long as Harry's ability to control himself depended on the presence and influence of but one person, no true control could be achieved. This was further illustrated about a year later, when his favorite counselor again left for a short time. During her absence of a few days' duration, Harry behaved exemplarily. On her return he was very happy to see her, and immediately told her that he had missed her a lot. "I dreamed about you all the time, about all the fun we had and will have, like bike riding and stuff." Although he was angry about her absence, he no longer could take revenge on her. But when a few days later another counselor, who was his favorite's close friend, went on a vacation, Harry went up a fire escape, broke a window leading into this counselor's room, stole a small camera and a coin purse containing about a dollar, and off he went. Later, on his return, he guiltily slipped the stolen money under his favorite counselor's door and made some noise to make sure she would hear him. When she opened the door, he handed her the purse and camera. He explained that he had done this because he was so angry at people who left the School that he had not been able to control his wish to get even with them.

Harry could control himself and act decently as yet only with those whom he liked; others were not yet persons in their own right to him, but just good objects upon which to act out his anger. Even the best experiences offered to Harry could become truly gratifying for him only after he had discovered that others, although less directly related to him, were also human beings, and with that, view this as a friendly world, and himself as one of its citizens.

Personality Integration

DISCOVERING HUMAN BEINGS

WHEN HARRY CAME to the School he did not know, in the psychological sense, what human beings were. This was epitomized by some of his remarks.

In a conversation that took place shortly after he came, Harry talked about no one but himself. There were no other people in his world, only ghoulish figures, which populated his life whether he was awake or asleep. He told about having spooky dreams in which a ghost spirited him away and "then I took a knife and stuck her in the belly. She was a lady ghost," he added, as if in explanation. He stuck the knife "in the head, if it was a man ghost." Asked whether he had any pleasant dreams he said that he did; they were dreams about sleeping with his mother, which he liked to do. He especially liked to sleep on the couch with her. Knowing Harry had slept with his mother in reality, we asked him whether these were good or bad "dreams," and Harry answered that it was a good dream when his father did not kick his mother. But when his father "gets drunk and beats my mother, I get scared and run away." Events in reality—sleeping with his mother, being frightened when his father came home drunk, and running away—all these and more, were experienced as dreams, which were on a par with those other dreams in which ghoulish figures carried him off and were knifed by him.

A few weeks later Harry told the psychiatrist that she was wearing "a horrid, bitchy mask" and he began to scratch her face to tear it off. But then he decided that her mask was sewn onto her head and could never be removed. When she asked him whether others wore masks, he said that everybody did—that I, too, wore a mask, but that mine could occasionally be removed. Asked to draw these masks, he drew something resembling the psychiatrist's face, and exclaimed, "It's horrid!" Then he drew my mask. "It's not so bad, not as bad as yours." Questioned again, he insisted that he was absolutely sure we all wore masks. Then he spontaneously offered to draw a face. It was that of his counselor. "She is my counselor. I like her." A few weeks of close and, in some small measure, satisfying contact with his counselor, during which she had protected and fed him and had not punished him for his misdeeds, was sufficient to change her into a person with a face of her own. Thus, feeling liked by a person and, to some degree, returning that liking, removed the horrible mask.

Only much later did we begin to understand that putting masks on human beings and experiencing them as ghosts were devices also used by Harry to protect others and himself from the consequences of his homicidal anger. He dreamed of running a knife through his parents and sisters; he had attacked his mother with a knife in reality. He feared that any day these wishes and threats might become real, either for his family or for us, who had taken their place. If we were only ghosts, dead anyway, or masks, then even if he put knives into us, no real damage would be done. Thus his hostile phantasies seemed less destructive when he did not see us as people.

That this may be a correct interpretation seems borne out by the fact that the more he liked a person, the more that person seemed to him to have a face. (I should better say, the less he hated a person, since liking anybody was still way beyond him. He may, at best, have liked what some of us did for him.) But as soon as Harry became afraid of someone, or hated him, which to Harry at this time were hardly separate emotions, this person wore a mask, and became a ghost. Thus, since one cannot kill a ghost, his destructive wishes seemed somewhat safer and more acceptable.

A further suggestion that Harry used the self-protective device of turning reality into dreams may be found in his remark about good and bad dreams. His mother began sleeping with him on the couch at a time when she had decided to discontinue sexual relations with her husband. To sleep with one's mother, particularly after she has left her husband's bed, is very threatening, even more so if one has an abusive father who beats anyone who goes against his wishes. But even a good child, let alone a bad one, may safely dream about it. Therefore, Harry declared that this real situation was only a dream, since it made him feel safer to believe this. And if this was necessary for his few "good" experiences, it was even more so for the bad ones. To see one's father drunk, and beating one's mother, is terrifying. It is much safer only to dream it. Thus, for Harry, turning reality into nightmares, and faces into horrid masks, made his life not more, but less threatening. It was better if one could view the nightmares of reality as mere dreams; therefore, Harry could recognize reality as such only after he became convinced that reality was permanently much safer for him than nightmares. To reach this point took many months. But in the meantime his world slowly became populated by human beings rather than ghosts.

Within three months, even the psychiatrist's mask came off.

"The masks are off everybody's face," he told her, though with more bravado than inner confidence. This new trust in the existence of human beings disintegrated immediately whenever he felt his security threatened. The world then turned again into a place populated by ghoulish, anxiety-provoking, inhuman figures. For a world that could not provide security for a child was not a human world.

Nine months at the School and Harry could talk freely about his belief in masks. On meeting the psychiatrist, who had spent time with another child that day rather than with him, he shouted at her that she was wearing an ugly mask. At that, she stopped and talked with him for a while to reassure him that she had not lost interest in him and would come soon to play with him. Then she asked him why he again thought she was wearing a mask. He replied, "You wear a mask. But I say, 'Won't you see me [play with me]?' and you promise it; and then you don't [wear the mask]." Thus if someone disappointed his hope for love, as the psychiatrist had done by paying attention to another child rather than to him, this person immediately changed again into a ghost.

But it was not only being disappointed in people that made Harry see them as inhuman. The same thing occurred when anything happened to increase his anxieties, even when it was not a particular person's fault. For instance, Harry had to be taken to the sick room because of a cold. Fearful and angry about his illness, he told his counselor that she looked as if she were wearing a mask. Then he spontaneously added, "You know, when I'm mad or scared, I think people wear masks." When she assured Harry that he was not very sick and that she would spend quite some time at his bedside, he asked her to tell him, every time she left, exactly when she would be back. Then he asked her to bring him her clock, so that he could watch its hands until they indicated the time of her return. "It's your clock, and it ticks so loud that when I hear it I don't feel alone." By this time, a symbolic representation, through one of her possessions, of the person he now loved was sufficient to provide him with security.

Harry was now able to stand off sufficiently from his anxieties to understand that his delusional distortion of reality, his impression of people as ghoulish figures wearing masks, was due to his fear of being deserted. And what was more important, he could spontaneously devise ways of overcoming this fear and tying himself securely to reality. He was able to master his anxieties by means of self-selected symbols (the clock), which reassured him that his relation with his counselor continued even during her temporary physical absence.

I said before that giving things when no mutual relation exists often satisfies little or nothing; now I should add that the younger, the more emotionally immature a child is, the less he is able to establish personal attachments without being given, generously, by an adult, time, concern, positive emotions, tender care, and objects. The infant's utter dependency makes it impossible for him to relate unless he feels assured that he will always receive tender care from this one person, usually his mother. And because of the primitive organization of his personality, this security can be conveyed to him most easily when the appropriate emotions are accompanied by tangible evidence of their existence.

Thus in all our work, success depends on whether we can offer tender care to the child so that it is acceptable to him, and can persuade him to avail himself of our offerings—be they of time, concern, services, or presents—not as things in themselves, but as appropriate expressions of our genuine emotions. The child who comes to us has been severely disappointed over such a long period that he is not ready to believe in our good intentions. Too often he was bribed to do not what was best for him, but what was most convenient for the giver; too often he was cared for not to increase his comfort, but to pacify the guilty feelings of a parent or the criticism of a neighbor. Too many times he was exposed to a parent's concern that he grow up into a being who should vicariously satisfy the parent's frustrated wishes, rather than his own desires. For these and many other reasons the child who comes to the School cannot accept as genuine what we try to offer him. The more we do for him, the more he is convinced that we are trying to lull his critical powers, to ensnare him, to persuade him to do something that we desire him to do, which will be to his detriment.

During his first weeks at the School it was very difficult for Harry, too, to allow himself to accept any satisfaction of his dependent needs. He would not even permit his counselor to protect him, because he feared that he would be thought weak. He had to maintain his tough, "big shot" act at all cost, because he felt secure only if he could intimidate others. Once, when some of the boys were infuriated by his behavior and threatened to beat him up, his counselor tried to protect him. Even in this dire situation, Harry shouted at her, "I don't want you to stick up for me! I'll sock you, I'll kick you in the ass, if you try to help me!"

When someone offered Harry candy or sweets, he threatened them most rudely with what he would do to them if they did not hand the candy over, although this was what they clearly intended to do anyway. He had to maintain, at least to himself, that what he received was given, not freely and in friendship, but because we feared him.

As mentioned before, the first gratification Harry could accept was connected with his truancies. When he returned at night, he was always so totally exhausted that he either immediately fell on his bed and went to sleep, or could put up no resistance to being fed. After several weeks of this reassuring feeding, he permitted himself to be undressed. But he was so tired that, while he gave up resisting it, he hardly recognized it as an act of friendliness, or did so only very dimly. After two months he allowed his counselor to prepare a warm bath for him before going to bed. He did not yet permit her to touch him, although he eventually asked her to sit and talk to him or to read him a story while he enjoyed the purely physical comfort of a warm bath. It took all of six months before he could not only grudgingly permit her to wash him, but could ask her to do so.

Before this point had been reached, at about the time his favorite counselor permanently "lost her mask," he began to find it possible to accept some other dependent gratifications from her. Even then, however, the nature and degree of his previous deprivations revealed themselves in both his resistance and his response to opportunities for receiving tender care. His resistance was well established when he came; a high premium had been placed on the "big shot" pose. But this was a School where children could readily behave like little shots, and where all efforts were made to have them enjoy their childhood as children. Each day, unless he were truanting, Harry witnessed such behavior in others. He withstood this unstressed persuasion for about one month, and then began, somewhat circuitously, to demand his share. At first he confined himself to manipulating situations in which he felt that receiving childish care would be so legitimate that no one would guess that he was really enjoying childhood pleasures or doubt his toughness.

Once, he hurt his foot, or at least claimed to do so, and the counselor carried him upstairs. Having experienced how good it felt to be carried by her, without in the least admitting this to others (or, as likely as not, to himself), he maintained for several days thereafter that he could not walk and would have to be carried everywhere he went. (When his favorite counselor was not there to carry him, he had no difficulty in playing active games or running about.) After a few days had passed, during which he continued to take advantage of his injury in this way, his counselor told him that she would gladly carry him even if his foot did not hurt, and this she did. But it was only several weeks later that he spontaneously asked her to carry him in her arms, without making any remarks about his extreme fatigue or his sore foot.

After this, Harry became more responsive to situations that allowed him to express and find satisfaction for his primitive, dependent needs. After some initial hesitation, he began to eat wolfishly; then he began to suck things. For example, in the bathtub he at first caught drops of water from the faucet in his open mouth, and later began to suck and lick the faucet. For a long time he regularly transformed his washcloth into a primitive form of pacifier, on which he sucked delightedly. At meals he showed marked preference for foods (sliced fruit, for example) that could be picked up and sucked. When taken out for a treat, he rejected the ice cream sundae or chocolate milk shake commonly preferred by children his age and selected two or more popsicles instead. The more he gained confidence in himself and trust in the world, he more he behaved, with his favorite counselor, like a very small child. He not only let her bathe and dress him, as described above, but also asked to be spoon-fed and cuddled by her.

How Harry's progress was intimately connected with this one close friendship was also illustrated by his use of toys. He had never learned how to play with toys, but he envied other children who could enjoy such play. His jealousy of those who, like his sisters, could play relatively peacefully, and his frustration at being unable to do this himself, which was aggravated as he watched others, made him want to destroy all toys. He preferred to bite them to pieces, when that was at all possible. It made no difference whether the toys were his own or belonged to some other child. The very first toy he did not destroy, but, on the contrary, carried with him for a long time, was one his counselor made for him in his presence. And for some time thereafter he accepted only toys that she made for him. This was probably due to his past experiences with gratification—treats, toys, physical care—that had been given him not for his own sake. He was too convinced that, when something nice was offered, it was done for the adult's benefit rather than his own. To his parents, it had been more important to receive, in return for their presents, expressions of love and gratitude, whether they were faked or not, than to see that Harry had a good time himself.

This was highlighted by an incident that took place after he had been with us for approximately two months. Harry came to me and insisted that I had to give him fifty cents so that he could buy a box of candy for his mother's birthday, which was several weeks off. I told him that I saw no reason why he should buy her a birthday present, since he would not be seeing her on her birthday. I emphasized that I would gladly give him the money to spend on himself, but not to spend on others. While I wanted him to have candy if he wanted it, I was not in the least interested in spending my money on his mother nor in having him spend my money on her. Therefore, I held out two quarters for him to take if he would agree to spend it on himself.

Exposed to such a temptation, Harry became very excited and abusive. He accused me of preventing him from being nice to his mother, and was righteously indignant that I should think he might wish to spend money on himself rather than on her. Screaming with anger, with tears in his eyes, he loudly affirmed his great love for his mother. I tried to reassure him that I did not doubt his emotional attachment and his good intentions, but that I, as well as the rest of the staff, liked Harry very much and hardly knew his mother. Therefore, it made good sense for us to wish him to spend money that we gave him on himself and not on her. Harry seemed unable to accept this at the moment. His excitement increased, so I thought it best to give him the fifty cents, without further ado. But I said one last time that, while he could spend the money as he liked best, I would prefer him by far to spend it on himself than on others, whoever they might be. With that, his excitement subsided and he left my office quietly.

From the window I could see him walk slowly out of the house. Gone was the agitation he had shown just a moment before. In what seemed a very concentrated and thoughtful mood, he crossed the street and walked a few steps. Then he stopped, and after thinking a while, walked deliberately to a sewer, and slowly and carefully dropped the two quarters into it. That done, his whole attitude again became very lively. He ran back to the house and stormed into my office; telling me that he had lost the money, he demanded more. I told him that I would give him another fifty cents, but this time only if he spent it on himself and no one else. He agreed, smiling happily, accepted the money and spent it on some candy. Afterward, he made a point of telling me how good it had tasted.

This episode illustrates both his ambivalent relation to his mother and his testing of the School's intentions. Our reassurance that we preferred him to have a good time (by spending the money on himself) rather than make a pretension of desirable behavior (by spending money on his mother) was used by Harry to test not only our sincerity but also our readiness to help him solve an ambivalent conflict. It seemed that at this moment Harry could enjoy himself only after he had first pacified his feelings of guilt by symbolically propitiating his mother. He had intended the money for her, and he could not spend it on himself despite our encouragement. But our understanding of his stronger desires was sufficient to permit Harry to act out his problem, i.e., to expend money on his mother (which pacified his guilt and was in line with his positive feelings for her) but in such a way that she would derive no pleasure from it (which was in accordance with his stronger, negative feelings about her). He behaved as his parents, who "lost money" when they bought toys that Harry could not enjoy because they were not really intended for his enjoyment. These may have been some of the motives that made Harry drop the money into a sewer.[22]

Many such experiences, similar in psychological meaning though entirely different in actuality, are needed before a child's testing of us and our intentions convinces him that, at the School, satisfactions are offered to him for his own sake and not for extraneous or ulterior considerations of our own—such as our temporary convenience, or our wish to mold him into some preconceived notion of what his personality ought to be. Harry was no exception. Again and again, he tested us and because he usually did not find us wanting, his view of the world slowly changed.

By the time Harry had been with us for eight months he had accumulated quite a number of toys, including stuffed animals, which he no longer tore to pieces. Now when the boys of his group planned to have a fancy zoo of stuffed animals he could join in their fun. Each boy dressed up his animals according to his own taste. Harry began with his elephant. He made a cage for it, to which he attached a sign saying that it was the biggest of all animals, the king of all elephants. Next came a cage for his favorite, the teddy bear; this he dressed in his very own clothes and labeled it, "Clumsy, a bear only seven years old who is still clumsy at times." Clumsy was followed by Hoppy, a lazy rabbit who "only kills carrots." Last came his dog, Lollipop, so named because "he loves lollipops and eats them all the time."

Seen in the sequence in which he arranged them, it seemed that Harry was stating that at first he had tried to derive protection from the idea of being the strongest and biggest, the tough "big shot," the animal king, because only then could the defenseless and inadequate "clumsy" boy he actually was feel safe. Behind all this tough-

---

22. The possible symbolic meaning of dropping money into a sewer suggests that Harry's bad relation to the mother may have originated partly in the way she handled him during his education in cleanliness. Since eating and elimination are closely connected, and since, in the young child's mind, giving up feces is often equated with giving a gift, the wish to buy his mother candy may have been part of a total emotional experience, which he acted out here.

ness and awkwardness, which he now recognized as normal for a child only seven years old, was hidden the real Harry—a boy who was not clumsy at all, but defenseless, as a rabbit whose only safety rests in always looking out for potential enemies, and who, as soon as he spies one, runs away as fast as he can without waiting to find out whether the danger is imagined or real. But what Harry wanted was not to be a fearful rabbit, but a lazy one, who would stay put, and do no more harm than "killing" carrots—although that even this rabbit "kills," may have had symbolic meaning for Harry. Fully childish, was Lollipop. He neither ran nor killed; but merely enjoyed the infantile pleasures of eating and sucking.

A few months later, at Easter time, Harry shared with his Easter bunny his newly acquired knowledge about how to behave. He admonished it, "Act like a real little boy and don't crawl around or climb on roofs. If you do that people will think you're a monkey and treat you like a monkey, and you don't want that to happen." The lazy and carefree Lollipop was slowly being replaced by a responsible citizen who recognized that running away and doing bad things was not worthy of a human being, and that it was, in part, this "monkey"-like behavior that had caused others to treat him as if he were an animal.

DEVELOPING A CONSCIENCE

Harry's desire to behave responsibly had developed in the course of a process in which a more reasonable superego replaced a primitive, self-punitive, sense of guilt. Harry's self-destructive acts had been the consequence of his guilty feelings, of his conviction that he deserved punishment. Originally, he may have been motivated by magical thinking along such lines: he dared fate to destroy him and, when fate did not oblige him in that respect, he concluded, optimistically, that his misdeeds had been forgiven or had not been very bad in the first place; or pessimistically, that he was spared this time only to be much more horribly destroyed the next.

It is a long move from such magical thinking to the establishment of true inner controls. It was almost a year before Harry began to succeed in this integrative task. Identification with his favorite counselor, adoption of her standards as the result of his very satisfying relation with her (which was aided by the efforts of other staff members), and last but not least, making his own the values of the School because they had proved their merit through the protection and satisfaction they provided—all permitted Harry to give up the physical self-punishment, of which we disapproved, and to replace it by conscience reactions, which we encouraged. Instead of retracing this process in detail, one characteristic example may illustrate it—an incident that was a major turning point in Harry's attitude toward staff members and himself.

In cases of staff sickness, vacations, or for other reasons, a substitute counselor temporarily takes the place of one of a group's two regular counselors. Staff members also often serve as substitutes during their initial training period. Harry had been at the School for about nine months when a young man was called in to substitute for one of the regular counselors of Harry's group. With newcomers, whose attitude he needed to test out to feel secure, Harry was characteristically on his worst behavior. The substitute, though relatively inexperienced, by and large was quite good with the boys and rather well received by the group. Nevertheless, at one point, exasperated by Harry's misbehavior, he lost his patience and gave Harry a token spanking.

The children know that any form of physical punishment by teachers or counselors is not permitted, and right away some boys came to tell me what had happened. They had little doubt that Harry had only received what he had asked for, and they probably enjoyed seeing him punished. So they told me about it not out of sympathy for Harry, but out of concern about their own safety, which depended on whether or not they could trust the School's promise that they need not fear physical punishment. Much as I dislike corporal punishment in itself, my actions in this case were at first motivated more by my wish to show these children that I meant to keep my promises than by my concern for Harry. I knew that he could overtax one's patience and that the School had already lost a few potentially good staff members because they could not take Harry during the anxious period when they served as substitutes, i.e., beginning counselors. Little did I know at the beginning of this episode that it would have far-reaching consequences for Harry. As I became aware of this, I carried my actions further, no longer mainly for the sake of the other children, but also for his benefit.

In any case, I immediately went back with the boys to their dormitory and in front of all the children in this group, including Harry, I relieved this substitute counselor and asked one of our experienced counselors to take his place.

This showed Harry, as well as the other children, that immediate action had been taken. A little while later, after tempers had cooled off, I discussed the event with the group. I reminded them that when they had come to the School I had made promises to them, one of which was that they should never be spanked. Therefore, both because I thoroughly disapproved of physical punishment, which all staff members knew, and because I wanted to live up to my promise, I had asked the substitute counselor to terminate his services to the School. I added that no other action was open to me in view of the School's policies in this respect and my own promises, but that I, myself, felt it was nevertheless not quite fair to the substitute. Harry's behavior had been so exasperating that it required considerably more than average patience, and it was understandable that the young man had lost his temper. Turning to Harry, I said that he, in particular, should understand how a person might lose his temper, since he continually did so himself. On the other hand, no misbehavior of a child at the School would be punished in kind, or by spanking.

To me this was just another of our innumerable efforts to convey our attitudes to Harry, to reach him with our emotions, to convince him that life at the School was different from what he had known before. Contrary to my expectations, all this made a great impression on Harry, and he began to cry violently. During the rest of the evening and until late at night, he came to see me several times, and made, in turn, extravagant promises about being good in the future and violent threats about what he would do if the counselor were not reinstated. I told him that his feelings were understandable and even commendable, but that there was nothing to be done now. I told him that he had good reason to blame himself for the substitute's difficulties, since he had provoked the situation in the first place.

Harry's behavior during this incident demonstrated to us for the first time that his conscience was definitely developing. His feeling of guilt was caused not by any direct act of violence, but by the fact that he had been instrumental in creating an act of injustice. From this moment on, he never again acted quite as irresponsibly as before.

Harry, himself, was quite aware that his "conscience" was a new acquisition. He felt a need to justify the fact that he had never had one before. When his counselor read the story of Pinocchio to the children, one boy remarked that Pinocchio was certainly dumb if he had to ask what a conscience was. At that, Harry became very defensive and said, "How could he know what a conscience is? He hadn't ever been to school yet." The school Harry had in mind was the Orthogenic School. It was the only place he knew where a conscience could be acquired. Again and again he requested that the story of Pinocchio be read to him, and particularly enjoyed the parts dealing with the problem of conscience and the fact that Pinocchio could become a real boy only when he had learned the difference between right and wrong.

Whatever feeble ego Harry had possessed had been subservient to his id, which only made him act out all the more. Now his ego became overpowered by his superego. Unfortunately the superego he had developed through identification with significant figures at the School was not free from previously acquired elements. For a long time he had been under the influence of a rigorous mother, whose demands had made their impact on his personality. At the same time his bad life-experiences had generated great violence in feelings and actions. This violence was not yet tamed. He no longer acted it out all the time, but it was still within him; and it attached itself now to his superego. He always had turned a great deal of hostility against himself, as could be seen from his self-destructive actions. But these had been more or less in the nature of crude discharges rather than conscience reactions. Now he acquired not only a conscience, but a violent, unreasonable one. By no means was an optimum harmony among id, ego, and superego yet reached. Paraphrasing a remark of Freud, one might say that where there had been id there was now superego, equally passionate and irrational.

So Harry kept demanding more punishment of all kinds because, as he put it, he was "bad." When annoyed or frustrated, he still felt his old, aggressive desires, still hated us and wanted to get even with us. But he could no longer afford to act out immediately if he had no more adequate reason for doing so than a feeling of frustration. So he wished to be punished. This would solve his emotional impasse. Either the punishment would serve as an externally imposed restraint, which would prevent him from acting out and thus solve the inner conflict; or it would aggravate his anger to such degree that he would feel justified in acting out, and in this way, too, resolve his inner conflict, at least for the time being. In desperation, he would shout at his counselor or me, "I want to hurt you so that you'll hurt me!" Thus he openly stated his aggressive wishes and his desire to be punished for them.

The next step was for his superego to become so strict that Harry felt guilty and tried to make amends when anything bad happened at the School. He seemed to wish to function as the conscience for all the children. A tentative explanation for this is that Harry had acquired his own conscience through appropriating the morals and mores of staff members who, to him, in their totality represented the "School." It was not yet his individual superego, based on his standards and controlling his behavior. Such individualization of introjected values took place at a later time.

There may also have been a much simpler explanation. Anyone who went against what he considered desirable standards tempted Harry to do the same. If another child ran away, he felt tempted to abscond. He was not so much interested in keeping the other person from truanting as in not being tempted to truant himself. In other words, in order to prevent himself from running away he had to prevent others from doing so.

The simplest solution again seemed to be to seek externally imposed restraints. He told me of other delinquents' plans to run away, and asked me to have them locked in or turned over to the police. When he finally realized I would do neither, he invented quite ingenious devices to gain his goal. Understanding only too well the psychology of the child who runs away, he knew that he must permit a token truancy in order to head off the real thing. He induced such a child to play games with him, the outcome of which would decide whether they would run away or not. In this way, they could maintain to themselves that they had not yet given up running away and that it was only chance, or fate, that decided against it. For example, Harry would ask the other boy, "What is the answer for tomorrow? No or yes?" that is, should they truant or not? The answer depended on which one reached first a prearranged goal. If the other boy won the race, the answer was "no," and they would not run away. If Harry won the race, they would. Harry usually selected a bigger boy and a faster runner for this game so that that boy would win. This was another way in which he tried to externalize his inner conflict by finding an external solution. But such devices did not always work. There was no certainty that he would not run away as long as his inner force to resist acting out remained weak. And its power depended on the degree to which he felt close to those he liked and by whom he wished to be liked.

A few months later Harry hit on another device to keep from running away. Gleefully he reported that another delinquent boy had truanted ten times while he, Harry, during the same time period, had not done so once. Now, even if he wanted to, he could not run away, he said, because this would ruin his record, which he wished to bring up to two hundred times of remaining at the School when other children ran away. Asked what he would do once he had reached the two-hundred mark, he thought it over and decided that he would just go on improving his record. But why did he want to establish this record? "Because it makes me feel good," and he added that he was looking forward with pleasure to a trip to the Chicago Natural History Museum on the coming Saturday. To remain with us just because it was the right thing to do was not yet a sufficient motive; he also had to assure himself continuously of the pleasures that were awaiting him as a reward.

We have already seen that, as late as a year and a half after entering the School, Harry still ran away and stole. However, the latter was done very rarely and then only if his relation to those close to him had broken down. Also, while the temptation to steal was still too great to avoid altogether, now his conscience bothered him so much that he had to make restitution afterward. On one occasion he had stolen some money from a counselor whom he disliked. He may have intended to return it, but his own counselor discovered the theft before he gave the money back. Right afterward he tried to call me on the telephone, but "I did not answer." He then made sure that a message was left for me urging me not to send Harry away from the School.

The arrival of a new child at the School was always threatening to Harry. Fearful that the newcomer would deprive him of something, even though they were not in the same group and did not share counselors or teachers, Harry would try to beat the other to it by stealing something and then running away. During his second year, Harry's fear that a new child would totally dispossess him (as his sisters had done) was no longer as acute, but he still feared that he might not get enough. Therefore instead of running away he began to revert to extremely infantile behavior. He claimed that he was a little baby, and requested uninterrupted attention.

A new girl had come to the School and, as usual, this tempted Harry to return to delinquency. His counselor's efforts helped him to combat the temptation. In addition, he concentrated on thinking and talking about his birthday, which was still many weeks away. He acted out his birthday party, and even sang "Happy Birthday" to himself. He reminded his counselor of the presents he expected to receive and of her promise to take him out to dinner. He asked her whether she would take him to his favorite eating place, which he did not call by its true name, "The Midway Huddle," but the "Midway Cuddle"; then he began humming the song, "Cuddle Up a Little Closer." So cuddling up to her, and cuddled by her he lost the need to run away.

Of course running away and stealing were not the only delinquent activities to which Harry was tempted. Given his inner violence, it did not take much on the part of others to induce him to act out their aggressions for them. For some time he rose to every dare, as much as we tried to prevent others from challenging him and him from accepting the dare. Things got better only after he acquired his conscience, which, as I have said, became so strict that it seemed to apply to the whole School. Once a boy tried to get Harry to break some windows, and even placed a stone in his hand. Previously, Harry would have complied, but things had changed, and now he became terror stricken. At about the same time, a boy in a fit of temper upset several chairs in the dormitory. Harry chanced to enter the room at this moment and, without saying anything or being asked to help, began to pick up all the chairs that had been overturned. Another day a boy proudly told him that he was flooding the bathroom, which had been one of Harry's favorite exploits in the past. But now, on hearing of this plan, Harry dashed into the bathroom and quickly turned off the faucets.

Eventually, Harry's guilt about present and past misdeeds became so acute that he could not permit himself to enjoy even gratifications that most children take for granted. When the morning of his birthday, to which he had been looking forward for weeks finally arrived, he banged his head against the wall in self-reproach, and cried, "I don't deserve any birthday presents." Again, in a favorite and often-repeated play, some crooks were trying to make a getaway in a car. They planned to reform, to be "good," but it was always too late. Their car crashed and they perished. This play was the expression both of his fear that it might be too late for him, also, and of his wish to stay on the right track by playing out in front of his eyes the dangers of asocial behavior. No longer was he the charmed one to whom nothing could happen. On the contrary, Harry now lived always in terror of being utterly destroyed for his sins.

WORKING THROUGH

While the basis of our work consists in satisfying a child's needs for gratification, and offering him good human relations, this, alone, is not enough. Deliberate efforts to help a child with his difficulties form only the foundation of our work. In Harry's case, we affixed the furniture to walls and floors; we tried to make running away less pleasant by not protecting him against the police, and staying with us more attractive through the giving of toys and tender care, and the withholding of punitive criticism. Without such foundations nothing could be achieved. But, on the other hand, foundations alone do not provide a child with all he needs for successful living. Simultaneously, with their establishment—and here our analogy with a building breaks down—must go the erection of that superstructure, which is the complex but at the same time integrated personality. Because our children come to us with personalities of their own, and are not *tabulae rasae* on which we can make the first impression, our work is the more difficult. We have to tear down crooked and dangerous walls while at the same time erecting new ones, but never can we let the child be without any walls, for they may be his defenses, for example, against suicidal tendencies. We may even have to buttress very shaky walls such as, for example, obsessional defenses against paranoia, so that they will not collapse and in coming down destroy or permanently cover up with their rubbish the new structure just started, which will provide more adequate protection against the difficulties of living. Once these new walls—the child's adequate tools for mastery—are ready, then tearing down the old ones may prove more difficult just because we had to re-enforce them temporarily.[23]

The child must not only be helped to give up his pathological behavior, which, by itself, would at best only result in a surface adjustment, and at worst, lead to permanent placement in an institution; but he must also free himself of the causes of his conduct. While in many of our children it would be easy to point to the parents' shortcomings as causative factors, the reality is that, by the time we meet them, the children have developed, on their own, attitudes and convictions that stand in the way of relating to people and meeting reality adequately. These have to be rectified, and when necessary replaced, often by an entirely different set of inner attitudes, hopes, and expectations; otherwise—to return to the analogy of the building—we would only be adding pretty plaster walls in front of the old crooked and rotten walls, which basically would remain as insufficient as before to carry the roof and keep the inhabitants comfortably protected.

It is easier to speak about such matters in similes than to spell out in detail how the process of ridding oneself of the bad effects of the past takes place, and the integration of one's personality is achieved. For example, sometimes it is necessary for a child to understand why he behaves asocially and what attitudes of his parents evoked his neurotic reactions, before he can relinquish such behavior. In other cases, and more frequently in young children, such insight into what went wrong in the past is not necessary, and help around everyday life-experiences without reference to the pathogenic past suffices to help the child master his difficulties permanently.

But one of the things all our children have to be helped with is

---

23. This may explain why our work is often so slow, and why in the process of rehabilitation some children have to become worse, or at least seem to become worse to the outside observer. It is not only because the pathology, which before was partly hidden, has to be brought out into the open, but also, occasionally, it has to be temporarily re-enforced.

to recognize the present as present, and the past as past. For example, when Harry rightly blamed his night fears as one reason for running away, we reminded him that nights at the School were peaceful and quiet—much more so than on the streets—and that a dependable adult whom he knew was his friend was ready to protect him in the event of any disturbance. Whenever possible he was shown how his own behavior, or his own unrealistic point of view, created or aggravated unpleasant situations.[24]

But such explanations or interpretations can be given only if the child is ready for them; otherwise they seem to be additional experiences of being pushed around by adults who are using their superior reasoning powers to put something over on a helpless child. Or, to quote one boy's reaction to an explanation for which he was not ready, "I hope telling me all that stuff did you some good, because I'm not the least bit interested in it."

For more than six months Harry was not the least bit interested in finding out more about himself. All he wanted was to live his old life a little more comfortably; he did not care about changing himself—and for a long time, this is true of all our children.

The process of personality integration is not dependent on a physical setting, but it is facilitated if one can concentrate on it without obstruction from deliberate or chance extraneous stimuli. Therefore, it is often best accomplished in the privacy of a treatment room, though no deep change in personality structure will occur if the efforts to achieve it are restricted to the treatment situation only. The fact remains that quite a few children make their first efforts at restructuring their personalities there, while others do better in group or real-life situations and use the privacy of the treatment room, rather, to relax from such efforts and to store up energy for the next trial.

Many acting-out delinquents cannot stand the confinement of a treatment room; others find the implied intimacy with an adult too overpowering to their limited abilities to relate. Applying the correct dosage of physical and emotional closeness to such children is a difficult task. To return from these general considerations to Harry,

---

24. One fear in regard to his security posed a difficult problem for Harry, in view of the real possibilities involved. He feared that his parents might want to take him back. Being a ward of the court was too difficult a concept to be fully comprehensible to him or to afford him true security. Moreover, by petitioning the court, parents can usually succeed in obtaining visiting privileges, which they sometimes misuse to promise the child that they will again make a home for him. This promise is seldom kept. In rehabilitating severe delinquents, it would seem desirable for juvenile courts permanently to restrain parents who remain untreatable from visiting their child, and thus remove this threat to the child's rehabilitation.

I might mention that only after living with him for more than six months did we dare suggest that he begin individual play sessions with his favorite counselor. Up to then it had been beyond his endurance to be in the same room with an adult in a situation that implied any emotional demand. And even after the play sessions started, for quite some time he came only very irregularly, and only when his counselor made very special efforts to get him to come.

In the sessions Harry did not dare give his imagination free rein, but used this time mostly to obtain quite basic satisfactions: eating quietly, curling up in the counselor's lap, being read to. It was several more months before he began to enjoy the sessions, and longer before he could act out what was on his mind through drawing, using toys, and so on. Still, for a long time whatever insight he was able to gain was derived more from actual situations, such as his behavior with other children, than from the play sessions, in which he used symbolic materials such as dolls and the playhouse. Nevertheless, one day he finally began to play act.

Why it took him so long to act out what was pressing on his mind, why he was so afraid to re-create and thus visualize it, became apparent as soon as he began to play with dolls. The very first use he made of symbolic toy material was to re-enact a scene in which a father came home drunk and destroyed the furniture, while a little boy fled over the roof. This basic plot he replayed many times with relatively few variations. Only much later did he begin to use soldiers fighting, airplanes dropping bombs, cars crashing, etc., to act out his anxieties and hostility in more general and childlike form. These play sessions proceeded pretty much along the lines of child psychoanalysis, a process that has been sufficiently described so that to include a detailed account of it seems unnecessary here. But it should be stressed that these sessions made only a supplementary contribution to Harry's rehabilitation; in the main, it was the result of living in an environment that through its total influence promoted the integration of Harry's personality.[25]

Much of his insight, Harry gained spontaneously. Once a story was read to him about a little beaver who went to a new place to establish his home. The story told how the beaver's parents, brother, and sister were to live with him, once the home was ready. At this point Harry suddenly interrupted: "I bet I know what happens. When he goes back to call for them to take them to the new home

---

25. Of course, in line with the philosophy and the structure of the School, these play sessions were closely interrelated with what went on during Harry's daily life, while insight gained into pressing problems during the individual sessions had an immediate influence on the way all of his life at the School was handled.

he finds out his mother, father, and sisters are all dead." (The story mentioned both brothers and sisters, but Harry himself had only two little sisters.) Then, after a moment, he added very softly, as if talking to himself rather than to the counselor, "That's why I was afraid of going back home when I ran away." His wish to kill them off had driven him to run away, but while he was gone, the wish itself remained with those against whom it was directed, and he feared to find out that it had killed even while he had been absent.[26]

Considerably later, in another play session, Harry brought out the hopes he had once attached to his father's drunken excesses. Again he enacted the familiar scene with dolls and play house: the father comes home drunk and beats his wife and children. But this time the father kicked the mother and sisters out of the house "for good," and asked the little boy doll to stay with him "forever." After he had repeated this scene several times, Harry added the explanation, "That's what I hoped he'd do." And thereafter this particular sequence was no longer repeated.

Events at the School often served to stimulate a better understanding of certain motives for his past behavior. Once when a newcomer ran away, much as Harry used to, he explained, "He runs away partly to show off, and partly because he's scared"—and again realized that these had been among the reasons for his own truancies.

But passing events did not always lead to better insight and understanding. The new situations in which Harry found himself provoked also new defenses, denials, and distortions. One day, when discussing how long he had been living with us, he said that it was six years—which was actually the number of years since his older sister was born and his father resumed drinking. Thus he tried to deny that the traumatic years at home had ever happened. He seemed to wish to forget that there was a long period of bad experiences between the first phase of his life, when he had known if not love, at least some measure of security, and the latest period, which began with his coming to the School and the consequent renewal of an orderly and safe life.

After Harry had used the dolls and doll house for quite some time to act out his anxieties, he gave up this play for a period of many months. Approximately two years later, he turned once more to these toys. Previously he had used them to relive in imagination

---

26. Harry was so impressed with the story about the little beaver that he repeatedly asked to have it read to him, and later, when his group decided to change their name, it was due to his influence that they agreed to call themselves "Beavers."

his traumatic past. Now he enacted the behavior of a good family in times of mild stress (the way his parents may have behaved before his father returned to drink). A little boy (the doll representing Harry) got into the type of mischief that small children are apt to create. Finally the boy knocked a table over, which was reminiscent both of the father's behavior and of Harry when he came to us. This really annoyed the father doll, according to Harry. But, compared with the previous behavior of the father when enraged, Harry now had him act reasonably and with control. He was merely made to say, "I'm mad at you," and there the matter ended.

The doll play must have reminded Harry that things had actually not been handled this way at his home. This thought made him angry and he returned to playing war with soldiers, which for so long had served as his favorite way of expressing his deep anger and hostility. But now the play with the soldiers soon fizzled out; he lost interest before any violent action occurred. Instead, he turned to a toy airplane. Before letting the plane go up, Harry said, "I must make sure that the plane has good brakes. That's important. Otherwise it might get out of control." Then he equipped the plane with radar, because "I have to see what's ahead." Forgetting, denying that there had ever been any bad times at home, and pretending that his father never showed more violence than merely saying, "I'm mad," were some of the emergency brakes he had forged for himself, as were also his fear of excessive punishment and, later, his demands for it. Now, however, these emergency methods of controlling his asocial behavior were no longer needed. At the end of this play session he said, "I want to turn off the emergency brake. We don't need it any more, because the war's over. It's really over and for good."

This runaway, impulse-ridden boy was not yet in full control of himself, but he now possessed brakes, which he could apply should he ever again get out of control. He dared to look ahead to the future (the radar) because he was now convinced that the future, unlike his past, would not be too horrible to face. Once secure in this confidence, Harry's war with society would be over.

DEVELOPING A NEW PERSONALITY

All these processes—disintegration of old patterns, development of conscience, mastering the traumatic past—which were made possible only by the formation and strengthening of true personal relations, proceeded simultaneously. It is hard to determine just when, in time, Harry's new personality slowly began to supersede the old.

It was all of a year before surface adjustments became anchored in a healthier balance between superego and id, and a strengthened ego could assert itself more successfully.

One day this "new" Harry bought an ice cream cone in a drugstore. The price was eight cents and he paid with a quarter. He was given nineteen cents in change. At first he tried to keep the extra money, but after a while he turned to the clerk, saying, "You gave me too much back," and returned the excess pennies. Harry was very proud of himself as he received the warm praise of his counselor. "I wanted to be honest," he said, "and I could." He was no longer able to keep mistakenly received change without serious qualms, as he would have been when he first came to the School, nor did he feel guilty about momentarily having tried to keep the pennies, as he would have later. But he could not yet be honest in a matter-of-fact way. It was something to be proud of, as proud as he had been before about being able to steal and get away with it. It was still a type of behavior that he could keep up only if he received special praise for it, and this he was always generously given.

As Harry's asocial desires became less pressing, they were easier to control. Because he lived at the School, his outer world became more orderly, and then, as a result, his inner world, also. With this achievement, external controls were less necessary. Even praise, which, in the last analysis, is only external control, or external support of inner controls, was not as vital to his growing mastery over himself. On the other hand, the greater order in his previously chaotic inner world influenced and helped change the nature of Harry's experiences with the outer world. Since he no longer was driven into serious conflict with society, society no longer retaliated. Consequently he was freed of his fear of such reprisal. With this, his whole picture of the world and of life became more benign. "You know," he said, "there aren't so many cops around now, because there aren't so many crooks left." To the "bad" boy, the world was full of "cops" and crooks, both equally dangerous to him. In a world crowded with "bad" people, Harry had felt threatened all the time: if the "cops" did not get him, the crooks would do him in. But once he had changed for the better, the whole world followed suit.

In addition, since the world had become a safe place, Harry no longer needed to be a big, "tough guy" in order to protect himself. He could be glad he was still young, with plenty of time to grow and change still more. His strutting, "big shot" behavior was replaced by genuinely childlike attitudes. For example, a stranger, as so frequently happened, made some "cute" remarks to him, including, "I suppose you're about through with school now." Harry replied with disgust, "Don't be silly!" A statement that would once have pleased him and fitted in well with his behavior, now struck him as disgusting. Another example of his newly-acquired childhood and his desire to enjoy it was his request to be transferred back from the group of older boys, with whom he was then living, to the group of his own age in which he had lived initially; and this change was effected with great success.

When Harry first came to us, at seven years of age, his academic achievement had been on the preschool level, although he claimed to be able to do fourth or fifth grade work. He also bragged that he could read everything, knew everything, and therefore had no need to do silly, stupid school work. Actually, since he was always "on the go" during his first year at School, he was never in class and had no time to learn. During the second half-year he slowly became acclimated to the classroom, by being permitted to play, run around, hide in the fireplace, and so on, as he liked. For the entire first year, no academic learning to speak of took place. Only after Harry had learned to "stay put" and the world had begun to seem orderly and comprehensible to him, could he make first efforts at comprehending it through learning. After that, he became one of the best and most effective workers in his class. From a beginning in which he learned almost nothing during his first year at School, Harry succeeded during the next eight months in mastering nearly two years of academic achievement. This was accomplished partly because, during this time, his overstrict conscience was forcing him to work unusually hard.

The change in Harry's behavior and personality became visible also in his appearance. The tight, harried expression disappeared from his face and the artificial grimacing was replaced for a time by an overserious, worried mien, and then finally by a childish grin. The boy who had always seemed too tense and distraught, as if he would at any moment fall to pieces, began to look well put together. Physical development and integration accompanied his emotional and intellectual growth. During the first ten months at the School he grew two inches and gained ten pounds. Then came the period discussed below, when overcontrol caused a storage of tension within him, when guilt imposed a rigid restraint upon his inner energy, which resulted in body rigidity. During these nine months Harry did not grow in height, and lost weight (altogether eight pounds). Then the storing of tension in his body was replaced by a definite somatic symptom, and with this concentration of tension in one symptom it seemed that his body could loosen up again. Harry again started to grow, and gained ten pounds in four months. After this symptom slowly disintegrated, which occurred simultaneously with the dissolution of his neurotically strict conscience, Harry grew three and a half inches in eleven months and gained weight accordingly.

SOMATIC SYMPTOMS: THE LAST TURMOIL

Long before Harry unconsciously began to use a physical symptom to deal with a seemingly unsolvable conflict, he had used a real or pretended bodily injury to justify his acceptance and enjoyment of infantile satisfactions. Eventually, like many other delinquent children, Harry developed one relatively long-lasting physical symptom. This arose during that period in his rehabilitation when his chief deterrent to asocial behavior was slowly changing from fear that his relation to one particular person would be damaged if he acted out, to an internal feeling of guilt. It was the period during which temporary restraint of misbehavior, achieved only because a loved person was present, was being replaced by permanent restraint, achieved through inner control.[27]

For a considerable time, Harry tried to live and act on a compromise basis. He controlled himself in the presence of persons who were important to him, in order to retain their affection and the tangible advantages offered by life at the School. This was best illustrated by the incident in which he dropped the rock he was

---

27. This raises the question of why the normal child succeeds in renouncing immediate discharge of tension during the process of superego formation without having to resort to physical illness or somatic symptoms of a definite nature, although he, too, may complain of "hurts" or be frequently tired and listless. The explanation for the relative absence of definite and observable somatic concomitants of superego formation in the normal infant and their frequent appearance in the rehabilitation of a delinquent child during the latency period, may be found in the difference in degree of maturity. The infant relies entirely on the parents for all the necessities of life; therefore, the affection of the parents is absolutely necessary for him to feel adequately protected. At the same time, any threatened withdrawal of the parent's love is an overpowering experience, which the child must avoid at all costs; thus he is forced to incorporate parental requirements within himself without delay.

By comparison, the delinquent youngster is quite independent, both because of his greater maturity and because of his delinquency. Harry, for example, had by the age of five or six acquired an amazing degree of self-sufficiency. At the expense of punishment, or the fear of it, he had learned to satisfy his most critical needs, and when necessary, to relinquish certain desires, such as for regular meals or a comfortable bed. He could satisfy his hunger independently of his parents, by stealing food or by begging; a basement or an empty garage provided sufficient shelter. When compared with the dependency of the infant, he was under no equivalent pressure to conform to adult requirements at all costs.

Thus to children like Harry for a long period the expenditure of psychic energy involved in developing inner controls and forming a superego seems unacceptable and unnecessary.

about to throw because he saw his favorite counselor coming toward him. But when out of range of the few persons he liked and respected, he returned to his acting-out behavior, or was at least very much tempted to do so. An impasse was reached when the number and importance of those with whom Harry had formed positive relations increased until he was always surrounded by meaningful persons—or at least their mental image. With this, our approval and criticism became even more important to him and he more often wished to control the strong temptation he still felt to act out.

One way out of this impasse was to somatize it, to become ill. If one is ill, one cannot run away or behave aggressively. It becomes much easier to conform to adults' requirements. Outside stimulations are restricted, and thus temptations to asocial conduct are reduced. Also, if one is sick one may temporarily become utterly dependent without losing the self-respect derived from being self-sufficient. In this way the pretense of independence can be preserved while one is actually enjoying complete dependence.

But since aggressive self-sufficiency had been Harry's main defense against his great need and wish for dependent gratification, giving it up left him vulnerable. Therefore, he took refuge in physical sickness. While being sick creates vulnerability, if one is sure to receive good care, such vulnerability is not very dangerous. Physical illness also permitted Harry to make great demands on us, demands that he had once been able to make readily enough, but could not now, while plagued with guilt. Making exaggerated claims upon us also offered an outlet for his hostility. Thus, by being ill, Harry could combine aggressiveness with a demand for dependency without losing status or creating guilt.

How he used physical illness to prevent himself from acting out may be illustrated by his behavior one day when he smuggled some paring knives from the kitchen into his bed in the dormitory. Immediately after doing so, he complained of a stomach ache, insisted that he had a temperature, and wanted to be taken out of the dormitory into the sick room. In this way he tried to prevent himself from having a chance to use the knives against anyone. After he had received a great deal of attention and care, he admitted that he had stolen the knives, brought them out of their hiding place, and handed them over to his counselor. Once the knives were removed, he no longer felt sick.

What kind of sickness a child succumbs to under such circumstances depends on physiological factors as well as on his life history. We have seen quite a few delinquents who developed colds or bronchial asthma to force themselves to stay put while at the same time making sure that they will receive tender care. Others go so far as to break a toe, or even an arm. Harry, too, at first experimented for some time with stomach aches and colds. Among the reasons he gave them up was that, for a stomach ache, a diet was required, and for a cold, staying in bed. Having to diet would have meant depriving himself of the pleasure of eating, which he could or would not forego; staying in bed would have deprived him of the chance to discharge tension through mobility, such as in sports; but he needed this discharge in order to control himself otherwise.

For these and many more complex reasons, during short periods Harry suffered from allergies, neuro-dermatitis, and athlete's foot. Finally he settled down to a very long siege of ringworm.[28] It seemed that the small child's repeated and insistent demand for careful treatment of real or imaginary bruises, and his happy wearing of band-aids, had been transposed into a more mature form of skin disease.[29]

At first Harry was violent in accusing us of causing his ringworm, of having "invented" it to deprive him, for example, of swimming in our pool. One may speculate on the degree to which this was due to insight: without our efforts to induce him to adopt inner controls, and without our offer to provide him with dependent gratification, this illness might have been unnecessary; certainly it would have remained unnoticed or at least untreated. He often accused us of not caring for him adequately, or not wanting him to get well. At the same time he hung on to his sickness for dear life.

After he had made much of this disability for many months, Harry finally decided how he had acquired the ringworm. It had been at the movies, while watching a picture about Robin Hood. (There was no basis for this statement in reality, nor had anybody intimated that this incident might have been the source of his infection.) As Harry told the story, Robin Hood had no parents, only friends, who helped him fight everybody, as Harry had fought everybody while roaming the streets. The morning after he saw the movie,

28. His ringworm persisted for almost two years. It nearly disappeared in emotionally quiet times, but flared up when the tension rose because of parental interference. During this period, it did not respond to treatment, despite twice-repeated, successful x-ray epilations and most careful medical care. (It is most unusual for ringworm to persist under such treatment, when regularly checked by a dermatologist, with the supplementary daily treatment administered by an R.N., and when the possibility of reinfection is excluded.)

29. Following an observation by Fenichel (O. Fenichel, *The Psychoanalytic Theory of Neurosis*, Norton, New York, 1945, p. 256), it may be said that dermatoses are particularly suitable symptoms because they can become sites for both the discharge and the damming up of tension.

he said, his head itched for the first time. He added, "Everybody would be much happier if there would not be any movie houses and people did not have to go to shows." Since he had seen Robin Hood, "I have to have my head bathed and salved twice a day," he said, "and that's very nice." (Actually as part of his treatment his head was bathed only once a day but was salved twice.) He added that he did not care whether he ever got rid of the disease. Thus the sickness was a warning that going to the movies, running away and stealing, which he connected with Robin Hood, were dangerous ventures.

So much for some of the psychological factors that made Harry want to be sick, and which aggravated and made him hang on to his sickness. During this period in his rehabilitation, as mentioned above, his bodily tonus changed in a way suggesting that a process of tension-storing was at work. Harry who previously had been wonderfully well coordinated, probably as a result of continuous exercise during his runaway life, became clumsy and even slow in movement. He felt this himself, since, as mentioned before, he called one of the animals with which he identified, "clumsy," and the other "lazy." His gait, which had been smooth and rapid, became leaden and slouching, as if his limbs were too heavy for him to carry. Although the whole body was involved, the parts of the body most affected were his legs; he complained of feeling tired all the time.

Harry's sickness, without being at all painful, entitled him to receive additional tender care, which he now permitted himself to enjoy without further justification. This he openly stated. While his ringworm infection persisted, he regressed to nightly enuresis. Therefore, the customary evening bath was replaced by what he considered "something special," a bath in the morning. This bath and the ringworm treatment took considerable time, during which our nurse devoted herself entirely to his care. He enjoyed this very much. In the tub he behaved like a little child, trying to submerge himself entirely, playing for long periods with small toys, the washcloth, or the soap. Once he suddenly declared, "Last year I fell a lot and was always covered with scratches, and I had to run to you for band-aids, but this is much better."

But then, in the middle of Harry's second year at School, when he was not yet nine years old, an unfortunate series of traumatic events took place. His parents' divorce became final. The proceedings had been prolonged while the parents fought for the custody of the children. Harry was informed of his parents' divorce just at a time when his overstrong conscience was making him feel

guilty about anything that went wrong. He felt that their separation
and contentiousness in court were his fault. He was convinced that
he had not only caused the parents' divorce, but had also succeeded in doing away with them, for which he deserved to be
destroyed. On receiving the news that his parents were divorced, he
said, "I don't have parents any more."

Shortly afterward he made several self-destructive efforts. He
tried to put his hand into an electric fan. He went to the kitchen
stove, blew out the pilot light, and then turned on all the gas outlets; his open explanation was that he wanted to kill himself. Later
he took an inner tube and rolled it down an incline; then, rushing
ahead of it, lay down so that it would roll over him: "This is a
car, running over me."

When he was not angry at himself for the divorce, he was
angry at his mother. For weeks afterward, whenever he saw a woman
walking down the street who was of his mother's build he would
throw snowballs at her because, as he said, he hated all women.

Eventually his counselor persuaded him to throw the snowballs
at posters showing women rather than at real persons. Then Harry
gave as the reason for his actions, "They don't like me." When it
was pointed out to him that he was throwing snowballs either at
strangers, who did not know him, or at mere images on posters,
which had no feelings, he explained, "But I don't mean them, I
mean my folks. They are mad at me."

For a long time he refused to accept the term "divorced," and
insisted that his parents had been "reversed." He had always felt
that his mother was the stronger one, despite the father's violence
toward her. The divorce seemed to have definitely "reversed" the
roles, perhaps because the mother had been put in charge of his
sisters, while the court had put him under his father's jurisdiction.
But this legal arrangement, while very much overstressed to him
by the mother, did little more than fortify his old distorted view of
his parents' roles, based on much earlier experiences. It added to
his confusion about sex and strengthened his conviction that his
mother had never been a mother, at least to him.

Matters were made worse because his mother, of whom he was
so afraid, managed to meet him secretly. She usually waited in a
parked car near the School. On spying Harry, she would jump out,
press some money in his hand (to have money was always a temptation for Harry to run away), and tell him that she would never
accept the court settlement, but would fight to get him back. Her
plan would succeed, she told him, because she was going to marry
a policeman, who would then arrange in court for Harry to be

returned to her.[30] This totally shattered Harry. A policeman was a most threatening figure to him—his own adversary in truancy, and the personification of his father's worst enemy. Once, the mother had had the father arrested when he was demolishing the apartment. In Harry's presence, the father attacked the policemen and was severely beaten by them. Now his mother was planning to marry a man who represented his and his father's common enemy.

On the next day after hearing of this, a severe case of *verruca plana juvenilis* was added to Harry's ringworm. We became even more accepting of his difficulties, and tried everything possible to reassure him and make him comfortable, both because of his upsetting experience with his mother and because of the unpleasantness of the cure for warts. Characteristically, these appeared on his foot (a further prevention against running away, which had become more threatening since a policeman-husband supposedly would be put in charge of him as a father) and on his hand, into which his mother had pressed the forbidden money (Harry knew that we do not approve of such money gifts). Under treatment, with which were combined our efforts to reassure him, the warts disappeared within two weeks. Then, as if this were not bad enough, Harry had a visit with his father shortly after the warts cleared up. His father informed him that he had wrecked his boss's car while intoxicated and had consequently lost his job. Bandages visibly indicated the seriousness of the accident. And all this at the time Harry was trying to master the ambivalence underlying his positive relation to his father. For example, Harry had spoken about his hope that his father might build up the business in which he was employed, but also had said that he, Harry, planned to take it away from him when he grew up. Now it seemed that the father had not only lost his "business" but had also been mutilated in line with what we might infer were Harry's more far-reaching, aggressive wishes.

Interestingly enough, he had reacted to the visit with the mother, in which she told him of her plans to remarry, with a symptom that was painful and incapacitating to him, as if she had revived her old punitive impact on him. The threat of the policeman-husband also may have influenced Harry to somatize his anger and fear. His reaction, however, to the impact of the father's visit and accident

---

30. As mentioned before, the mother later married a man who owned and ran a tavern. We never found out whether she really planned to marry a policeman, as she told Harry, or whether she just invented the story to impress Harry that the court order giving his father custody of him did not mean much. The latter turned out, in fact, to be true, because shortly after her remarriage the mother went to court with the request that she be given custody of Harry, and after some litigation, Harry's father, influenced by his second wife, agreed to this change.

was just the opposite: he again acted out. He ran away for two hours, during which time he attacked a little boy severely, both aggressively and sexually. His victim received several bad cuts, which required sutures. When Harry returned, he was subdued and anxious to please. He did not know why he had attacked the boy, except that he was so angry he could not do otherwise. Anxious and full of guilt, he retired even further from the world than his sickness made possible. Through a short siege of agoraphobia Harry tried to make sure that he would not meet his mother again by chance, or hurt others in anger.

A much more far-reaching consequence of the repeated, secret meetings with his mother was that the coordinated process of the disintegration of delinquent patterns and the development of an integrated personality was thrown out of gear.

The next two years of Harry's life were shadowed by the evil spectre of the parents' fight over him. Every clandestine meeting with the mother, every officially arranged visit with either parent, was a traumatic experience from which it took Harry weeks to recover. Much of our work had to be concentrated upon helping Harry pick up the pieces of his integration each time it was shattered by a visit with the mother. Fortunately, that he was always able to do this, in the long run became strengthening and reassuring to him.

There seems little point in recounting the repeated ups and downs caused by the way the parents kept tearing Harry apart; basically, this was nothing but the consequence of the same acting out that in Harry's earliest years had kept him from living a normal life. We were aware of the destructive influence of the parents' behavior, but there was little we could do except protect Harry from the consequences as well as we could. Before their divorce the agency had offered the parents a chance to have psychiatric treatment. The parents could not avail themselves of this opportunity. Even casework treatment was too threatening to them. The divorce and the resultant increase in acting out on Harry's part motivated the agency to renew its efforts to do something for the parents. All that could be achieved was having the mother see the agency's psychiatrist twice. But she reacted with violent hatred and could not be induced to return. The father did not even get that far. Either because acting out offered the parents too much gratification, or for other reasons, they were unable to do anything to straighten themselves out.

The parents continued casework relations, but irregularly, and mostly in order to involve the agency in their quarrel with each other. They just could not give up fighting over Harry. Their emotional ties to each other, though most ambivalent and predominantly negative, were by no means dissolved by the divorce, or even by their remarriages. The mother, after her second marriage, on the surface settled into the middle-class respectability she had always desired. But with this came even greater rigidity in her emotional life and she felt deprived of the excitement and color she had known as a child through her alcoholic father, and later through her alcoholic husband. Visits with her former husband or arguments about him were the excitement in her otherwise drab life after the divorce. Harry was the presumed reason for their continued contacts. And Harry knew this. He knew that as much as he had been the cause of the parents' divorce he now was the cause of their continuing relation.

Each parent on each visit told him in detail about their arguments and their efforts to make sure that Harry would live with one rather than the other parent. Thus every visit tore at Harry's tenuous security. True, he liked the father better, but he was afraid that with him he might fall back on acting out and running away. He did not like the mother, but she seemed to offer more protection against his delinquent tendencies, a control that he felt he needed even more than an accepting and possibly loving father. To complicate matters further, at the time, the economic condition of the mother was strained. Harry's father contributed toward his support. Small as the sum was, by comparison it seemed to offer to the mother a considerable additional income, so that for economic reasons, also, she wanted to have Harry live with her.

Harry was drawn into all these conflicts. After one visit he told us, "My mother told me when I saw her that she is going to try to get me out of here. She told me not to tell anybody. But I'm thinking about it and worrying about it all the time. I don't want to leave here, but I'm afraid she'll drag me out."

He wondered why his mother had received custody of both girls but not of him. He complained that each time he saw her "my mother asks about when I'm going to see my father, what he said, how he lives, what I'm going to do with him, and if I want to see him. I usually get out of it by saying I don't know." He felt very unhappy about this. "It doesn't seem right. My mother always tells me my father doesn't treat the girls and her right."

The mother informed him in detail of the father's duty to contribute to the girls' care and complained to him that the father was in arrears in paying for the upkeep of the children.

The mother's pressure upon him to take her side against the

father, her threats to take him out of the School—the only place in the world he had found security—and her criticism of all he did and liked, revived Harry's old anxieties. Particularly, his castration anxieties were intensified each time he was with his mother. So vivid was his conception of his mother's unconscious aggressiveness toward him that immediately after a Christmas visit with her of a few days' duration he seriously believed that his penis had been operated on, that part of it had been cut off. Assurance was no comfort. If it had not happened, he was convinced it would happen soon. "I'm afraid that someone will cut off my penis," he said. "I'm afraid someone will come with a hatchet, or something, and cut it off." He again had nightmares, of which he had been free for quite some time. And he again called them his "night visits with my parents." About one of these bad dreams, he told us, "I had a dream last night that I had an electric penis." In reply to our question about what he meant, he went on, "I had an electric penis. Someone came and cut off my penis. They put a bulb in the hole where the urine comes out and it lit up." Several times he acted out that he was cutting off his penis and putting it away in a drawer for safe-keeping. Only much later did we learn that he did this on the days his mother had told him she would be waiting around the School to meet him on the sly.

Thrown into deep anxiety by the mother's pressure on him, it was only to be expected that he would try to "forget it all" by the old device of seeking such great excitement through running away that he could not think of how precarious his life had again become. Still he manfully withstood the temptation and did not return to delinquent behavior. He recalled that once, when he had run away from home because he was scared of what his mother might do to him, he had been so furious that he had killed a big cat with a pop bottle, "a mother cat that was going to make babies. The babies were still inside of her."

Now he had to take recourse to scaring himself in dreams so that he would not run away during the waking hours. He dreamt that he was running away and was taken to a detention home. "It was very scary. I was sure glad when I woke up and found I was still here." And as before, he again tied up with another formerly delinquent boy, and invented games in which one of these two runaway boys served as the conscience for the other. In this way, in times of great stress each boy could safely embark on phantasies about running away, and even plan to do it, while at the same time each could be certain that the other boy, who played the role of the conscience, would prevent this.

Harry's deep wish for a quiet life of infantile gratifications, which was opposed by his equally great need to be tough in order to resist the parental pressure to which he was exposed and which tempted him to return to delinquency, may be illustrated by one example. Once, when life had been more peaceful for a period because he had seen neither parent for some time, he could afford to do some finger painting, which up to then he had never dared to try. Harry was in a very contented mood, and, looking around the room, his eyes rested on another child's finger painting. "I want the kind of paint you mess with your hands," he said. His counselor brought him jars of all different colors, but he picked out brown and immediately began messing with it with both hands. Then he mixed in a little green, saying, "Isn't this icky?" He poured the mixture on paper and smeared it all around, and then he started to make patterns with the paint. After a while he became interested in folding the paper. He folded it several times in different ways. Nothing seemed to satisfy him, until finally he folded it exactly like a used diaper. His counselor remarked on the resemblance. Harry did not answer, but unfolded the paper, only to fold it again in the same diaper fashion. Then he said, "This is the most beautiful design I've ever made. I want to keep this one."

For a few minutes he continued deeply immersed in this play, but then suddenly stopping it, he picked up a cup that was on the table and darted out of the door of the session room. "I'm going to get some whiskey." He came back with the cup filled with water. Swaggering around, he pretended to be drunk, and played the "tough." Going to the doll house, he threw the furniture around, and exclaimed, "I'm apt to kill somebody when I'm like this!" After he had gone on in this way for several minutes, the counselor asked, "How does a little boy feel about that, Harry?" At that he dropped the act completely, walked up to her and said, "No good, Gayle." With this he crawled on her lap and asked for assurance that he would remain at the School for a long time.

He always needed such reassurance to be able to give up the "tough guy" act and let himself enjoy infantile pleasures. From remarks he made afterward, in different contexts, it seemed that playing with the diaper he made and enjoying it had reminded him of the mother's compulsive demands for compliance with rigidly enforced standards of orderliness, against which he knew only one defense, that used by his father—delinquent acting out.

Against threats to his newly won integration, which originated both in the repeated experiences with his parents and the fear that

he might have to return to one of them, Harry defended himself
by strengthening his most recently acquired attribute, his superego.
He turned against himself all the frustration and hostility generated
by the traumatic meetings with his parents. Unable to integrate his
hostility and unable to discharge it (which his now overpowering
controls prohibited), he at first tried to store it even more in his
physical (psychosomatic) symptom, to which he clung the harder.
But this was no longer so easy. The more he suffered from ringworm, the more tender care he received; but the more he enjoyed
this, the greater his anxiety became at the possibility of losing it.
So he tried to be hard with himself, as his mother had always wanted
him to be. He felt guilty for every misdeed he heard about, feared
that every crime he read about was his doing, or that he somehow
was implicated in it. He castigated himself severely for the slightest
misbehavior, which might, in fact, have been entirely permissible at
the School but not at home with his mother, which was the life he
was trying to brace himself for.

At this time Harry clung even more desperately to his symptom,
and now connected it definitely with "being good" and "being bad."
One day, when he was being taken to the dermatologist, he made a
statement showing that he knew he was taking advantage of a
spurious ailment in order to support his wish to stay at the School
as an invalid and secure infantile care for himself. Turning with
real anxiety to the nurse who had devoted herself almost exclusively
to him during the past few months, he said, "The doctor is going
to say, 'It's all a fake and baloney; you're all right.' " At other times
he also recognized that he needed this symptom so long as he was
not really "good," and that once he was "good" it would disappear.
In anticipation of another visit to the clinic he remarked that he
expected the dermatologist to say, "You've been so good that it's
all gone."

As has been mentioned, the problem of identifying with his
father and with father figures was one of Harry's major psychological
preoccupations. The news of his father's accident, and his fear that
his father might possibly die, lent new significance to Harry's ringworm. His father was wont to wear a sailor cap, the only reminder
of his time in the Navy. At this period, under the influence of his
strenuous fight against his own delinquency, Harry's recollections
of his father were unfavorable, with the exception of the latter's supposed heroism while in the Navy (from which, as mentioned before,
the father had actually been dishonorably discharged). The father
used to tell Harry tall stories about his feats in the Navy, and at
such times, he seemed a hero to the boy. Because of his scalp treat-

ments Harry was never without a sailor cap on his head, so that identification with his father was indirectly facilitated by the symptom. But he also professed to fear that he might become bald because of the infection (the x-ray treatment actually had made him bald temporarily), as bald, in fact as I—who was for him, at the time, the embodiment of all superego demands.

That identification with a father figure still had both fearful and protective connotations, was suggested by a dream about which Harry told the nurse one morning as she bathed him and treated his scalp. He had dreamt that another boy (with whom he had played truant, and whose continued delinquency was a great threat to his own newly acquired control) had run away, and had induced all the other children and the staff members, including myself, to run away with him. Only Harry and the nurse who took care of him remained. As a reward, he received many presents. Then finally the nurse ran away also and he was all alone. Harry, too, was about to run away when a voice warned him that he would lose all his presents if he did. So he decided to stay. Just then I returned. But I had turned into a crook; I had murdered all the rest, "but the cop got him." Thus in his dream, as in his efforts toward superego formation, the two father figures—the protective, gratifying one and the delinquent one—were merged, and both were arrested by the "cop." (This dream occurred at the time he believed the mother's claim that she would marry a policeman.)

Because of the mother's constant interference with our work, Harry's integration developed much more slowly than it might have under more favorable circumstances. However, he did make progress, and with it, the psychological connotations of his physical symptom changed. He no longer needed it to insure receiving tender care. He felt confident that his needs would be met at the School. Thus the physical symptom and all it involved became a handicap in the more mature activities for which his superego and ego were beginning to press. Harry now wished the ringworm would disappear. To speed up the process, he set himself a particular goal in connection with the more mature sports activities he had often enjoyed with his favorite counselor. This goal was truly self-set—one that he felt certain he could achieve. He stipulated, for example, that when his ringworm disappeared, he should be taken to certain ball games, and that long bicycle rides should become a regular weekly event. He thus concentrated on activities in which his formerly unintegrated, runaway tendencies could be gratified in an integrated, socially acceptable form, and which also permitted socially acceptable satisfaction for his old desires to throw and hit. This plan was agreed upon, and the ringworm infection cleared up permanently.

Harry Leaves Us

BY HIS THIRD YEAR with us Harry had freed himself of his deep-seated character disturbance; he was no longer a delinquent. And with the disappearance of his physical symptom, too, all Harry now needed was a well-protected, quiet life, free of seriously traumatic events, in order to carry on, undisturbed, the process of finding himself and developing a mature personality. He was neurotic, but not seriously so. If, at this moment, he could have been provided with a good home, he could have left the School. Unfortunately such a home was not available to Harry, since neither parent would accept the idea of a foster home placement. So it seemed best that he should remain with us. Most of our work consisted in helping him cope with the difficulties created by the parents. From this point until he left the School, our main task was to prolong as much as possible the time he could spend under its protection.

During the next two years, which brought Harry to the age of nearly twelve, much of our time was devoted to helping him deal with problems that confront normal children of his age. He worked, for example, on accepting his masculinity and combating his fears about feminine tendencies. Another problem, which he had not fully solved and to the resolution of which he now set his mind, was his tendency to copy other peoples' behavior instead of developing an integrated personality of his own. Many of his thoughts were devoted to his future. "I think a lot about what is going to happen to me. Not worry about it, but I just think about it all the time. You know I really like to think about the future. I guess it's up to me if it's going to be a happy one. I sure hope it is." He was very serious about his school work and applied himself arduously to studying. He wanted to do well in high school so that he could become a pilot. Academic learning occupied most of his interest and energy; truly making up for lost time, he was up to grade level on leaving us.

He learned to be realistic about his parents' marital difficulties and to accept the fact that they were not his fault. He even became able to face up to the parents' divorce. "I used to think of my parents marrying again. For a long time I used to pretend that they weren't divorced and that they would be together again. But now I don't pretend it any more. But I wish all this hadn't happened." Recognizing that his parents had made a mess of their marriage, he wanted his to be different. "I want my life to be a happy one, for me and for my wife, too. I'm not going to drink. If I get mad I'll tell somebody. I won't just try to run away by drinking." He was convinced that that was what alcoholics did, run away by drinking. As a typical preadolescent, he became more and more interested in being with boys his age. Mostly it was a period of quiet and peaceful expansion, when not interrupted by the traumatic impact of the parents. Most of all, he did not "want to go out of here the way I came in. I walked like a drunkard when I came, but when I go out, I want to be a respectable person. When I get married I'll know that you don't live together by fighting all the time, and when I go to high school I'm going to tell the principal what I want to be, so he'll help me pick the right courses. Then when I am a pilot of course I won't drink at all, because if you ever drink on the job, you'll just lose it. Of course I might take a drink once in a great while, because that's what most people who ever drink do. But I never want to drink and get drunk. In fact, I don't think I'll drink at all."

Toward the end of his fifth year with us a new court fight threatened between the parents about whom he would live with on leaving us. Rather than have Harry appear in court, I put it up to him to tell us what his choice was. After much thought he decided to go to his mother; he seemed conscious mostly of the great promises she had made him and of the fact that his sisters lived with her, while there were no children in his father's house. Also, and this was true to fact, his stepfather showed much greater interest in him than did his stepmother. Unconsciously, it was his old fear that his father might return to drinking that motivated his decision.

After it was made, and he knew he would leave us soon to live with his mother, he repeatedly reminisced about his past. "I used to be bad; I ran away and stole lots of things. I used to go to lots of movies all the time. How come I can get along without them now? For a long time after I gave up running away here at the School I still thought of running away. But then later I felt different about it. I felt so funny that I just couldn't run away. I thought of my record and I would have to start it all over and I had a good record for so long. I just couldn't see breaking my record and ruining it. But sometimes I still would get so mad that I would want to run, but I just couldn't. I'd get so mad at Dr. B. I used to think, 'when I get big I'm going to sock you.' And then later I thought, how silly to get so mad at Dr. B. He never did anything but good to me. I had a hell of a lot of trouble; I know that now. Now I want to get through school and then I'm going to fly a plane someday." He also thought back on how he used to punish himself. "When

I did something bad I kept wishing I would get sick. 'Everybody else gets hurt, why don't I get hurt?' I asked myself. Then I used to hurt myself. I don't really hurt myself any more, but I still think about it a lot. I used to go and hurt myself any time anything happened. Lots of times I hurt myself. I would find a piece of glass and cut my finger with it. It isn't the same thing to think about something and do it. I wouldn't really do it any more. I used to think it would help and make everything all right if I just could hurt myself. Now I don't believe that helps any more."

Despite such serious thoughts, Harry was really bubbling over with vitality and good spirits. Never had he been so happy before, and he looked it. He really accepted the fact that many adults liked him; he went from one to the other very freely and was able to stay on good terms with them all—with both men and women and, most of all, with boys his age.

At his farewell party, Harry made a little speech to the assembled School. Although when he volunteered to speak I had asked him to tell us about himself and his experience with us, he chose rather to talk mostly about me. The most important statement he made was, "Dr. B. is a very cautious man. Because Dr. B. does not want anybody to get hurt, or hurt himself or hurt others." Perhaps he went a bit too far in identifying with me, but in a way it summed up what he had achieved. Harry, who had been a violently acting-out delinquent, now wanted to have a safe and peaceful life. He wanted to protect himself well, and he did not want to get hurt, or to hurt others.

Out in Life

HARRY'S DECISION TO LIVE with his mother had not been an easy one. He had great anxiety about leaving the School and many misgivings about living with his mother. He did not feel quite sure that he had made the right decision. Still, once the move was made, he tried very hard to please her. He did not succeed. Despite our warnings, the mother, out of anxiety that Harry might grow up to be like his father, immediately began imposing much too rigid discipline on him. Moreover, she forced him into activities that were suitable for his little sisters but hateful to him.

Within a year after Harry went to live with his mother, a sudden change occurred in his father. He became ill with incapacitating allergies and asthma and had to give up his job. He was no longer able to contribute to Harry's upkeep. The mother, who had counted on the father's contribution, complained bitterly to Harry about this. It is hard to know to what degree she also lost interest in Harry and the link he represented to his father when the latter no longer provided excitement by changing from an acting-out, violent person into one who was drab and dependent. In any case, the difficulties between her and her son increased with the father's non-support and the resultant loss of income to her, and she lost interest in keeping Harry with her. She encouraged Harry to ask his father to take him in, and when the father accepted this, she readily agreed to the move. So after a year and a half of living with his mother, Harry moved in with his father, and on this writing has been living with him for over two years.

Harry's reason for leaving her was the mother's constant criticism of him, although he actually did very well in school and in YMCA activities. He said that he just could not stand the many arguments about his behavior and her continual complaints about his father. So Harry, who as an infant had run away and become a delinquent to get away from the arguments of his parents, ended up by being exposed again to nothing but arguments in his mother's home.

As long as Harry was with her, the mother lived in a poor, run-down neighborhood. But as soon as he left, she and her husband bought a new house in a nice, middle-class neighborhood and moved there. Harry resented bitterly the fact that when he was with her she lived in a delinquent neighborhood, the temptations of which he feared, only to move as soon as he left into pleasant, middle-class surroundings—thus providing that nice home he had longed for, and which she had promised him, not for him but for his sisters. Harry was also deeply hurt because the mother, who had made such tremendous efforts to convince him that he should live with her, was no longer interested in keeping him once the father stopped his support.

He was still very bitter while talking about it some two years later, on one of his rather frequent visits to the School. He repeated how his decision to live with his mother was due to her glowing description of the wonderful life she would make for him. He was still angry at her for marring his last years at the School by prodding him not to listen to anything we said, and for trying to convince him that all the School wanted to do was keep him from her. It was painful for him to realize that, after all she had said about the miserable life his father was living, she was willing to send him to such a life.

Looking back from a vantage point two years distant from his experience with his mother, Harry said, "As soon as I came to live with her, I couldn't do nothing. All of a sudden all playing stopped for me. The only thing she let me do was to go to the "Y," but all of a sudden everything else was stopped. I was always cooped up in the house all the time. And always there were arguments. I got along with my sisters and my stepfather all right—pretty well anyway—but my mother, she always started arguments. I was always doing something wrong." Then he reminisced about leaving her. "I often wondered why she let me go so easily. I thought, well, now we'll really see whether she wants me or the money. I guess it sure looked like she wanted the money because a good mother wouldn't just let her child walk out like that without anything to say. It was mighty fast, and at the time she'd been looking for a house. A two-bedroom house would be much cheaper than a three-bedroom—a couple of thousand dollars cheaper." Fortunately, despite the father's illness, he could say, "Ever since I've been with my father things have been better. He set a time to come in, but I can go out and play, and he let me meet the fellows and I could do stuff like that."

When Harry told us all this, four years had passed since he left the School—four years full of difficulties for him. But he had managed them well. He had just finished his freshman year in high school with good grades. He still planned to become a pilot and worked hard to achieve this. He knew he would need good marks in such subjects as algebra and in these he received the highest possible grade. In addition, during the last two years he had worked two or three hours every day to help support himself.[31]

Harry resented the way his mother continued, on his occasional visits with her, to tear down his father. She would say that his sickness "serves him right. That's what he gets for drinking. He is a rotten father." Harry added, "Whenever I see her she brings up all the time the money my father owes her. Every time I see her she's griping about the money and I don't want to say anything to start no arguments."

But despite this difficult life, Harry kept on working for a better future for himself. "Well, up to now I guess I'm coming along all right. I don't get into trouble with anybody. I'm not running away or anything. But one thing I'll say is that when a couple is divorced it's not the couple that suffers, it's the children. I found that out already. Even my sisters suffer, the way they are moved around from school to school. If I ever have kids that won't happen to them." Harry's life after leaving us had been most difficult. But

---

31. Since the father, as mentioned before, could work only irregular hours, he tried to make a living driving a cab.

since he now knew that there were people who cared very much for him, despite all hardships, he was able to turn his life toward success.

Epilogue

THIS REPORT would not be complete without mentioning more specifically those who helped Harry at the School—the staff, and the children. The School's work is built on personal relations which, by definition, are reciprocal. Harry's progress was so steady and so rapid despite all difficulties only because the intense efforts of various staff members were kindled by the keen satisfaction they felt at each step Harry took toward socialization. This is so necessary for success in our difficult work that we can keep a child only if at least two, and preferably more, members of our staff feel capable not only of taking care of him but of forming a truly positive relation to him.

In Harry's case, deep empathy and strong, positive rapport were re-enforced by the fact that several of us saw in his violent and actually threatening behavior a challenge to our therapeutic and educational philosophy. Here was a child who seemed obviously in need of physical restraint if the staff and other children were to be safeguarded. On the other hand, our philosophy was firmly opposed to all physical restraint. Yet we realized that to give Harry free rein meant running grave risks indeed. That our living together proceeded without untoward events, despite our own fears, and the warnings of others, was most gratifying to all who worked with him.

The children, too, after his first violent period was over, took great pride in Harry's progress and thus played an important supporting role. Their joy was unmistakable when Harry began to return very quickly after running away, and when he started to learn in class. They gained vicarious strength in mastering their own problems from watching and taking a hand in the improvement of such a seriously disturbed child. Compared with his difficulties their own often appeared minor.

Similarly, Harry's teacher and counselors were encouraged by the pleasure they derived from each advance in his rehabilitation. It gave them the strength to endure the next tribulation that Harry was so sure to present. Each step forward seemed another demonstration to all of us that our basic assumptions were sound, that we were indeed building a setting that was therapeutic through the totality of activities and personal relations taking place within it. In this sense, Harry lived out for us the validation of our theories, the proof that they could be applied in practice. With each success we gained further strength to go on and try harder and this strength was transmitted to Harry. All this was particularly important to us because it happened at a time when we were still building up the School according to as yet barely tested convictions.

While this was true for all staff members, individual workers maintained their strong, positive attachments to Harry, despite trials and tribulations, for personal reasons. Some seemed able to make up for their own unfortunate childhoods by providing a more fortunate one for a child who had once seemed incapable of happiness. Others were initially attracted to Harry because he dared to act out delinquent desires that they needed to suppress in themselves. But as the picture slowly unraveled, they learned at what price, in anxiety and unhappiness, such delinquent bravado is bought. It reassured them that they had given up nothing desirable by controlling their own delinquent desires. Thus the pressure on their egos was relieved, and this made it possible for them to bear up under the continuous strain of working with Harry, and even to enjoy it.

Why the author was able to maintain his positive attachment should be obvious by now: I wanted Harry to be able to live a relatively happy life because this meant for me, also, self-realization through my chosen work.

Appendix

On Writing Case Histories

SOME OF THE DIFFICULTIES confronting the writer of case histories were mentioned in the Introduction. But there are many more, which are peculiar to the compilation of clinical case material if and when the person writing the history is, or has been, deeply involved with the individual about whom he writes. The therapist's emotional involvement in the patient and his problems has received well deserved recognition as a central issue in treatment. It has been discussed from various angles and under different names—most frequently as counter-transference. If counter-transference is a serious problem in the well-controlled situation of the psychoanalytic treatment room, one can imagine how much more difficulty it creates when the therapist actually lives with the child.

Despite efforts to analyze and control counter-transference phenomena, it probably will never be possible to do away with them entirely; it is doubtful, in fact, whether this would be desirable. In order to succeed in the rehabilitation of, for example, severely disturbed children, the therapist must have a deep emotional investment in his work and in the child. But this tends to interfere with his ability to be an unbiased observer of specific events and over-all trends in the child's development. His objectivity suffers from his involvement when he reports on the child's relations with him, or with others, and when he selects and describes the experiences that were significant in promoting mental health. The best checks on this tendency to distort, which may be due not only to emotional involvement in the child but also to narcissistic pride in having been the person best able to help him, are: a clear recognition of the danger, a watchfulness based on this realization, and a desire for scientific honesty. I have tried to remain aware of the factors that interfere with objectivity, and to control as much as possible any misinterpretations that might enter the writing of these histories.

As head of the institution, naturally I have a deep interest in the children; but my emotional involvement with any particular child is less intense than that of the staff members who work most directly with him. My function as supervisor and arbitrator of the staff requires and implies greater objectivity; differences of opinion about any one child or any situation force me, in fact, to be less subjective than I might be otherwise. Most of all, even if I should be deeply and subjectively involved in a child—as I frequently am —this could not directly and uniformly influence the reports of other staff members about this child. While some of them might sometimes wish to reflect my particular emotional investment and hence slant some observations and reports, other staff members, or the same workers at different times, might resent my personal interest as alien to their relation with the child and thus remain uninfluenced by it.

For this and many other reasons, it seems to me that using the observations of others gives a somewhat better chance, if not to be ideally objective, at least to avoid gross distortions. Therefore, with one exception, in these case histories I have not described and evaluated my own contacts with the children unless they were observed and recorded by another staff member. This one exception is in the case of the follow-up interviews that took place more than three years after the children left us. By then most of the staff members who had been especially significant to each child were no longer with us—a good reason why I should be the one to talk to the children about how they had been getting along. It may also have seemed logical for them to tell me about matters relating to their experiences, in view of my special role in planning for the children's lives after they leave us. But these interviews, with the children's knowledge, were electrically transcribed, and the reports on them were based on these transcriptions.

As for these youngsters' lives with us, I feel that it has been possible to be relatively objective in rendering and analyzing the reports of other staff members about them. Anything that was mere hearsay, that is, events told to others or to me but not dictated and transcribed, has been excluded from the histories. Similarly, I have not used data that did not seem worth recording when they occurred but were only reported later, when subsequent events evoked their memory. It is too easy to have distorted recollections of what has happened when one knows its consequences, or wishes to find in a particular experience the cause for important events that followed. I cannot say with full confidence that such hindsight has never influenced our evaluations of a child's over-all development at the School or his particular interactions with a staff member. But to the best of our ability, the actual events mentioned in the case histories (though not always the discussion based on these incidents) are reported objectively, in the sense that the person recording the events was in no position to know what their future role might be in understanding the child's development. The raw material used consists solely of observations dictated by various staff members a few hours or (at the longest) days after the events took place— recordings that could have been influenced only by evaluations of the child's difficulties and developments that were made up to that time in various staff meetings and discussions.

Perhaps at this point I should describe briefly the materials on which these case histories are based. At least three staff members— a teacher and two regular counselors—report continually their observations of and experiences with each child. In many cases the child has individual play sessions several times a week with another, fourth staff member who, of course, reports regularly also. Each child is seen, on the average, once every other month by our consulting psychoanalyst, who reports his impressions. In addition to all of these, other staff members, such as the counselors of other children, substitute counselors, the nurse, etc., record their observations when a child becomes involved in some seemingly significant way with them or if they feel that by chance they have observed some important incident.

These reports are not a continuous narration, but rather a description (and sometimes also evaluation) of specific interactions, which, at the time they occur, seem typical of the child's emotional difficulties, or of his response to the world. They may for example, reveal new developments in him, which are significant for his relation to the adult, or meaningful in some other way—or simply baffling. Such events are dictated in some detail, as soon as possible after they happen.

Ideally, every worker should report on each day in which he has contact with a child. In practice, this ideal is not often fully achieved. What the children actually do and say, the very words and intonation they use, their facial and bodily expressions, are easily forgotten or distorted unless they are quickly written down.

Therefore, our best reports are derived from notes taken immediately following an interaction, after a play session, or when coming off duty after half a day spent teaching or with a dormitory group. These notes aid in recalling the events when the worker dictates, on the same or the following day, a more complete account of what has happened.

Dictation that is separated by a week or longer from the observations reported, tends to be stale and of much less value in helping us understand the child's and our own behavior. The reason for this is that the emotional climate, the mood, leading up to, accompanying, or following the episode, soon evaporates and is replaced by a somewhat sterile objectivity, which is devoid of the overtones that gave the events their full meaning. Instead of reflecting the impact of a symphony of feelings, interactions, and experiences, played, so to speak, by full orchestra, a stale report recalls to mind only selected motifs played by but a few instruments.

Given the variety of observers and observations, and the fact that the same occurrence or development is reported by different observers in different contexts, it is relatively easy to detect whether anyone, in his tale, is being carried away beyond the facts by his emotional involvement. Except for the time spent in play sessions and in the classroom, each child is observed most of the day by more than one staff member. All of these workers do not necessarily dictate their observations, but they read the reports of those who are most concerned with a particular child. Staff meeting discussions based on these reports, supervisory conferences, as well as more casual conversations, help workers to differentiate between what has actually happened and what they may have wished to see take place. Over the years, we have found that such discussions exercise a corrective influence and are an added motivation to be as honest as possible in reporting. Even if a staff member, despite his and our best efforts, should view events in a biased way—either because of a special, personal difficulty or because of his emotional involvement with the child—such distortion tends to be rectified since two or more other observers will simultaneously report their experiences with the same child. Such multiple accounts create an impression of the child and his relations to others that is based on many more dimensions than would be possible if observations or memories of only one person had to be relied upon, particularly if this one person should happen to be, at the same time, therapist and evaluator of what goes on in therapy.

This may be further illustrated by the example of one of the children whose history is given in this volume. Recorded observations were made on this child by a total of twenty-one different staff members. Some of them reported only occasionally over a period of years; others reported rather fully over a shorter period of time. Four staff members recorded observations on this child continually throughout his whole stay with us, which extended over several years. This record easily contained several thousand pages, typed single-spaced. Even that could not cover all the child's experiences with us, but it offered ample material on which to draw when writing his history. In preparing it for publication, I relied to some degree on all reported observations, though mainly on those of the four staff members who worked most intensively with the child. Next in importance as source material were the comments of the consulting psychiatrists, various test findings, and the observations of others. Those whose reports were used to an appreciable extent are credited at the appropriate places in the text.

These participant-observers varied widely in age and training, life history, personality makeup, and in the individual tinge of their involvement with the child. As the writer of these histories, I am in turn different from those who recorded the material on which these studies are based. Thus while personal bias and involvement can never be totally avoided, it seems likely that any one personal entanglement was cancelled out by that of other participant-observers. My own wishes and prejudices could not exercise too much of a distorting influence, since I deliberately used none of my own observations but only those recorded by others.

The histories presented in this book were read by all staff members who in some major capacity worked with the child described. Their criticisms and suggestions were discussed and incorporated into the narrations. As here presented, the histories met with the full approval of those about whose work they tell. The children who are described gave me at one time or another permission to publish an account of their lives with us, but did so without having read them first, or having knowledge of the details presented.

Efforts, such as I have described, to control distortions are, of course, desirable in order to assure the greatest possible objectivity. But they also interfere with rendering a true picture of the emotional involvement of the staff, and therefore tend to reduce the liveliness of the accounts of the child's life with us. Impressions of personal feeling and tone would have been greater in these histories if fewer efforts had been made to control bias based on individual emotional involvement. If the reading of the four histories is therefore less attractive, I hope this will be considered a reasonable price to pay for greater objectivity. Sometimes the staff members and I were sorely tempted to include in a child's story vividly remembered events that had great emotional meaning for us and the child but which, unfortunately, for one reason or another, were not reported at the time they occurred. Perhaps they seemed unimportant to the participant-observer when they took place, and their far-reaching significance emerged only later. But we withstood the temptation to tell about these occurrences—though sometimes with much regret. I only hope that, despite such efforts to prevent our very personal involvement from influencing our objectivity, the deep dedication of staff members to each of the children described has not been obscured.

Only a work of art, and not a case report, could give full life to each human being whose history is presented here. Although some blurring of highly individual relations may have occurred in the process of weaving a composite picture, it is hoped that enough has been said about each child so that he comes to life—still without encumbering the stories with too much detail. Even such lengthy histories as form this book can give a relatively adequate picture of only a few of the more important events in each child's life; it has been necessary to concentrate mainly on what seemed the most significant developments. I hope, however, that by steering a middle course between too much and too little I have made it possible for the reader to experience each child as a person. Only thus may the reader fill out the many gaps that remain, fathom reactions and motives of the child and staff even when they are not explicitly stated, and apply his own critical judgment in evaluating the events described.

The Children's Families

WHAT BRINGS OUR CHILDREN to the School in the first place? Why do they fail in life so signally and at such an early age that outpatient treatment, such as child psychoanalysis, is insufficient and residential care becomes necessary? This question is even more difficult to answer than queries about the success of our treatment efforts. It is easy to blame the parents, or at least the parents' emotional disturbances, for the problems of their children. This is so suggestive a factor, particularly to persons, like ourselves, who are strongly identified with the children—either because of their work with them or because of the personal life experiences that led them to make the rehabilitation of disturbed children their vocation— that we, too, have sometimes been guilty of looking to parental difficulties for an easy explanation of a child's disturbance. But when we first meet the parents they have been living with their trying children for years. How can we be sure that apparent parental disregard for the emotional needs of a child was originally the cause of the child's disturbance? On the contrary, may it not in fact be a response to the terrible strain inherent in any close relation with a delinquent or schizophrenic child?

In the literature on severely disturbed children much attention has been given to the way parents, particularly mothers, cause or aggravate their children's emotional disturbances. There is no doubt that family disorganization, neurotic attitudes, and other personal problems of parents contribute heavily to the emotional troubles of their children. A number of our youngsters, for example, have had mothers who underwent psychotic episodes. In some cases, such as Mary's, it can be concluded beyond a reasonable doubt that the mother's psychosis, if it did not cause this child's disturbance, contributed largely to it. But we cannot generalize from these few cases and conclude that the parents' disturbances are therefore necessarily the only or main cause of the children's illnesses.

Very recently there has been occasional discussion of the great emotional problems that may be inherent in the child, and of the creation of emotional difficulties in the parents by the child. Attention has been paid to the pernicious effect of watching or participating in a young child's unintegrated behavior on a parent whose own integration is tenuous to begin with. Nevertheless, comparatively little is known about the parents of schizophrenic or autistic children. The reports published on them[1] are often based on recollections of adult schizophrenics about their childhood or parents. Or they are derived from the psychiatrists' evaluations of parents after the latter have lived with their autistic children for several years, by which time it is difficult to determine how many of the self-accusing remarks or statements totally devoid of feeling made by the parents are prompted by their guilt at having failed. We have often observed the same guilt in anxious parents of brain-injured children, although it is obvious that the parents have not contributed to the problem.[2]

Our own emotional experience with severely disturbed children has also taught us not to make oversimple evaluations about parent-

---

1. For example, S. Reichard and C. Tillman, "Patterns of Parent-Child Relationship in Schizophrenia," *Psychiatry*, XIII (1950), 247-257; and the literature quoted by them.

2. We do not accept such children for enrollment, but since many of them are brought to the School we have ample opportunity to observe the attitudes of their parents.

child interactions. The children often manage, particularly during their first year at the School, to keep us at a distance despite our deep wish and best efforts to make contact with them, to reach them emotionally. They have an almost uncanny ability to frustrate even our best-intentioned, most genuine attempts to establish rapport. To what degree does the tendency of parents, for example, to bring up their children according to deadly routine stem from the child's own lack of spontaneous response? Failure to experience such response during the first months of the infant's life may cause a mother to despair of her ability to act correctly toward her child. Because of her insecurity, or in an effort to protect herself against frustration and guilt, she may turn to mere routine or may follow exactly the advice of so-called experts.

Certainly our data, conclusive as they are regarding the detrimental influence of some of our mothers on their infants, do not permit us to rule out the possibility that the absence of positive or appropriate responses on the part of the autistic child is the crucial factor toward changing a merely anxious or insecure parent into an indifferent, sometimes a rejecting one. The mother may well evolve these reactions in defense against the unbearable pain and anxiety inflicted by the indifference or strange responses of the infant. In many cases we have arrived at conclusions similar to those reported by Escalona. Hers is a concise and exact statement of the case:

". . . Wherever the life histories of severely disorganized children were given adequate scrutiny, it was noted that disturbances in the earliest and most basic interpersonal relationships were present. Early feeding difficulties, resistance to weaning, traumatic toilet training, difficulties over physical restraint, sleeping disturbances— all the familiar landmarks of infantile maladjustment—cropped up with monotonous regularity. Furthermore, most of the mothers or other persons in close contact with these children, spontaneously commented that there was something puzzling and different about these children from a very early age on. Mothers felt that they never knew what to expect, that they lacked a sense of intimacy and close rapport which they had known with their other children. One gains the impression that either remoteness or an exceptionally high degree of irritability (or both) in the child prevented a close interdependent relationship between mother and child in many of these instances.

"This is one of the points at which we wish to call attention to a possible source of error in our thinking about the nature of this illness and hence about the appropriate therapeutic approach. From experience with nonpsychotic children it is well known that behavior deviations of the kind just enumerated are often produced by parental attitudes. Hence, it is easy to assume that in these severely disturbed children, maternal rejection is at the root of the trouble. Yet, the more one studies the early life history of psychotic children, the more one is impressed with the atypical and pathological reaction of the children to perfectly ordinary maternal attitudes and to the inevitable daily routines. A baby who will not eat when food is offered, who cries when he is expected to sleep, who is incessantly active or pathologically lethargic, who reacts with panicky resistance to routine procedures such as bathing or being dressed, and who rarely provides for the mother the emotional gratification that comes from having the baby respond to her positively cannot help but be upsetting to even the most loving mother. Finding the usual methods of baby care unsuccessful with their atypical children, these mothers will, of course, try everything and thus go to extremes in both strictness and indulgence. They will seek and receive contradictory advice and act upon much of it, and when we come along to take a developmental history it is found that the child has been managed inconsistently. After years of more or less unsuccessful attempts to manage the child effectively, feelings of ambivalence and guilt must of necessity develop in mothers of such children, and the presence of such maternal attitudes is apt to lead the therapist to think of the disturbed mother-child relationship as the cause of the child's illness. It seems possible to the writer that we may sometimes be confusing end-results with causes."[3]

In view of these considerations, even "objective" data—for example, on family disorganization, which Table III shows is common in the homes of our children—should be interpreted with great caution. Family dissension might be not the cause but the consequence of the child's disturbance. The breakup might not have occurred if the parents had not suffered because of the child or blamed each other for his unhappiness. That this is a real possibility is suggested by the fact that a few marriages, which were at the breaking point, improved considerably after the child had been at the School for some time. This improvement relieved the guilt and anxiety of the parents, and thus permitted them to get along better with each other.

But it would be hazardous to base conclusions on so few cases. Indeed, we can match cases in which removal of the child from the home led to better integration of one or both parents, or to improvement in their relations, with other instances in which a child's coming to the School had the opposite effect. More than once a mother

3. S. Escalona, "Some Considerations Regarding Psychotherapy with Psychotic Children," *Bulletin of the Menninger Clinic*, XII (1948), 127-128.

has had a schizophrenic break after realizing that her hold on her child was lost, or after the former symbiotic relation, or *folie à deux,* became impossible as the child improved and grew independent of the mother. In these situations it seemed that the mother could maintain her tenuous integration only so long as she could discharge, act out, or otherwise satisfy some of her pathological needs through her child. When these satisfactions were blocked by the removal and subsequent improvement of the child, the mother lost her weak hold on reality and had to be hospitalized. At present there are two children in the School whose mothers have reacted in exactly this way, and it has also happened a few times in the past.

Our experience with fathers has not been quite the same. Nevertheless, the father of one child presently enrolled in the School reacted to being separated from him by resorting so heavily to alcohol that he had to be hospitalized. Similarly, the fathers of two other children who are no longer with us turned to drinking when deprived of the children who had been the objects of their acting out.

The parents of many of our children received psychotherapy before their children were enrolled. (This is tabulated on pages 489-90.) Some of them placed their children with us only after they had come to realize in their own treatment how seriously disturbed the children were. Other parents sought psychotherapy after their children had been with us for several years. In a few instances I suggested to these parents at the time their children were admitted to the School that they, as well as their children, were in need of therapy. Some had one or two interviews with a psychoanalyst but went no further; this was so frequent a behavior pattern, in fact, that it appears to be useless to suggest therapy to parents when they enter their child in the School. Probably they feel that separating themselves from the child will also alleviate their own emotional difficulties, some of which they freely bring out in conversation. Eventually, however, they may learn that this has not solved their problems, and then it becomes possible for them to accept the idea that they, too, need treatment.

On the other hand, five of the fathers and four of the mothers of the forty children now enrolled began treatment several years after their children entered the School. For at least two of them, the reason was that the child's improvement gave the parent confidence that psychotherapeutic measures were beneficial and might improve his situation, a belief that previously had been absent. Similar factors may have been at work in other parents who sought treatment some time after they placed their children with us; but in the majority of these cases it seems that the removal of the child interfered

so much with the parent's ability to discharge or satisfy his emotions through the child that the parent found it necessary to do something about himself.

All this is suggestive; however, it ought to be taken with a grain
of salt. After all, we do not know that these mothers might not have
had schizophrenic episodes anyway. We do not know how many
other influential factors impinged on their lives after their children
left home. Neither do we know whether the fathers' alcoholism was
brought on by other factors than their children's removal. Perhaps
the parents who secured therapy for themselves would have done
so anyway. Although we cannot answer these questions, they warn
against jumping to conclusions when studying the tables on family
disintegration and the parents' apparent symptoms or disturbances.
Many of these symptoms may have developed as neurotic defenses
against the sharp narcissistic hurt caused by having a severely disturbed child; or the parents may have developed these defenses in
order to be able to suffer the child's extremely hostile behavior
without retaliation (many parents had been advised by experts to
adopt such "no reaction" attitudes).

We feel that only very careful investigation of the families of
these extremely disturbed children can lead to a correct evaluation
of the extent to which the pernicious interaction between each child
and his parents—which has been reported so frequently in the literature, and which we observe constantly in our children—was due
to the parents' neuroses or psychoses or to the emotional disturbance
of the infant or child.[4]

FAMILY STATUS

Statistical tables can hardly bring children or parents to life
in the mind of the reader. But we hope that the first book on the
School, together with the histories presented on the preceding pages,
have offered sufficiently vivid pictures of the children and their life
at the School, and that the following data may help by sketching at
least a few additional facts about them.

In the spring of 1954, forty children (our average enrollment)
were living at the School—twenty-seven boys and thirteen girls.
Obviously, their family constellations underwent changes both before
and after these children came to the School. Since the effect of these
changes was much more profound while the child was still living at

---

4. At present we are studying childhood schizophrenia with emphasis on our
own reaction to schizophrenic children. This study we hope will lead to better
understanding of the interaction between the schizophrenic child and his parents.

home, we based the following table on critical family events that occurred before the child came to us. A family was listed as broken even if a divorced parent (either mother or father) with whom the child lived happened to remarry, or if a stepfather, for example, adopted the child after marrying the child's mother. While this made for a legally intact family, the child during his formative years still suffered from the dissension within the family prior to the divorce and from the loss, for a time, of one parent.

TABLE III—*Family Status*

	Number	Per Cent
Family intact	26	65.0
Parents divorced; neither remarried	6	15.0
Mother dead, father remarried, child living with father and stepmother	1	2.5
Father dead, mother not remarried	1	2.5
Divorced father remarried, child living with father and stepmother	2	5.0
Divorced mother remarried, child living with mother and stepfather	1	2.5
Unmarried mother	1	2.5
Child abandoned immediately after birth; reared by social agency	2	5.0
TOTAL	40	100.0

Divorce and separation do not necessarily indicate the whole picture of family disintegration, since a divorced parent may continue to play a positive and meaningful role in the child's life. However, of the seven cases in which the fathers left the family, only one continued to take an active interest in his child. Two of the fathers were complete strangers to their children, since they left before or shortly after the children's births. Thus, on entering the School, nine of our forty children had experienced no relations with their fathers, as Table IV shows.

Seven of our children had no mothers to whom they could relate, as may be seen from Table V.

Thus sixteen of our children, or forty per cent, had only one functioning parent. And even this does not tell the whole story. Most of our children grew up during the war. Of those whose families were listed as intact, six were deprived of their fathers during their most important formative years, while some mothers lived under the added strain of following their husbands from camp to camp and knowing them exposed to the vagaries of war.

TABLE IV—*Fathers' Participation in Family Life*

	Number	Per Cent
Fathers participating	31	77.5
Fathers not participating		
Father dead	1	
Father unknown to child; child either given up at birth and never adopted or remained with mother	4	
Father divorced; took no known interest in child	4	
Total fathers not participating	9	22.5
TOTAL	40	100.0

TABLE V—*Mothers' Participation in Family Life*

	Number	Per Cent
Mothers not participating	33	82.5
Mothers not participating.		
Mother dead	1	
Mother gave child up at birth, or soon after. Child turned over to social agency but never adopted	3	
Mother left father and child, took no further interest in child	2	
Mother incurably sick and unable to care for child, who was from infancy in series of nurseries and foster homes	1	
Total mothers not participating	7	17.5
TOTAL	40	100.0

Listing a family as intact at the time the child came to the School tends to give an erroneous impression for other reasons also. The parents of one child had been once legally separated and once divorced before the child came to the School, but had been reunited both times; they were divorced a second time after the child came to live with us, but again they remarried. In line with legal facts, this family had to be listed as intact. The same was true for the family of the child whose mother was incurably sick. Although legally intact, this family provided no physical setting for the child's life and made no contribution to his emotional well-being. In another case, the father of one of our children had been away in the war; on his return he was slowly dying of an incurable disease. This situation was further aggravated by the fact that the mother was so severely handicapped that she was barely able to fulfill her functions as a mother. The father died shortly after the child entered the School. The parents of six other children whose families were listed as intact contemplated divorce many times. In two of these cases prolonged separations took place, with divorce in mind. But since the parents were living together when their children entered the School, these families, also, were listed as intact.

What may be screened by such a listing is illustrated by a last example. One of these children was born in Europe in a dugout; neither parents nor child could leave this during the latter's first years of life, for had they done so, and been discovered by the Germans, they would have been executed immediately. This child spent the next four years of his life partly with his parents and partly separated from them in various displaced persons camps. In this case, too, the parents remained legally married, and since the child was temporarily with them prior to entering the School, the family had to be listed as intact.

EMOTIONAL DISTURBANCE OF PARENTS

When discussing family disorganization we are on safe grounds, at least as far as the data are concerned, since we are dealing with facts. But evaluating the emotional disturbance of parents is quite a different matter. Classificatory terms such as "neurosis" or "schizophrenia" do not necessarily mean much for our purposes. Even the classification of a parent as "normal" has little meaning when we are interested mainly in his effect on a specific child. A relatively "normal" parent may from time to time, or for a short time under particular stress, act irrationally with one of his children—be excessively punitive or permissive or behave chaotically or unpredictably. Such temporary reactions may tell little about the parent's real personality. But if the brief impairment of the parent's personal integration or relation to the child occurs at a critical time in the life of the child, at a moment when he is emotionally most vulnerable, then deep and lasting damage may result. A temporary but serious lack of consistency in an average parent sometimes can be more damaging than, for example, compulsive enforcement of cleanliness within an otherwise good parent-child relation.

For these and many other reasons our evaluation of parents was based not on an estimate of their disturbances in the past, but on their personality structures as they seemed to us during the time we knew them. When a diagnosis on the basis of recent, independent examination was available, it was used; when no such diagnosis was known to us, the parent had to be classified on the basis of our impressions. Such an appraisal has its shortcomings. Though we may, over several years, have many contacts with the parent, we recognize that he labors under great emotional stress when meeting the staff members of a treatment institution to which he must entrust his child. Therefore, unless the diagnosis of severe neurosis was made by an outside psychiatrist, a parent was counted as "neurotic" only if there existed no doubt that he was severely neurotic not only in his relations to his child but also in most of his other relations and activities. On the other hand, parents who showed even rather strong neurotic tendencies in relation to the child were classified as "normal" as long as they functioned adequately in other aspects of their lives. Even if this was done mainly by means of neurotic defenses, these parents were tabulated as "normal" when the defenses were suitable to their way of life and had no seriously crippling consequences.

TABLE VI—*Diagnoses of Mothers*

	Number	Per Cent
Schizophrenic mothers		
Mother underwent shock treatment in mental hospital	3	
Mother untreatable, ambulatory schizophrenic, as diagnosed by psychiatrist	5	
Mother ambulatory schizophrenic, possibly treatable, as diagnosed by psychiatrist	5	
Total schizophrenic	13	32.5
Neurotic mothers		
Mother diagnosed neurotic or borderline schizophrenic by psychiatrist	2	
Mother diagnosed neurotic by psychiatrist	12	
Mother declared by law unfit to be a mother	1	
Mother sex delinquent	1	
Mother incurably sick, bedridden, with severe consequences for her psyche	1	
Total neurotic	17	42.5
Mother normal	6	15.0
Mother unknown to us	3	7.5
Mother dead	1	2.5
TOTAL	40	100.0

The fathers appeared to be, by and large, better integrated. Perhaps this was so because the children of very disturbed mothers are more likely to need the School than those of equally disturbed fathers. The more disturbed a mother is the more likely it is that she may contribute to an early and profound disturbance in the child. In general, the impact of an equally disturbed father might be apt to interfere with the child's normal development at a later stage or, if earlier, indirectly through his impact on the mother. Of course such an explanation of the differences in degree of disturbance between fathers and mothers, which may be seen from a comparison of Tables VI and VII, is only tentative. Many more extensive and careful studies are needed.

TABLE VII—*Diagnoses of Fathers*

	Number	Per Cent
Schizophrenic father	2	
Borderline schizophrenic	1	
Total schizophrenic	3	7.5
Neurotic fathers	12	
Alcoholics	3	
Total neurotic	15	37.5
Fathers normal	14	35.0
Fathers unknown to us	6	15.0
Fathers dead	2	5.0
TOTAL	40	100.0

A more reliable estimate of the parents' personality integration can be derived from the results of their experiences with psychotherapy. Tables VIII and IX reveal something of this.

In view of the previous statement that the fathers' personalities seemed better integrated than those of the mothers, it might be expected that they felt less need to seek psychiatric treatment before bringing their child to us. The following tables indicate that this was indeed the case.

These tables also shed light on another question often raised about the School's work. Many observers have maintained that psychotherapy of children without simultaneous treatment of the parents, or at least of the mother, serves little purpose, since neurotic parents will undo any benefits the child may derive from therapy. If the child continues to live with his parents, this is a valid argument. Even with children much less disturbed than ours, parental attitudes often

TABLE VIII—*Therapy of Mothers**

	Number	Per Cent
PSYCHOANALYSIS		
Began at least one year before child came to School and continued for some time after	7	
Began after child came to School and continued for a prolonged period of time	2	
Total psychoanalysis	9	22.5
PSYCHOTHERAPY		
Treatment in child guidance clinics at least one year before child came to School; continued while child was at School	5	
In psychotherapy with psychiatrists at least one year before child came to School; continued while child was at School	3	
Casework treatment by placing agencies before child came to School; continued while child was at School	2	
Total psychotherapy	10	25.0
TREATMENT ATTEMPTS THAT FAILED		
Attempts at psychotherapy with psychiatrist failed	2	
Two attempts at psychoanalysis failed (one before child came to School; a second afterward)	1	
Total failures	3	7.5
UNTREATABLE		
Mother declared untreatable after sustained psychotherapy or psychoanalysis		
Received shock treatment	3	
No further treatment attempts made	2	
Mother incurably sick, bedridden, with serious psychological consequences	1	
Total untreatable	6	15.0
Mother unknown to us; declared by law unfit to be a mother	1	2.5
Mother unknown to us; child reared by series of foster mothers	2	5.0
No treatment attempted; never examined by psychiatrist	9	22.5
TOTAL	40	100.0

* This table does not include two mothers who died, but gives information about stepmothers who had assumed their roles some time before the children came to us.

TABLE IX—*Therapy of Fathers*

	Number	Per Cent
PSYCHOANALYSIS		
Father began treatment some time after child came to the School; is still continuing	3	7.5
PSYCHOTHERAPY		
With psychiatrist in private practice before child came to School	3	
Begun in child guidance clinic before child came to School	2	
Total psychotherapy	5	12.5
UNTREATABLE		
Father had short schizophrenic break requiring institutionalization	2	5.0
Father dead (mother did not remarry)	2	5.0
Father unknown to us	5	12.5
No treatment attempted	23	57.5
TOTAL	40	100.0

make it necessary to remove the child from the home during the period of therapy, as was pointed out by Anna Freud.[5]

The question of therapy while the child lived at home was not pertinent to our children, because they could not be maintained in their homes or in foster homes. Many of them were exposed to therapy while living with their parents, and several to simultaneous treatment of mother and child. Nevertheless, the children failed to improve, and in many cases got worse. Still, it might be argued that once the child moved into the School, therapy of the parent might have proved successful. Theoretically this is true. But in practice many of the mothers were not able to accept therapy, while a few did not need it because they became "normal" after the child left home, particularly if the child improved significantly.

The problem of what should be done for very disturbed parents remains unsolved, at least at the present stage of our knowledge. It seems pointless for an institution such as ours to attempt therapy of fathers or mothers. Several of the parents of our children underwent extensive psychotherapy or psychoanalysis (often with outstanding therapists), which failed as far as having a salutary effect on the disturbed child was concerned. The cases of John and Harry

---

5. A. Freud, *The Psychoanalytic Treatment of Children* (London: Imago Publishing Co., 1946), p. 36.

are characteristic examples of our failure to persuade parents to accept therapy and of the psychoanalysts' inability to keep them in therapy once started. A majority of our mothers either sought treatment before their children came to live with us (often for reasons other than desperation over their failure as mothers) or were found to be inaccessible to therapy. Of course there were exceptions. We succeeded in inducing a few parents to seek help for themselves after their children were admitted to the School, and the treatment proved successful for both the parent and his relation to the disturbed child. But these cases formed a small minority.

On the other hand, I should like to comment again, more emphatically, on what the removal of a very disturbed child from the home can do for his parents' integration. Several parents who seemed very disturbed when they brought their children to us recuperated in a year or two and then appeared "normal." When we began our work we underestimated the severity of the children's influence on their parents. But we learned that often the parents' integrative powers, although inadequate to cope with their difficulties while the children lived at home, were sufficient to re-establish and maintain their integration once the children were removed. Later, these parents seemed to gain further strength from the children's improvement.

Despite the apparently severe disturbance of many of our parents at the time they brought their children to us, their cooperation with us after the children were at the School for a while was most gratifying. This seemed to be, at least in part, the result of our policy of coupling long-term treatment with rare home visits. The latter are strictly controlled by what seems best for the child and are rarely arranged more than a few weeks in advance. Uncertainty about when the child will be available prevents the parent from simply postponing gratification, through the child, of his neurotic needs until the time of the next visit. The parents are not able to keep their neuroses in "deep-freeze" until their children come home. Restriction of visits, control over presents that are intended to bribe or induce feelings of guilt, a censorship that prohibits letters containing criticisms of the child or warnings and admonitions about what he ought and ought not to do, and absolute protection of the child against his parents' knowing how he misbehaves at School, all serve first to reduce, then to eliminate the child's and the parents' ability and need to act out against each other. Neurotic desires that can no longer be satisfied in this way are directed against other, less susceptible figures (the School's staff) and eventually can be mastered in constructive ways.

Similarly, our fears that the parents might undo the School's work after a child left us turned out to be grossly exaggerated. Most parents continued to cooperate with us to the fullest. After suffering so much from their children's behavior and their own guilt, most parents were more than willing to avoid anything that might again create an insufferable condition for themselves. Their self-interest combined with that of the child, and only rarely did they disregard our advice.

We also found that neurotic tendencies, which could no longer be discharged on the child placed with us, were only rarely transferred to another child in the family. Our experience was practically uniform in this respect. Indeed, there was every indication that the removal of the sickest member of the family benefited the other children, as well. While we have no reportable "objective" data on this, again and again we saw depressed or neurotic siblings blossom out within a year or two—sometimes within months—after the very disturbed child left home. Thus it seemed that parents could not or did not simply transfer neurotic attachments from one child to another of different age, who had a different life history and a different relation to his parents.

The only family situation where this did not seem generally to hold true was in two cases of twins. In both these situations, as the "bad," delinquent twin became rehabilitated during his stay at the School, the previously "good" sibling slowly turned into the "bad" one. In these cases, where both children probably had very similar life histories, neurotic attachments and needs were seemingly more readily transferred from one to the other. Even then, however, the neurosis or delinquency of the "good" twin who turned "bad," though of the same type, was relatively mild compared with that of the twin placed in the School. Apparently, the original "bad" twin shielded his twin sibling during their earlier years from the full impact of parental neurotic involvement. When, on removal of the "bad" twin, these neurotic feelings were directed against the one remaining at home, the latter met this crisis with a personality much better able to withstand it, because of his previous, more fortunate life experiences.

To sum up these observations: Contrary to our *a priori* expectation that the parents would be very difficult and would interfere with our work or undo it afterward, we found them amazingly cooperative, considering their own serious emotional difficulties.

Most of our children were always under the custody of their parents, a situation that was not changed by their placement in the School. If the parents were divorced, the mother was the guardian—

with one exception: in one case, she was declared unfit and the father was the child's guardian.

Three children were adopted by stepparents after their own parents' death or divorce. Four were adopted during earliest infancy, in two cases because the mothers were told that they could not bear children. Both these mothers became pregnant after the adoption, however, and thereafter tended to take greater emotional interest in their own children, or to defend themselves against this tendency by remaining "objective."

Eleven children were placed in the School by five different private social agencies, three of which were located in Illinois and two in other states. These agencies in most cases took major responsibility for the children before they were placed with us, but only five of the children were actually under agency guardianship. Of the children placed with us by agencies, two had no living parents; the mothers of three were divorced and were not remarried. Six children placed by agencies had legally intact families, and one was originally adopted by the parents from the agency.

We make special efforts to see that no religious, social, or status group of the general population is exclusively represented at the School. Our tuition is comparatively high (at present $4,500 yearly), which means that only upper- or upper-middle-class parents can afford to pay the fees. So that lower-than-middle-class children can also attend the School, we try to secure scholarships for children whose parents cannot meet the tuition.[6] On the day selected for reporting, sixteen of the children, including children placed by agencies, were receiving financial help. Nine were underwritten by agencies, while scholarships were granted directly to seven other children. For two children, the placing agencies paid full tuition.

The socio-economic status of the children's families may be further illustrated by the occupations of the fathers, which are summarized in Table X.

Although children from all states are accepted for enrollment, geographical proximity facilitates preliminary investigations, visits, etc. Therefore, the homes of a large percentage of the children were

---

6. Funds for scholarships have been provided in the past mainly by the Foundation for Emotionally Disturbed Children of Chicago, and more recently also by the Ray and Charles Newman Memorial Foundation of New York and a few private donors. Since these funds are limited, we offer only part-scholarships so as to increase the number of children from lower-income groups who can attend the School. In these cases the referring agencies provide part of the tuition and scholarships cover the rest. Middle-income-group parents pay as much as they can afford and scholarships cover the balance of the fees.

in the Middle West, particularly the Chicago area. Table XI shows the geographical distribution of the homes of the children at the time these data were collated.

TABLE X—*Fathers' Occupations*

	Number	Per Cent
Manufacturers, business executives, and owners of business enterprises	14	35.0
Physicians	4	10.0
Salesmen	4	10.0
Laborers	3	7.5
Fathers unknown	3	7.5
Stockbrokers	2	5.0
Lawyers	2	5.0
Artists	2	5.0
Civil employees	2	5.0
No occupation	2	5.0
Scientist	1	2.5
Farmer	1	2.5
TOTAL	40	100.0

TABLE XI—*Geographical Distribution*

	Number	Per Cent
ILLINOIS		
Chicago	11	
Illinois (outside Chicago)	5	
TOTAL	16	40.0
NEW YORK		
New York City	3	
New York State	2	
TOTAL	5	12.5
CALIFORNIA		4	10.0
WISCONSIN		3	7.5
KENTUCKY		2	5.0
OHIO		2	5.0
ARIZONA		1	2.5
INDIANA		1	2.5
MARYLAND		1	2.5
MICHIGAN		1	2.5
MINNESOTA		1	2.5
TENNESSEE		1	2.5
TEXAS		1	2.5
WASHINGTON		1	2.5
TOTAI		40	100.0

The Children

SOMATIC DISTURBANCES

WE ACCEPT ONLY THOSE CHILDREN who do not suffer from any organic disease, unless we are convinced that removal of the psychological factors aggravating the somatic disturbance would reduce it to a matter of small consequence. So far, we have found that most somatic disorders cleared up within one year or less, although they tended to reappear during or after home visits.[7] Symptoms such as stuttering, enuresis, and strabismus were the most persistent ones.

The following list (Table XII) includes only the more serious physical symptoms from which these forty children suffered when they came to us. For example, bronchial asthma as an occasional affliction or as a seasonal concomitant of hay fever occurred more frequently than the list indicates. Only chronic cases, which required repeated medical attention, prolonged bed rest, or hospitalization, are mentioned. Upper respiratory infections and allergies are not listed if they did not seriously and chronically interfere with the child's total life. Simple bed-wetting was so common among our children that where soiling or wetting is mentioned, it indicates absence of bladder or bowel control during both day and night. "Vomiting" means persistent emesis several times a day (usually at each meal) over a period of years. "Accident proneness" is included among the physical symptoms when it led to long periods of incapacitation, including hospitalization, and hence to psychological consequences similar to those of some of the chronic illnesses. Since several children suffered from more than one symptom, there are more symptoms than children. The number of children who were free of physical symptoms is also shown in Table XII.

INTELLIGENCE

We do not serve mentally defective or brain-damaged children. However, this needs to be qualified in the same way as the preceding remarks about children who suffer from organic physical disorders. We do accept children regardless of their ability to function mentally, including academically, if we expect that the intellectual blocking

---

7. For further discussion of the disappearance of physical symptoms in children living in a treatment institution, see B. Bettelheim and E. Sylvester, "Physical Symptoms in Emotionally Disturbed Children," *The Psychoanalytic Study of the Child*, III-IV (New York: International Universities Press, 1949) pp. 353-368.

TABLE XII—*Physical Symptoms*

	Number	Per Cent
ALLERGIES		
Hay fever (allergy to dust, pollen, etc.)	6	
Chronic eczemas and dermatitis	3	
Food allergies in addition to pollen allergies	2	
Total allergies	11	
DISTURBANCES OF ELIMINATION		
Soiling (day and night)	8	
Pyloric spasm	1	
Elongated colon	1	
Total disturbances of elimination	10	
EATING DISTURBANCES		
Obesity (30 lbs. or more overweight)	4	
Vomiting	2	
Anorexia	1	
Total disturbances of eating	7	
SPEECH DIFFICULTIES		
Aphasia	2	
No speech because of autism	2	
Infantile speech (incomprehensible)	2	
Severe stuttering	2	
Total speech difficulties	8	
RESPIRATORY AILMENTS		
Bronchial asthma	3	
Incapacitating colds	2	
Total respiratory ailments	5	
ACCIDENT PRONENESS (including repeated severe burns, frequent broken bones, etc.)	5	
STRABISMUS (inability to focus)*	3	
MIGRAINE	1	
Total number of children with physical symptoms	25	62.5
Children with no serious or prolonged physical symptoms	15	37.5
TOTAL	40	100.0

* Why physical symptoms do not improve while the child lives in the environment where he needs them as protective devices, but clear up at the School once the child feels secure in this new setting, may be illustrated by quoting a boy whose severe strabismus had not improved while he lived at home, despite an operation and psychoanalytic therapy. The boy was telling other children about his eye operation and how it had been a failure. Another boy, with the unconscious understanding of the first child's emotions and empathy for his need so often possessed by schizoid children, asked him why he was still crossing his eyes, particularly when he talked to others. To that the cross-eyed boy replied, "Yeah, I do it on purpose. I don't want people to know that I'm looking."

will eventually dissolve under treatment. This applies also to children who are at the time of entrance untestable because of their inability to cooperate, for example, autistic children, or who test very low because of their unwillingness to cooperate in the testing situation.

Test results on emotionally disturbed children, while they suggest the children's present functioning, do not do justice to their potential abilities. For example, one child tested in the low nineties but an evaluation of subscores indicated that his potential I.Q. was 130. Another child earned an I.Q. of 105, but only because he blocked on all tasks that created anxiety in him. His performance on items not creating anxiety suggested that his potential I.Q. was 149. Table XIII shows the intelligence level at which the children were functioning when these data were compiled. The children who could not be given objective tests, because of autistic withdrawal or extreme negativism, were grouped under the heading "I.Q. not yet established." Of the five children in this category, four were at the School less than a year—the fifth less than two years.

TABLE XIII—Intelligence

I.Q.'s of	Number	Per Cent
81-90	3	7.5
91-100	5	12.5
101-110	10	25.0
111-120	5	12.5
121-130	6	15.0
131-140	3	7.5
141-150	1	2.5
151-160	1	2.5
161-170	1	2.5
I.Q. not yet established	5	12.5
TOTAL	40	100.0

Median I.Q. *including* the children whose I.Q. could not be established   106
Median I.Q. *excluding* the children whose I.Q. could not be established   110

This table may be compared with intelligence evaluations made of the children before they came to us. Repeated testings had shown nine children as morons and six as feeble-minded. Of these fifteen children, eight now have normal I.Q.'s (90 or above), two still test between 80 and 90, and five are in the category of "I. Q. not yet established."

Closely related to the impairment of intelligence by emotional disturbance is the blocking that prevents learning. Most of our children had a history of more or less serious academic difficulty, though a sizable minority excelled in at least a few subjects. Including those who were classified as mentally deficient, twenty-seven of our children were declared more or less unable to learn and came to us seriously retarded (more than two academic years). Twelve of these had earned normal or superior I.Q.'s in intelligence tests before they came to us, but nevertheless had been academic failures before their rehabilitation began.

EMOTIONAL DISTURBANCES

We finally come to the question that is hardest to answer, namely, what were the emotional disturbances that led to the children's placement in the School? Diagnosis of a severely disturbed child is difficult, since the diagnostic categories are not well established. It often happens that a child who comes to us as a delinquent, on more careful examination turns out to be schizophrenic or psychotic. Moreover, it is often very difficult to determine whether a young child is autistic or feeble-minded. We cannot always rely on the diagnoses made by psychiatrists who have examined the children previously. John is typical of a large group of children who were

TABLE XIV—*Psychiatric Diagnoses**

	Number	Per Cent
Schizophrenic		
Psychotic	5	
Paranoiac	5	
Mixed forms	9	
Total schizophrenic	19	47.5
Severely neurotic with marked schizophrenic elements	11	27.5
Autistic (including diagnosis of childhood schizophrenia and infantile marasmus)†	10	25.0
TOTAL	40	100.0

* All children classified here as autistic and schizophrenic, and several of the severely neurotic children, came to us with such psychiatric evaluations as "hopeless," "outlook uncertain," or "prognosis very guarded." Ten of them at one time or another were declared to be untreatable.

† Among these ten children we considered one as possibly brain-injured. Five had been diagnosed at one time or another as brain-damaged and three as psychotic.

diagnosed as suffering from brain injury, cerebral agenesis, or cerebral palsy.

Despite the variety of presenting symptoms, each child on arrival seemed to show more markedly the characteristics of one diagnostic group rather than another. Table XIV is presented with the warning that the classifications should not be considered conclusive; the diagnoses are the ones that seemed most likely.

While here each child is subsumed under one category only, Table XV sets forth the most marked symptoms of disturbance shown by each child before enrollment. In most cases it was these symptoms, and not the psychiatric diagnoses, that forced parents or society to place the child with us. Among the symptoms precipitating enrollment were serious delinquency, homicidal attempts, incendiarism, etc. Since some of the children showed several symptoms, the total is greater than the number of children. Feeble-minded behavior was very marked in many cases, and it is here listed again.

TABLE XV—*Presenting Symptoms*

		Number
Delinquency		
Sex delinquency	4	
Stealing, robbing	4	
Homicidal attempts	3	
Incendiarism	2	
Mixed types of acting-out delinquencies	10	
Total delinquents		23
Inability to learn		27
Feeble-mindedness		15
Soiling		8
Severe compulsions (including claustrophobia, agoraphobia, anaclitic behavior, etc.)		7
Transvestism		3
Suicidal attempts		2

TREATMENT BEFORE ENROLLMENT

Considering the severity of the children's symptoms and the normal reluctance to entrust a child to institutional treatment, it is only natural that efforts were made to treat the majority of our children previous to their enrollment. In many cases it was the child's therapist who referred him to us and who convinced the parents or agency that he should be placed at the School, either because psychotherapy failed to yield the desired results or because the child was found to be inaccessible to therapy. In Table XVI only psychotherapy of a year's duration or longer before enrollment is mentioned. Brief psychotherapy or a series of diagnostic psychiatric interviews are not listed, since nearly all the children were exposed to them. Several underwent more than one type of psychotherapy, as, for example, psychoanalysis followed by residential treatment; therefore, in Table XVII, all children who came to us, with or without previous, sustained efforts at psychotherapy, are listed; and those for whom no treatment was attempted because they were declared untreatable are separated from those who were referred to us immediately without an intermediate treatment period.

TABLE XVI—*Psychotherapy Preceding Placement - I*

		Number
Psychoanalysis		11
Residential treatment, including psychotherapy in psychiatric hospitals		7
Psychotherapy		
In child guidance clinics	10	
With psychotherapists in private practice	6	
Casework treatment	3	
Total psychotherapy		19
TOTAL		37

TABLE XVII—*Psychotherapy Preceding Placement - II*

	Number	Per Cent
One or more sustained efforts at ambulatory psychoanalysis or psychotherapy	27	67.5
One prolonged placement in a residential treatment institution with therapy	4	10.0
One or more sustained efforts at psychoanalysis or psychotherapy, and in addition placement in a residential treatment institution with psychotherapy	3	7.5
No previous effort at psychotherapy because child was considered untreatable	3	7.5
No previous effort at psychotherapy because referring psychiatrist felt only residential treatment could succeed	3	7.5
TOTAL	40	100.0

SIBLINGS

It is often thought that the only child is more likely to suffer from emotional disturbance than the child with siblings, either because of his parents' concentrated attention upon him or because of his lack of play companions. This theory does not hold true for children who are so severely disturbed that they must be placed in the School. As can be seen from the following table, only four of the forty had no siblings (the two children given up at birth should not be considered only children, since they lived from infancy in foster homes along with other children).

TABLE XVIII—*Number of Children in Family*

	Number	Per Cent
Two children in family	21	52.5
Three children in family	11	27.5
Only children	4	10.0
Four or more children in family	2	5.0
Brought up in foster families with other children	2	5.0
TOTAL	40	100.0

Study of the sibling relationships among our children, as shown in Table XIX, reveals a preponderance of older children. Of thirty-four children who had siblings, twenty-one were the oldest in the family and only twelve were younger children. This suggests the possibility that the oldest child is more likely to suffer from the parents' inexperience or from their disturbances, which may be discharged so thoroughly on the first subject who offers himself that perhaps no similarly intensive pathological involvement in another child occurs. Another possibility is that the very insecure parent gains some strength from the fact that the oldest child survived despite the parent's insecurity, anxiety, and perhaps hostility, and this gives him a modicum of security in dealing with succeeding children.

TABLE XIX—*Position Among Siblings*

	Number	Per Cent
Oldest children	21	52.5
Youngest children	8	20.0
Middle children	4	10.0
One of twins	1	2.5
(Only children)	(4)	(10.0)
(Children brought up in foster homes)	(2)	(5.0)
TOTAL	40	100.0

Still, the brothers and sisters of extremely disturbed children are likely to suffer emotional disturbance to some degree, because of the same parental problems that affected the older child or because of the disturbance of the older child, or through a combination of both. That the older child's disturbance may contribute importantly to that of his younger brothers or sisters is suggested by the fact that none of the children at the School had older siblings who needed (or, to the best of our knowledge, underwent) psychotherapy; perhaps older children can protect themselves better against the pernicious effect of the seriously disturbed younger sibling's behavior. On the other hand, in five cases in which the oldest child was enrolled at the School, all the younger siblings needed and received psychotherapy. In one of these families, three younger children underwent treatment; in another family, two did so; and in the remaining three families, with only two children each (the older being at the School), the younger sibling received psychotherapy.

AGE AND LENGTH OF STAY

In general, the activities and scheme of life at the School are geared to the needs and desires of children of grade-school age. Much as we should like to be able to serve children younger than six—since the younger the child the better the chance for full recovery—we feel that we cannot administer nursery age and grade-school age programs within the same milieu. Similarly, we do not accept children older than eleven or twelve, since it is desirable that they stay with us for at least three years before they begin to outgrow our program (we can keep children with us up to about the age of sixteen, if they come to us before adolescence). We are prepared to teach subjects from preschool up to and including ninth-

TABLE XX—*Age Distribution*

Age on Enrollment	Number	Per Cent	Present Age	Number	Per Cent
6 years	2	5.0	8 years	2	5.0
7 years	8	20.0	9 years	0	0.0
8 years	7	17.5	10 years	6	15.0
9 years	7	17.5	11 years	9	22.5
10 years	7	17.5	12 years	6	15.0
11 years	5	12.5	13 years	8	20.0
12 years	3	7.5	14 years	6	15.0
13 years	1	2.5	15 years	3	7.5
TOTAL	40	100.0	TOTAL	40	100.0

Median age on enrollment: 9 years   Median age at present: 12 years and tenth-grade work. The preceding table on age distribution (Table XX) sets forth the children's ages on enrollment and at the time of writing; Table XXI shows their length of stay.

TABLE XXI—*Length of Stay*

Period at the School	Number	Per Cent
Less than one year	8	20.0
One to two years	7	17.5
Two to three years	5	12.5
Three to four years	9	22.5
Four to five years	6	15.0
Five to six years	3	7.5
Six years and more	2	5.0
TOTAL	40	100.0

Median length of stay: 3 years

Index[1]

academic
  difficulties, 498
  progress, 56, 110-11, 119, 124, 126, 147, 149, 182, 452, 469
accident proneness, 495-96
adequacy, pseudo, 204, 226
adjustment, surface, 182
adolescent problems 123-25, 132, 135, 152
adopted children, 493
age distribution of children, 502-03
aggression, 26, 91-92, 94-95, 97, 99-100, 102-03, 108, 112, 114, 117, 140-42, 157, 296, 374, 403, 406-07, 426, 454, 499; *see also* controls
agoraphobia, 459, 499
Aichhorn, A., 13

Aid to Dependent Children, 156
allergies, 455, 496; *see also* hay fever
alter ego, protective, 418
ambivalence, 161, 176, 353
anaclitic behavior, 499
anal preoccupation, 106, 214, 307-08, 317-18
anger; see aggression, *and* temper outbursts
animals, 187, 194, 199, 202, 204, 211
  cruelty to, 157
anorexia, 305-06, 308, 373, 377, 496
aphasia, 496
Art Institute of Chicago, 110-11, 131-32, 143
asthma, 495-96
athetoid movements, 286, 343
athlete's foot, 455

1. The histories forming this volume deal, throughout their entirety, with aggression, ambivalence, anality, anxiety, control, delinquency, dependency, desperation, emotional disturbances, the children's families, games, guilt, problems of identification and identity, infantilism, integration, masochism, masturbation, psychoanalytic and psychotherapeutic procedures, oedipal and oral problems, the Orthogenic School and its procedures, phallic and urethral disturbances, phantasies, play, regression, human relations, residential treatment, safety, self-assertion, destruction and self-destructive tendencies, sex, the staff, the institutes of the mind (id, ego, and super-ego), temper tantrums, different types of therapy, toilet training, emotional difficulties and attachments of every kind. It seemed pointless to mention all of these in the Index; therefore, only a few entries are made under these headings, and not every page is referred to in which these problems are mentioned either directly or by implication.

aunts; *see* families, the children's
autism, 62, 77, 116, 121, 141, 152, 257, 479-80, 497-98
autobiography, 229-30
Axford, C., 349, 401

babies
concern with, 213, 222, 226-28, 231-32
desire to be, 218, 225, 243, 247
baby bottles, 89, 143, 189-90, 200, 212, 219, 222, 230, 237, 319, 336, 354
Beck, A., 302
Beck, S. J., 57, 120, 207, 271, 302
Bergquist, L., xvi
Blustein, E., 165
body
appearance, 48, 64, 70, 174, 184, 186, 214, 225, 243, 247, 452
coordination, 62, 70, 73, 81, 100, 214, 292, 296, 312, 319, 339, 343, 345, 349, 357, 369, 372-73, 376, 456
bombs, 216
Bradley, C., 257
brain-damaged children, 495, 498-99

camp, 129
cannibalistic phantasies, 216, 249, 305, 315; *see also* oral incorporation
case histories
validity of, 4
writing, 4, 5, 473-78
casework, 47-49, 55, 65, 145, 150, 152, 159, 199, 459, 500
case workers; *see* casework
castration anxiety, 192, 208, 213, 232, 397-98, 408, 461
cerebral agenesis, 499
cerebral palsy, 499
Chicago Child Care Society, xv, 389
childbirth, 225-26, 228
Christmas, 92-93, 178, 184, 201, 223
claustrophobia, 499
clinics, child guidance, 500
Cohen, L., 165
colon, elongated, 496
comic books; *see* mass media
constipation, 281-82, 307-08

controls
anxiety about lack of, 66-69, 74-76, 84, 162
external, 184, 405, 419, 425-30, 443
inner, 191, 196, 293, 450, 453
symbols of, 420
cooking, 76, 84, 88-89, 113, 127, 152
counselor
night, 34
substitute, 440-41
counter-transference, 473

darkness and light, 33-34
death, 220, 224
delinquency, 390-91, 399, 451, 459, 498-99
delusions of grandeur, 406
dentist, 41
depression, 58-60, 69, 76-77, 83, 86, 105, 111, 116, 124, 136-37, 187-88
dermatitis, 455-56, 458, 463-64, 496
desperation, 185-86, 298
detention home juvenile, 415-17, 461
diagnoses of children
psychiatric, 498-99
unfavorable, 302
dictation, 476
divorce of parents; *see* families, the children's
doll play, 173, 176, 180, 194, 199, 448-50
doors, locked, 29, 419
drawings, 48, 63, 76, 86-87, 94, 97-98, 100-01, 105, 107-08, 111, 114-15, 119-20, 123-24, 126-27, 131-33, 143, 147, 149-52, 168, 182, 188, 196, 221
dreams, 90, 93, 158, 211, 216, 220-22, 232, 236, 247, 308, 374, 431-32, 464; *see also* nightmares
duration of children's stay, 503

Easter, 110, 353
eating problems, 64, 67-69, 71, 75-76, 78-79, 82, 84, 88, 100, 106, 138, 144, 294, 376
eczema; *see* dermatitis
"El" trains, 390, 393; *see also* trains
emotional disturbances
of children; *see* diagnoses of children, *and* psychiatric examinations

of parents; *see* families, the children's
Empire State Building, 77, 125-26
enuresis, 316-18, 427-28, 456, 495; *see also* incontinence *and* urination
Erikson, E., 307, 333
Escalona, S., 480-81
excursions, 37
exhibitionism, 113-14, 123, 188
exploring, 38

families, the children's
aunts, 214, 219, 221-22, 229, 234-37, 244, 249-50, 252
fathers, 46-47, 59, 61, 76, 129-30, 151, 177, 245-46, 265, 273, 304, 310-11, 315, 338, 345, 351, 376-77, 381, 390, 392, 394-98, 403, 412, 431-32, 457-58, 460, 463, 467-69; psychosomatic disturbances of, 274-75; therapy of, 490
grandmothers, 47-48, 65, 283-84, 329
mothers, 43, 46-54, 59, 61, 65, 80, 99, 128-30, 135, 143, 145-46, 150-51, 176-77, 197-98, 215-16, 221-29, 231-37, 240, 243, 246, 250; 275-77, 284-85, 288-89, 304, 314-15, 318, 320, 329, 334-35, 341, 345, 351, 377, 379, 390-92 394-99, 431-32, 438, 457-62, 466-69; all-giving, 204; birthdays of, 436-38; "good," 410; melancholic, 169; psychotherapy of, 277-79, 489; secret meetings with, 457, 459, 461, 463
parents, 9-11, 16, 24, 38, 158, 180, 197, 274, 287, 468, 478-86, 493-94, 501-02; divorce of, 392, 456-57, 460, 465; emotional disturbances of, 486-88, 490-92; psychiatric treatment of, 459, 482-83; remarriage of, 460
stepfathers, 466, 469
stepmothers, 466
family life, 114-15, 128-29, 139, 142, 145
farewell party, 171, 467
farming, 101, 122
fathers; *see* families, the children's

fear
of bodily harm, 247-48
of death, 58, 60, 72, 76
of desertion, 31, 58, 80, 198-99, 206, 209, 213, 219-20, 243, 249
of distances 32
of falling, 33
of future, 110-11, 114-15, 124-25, 127-28, 135, 143
of poverty, 60
of retaliation, 175
of separation; *see* fear of desertion
of sickness, 88, 174, 215-16, 232, 408
of starvation, 59-60, 63, 75, 82-83, 86-87, 89, 106, 143
of strangers, 31
feeble-mindedness; *see* diagnoses of children
feeding
early, 280-81
with eye dropper, 271, 280-81, 294, 354
forced, 283, 313, 364, 377
self-feeding, attempt at, 424
feminine strivings, 398; *see also* transvestism
fences, 23-30, 196
Fenichel, O., 259, 455
Flapan, D., 165
folie à deux, 482
foster homes, 145, 149-53, 181, 266-69
Foundation for Emotionally Disturbed Children, 493
Fourth of July, 88
Frances, 156-57, 181, 197-98, 206-07, 213-14, 216-19, 222-23, 229, 232-37, 241, 243, 246-51, 253, 264-65, 269; her husband, 211, 218, 222, 229, 241, 264-65; her marriage, 208, 210; her pregnancy, 232, 243; her son, 252, 265
Freud, A., 490
Freud, S., 442

games, 82, 91, 93, 100, 102, 104, 112-13, 126, 137, 356
punitive, 174-5
gardening, 76-77, 87, 94, 139
ghosts, 431-33

God, 299, 301, 308, 327
Goldfarb, W., 63
Goldstein, K., 64
grandmothers; see families, the children's
Great Dictator, 71-72, 74, 84, 94, 116, 133
greed, 165
grievances, 177, 190, 195
group living, 27, 425
guilt, feelings of, 50-54, 74, 85, 91-97, 99, 102, 113, 130, 175-76, 199, 442

Hallowe'en, 88, 220, 313
Harper, L., 61
hay fever, 495, 496
Henry, J., xvi
high school, 149, 151, 153
homicidal attempts, 499; see also aggression
hospitalization, 285
hostility; see aggression
housework, 25
Howard, K., 165

identification, 183, 205
  with destructive aspects of parents' personalities, 399
identity, personal, 112-14, 152; see also negative identity
incendiarism, 499
incontinence, 34, 495-96, 499; see also enuresis
incorporation, 183, 244, 247
infantile
  behavior, 75-76, 80-83, 89, 93, 100, 111, 113, 115, 118, 137, 142-43
  experiences, 33
inferiority, feelings of, 57, 60, 120, 127, 140-41
initiations, 335-36, 342-43, 347, 353
institutional treatment, 262-64
integration, 113, 118, 137, 146, 446-47
intelligence, 56, 119, 147, 182, 495, 497
intercourse, 180, 209, 213, 225, 246
interviews, follow-up, 474
introjection, 227, 253, 265
isolation, 48-50, 53, 55, 57, 61, 63, 65, 66, 72-73, 77-80, 87, 105, 116, 140-42, 158, 185-86, 209, 304

jackstraws, 356; see also games
Janowitz, G., xvi, 61, 96, 106, 109, 165, 269, 401, 429, 462
Janowitz, M., xvi
Jewish Children's Bureau of Chicago, xv, 157

Kaiser, G., 61
kaleidoscope, 354
Kanner, L., 8, 256-58
kindergarten, 48, 110, 284
kitchen raid, 406

Labor Day, 88
lactation, 193
latency period, 195
Leer, J., 165
Leviton, I., 401
lex talionis, 195, 313, 427
light; see darkness and light
Lukes, A., 61, 165, 269, 401

marasmus, infantile, 498
masks, 431-33
masochism, 295
mass media, 63, 85, 97, 104-05, 116, 127, 136, 244, 390, 393, 400, 409-12, 455-56, 466
masturbation, 156, 172, 178, 192-93, 196, 198, 200-01, 213, 215, 220, 269, 292, 328
McKnight, P., 61
Marquis, R., xvi
megalomania, 61, 73, 83, 84, 99, 108-09, 116, 124, 126, 130, 132, 136-37, 210
menstruation, 214-15
menu, 28
messing, 105-06, 162, 221, 317, 339
migraine, 496
Milne, A. A., 321
Mississippi River, 210
monsters, 193
mother figures, 80, 81, 94, 96-97, 106, 114
mothers; see families, the children's
mousetraps, 408
mouth noises, movement, 62-63, 71, 73, 76, 82, 118, 154
movies; see mass media
Museum of Science and Industry, 52, 86

Mussolini, 310

negative identity, 333
neighbors, 222, 234
Nelson, P., xvi
nightmares, 40, 158, 182, 193, 197-99,
    201, 206, 208, 214, 400, 413,
    447, 461; see also dreams
Noah, 299
noise, 25, 172
noses; see Tristram Shandy
nurseries, 47-48, 82, 104, 132, 156,
    198
nursing, 226-28

psychiatrist, 157, 167, 181, 207
psychoanalysis, 13, 487-88, 500
psychoanalyst, consulting, 475
psychological institutionalism, 44-46
psychoses of children, 481; see also
    diagnoses of children
psychosomatic disturbances of fathers;
    see families, the children's
psychotherapy
    of children, 500
    of mothers; see families, the chil-
        dren's
punishment, wish for, 442
pyloric spasm, 496

Oberndorf, C., 12
obesity, 496
objectivity, 477-78
oedipal conflicts, situations, phantasies,
    80-81, 95, 264-65, 315-16, 335,
    345, 394, 396
onions, 177, 188
oral
    anxieties, 76, 88, 94, 101-03, 127,
        133
    experiments, 335-36, 353-54
    incorporation, 226-27, 304, 309,
        315, 397; see also cannibalistic
        phantasies
    phase, 106
    trauma, 283, 314
orderliness, 25, 163
organic disease, 495
orphanage, 48-51, 53-55, 62, 64-66,
    69, 74-75, 77, 79, 88, 90, 93, 96,
    103-04, 109, 117-19, 131-33, 137,
    154, 192

"Orthogenic jail," 340
Orthogenic School
    bathrooms, 34
    beds, 32
    buildings, 18, 23, 28, 32, 37, 39, 41
    classrooms, 23, 31
    decorating, 28
    dormitories, 12, 19, 21-22, 24, 31,
        33-34, 39-41
    furniture, 27-28, 33, 35
    ideal, 336-37
    night lights, 34
    physical setting, 17-19, 29, 34-37,
        39, 41
    playgrounds, 18, 20, 31
    reorganization of, 321
    spatial closeness and distance, 31
    wall colors, 27

pacifier, 436
paintings; see drawings
paranoia, 50, 141, 498; see also diag-
    noses of children
parents; see families, the children's
    foster; see foster homes
participant-observers, 477
passivity, 295
penis, female, 397
Perkins, G., 165
permanence, 203
persecution, feelings of, 175
personalities,
    borrowed, 261-63
    expression of, 25
phallic aggression, 397
phantasies, 57-58, 81, 86, 96-97, 114-
    16, 120-24, 130, 132-33, 140-41,
    192-93, 196
    of destruction, 52, 54-55, 59-61, 66-
        71, 74, 77, 93-97, 102-07, 115,
        118, 126, 220, 224, 236, 249, 267
    of poisoning, 75, 106, 335
    of world destruction, 299
    see also masturbation, 198, 200-01
phobias, 283, 296
Pinocchio, 441
play, 56, 93-94, 96-97, 104, 195; see
    also games
police, 164, 199, 390, 408, 415-17,
    443, 451, 457-58, 464
pregnancy, concern with, 213-15, 217,
    225-26, 228, 243-44, 246-47, 251

privacy, 27, 35
psychiatric examinations, 55, 119, 286, 356, 359, 375, 431-33; *see also* diagnoses of children
psychiatric treatment of parents; *see* families, the children's

radio; *see* mass media
railway depot, 39
Rallahan, 304, 346
Rapaport, D., xvi
Ray and Charles Newman Memorial Foundation, 493
Ray, K., xvi
reading, 56, 110, 114-15, 118-19, 134, 152
records, 477
Redl, F., 13
regression, 214
Reichard, S., 479
relate, inability to; *see* isolation
relations
    to other children, 62, 65, 70, 71, 77-78, 84-85, 90-91, 95-96, 100, 102, 104, 111-12, 118-19, 120, 131, 133, 151-52, 162
    to men, 117-18, 121, 136, 152
remarriage of parents; *see* families, the children's
removal of child from home, 491
reports, 475
residential treatment, 9, 13, 500
resting, 162
ringworm, *see* dermatitis
robberies, 422, 499
robbers, stories about, 340-41, 343-44, 352, 360
Robin Hood, 455-56
Rorschach tests, 57, 120-21, 140-41, 151, 207, 248, 302-03, 360-61, 382, 384
"round square," 194
running away, 389, 393-95, 397, 399, 400-02, 404-5, 409, 412-17, 419-20, 431, 435, 443, 449, 466
    efforts to prevent, 420-24

safety, physical, 30, 32, 41
schizophrenia, 57, 121, 141, 209, 256-61, 482, 498
scholarships, 493
school, public, 50, 110

Schroeder, B., 401
screaming, 51, 62, 65, 70, 73-74, 78, 164, 169, 184-86, 205, 231, 243, 269
self-assertion, 312
self-destructive tendencies, 390, 399, 407-08, 428, 457; *see also* suicide attempts
sex
    anxieties, 159, 200, 208, 212-13, 215, 219
    experiences, 157
    relations, 198, 209
shelter, 37, 41
shopping trips, 165
siblings, 49-51, 54, 80, 213, 274, 276, 325, 390-91, 393, 395-96, 398, 400, 449, 467-69, 492, 500-02
snout, 200
snow man, 397, 421
social agencies, 47, 53-55, 130, 135, 142-43, 145, 150-52, 155, 181, 199, 207, 231, 242-43, 246, 253-54, 266-67, 459, 493
social customs, ignorance of, 134, 139; *see also* table manners
social sensitivity, 111, 126, 133, 144
soiling; *see* enuresis, incontinence, messing
Solomon, King, 212
spanking, 175, 440-41
spasticity, 292, 343
speech, 49, 53-54, 56-58, 62-63, 86, 111, 129, 134, 143, 154, 496
spelling, 53-54, 56, 110
spitting, 305-06
Spitz, A., 322
stability, 35
staff, 95, 100, 108, 125
    changes, 35
    length of association, 36
stamp collecting, 127-28
statistical analyses, 13
stealing, 155, 157, 175, 422, 499
stepfathers; *see* families, the children's
stepmothers; *see* families, the children's
Sterba, E., 257-58
strabismus, 495-96
stuttering, 495-96
sucking, 62, 89, 90, 138, 200, 218-19, 221, 224, 319, 355, 436

suicidal attempts, 55, 61, 66, 69, 77, 104, 126, 133, 499; *see also* self-destructive tendencies
superego, 95, 98, 191, 195, 418
Sylvester, E., 44, 61, 165, 319, 346, 401, 495
symptoms, physical, 174, 200, 247, 453-54, 463-64, 495-96, 499

table manners, 291, 306-07, 311, 317, 350, 369; *see also* social customs
teachers, 95
telephone, toy, 52-53, 86, 91, 94, 117
television; *see* mass media
temper outbursts, 51, 53-54, 62-63, 65, 70, 71, 75, 77-78, 82, 100, 142
Thanksgiving, 87-88
Thematic Apperception Tests, 57-60, 121-24, 238, 296-99, 300-01, 323-27, 379-82
therapeutic team, 258
therapy of fathers; *see* families, the children's
thrush mouth, 271, 280-81
thumbsucking, 48, 62-63, 83, 90, 100, 116, 156, 189-90, 192, 198, 205, 211, 339
tickling, 296, 374
tics, 208, 214
Tillman, C., 479
time, sense of, 297-98
toilet training, 67, 281
touch, reaction to, 295-96, 312, 343, 349
trains, 39; *see also* "El" trains
transvestism, 398, 499; *see also* feminine strivings
treasure hunts, 37

treatment
  procedures, change in, 263
  success, 9-16
Treiman, J., xvi, 165, 230, 268-69
Tristram Shandy, 201
trust, 38
tuition, 493
twins, 492

United Nations, 118
United States National Institute of Mental Health, xvi
University of Chicago, xv, 1, 17, 108, 149, 153
urination, 156, 167, 179, 221; *see also* enuresis *and* incontinence
  aggressive, 427-28

Valentine's Day, 72
visits
  birthday, 365-68
  with parents, 10, 38, 47-53, 128, 150, 287-90, 292, 307, 311, 315-16, 318-19, 328-29, 334, 337-38, 341, 350, 352-53, 358, 363, 369, 371, 400, 460, 491, 495
  pre-placement, 254
vomiting, 280-83, 289, 291-94, 296, 305-08, 315, 317-19, 329, 353, 368-69, 377, 495-96

warts, 458
Wexler, M., xvi
White, F., xvi, 347, 372, 377, 385
"wild critter," 71, 72, 74, 77, 84, 86, 92, 98, 108
Wingo, J., xvi, 349, 357, 401
withdrawal; *see* isolation

zoo of stuffed animals, 438

suicidal attempts, 45, 61, 66, 69, 77,
104, 126, 436, 499; see also self-
destructive tendencies
superego, 95, 98, 191, 195, 418
Sylvester H., 44, 61, 165, 319, 366,
401, 495
symptoms, physical, 174, 200, 247,
453-54, 463-64, 495-96, 499

table manners, 291, 306-07, 311, 317,
350, 368; see also social customs
teachers, 95
telephone, toy, 52-53, 86, 91, 94, 117
television; see mass media
temper tantrums, 51, 53-54, 62-63,
65, 70, 71, 75, 77-78, 82, 100, 142
Thanksgiving, 87-88
Thematic Apperception Tests, 57-60,
121-24, 238, 296-99, 300-01,
325-27, 379-82
therapeutic team, 258
therapy of fathers, see families, the
children's
thumb motor, 271, 280-81
thumbsucking, 48, 82-83, 85, 90, 100,
110, 156, 189-90, 192, 198, 205,
211, 339
toileting, 250, 374
ties, 208, 214
Tillman C., 479
time, sense of, 207-08
toilet training, 63, 281
touch, reaction to, 295-96, 312, 343,
349
trains, 29; see also "HO" trains
transvestism, 358, 499; see also feminine strivings
treasure hunts, 37

treatment
procedures, change in, 263
success, 9-16
Treiman J., xvi, 165, 230, 265-69
Tristram Shandy, 201
trust, 2X
tuition, 493
twins, 492

United Nations, 113
United States, National Institute of
Mental Health, xvi
University of Chicago, xv, 1, 17, 108,
149, 153
...ination, 156, 167, 179, 221; see also
enuresis and incontinence
aggressive, 427-28

Valentine's Day, 72
visits
birthday, 365-68
with parents, 10, 35, 47-53, 128,
150, 287-90, 292, 307, 311, 315-
16, 318-19, 323-29, 334, 337-38,
341, 350, 355-53, 358, 362, 364,
371, 400, 460, 491, 495
pre-placement, 231
vomiting, 280-83, 289, 291-94, 296,
303-08, 315, 317-19, 329, 553,
368-69, 372, 495-96

wants, 458
Wexler M., xvi
White F., xvi, 347, 372, 377, 385
wild critter?, 71, 72, 74, 77, 84,
86, 92, 98, 168
Wingo, 1, xvi, 329, 357, 401
withdrawal; see isolation

zoo of stuffed animals, 438